THE TEXAS THAT MIGHT HAVE BEEN

NUMBER THIRTY-THREE
Elma Dill Russell Spencer Series in the West and Southwest

Andrés Tijerina, General Editor

Series Board:
Alwyn Barr
James E. Crisp
Rebecca Sharpless
Eric Van Young

THE TEXAS THAT MIGHT HAVE BEEN

Sam Houston's Foes Write to Albert Sidney Johnston

Collected by Margaret Swett Henson

Edited and with an Introduction by Donald E. Willett

Texas A&M University Press | College Station

This paper meets the requirements of ANSI/NISO Z39.48-1992
(Permanence of Paper).

Binding materials have been chosen for durability.

Library of Congress Cataloging-in-Publication Data

The Texas that might have been : Sam Houston's foes write to Albert Sidney
Johnston / collected by Margaret Swett Henson ; edited and with an introduction by
Donald E. Willett. — 1st ed.

    p. cm. — (Elma Dill Russell Spencer series in the West and Southwest ; no. 33)
  Includes bibliographical references and index.

  ISBN-13: 978-1-60344-145-2 (cloth : alk. paper)

  ISBN-10: 1-60344-145-X (cloth : alk. paper)

1. Love, James, 1795–1874—Correspondence. 2. Houston, Sam,
1793–1863—Adversaries—Correspondence. 3. Johnston, Albert Sidney,
1803–1862—Correspondence. 4. Texas—Officials and employees—
Correspondence. 5. Lamar, Mirabeau Buonaparte, 1798–1859. 6. Texas—History—
Republic, 1836–1846. 7. Texas—History—1846–1950. I. Johnston, Albert Sidney,
1803–1862. II. Henson, Margaret Swett, 1924–2001. III. Willett, Donald. IV. Series:
Elma Dill Russell Spencer series in the West and Southwest ; no. 33.

  F390.T44 2009

  976.4'04—dc22

                  2009018523

For Margaret Swett Henson,
a great Texas historian

CONTENTS

PREFACE

O n January 22, 2001, Texas lost one of its favorite daughters, Margaret Swett Henson. Margaret was a loving wife and devoted mother. She was also a gifted teacher, researcher, and author of historical works on early Texas. This gentle soul who loved all things Texan was a prolific writer who published twelve books in her lifetime.[1] Her first work, *Samuel May Williams, Early Texas Entrepreneur* (1976), won the Summerfield G. Roberts Award for the best book on the Republic of Texas. Her 1988 book, *Chambers County: A Pictorial History*, won that year's T. R. Fehrenbach Award from the Texas Historical Commission. At the time of her death Margaret was working on what she believed would be her magnum opus, a lengthy biography of Texas entrepreneur Thomas McKinney. The unfinished manuscript, along with her extensive research material on the topic, lies among her personal papers at the Texas Collection of the Rosenberg Library in Galveston.

Margaret's work on Texas history did not go unnoticed. *The Directory of American Scholars*, *Who's Who in the South and Southwest*, and *The World Who's Who of Women* included her accomplishments in their publications. In 1986 the East Texas Historical Association named her a Fellow of that organization. The following year the oldest learned society in Texas, the Texas State Historical Association, also selected her as a Fellow. In 1997 Texas historians elected her president of this prestigious organization. At the time of her death many scholars considered Margaret Swett Henson the first lady of Texas history.

During the twentieth century Texas produced its fair share of noted historians. Scholars such as Herbert Bolton, Eugene C. Barker, Carlos E. Castañeda, Walter Prescott Webb, and T. R. Fehrenbach viewed Texas history as an epic adventure, bigger than life itself. They wrote on a grand scale that fascinated the world. Their stories about cowboys and Indians, swashbuckling buccaneers, brigands and banditos, intrepid European explorers, pious padres, Anglo revolutionaries, and the Republic of Texas grace libraries worldwide. I believe that Margaret Henson's work followed in their giant footsteps.

Margaret Louise Swett was born in Chicago, Illinois, on January 3, 1924. She was the only child of Clara Kaufman Swett and William Claude Swett. Shortly after little Margaret arrived, the Swett family moved to Glen Ellen, a suburb of the Windy City. She attended nearby Glenboro High School and graduated with honors. Even though her father was a graduate of the University of Illinois, she turned down several local scholarships. Instead she boarded a train and headed south. She first arrived in Austin, Texas, in September 1941 and made the Littlefield Dormitory on the University of Texas campus her new home. Her high school grades and excellent entrance exam scores quickly caught the attention of the school's honors program committee. Much to her surprise Margaret found herself in the University of Texas' "Plan II" honors program. Her first mentors included legendary professors Harry Ransom, Frederick Duncalf, Martin Ettlinger, and Clarence Ayers.

In October 1943 Margaret, for the first time, put her formal education on hold when she married a fellow student, William A. "Bill" Nowotny. For the next eight years she followed her husband's work in the oil patch. Stops along the way included Houston, San Antonio, Bogotá, Colombia, and Lake Charles, Louisiana. She bore her first two children: Kathleen in 1946 and Patricia in 1949. Tragically, doctors soon diagnosed Patricia with cystic fibrosis. For the next fifteen years Margaret and Pat fought the ravages of this deadly disease. Pat died on March 7, 1964.

Two years after Pat's birth Margaret married J. Scott Henson and moved to McGehee, Arkansas, in the southeastern corner of the state. Her husband worked at an oil pipeline terminal on the Mississippi River while Margaret worked as a full-time stay-at-home mother. The Henson family lived there for nine years and grew by three members: Mike, born in 1952; Peter, born in 1955; and Steve, born in 1957. While in McGehee Margaret returned to academics. She enrolled in several college classes at nearby Arkansas A&M at Monticello, later renamed the University of Arkansas at Monticello. In 1959 she took a fateful step and enrolled in a U.S. history to 1865 correspondence course from the University of Texas. One of her instructors in this class was a junior faculty member who would earn his doctorate in history from Harvard University the following year: Robert C. Cotner.

In 1960, with five kids in tow, Margaret and Scott returned to the Lone Star State for the last time. While the movers unpacked their belongings she enrolled at the University of Houston and completed her bachelor of science degree in education two years later. With her teaching certificate in hand she found her first job with the Houston Independent School District. For seven years she taught Texas, U.S., and world history to junior high school students. At night she took graduate history classes at her alma mater. In 1969 she earned her master of arts degree in American history, with a minor in Latin American history.[2]

When the University of Houston announced a new PhD degree plan in history Margaret was the first in line to enroll in the program. From 1969 to 1971 she served as a teaching fellow for the department. The next year she took an instructor's job at the old South Texas Junior College campus in downtown Houston. Between 1972 and 1974 she taught at the Houston Community College. During this time Margaret continued her studies and perfected her ultimately legendary research skills.

In 1974 Margaret, by then a fifty-year-old grandmother, literally and figuratively made history. Thirty-three years after she first entered college Margaret Henson earned the highest degree a university can bestow upon a student: the doctor of philosophy. She became the first student to earn a doctorate in history from the University of Houston. Professor Stanley Siegel, a renowned scholar in the political history of the Republic of Texas, directed Margaret's dissertation, "Samuel May Williams, 1795–1858: Texas Entrepreneur." It became an instant classic in Texas history.

After completing her PhD, Margaret found work as an archivist for the Houston Metropolitan Project. This undertaking, funded by the National Endowment for the Humanities and cosponsored by the University of Houston, Rice University, Texas Southern University, and the Houston Public Library, surveyed public documents in Houston and Harris County and located other important local history collections that related to this area. Margaret helped to sort these important papers and develop a computerized finding aid that directed scholars to new source material. Along the way she studied at the National Archives in Washington, D.C., and visited the archives of the Wisconsin and Ohio state historical societies. These trips taught her how to collect, arrange, and preserve historical documents. Working as an archivist also fine-tuned her historical research skills.

Margaret believed that one way to improve her chances of finding a teaching job at a university was to publish a book. She reworked her dissertation and sent the manuscript to College Station. Frank Wardlaw, director of Texas A&M University Press, appreciated the quality of research and writing style and quickly offered Margaret a book contract. Margaret finished *Samuel May Williams, Early Texas Entrepreneur*, in 1976. It immediately received rave reviews and won the Summerfield G. Roberts Award. These accolades established her as one of the leading scholars of early Texas history.

Her strategy paid off. In 1977 the University of Houston at Clear Lake hired her as an adjunct assistant professor. Although not a tenure-track position, this job affected her career in three areas. First, permanent academic employment allowed her to end her status as an itinerant academic. She no longer had to search for part-time jobs at local campuses to pay the bills. Second, the University of Houston at Clear Lake offered junior-, senior-, and graduate-level classes. This allowed Margaret to mentor and teach students who shared her love of early Texas history. Third, her newfound professional and financial stability allowed her greater flexibility to study, conduct research, and publish in her areas of interest.

On July 20, 1970, Margaret contacted the Howard-Tilton Memorial Library at Tulane University and asked if their archive contained any documents that pertained to Samuel May Williams.[3] Connie G. Griffith, director of the Special Collections Division at the library, reported that her archive contained no material on Williams, but she noted that "we have a very extensive collection of Albert Sidney Johnston and his son, William Preston Johnston. There are quite a few letters for the period of Johnston's service in Texas."[4] Margaret put this tidbit of information on the back burner for future reference.

Sometime before 1974 Margaret again contacted Griffith and asked for permission to publish part of the Johnston Collection. Griffith never responded; she retired in 1974, and someone misplaced Margaret's letter. With no permission to publish the Johnston materials Margaret concentrated instead on finishing her dissertation and turning it into a book manuscript. After she published the Samuel May Williams book Margaret did two things that brought her back in contact with the Johnston Collection. First, she refocused her scholarly attention on Samuel May Williams's associate and fellow entrepreneur, Thomas McKinney. Second, she sent a copy of her book to the Special Collections Division at the Tulane library.

On June 16, 1978, Ann S. Gwyn, the new head of the Special Collections Division at Tulane's library, wrote to Margaret and indicated that, "if you are interested in pursuing the publication of the [James] Love-Johnston letters, we should be delighted." Gwyn stipulated that the letters should be "published in a scholarly journal or as part of a scholarly book."[5] This was all the encouragement that Margaret needed.

It was eight years before Margaret returned to the Johnston Collection, however. In November 1978 she attended the Southern Historical Association's annual meeting in New Orleans. While there she stopped at the Special Collections Division at Tulane's library and copied the index of correspondence for the Johnston Collection.[6] Six months later, while Margaret was in New Orleans for the annual meeting of the Organization of American Historians, she once again visited the Special Collections Division.[7] One of the collections that she researched was the Mrs. Mason Barrett Collection, part of the Albert Sidney Johnston and William Preston Johnston papers. The Johnston papers fascinated her. She found new material on Thomas McKinney, but something else in the collection caught her eye.

She noticed that a large number of prominent Texans used Albert Sidney Johnston as a sounding board for new political and economic ideas. Something about Johnston's demeanor and persona must have prompted them to confide in him on a wide variety of topics and shared interests. Had Margaret stumbled upon new archival material that proffered a new view of the Republic of Texas and early state of Texas? Could a collection of these letters somehow provide Texans with a new window on their history and culture? Margaret decided to pursue those questions. On June 6, 1979, Tulane University's library sent her an invoice for "Xeroxing of Barrett and Johnston Collection."[8] Margaret Henson and General Albert Sidney Johnston were about to meet on the field of historical scholarship.

That summer Margaret organized and documented the James Love–Albert Sidney Johnston correspondence and submitted the resulting manuscript to Texas A&M University Press. In commenting on the project, Lloyd G. Lyman, the new press director, wrote, "There is no denying that his [James Love's] letters shed much light on the viewpoint of southern Whigs and the maneuvering of early Texas politicians." He encouraged her to reassess the material and expand the scope of the work.[9]

Margaret heeded Lyman's advice. In 1980 she rechecked her folder of photocopied letters from the Albert Sidney Johnston Collection and incorporated a large number of letters from other prominent Texans into her expanded text. She titled this new manuscript "Dear General: Letters from Texas to Albert Sidney Johnston concerning Politics, 1836–1861," but she could not find a publisher. Margaret put the manuscript in a dark-brown envelope box and placed it in the middle drawer of a rusty old file cabinet. It remained there for twenty-one years.

I do not remember when I first met Margaret Swett Henson, but it was probably in the mid-1980s, either at an East Texas Historical Association meeting or the annual convention of the Texas State Historical Association. I do remember, year after year, pleasantly talking with her and with J. Milton Nance and Archie McDonald—three renowned historians of early Texas history—in the lobby of the Fredonia Hotel in Nacogdoches, Texas. I always looked forward to these spirited conversations. I appreciated the sage advice and genuine interest they showed in this junior faculty member's fledgling career.

My first professional contact with Margaret occurred in 1996, when she agreed to participate in a local history lecture series that I helped to run. That year the series focused on Galveston history, and Margaret talked to a standing-room-only audience on the founding of Galveston. Later I asked her to write a chapter on that topic for a book on Galveston history that I hoped to publish. She happily agreed to the project. Prior to her death Margaret informed me that she had completed the article and would mail it to me.

Of course, I never received the packet. I contacted Margaret's daughter, Kathleen Duncan, and asked permission to inspect her late mother's study for the missing work.[10] After several hours of searching through hundreds of folders and files I found the article, which Margaret had titled, "Founding the Galveston City Company: Nineteenth Century Politics, Entrepreneurs, and Land Speculation." And I found much more. Stuffed in the bottom of that rusty old cabinet was a lost Margaret Henson manuscript. When I opened the box, I expected to find a draft of one of her early books. After all, the box was aged and moldy (an appropriate condition for anything that resides in coastal Texas). I was wrong. The title page did not remind me of any of Margaret's book-length works. I showed this treasure to her daughter, who agreed to allow me to examine the work and evaluate its merit.

After some discussions Kathleen Duncan permitted me to re-edit the manuscript and seek a publisher for this important work. The Henson heirs also agreed to donate their mother's papers to the Texas Collection of the Rosenberg Library in Galveston. They also agreed to donate her extensive collection of Texas history books to the Jack Williams Library at Texas A&M University at Galveston. I also agreed to donate any royalties generated from book sales to the Margaret Henson Fund. The Williams Library will use this fund to purchase books on early Texas in Margaret's honor.

I took the manuscript home and began to read. I soon realized why so many people around the world love to study early Texas history. This was great stuff—political intrigue, bloody battlefields, a bold and intrepid navy, "good guys" (Albert Sidney Johnston, James Love, and their friends), and plenty of "bad guys," including Sam Houston, his Indian allies, Mexican brigands, and Santa Anna, the "butcher of the Alamo." The stories in these letters told the story of Texas. Or did they?

As I began to re-edit the letters and expand Margaret's footnotes some lingering questions began to bother me. Why did she select only these letters from the Albert Sidney Johnston Collection at Tulane? Why not include some letters from other famous individuals? For instance, why not add more letters from Republic of Texas presidents Sam Houston and Mirabeau B. Lamar? Their musings could generate more interest in the book and maybe sell more copies. I quickly dismissed this thought. This was, after all, Henson's second manuscript and her first and, as it turns out, only attempt to edit such a collection. Margaret was a gifted writer, but she was first and foremost a great scholar with something to say. I concluded that Margaret Henson did not collect these letters just to tell a story or sell books.

I now faced two questions: Why did she choose only these letters? And what was she really trying to say? Maybe the answer lay in her introduction. Margaret believed that the letters were "a valuable source of information about the political, social, and economic conditions there [in Texas] from the days of the Republic to the Civil War." The letter writers vividly commented on most of the major historical events that occurred in Texas during this time period. And their penchant for detail adds to our understanding of these individual events. She also pointed out that this correspondence "allows the reader to glimpse what opponents of Sam Houston thought about the tactics the Old Hero used while twice president of the Republic (1836–1838, 1841–1844) and U.S. senator (1846–1859)." It is obvious from the first letter to the last that these gentlemen had no use for the "Hero of San Jacinto" and the vision of Texas that he championed. Once Albert Sidney Johnston broke with President Houston over military policy in 1838 these letter writers no longer viewed Johnston simply as a friend. They now saw him as a like-minded political ally and confidant.

Margaret also believed that some scholars could use "these letters, combined with other sources," to "produce a study evaluating the relationship between national politics and the Texas factions." It is obvious from the letters that these men understood the symbiotic relationship between Texas and the

United States. That the politics of Washington steered the course of Texas events was an unquestioned truth. She also hoped that others would some-day use these letters to study "the use of political patronage available to both the Houston and anti-Houston factions when each was in office."[11] The classic example of someone who understood and availed himself of the benefits of this patronage was the recipient of these letters. Between 1838 and the end of the republic Albert Sidney Johnston's career in Texas flourished only when Houston did not sleep in the executive mansion. When Texas joined the Union in 1845 and "Ole Sam" became a U.S. senator, Houston's machinations in Washington kept Johnston out of the regular army during the U.S.-Mexico War and underemployed once he returned home with his state militia unit. After that war Johnston labored as a yeoman farmer until the Whig Party victory in 1848 enabled the impoverished West Point graduate to become an army paymaster. Patronage and politics, opposition as opportunity, independence or dependence—were these the central concepts in these letters that Margaret wanted future historians to reexamine and possibly reinterpret?

To answer this question I reread Margaret's major works, especially her books on Samuel May Williams, Juan Bradburn, and Lorenzo de Zavala. I noticed several patterns in her work. She was never afraid to take a risk or butt heads with fellow historians. If she found factual errors or an interpretation that did not gel with her research Margaret never backed down. She used her clean writing style to tell an interesting story and solidify her interpretation.

Prior to Margaret's research most Texas historians viewed Samuel May Williams as a somewhat unscrupulous businessman with an unsavory reputation. At best he played a secondary role in early Texas history. Certainly he did not warrant a book-length biography. The same could be said about Juan Bradburn. Until Margaret studied him, most scholars portrayed Bradburn as a power-hungry lackey who abused power, betrayed his heritage and culture, and caused the Anahuac War. And when Margaret reexamined Lorenzo de Zavala she not only found a Mexican liberal who opposed the rise of central-ism in the Mexican government but also discovered a pragmatist who helped to mold the Republic of Texas. She reexamined these three men's careers and rehabilitated their reputations. Or, citing the old historical cliché, she rescued them from the trash bin of history and portrayed them instead as major figures in Texas history.

So, what was Margaret Henson's modus operandi as a historian? She was a great writer, a great researcher, and a great storyteller who spent her scholarly life resurrecting forgotten figures and elevating them to near heroic stature. Margaret sometimes liked to swim against the current tide of historical interpretation. If her meticulous research indicated that a historical work contained flaws Margaret would contradict that rendering. She made the unknown known and the forgotten famous. And she placed them solidly on the mantel of mainstream history.

I believe the contrarian in Margaret helped her choose these letters. Certainly, she believed that these letters were important for all the reasons she mentioned in her introduction. Unfortunately, however, the contrarian in her never articulated the more profound meaning of these letters. I think she chose these letters because they represent, as well as any collection that she studied, an alternative vision of Texas. These letters are important because they give the reader access to, for the first time, the thoughts of some powerful individuals who dreamed of a Texas that never unfolded. These letters are the musings of a group of men who throughout most of their lives constituted the opposition's point of view within Texas. Thus, these letters to a certain extent present the vision of a Texas unfulfilled, a vision of a Texas where the victorious General Sam Houston after the Battle of San Jacinto did not throw his hat into the political arena. He instead went home and did not try to reshape Texas to suit his own image of it.

After their victory at San Jacinto most Texans, including these letter writers, favored a quick marriage with the United States. When Andrew Jackson rebuffed this Texan marriage proposal for political reasons and substituted diplomatic recognition for political wedlock some Texans, including these letter writers, reexamined their position. Was abandoning their Texas revolution for a back-row seat within Jacksonian democracy such a good idea? And where was Jacksonian America headed—toward the ideals of the American Revolution and Jeffersonian democracy or toward political chaos and mob rule? Did they want to exchange the political abuses they had experienced at the hands of one petty dictator, General Antonio López de Santa Anna Pérez de Lebrón, for the chaos and corruption of the illiterate masses and their illegitimate leader, "King Andrew" Jackson? Should they follow the dictates of an American mob, or should they plot their own destiny? When Texans placed Andrew Jackson's protégé, Sam Houston, in the executive mansion these letter writers had their answer.

James Love, a close friend of Albert Sidney Johnston and a prolific commentator on Texas politics, summarized these strong feelings about this perceived early Texas/United States paradigm in a telltale 1839 letter to Senator John J. Crittenden of Kentucky. In part the Texan noted, "We are sorry for our brethren in the U. S. The Florida War not ended. The riots in your legislative halls, your runaway depositers [sic], your abolition etc. etc., all indicate that you are not well governed or cannot govern yourselves."[12] Love then chided his friend and political mentor, "The tide of prosperity is setting in strong upon us, our government is a sober one, our laws well administered, our lands rich, our climate fine, our people brave and our independence no longer doubtful. We are young and thrifty, no *money* stolen, no riots, no abolition, we are building up churches, colleges, we observe the laws, we hang murderers, and punish th[iefs.] *Take from us a lesson.*"[13]

After the United States rebuffed Texas' early calls for annexation James Love and friends began to dream of a new Texas that was the polar opposite of Sam Houston's vision. Houston's Texas, bounded on the west by the old San Antonio Road or El Camino Real, and on the east by the Gulf of Mexico, approximated Spanish Texas and looked eastward to the United States for guidance and stability. Houston did not believe that Texas could permanently exist on its own. He believed that the future of Texas was the future of the United States. Houston wanted to wait for the United States to allow Texas somehow to enter the Union. Protected by an umbrella of Jacksonian democracy, Texas would fulfill its destiny within the federal Union.

Love and friends imagined a Republic of Texas that would range westward from the Gulf of Mexico to the Pacific Coast and southward from the New Mexico territory to the Valley of Mexico. To them the Republic of Texas, not Jacksonian democracy, was the new harbinger of the American Revolution and Jeffersonian democracy. Once the masses assumed power in Washington on the Potomac, Texas became the new "Republic on the Hill" that exemplified American democracy to the rest of the world. Texas, not the United States, was the new beacon for democratic reform. With luck, audacity, and gallant leadership they believed that Texas could become a major force in North America that would bow to no one. Love and friends wanted to build Texas into a physical and philosophical empire. They, not Sam Houston or Andrew Jackson, would re-purify the democratic spirit.

Love described his vision of Texas to his old Kentucky friend, J. J. Crittenden: "We are getting along *swimmingly* there. The Mexicans at war with each other. The eight eastern provinces (Federal) in rebellion, and heretofore successful, they are anxious for an alliance. We will not disturb them, but will have as little as possible to do with them. The Indians on the frontier the past winter have been some what troublesome, so soon as we get money, they will be driven across the mountains, after a while down the vallies [sic], and then *into* the pacific, That is our line of march."[14]

The authors of the letters in this book noticed that during Houston's first administration he made no effort to expand Texan hegemony to its legal boundaries or beyond. Instead he championed peaceful relations with his Indian allies in East Texas, downsized the army, disassembled the navy, quieted calls to invade northern Mexico, continued to press for annexation to the United States, allowed the government to pursue a disastrous fiscal policy of inflated paper money and unsecured loans, and did little to encourage European recognition of Texas independence. He left Texas a weakened child seeking a foster parent.

After Love and friends in 1838 failed to persuade Albert Sidney Johnston to run for president, they endorsed Mirabeau B. Lamar's campaign for chief executive. And they believed, for a while, that they had found a like-minded visionary. According to these letters they supported Lamar's relocation of the new capital to Austin because Houston opposed such a move and because it could serve as a jumping-off point for further westward expansion and land speculation. They viewed the failed Santa Fe expedition in a similar fashion. To them Santa Fe should have been the next Texan outpost on the road to the Pacific. They did not embrace Houston's multiethnic view of Texas. Instead they supported Lamar's Indian removal policy in East Texas and called for continual military campaigns against the Plains Indians. They loved the Texas Navy, especially the steam-powered warship, *Zavala,* and wanted President Lamar to implement Secretary of War Albert Sidney Johnston's calls for a more aggressive use of the Texas Army to enforce the government's expansionist policy. They agreed with Lamar's call for a national bank and mourned its defeat. They also believed that large foreign loans could halt runaway inflation and allow the government in the long run to finance its aggressive expansionist policy. They liked Lamar's attempts to buy diplomatic recognition from centralist politicians in Mexico, and they smiled when Lamar tacitly supported the formation of breakaway federalist governments in the Yucatán Peninsula and northern Mexico. Lamar's failure to implement most of his policies sounded a death knell for Love and friends' vision of Texas. It also opened the door for their archenemy, Sam Houston, to seize control of the government again and shatter this vision forever.

In 1841 James Love and friends again begged Albert Sidney Johnston to run for president, and once again he let them down. This refusal opened the door for the "Hero of San Jacinto" to crush the opposition's dreams. According to these letters they believed that once Houston settled into the executive mansion he systematically began to destroy the republic's ability to stand on its own two feet and exist independently within the family of nations. Love and friends believed that the Texas Navy was the first line of defense against Mexican military and political attack. When Houston declared his nation's navy to be a band of pirates, Love and others believed that he had paved the way for the centralists in Mexico to crush the federalist insurrections in northern Mexico and the Yucatán Peninsula, uprisings that they supported, and to re-unify the Mexican government. Houston's move also paved the way for the Mexican navy to pillage the Texas coast and reconquer the rebellious province of Texas. Two Mexican incursions onto Texas soil in 1842, the Vásquez raid on San Antonio in March and the Woll invasion in September, and Houston's timid military responses to these events confirmed their earlier suspicions about Houston's intent. And when the Texas government begged the United States to use its army and navy to protect Texas' sovereignty, they knew that their vision of the Republic of Texas was lost forever.

Still, these letter writers benefited from the stability and prosperity that statehood bestowed upon the erstwhile republic. And they reveled in Sam Houston's new focus on national politics at the expense of his local hegemony. However, a booming export economy fueled by land speculation, cotton, and slavery endeared these letter writers to their southern brethren and their way of life. The new enemy was no longer Andrew Jackson and his ignorant mob. It was northern industrialists and their Republican political allies. To these Texans the majority of Americans had once again drifted away from the ideals of the American Revolution and Jeffersonian democracy. These Texans wondered if the Confederacy was a second chance to purify American democracy. Was the rebellious South the new "Republic on the Hill"? And should Texas become its leader?

Historically, Houston's vision of Texas prevailed. He championed Texas' marriage to the United States, and Texas joined the Union in 1845. In 1861 he pleaded with his fellow Texans to remain in the Union, but they did not listen. Ironically, James Love agreed with Houston on this issue. However, when Texans voted to secede, Love and friends shifted their loyalty to the Confederacy. After the Civil War, repentant Texans confessed their sins and reluctantly re-embraced Sam Houston's vision of Texas as a part of the federal union and his belief that Texans are first of all Americans. But have future generations of Texans completely accepted Houston's political and philosophic vision of

Texas and Texans? Obviously, almost all Texans embrace the United States of America as their nation of origin and they accept the geographical boundaries of the state of Texas. But do Texans completely embrace Houston's philosophical vision of Texas? In other words, how do Texans view themselves?

Have Texans since Houston's era embraced Love and company's romantic vision of Texas as an independent state of mind that represents the ideals of the American Revolution and Jeffersonian democracy? An interesting argument can probably be generated to support the idea that many Texans embrace these letter writers' view that Texans are *über*-Americans who faithfully guard the country's ideals and beliefs. And Texans believe that they are larger than life. If you embrace citizenship within the Lone Star State you must naturally concur, like Love and friends surmised a century and a half ago, that you are a Texan first and an American citizen second. And you see no contradiction in this duality. Sam Houston was right, however. Texas as a bounded area and a political entity can survive only within the federal union. But, James Love and friends were also right. Texans are Americans, but Americans are not necessarily Texans. The "Empire of Texas" is a state of mind that exists within the federal union. And that is the Texas dialectic.

ACKNOWLEDGMENTS

When I opened the middle drawer of Margaret Swett Henson's rusty file cabinet and discovered her unpublished manuscript of the letters to Albert Sidney Johnston, I did not know I was beginning a long personal journey, one that allowed me to befriend many wonderful people, both past and present, and to explore an era of Texas history that I wish I had discovered earlier.

To complete this project required funding, research, and guidance. Luckily, I found plenty of each. Terry Jones, a professor of history at the University of Louisiana at Monroe who specializes in Civil War history, and Archie McDonald, Regents Professor of History at Stephen F. Austin State University in Nacogdoches, Texas, read Margaret's original manuscript and encouraged me to expand her work and find a publisher. Dr. John Huddleston, a professor of history at Schreiner University in Kerrville, Texas, acted as my Texas history sounding board and critiqued my early drafts.

I especially wish to thank Wilbur E. Meneray, assistant dean for special collections at the Special Collections Division of the Howard-Tilton Memorial Library at Tulane University, for allowing me to research that wonderful archive. He helped me navigate the Albert Sidney Johnston Collection and encouraged me to continue Margaret Henson's work. Director Casey Green and the staff at the Texas Collection of the Rosenberg Library in Galveston, Texas, provided the illustrations for this book and a permanent home for Margaret Henson's papers. And the interlibrary loan staff, especially Ramona Treviño, at the Jack Williams Library at Texas A&M University at Galveston performed wonderfully in spite of my incessant rumblings about long-forgotten books. I also wish to thank John W. Crain, the director of the Summerlee Foundation, who awarded this project a grant to support the publication of this manuscript. A generous research grant from the Texas A&M University at Galveston Research Office allowed me to travel to New Orleans, Louisiana, and examine the Albert Sidney Johnston Collection at Tulane University.

Special thanks go to the staff at the Texas A&M University Press. I want to sincerely thank Maureen C. Bemko, my copy editor, for her spectacular editing job. And somehow Thom Lemmons, my managing editor, brought all the pieces together. I owe a huge debt to my editor, Mary Lenn Dixon. Her sage advice and constant encouragement helped me complete this work.

Had Margaret's family, her daughter Kathleen Duncan and sons Mike, Peter, and Steve, not consented to this project, I would not have taken this voyage of discovery through early Texas history. Thanks for the memories. And finally, without Bernie's help I would have never finished this project.

THE TEXAS THAT MIGHT HAVE BEEN

EDITOR'S INTRODUCTION

Donald Willett

Shortly after I agreed to bring this project to press it dawned on me that I am by training a maritime labor historian, not a scholar of early Texas history. However, the personal contacts that I made over the years with Margaret Swett Henson convinced me that I needed to finish her work, even if it was in a new field of study. Undeterred, I vowed to do my best to honor and complete the scholarship that Margaret so nobly launched. And I thought that, along the way, maybe I too would befriend some of the greatest figures in the historiography of early Texas and learn from their stories. Heeding the mantra "read the classics" helped me to commence this project. I soon developed another mantra: "If you can't find it in the *Handbook of Texas Online*, Google it."

As a novice historian of early Texas I quickly learned two things. First, I realized that Margaret had a keen eye for important documents in early Texas history. These letters she selected are a treasure trove of information and insights that both the specialist and general reader should enjoy. Second, I realized that I was totally ignorant of many of the persons, places, and events that the letter writers mentioned in their correspondence. To overcome this failing I have tried to implement the following sage advice from my graduate school mentors: "If you don't know it, find it, then footnote it."

In reediting this manuscript I tried to follow Margaret's original intent, but I have also attempted to apply my own personal touches. I visited the Special Collections Division at the Tulane University library and viewed the Albert Sidney Johnston Collection. There were several very interesting letters in that collection that I wanted to include in this book. However, I chose not to compromise the integrity of Margaret's original research. Therefore I only included those letters that she selected for her 1980 manuscript.[1] Since I am a self-confessed novice in this area of historical knowledge, I felt it necessary to flesh out her secondary research, not only for my own edification but for those readers who might not be as well versed in Texas history as Margaret and her peers. So with rare exceptions I deleted Margaret's original footnotes and started from scratch, providing a brief sketch the first time most new persons, places, or events appeared in a letter. Later I tried to update the biographical information on individuals each time a letter writer mentioned them. Still there were numerous persons, places, and events that I could not find. I hope that my limited expertise on this topic will not deter the reader from enjoying these important letters written to the "Dear General." It is my hope that everyone will enjoy these letters because they are a window, sometimes smudged, that opens upon an exciting period of Texas history.

There are a number of topical threads that are woven into the fabric of these letters. Many are serious, others are interesting, and some are comical. One major thread concerns the economic well-being of Texas. Until 1846 the economic news in Texas usually was bad. Most letters bemoan the chronic insolvency of the Republic of Texas' national treasury. One could almost judge the mood of the nation by the success or failure of various government agents in their attempts to sell government bonds or find economic entities that would lend money to the struggling republic. Interestingly, no one in these letters ever called for a tax hike to stabilize the government's expanding indebtedness. Most letter writers expected that a growing economy would balance the government's budget. It never happened.

Another topic that seems to have prompted great despair was the continual disintegration of the republic's various issues of currency. The writers meticulously noted the rise and decline of various Texas notes. Interestingly, any rumor that a Texas agent had negotiated a loan for the Texas government temporarily improved the currency's exchange rate. But each rejection of a Texas loan sent the republic's currency crashing to a new low. As the local currency collapsed in value, most Texans, including these letter writers, engaged in barter or land speculation.

These letters clearly point out that friend and foe in Texas eagerly engaged in land speculation. The "Texas Troika" of James Love, Albert Triplett Burnley, and Albert Sidney Johnston bought and sold land with the best of them. These men used their political contacts, insider information, and Johnston's sterling reputation to buy land throughout Texas. Speculations in Galveston, San Luis, Oyster Creek, Austin, Houston, East Texas, and the area around San Antonio sometimes turned a profit but other times produced a loss. And anyone was fair game. When agents for the German Emigration Company landed in Galveston and toured Texas looking for a potential colony, the Texas Troika and others followed the Germans' progress like hungry wolves.

Clearly Albert Sidney Johnston was a magnificent warrior and an able administrator, but personal finance was not one of his strong points. Both of his biographers briefly note his financial woes but do not elaborate on this aspect of his life. These letters suggest that Johnston's time in Texas was a financial disaster. He spent much of his stay in Texas one step ahead of the debt collector. His family lived in near-squalid conditions. Without constant financial aid from Burnley and Love and their devotion to his economic well-being, Johnston and his family would have resided in a debtors' prison. The nadir of Johnston's land speculations occurred in 1849 when he lost his beloved plantation, China Grove, to foreclosure.[2] Fortunately, timely intercessions that year by Burnley and Love persuaded President Zachary Taylor to hire Johnston as an army paymaster. This job saved the family from bankruptcy.

The Kentucky connection is another interesting thread that runs throughout these letters. James Love and Albert Sidney Johnston spent their formative years in Kentucky. When they immigrated to Texas, neither man cut personal, political, or social ties with their acquaintances in the Bluegrass State. Both men maintained contact with a large number of Kentuckians, including the two most powerful politicians in that state, Henry Clay and John J. Crittenden. One wonders if Clay in 1844 sought Johnston and Love's advice before he made the fateful decision during his presidential campaign to oppose the admission of Texas into the federal union. Love's comment in the last letter of this collection, "If I met John J. Crittenden in conflict, I would prefer killing him to a Comanche," graphically illustrates the anger and disappointment Love felt toward his mentor when he learned that the old Kentuckian refused to take an oath of loyalty to the Confederacy.[3] Love and Johnston also kept in constant contact with other important Kentuckians, including General Leslie Combs, who served with Love in the Kentucky state legislature; James Erwin, Henry Clay's son-in-law; and Aaron K. Wooley, who was Johnston's fellow cadet at West Point and also served in the Kentucky state legislature with James Love. These men were the core of a group of Kentuckians I affectionately refer to as the "Kentucky Brotherhood." The other members of this gang, including Love and Johnston, called Texas their home.

These letters mention a number of former Kentuckians who maintained contact with Love and Johnston while they resided in Texas. The first Kentuckians to gain credence in the Lone Star State entered during the Texas Revolution. Led by Sidney Sherman these Kentucky volunteers won fame and martial glory at the Battle of San Jacinto. Other Kentuckians who served Texas after the revolution included Peter Wagner Grayson, the first attorney general of the republic, and General Felix Huston, who shot Albert Sidney Johnston in a duel but later became his friend. Another Kentuckian of note was Richard Fox Brenham. He served as a civil commissioner for Texas on the ill-fated Santa Fe expedition. When he returned to Texas he volunteered for the Somervell expedition to northern Mexico and later participated in the Mier expedition. He died while trying to escape his Mexican captors. Another prominent Kentucky-Texan whose name appears in these letters was Thomas McKinney. He helped both to finance the revolution and found the city of Galveston.

After the revolution a second wave of Kentuckians moved to Texas. This younger cohort gravitated toward Love and Johnston and sought their advice and approval. One of these was Alexander Parker Crittenden, a distant relative of John J. Crittenden. Alexander Crittenden was an ambitious lawyer who lived in Galveston and socialized with Love and Johnston. A third Crittenden in this gang was John J. Crittenden's eldest son, George Bibb Crittenden. A graduate of West Point, he entered Texas in 1842 and quickly accepted a commission in the army. He soon found himself on the losing side during the Mier expedition. The youngest member of the Kentucky Brotherhood was James Love's nephew, a law student named William Pitt Ballinger. He lived in Galveston and served under Albert Sidney Johnston during the U.S.-Mexico War.

These Kentucky-Texans wanted Albert Sidney Johnston to seek political office and use his potential power to mold Texas politics. From 1838 to the end of the republic they encouraged Johnston to run for the presidency. However, their pleas for him to campaign in 1841 and in 1844 fell on deaf ears.[4] As late as 1860 James Love encouraged Johnston to "take care, old fellow, or you will be [U.S.] President after awhile, a station that no honest man in these desperate days ought to hold, but I dare say that Madam [Mrs. Johnston] (my very good friend, I hope) would have no objection in the White House to receive the Congress & their ladies."[5] The mention of so many Kentuckians in these letters, their powerful connections with Albert Sidney Johnston, and their Machiavellian political ambitions may suggest that the Kentucky Brotherhood warrants further investigation.

And what about Texan migrations to California? At the end of the U.S.-Mexico War several of Albert Sidney Johnston's closest friends migrated to California. They included Alexander Parker Crittenden, who left for California in 1848 and soon became involved in state politics. He served four years in the state legislature and chaired its judiciary committee. He later moved to San Francisco and became one of the state's leading lawyers. In 1870 he died at the hands of his spurned mistress, Laura D. Field.[6] Another friend was Tod Robinson, who moved to California in 1850 and served one term as a state district judge. He later made his home in Sacramento and established a successful law practice there. In 1865 Robinson moved to San Francisco, where he undoubtedly socialized with Alexander Parker Crittenden. Another Texan who moved west was James Robinson. A veteran of the Battle of San Jacinto, Robinson moved his family in 1850 to San Diego, California, and served as district attorney from 1852 to 1855 and as school commissioner in 1854. He purchased a large amount of property and helped to promote a railroad from El Paso to California. Robinson died in San Diego in October 1857. Another Texas émigré to the Golden State was General Thomas Jefferson Green. He moved to California in 1849 and served in the first state senate. He cosponsored legislation to establish the University of California. After his legislative career ended he served as a major general in the state militia. Another Texan who briefly moved to the Golden State was Ben McCulloch. This former Texas Ranger arrived on the West Coast in 1849 and promptly headed for the gold fields. He did not strike it rich, but he did serve one term as sheriff of Sacramento. Another Texan mentioned in these letters who migrated to California was John Coffee Hays, probably the most famous Texas Ranger. He arrived in San Francisco in 1850, and that same year San Franciscans elected Hays their new sheriff. He took the oath of office on the same day his dear friend, Ben McCulloch, took the oath as sheriff in Sacramento. All of these men had several things in common. They knew and admired Albert Sidney Johnston. They were members of the Whig Party. They helped to shape the early history of Texas. And they helped to shape the early history of the state of California. Is there a larger California-Texas historical connection? These letters suggest that such a connection exists, and further research should be undertaken to uncover it.

Another thread running through these letters is "aches and pains." Almost every letter comments on health issues. Constant queries about family health and well-being were more than courteous inquiries. They were pleas to know if dear friends were still healthy. During this letter writing period disease was rampant in Texas. Most somber were the comments on the frequent outbreaks of yellow fever. Letters written during the 1844 epidemic posted long lists of victims of the so-called "Black Vomit." Many were friends of Johnston and Love. Some names tragically appeared in earlier letters. Comments by James Love on the loss of his beloved son-in-law, Richard Morris, were most telling. Love actively participated in the Howard Association, an organization founded to help victims of the yellow fever epidemic, and his willingness to render aid and comfort to fellow Galvestonians during this outbreak was saintly and heroic.

The practice of medicine in Texas during this period was quite primitive. There were some good doctors. Ashbel Smith of Galveston and Anson Jones of Brazoria, both mentioned in these letters, were examples of skilled practitioners. But most families used home remedies to battle illness. These letter writers sometimes followed what were known as Thomsonian medical theories, which promoted the use of local herbs to treat illness. Examples included drinking a tea made from the Jerusalem artichoke to cure bronchial problems and ingesting tobacco products to heal nervous exhaustion, a treatment prescribed for President Mirabeau B. Lamar. These letters suggest that alternative medical practices were an integral part of everyday life in Texas.

Another startling thread that appears in these letters was the frequent practice of dueling. In twenty-first-century Texas when someone sullies your honor, a civilized person threatens to sue them in court. In early-nineteenth-century frontier Texas when someone tried to blemish your good name, a solid citizen challenged the antagonist to a duel. The most dramatic example is Albert Sidney Johnston's letter challenging Sam Houston to a duel.[7] One can only speculate how Texas history would have changed if this duel had actually taken place and one of these men had died. The most tragic duel mentioned in these letters occurred when Lysander Wells accused William Redd of ruining the moral reputation of a young woman from Georgia. A certified marriage license in Redd's bloodied pocket proved Wells wrong and cost both men their lives.[8] Even James Love agreed to a duel. He challenged Commodore Edwin Moore "to fight at sundown on the beach [in Galveston] with rifles at 40 paces back to back, to fire when you pleased and as you pleased," after Moore supposedly attacked Samuel May Williams's good name.[9] And how can anyone forget the infamous Memucan Hunt–James S. Mayfield feud? The eight-letter interchange between these potential combatants is a humorous episode of frontier honor.[10]

The most important thread running through these letters is Love and friends' attitude toward Sam Houston and his views on Texas. At one level these letters testify to the sheer personal hatred between these correspondents and Houston. Constant name-calling and stinging criticism of Houston and his political machinations punctuate these letters and grace other written documents.[11] Obviously, many of these attacks were personal, and we do not know how many were true. Simply stated, these men did not like Sam Houston.

Not all of the writers' antipathy toward Houston was personal. On another level these stinging observations suggested displeasure with Houston's philosophy and politics. In letters written during the Republic of Texas period the many references to conflicts between Whigs and Jacksonian Democrats in the United States (and to their Texas equivalents, that is, Houston versus anti-Houston clashes in the republic) suggested a growing political and philosophical polarity within Texas. Love and friends wanted Texas to remain independent and chart its own course among the nations of the world. Houston did not.

How far would these men go to preserve their vision of Texas? In an 1844 letter to a friend in Kentucky James Love speculated that Texas could chart its destiny if it could win diplomatic recognition from Mexico, open Texas to large-scale European immigration, and end the institution of slavery. He noted, "If Texas could be tempted to abolish slavery, by the adoption of organic laws, her best and most generous patron and friend would be England. The abolition society there, backed by her Majestys [sic] ministers are ready to pay us their face value and apprentice them for a term of years, at nominal wages only, and to take public lands at U. States prices in payment of the money advanced. Added to this the guarantee of our independence by Mexico, and the certainty of an immense European emigration to purchase these lands already appropriated." In his opinion the only barrier to achieving this goal was the land of his birth. "If she [the U.S. government] would let us alone, we could soon settle our affairs in a manner to suit us, but it seems she will neither do that, or take any decisive steps to give us peace. And the first moment we engage in negotiations with other powers to give us peace, she forbids it, and then leaves us to our fate."[12]

And what was that fate? Texans did not abolish slavery in 1844, but they gave up their political independence the following year. They joined the

Union and embraced American citizenship. But to this day Texans remain philosophically polarized. Are they Texas-Americans or American-Texans? Is James Love and friends' view—that Texans are distinct—correct? Or was Sam Houston more accurate in his view that Texans are Americans who live in Texas? Nobody really knows.

You see this polarity in the way historians interpret Texas history. Most twentieth-century historians, including Eugene Barker and T. R. Fehrenbach, portrayed Texas as a land inhabited by larger-than-life villains and heroes. When they entered Texas they somehow changed. And this metamorphosis molded Texas history and changed the world. Recent historians have revisited these epic figures and events, and these later scholars do not agree. They portray these figures as mere mortals who possessed human frailties and fatal flaws. They sometimes acted in a heroic fashion, but usually they did not.

You see this polarity in institutions of higher learning. Some Texas universities, public and private, view themselves as institutions of academic excellence that are by chance geographically displaced. They believe that they could, and probably should, excel on either coast. Others Texas universities are proud of their Texas roots and believe other American universities should emulate their goals and traditions.

You can see this polarity in Texas urban centers. Some Texas cities tout their urbane sophistication and compare themselves to other American centers of culture and cuisine. Other large Texas towns fully embrace all things Texan. They like their cowboy fashions, Texas music, and Tex-Mex barbecue, and they do not care if anyone else agrees with them.

Finally, and most importantly (if you are from Texas), there is professional football. One football franchise in Texas proudly proclaims that they are "America's Team." The other football franchise calls themselves the "Texans," and each team annually challenges the other for the athletic and philosophical supremacy of Texas. Truly, James Love and friends and Sam Houston would be impressed that their differing views still linger in twenty-first-century Texas. It is a Texas dialectic that continues to march through time.

INTRODUCTION

Margaret Swett Henson

These selected letters to Albert Sidney Johnston from his Texas friends are a valuable source of information about the political, social, and economic conditions from the days of the republic to the Civil War. This correspondence offers new views and details about events and personalities that shaped the Lone Star State and most importantly allows the reader to glimpse what opponents of Sam Houston thought about the tactics the Old Hero used while twice president of the republic (1836–1838, 1841–1844) and U.S. senator (1846–1859).

The bulk of the letters, sixty-seven to be exact, are from James Love, a transplanted Kentucky Whig who settled in Galveston in 1838. Born in Nelson County, Kentucky, on May 12, 1795, he was eight years older than Johnston. At the age of seventeen Love volunteered for service in the War of 1812. After the war he studied law and passed the bar exam. He served in the Kentucky House of Representatives from 1819 to 1831 and served one term as the Speaker of the House. In 1833 he served one term in the U.S. House of Representatives. In 1837 he moved to Houston and opened a law office in the then-capital of the republic and became well acquainted with all the prominent figures of the day. Like the others, he dabbled in land speculation and acquired large tracts of land along Oyster Creek in neighboring Brazoria County. He built a plantation on this rich alluvial land that produced cotton and later sugar. He invested in stock in the newly formed Galveston City Company and was a member of its original board of directors. This board was a powerful force on the Island because it controlled the forty-six-hundred-acre site of the new port city. Except for a single term as district judge and service at the state annexation convention of 1845, Love took no active role in Texas politics. However, he was a bitter enemy of Sam Houston and devoted his energy to any individual who opposed the Old Hero. This mutual antipathy apparently reached a crescendo in 1842 when Houston, in a speech to some militia volunteers, suggested that Love and several of his friends should immediately be executed as traitors. Not to be outdone, Love, speaking to this same group, threatened to deport Houston back to the United States.

During the nine years of the Texas republic, no real political parties existed, and partisan activities centered around factions supporting Sam Houston or opposing him. Loyal Whig as he was, Love admitted in 1840 that "we are not ripe in Texas for making parties, nor is it in the power of anyone to form any."[1] Love and Johnston became Houston's enemies, and in 1838 they supported the candidacy of Mirabeau B. Lamar for president. Love hoped to make Johnston president of Texas, but circumstances prevented the culmination of this dream. The pair supported whoever ran in opposition to the Old Hero of San Jacinto. This collection of letters offers illustrations of the power brokering and the use of the patronage during the years of the republic and early statehood.

Until after annexation to the United States in 1845, Texans were unable to take part in party politics in the United States, but Love, Johnston, and their acquaintances retained a lively interest in Whig politics. Organized in the early 1830s from remnants of the National Republican Party and all those who opposed Andrew Jackson's Democratic Party, the Whigs looked to Henry Clay of Kentucky and Daniel Webster of Massachusetts as their main spokesmen. Neither of the pair achieved the presidency, though the party captured the White House in 1840 with William Henry Harrison and again in 1848, with Zachary Taylor. Clay was the party's candidate in 1844. He lost to Democrat James K. Polk over the issue of Texas annexation. Clay, trying to keep peace with northern abolitionist Whigs, stated that the time was not yet right for annexation. Polk and the Democrats championed an expansionist plank that favored Texas annexation. In the 1850s the question of slavery finally killed the Whig Party when sectional loyalty prevented the formation of national party platforms. Former Whigs drifted into other parties or coalitions before the Civil War.

Albert Sidney Johnston had family ties with the Whig Party. Born in Kentucky in 1803, he was named for the English Whig martyr, Algernon

Sidney, though protests from some family members changed Algernon to Albert. With help from his older stepbrother, Josiah Stoddard Johnston, who was a National Republican congressman (and later senator) from Louisiana and friend of Henry Clay, Albert Sidney entered the United States Military Academy at West Point and graduated in 1826. For the next eight years, Lieutenant Johnston served near the Great Lakes and in the Mississippi Valley. During the Black Hawk War he acquired a reputation for cool thinking and competent command. In 1834 he reluctantly resigned his commission in order to care for his dying wife. After her death the following year he left his two small children with their maternal grandmother in Kentucky and sought solace in military adventures in Texas.[2]

He arrived in the newly independent nation several months after the revolution ended. Even so, Texas welcomed a man of his experience. When Sam Houston became president in September 1836, he named Johnston senior brigadier general of the Texas Army to replace Felix Huston. Huston refused to surrender his command, and a duel between the two men ensued. Johnson was severely wounded and could not take command. He continued to serve as the senior brigadier general from February 1837 until the end of 1838. It was during this period that Johnston became disillusioned with Houston over the conduct of the army. The Old Hero, partly because of a lack of funds and partly due to diplomatic negotiations in progress, refused to authorize a campaign against the remnant Mexican army along the Rio Grande or the Indians who preyed on the western frontier. Disgusted with the inactivity and the lack of military supplies, Johnston wanted to resign, but each time his friends persuaded him to take an extended furlough.[3] This brief service as general permitted Johnston's friends to use this military title for the rest of his life although he did not achieve that rank again until 1861.

In December 1838 President Mirabeau B. Lamar named Johnston secretary of war in his cabinet, the position the Kentuckian held when this series of letters commences. But inactivity, with the exception of one campaign against the Cherokees in eastern Texas, and the continuing lack of money for the military department frustrated the former West Pointer. In March 1840 he resigned and returned to Kentucky to put his personal finances in order. Except for brief annual visits to Galveston and Brazoria to oversee his land speculations and visit with James Love, Johnston did not return to Texas until 1846, when the Lone Star State was annexed into the Union and the United States went to war with Mexico. Senator Sam Houston and other Democratic Party politicians from Texas made sure that the U.S. Army rejected Johnston's request for a command. Instead, Johnston served with distinction as a colonel in the First Texas Rifle Volunteers. In 1847 Johnston moved to his plantation, China Grove, northeast of Brazoria, where he remained until 1850.

In late 1849 his former commander, Zachary Taylor, now president, appointed Johnston paymaster for the U.S. Army in Texas. Five years later, the army promoted Johnston to the rank of colonel and placed him in command of the newly formed Second Cavalry and stationed him on the Texas frontier. He secured this choice appointment through the timely intercession of his close friend, Secretary of War Jefferson Davis. In 1857 he was detached from that command and sent to Utah to quell the Mormon rebellion, a task he completed in 1859. An assignment to the Pacific Department followed, but in 1861 the firing on Fort Sumter and the secession of Texas, his adopted state, forced Johnston to choose his homeland over his love of the U.S. Army. He submitted his resignation. The Confederacy quickly offered him command of the Western Department as a full general, thus restoring the rank he had first earned in Texas. On April 6, 1862, he died while leading his troops at Shiloh.[4]

Johnston inspired respect and admiration among his friends, who always addressed him as "Dear General." In his first four letters to Johnston in 1838 and 1839, James Love employed the formal "Dear Sir" but soon changed to the more warm and familiar "Dear General." In some ways, the use of "General" was like a first name. It retained the formality required by proper nineteenth-century manners and reinforced the southern love of military titles. First names were reserved for close family members. Johnston would never call Love "James." Instead he used "Dear Love," or even "My Dear Sir."

While it is impossible to positively identify the political affiliation of each of the letter writers, most seem to have at one time been Whigs. By the 1840s, some southern Whigs in the United States had become disillusioned with the growing influence of the abolitionist wing of the party and joined local Democrats. In Texas many Whigs jumped ship after annexation and joined the Democrats. There was a pragmatic political reason to identify oneself with the Democratic Party—the party of annexation. If a man had political ambitions in Texas he knew that the average voter viewed Whigs as elitists who opposed annexation. The editor of the *Telegraph and Texas Register* announced that some "pewter Democrats," his term for turncoat Whigs, changed parties for mere expediency.[5] In addition, after the party died in the early 1850s, and after Reconstruction, southern men preferred to identify themselves with the Democratic Party and to hide the fact that they had ever belonged to anything else. Except for isolated articles in newspapers or fugitive letters, this sleight of hand made it difficult to establish who was a Whig. Among the letter writers in this book Albert Triplett Burnley and James Reily in 1848 and again in 1852 were connected with the Whig Party. This confirmed the assumption that they were Whigs because their wives were daughters of prominent Kentucky Whig families.[6] The witty Alexander Parker Crittenden, a relative of Kentucky's John J. Crittenden, doubtless supported the party, as did Love's son-in-law, Richard Morris, and his nephew, William Pitt Ballinger.

It is tempting to label many of those who served in the Lamar administration as Texas Whigs, and the fact that James Love and Albert Sidney Johnston took such an active interest in the Lamar, or anti-Houston, faction seems to lend credence to this assumption. However, it is equally as easy to place Sam Houston in the Democratic Party; after all, he was Andrew Jackson's protégé, and when he entered the U.S. Senate, he sided with that party. Nevertheless, even if he had espoused Democratic Party principles in 1836–1838 and 1841–1844, he drafted into his service two men later identified as Whigs—Albert Triplett Burnley and James Reily—to serve as emissaries to the United States, and in the case of Burnley, to Europe. Evidently in Texas the problems of the new republic transcended nascent party lines, although James Love's letters strongly suggest a current of Whig Party loyalty pulsating below the surface. Perhaps these letters, combined with other sources, will produce a study evaluating the relationship between national politics and the Texas factions.

Another area ripe for study is the use of political patronage available to both the Houston and anti-Houston factions when each was in office. These letters only confirm and enhance what is obvious in the collections of correspondence of both Lamar and Houston. In 1839 Lamar "turned the rascals out" in a style usually associated with Andrew Jackson. He even removed innocuous and apolitical Gail Borden from the Galveston Custom House, a change Lamar regretted when his appointee became involved in a scandal. Moreover, these letters suggest that an appreciative Whig Party doled out considerable political patronage to Texas Whigs after Zachary Taylor won the presidential election of 1848. For example, in May 1848 James Love visited the future president. After this friendly meeting Love helped to draft the letter that secured the party nomination for Taylor. In exchange for this loyalty the new president named James Love clerk of the U.S. District Court in Galveston and appointed his nephew, William Pitt Ballinger, the new district attorney. And of course the Taylor administration named Albert Sidney Johnston the new paymaster of the U.S. Army in Texas.

Love may have turned to the American Party (Know Nothings) from 1853 through 1856, and in 1860 he definitely supported John Bell and the Constitutional Union Party. A strong Unionist, Love disliked the idea of secession and was one of only thirty Galvestonians who voted against secession. However, when his beloved Texas left the Union Love swore an oath of loyalty to the Confederacy and, although he was over sixty-five, joined the Eighth Texas Cavalry (Terry's Texas Rangers) and served for two years. In 1867 Texans elected him the first judge of the newly created Galveston and Harris County Criminal District Court. Shortly after Radical Reconstruction commenced, the military commander in Texas, General Charles Griffin, removed Love, along with the governor and most other Texas officials, from office and labeled him an "impediment to reconstruction." Ill health clouded his last years. He died at his home in Galveston on June 11, 1874, just past his seventy-ninth birthday.[7] These letters to Albert Sidney Johnston constitute the bulk of his papers on deposit in the Johnston Collection at Tulane, although there are scattered letters from him in other collections. His wife and oldest daughter died soon after he did, and what became of Love's personal papers remains a secret.

These letters detailing early Texas politics have remained almost unused by Texas historians. Only Llerena B. Friend, Tom Henderson Wells, and Marilyn Sibley visited Tulane University in New Orleans, where the collection is housed, and each utilized a portion of the correspondence in their works on Sam Houston, Commodore Edwin W. Moore, and Albert Sidney Johnston. In 1964 Charles P. Roland wrote a biography of Johnston based on the collection.[8]

In 1942 a great-granddaughter of Albert Sidney Johnston deposited the large collection of papers in the Howard-Tilton Memorial Library. Immediately following the Civil War, Johnston's eldest son, William Preston Johnston, began gathering his father's papers in order to write a biography, which he published in 1878: *The Life of Gen. Albert Sidney Johnston*. Young Johnston had been educated at Yale, and following service in the Confederate army, he joined the faculty at Washington (later Washington and Lee) College. In 1880 he became president of Louisiana State University and, in 1884, the first president of Tulane, where he remained until his death in 1899.

In editing these letters, the spelling and syntax of Johnston's nineteenth-century correspondents was preserved, but the editor [Henson] added punctuation to make the gossipy, informal phrases and sentences more readable. In a few instances, words were indecipherable due either to illegible handwriting or injury to the document, and such cases are indicated by brackets. All bracketed materials are editorial additions, but parentheses were in the original correspondence. People, places, and events are fully footnoted so amateur historians may read the document with ease. Errors of interpretation and identification lie totally with the editor, who hopes they have been kept to a minimum. The factual material in the footnotes is not accompanied by source citations but is from standard sources.

PART I

"The Glorious Excitement of Uncertainty"

1. Albert Sidney Johnston. Courtesy Prints and Photographs Collection, CN02281A, Dolph Briscoe Center for American History, University of Texas at Austin.

2. Sam Houston. Courtesy Special Collections, Rosenberg Library, Galveston.

3. Memucan Hunt. Courtesy Special Collections, Rosenberg Library, Galveston.

4. Mirabeau Buonaparte Lamar. Courtesy Special Collections, Rosenberg Library, Galveston.

5. William Pitt Ballinger. Courtesy Special Collections, Rosenberg Library, Galveston.

6. Hugh McLeod. From *Forgotten Texas Leader: Hugh McLeod and the Texan Santa Fe Expedition*, Texas A&M University Press, 1999.

THE LAMAR YEARS, 1838-1841

B y April 1838, when this collection of letters begins, the Republic of Texas was in a period of rapid transition. For two years this former Mexican territory had claimed its place among the other nations of the world. The results were unclear. After twenty-four months of independence the government worked within the legal limits prescribed by its constitution. Sam Houston, the first elected president of the republic, called for new elections and promised to hand over the reins of power to his legally elected successor. The resulting campaign was hard fought, but no one cried foul when the electoral committee proclaimed Mirabeau Buonaparte Lamar the winner. The political infrastructure of the Republic of Texas was stable and grounded.

On paper the newly formed Republic of Texas was massive. In reality most of the territory was uninhabited or underutilized. Between the Sabine and the Nueces rivers Euro-Americans settled near the coastline or cleared farmland close to the adjacent river valleys. Hispanics clustered near San Antonio, Nacogdoches, and the banks of the Rio Grande. "Civilized" Indians resided in East Texas. Everywhere else nomadic Indians reigned supreme. The Republic of Texas was a rough-and-tumble western frontier waiting to be civilized or at least tamed.

Texas' place among the other nations of the world was neither stable nor grounded. By April 1838 the only nation that diplomatically recognized the existence of the Republic of Texas was its northern neighbor, the United States of America. The Republic of Mexico, its former ruler and neighbor to the south, adamantly refused to acknowledge the independence of Texas. Instead Mexico claimed that this errant territory was in a state of rebellion and threatened to send military forces northward to crush the uprising. All of Europe agreed with Mexico's position. De jure and de facto Texas were not yet one. As evidenced by James Love's characterization of Texas' situation, written to Albert Sidney Johnston in his letter of May 15, 1843, it truly was a time dominated by "the glorious excitement of uncertainty."

"My brother will hand you this."[1] Thus begins this series of letters, most of which were written to General Albert Sidney Johnston by a group of friends from Texas.[2] In April 1838, when the first of these letters was written, Albert Sidney Johnston was the senior brigadier general in command of the army of the Republic of Texas. That December he became secretary of war under President Lamar. He held this position throughout 1839. During the period in which this first group of letters was written, 1838–1841, Johnston received letters from James Love, Albert Triplett Burnley, Charles Harrison, James B. Ransom, James Reily, Mirabeau Buonaparte Lamar, Thomas Jefferson Rusk, Hugh McLeod, Louis P. Cooke, Tod Robinson, Richard Morris, Alexander Parker Crittenden, and Samuel Alexander Roberts. In April 1838 James Love still resided in Houston. Later that year he moved his family and law practice to Galveston. Burnley, in April 1838, served as a loan agent in the United States and Europe for President Houston's administration. Burnley held a similar position during Lamar's presidency. Charles Harrison resided in Kentucky. James B. Ransom was President Lamar's private secretary. In 1838 James Reily was a law partner of Thomas Jefferson Rusk, and the following year he partnered with James Love. In 1839 President Lamar sent Reily to the United States to sell Texas government bonds. Hugh McLeod resided in East Texas and served actively in the local militia. Louis P. Cooke was a member of the Third Congress of Texas and in 1839 served as Lamar's secretary of the navy. Tod Robinson immigrated to Texas during this period and quickly established and edited the San Luis *Advocate*. In 1838 Richard Morris practiced law in Houston. He moved to Galveston in 1840 and successfully courted James Love's daughter. Alexander Parker Crittenden practiced law in Galveston. Samuel Alexander Roberts was a family friend of President Lamar and during this time period was the secretary of the Texas legation in Washington and later headed Texas' Department of State.

Unlike Sam Houston, his presidential predecessor, Lamar vigorously pursued diplomatic recognition from any or all nations. France in 1839 became the first European nation to recognize the Republic of Texas. Texas ministers also proposed treaties with England, the Netherlands, and Belgium. However, all attempts to cajole Mexico into recognizing Texas' independence met with fatalistic indifference. When Lamar left office Texas' place among other sovereign nations, although improved, remained unclear.

Government finances were a major concern during the Lamar years. Texans believed that the only way the newly created republic could establish any type of financial stability and meet its growing fiscal obligations was to sell government bonds on the open market and print money. Beginning with the first Houston administration, the government of Texas sent special financial agents to the United States and Europe. If we are to believe these letter writers, all Texans, friend and foe alike, followed these financial missions with a keen eye. The slightest hint of a successful bond sale or bank loan boosted morale and improved the Texas currency exchange rate. When a special agent returned home empty handed the republic fell into a state of economic and mental depression. The Lamar administration continued the practice of sending out representatives to purvey government bonds. These agents included Albert Triplett Burnley, James Reily, and General James Hamilton, a former governor of South Carolina. In general these missions failed, and the Texas economy continued to spiral rapidly toward bankruptcy.

Another topic that excited these men's fancy during the Lamar years was the Texas Navy. These letter writers strongly disagreed with Sam Houston's hostile naval policy. They believed that Houston's dismantling of the navy during his first term left coastal Texas communities vulnerable to a Mexican naval blockade and opened the rest of the republic to another invasion. Lamar's friends believed that if he built a navy with offensive capabilities the Mexican military threat would evaporate. Command of the sea would allow the Texian Navy to engage and defeat the Mexican navy and blockade Mexican ports. These decisive actions would stifle Mexico's economy, bankrupt its government, and force it to acknowledge Texas' independence. For these gentlemen, a strong Texas navy, not annexation to the United States, was key to the survival of Texas.

These letter writers also supported Lamar's policies regarding Indians. Earlier they had opposed Houston's attempts to grant a deed of title to "civilized" Indians who had lived in East Texas since the late 1820s. When President Lamar ordered the Cherokee Indians to abandon their tribal lands or face military reprisals these letter writers applauded loudly. They encouraged their friend Albert Sidney Johnston to hurry into harm's way and grasp his fair share of martial glory before the saber and pistol determined these Indians' fate. When Lamar reversed Houston's pacific policies toward the Plains Indians and ordered the Texas Rangers and the frontier militia units to take the offensive and drive these Indians from their ancient homelands, many of these letter writers volunteered for action. For these men, and for most other white Texans, Lamar's Indian removal program was good government policy.

For Albert Sidney Johnston and his dear friends, the Lamar presidency, from 1839 to 1841, was their last chance to mold the Republic of Texas into a stand-alone nation. They failed. For most Texans Lamar's ethnic cleansing policies were a resounding success. The Indian removal policy in East Texas and the aggressive military operations against hostile frontier nomads transformed the republic into a racially homogeneous democratic republic for slave owners. Certainly, during the Lamar years the diplomatic status of the Republic of Texas improved dramatically. However, until Mexico recognized Texas' independence, it would not stand as an equal in the eyes of the world. On the high seas, or at least in the western Gulf of Mexico, the Texas Navy asserted command of the seas and complicated any attempt by Mexico to find a military solution to the Texas question.

Lamar's aggressive policies asserted temporary hegemony over Texas' boundaries, fostered growing diplomatic clout within the international community, gained command of the seas, and bankrupted the republic. The "no reelection" clause in the republic's constitution left Albert Sidney Johnston and friends facing their worst nightmare—no popular, like-minded presidential candidate to face their archnemesis, Sam Houston.

James Love to Albert Sidney Johnston

City of Houston[1]
April 28th 1838

Dear Sir,

My brother[2] will hand you this. I have asked him to look to you as a friend in all emergencies. I feel confident he will feel disposed to avail himself of your friendly advice on all occasions.

It was my intention to have seen you in San Antonio, but business of one sort or other will prevent me making that trip this present season.

I have heard you were greatly dissatisfied, and have no doubt you have sufficient cause. But still, I am clearly of opinion you ought not to leave the service at present.[3]

I think I see brighter prospects for Texas, and another will certainly place our affairs in a condition to assume the offensive. The next administration will feel disposed to distinguish itself in some way or other.[4] And nothing, you know, is so captivating as military renown and no way so sure a road to the favor of the *sovereigns*. Therefore, I think every exertion will be used to assume the offensive. From what I know, I incline to the belief we will, in the course of the summer, obtain the *success* of war and we will have on the Gulf a force sufficient to drive the Mexican fleet out of the waters.[5]

Grayson[6] will leave in a few days for the U.S. with full powers to negotiate on all these subjects. Application for admission will be withdrawn,[7] and I entertain but slight hopes that it will ever take place. Indeed, I do not know that any great good would result to us from it now. I have no news of particular importance.

Sincerely yours
Jas Love

Grayson sends his most particular compliments & says he backs all I say in this letter & consider his name as signed to it.

JL
Genl. A. S. Johnson [*sic*]
San Antonio

1. Houston, founded in 1836, served as the capital of the Republic of Texas from May 1837 to September 1839. "Houston, City of," *Handbook of Texas Online*, http://www.tsha.utexas.edu/handbook/online/articles/HH/hdh3.html [accessed September 5, 2007]. The *Handbook of Texas Online* has since moved to a new site: http://www.tshaonline.org/handbook.

2. "My brother" refers to Pallas Love, who died prior to December 1839. See Brazoria County Death Records, A, 243, Brazoria County Courthouse, Angleton, Tex.

3. In August 1836 Thomas Rusk appointed Albert Sidney Johnston adjutant general in the Texas Army. On January 31, 1837, President Sam Houston promoted Johnston to senior brigadier general in command of the army. "Johnston, Albert Sidney," *Handbook of Texas Online* [accessed September 20, 2004].

4. Since the constitution of the Republic of Texas did not allow a sitting president to succeed himself, three candidates—Mirabeau B. Lamar, Peter Grayson, and James Collinsworth—vied to succeed Houston in office. Tragically,

the latter two committed suicide before the election, Grayson on July 9, 1838, and Collinsworth on July 11, 1838. "Lamar, Mirabeau, Buonaparte," *Handbook of Texas Online* [accessed December 23, 2006]; "Grayson, Peter Wagener," *Handbook of Texas Online* [accessed January 2, 2005]; and "Collinsworth, James," *Handbook of Texas Online* [accessed December 23, 2006].

5. Love was wrong. No land battles between Texas and Mexico occurred that summer. The second Texas Navy did not commence operations until March 1839. "Texas Navy," *Handbook of Texas Online* [accessed December 31, 2006].

6. Peter Wagener Grayson was born on 1788 in Bardstown, Virginia (later Kentucky). He came to Texas in 1830, became involved in the revolutionary movement, and then helped to recruit volunteers in the United States. He served as attorney general during David G. Burnet's ad interim presidency and Sam Houston's first term. In 1838 Houston sent Grayson to the U.S. capital to procure a loan to purchase naval vessels and to negotiate an annexation treaty with the United States. He committed suicide in Tennessee in July, and Samuel May Williams assumed his mission. "Grayson, Peter Wagener," *Handbook of Texas Online* [accessed January 2, 2005].

7. In September 1836 Texans overwhelmingly voted for annexation to the United States, but the Martin Van Buren administration refused to consider the application. The administration feared Mexican retaliation and believed that bringing Texas into the Union as a slave state might persuade many voters to turn against the Democratic Party's presidential candidate in 1840. In October 1838 Anson Jones, the Texan minister to the United States, withdrew the application. "Annexation," *Handbook of Texas Online* [accessed December 16, 2004].

James Love to Albert Sidney Johnston

New Orleans
Feb 10th 1839

Dear Sir,

The *Cuba*[1] goes out in the morning and I regret that I cannot come with her. I am detained on account of private business, and a matter connected with the future as regards myself in Texas.

I have understood from Maj. Reily[2] this morning that he will return in the *Cuba*. And you will, of course, know the reason why he returns sooner than he contemplated when he left Texas. I am not in possession of such facts in regard to his powers touching the negotiation for the loan as to enable me to say certainly why the effort to obtain money has not succeeded. The general instructions would seem to give him full power to negotiate on any terms he might choose, and the only inference I can draw is that his *private* instructions are such as prohibits him from accepting terms that has been proposed. I have said to you in Texas, from knowledge I had of monied affairs in the South, and the effort required on the part of the Banks to sustain themselves under the operation of causes so disastrous to commercial pursuits,[3] would render the probability of any negotiation here founded on Texian security very remote. I know a different opinion has, and may still prevail in Texas, but the future will show that with one single exception, there does not exist the most remote possibility of obtaining money in the South upon almost any terms whatever in any reasonable time—if at all. I am not so familiar with the wants of the government as to express any opinion on the necessity of having money now, or how far that necessity should [illegible] in the sale of bonds at a depreciation that might be considered oppressive. But I do know from diligent inquiry from every source where money was likely to be had, with the exceptions I have named, you could not cash $500,000 of Texas bonds at 30cts the dollar. Nor do I believe even that sum could be had. In conversation on this subject with the Presidents and directors of Banks, there is one universal answer, and that is "we have our hands full, we must take care to sustain ourselves, and the times will not justify any risk in dealing in securities upon which we are not certain we can realize. We do not doubt your ultimate triumph, but we do not know *when* you may be able to consumate [sic] your revolution and establish the *credit* of your government on a basis to enable us to realize."

I have given Maj Reily all the aid in my power and every avenue has been opened to him to see if he could obtain money on terms advantageous to the government. And I do not believe one single offer has been made him except that from the Vicksburg Railroad and Commercial Bank through their agent, Mr. Beal, to whom they have delegated the power to treat. Mr. Beal, you know, has dealt largely in our funded debt and contemplates making further investments there. He seems to entertain confidence in our success and ultimate prosperity than almost any other. And as a matter of course, feels an interest in promoting any measure that may give confidence to the country. He has made the offer to give $210,000 in equal proportions of funded debt and promissory notes and $200,000 in cash and checks bearing an interest of 8 pr cent on Philadelphia, which of course, are equal, perhaps better than southern money in the North in all purchases the government of Texas may wish to make there—or he proposed to give $300,000 in cash and checks for the bonds of $500,000. Both these propositions have been declined by Mr. Reily. I do not say the government should accept these propositions, but I do say it is the best that can be done here. The only reason why checks are substituted for cash is to prevent the immediate return of those notes on the Bank to be cashed. If the money was to be paid out and circulated in Texas, they would prefer giving cash—because the return of the notes to the Bank would be slow & could be met without inconvenience. But to issue $300,000 and the government to use it in a short time, as they certainly would do, it would return immediately to the Bank and subject them to great inconvenience. No Bank that regards their credit and standing in these critical and doubtful times will do it. Connected with this subject, I will make a remark or two on another matter that seemed to have some bearing on the question of negotiations that was in relation to the circulation of the notes of the Bank loaning the money in Texas. Maj Reily objected to the privilege being given to the Bank for a longer period than two or three years. That restriction would at once put a stop to all negotiation. You will understand that Banks in the South do not want Texian bonds at any price [in] order to retain them for the *interest* they will receive on them. And the main inducement held out to influence them to take the bonds at all was the great advantages that would accrue to them at a future day by enlarging their circulation, in having their notes received in payment of dues to the government. It is to secure these *supposed* advantages (and I think they are only imaginary, they cannot be *real*) that the thought of buying the bonds has for a moment been entertained.

We have but to reflect one moment to know that Texas will establish a national Bank so soon as she can obtain the necessary capital for doing so. Whenever that is done, provided it is established on a solid basis, the circulation of the notes of that institution will drive all other bank notes from the Republic. We have a practical illustration of this in the fact at this moment, United States Bank notes are not bankable in this City, nor are the notes of the banks in this City bankable in Philadelphia. The notes of the Mississippi banks are not bankable here, and the notes of the banks here not bankable in Mississippi. Hence we see that the notes of specie paying banks in Texas will never circulate at par in the United States, nor will the notes of the banks in this country ever circulate to any extent in Texas. You must be aware that so long as ours is a depreciated currency, the notes of banks in this country will not *circulate* with us, and it is equally certain that the same thing will exist when a National Bank is established in Texas. If, however, those who *have money* will argue themselves into the belief that they see great advantages "*ahead*," which exist soley [sic] in the imagination, I have no objections if it helps us to the money. Our promissory notes are now worth no more than 40cts the dollar. And I beg nothing in saying that if it were necessary to lay out in this market $100,000 in Texas Treasury notes, to supply the absolute necessities of the Government, they would suffer a still greater depreciation. And I am not certain they could be sold at any price. I am fully confirmed in this opinion from the fact that I have made inquiry here at what price they would be received as collateral security upon six or twelve months time, and could not obtain anything from merchants upon them. If an arrangement of this kind could have been affected, it would have afforded the government relief from its temporary embarrassment, and the notes, before expiration of the time, could have been redeemed without loss. I have felt some anxiety that our government should be placed in a condition not only to protect herself at home, but to give us consequence abroad. This we all know cannot be done without the *sinews* of war. The best *sinew* is money.

Your department[4] is daily suffering no reputation from the want of the necessary means to defend the country. You cannot make it *respectable* without money, and altho[ugh] I have volunteered to write the History of *your* campaigns, I am of the opinion the less is written on that subject, the better, unless you can raise the means to justify a *demonstration*.

I will not disguise from you that some effort has been made here to discredit the President and to weaken that confidence in him which all here see disposed to entertain. I do not know from what quarter this effort has originated, but it has no effect. And all here who *really* love Texas have united not only to give confidence to him, but in doing so, to benefit their country.

Genl Lamar has the finest field open before him to acquire fame of any man on the continent. And altho his path may not be strewed with roses, I yet feel confident he will triumph, and the cause of the country with him. He has the confidence of the people at home, his reputation is high abroad, and give him the means, and I have no doubt he will render a good account. But how can the country prosper? how can he put in motion the necessary elements upon which success can alone be commanded without

means and credit? It is idle, in my opinion, to be *stickling* [sic] whether we get
a few thousand dollars more or less, whilst our citizens are slaughtered on the
frontier by the savage, whilst we are daily open to the insult of the Mexican,
and whilst our money is daily suffering a still more rapid depreciation, and
all the means of improvement in our condition is absolutely cut off. I know
his blood must chafe under these discouraging circumstances, and were I the
President, I would *cut* the knot at once, and not await the slow operation.
Of course, that may never take place. I *would* have money to begin with, and
every *honest* man in the country will approve the deed. When the first loan
of $500,000 is taken, I am sure there will be less difficulty in the next. And
in order to relieve the difficulties arising from selling the bonds at a low rate,
I send you a calculation based on the supposition that you will prefer the
loan at $200,000 in par funds and $210,000 in Texas, which will make the
price of the bonds at 94 5/20 the dollar. This is the price that will go to
the world, and it would not in any manner discredit the government. [See
the end of this letter for Love's computation of the interest.]

  I have written to you without disguise on this subject, because I
know you freely understand the relation I bear towards the whole affair,
and that I am not in the most remote manner connected in interest with it,
except so far as the negotiation of a loan by the government might be beneficial to the credit of the country. I make this remark because circumstances
transpired before I left Houston that made this impression on my mind. That
others thought as I was the avenue of communication to the government, I
was interested in the profits if any should arise. I disclosed to the Secretary
of the Treasury[5] and the President all I know, and results show that the terms
proposed are such as I represented they would be. And how the determination on my part to decline altogether the kindness of the President in
tendering me the appointment of Commissioner. I still feel grateful for the
confidence shown by this offer, but could not consent to place myself in an
attitude to be *suspected*.

  The whole case, as it stands, is at best comprised in a nutshell. If
discounts exist to make it necessary for the government to have money,
and they believe the terms are the best that can be had, they can avail
themselves of the proposition. If, on the other hand, they decide on reject-
ing the terms proposed, there is one end of the matter. And the agent here
will return the money and checks to the Bank. It is time matters should
be closed in some way, and unless such instructions are given as will make

the proposition sent, the basis of negotiation, the avenue now open will be closed forever.

You will have learned that the State Bank of Alabama and its branches have suspended specie payments. This has increased the timidity in money matters here, and general distrust seems to prevail. The banks all settle at the end of each week and keep no interest account.

I have seen a letter from Genl. Hamilton.[6] He does not propose being here before the 20th Inst. And will not come out in the *Charleston*,[7] which is expected on the 12th and is consigned to Reed.[8]

My family are in tolerable health. That of my daughter is yet precarious. We will leave on the 15th for Houston.[9]

My best respects to the Col. And say I hope his melancholy has left him and that the rumor of his rejection by Miss L has not increased it.[10]

Your friend
James Love

The difference betwixt the Interest on
$210,000 at 8 per cent and ten
per cent per annum is 4,200
and after Ten years is $42,000
To compound the Interest which we must
do to arrive at the *real* difference, we must
calculate the *annual* payment of Interest
say. $4200
9 Years Interest @ 10 % on 4200 is $3780
8 " " " " 3360
7 " " " " 2940
6 " " " " 2520
5 " " " " 2100
4 " " " " 1680
3 " " " " 1260
2 " " " " 540
1 " " " " 420 18,900
Saved in Interest 60,900
Price of Bonds 410—
Bonds at par 500,000 $470,900
500.000 Bonds @ 94 5/20 is 470,900

1. The *Cuba*, a 600-ton, 177-foot steamer that drew 13 feet, was built in Baltimore in 1837 and served as a regular packet between New Orleans and Texas. James E. Winston, "Notes on Commercial Relations between New Orleans and Texan Ports, 1838–1839," 34, no. 2 *Southwestern Historical Quarterly Online*, http://www.tsha.utexas.edu/publications/journals/shq/online/v034/n2/contrib_DIVL1372.html [accessed December 3, 2007].

2. James Reily was born on July 3, 1811, in Hamilton, Ohio. He graduated from Miami University (Ohio) and studied law at Transylvania University in Kentucky. He read law with Robert Todd in Lexington, Kentucky, and married a grandniece of Henry Clay. In 1836 they moved to Texas, where he served as a major in the Army of the Republic of Texas and aide-de-camp to Thomas J. Rusk. He became Rusk's law partner in early 1838. Later that year he joined James Love in a law partnership in Houston that lasted until Love moved to Galveston. President Lamar appointed him loan commissioner to negotiate the sale of $1 million in Republic of Texas bonds in the United States. The government instructed Reily to sell the bonds only to specie-paying banks and forbade him from accepting promissory notes or funded debt as payment. Lamar recalled him in April when no banks could offer terms acceptable to the Texas government. "Reily, James," *Handbook of Texas Online* [accessed September 29, 2004]. For Reily's instructions, see Charles Adams Gulick et al., *The Papers of Mirabeau Buonaparte Lamar*, 6 vols. (Austin: Von Boeckmann-Jones, 1921–1927), 2:458–59, 526.

3. Southern banks were still suffering from the effects of the Panic of 1837, which had resulted from inflation, land speculating, and President Andrew Jackson's monetary policies against the Bank of the United States. A bill to establish an Independent Treasury System, a federal depository system outside of regular banks, had passed the U.S. Senate in January and was pending in the House. Love and other Whigs (many of whom were bankers) deplored this scheme sponsored by the Democrats. It became law in June 1838.

4. Lamar appointed Johnston secretary of war on December 13, 1838. He served until March 1840, when he resigned. He believed that a lack of funds hampered any real show of force against the Mexicans and Indians. "Johnston, Albert Sidney," *Handbook of Texas Online* [accessed September 20, 2004].

5. This was Richard G. Dunlap, who was born in Knoxville, Tennessee, and served in the War of 1812 and the 1817 Seminole campaign in Florida. He moved to Texas in 1837, became secretary of the treasury in December 1838, and served until April 1840. He then served as minister from Texas to the

United States. "Dunlap, Richard G.," *Handbook of Texas Online* [accessed October 1, 2004].

6. James Hamilton was born in Charleston, South Carolina, on May 8, 1786. After completing his academic studies and passing the bar he established a law practice in his hometown. He fought in the War of 1812 and later served as mayor of Charleston. From 1819 to 1823 he served as the city's representative in the South Carolina House of Representatives. He next served the Palmetto State in the U.S. House of Representatives from 1823 until 1830, when he won election as governor of the state and served one term (1830–1832). While in the governor's mansion he, along with John C. Calhoun, led the state through the Nullification Crisis. While in South Carolina he strongly supported Texas independence. In late 1836 President David G. Burnet offered command of the Texas Army to Hamilton, but he respectfully declined. President Lamar appointed Hamilton a loan commissioner for the republic. "Hamilton, James," *Handbook of Texas Online* [accessed October 1, 2004].

7. The *Charleston*, a sidewheel steamer built in 1838, was designed as a packet that could carry 120 passengers. With the aid of James Hamilton and his British friend, James Holford, Texas acquired the steamer in November 1838 for $120,000. It underwent alterations that converted the vessel into a troopship. The Republic of Texas renamed it the *Zavala* in honor of the vice president of the ad interim government, Lorenzo de Zavala. He was a Yucatecan supporter of Texas who died in 1836. "*Zavala*," *Handbook of Texas Online* [accessed September 5, 2007].

8. James Reed was a commission merchant in New Orleans who, in partnership with James Morgan, operated a store at Anahuac in 1834 and whose schooner, *Flash*, aided in the Texas Revolution. "*Durango*," *Handbook of Texas Online* [accessed September 5, 2007].

9. Love resided in Houston at this time with his wife, daughter Mary, age about fifteen, and infant son, Joseph Eve Love. "Love, James," *Handbook of Texas Online* [accessed September 6, 2004].

10. Lieutenant Colonel Benjamin F. (or H.?) Johnson, who was assistant adjutant general, was courting President Lamar's younger sister, Loretto Rebecca. He fought alongside Lamar at the Battle of San Jacinto. Johnson later died in northern Mexico while on a diplomatic mission for President Lamar. A. K. Christian, "Mirabeau Buonaparte Lamar," 24, no. 3, *Southwestern Historical Quarterly Online* [accessed September 5, 2007].

James Love to Albert Sidney Johnston

N Orleans
Feb. 11th 1839

Dear Sir

I wrote you a long letter on yesterday on the subject of our prospects in negotiating a loan. Since I wrote, I learn it is uncertain whether Mr. Reily will return in the *Cuba* to Texas. Altho I inflicted on you a letter of such prodigious length yesterday, I will say once again this morning, that the only chance of obtaining money in the South is the one now under consideration. The future may bring better terms, but can we wait? If we can, it might be better to let the whole matter pass. But I do think we lose more by delay than we might gain in terms. I have now done with this whole subject and whatever may be the result, I content myself in the belief that the prevailing motive was a desire to serve the country. The Secretary of the Treasury[1] did not treat me with sincerity in this matter. He has *supposed* a state of case that did not exist, and taken for *granted* things, which if he had known me well, he would have believed impossible. We will let that pass. It only serves to give me another admonition that all who touch political matters wade in troubled waters. I assure you if you were out of the concern, my interest and feeling for the success of the administration would be greatly lessened.

The *long* letter you will see is confidential, but on reflection, I say if it can be of any service, you may read it to those who would likely be *benefited* by it. But this I leave to your own discretion.

Combs[2] has gone up the river. He has acquired the soubriquet [sic] of the Itinerant Storyteller and seems to be succeeding in his profession. Beal is sick and is taking *Thompsonian* [sic] medicine.[3] His friends think he will convalesce. He thinks not—we shall see.

We have a great deal of gaiety, hard times, and bad weather in the City. I will be with you as soon as I can. In the meantime, I hope you will not let the reputation of the office grow into disrepute, but will always keep a good supply of the *raw* material for friends.

Sincerely
Jas Love
Genl. A. S. Johnston
Houston

1. Richard G. Dunlap was secretary of the treasury at this time. "Dunlap, Richard G.," *Handbook of Texas Online* [accessed October 1, 2004].

2. Leslie Combs was born in 1793 in Clark County, Kentucky. He served in the War of 1812 and was a member of the Kentucky legislature (1827–1829 and 1833). In 1836 he was directed to lead ten companies of the Kentucky militia to the Sabine River, but the force disbanded before marching. General Combs was a Henry Clay Whig through 1848. http://www.combs-families .org/combs/families/c-les.htm [accessed September 10, 2007].

3. "Thomsonian medicine" was popular among early-nineteenth-century Americans. Samuel Thomson (1769–1843) believed that disease was the result of a decrease in "vital fluids" brought about by a loss of animal heat. He believed that vital heat could be restored by taking steam baths and ingesting cayenne (*Capsicum annum*). This would force toxins into the stomach, where they could be eliminated by emetics. http://www.steven-horne.com/Articles/ samuelthomson.htm [accessed September 10, 2007].

James Love to Albert Sidney Johnston

N. Orleans
Feb 17th 1839

Dear Genl

I will not leave this until the first of March. That is the longest *possible* time of postponement.

I do not know that I have anything to write to you either of general (or) of special interest. There seems to be increasing confidence in the certainty of our success as a nation. I meet daily with many who say they have changed their opinions and express regret that they ever were opposed to annexation and wish it had taken place. On the other hand, all who are in any degree conversant with Mexican affairs entertain the opinion that she must fall sooner or later, and in any event, the confused state of affairs there must result in benefit to us. We must look, of course, to the conflict that sooner or later must take place between the government forces and the Federalists. I think it probable that the Federalists will be subdued and that centralism will prevail. The only possible danger arising to us from the present state of things exists in the probability that the government forces will subdue the rebellion in the Eastern provinces,[1] and having a large force at their disposition, may again take it into their head to invade us.

I have no means of judging of what will probably be the decision of the President on the subject of the proposition to take the loan of $500,000. Judging from what occurred here, I suppose the terms proposed will not be acceded to. I do not now believe it is a matter of much consequence whether the authority be given or not. Circumstances have arisen which makes it improbable that it will be taken on any terms. I wrote to you before that the Southern Banks were in a condition that requires great sagacity to enable them to sustain themselves. That state of things seems to be on the increase, and they all show great timidity in extending their operations. And from what I know of this particular transaction, I am of the opinion they will for the present decline taking the loan.

Genl Hamilton has not yet arrived and it would not surprise me if he did not come at all. It seems to be certain that "Holford of Holford Place, Regent Street, London" will not.[2] So much for one great pillar of support from whose magic name gold was to be scattered sufficient for all our wants.

We have had a gay time of it in the City. Ladies balls, batchlor [sic] balls, masked balls, Monday evening *soirees* etc The *Great Western*[3] is here and dims other Ky belles.

Sincerely yours
Jas Love

Genl Hamilton writes that the *Charleston* will be here the 25th. She will leave Savannah on the 11th.

JL
Genl A. S. Johnston
Houston, Texas

1. The eastern provinces of Mexico that bordered Texas were Coahuila, Nuevo León, and Tamaulipas. Love's assessment was correct; the government forces (centralists) won.
2. James Holford was a banker whom General James Hamilton met in London. Expecting to profit from Texan securities and land, Holford provided funds to purchase the *Charleston*. Jim Hill, *The Texas Navy in Forgotten Battles and Shirtsleeve Diplomacy* (Austin: State House Press, 1987), 108.

3.   Love's comment about the Great Western dimming other Kentucky belles
      suggests that he meant Sarah Bowman, whose nickname was the "Great
      Western." However, there is no record of Sarah Bowman visiting New Or-
      leans in 1839. The *Great Western* was also the name of a steam packet run-
      ning from New York to New Orleans.

Albert Triplett Burnley to Albert Sidney Johnston

Galveston
Feby 25 1839

Dear Genl

Finding Mr. Reily here on my arrival & consequently that my letter by him requesting Genl Hamilton to remain in Orleans until my arrival
there had not gone out, I[1] concluded it probable Genl H[amilton] would
come out in the *Cuba,* & therefore determined to wait her arrival. She
arrived this evening, & by Mr. Monroe Edwards[2] I learn that Genl Hamilton
had not reached New Orleans when he left there; that the *Charleston* had
not left New York on the 9th in consequence of the ice in the Bay; & that
Mr. Holford had returned to England. He has, no doubt, left his business to
be closed by Genl H.

The *Columbia* departs for Orleans tomorrow, & I go in her. I shall
probably meet Genl H in Orleans, & I think it doubtful whether he will
come to Texas —tho he may. Unless there is some special reason for his coming, I shall urge him to proceed on our mission without further delay.[3]

Enclosed I hand you the petition of my friend, T. W. Gilmer,[4]
addressed to Congress, praying for compensation for his services or expenses
as his *first* Commn [Commission] *with me* in attempting to negotiate the
loan. Congress having adjourned, I thought the petition too late, but thinking on the subject since I left you, it seems to me, the auditorial [*sic*] court is
vested with full power to settle the claim. I shall therefore esteem it a favour
if you will present it for Mr. Gilmer. You will find it placed by my endorsement under your control. Mr. Gilmer was in [the] Commission upwards of
12 months—and actively engaged in trying to negotiate the loan only 6 or 7
months. I feel confident he must have spent $2,000 in good money—besides
which, the allowance to Manard [Menard] & Yates,[5] the first commrs [com-
missioners], will afford a precedent by which to determine the allowance

to him. *Any* settlement which the government may think equitable, I am authorized to say, will be satisfactory to Mr. Gilmer.[6] Any allowance made him in Tr[easur]y Notes, please invest in Military scrip & hence into funded debt & hold it subject to my order.[7]

If Col. Bee[8] pays you the 100$ I gave you the order on him for, please send it by the first safe conveyance to Mrs. Bell[9] & say to her I sent it to her on account of, & at the request of Mr. Geo. B. Clelland, and who, I believe, owes her that amount or near it.

As to the claim which I left you on the Treasury amounting to $10,581.20, I wish you to retain [it] in your hands in Treasury notes subject to the order of the Reeds (the assignment of B. S. Reed) or to my order if I send you their authority to me to control it.

The amount of Reed's claim—say

-1,156
_____
9,424

I have already desired you to pay Gray[10] $200 & Sawyer[11] $1000

-1,200
_____
leaving $8,224.79

I wish you to purchase Military scrip immediately at the best price you can (you can purchase of Robinson[12] for 60cts and I think you had better not wait to get it lower, to say nothing of the trouble of buying it in small quantities) to the value of

5,224.79
_____
leaving $3,000.

The remaining $3,000 I wish you to retain until Dr. Jones[13] informs you whether he can purchase 5 shares of Galveston stock at $600. If he can, pay it over to him, & if I can get the use of the money from those to whom it belongs, you shall [have] half of it. If I cannot, then the purchase must be for the benefit of the owners of the money. If Jones says he cannot purchase the stock, then purchase Military scrip with the $3000 also & convert the whole $8224.79 into funded debt & hold it subject to my order. When converted into funded debt, if *that* can be converted into Galv.[eston] Stock at a sale equal to $600 per share in Treasury notes, I wish the whole of the funded debt disposed of in that way whenever an opportunity offers.

I will write you again from Orleans & *hope* to inform you of some arrangement *made* by which the $6000 will be ready for Karnes.[14] By the way, had you not better write to Van Ness[15] to examine critically the title to the property which we propose to buy? Most of the titles about Bexar are bad or doubtful, & our friend Karnes may not be a very good judge, & it would be *hell* to *borrow* this money to buy a bad title.

Make the best respects to Watrous,[16] Robinson, Col Johnson, McLeod,[17] in fact, all my friends, & I will do the same favour for you in Louisville. I will see your children[18] & give your love to Miss ____. Let me hear from you often & believe me

yr friend
A. T. Burnley

P.S. Please remind Judge Webb[19] (with my best respects) to send me to Phila[delphia]. to care of N. Biddle[20] a copy of the acts of the last session of Congress when presented, also an impression of the New Seal of State.

Genl A. Sidney Johnston
Houston Texas

1.   Albert Triplett Burnley was born in 1800 in Hanover County, Virginia. He read law with Judge (later Senator) George M. Bibb of Kentucky and married Bibb's daughter. He invested in a coal mine at Owensboro, Kentucky, with his uncle, entrepreneur Robert Triplett, and started a commission business in New Orleans. Burnley became interested in Texas when Triplett invested in the first Texas loan negotiated by Stephen F. Austin in January 1836 in New Orleans. In 1837, President Houston commissioned Burnley to seek a $5 million loan for the republic, but the attempt failed. He visited bankers in the Northeast in 1838 and later visited Europe, but his efforts were still unsuccessful. President Lamar recommissioned him in February 1839, and he accompanied James Hamilton as they continued to seek funds. These efforts also failed. He returned to Texas in January 1840 and purchased a plantation in Brazoria County, in the general vicinity of Albert Sidney Johnston's plantation. In 1850 he moved to Washington, D.C., and became heavily involved in Whig Party politics. "Burnley, Albert Triplett," *Handbook of Texas Online* [accessed October 4, 2004].

2.   Monroe Edwards was born in 1808 in Danville, Kentucky. He immigrated to the Galveston Bay area around 1825 and occasionally engaged in the illicit

importation of Africans to Brazil. He obtained a large land grant in Brazoria County and used his plantation as a base of operations for his illegal slave trade. At the time Burnley wrote this letter, Edwards was under indictment in Texas for forging his partner's name to a bill of sale. Within a few months he would jump bond and flee to Europe. "Edwards, Monroe," *Handbook of Texas Online* [accessed October 4, 2004].

3. Lamar appointed Burnley and Hamilton to negotiate with bankers in Philadelphia and/or Europe to secure the $5 million loan.

4. Thomas Walker Gilmer was born on April 6, 1802, in Albemarle County, Virginia. Gilmer studied law, practiced in Charlottesville, Virginia, and served in the Virginia House of Delegates (1829–1836, 1839–1840), including two sessions as Speaker. From 1840 until 1841 he served as governor of Virginia. In 1841 he entered the Twenty-seventh U.S. Congress as a member of the Whig Party and served until February 15, 1844. President John Tyler appointed Gilmer secretary of the navy. Gilmer was a member of the ill-fated party of visitors who died when an experimental gun on board the USS *Princeton* exploded while on a tour of the Potomac River. His death meant the loss of a valuable ally for President Tyler. Some historians suggest that his death may have delayed the Texas annexation effort. Naval Historical Center, http://www.history.navy.mil/photos/pers-us/uspers-g/t-gilmer.htm [accessed September 5, 2007]; http://bioguide.congress.gov/scripts/biodisplay.pl?index=G000218 [accessed September 5, 2007].

5. Michel Branamour Menard was born in December 1805 in La Prairie, near Montreal, Canada. He entered Texas in 1829 and became a land speculator and Indian trader. During the Texas Revolution he represented Liberty County at the 1836 Convention and signed the Texas Declaration of Independence. After the war he, along with Samuel May Williams and Thomas F. McKinney, founded the Galveston City Company. Andrew Janeway Yates was born in 1803 in Hartford, Connecticut. He arrived in Texas in 1835 and received a land grant in Liberty County. When the Texas Revolution broke out Yates joined the Texas Army. In late 1835 and 1836 the government sent him to the United States, where he served with Menard as a loan commissioner. Their efforts failed to raise money in the United States. "Menard, Michel Branamour," and "Yates, Andrew Janeway," *Handbook of Texas Online* [accessed October 4, 2004].

6. Gilmer's connection with Albert Brumley and their involvement in Texas' attempts in 1838 and 1839 to negotiate loans from U.S. banks explains why he, along with U.S. Secretary of State Abel Upshur and President John Tyler, in 1844 fought so hard for the annexation of Texas.

7. The funded debt of the republic was the long-term securities issued in the form of interest-bearing promissory notes from the government. They first appeared in the fall of 1837, payable in twelve months and carrying 10 percent interest. Issued in $1, $2, $3, $5, $10, $20, $50, $100, and $500 denominations totaling $500,000, the notes were known as "star money" because of the star printed in the center. A second issue in December increased the total in circulation to $650,000. An engraved series followed in January 1838, raising the total to $1,165,139. The printed notes circulated at par in specie, but by January 1839 the engraved interest notes dropped from 65 cents on the dollar to 40 cents specie. The investment character encouraged circulation in the United States. The government also issued military scrip as promissory notes for the payment of supplies and services. All of these notes circulated like money, although the name of the payee and endorsement were required. "Money of the Republic of Texas," *Handbook of Texas Online* [accessed November 3, 2007].

8. Barnard E. Bee was born in 1787 in Charleston, South Carolina. He served on the staff of his brother-in-law, Governor James Hamilton, and influenced Hamilton to leave South Carolina and come to Texas in 1836. During the Texas Revolution he served as secretary of the treasury and later as secretary of state under the ad interim administration of David G. Burnet. He was one of the three commissioners who accompanied the defeated General Santa Anna to Washington, D.C., after the Battle of San Jacinto. Bee returned to Texas in 1837 and served as secretary of war in Houston's first administration. Lamar made him secretary of state. In February 1839 he resigned his cabinet position and traveled to Mexico as a special negotiator, hoping to secure recognition of Texas independence. This mission, the first of three sent by Lamar, ended without success. In 1840 he replaced Richard G. Dunlap as Texas minister to the United States. Sam Houston, after his second inauguration as president, replaced Bee with James Riley. "Bee, Barnard Elliott, Sr.," *Handbook of Texas Online* [accessed October 4, 2004].

9. Mary Eveline McKenzie Bell, widow of Josiah Hughes Bell, came to Texas with her husband in 1821. Bell owned land near Columbia on the Brazos River. He developed a sugar plantation along the banks of the river and subsequently laid out the two towns that came to be known as East Columbia and West Columbia. "Bell, Josiah Hughes," *Handbook of Texas Online* [accessed November 7, 2007].

10. William Fairfax Gray was born in 1787 in Fairfax County, Virginia. In 1835 he first visited Texas while acting as a land agent for Albert Burnley and

General Thomas Jefferson Green. He attended the Convention of 1836 at Washington on the Brazos. In 1837 he moved his family to Houston, where he practiced law and served as clerk in the Texas Congress (1837), secretary of the Texas Senate (1838), and clerk of the Texas Supreme Court (1840). "Gray, William Fairfax," *Handbook of Texas Online* [accessed October 4, 2004].

11. Frederick A. Sawyer, a lawyer from North Carolina, came to Texas in 1836 as an aide to General Thomas Jefferson Green and served as secretary of war in Burnet's cabinet. He settled at Velasco and represented Brazoria County in the Texas Congress. "Sawyer, Frederick A.," *Handbook of Texas Online* [accessed October 11, 2004].

12. Tod Robinson was born in 1812 in Anson County, North Carolina, grew up in Alabama, and later lived in New Orleans. In 1839 he immigrated to Texas. He served in the Texas House of Representatives for Brazoria County, which was Albert Sidney Johnston's home county, from 1841 to the end of the republic. He chaired the House's finance committee. He later became a prominent Whig politician in California. "Robinson, Tod," *Handbook of Texas Online* [accessed June 11, 2004].

13. Dr. Levi Jones was born in 1792 in Virginia. He came to Texas in 1833 to speculate in land. In 1837 he was an original investor in the Galveston City Company and became its agent in April 1838 until replaced by Gail Borden Jr. in 1839. "Jones, Dr. Levi," *Handbook of Texas Online* [accessed October 11, 2004].

14. Henry Wax Karnes was born in 1812 in Tennessee. He first came to Texas from Tennessee in 1828 and returned in 1835. During the revolution he served in the Texian army and fought at Concepción, the siege of Bexar, and San Jacinto. He continued to serve the republic as a scout and military leader against Mexicans and Comanches west of San Antonio. Like many others, he engaged in land speculation. "Karnes, Henry Wax," *Handbook of Texas Online* [accessed October 11, 2004].

15. Cornelius Van Ness was born in 1803 in Burlington, Vermont. He was the son of the governor of Vermont, and in 1829 he accompanied his father to Spain, where the elder Van Ness served as the U.S. minister until 1837. The younger Van Ness returned home in 1836. Fluent in Spanish, in March 1837 he immigrated to San Antonio, where he practiced law. In 1837 he served as district attorney for the city, and from 1838 to 1842 he represented Bexar County in the Texas Congress. "Van Ness, Cornelius," *Handbook of Texas Online* [accessed October 11, 2004].

16. John Charles Watrous was born in 1806 in Colchester, Connecticut. He studied law in Knoxville and in the 1830s practiced law in Tennessee, northern Alabama, and Mississippi. In 1837 he immigrated to Texas, where he served as a land agent for several Texas land companies and accepted stocks in lieu of fees. In 1838 President Lamar appointed him attorney general, and he served in that office until conflicts of interest in 1840 forced him to retire. "Watrous, John Charles," *Handbook of Texas Online* [accessed October 11, 2004].

17. Hugh McLeod was born in 1814 in New York City and graduated from West Point in 1831. He resigned his commission and arrived in Texas shortly after the revolution ended. He served under General Albert Sidney Johnston as adjutant general of the Texas Army. Later he fought and was wounded at the Battle of the Neches, participated in the Council House Fight, and led the military leg of the ill-fated Santa Fe expedition. "McLeod, Hugh," *Handbook of Texas Online* [accessed June 16, 2004].

18. Johnston's children by Henrietta Preston, who died in 1835, lived with their maternal grandmother. They were William Preston Johnston, age eight, and Henrietta Preston Johnston, age seven. An infant daughter, Maria, had died in 1834.

19. James Webb was born in 1792 in Fairfax County, Virginia. He practiced law in Virginia, Georgia, and Florida, where he was named district judge in 1825. He served in that capacity until 1838, when he resigned and immigrated to Texas. In Austin he became friends with President Lamar, who appointed Webb secretary of the treasury and later secretary of state, when Barnard Bee resigned from that position to accept the mission to Mexico. Webb served as secretary of state until May 1839, when Lamar appointed him attorney general. "Webb, James," *Handbook of Texas Online* [accessed October 11, 2004].

20. Nicholas Biddle was the president of the United States Bank in Philadelphia and a target for loan commissioners from the Republic of Texas.

James Love to Albert Sidney Johnston

N Orleans
Feb 27ᵗʰ 1839

Dear Genl

I expected to have left on the boat by tomorrow, but await the arrival of Mr. Burnley who writes he will come over on the *Columbia*. I shall then leave as soon as I can. The last letter from Genl Hamilton states that he will be here on the 1st certainly. There is no news of the *Charleston;* I presume she is on her way.

You will naturally feel some anxiety about the loan and I wish I could give you something definite on that subject, or in other words, say you would be *certain* to get it. I wrote you before that I was fearful of delay, and circumstances have taken place that places the whole matter in a *doubtful* attitude. It will require eight days to have it determined. I cannot write you the particulars, because I am not permitted to do so. It is sufficient to say that every means have, and will be used to consumate [*sic*] the arrangement. However high our credit should be, there yet exists some fear and trembling on the subject of Texian securities. The basis of our credit is not as yet sufficiently established to induce capitalists to advance freely. You will recollect that this subject has cut a prominent figure in our affairs for more than two years, *and we have not yet borrowed a dollar.* I cannot say when we will be able to do so. But I have said enough about this, more than I shall ever again say on any subject connected with our affairs.

I am sorry too, to hear there exists so much dissatisfaction with Genl Lamar. I had hoped his administration would have been supported by the united voice of the whole people, as I feel confident his desire is to serve his country. I am *certain* that a powerful and organized effort will be made to prostrate him; let his friends prepare for it in time. A minority in Congress wants [to] so cripple him, that all his efforts would be unavailing. *You,* I know, will "stand up to the rack" in all honest things, but it is hard to say who else will.

Hancock[1] is here and will probably come over with me to Houston, or before me.

The price of our money is something better today. It is worth 25c[en]ts. I bought yesterday $4,000. I would have bought a considerable sum, but I was really afraid that the price in Texas would be so large as to reduce its value.

Sincerely yours
Jas Love

I shall take care to have our *tavern* supplied with the needful when I return.

Will you tell Mr. Harrison[2] it is of vast importance for me to demand all my funds immediately on my return, and the note he sent me cannot be collected. The man is gone.

Genl A. S. Johnston
Houston, Texas

1. George Hancock of Shelbyville, Kentucky, was the uncle of Johnston's first wife, Henrietta Preston, and his second wife, Eliza Griffin. "Hancock, George," *Handbook of Texas Online* [accessed June 15, 2004].
2. Colonel Charles L. Harrison led a group of volunteers from Kentucky to Texas in July 1836 and remained with the army through 1837. James E. Winston, "Kentucky and the Independence of Texas," *Southwestern Historical Quarterly Online* 016, no.1 [accessed October 5, 2007].

Albert Triplett Burnley to Albert Sidney Johnston

New Orleans
March 6th 1839

Dear General

I wrote you from Galveston—had a pleasant trip over in the *Columbia,* & am here waiting for Genl Hamilton who has written that he will be here today & intends making a short trip to Houston. Whether he will do so after seeing me is uncertain, unless he has Holford's business to settle with the Government. The *Charleston* was to have been here yesterday or today & is advertised for Galveston on Mr [March] 10[th]. If she or Genl H arrive before the *Columbia* departs this evening, I will add a P. S. to this letter.

I am happy to inform you I have made an arrangement with my friend, James Erwin,[1] which secures the $6,000 by 15 Sept. To wit—I am to go on to Kent[uck]y, & if I can, raise the money there—or if not, in Phila. through my friend, N. Biddle, I am to do it, & place it at Erwin's disposal, & he will, with pleasure, inform you of it & provide the funds here to your order. If *I* fail in Kenty & Phila, then I am to inform you & Erwin, & he will advance the $6,000 & hold it subject to your order & send you authority to draw for it—we permitting him to take an interest, of 1/3 in the purchase. This arrangement secures the money in any event, & you may go on to close the purchase with full confidence of getting the money here 15th Sept if I don't make some arrangement to raise it earlier. If Erwin has to advance us the money, then let our interest be to you 1/2, to Erwin 1/3, & to me 1/6; or to each of us 1/3—exactly as you please. I think you would prefer to have not less than 1/2 the purchase, & I shall be perfectly satisfied with 1/6th, & so let it be unless *you prefer* its being held in equal thirds. Let me hear from you directed to Phila care of N. Biddle what Karnes[2] has done, & whether the above arrangement is satisfactory, if better can't be done.

      Tell Genl Rusk[3] and Tod Robinson I subscribed for the *Picayune*[4] as they requested.

      Say to McLeod[5] I sent him 5 lbs Tobacco. Your winter clothes go out by the *Columbia,* the summer clothes are sent for to New York & will be sent shortly. The silk drawers & shirts St. John[6] had not of large size. He has promised me to look for some large enough for you & if they can be got, they will also be sent with the clothes by the *Columbia.*

      Reily has done nothing yet. Beal has gone to Vicksburg to see the Bank & is expected back today or tomorrow. I fear nothing will be done.

In haste yr friend etc
A. T. Burnley

    P S

      Nothing of Genl H or the *Charleston.* Mr. Love will take out the clothes in the next boat.

ATB
Genl A. Sidney Johnston
Scy of War
Houston Texas

1.   James Erwin, son-in-law of Henry Clay, divided his time between business interests in New Orleans and Lexington, Kentucky.
2.   Henry Wax Karnes apparently acted as an intermediary for Johnston and Brumley's attempts to purchase land around San Antonio and Austin. "Karnes, Henry Wax," *Handbook of Texas Online* [accessed October 11, 2004].
3.   Thomas Jefferson Rusk was born in 1803 in Pendleton District, South Carolina. He moved to Georgia, where he practiced law until 1835. Coming to Texas on business, he decided to remain in Nacogdoches and in late 1835 became a contractor and inspector general of the volunteer army. He attended

the Convention of 1836 and signed the Texas Declaration of Independence. He participated in the Battle of San Jacinto and, in May 1836, assumed command of the army when Houston left Texas for medical treatment. He refused to run for the vice presidency on the Houston ticket in 1838 and instead became chief justice of the Texas Supreme Court. "Rusk, Thomas Jefferson," *Handbook of Texas Online* [accessed October 13, 2004].

4. The New Orleans newspaper, now the *Times-Picayune,* was established in 1837. http://www.nytimes.com/2005/09/05/business/media/05picayune.html?_r=1.

5. Hugh McLeod.

6. St. John, Fabre & Co., tailor and clothing merchants, was located at 61 Canal Street in New Orleans.

James Love to Albert Sidney Johnston

N. O.
March 9th 1839

Dear Genl

I have again to say that I will not be over this trip.

Genl Hamilton arrived yesterday. He left the *Charleston* at Mobile and she will be here today. I will leave for Texas on Tuesday morning, and will be in Galveston Bay on Thursday night or Friday morning. She is represented to be a splendid vessel & every way adapted to the purpose for which she is intended.[1]

Mr Reily is now engaged in conversation with Genl Hamilton on matters touching the loan and whether it will be had or not as yet rests in *dubio.* I cannot explain *why* this is so, but time has an important bearing on this matter, and time can alone determine what it will end in.

We have no general news of interest. Can't you come down the bay and meet the Genl & the *Charleston* [?] *Holford has gone to England.*

Sincerely yours
Jas Love
Genl A. Sidney Johnston
Houston Texas

1. For a quite different assessment of the *Charleston/Zavala,* see R. G. Dunlap to M. B. Lamar, April 4, 1839, in Gulick et al., *Lamar Papers,* 2:514.

Albert Triplett Burnley to Albert Sidney Johnston

Louisville
Apl 12th 1839

Dear Genl.

Yours of 12th March has been recd. I have written to Gilmer[1] to send you his Commn [Commission]. In regard to the claims on the Government which I left in your hands—when collected, retain in your hands in *Treasury notes* the am[oun]t of Read's claim. The balance I wish you & Love to dispose of in the way you think most advantageous without reference to any previous instruction from me, for I consider it nonsense for a man here to undertake to control a man of sense in Texas about matters to be accomplished there.

I consider Galveston stock & funded debt as now the most desirable speculations in Texas, especially when the fund, like the one in your hands, belongs in small parcels to a good many persons. If you can't buy these stocks for the price they are going at when I was there—why give more.

I am a little afraid our friend Karnes[2] will fail in the San Antonio purchase. Any arrangement you make other than the one spoken of, I will agree to, & do my best to comply with it when you tell me what it is.

I have seen Hobbs[3] since I wrote you last. He has done nothing, but is trying & says he is going to St. Louis shortly, principally with a [view?] to dispose of your property & I hope he may succeed for I fear Biddle's resignation will interfere with my raising money through his bank, which I had hoped to do.

I am also a little apprehensive his resignation will have an unfavorable effect upon our negotiation. Mr. Dunlap,[4] his successor, is his intimate & particular friend & connection, & I doubt not was appointed at his instance. He told me himself, Dunlap was the only man he consults with about Texas matters, & on that subject, he agreed with him in every particular & was the most judicious and sensible man in Phila. If Biddle retains his influence in his Bank, he can do some things we want him to do better out of the board than in it. & I cannot but *hope* he may have resigned somewhat in reference to our affairs. We shall soon see.

Genl Hamilton desires me to meet him in Phila[delphia] on 10th May. I have made my arrangements & shall be there on the 1st.

If you & Love receive too many introductory letters from me, you must bear it. I can't help it. *She*[5] & your friends are all well. Hancock[6] has got home—nothing new—remember me to all acquaintances & belive [*sic*] me in much haste

> Very truly yr friend
> A. T. Burnley
> Genl A. Sidney Johnston
> Houston, Texas

1. Thomas W. Gilmer.
2. Henry Wax Karnes. Johnston did not purchase any land in San Antonio, but he did buy some land in Austin.
3. Burnley is referring to Edward Dorsey Hobbs of Louisville, Kentucky.
4. Thomas Dunlap, assistant cashier in 1838, was left in charge of the bank when Biddle resigned on March 29, 1839.
5. "She" is Eliza Griffin, Johnston's future (second) wife. "Griffin, Eliza," *Handbook of Texas Online* [accessed June 15, 2004].
6. George Hancock was an uncle of Albert Sidney Johnston's first wife, Henrietta Preston. Hancock resided at Hayfield, about five miles from Louisville. "Hancock, George," *Handbook of Texas Online* [accessed June 15, 2004].

Charles Harrison to Albert Sidney Johnston

[n.d., n.p.; ca. June 1839]

My Dear Sir

I regret to hear that there is much difficulty with the Executive & his cabinet. How is it that Watrous[1] has left when you were under the impression that he was more attached to the President than any other. I am not surprised that he is not able to procure the talents of the country because they *can all make more* money by prosecuting any other business. He will find but few in *that* country[2] willing to live at the seat of Govt for $1500 or 2000 a year! Situated as you are, you, I suppose, will be compelled to hang on for some time. Your own fame is identified in the success of the administration, at least so far as the protection of the frontier & supression [*sic*] of Indian hostilities which I am satisfied you will effect if funds can be procured.

Mr Davis[3] will tell you the news of Ky. Money is hard to procure & the times growing worse.

There is a report here that you are to be married which I have ventured to contradict.

Should you have any use of service for me there or here—command me. Any number of men can be had if you have the means of transportation etc etc.

I am, dear sir, with high consideration of esteem

> yours
> Chas Harrison
> Genl A. Sydney [*sic*] Johnston
> Secy of War
> Houston Texas
> H. W. Davis

1. John Charles Watrous at this time served as President Lamar's attorney general.
2. Many people believed that the moving of the capital from Houston to Austin was a grave mistake. They feared that Indians and Mexicans would attack the city because it was so far inland and on the frontier. The Third Congress adjourned in Houston in May 1839, and the Fourth Congress assembled in Austin in November. The executive branch and all government offices moved during late summer.
3. Harrison W. Davis of Kentucky carried this letter to Johnston.

James Love to Albert Sidney Johnston

> Galveston
> June 23rd 1839

Dear General

I am still occasionally thinking of the affairs of state, and whether suggestions I may make shall be worth anything or not, you can always take them for what they are worth.

You will have heard by the arrival of Jones,[1] Williams,[2] and Bryan.[3] We are to give them a dinner on Thursday.[4] I am a subscriber and will attend, and matters are so arranged that conviviality will not be interrupted by any display of spite or malevolence. I have joined readily in this thing and made it a condition.

I have conversed freely with Jones and Williams, and if the President shows the least disposition on his part, they will meet him more than half way, and the opposition that the President expects here, if not subdued, will be trimmed. Even McKinney[5] will not attempt to revive it. Whatever the personal feelings of the President, it is his *duty* not to excite any particular hostility because by it, the country may suffer. I have ever been confident that someone has made statements to him in regard to others that is untrue, and both Jones & Williams declare to me that in no instance have they ever spoken disrespectfully of him. I am sure in regard to Gail Borden[6] this information was not correct, knowing Borden well as long as anyone in the country. I declare I have never hear [sic] him speak evil of anyone. I am particularly desirous now that all these feelings of asperity should subside because it injures us abroad. I have recd several letters on this subject and some who have professed to be his best friends have disclaimed in the U. States their having anything to do with removals, etc. I think I know Genl Lamar, and am sure he is patriotic and means to serve his country faithfully. To enable him to do so, he must conciliate, not as a man, but as a *politician*. He is called to preside over a nation composed of his disjointed materials. Time and expediency may enable him to erect a decent superstructure. The least haste or unskillfulness will disorganize.

I venture to predict that he may without any extraordinary effort control the next congress except upon some nominations that is a matter of no consequence. It is a time for his friends to be active, and he is a recusant that would desert now when the tide seems to be against him. I will take upon myself to mitigate or destroy opposition here, if he will give me the least assistance. I intended to have had a conversation with him before I left Houston on this subject, but was prevented by his ill health. He cannot misconstrue my motives as I am not in the line of politics at all. Confiding, as I do in you, I leave to your discretion this letter—and write to me about it. I did not know that Dr. [Levi] Jones was going up or I would have written.

Sincerely yours
Jas Love
Genl A. S. Johnston
Houston

1. Dr Anson Jones was born in 1798 in Seekonville, Great Barrington, Massachusetts. As a young man he practiced medicine, but he never prospered.

In 1832 he gave up his medical practice, moved to New Orleans, and worked as a commission merchant. He then immigrated to Brazoria, Texas, and once again practiced medicine. He became involved in the revolutionary movement, he fought at the Battle of San Jacinto. During Houston's first term as president, Jones served as minister to the United States, but President Lamar recalled him in May 1839. During Lamar's presidency Jones served in the Texas Senate and chaired its foreign relations committee. During Houston's second presidential term he served as secretary of state, and he was later elected the last president of the Republic of Texas. "Jones, Dr. Anson," *Handbook of Texas Online* [accessed October 13, 2004].

2. Samuel May Williams was born in 1795 in Providence, Rhode Island. He came to Texas in 1822 and became a clerk and translator for Stephen F. Austin. In 1833 he and Thomas F. McKinney established a commission house in Quintana, at the mouth of the Brazos River. During the revolution he and McKinney traveled to the United States and obtained funds and arms for the war; the republic never reimbursed them for their expenses. Together with McKinney, Williams founded the Galveston City Company. In 1838 Williams, a staunch supporter of Sam Houston, received a commission from President Houston to negotiate a $5 million loan in the United States and to purchase seven ships for the Texas Navy. When Lamar assumed the presidency in December 1838 he quickly replaced Williams. "Williams, Samuel May," *Handbook of Texas Online* [accessed October 13, 2004].

3. Moses Austin Bryan was born in Herculaneum, Missouri, on September 25, 1817, and was Stephen F. Austin's nephew. His family arrived in Texas in 1831, and he fought at the Battle of San Jacinto. Bryan served as Anson Jones's secretary at the Texas legation in the U.S. capital. "Bryan, Moses Austin," *Handbook of Texas Online* [accessed October 15, 2004].

4. This dinner in Galveston honored former Sam Houston appointees who were relieved of duty shortly after Lamar took office.

5. Thomas Freeman McKinney was born in 1801 in Lincoln County, Kentucky. He first arrived in Texas in 1824, and the following year he opened a store in Nacogdoches. By 1834 he and Samuel May Williams were business partners, and during the revolution the two traveled to the United States to secure funds and arms for the war. He was a cofounder of the Galveston City Company with Williams and, also like Williams, an ardent supporter of Sam Houston. "McKinney, Thomas Freeman," *Handbook of Texas Online* [accessed October 15, 2004].

6.   Gail Borden Jr. was born in 1801 in Norwich, New York. He came to Texas in
     1829 and served as a surveyor, publisher, and inventor. He was eccentric and
     above politics, but in June 1837 Houston appointed him collector for the port
     of Galveston. In December 1838 Lamar replaced him for political reasons, a
     move that was unpopular in Galveston, even among the pro-Lamar faction.
     "Borden, Gail, Jr.," *Handbook of Texas Online* [accessed October 15, 2004].

James Love to Albert Sidney Johnston

Galveston

June 26th 1839

Dear Genl

Since I wrote I have visited the vessel of war, *Viper*.[1] I do not profess
to be much of a judge, but think she is an elegant vessel and will do service
and she is ready for it.

You will see Plummer. He has arranged for $5,000 good money on
condition that Genl Lamar & yourself will guarantee its punctual payment.
Will you do it?

Nat Watrous[2] is sick; he has the fever. He was better yesterday evening. I have not heard from him this morning. I will be up in a few days.

J. Love

PS

I send some money & letters for Reily. If he has gone, retain the
money for me.

Genl A. S. Johnston
Houston

1.   The *Viper* was a schooner of war that was purchased by the Republic of
     Texas and renamed the *San Jacinto*. Built by the firm of Schott and Whit-
     ney in Baltimore, the *Viper* was 66 feet long with a 21.5-foot beam, drew 8
     feet of water, and displaced 170 tons. It carried a complement of thirteen
     officers and sixty-nine sailors, with armaments that included four 12-pound
     medium-barrel and one 9-pound long-barrel brass pivot cannons. The gov-

ernment commissioned the vessel the day after Love mailed this letter. Love probably attended the ceremony. *"Viper," Handbook of Texas Online* [accessed October 15, 2004].

2.   Nathaniel H. Watrous was John Charles Watrous's brother. Nat later moved to Bastrop.

James Love to Albert Sidney Johnston

Houston
July 11th 1839

Dear General

      I have written to Reily by this mail giving him the intelligence of the indisposition of Mrs. Reily. She has had the 2nd chill today accompanied by some fever. The Dr. is of opinion the attack is not serious. She cannot now go down [to Galveston] with us, but I will return next boat for her in the hope she will be sufficiently well to return with us. I write to you these particulars (and they are just as I have state [*sic*] them) because if there is not some urgent necessity for Maj Reily to remain, he had better return. Not because I think she will be seriously ill but because I believe his absence is the *cause* of her illness. She is devotedly attached to him, & it has created a nervous excitement and a weakness that *may* induce bad health. I have not written this much to him, & I leave you to judge whether he can in honor return. In the meantime, you may be assured that every care will be taken of her and information given him of the state of her health, should it become worse.

      We have no news. Karnes is here on his way to N.O.

      Bee[1] wishes to be sent to Washington to *open* a negotiation with Mexico. The President will *not* send him & he is right.

Sincerely
Genl A. Sidney Johnston
Jas Love
Nacogdoches Texas

1.   Barnard Elliott Bee. In April 1840 he became the Texas minister plenipotentiary in Washington.

James Love to Albert Sidney Johnston

Galveston
July 20 [1839]

Dear Sir

If you have made no other arrangements in relation to your contemplated purchase in the North, let me suggest to you, whether they had not better be made through Williams[1] at Baltimore. I do not mean by any means to supersede Daingerfield,[2] but the idea is this: let Daingerfield ascertain the current prices & give to Williams the privilege of purchasing at those prices. The object I have is this: it places in his hands funds that will enable the house here[3] to do more business, which benefits us all.

The subject of our currency is one I have reflected upon much. The exceeding low rate at N. O. is ruinous. I am confident if the President would "take the responsibility" and permit the use of 30 or 40 thousand dollars on account of the Government secretly, the currency can be raised at N. O. to 60 or 70 cents. Think of this seriously. The people suffer immensely on account of the ruinous depreciation.

Yours
Jas Love

Will you send the papers, or better, to get the money to pay for our lots in Galveston. I will be up next week.

JL
Genl A. S. Johnston
Houston Texas

---

1. Henry Howell Williams was Samuel May Williams's brother. He resided in Baltimore. "Williams, Henry Howell," *Handbook of Texas Online* [accessed October 15, 2004].

2. William Henry Daingerfield was born in 1808 in Alexandria, Virginia. In 1837 he moved from Virginia to San Antonio, Texas, where in 1838 he was elected mayor. In 1839, President Lamar and Secretary of War Albert Sidney Johnston appointed him commissary for the Republic of Texas Army. "Daingerfield, William Henry," *Handbook of Texas Online* [accessed October 15, 2004].

3.   McKinney and Williams were suffering from the hard times following the Panic of 1837, but of even greater concern was the fact that the firm had financed the Texas Revolution during 1835–1836 and the republic was unable to repay the debt. Love was trying to win McKinney over to the Lamar faction by providing more business for their banking house. Sam Williams was less partisan, but his brother Henry was active in Whig politics in Baltimore and thus acceptable to Love.

James Love to Albert Sidney Johnston

Houston
July 24th [1839]

Dear Genl

I arrived ten minutes since and have recd the glorious news contained in your letter. The impulse given by this fight will be irresistible and we will soon be rid of a troublesome enemy. I rejoice you were present and I am *sure* it contributed in no small degree to success. I am almost malicious enough to wish you were among the wounded, but *not the slain*. I have taken the liberty of having your letter published; these things contribute greatly to encourage the business. Give me the benefit of a good honest fight, and all the stump orators in the universe could not resist me. The troops depart immediately and the officers will long be remembered by their countrymen. He that killed Bowles will be Vice President.[1] The Judge, I suppose, will not quit the field having a taste once of military fame.[2] It is irresistible.

I have letters from Burnley. He is off for Europe [and] prospects of success most flattering. The money, $400,000, you will have learned is at your service, and a better state of things exists everywhere for us.[3]

We have no neighborhood news but the death of Judge Birdsall.[4] He died day before yesterday. I left my family well. Miss Gray is with us, her & many full of mischief; many poor fellows suffer in a war of words. Jo is a captain and talks of you very frequently.[5]

You should come back so soon as you can in honor. There must be someone here to *direct* affairs. Young Hamilton[6] is here on matters touching the loan. Mr. Treat[7] of NY on matter of Mexico. I came in on this business.

Yours truly

My respects to the Judge, McLeod, and all of your gallant comrades that I know.[8]

Say to Reilly[9] [sic] that Mrs. Reilly [sic] is at my house, decidedly convalescent but unhappy about him. Send him home when you can (*with honor*).

> J L
> Genl A. Sidney Johnston
> Nagodoches [sic]

1. Love had just received news about the defeat on July 15–16 of the Cherokee Indians at the Battle of the Neches in which the elderly principal chief, Bowles (Chief Duwali), was killed. President Lamar had sent a commission of five, including Johnston and Vice President David G. Burnet, to remove the Cherokees from their land near Nacogdoches. The Indians agreed but wanted first to harvest their crops, a delay not approved by the commission. Although not in command, Albert Sidney Johnston and Vice President Burnet actively participated in this Texan victory. Robert W. Smith fired the shot that killed Bowles, but Love considered the victory a stepping stone toward the presidency for Johnston. The letter from Johnston appears in the Houston *Telegraph and Texas Register*, July 24, 1839. "Neches, Battle of the" *Handbook of Texas Online* [accessed December 3, 2007].

2. The judge that Love refers to is probably Thomas Rusk, who in December 1838 was elected chief justice of the Texas Supreme Court and commanded some of the troops at the Battle of the Neches.

3. Texas' loan commissioner, James Hamilton, had arranged for a $400,000 loan through the Bank of the United States. This "loan" proved to be a great disappointment. The Lamar administration had expected to receive the loan in the form of cash, which would alleviate the republic's financial problems, but the loan consisted only of U.S. postal notes and had to remain on deposit in New Orleans.

4. John Birdsall was born in 1802 in Green, Chenango County, New York. He arrived in Texas in 1837 and set up a law practice in Houston. President Houston appointed Birdsall attorney general of the Republic of Texas. He later served briefly as the chief justice pro tempore of the Texas Supreme Court, but the Texas Congress never confirmed that appointment. In early 1839 he became a law partner with Sam Houston. That partnership lasted until Birdsall's death later that year. "Birdsall, John," *Handbook of Texas Online* [accessed July 11, 2005].

5.   "Jo" refers to Love's two-year-old son, Joseph E. Love.

6.   "Young Hamilton" was General James Hamilton's son.

7.   James Treat was a mysterious New York real estate speculator with extensive ties in Mexico and Central America. President Lamar appointed Treat as a special agent to negotiate peace with Mexico. He arrived in Mexico City in December 1839 and continued negotiations with the Mexican government for more than a year. His efforts failed, and he died at sea in November 1840 while en route to Galveston. "Treat, James." *Handbook of Texas Online* [accessed October 18, 2004].

8.   The "Judge" is a reference to David G. Burnet. "McLeod" was Hugh McLeod. Both participated in the Battle of the Neches.

9.   James Reily had just ended his law partnership in Houston with Thomas Rusk and had begun a new partnership with James Love in Galveston.

James Love to Albert Sidney Johnston

Houston
July 24th [1839]

Dear Genl

I wrote you this morning in the expectation that the express was about to start.

Mr. Treat from N. York on a confidential mission in relation to negotiation with Mexico for peace [is] proposing a change in the mode, making it strictly confidential and secret. It is the only way it can be done. The consideration to be given is money. The prospect of success is flattering, the boundary and the amount to be paid, the only difficulty. Bee[1] mis managed the whole affair, but still desires to proceed in it.

Young Hamilton is here with dispatches on the subject of the loan, proposing some change in the bonds, and presenting a new feature in the nature of a sinking fund, all which is calculated to give credit to the operation. I came up, as I wrote you, to assist in these things. We have not been able to do anything today. The President's mother[2] is ill, and is supposed to be on her death bed. The President is with her, sick and in bed himself. I must go down tomorrow, but have endeavored to have matters so arranged that the objects can be accomplished. I regret exceedingly you are not here. Judge Webb[3] is gone to Austin, Cook[4] is not here, and all is left to Dr. Starr.[5]

Whenever you receive this, you must hasten the return of Judge Burnet, his talent is wanted now.

Santa Anna has abdicated & his friend, Genl Bravo, succeeds him.[6] This, no doubt, is part of the plan preliminary to making him, Santa Anna, dictator. Congress has invested the President with full power for the "pacification" of Texas, and authorizes the raising of 60,000 men. This I consider a mere blind and means nothing. We will have no invasion.

Your success with the Indians will give a new impulse to things. It strengthens the government every way. You have $400,000 for your summer work. You must carry out the operations you have commenced, a force must be raised and sent west, of at least 300. The campaign against the Comanches must be on foot by the 15th of Sept. You meet them as they come down. You should be in a position to direct these things. Do your business quickly in the East & return.

> Sincerely yours
> Jas Love
> Genl A. Sidney Johnston
> Nacogdoches

1. Barnard Elliott Bee resigned as Lamar's secretary of state and joined the diplomatic service as a minister to Mexico. On February 20, 1839, he departed for Mexico City in hopes of negotiating Texas' independence. The Mexican government refused to recognize his credential, and they sent him packing on May 24. "Bee, Barnard Elliott," *Handbook of Texas Online.*

2. Rebecca Lamar died July 26, 1839, at Oak Grove, her son's plantation southwest of Houston (north of Rice University), attended by Dr. Ashbel Smith. That summer yellow fever raged throughout Texas, but Smith did not believe that her death was due to the epidemic. "Lamar, Mirabeau B.," *Handbook of Texas Online.*

3. At this time Webb, the former district judge from Florida, was several months away from becoming the attorney general of Texas. "Webb, James," *Handbook of Texas Online.*

4. Louis P. Cooke was born in 1811 in Tennessee and arrived in Texas shortly after the Battle of San Jacinto. He served as President Lamar's secretary of the navy from May 1839 to December 1841. "Cooke, Louis P.," *Handbook of Texas Online* [accessed October 18, 2004].

5. James Harper Starr was born in New Hartford, Connecticut, on December 18, 1809. A self-taught physician, he first practiced medicine in 1830 in Colum-

bus, Ohio. He arrived in Texas on January 17, 1837, and settled in Nacogdoches. In May 1839 President Lamar appointed Starr secretary of the Texas
treasury. He served in that office until August 1840. "Starr, James Harper,"
Handbook of Texas Online [accessed October 18, 2004].

6.   Santa Anna was Mexico's president ad interim while Anastasio Bustamante
led the army from May to July 1839. Santa Anna "resigned" for reasons of
health on July 11 and turned the government over to the president of the
Council, Nicolás Bravo. "Santa Anna, Antonio López de," *Handbook of Texas
Online* [accessed December 27, 2006].

J. B. Ransom to Albert Sidney Johnston

Houston
25th July 1839

Genl A. S. Johnston
Dear Sir.

As the express is about leaving, I[1] have just time to say to you that
the news of your operations against the Indians has given unusual satisfaction.

Genl Lamar would have written but his mother lies at the point of
death & his health is exceedingly delicate.

We are full of news; accounts from N Orleans state that Bravo has
superceded [*sic*] Santa Ana. Mr. Hamilton, son of the Genl, in company with
Mr Treat of N York have arrived with the loan, & the best hopes are entertained by Genl H that he will early succeed in England (these matters are, of
course, private). Col Love has just left here; I gave him your letter. He is in
high spirits & goes it in full, for Genl Lamar has succeeded in conciliating matters with the Galvestonians, & thinks all matters will go right in a few weeks.

Politics begin to run high & men begin to exhibit their hands. This
evening the candidates speachify [*sic*] at the Capital, Thurston[2] leading the way,
followed by Cock,[3] who is no less warm against the Administration & bitter in
his personality towards Genl Lamar. I think parties are cooling off, however, &
would become quiet but for such Demagogues as only subsist in the midst of strife
& discontent. Doubtless, the Administration is gaining & its friends have everything to hope, particularly since your operations against those rascally savages.

To change & improve the subject. I must tell you that your friend,
C. Watrous, was up last week and stood up to his fodder like a man, frequently

disclosing his determination to *wed Miss M* if he possibly *can*, & I think he *will*.
Miss Gray is at the Island & owing to the ill health of Cate & Alice,[4] Mrs. Gray
went down with Col Love today. Col Johnson has just returned from there
& says that two gents, Mssrs Foster & Gaines, have recd their walking papers
from the hands of Miss Love[5] (as a matter of course). You must have heard
of Judge Birdsall's death; in a state of despair, he cut his throat a few hours
before his death, a circumstance much regretted. He was a worthy man.

Judge Webb & Col Cook[e] have gone to the City of Austin, & so
many others have left that Houston is nearly deserted.

As I am not on terms of correspondence, I must apologize for
obtruding so long a letter on your attention which was not intended when
commenced. Genl Foot[e][6] is by my side and sends his compliments.

> With due regard
> Very Respectfully yr[paper torn]
> J. B. Ransom

P. S.

I send you the paper of 11th containing a "communication" which I
put in clandestinely as a matter of policy.[7]

> JBR
> Genl A. S. Johnston
> Head Quarters Texan Army

1. James B. Ransom was President Lamar's private secretary. "Ransom, James
    B.," *Handbook of Texas Online* [accessed October 18, 2004].
2. Algernon Sidney Thurston was born on May 19, 1801. He arrived in Houston
    in 1837 and established a law practice in the Bayou City. He served as com-
    missary general for the republic and also as quartermaster general in 1838.
    President Houston nominated him to serve as attorney general in the last
    weeks of his administration, but President Lamar rejected the nomination.
    "Thurston, Algernon Sidney," *Handbook of Texas Online* [December 27, 2006].
3. James Decatur Cocke was born in 1815 near Richmond, Virginia. He moved
    to Texas in 1837 and befriended Lamar. He backed Lamar's aggressive mili-
    tary policy toward Mexico. He participated in the Mier expedition and was
    the first man to draw a black bean in a lottery the Mexican army held to
    determine which of the captured Texans to execute. His last words reportedly
    were, "Tell my friends I die with grace." "Cocke, James Decatur," *Handbook*

of Texas Online [accessed October 18, 2004]. See also "Black Bean Episode," *Handbook of Texas Online* [accessed February 6, 2007].

4. "Cate & Alice" refers to Catharine D. and Susan Alice, ages seven and four, the youngest daughters of William Fairfax Gray.

5. Foster has not been identified, but "Miss Love" is James Love's daughter Mary, and Gaines is William B. P. Gaines.

6. Henry Stuart Foote was born in 1804 in Fauquier County, Virginia. In 1839, as a member of the Mississippi legislature, he visited Texas to conduct research for a history of the republic. In 1841 he published a two-volume work, *Texas and the Texans.* "Foote, Henry Stuart," *Handbook of Texas Online* [accessed October 18, 2004].

7. This "communication" refers to a letter printed in the Houston *Telegraph and Texas Register,* May 11, 1839, from President Lamar to "Colonel" Bowles, chief of the Cherokees, expressing his displeasure that the Cherokees had denied Anglo Texans access to the Cherokee town of Neches Saline. This incident sparked the subsequent war against the Cherokees in July.

James Love to Albert Sidney Johnston

Galveston
Sept 17th [1839]

Dear General

I wish you to see the last *Civilian.* There is an article there that I think might be published in the *Telegraph.*[1]

I do not think I shall be up before you leave, but will see you early in November.[2]

Yours
J. Love
Genl A. S. Johnston
Houston

1. The article referred to was an exposé of Lamar's appointee and friend, Dr. Willis Roberts, collector of customs at Galveston. It appears in the Houston *Telegraph and Texas Register,* October 9, 1839. The files for the Galveston *Civilian* for 1839 were destroyed.

2.   Johnston was moving the War Department from Houston to Austin, and
     Love planned to attend the upcoming session of Congress scheduled for No-
     vember and to lobby for his interests.

Albert Triplett Burnley to James Love

London
Sept 20th 1839

Dear Love

Your letters of 23rd June & 13th July I recd at the same time by the
last packet & are the only letters I have recd from you since I have been in
England. The most surprising thing you tell me is that you have not heard from
me since I left Louisville. I have written frequently to you & Jones,[1] & the loss
of the *Cuba*[2] to which you refer as the grave of my letters, cannot account for
them all, for I have written too many for all to have been on board the *Cuba.*

So it is, I *cannot nor* even *try* to recapitutlate [sic] all I have written.
Suffice it to say, we raised the money we sent to Texas in Phila by d[ra]fts
on England, which besides the security of a pledge of Texas Bonds, involves
a personal responsibility on Genl Hamilton & myself as the Drawers of the
dfts. This we were compelled to do or fail to get you any money in consequence of the absurity [sic] in the Loan Law of requiring the Commssrs to
deposit the Bonds in a bank, then transissue by the bank when the money
was paid into the credit of the Government. Thereby discrediting the Com-
msrs on the face of the law & preventing them from raising money for the
pressing wants of the Government in any other way than by a sale (which
may be, & in times like these, is sufferable) or by incuring [sic] heavy personal responsibilities.

On reaching this country, I found everything in a horrid condition. The Bank of England, like our bank, had overtraded. The country had
incurred a debt of 7,000,000 for grain in consequence of the short crop last
year, & which had to be sent to the Continent in bullion. And the whole
country had speculated in American securities to an extent that was perfect
gambling (in all about $200,000,000) besides which the market was flooded
with other American securities seeking purchasers. Under these circumstances, the Bank of England & all her private bankers & capitalists had to
contract themselves suddenly & violently, hereby producing convulsions

that were horrid & alarming. Everything fell to price. Many manufactories were obliged to suspend or diminish operations. The opperatives [sic] were thrown out of employment & thousands & tens of thousands actually suffering for the necessaries of life with a prospect of starvation before them. & these men driven to desparation [sic], would have resorted to revolution & bloodshed for relief, but for the strong, organized, military power of the government. All I saw & know that money commanded 18 per cent on a pledge of the best American securities.

Under these circumstances, it was folly to talk about the bond of a new country like Texas which 9/10s of the people never heard of. We, therefore, say: we do not offer or expect to sell our bonds now, but simply to pledge them for an advance on them until times get better.

In the meantime, our friends here advise us to reduce the rate of interest & sell the bonds at a corresponding discount, which, they say, will make them more saleable. The objection to this is that $5,000,000 reduced to 5 percent Int & sold for 50 or $60 on the 100$ would only produce 2 1/2 to 3 million of dollars, which is but little more than 1/2 the government wants & the present law authorises the issue of only $5,000,000 however low the rate of interest may be.

Under such circumstances, it has been determined that I shall remain here & try to talk & write up the credit of the country & if possible, procure an advance on a pledge of our bonds for 10 or 12 months until the times get better. In the meantime, the Genl starts back tomorrow in the *Liverpool* to present some alternatives in the Loan Law in relation to the sale of interest, the sinking fund, etc which he will explain fully to you. Also to urge the adoption of some measure to procure our recognition by Mexico, in all which I beg you & all our friends will aid him to the utmost of your ability, for I assure your [sic], these things are necessary to our success. And even if I succeed in getting an advance on our bonds (& I entertain a good deal of confidence I shall do so here, in France, or in Holland before 1ˢᵗ Nov) it will be upon the faith that we will be able to proceed in all I have alluded to. Depend upon it, negotiating a loan for Texas is no sinecure. I have now been five months from my family, at a heavy expense, & my present expectation is that I shall have to remain all the winter. Love and my other friends & the government may rely on one thing; I shall leave *nothing* honorable undone to accomplish our object & I will not desert my post while there is a hope of doing anything.[3]

We have powerful influences at work for us. France has recognized our independence;[4] England expresses the most friendly feelings &disposi-

tions & I doubt not will recognise, so that if times get better here (& they are improving & I think will continue to improve), I have but little doubt we shall accomplish our mission in the spring. I hope, by the *British Queen* on the 1ˢᵗ Nov, to inform you I have procured an advance of some more money on a pledge of our bond.

You say my friends are amazed that Genl H[amilton] should run away with all the credit of our success. Let them not be, for it does not amaze me. If we can succeed, & I escape censure, I shall be satisfied. I have nothing to ask or wish for from popular applause. The General & I are excellent friends. I never advise any step that is not adopted & I oppose nothing that is not abandoned. He consults me about everything & I know has the highest respect for my judgement & opinions. And it must be conceded (& I bear cheerful testimony to the fact publickly & privately) that Genl H's high character & standing here & in the U.S. gives him an influence which I do not pretend to, & I feel that I should be wanting in my duty to Texas if I did not secure that influence to promote such plans, views, & opinions as I work for the interest of the country—even at the sacrifice of being considered as playing Mr. Second Fiddle. Besides which, the genl is really a man of much tact & ability—more than I thought and altho' I do think his ambition for distinction (the vanity which is inseparable from all great men) make him say & write "*I*" rather more than *strict* justice would warrant, yet still, it amuses more than annoys me & I beg you to discount the idea of any claim of merit by me or my friends inconsistant [*sic*] with any claim advanced by him or his friends. On the contrary, let it be understood (as is true) that we are excellent friends and acting most harmoniously together & I beg you & all my friends to treat him as my friend & to promote his views and wishes as much as possible.

I need hardly say that the unprecedented pressure for money here has prevented me from selling the land scrip I brought out, or from making any arrangements for a commercial establishment. When times get better & we negotiate the Loan, I shall try to accomplish both objects.

You tell me not to fail to move out to Texas this fall & to bring Judge Bibb⁵ with me. Would to heaven I could do so. But this Loan business has already prevented me last fall & the fall before from moving to Texas, & will, of course, prevent me from moving this. As upon a full view of the whole ground, I have very reluctantly determined that the chance of my getting an advance on our bonds, makes it my *duty* to remain.

I believe this loan will be the ruin of me if we do not get through with it shortly & I think it has caused me to neglect my family in a way that would justify my wife in applying for a divorce. As to Judge Bibb, you must write to him & if he can raise money enough,[6] I know he will join you, for I left him very full of Texas & sick of judging. He said he would wait for me no longer than this fall.

  Not going to Texas this fall also plays the Devil with me about opening a plantation there next year. I have not heard a word from Geo. Crittenden.[7] Where he is—or what he is about & it is uncertain what he can do with the means he has. That I shall make some arrangement with Hamilton to put the Negroes to work which he will explain to you & George, & you must aid in carrying it into effect as much as you can. George must come into the scheme, even tho' he may have formed some others of his own because I was obliged to make it in ignorance of what he would be able to do.

  Times had begun to get better when a week ago the weather became, & has continued, very unfavorable for the crops here, which affects injuriously the money market more than anything else. Add to which, 4 days ago, news arrived from Paris that Hottinguer and Co. had refused to accpt [sic] bills drawn by the Bank of the U.S. To the amount of 1,200,0000 [sic], which has produced a tremendous excitement there & here, & will produce the same in the U. S. The thing is yet unexplained. We look for news from Paris tonight. Unless the bills are taken up by somebody for the honour of the Bank, & that intelligence goes out in the *Liverpool* tomorrow, along with the news of the protest, the consequences may be very serious in the U.S.

  Please show this letter to Jones & Genl Johnston & beg each to consider it as similar to himself. My best respects to your family. Believe me in haste

       Very truly & sincerely you friend
       A. T. Burnley

  Direct your letters to me, ATB, care Jas Treat, New York. They will there be enclosed to me here by his clerk.

       Col James Love
       Galviston [sic] Texas
       care of Saml Riker, Jr.[8]
       New Orleans

1. This refers to Dr. Levi Jones.
2. The *Cuba* sank on June 12, 1839, after leaving Galveston for New Orleans.

3. Burnley failed to secure any bond money in Europe. Lamar recalled him in January 1840.

4. On September 25, 1839, France recognized the independence of the Republic of Texas.

5. Judge George M. Bibb, who was chief justice of the Kentucky Supreme Court and very active in Whig politics, was Burnley's father-in-law. "Bibb, Judge George M.," *Handbook of Texas Online* [accessed October 4, 2004].

6. Burnley purchased land in Texas for his father-in-law, Judge George M. Bibb.

7. George Bibb Crittenden was born on March 20, 1812, in Russellville, Kentucky. The son of Kentucky senator John J. Crittenden, George Bibb Crittenden graduated from West Point and served in the Black Hawk War. He entered Texas in 1842 and received a commission in the Army of the Republic of Texas. "Crittenden, George Bibb," *Handbook of Texas Online* [accessed October 18, 2004].

8. In the 1838 New Orleans city directory Samuel Riker is listed at 36 Camp Street.

James Love to Albert Sidney Johnston

Galveston
Novr 6th 1839

Dear General

I recd your letter by Capt Moore[1] and was happy to learn you were well. The prevalence of fever[2] here has so interrupted my private business that I cannot be at Austin until the 1st of Decr. We have escaped entirely and it is now in a manner gone.

I have recd a letter from Burnley [and] I have given it to Williams[3] who will show it to you. You will see from its contents that the prospect of getting money is not the most flattering, altho I suppose some will be had. Genl Hamilton writes that he will leave N. O. on the 20th. I will come up with him; his object is to procure some amendment to the loan bill. Whether he will succeed or not, remains to be seen.

I did not choose to tattle or I could have told you when we last met that it was determined by those high in power that Burnet was the *available* candidate. You expressed your intention to retire, which I thought best for you, even if you had political aspirations. *For he that unites his fate with this administration will fail.* We will talk all this over when we meet.

The examination of the custom house has closed. It is not certainly known what the report will be, altho it is said, he will report a default of $14,000. He proceeded throughout without asking for any information out of the Custom house. What is the result I know not, but I do know that the proof is here of malpractice & default.[4] And I also know that the matter will be investigated by Congress. I hear the opposition will go [to] unwarrantable lengths; the ostensible grounds will be the Velasco cotton, and a late speech at Austin said to be violent. You know, however, that opposition will always find causes.

Our city improves and winter has fairly set in. I see by the papers your nephew, the probate Judge, is dead, and no particular news from Ky.

The ladies send their regards and all your friends here have escaped [yellow fever] and wish to see you.

> Sincerely yours
> Jas Love
> Genl. A. Sidney Johnston
> Austin

1. Edwin Ward Moore was born in 1810 in Alexandria, Virginia. He joined the U.S. Navy in 1825 and was promoted to lieutenant in 1835. In July 1839 he resigned his commission and became the commodore of the newly organized Texas Navy, which had its home port in Galveston. "Moore, Edwin Ward," *Handbook of Texas Online* [accessed October 22, 2004].

2. The yellow fever epidemic began in Galveston in September 1839, apparently brought to the city by a vessel that had sailed from Vera Cruz. Yellow fever also raged in New Orleans and Houston and lasted until the first frost.

3. Samuel May Williams represented Galveston in Texas' Fourth Congress, but he had to attend to business in Houston on the way and thus arrived after the session began. The letter he carried was from Burnley to Love, dated September 20, 1839. See "Williams, Samuel May," *Handbook of Texas Online*.

4. Upon assuming the presidency Lamar dismissed Gail Borden as the customs collector for Galveston. In his stead Lamar appointed an old family friend, Dr. Willis Roberts, a recent arrival from Mobile, Alabama. This appointment angered most Galvestonians. Letters soon appeared in the local newspapers claiming fraud and malfeasance by the new collector. A later government investigation determined that two clerks, not Dr. Roberts, stole from the government.

James Reily to Albert Sidney Johnston

Houston
Nov 14th 1839

General Johnston
Sir

This letter no doubt finds you deeply engaged in divising [*sic*] the best way to protect the frontier, or in impressing upon some members of Congress the necessity of voting supplies for the payment of an increased military. If it intrudes upon you, please pardon the trouble it gives, for rest assured, the writer wishes you all success, whether your brow wears the sternness of a military chieftain dreaming & cogitating upon plans of bloody war, or whether most anxiously enquiring from some poor limb of the law whether he has any *poetic work amongst* Blackstone, Kent, Peters, & Wheaton.[1]

It was my intention instead of writing to have visited Austin in order to have rendered in my own person, an account of my Cherokee agency. At present, I could not well leave. My accounts are made out & I have no fear but they will pass muster. The office of *cashier*, once laid down, will never again be resumed, at least in times of war.

I reached Houston last Sunday, two weeks ago. Your friends in the East [Texas] (& I am gratified to know you have many warm ones there) were at peace & in comfort—Rusk, Mayfield, Taylor, Hotchkiss, Hart,[2] Capt Smith,[3] et al sent their kindest wishes to you. Even the lovely Miss Anna,[4] who felt satisfied she failed in what she never failed before, to win in captivating the hearts of all widowers & bachelors, made me the messenger of her good wishes to Genl Johnston. The *toast* & the *dream* were frequently the themes of her conversation, altho you were ungallant enough to leave her dominions with a heart unscathed.

Death & disease, as you have heard, played & are still playing a terrible game in Houston. They call it healthy here now, but the frequent outgoings of a certain little *black buggy* every day gives the lie to the assertion. On my arrival I found Mrs. R[eily] very sick indeed, & had she been able to travel, should have left Houston the very day I arrived.[5] As it is, my residence in Houston shall be short. I am most comfortably fixed, but am utterly isolated from the men whose society last summer I so much enjoyed.[6] With the people of H[ouston], I have but little intercourse & no intimates.

I am living in our old quarters,[7] but as Austin would not afford me a living at present at the law, I expect to return next spring to Nacogdoches & visit you next winter at the expense of the public as an Hon[orable] M[ember of] C[ongress].[8] *What a gratification to mans' [sic] ambition!* In that old place I shall find many & warm friends.

> I remain yours
> James Reily
> Private
> Hon. A. Sidney Johnston,
> Secy of War
> Austin Texas

1. Reily is referring to the law commentaries by English jurist William Blackstone, New York chancellor James Kent, and to Richard Peters and Henry Wheaton, the compilers of the Supreme Court *Reports* (1827–1843 and 1815–1827, respectively).

2. At this time Thomas J. Rusk served as chief justice of the Republic of Texas Supreme Court and resided in Nacogdoches. James S. Mayfield was born in 1809 in Tennessee and moved to Texas in 1837. Earlier in 1839 Mayfield aided Albert Sidney Johnston during his discussions with the Cherokee Indians over land grants in East Texas. He resided in Nacogdoches. Charles S. Taylor was born in London in 1801. He came to Texas in 1830 and established a mercantile business in Nacogdoches. He signed the Texas Declaration of Independence. Archibald Hotchkiss was born in 1794 in Washington County, New York. He immigrated to Texas in 1833 as an agent for the Galveston Bay and Texas Land Company and settled in Nacogdoches the next year. In 1835 he wrote to Mirabeau B. Lamar, urging the expulsion of the Cherokee Indians from East Texas. Apparently, the future president took note; Indian removal became a cornerstone of Lamar administration policy. William Hart was a resident of Nacogdoches. "Rusk, Thomas J.," "Mayfield, James S.," "Taylor, Charles S.," and "Hotchkiss, Archibald," *Handbook of Texas Online* [accessed October 22, 2004].

3. Robert W. Smith was born in 1814 in North Carolina. He came to Texas in 1836 and fought at the Battle of San Jacinto. During the Cherokee War he served as a captain in the Texas Army. Smith killed Chief Bowles at the Battle of the Neches and is the same person that James Love suggested should

serve as the vice presidential candidate for anyone (Albert Sidney Johnston, he hoped) who would run against Sam Houston for president. See letter above from Love to Johnston dated July 24, 1839. "Smith, Robert W.," *Handbook of Texas Online* [accessed October 22, 2004].

4. Anna Raguet, the eldest child of Henry and Marcia Ann Raguet, was born in 1819 in Pennsylvania. Her father brought the family to Texas from Cincinnati in 1833. She was the belle of Nacogdoches until her marriage on March 29, 1840, to Dr. Robert A. Irion. Her suitors included Sam Houston, but even his divorce in 1837 from Eliza Allen, from whom he had been separated since 1829, failed to overcome Miss Anna's scruples about marrying him.

5. See above James Love's letter to Johnston, dated July 11, 1839.

6. Love had moved to Galveston and the government had moved to Austin, so Houston seemed deserted to him.

7. Reily and Love had maintained an office opposite the courthouse and perhaps lived there.

8. Reily successfully ran for a seat in the Fifth Congress, where he represented Harris County.

Mirabeau Buonaparte Lamar to Albert Sidney Johnston

[n.d., n.p.; Austin,
November 1839]

Genl Johnston

I have just recd the report of the agent appointed to inspect the condition of the Custom House at Galveston, and feel constrained from a sense of duty to the public interest to remove the present collector.[1] I wish to make an appointment immediately, and I know of no one in whom I can place greater reliance nor for whom I have greater personal attachment than Col Love. I have therefore an idea of sending in his name to the Senate as successor to Dr. Roberts. What do you think of it? He is going to settle permanently on the Island, and the duty of the office will not conflict with his private affairs. He will be here in a short time, but I do not want to delay until his arrival. I wish to make a nomination to the Senate forthwith. If the Col, on his arrival, should not choose to accept, it will only give me little more time to look about & make another selection.[2]

Yours

M. B. Lamar

1. Dr. Willis Roberts resigned as the chief customs collector for the port of Galveston in December 1839.
2. Love, of course, refused the appointment. Alden A. M. Jackson became the new customs collector.

James Love to Albert Sidney Johnston

Houston

Nov 18th 1839

Dear General

I regret that I cannot as yet take my departure for the frontier *diggins* [*sic*]. You are, you know, a frontier Government. I expect to be off about the 25th. I am all anxiety to see how affairs will be managed by the sages of the land. They have met there with but one predominant idea, and that is opposition. When they have satisfied that feeling, they must, of necessity, take some ground to *redeem* the country. I want to know what it is. When they repeal the taxes, the tariff, disband the army, & navy and stop the issues, reject the loan—I want to know the substitute.[1]

It would have given me great pleasure to have been there and rendered what assistance I could in sustaining the Executive in measures I know to be right. But let me take things calmly, and I predict that before the session closes, he may have things as he wishes.

The last arrivals did not bring any news of interest. We are looking for boats from the *Neptune*[2] & *Columbia*—when we may learn some things new.

I came up yesterday and will go down the first boat. I left my family well, and the fever had disappeared entirely. There has been awful mortality here, and still dying two or three a day.

They sold 100 lots at San Luis[3] the other day for $75,000, a fair sale [and] one-third cash.

I write in haste & have nothing to write.

> Yours truly
> Jas Love

Present my respects to his Excellency [Lamar], and tell him that the greater the difficulties that surround one, the greater the triumph when overcome.

> Genl A. Sidney Johnston
> Austin

1. The Houston faction dominated the House and included the Old Hero, who represented Nacogdoches. The Houston faction opposed the recent Cherokee War, the removal of the capital to Austin, and the costly army and navy. They favored retrenchment and fiscal caution. They viewed the Lamar administration as irresponsible and extravagant.

2. The *Neptune* was a 745-ton wooden steamer, 215 feet long, and was built in New York in 1836. It began serving the Texas coast in October 1839. On January 1, 1863, the ship sank while attacking the Union warship *Harriet Lane* at the Battle of Galveston. "Galveston, Battle of," *Handbook of Texas Online* [accessed December 3, 2007].

3. Land speculators plotted a new town on San Luis Island just west of Galveston. Its promoters included Tod Robinson and William H. Jack of Brazoria. Love considered investing. Within a few years, the channel between the two islands silted up, and the town of San Luis, described by its promoters as a rival to Galveston, died. See "Robinson, Tod," and "Jack, William H.," *Handbook of Texas Online* [accessed October 27, 2004].

James Love to Albert Sidney Johnston

> Houston
> Dec 29th 1839

Dear General

I reached Houston in five days [returning from Austin]; had a pleasant journey and the "Poor Gentlemen" [*sic*] stood up like a soldier. I have already had the pleasure three times in refusing to loan him.[1]

I enclose a copy of Burnley's letter to the President[2] to Williams which of course you have seen. There is one clause omitted in the copy for reasons you will comprehend. You will see that the issue is uncertain; I hope it will be favorable. Burnley's temperament is not so sanguine as the General's, but in his private letter to me he says he thinks they will succeed. *It is doubtful.*

The General arrived two days after I did and left yesterday in time for the *Neptune* today. He will leave the U.S. in February and Burnley will return with him. He is now at Louisville awaiting orders.

We have no news from Kentucky of interest. Out friends still inquire for us and begin to look towards Texas. The Harrisburgh [sic] Convention has nominated Harrison; Old Hal, of course, laid on the shelf.[3] You will see the disgraceful scene in the U.S. Congress arising from the N. Jersey election. The truth is these petty states are not fit to govern a people, *and they will not.*

The advance on lots at Galveston this last sale was considerable & mostly purchased by strangers. The concourse of people there is great, and the improvement rapid, as I am told.

They are getting along here much in the old style. With great effort they drummed up a cotillion party the other night, but few ladies and they ugly. As a matter of interest to you, I may say the young ladies hearing of your difficulty for want of a shirt at the Levee, have it in contemplation to make up by subscription a sum sufficient to obtain another for you.

Reily goes up and can give you all the news.

> Yours truly
> Jas Love

pr Ikin to whom I have given a letter of introduction to you. [He is] the son of a wealthy English gentleman who has been imposed on by old Woodward. I would be sorry to see him cheated again.

> Genl A. Sidney Johnston
> Austin

1.   The "Poor Gentleman" is Memucan Hunt; see below, Love to A. S. Johnston, January 12, 1840. Memucan Hunt was born in 1807 in Vance County, North Carolina. He entered Texas shortly after the Battle of San Jacinto, and President Burnet commissioned him brigadier general. President Houston sent

Hunt and William Wharton back East, to Washington, to procure diplomatic recognition of the Republic of Texas. Hunt served as the first Texas minister in Washington. Under President Lamar, Hunt served as secretary of the Texas Navy. Later he served on the Texas–United States Boundary Commission. See "Hunt, Memucan," *Handbook of Texas Online* [accessed October 25, 2004].

2.   This letter is in the Comptrollers' Letters collection, Texas State Archives. Also see Gulick et al., *Lamar Papers*, 3:201, 209.

3.   The Whig Party held its first national convention in Harrisburg, Pennsylvania, on December 4, 1839. Henry Clay (nicknamed "Old Hal") was the favorite to win the nomination, but recent Whig Party defeats turned many party members against Clay. Convention delegates nominated a dark horse candidate, General William Henry Harrison, on the fifth ballot. "Clay, Henry," *Handbook of Texas Online* [accessed September 29, 2004].

Albert Sidney Johnston to Sam Houston

City of Austin
5th of Jany 1840

Genl Sam Houston
Sir

I have just been informed that on last evening and also on this morning you thought it necessary to use the most vituperative language with regard to me, for what cause I know not. In doing so, you bore in mind the responsibility you incurred, and you will be surprised that I inform you that *immediately* after the termination of the present session of Congress, I will hold you accountable.[1]

A. Sidney Johnston

[notation below added in Johnston's hand]

Genl Houston, on this note being presented by my friend, the Hon. S. M. Williams, disclaimed having at any time spoken in disrespectful terms of me, and gave a list of name[s] of the persons present at the times specified who could be referred to. He said to Mr. Williams [that] he would write to me to that effect. On being told so by Mr. Williams, I said he, Genl Houston, would not consider my note before him in writing to me, and it might be returned with the Genl's answer, which if in accordance with his verbal statement, I will consider satisfactory.

1.   Houston denied any insult toward General Johnston. Houston's reply to this
     letter can be viewed in William Preston Johnston, *The Life of General Albert
     Sidney Johnston: His Service in the Armies of the United States, the Republic of
     Texas, and the Confederate States* (New York: D. Appleton, 1878), 121–22.

James Love to Albert Sidney Johnston

Galveston
Jany 12th 1840

Dear General

I have recd your favor and do not feel any disappointment that the
lots were not sold, because I did not expect they would. I am sure now of
what I thought before; that the new bargains were put on me, and the lots I
recd were not the lots actually purchased for me.

The *Neptune* arrived yesterday and Genl Henderson in it.[1] I was
introduced to his lady,[2] and think from what little I saw, that she has sense
enough not to expect too much, and will conform as near as may be to things
as she finds them. We give him a dinner tomorrow. Hunt left yesterday for
Sabine. It is said there, he has announced that he will be a candidate for the
Presidency. What a world we have.

I saw dispatches from Treat from Vera Cruz.[3] In his letter to me, he
speaks with some confidence of success, altho he says that the late movements on the Rio Grande has [sic] lessened considerably the probability of
success. It has created a great sensation in Mexico, and the effort is made
to place a large force in the field to operate in that quarter. Bustamante[4] *is*
becoming, or is unpopular. Santa Anna is sick and that miserable country in
a miserable condition.

I have just heard of Burleson's success. These things do us great service, and you too, whilst on this subject, I may say I think you should ponder
well on the subject before you retire. You are now, for the first time, in a condition to enable you to reap the just reward of your exertions. Take the leave of
absence and be governed by circumstances hereafter. In relation to any little
cabal that may be on the tapis [table] as to whom may be next President,
amounts to just nothing at all. We are not ripe in Texas for making parties, not
is it in the power of anyone to form any. The only competition you could have
of a dangerous character is Houston; so far as he is concerned, except for him-

self, he would prefer you. *Abide your time*, and the reason I now have for saying you ought not to retire just now is: that your position is better than anyone in the country, and ought not to be abandoned hastily. I speak as a politician, and on such subjects I generally think right. In relation to your private affairs, I can have nothing to say only that if my services in arranging any business on your return that interrupt the duties attached to your office, they will be freely given.

The price of lots here is on the advance, [and] you could sell out now at a handsome profit. I think with you about Texana,[5] but really have no time to attend to such matters, but will see if anything can be done. I have paid Menard[6] $405 for you; he takes Franklin's[7] for the valorem. Our money is worth 40 [cents to the dollar] in N. O. & on the rise.

I shall not go to NO until the 27th. Business brisk in our city, advancing rapidly.

> J. Love
> Genl A. Sidney Johnston
> Austin

1. James Pinckney Henderson was born in 1808 in Lincolnton, North Carolina. He arrived in Texas shortly after the Battle of San Jacinto. Interim president David G. Burnet commissioned Henderson as a general in the Texas Army, and he served briefly in Houston's first administration as the attorney general and secretary of state. Later, in 1837, he served as Texas' minister to England and France and worked to secure diplomatic recognition and commercial treaties. He believed that James Hamilton's activities as President Lamar's loan commissioner interfered with his own mission. In 1840 he returned to Texas with less than he thought he could have secured. "Henderson, James Pinckney," *Handbook of Texas Online* [accessed October 25, 2004].

2. In October 1839 Henderson had married Frances Cox of Philadelphia in London.

3. At this time James Treat was in Mexico City trying to persuade the government of Mexico to recognize the independence of Texas. See "Treat, James," *Handbook of Texas Online*.

4. Anastasio Bustamante was president of Mexico from 1837 to 1839. "Bustamante, Anastasio," *Handbook of Texas Online* [accessed December 3, 2007].

5. Founded in 1832 and originally named Santa Anna, Texana was a village on the Navidad and La Vaca (later Lavaca) rivers. During the revolution it served as a staging ground for volunteers from the United States. In 1837 the repub-

lic established Camp Independence near the newly renamed city. In 1838 real estate agents sold the first city lots, and the city incorporated in 1840. "Texana, Texas," *Handbook of Texas Online* [accessed October 27, 2004].

6. Michel Branamour Menard.

7. Benjamin Cromwell Franklin was born in 1805 in Georgia. Franklin came to Texas in 1835 and fought at the Battle of San Jacinto. In December 1836 Houston appointed him judge of the Second Judicial District in Brazoria, and he served until November 1839, when he resigned and established a law practice in Galveston. "Franklin, Benjamin Cromwell," *Handbook of Texas Online* [accessed October 27, 2004].

James Love to Albert Sidney Johnston

Galveston
Jany 24th 1840

Dear General

The arrival of the *Neptune* on yesterday did not put us in possession of any news. Our money is still at 25 or 30. Saligny[1] came over and I suppose will be with you. Genl Henderson, in his speech, has said he would recommend that discriminating duties should be laid on British importations because they did not recognize us. This will not do for the very simple reason that it injures us more than them. The trade to the U.S. bears heavily upon us & we pay nearly 50 per cent more for goods there than we would from G. Brittain [sic], besides it is a better market for our cotton. We are not *quite* strong enough to threaten a power like G. B., time & perseverance will accomplish our object. If we are rash, we only bring trouble on ourselves.

We have heard of the success against the Indians. These things do us much service and the country is already deriving the benefits resulting from such a course. The expense should not be regarded. That will be overlooked for the good achieved.

Our city improves wonderfully. I am anxious to see some of you interested in Jack's purchase. The next payment falls due in April, [and] it is time some definite arrangement should be made to meet it. *Entre Nous* If Watrous[2] is still anxious to sell out, buy of him at any rate not exceeding $2000 (current notes [?]). We will share the purchase, [take] upon yourself no concern about the payment. Draw on me for it at sight.

I shall go to N. O., I think, on the return of the *Neptune* next Friday and will return early in March.

I will be glad to see you down here. The times are ripe for investments & sales [illegible].

No late news from Mexico. Dr. Jones[3] can give you all the news.

Yours truly

Jas Love

Will you ask Mr. Shaw[4] if he has arranged my stock agreement & send the result.

1. Jean Pierre Isidore Alphonse Dubois (or A. de Saligny) was born in 1809 in Caen, Normandy, France. In 1839, while serving as one of the secretaries at the French legation in Washington, Saligny made an inspection tour of Texas just after Lamar took office. His report influenced France in 1839 to become the second nation to recognize the independence of Texas. France appointed Saligny as the first French chargé d'affaires. He arrived in Texas in January 1840 and established the French legation in Austin. "Dubois de Saligny," *Handbook of Texas Online* [accessed October 27, 2004].

2. John Charles Watrous.

3. Dr. Levi Jones.

4. James B. Shaw was born in 1820 in Ireland. In 1837 he immigrated to New Orleans and then to Texas. He rose from chief clerk in the Treasury Department to comptroller, a position he held from 1839 until 1859. "Shaw, James B.," *Handbook of Texas Online* [accessed October 27, 2004].

Thomas Jefferson Rusk to Albert Sidney Johnston

Nacogdoches

22nd Feby 1840

Dear Genl

I[1] was sorry that I did not overtake you on the road, and more so that I had not time to come home by way of Galveston as I desired to have many *talks* with you. On my arrival here, I found very great excitement prevailing in relation to the Cherokee bill.[2]

It was also currently reported here that you had resigned in disgust and was on your return to the United States which I promptly contradicted.[3]

Our frontier, so far, is perfectly quiet and emigration is still rapidly pouring in. If you can make it convenient on your return from New Orleans, I would be glad to see you in Nacogdoches.

I know your aversion to writing letters, but if you can spare an hour, be sure to write me. Let me know where you will be through the spring and summer and you shall occasionally hear from me. Give my respects to McKinney, Williams, & Menard.

> I am Sir Truly Your friend
> Tho J. Rusk
> Genl A. Sidney Johnston
> Galveston
> Dr. Jones

1. At this time Thomas Rusk served as chief justice of the Texas Supreme Court. He served until June 1840. See "Rusk, Thomas," *Handbook of Texas Online*.
2. The Cherokee Bill, introduced and guided through the Fourth Congress by Sam Houston, the representative from Nacogdoches, did not reflect the wishes of his constituents. Instead of allowing white settlers to appropriate the former Cherokee lands granted to the Indians by Mexico and abandoned since the Battle of the Neches in July 1839, the bill declared that this territory was the property of the republic, that it would be sold to settlers, and that the funds resulting from the sale would go into the treasury.
3. Johnston soon did resign as secretary of war, in March 1840.

James Love to Albert Sidney Johnston

> N Orleans
> March 1st 1840

Dear General

I have recd your letter and was glad to hear from you, and much pleased that you had made the purchase of Watrous and forfeited the Austin lots. I think that purchase was no go.

Texas money here is not worth more than 20 [cents to the dollar]. It does not proceed so much from want of confidence, as a want of cash to invest, and besides, the great advance the money holders have it in their power to make on Speculation here. The truth is no matter what the emergency may be, the issues ought to be stopped. It lessens our credit and injures our people at the same time without any corresponding benefit.

It is my intention to leave on the 5th certainly, and pass the summer at Galveston, and I shall hope to meet you there before you come to the States.

I have endeavored to effect an arrangement to procure money to pay Jack. Those who hold it in large sums, require a great advance, more than I would give, and they [the] only way to buy it cheap is to have cash & purchase in small sums.

The first note of Jack's falls due in April. I am prepared to pay that, and you would give yourself no uncertainty about it. I prefer paying the money to selling lots to raise it. The property now being ours, I have my own views about it which I will explain when we meet.

The monied affairs of this country [the United States] are in a wretched condition. They are worse than anything else but the *morals* of the people. The Banks are failing one at a time, & almost in every instance there is defalcation by the officers.

I consider that Harrison's prospects is good, indeed, I feel almost certain of his success.[1]

Col. Harrison[2] goes over in this boat and will give you all the news from Ky.

I forwarded by last boat numerous letters from Treat to Genl Lamar. There are indications that we may have a brush with Mexico. Let it come.[3]

> Yours truly
> Jas Love
> Genl A. Sidney Johnston
> Galveston, Texas

1. William Henry Harrison was the most popular candidate for the Whig nomination for president in the November 1840 election in the United States.
2. Charles L. Harrison was returning to Texas from Kentucky. He apparently is no relation to William Henry Harrison.

3. Each Mexican political faction, the federalists and the centralists, positioned
    troops along the Rio Grande. On one occasion more than six hundred cen-
    tralist cavalry, with some Caddo and Cherokee guides, penetrated as far
    north as the Nueces River, but they did not engage any Texas citizens. See
    J. Milton Nance, *After San Jacinto* (Austin: University of Texas Press, 1963),
    275–76.

Hugh McLeod to Albert Sidney Johnston

Houston
April 17th 1840

Dear General

The only token of your remembrance, or indication of your particular topography after leaving us, was a letter to Col Cooke[1] respecting Cavalry, and a promise in it to write to me. Since then, until the arrival of Mr.
Jones yesterday (and Carey),[2] I was under the impression that you had gone
to the States.

We have had some busy times lately, and the horoscope[3] promises
more. You have doubtless heard everything about the Comanche affair,[4] and
their subsequent return to San Antonio with a few more captives. They cannot do us *more* injury than before, and we have a prospect of recovering all
our friends.

We have nothing from Bexar later than Fisher's[5] & Van Ness's[6] letters. A draft of one third of the Militia of the two Western Brigades has been
ordered to be held in readiness—and I presume the Major Genl of Militia[7]
will again *resume* citizenship and endeavor to *assume* command. How I hate
that man! I wish, Genl, you had not left us.

If this reaches you at Galveston, come up here immediately and
ascertain for yourself what the probabilities of a campaign are. I think it
inevitable. You will not, I understand, leave the country until it is decided,
and you cannot know in time at that distance. And if Felix Huston comes
(which of course he will, with the "Gilded palaces of the Montezumas" in his
pocket), *you* must be here to throttle him. We are all willing to attack the
demagogue, but we can't destroy him—he's too slippery for us.

A stockade has been thrown around the Capital, and in case

of necessity here, we can place the archives in it, and at least die with decency.

Come up immediately & see us, and all will go straight again.

> Yours truly
> H. McLeod
> General A. Sidney Johnston
> Galveston
> Fav of Commodore Moore

1. William G. Cooke was born in 1808 in Fredericksburg, Virginia. He came to Texas in 1835. He participated in the siege of San Antonio and fought at the Battle of San Jacinto. He remained in the army until September 1837, but after a brief venture in the drug business in Houston, he reenlisted in October 1838. President Houston appointed him quartermaster general of the republic. In January 1840 President Lamar appointed him commissioner to sign treaties with the Comanches. On March 19, 1840, he participated in the Council House Fight in San Antonio. "Cooke, William Gordon," *Handbook of Texas Online* [accessed October 27, 2004].

2. This refers to Dr. Levi Jones and probably to a free man of color named Carey McKinney. The latter had been a slave to Thomas F. McKinney. During the Texas Revolution he served as a dispatch rider, and for that service the Fourth Congress granted him his freedom.

3. Interest in horoscopes must have been popular at this time. Antonio Canales, the leader of the Mexican federalist army, never made a move without consulting his. See Nance, *After San Jacinto,* 214; "Canales Rosillo, Antonio," *Handbook of Texas Online* [accessed November 1, 2004].

4. The Council House Fight took place on March 19, 1840, in San Antonio. That day twelve Comanche chiefs, accompanied by their families, promised to bring in a number of white captives. The chiefs arrived with only one, saying that they had no influence with the tribes holding the other captives. The Texans did not believe the story and announced that they would hold the chiefs for ransom until the other white captives were released. The Indians tried to resist, and a slaughter took place inside the Council House. Thirty-five Indians died and eight received wounds. Seven Texans also died. At this time Hugh McLeod was adjutant inspector general of the Texas Army. He was one of two officials assigned to negotiate with the Comanches when the fight

commenced. "Council House Fight," *Handbook of Texas Online* [accessed December 30, 2006].

5.   William S. Fisher came to Texas from Virginia in 1834 and settled near Gonzales. He served with the Texas Army in 1836 and fought at the Battle of San Jacinto. After the revolution, from December 1836 to November 1837 he functioned as secretary of war, but the Texas Congress never confirmed his appointment. In March 1840, at the time of the Council House Fight, he commanded two companies of regular cavalry in San Antonio. "Fisher, William S.," *Handbook of Texas Online* [accessed November 1, 2004].

6.   At this time Cornelius Van Ness lived in San Antonio and was its representative in the Texas Congress. See "Van Ness, Cornelius," *Handbook of Texas Online*.

7.   Huston was born in 1800 in Kentucky. In October 1839 President Lamar appointed Huston major general of the militia. He and Johnston had long been enemies and had fought a duel in February 1837 in which Johnston had been severely wounded. Afterward Huston was contrite, and for a time, cooperative, but his overbearing personality and prolonged absences from Texas did not increase his popularity with most Texans. "Huston, Felix," *Handbook of Texas Online* [accessed November 1, 2004].

Louis P. Cooke [Secretary of the Navy] to Albert Sidney Johnston

City of Austin
April 20th 1840

Dear General

I sit down this morning to write you a few lines and I feel that I am not in the proper mood of mind to write to any person, much less yourself. Gen Lamar has just been in the office and changed the name of the ship and two brigs from Texas, Brazos, and Colorado to Austin, *Archer,* and Wharton, the first and last of these names were resorted to, mainly to afford an excuse for using it appropriately the one underscored. In this matter I have not been the least consulted. Gen came into the office whilst I was out and instructed Comore [sic] Moore to make the changes. The *Austin City Gazette*[1] is giving hell to the administration and Lamar. The Colorado people are much displeased at it.

Burnett's [sic] chances for the presidency looks more and more gloomy, his pieces against Old Sam have done him no good whatever. I knew they would not. [illegible] Malicious like I advised him to write. I do not admire Burnett, and my creed is death to my foes and life to my friends.

I know but two classes of men—friends and foes. One I *love*, the other I *hate*. Your successor [Branch T. Archer][2] is imbicile [*sic*] and visionary. Doctor Starr[3] I hate, but still respect. Webb[4] I fain would love, but he is cool, and I feel that he is daily fading away my scant countenance [favor?]; and Lipscomb[5] is in equipoise. He is now one, now the other—he cannot feel in old age, the ardour [*sic*] of youth. I am unpleasantly situated.

I do not think we shall have any active service; the reports from the west all appear to be a hoax for the purpose of drawing troops to the western frontier. It is time, however, that cavalry is in San Antonio. He[6] was not down there, however; he censures more for the purpose of exiting [exacting?] sympathy than from necessity.

I am progressing in my profess. with satisfaction to myself. I have given up the idea of running for Congress for my profession's sake.

Little Bosun [?] has not yet forgotten your name. Whenever we ask him where Gen Johnston is, he climbs upon the sofa or goes to the window to look for you. Mary[7] and Miss Charity [?] send the warmest wishes of welfare and happiness to you.

God Bless you, Yours forever
Louis P. Cooke

PS There is some talk of sending Green[8] minister to Spain—ridiculous. I know this as I have most things from report.

Gen A. S. Johnston
Galveston

1. The *Austin City Gazette* was the first newspaper published in Austin. Its first edition went to press on October 30, 1839. At first the newspaper supported President Lamar, but in January 1840 the newspaper changed editors and shifted its support to Sam Houston. "Austin City Gazette," *Handbook of Texas Online* [accessed November 1, 2004].

2. Branch Tanner Archer was born in 1790 in Fauquier County, Virginia. He arrived in Texas in 1831 and quickly sided with Texians favoring independence. During the revolution he, along with William Wharton and Stephen F. Austin, traveled to the United States and lobbied for American support. In

March 1840 he became secretary of war, a position he held until 1842. "Archer, Branch Tanner," *Handbook of Texas Online* [accessed November 1, 2004].

3.   At this time James H. Starr served as secretary of the treasury. See "Starr, James Harper," *Handbook of Texas Online*.

4.   James Webb served as attorney general. See "Webb, James," *Handbook of Texas Online*.

5.   Abner Smith Lipscomb was born on February 10, 1789, in Abbeville District, South Carolina. He studied law under John C. Calhoun and established his first law practice in Stephens, Alabama. From 1823 to 1835 he served as chief justice of the Alabama Supreme Court. He moved to Texas in 1839, and on January 31, 1840, President Lamar appointed him secretary of state. He served until December 13, 1840. "Lipscomb, Abner Smith," *Handbook of Texas Online* [accessed November 1, 2004].

6.   "He" refers to President Lamar. See his Address to the Army, March 14, 1840, in Gulick et al., *Lamar Papers*, 3:352–53.

7.   "Mary" is Cooke's wife. They had four children.

8.   Thomas Jefferson Green was born in Warren County, North Carolina, in 1802. He organized the Texas Land Company and moved to Texas in 1836. Once the revolution began Green returned to the United States and raised troops, money, and supplies for the cause. He was a senator for Bexar County in the Second Congress. He did not receive the appointment as minister to Spain that Cooke mentions. "Green, Thomas Jefferson," *Handbook of Texas Online* [accessed December 30, 2006].

James Love to Albert Sidney Johnston

Galveston
May 20th 1840

Dear General

We have not much news since you left. Four or five hundred Comanches are around San Hosea[1] demanding their prisoners or a fight. Burleson has gone on & will probably take them in the rear. They do not mean to fight, in my opinion, until their women & children are free.

Canales[2] is here and is sanguine of success. Arms and ammunition is all he wants.

I recd a letter yesterday from Treat. He has been formally recd as agent of this country, and is in Treaty for peace. He thinks, if not successful at once on the basis of independence, he will place matters on such a basis as will secure the object hereafter & peace now. For some reason all this is given in confidence to me.

General Douglas[3] was here a day or two after you left; I am sorry you did not meet. He is a little sore, but still prefers you as a candidate to other, eg the gentleman now actually in the field. I do not believe that Houston will be a candidate, and I am sure you can be elected if he is not.

If you are ambitious and desire so distinguished a station as President of this great *nation,* your chance of success is good, and you should by all means be at Austin at the meeting of Congress and so arrange matters as to travel through the East. The immigration there has been prodigious.

We are getting along in our usual quiet way here. Mrs. L[ove] is well, Mrs. Davis at Quintana,[4] Mary [Love] at Houston; I am sharing the perfection of housekeeping. We will reassemble the last of the week. The Commodore [Moore] has returned & will go to sea with two vessels in a few days, his object I know not.

Present me to my old friends. Old *Throg*[5] at the head of the list.

> Yours truly
> Jas Love
> Genl A. Sidney Johnston
> Louisville, Kentucky

I open this to say that Wells[6] & Redd[7] fought a duel at three paces. The former shot thru the belly, mortal. The latter through the hair. W charged R with cowardice in not fighting the Comanches.

L

1.   Founded in 1720, Mission San José y San Miguel de Aguayo is located about five miles downstream from the Alamo, or Mission San Antonio de Valero, as the complex was originally known. The Catholic Church closed the mission in 1824. At the time James Love wrote this letter a detachment of the Texas Army's First Infantry under the command of William S. Fisher operated out of the mission. The Texans did not return the Comanche prisoners captured in the Council House Fight. These Comanches escaped and retaliated by raiding toward the coast. They eventually attacked Victoria and plundered Linnville. "San José y San Miguel de Aguayo Mission," *Handbook of Texas*

Online [accessed February 20, 2006]; see also "Council House Fight," *Handbook of Texas Online.*

2. Antonio Canales Rosillo was born in 1802 in Monterrey, Nuevo León. As a Mexican federalist he opposed Santa Anna's centralist government. The federalists had suffered defeat at the end of 1839 but nevertheless organized the Republic of the Rio Grande on January 18, 1840. They based their government on the federal constitution of 1824 that had been destroyed by Santa Anna and the centralists in 1835. The capital of the republic would be Laredo, but because there was a printing press at Guerrero, it served as the temporary seat of government. Jesús Cardenas became president, with Francisco Vidaurri y Villaseñor, vice president, and Canales as commander-in-chief of the army. The boundary of the new republic included the Mexican states of Tamaulipas and Coahuila north to the Nueces River and southwestward to Nuevo León, Zacatecas, Durango, Chihuahua, and New Mexico. While some Texans considered a portion of this land to be part of Texas, the new republic sought aid from the Lamar administration. At the time Love wrote this letter Canales had already visited San Antonio, Victoria, and Austin. See "Canales Rosillo, Antonio," *Handbook of Texas Online*; Nance, *After San Jacinto,* 252–315.

3. Kelsey Harris Douglass of Nacogdoches was a merchant and a member of the Second Congress. He commanded Texas troops at the Battle of the Neches against the Cherokees. He died at his home on October 20, 1840. "Douglass, Kelsey Harris," *Handbook of Texas Online* [accessed November 1, 2004].

4. Mrs. Mary Jane Hawkins Davis was the wife of James H. Davis, the law partner of Richard Morris in Houston. Mrs. Davis, married in January 1840, was the daughter of Joseph H. Hawkins of Kentucky and New Orleans. He was Stephen F. Austin's law partner. Hawkins died in 1824, and by the contract with Austin, was entitled to one-half of Austin's premium land for settling the first three hundred settlers, an area that amounted to more than twenty-five thousand acres. Under Mexican law, heirs had to reside in Texas, which Hawkins's widow was unwilling to do, but in 1833 Edmund St. John Hawkins came to claim the land. He died several years later, and his brother, Thomas J., and sister, Mary Jane, came to Texas to secure the land. She lived with the Loves in May 1840 while her husband attended court and was visiting someone in Quintana, on the west bank of the mouth of the Brazos River. "Hawkins, Joseph H," *Handbook of Texas Online* [accessed November 1, 2004].

5. "Old Throg" possibly was Avis Throckmorton from Louisville, Kentucky. See "Throckmorton, James Webb," *Handbook of Texas Online* [accessed February 9, 2007].

6. William Davis Redd was born in 1810 in Georgia. He came to Texas with Mirabeau B. Lamar and fought at the Battle of San Jacinto. He returned to Georgia but came back to Texas in January 1839. Lamar appointed him captain of Company A, First (Frontier) Regiment, stationed at San Antonio. He participated in the Council House Fight. "Redd, William Davis," *Handbook of Texas Online* [accessed November 3, 2004].

7. Lysander Wells was born in 1812 in Middletown, Connecticut. In 1835 he joined Sidney Sherman's company of Kentucky volunteers and came to Texas in January 1836. He fought at the Battle of San Jacinto. He remained in the army and commanded the First Texas Cavalry at the Council House Fight. After the battle Wells claimed that William Redd had failed to attack the fleeing Comanches. He also accused Redd of immoral activities with a young woman who lived with him. The two men met in a duel on May 7, 1840. Redd died instantly. Wells died twenty days later. After the duel bystanders found a marriage license in Redd's pocket. "Wells, Lysander," *Handbook of Texas Online* [accessed November 3, 2004].

Tod Robinson to Albert Sidney Johnston

Galveston
June 4, 1840

Dear General

Since your departure,[1] matters have gone in one undeviating round of uniformity without change or shadow thereof. It would be an interesting subject for study for a statistical philosopher to learn the ways & means by which the population of Galveston (and as far as I know, the whole of Texas) obtain a livelihood. Money, you know, was scarce when you left. It has become scarcer since. The weather warm, sultry, & oppressive. The people dull and lacking money to support existence through the summer. There is some sickness, I understand, in the City. The only case I know of among our acquaintance is Miss Jones[2] who is quite sick with brain fever. All the others are very well. At Houston they are dying rapidly, I am informed.

The President & Secy of State[3] are at present here; they create no excitement. Genl Houston is said to be quite sick; we hope he'll die. If he does, how we will ring the changes upon the name of A. Sydney [sic] Johnston ! We'll give it a "log cabin & hard cider"[4] run in Texas. In anticipation of an opportunity of manifesting my authority to promote so desirable an object, I have negotiated for a newspaper press of which I shall act the Editor. Do not be surprised if you receive "The Thunder and Lightning Exposition" with the flag of Johnston unfurled and floating broadly, freely, & gloriously, underwhich auspicious folds we march to victory. There now, what think you of that, Master Brookes[?]

Have you heard of the death of Wells? He was killed at San Antonio in a duel with Capt Redd. The eagle towering in his pride of place has been by the mousing owl hawked at & killed. One comfort, however, Redd was killed also.

Is there a chance for a decent man like myself to woo & win a decent woman for a wife in Kentucky? I wish you would make some inquiries on that score & correspond with me on the subject. If any chance of success offers, I will forward you a power of Atty duly authenticated to make proposal, enter into contracts, ratify arrangements, etc. etc.[5]

I have nothing of interest to communicate. I hope you will get this letter by private conveyance. It will be toll enough to read it and needs not the additional drawback of postage.

> Yours with respect
> Tod Robinson
> Genl A. Sidney Johnston
> Louisville, Kentucky
> Col [Charles] Harrison

1. Johnston resigned his post as secretary of war in March 1840 but did not leave Galveston until the end of April or the first of May.
2. Robinson is referring to Martha Jones, the daughter of Dr. Levi Jones and his wife, Lucy. Martha died a few weeks later.
3. Mirabeau B. Lamar was president at this time, and Abner S. Lipscomb was secretary of state.
4. "Log cabin & hard cider" is a humorous reference to the 1840 Whig Party campaign in the United States to elect William Henry Harrison president.

5.   This attempt at matchmaking failed. Robinson later married a young lady
     from Galveston, Judith Crittenden. He abandoned her in 1850 and headed
     for the gold fields of California.

James Love to Albert Sidney Johnston

                                                  Galveston
                                                  June 4, 1840

       Dear General

              Since you left, the government as well as myself have recd letters
       from Treat announcing that he has been officially recd in Mexico as agent
       to negotiate for peace. He is acting within the advice, and has recd the aid
       of the British Minister. Although he does not speak with great confidence of
       success, still it is a point gained. And I believe that nothing but fear of the
       Federalists prevents them from concluding the treaty at once. To the public,
       the cause of the Federalists may seem at its lowest ebb, but it is not so. They
       were never stronger, because the whole population west of the Rio Grande
       advocate the cause and they are daily making demonstrations that will, in
       the end, secure triumph. A general feeling exists with us to aid them, and
       hundred[s] of our citizens are preparing to assist. Nothing but the pending
       negotiation prevents the government from opening the offensive at once [to]
       give aid to the *Rebels,* and thereby secure us from further molestation.
              Canales[1] was here some time & has now encamped on the Island
       some sixty Americans. He is to return in a short time. Many have gone west,
       & do not be surprised if you hear before the summer is over of the capture of
       Matamoros.
              The President is here, is very much my friend, and actually *asks
       advice.* He will direct Treat forthwith to bring his negotiation to a point.
       If unsuccessful, he will send out the fleet, order out the troops to the Rio
       Grande, and then [away] goes Centralism forever.
              Old Sam has just arrived with his bride. I called yesterday evening.
       She is good looking, & strange to say, seems to love him. The ladies have not
       yet decided whether they will call, I supposed they will.
              Burnet's "Publius" against "Big Drunk" has killed him.[2] Rusk is a
       candidate for Congress & so is Old Sam. Harrison[3] does not take very well

in the East, and will soon return to Galveston. You will be brought out in the newspapers for Vice-President. It is not wished that you will say you will or you won't. The object at present, is to secure the Houston interest in the west. He shall not be a candidate, [and] if he is, you can say in all modesty, that you are not qualified. If he is not, then we will make you President, modesty notwithstanding. Williams and McKinney have no doubt Houston will *not* run. They are your friends, & the place is thine.

We will all assemble at the meeting of Congress, and you must, or should, be there, and it would be strange if matters cannot be arranged to suit us. I am still resolute in my determination to avoid politics, altho it is hard to do so.

We have health in Galveston. It is sickly at Houston, and there is no domestic news of any interest. A few days since we were encouraged in the hope that Wells would recover, [but] I learned yesterday that his case was hopeless.

Burleson is out there in some force and will make a Comanche campaign. The situation of the frontier proves the correctness of the Indian policy. Three years hence you will say "They were."

My family are all well and send their regards. Capt Jo[4] is still running and often talks of you.

You will present me kindly to all my old friends. I am sorry for them. What a disgraceful government, building log cabins to secure an election[!] Now you know I am a Whig and abhor the action of the present government, but still until lately, I did believe there was intelligence enough in the U.S. to vote on principle without resorting to tricks that would disgrace a mountebank. Tell them to come to us when humbug is gone down and put down, and when an honest man is not afraid of expressing his principles.

By the bye, the new American chargé has arrived; he is a vulgar blackguard, a drunken brawler in a barroom, and gentlemen here would not call on him. He will die the first summer,[5] and God send he may[!]

If the U S Government does not conduct itself better, we will turn out conquests the other way. The only use we will have for Ky, is to levy contributions upon her in the way of supplies.

Write to me & return so soon as you can.

Yours truly
Jas Love
Genl A. Sidney Johnston
Louisville, Kentucky

1. See "Canales Rosillo, Antonio," *Handbook of Texas Online.*
2. Love is referring to an open letter, written by Burnet and signed "Publius," in which he attacks Houston, his opponent in the presidential campaign.
3. Colonel Charles L. Harrison.
4. Joseph E. Love, James Love's three-year-old son.
5. In early 1840 the Van Buren administration appointed George Flood from Ohio to be the new U.S. chargé to Texas. He was recalled when the Whig Party candidate assumed the presidency in March 1841. Love's comment was prophetic because Flood died on August 1, 1841, of congestive fever, before he could leave Galveston.

James Love to Albert Sidney Johnston

Galveston
June 27, 1840

Dear Genl

The fleet is now on the Gulf; the *Zavalla* goes in the morning to N. O. for sailors. I will join the Commodore whose destination is as far as Campeachy, and to be governed by *circumstances.* He is ordered to rende-vous [sic] off Matamoros in fifty days for further orders. The reasons is this: You will have heard that during the President's visit (& he is yet here), Dr. Archer [Secretary of War] and the powers left at Austin became alarmed at reports of large force of Centralists at Laredo, and Indians assembled at the Waco village, and in his zeal, issued his call to "Arms," a levy *en masse* of Morehouse[1] & Somerville's brigades.[2]

Just preceeding [sic] this extraordinary call, it was known that Felix[3] was on his way to Austin, and did arrive there a few days after. The Presi-dent disapproved the whole proceeding and was anxious to get out of it as smoothly as possible. The order to Morehouse was countermanded, [but] just at this time, Karnes arrived; he & Van Ness[4] suggested to me a plan of rais-ing 1,000 volunteers for immediate service and to march at once to the Rio Grande. I presented the plan to Lipscomb who approved it, and we went to see this Excellency, who gave the order.

The feeling west is for the Federalists [and] it is universal. The movement is to encourage them and attack the Central force at Laredo & drive them across should Treat not succeed & information be recd in 20 days.

The instruction is to send out all the Regular force under Burleson to make a descent on Matamoros, to have the fleet there to cooperate, and if successful, to hold that city against both parties. In that event (of going there), the President will give command to a Brigadier to be appointed, and you are the man.

Karnes left last night [and] 500 volunteers are already with foot in stirrup. There seems to be no doubt the force will be raised, and I entertain as little that it is, the commencement of a war that give success to the Fed. & establishes outposts on the Rio del Norte. They all want you. I need enter into no explanation of my views, as you know them. I altogether approve of the movement, and believe before you receive this, the troops will be in the field. *Genl Houston will be ordered to raise troops in the East and go against the Indians.*[5]

The President will leave here in a few days. He is improved in spirit and made friends here. I am high in favor, and have promised him a *glorious termination* of his administration. Canales leaves tomorrow to collect together his scattered Mexicans and the whole thing will be promptly done. I do not speak of all these things doubtingly. I have been in daily communication with the President and have seen all the orders dispatched, and the officials, too. I make no suggestions to you, you must decided for yourself. Of this I feel certain, the war is at hand.

I write in haste & late at night. Mr. [William] Maury, the purser of the *Zavalla*, waits for this & has promised to put it into the P Office in N O. We will have troublous times. We have no domestic news but the death of Miss Martha Jones of fever. My family are all well.

> Farewell
> James Love

In addition, I say Treat is ordered to bring his negotiations to a close at once.[6]

> Genl A. Sidney Johnston
> Louisville
> Ky

1.   Edwin Morehouse was born in 1801 in New York. He came to Texas in 1826 and fought in the Texas Revolution. In 1838 he was named brigadier general of the Second Brigade of the militia. This unit consisted of volunteers from

Harris County. "Morehouse, Edwin," *Handbook of Texas Online* [accessed November 3, 2004].

2. Alexander Somervell was born in 1796 in Maryland. He immigrated to Texas in 1833 and soon formed a mercantile partnership in San Felipe with Stephen F. Austin's brother-in-law, James F. Perry. During the revolution he served during the siege of Bexar and fought at the Battle of San Jacinto. After the revolution he served briefly as President Burnet's secretary of war. In November 1839 troops elected Somervell brigadier general. "Somervell, Alexander," *Handbook of Texas Online* [accessed November 3, 2004].

3. Major General Felix Huston received orders from Secretary of State Abner Lipscomb to command troops in a campaign against the Indians on the upper Brazos River. See "Huston, Felix," *Handbook of Texas Online.*

4. Henry Wax Karnes and Cornelius Van Ness. After consulting with Lamar, Karnes called for volunteers on June 24, 1840.

5. Nothing developed from this excitement, partly because of events and partly because Karnes died on August 16, 1840, of yellow fever.

6. President Lamar sent James Treat to Mexico City to negotiate diplomatic recognition of Texas from Mexico. Mexican officials engaged in fruitless negotiations for over a year. As long as negotiations continued President Lamar did not allow the Texas Navy to engage the Mexican navy, blockade Mexican ports, or link with federalist rebels in the Yucatán. See "Treat, James," *Handbook of Texas Online.*

James Love to Albert Sidney Johnston

Galveston
July 7th, 1840

Dear General

Since I wrote you nothing has occurred of much importance. The President is yet here, but will leave in a day or two. I believe in truth that he dislikes to return, and would gladly abandon the honor to get rid of the trouble of playing President.

The news today is & it is true, that the levy *en masse* of the Dr [Archer, secretary of war] dissolved itself on the Colorado with as little ceremony as the President dissolved it here. He anticipates a rupture with Archer on his return.

Hunt[1] had a dinner given to him at some place in the East. He is greeted as one who gave all for his country, who has made the greatest sacrifices, and has been most ungratefully sacrificed. He has gone to Austin, and is engaged in spreading his injuries before the world. The President thinks Henderson is in dudgeon because he will not give McIntosh[2] the appointment of minister. He says he will not. Old Sam left here a day or two since on his way to the East; his lady love is here. He is about as usual, altho he was not drunk when he was last here. The American Minister is yet here, drunk every day, staggering about, and in the lowest associations. Felix[3] is up the country *waiting for orders* which he will never get for anything from the President. You will know from the enclosed morceau [morsel] what he is for.

I am obliged to you for the news of peace, and am only sorry it is not true and no foundation for it more than you knew before you left. The truth is Granny Bee[4] writes about, and talks about everything, without knowing anything. I recd letters from Treat yesterday & have read his to the President, they are of 10th June. He thinks his prospects more flattering & is certain the cabinet approves it. It is before the council of state, composed of 13, nine of whom make a quorum. If they approve, it will then be recommended to Congress, and not without. Such is the law of Mexico. The Minister of State observed to Treat that he considered two-thirds of the difficulties surmounted. I do not. The American consul at Liverpool has given information that negotiations are going on there for the purchase of steam ships, & that the *Argyle*[5] was purchased to transfer troops from Vera Cruz to Texas, but found none to transfer & did not change owners. The fleet is on the waters and is now looking down the coast. Canales is yet here, endeavoring to raise means to assist his movements. Karnes has issued a call for six month volunteers [and] I have no doubt about the result if he gets them. Van Ness, himself, and everyone from the west says he will. I confess, I have doubts, but have no reason for them that I know of.

To sum up. If Karnes raises his men and makes a move to the Rio Grande, the war will have begun. If on the back of this, any part of the loan should be had, an additional number of troops will be forthwith ordered out. Matamoros and Tampico will fall. If we do not further interfere, the fact of 1,000 troops American being on the line, enables the Federalists to organize, to assume the offensive, and organize the Republic of the Rio Grande. I need not repeat in the event of war, you are looked to by the President to command.

I have a letter from Burnley[6] of the 3rd June. He writes that our friends think the chance of success better than last year, but does not speak with any certainty. He was to leave on the 4th for Paris.

We are all well. The City is healthy.

Yours truly
Jas Love

1. At this time Memucan Hunt served as the Texas representative for boundary negotiations with the United States. See "Hunt, Memucan," *Handbook of Texas Online*.

2. When James Pinckney Henderson left the Texas legation in Paris and returned to Texas, he promised that George S. McIntosh, the secretary of the legation, would become the new chargé.

3. Felix Huston.

4. At this time Barnard E. Bee served as Texas minister plenipotentiary in Washington, but because of ill health he resided in South Carolina. Bee maintained correspondence with a friend in Mexico and continued to make pronouncements about Texas although he held no official status. See "Bee, Barnard E.," *Handbook of Texas Online*.

5. The *Argyle* was chartered by Mexico as a towing vessel for use at Vera Cruz. The steamships ordered in England were not delivered to Mexico until 1842.

6. Albert Triplett Burnley.

James Love to Albert Sidney Johnston

Galveston
July 22, 1840

Dear General

Since I wrote you, Genl Canales has left with 120 recruits for Aransas. He states, as well as others, there were 2,400 Americans in that quarter, ready & in camp for service, and about 1,000 Mexicans [federalists], and they intended to take the field immediately. The levy *en masse* have been disbanded some time, as four hundred assembled on the Colorado according to orders [and] met no orders, no officers, & no provisions. They left in disgust mingled with execrations. Rumor says Karnes[1] *is* raising his men. I have not any certain or definite information from him, and I think it more than probable that both he and Van Ness[2] are mistaken in their opinion of the certainty of doing so.

Three days since, the fleet rendezvoused at the Balize.[3] The Commodore wrote he would be off next morning. I do not look for any good growing out of the expedition other than showing strength.

Dr. Archer has given Felix[4] orders to raise a force and subdue the Indians on the upper Brazos. The President is angry about it & swears Felix shall never have any command and anticipates a scene with the Doctor. The President is yet here, and says he will *soon* leave. Judge Lipscomb[5] went yesterday. We have no additional news from Treat nor any from Burnley.

There has been some skirmishing with the Indians on the frontier, nothing decisive—horses stolen, a few killed, amongst them Bird Lockhart.[6]

Rumor here says that the President will make Sam Roberts[7] consul at N. Orleans; he will be a God in spite of the devil.

Nearly 800,000 dollars has been funded under the last law. It has produced a rise of a few cents in Texas money, and will continue to rise I think. The quotations in N. O are not materially different, yet sales have been made there at 18 [cents on the dollar?] by citizens of Galveston.

You will see from this that I do not now think the same necessity exists for your immediate return as formerly, altho I think y[ou] ought to be here certainly by the 1st November. We will have stormy times in Congress.

My family are all well, and no citizen of Galveston has fever, think of that; No scandal or any gossip.

> Yours truly
> James Love
> Genl A. Sidney Johnston
> Louisville Kentucky

1. Henry Wax Karnes did not raise an army to invade northern Mexico. Weakened by a wound he received a year earlier at the Battle of Arroyo Seco, Karnes died of yellow fever in San Antonio on August 16, 1840. See "Karnes, Henry Wax," *Handbook of Texas Online*.

2. At this time the Van Ness brothers, Cornelius and George, practiced law in San Antonio. Cornelius also represented Bexar County in the Texas Congress.

3. The Balize light was a navigational lighthouse first established by the French in 1699. Located southeast of Pilottown, Louisiana, it was near the various passes

that branch from the main channel of the Mississippi River near its mouth. http://www.lighthousedepot.com/database/uniquelighthouse.cfm?value=2363

4. "Dr. Archer" refers to Branch T. Archer, the secretary of war. "Felix" refers to Felix Huston.

5. "Lipscomb" refers to Abner Smith Lipscomb, Lamar's secretary of state.

6. Byrd Lockhart was born in Virginia in 1782. He immigrated to Texas in 1826 and made a living as a surveyor. During the revolution he participated in the siege of Bexar and was a defender in the Alamo. Sometime before the final attack Colonel Travis ordered Lockhart and Jackson Sowell to leave the fortress and search for supplies. He was in Gonzales when the Alamo fell. "Lockhart, Byrd," *Handbook of Texas Online* [accessed November 3, 2004].

7. Samuel Alexander Roberts was born in 1809 in Putnam County, Georgia. In 1837, at the urging of an old family friend, Mirabeau Lamar, Roberts immigrated to Houston, Texas. In 1841 he served as Lamar's secretary of state. Roberts did not become consul at New Orleans. "Roberts, Samuel Alexander," *Handbook of Texas Online* [accessed November 3, 2004].

Richard Morris to Albert Sidney Johnston

23rd July 1840
on board Steamer *Empress*[1]
[at New Orleans]

Dear General

Mr Pearce, who is going to Louisville, has kindly offered to take charge of this letter, as also of one entrusted to my care by Colnel [sic] Love & directed to you. I[2] left Texas on the 8th of this month. Our mutual friends were all well & nothing remarkable in the way of news stirring. Lamar & Lipscomb were at the Island where they have been staying some weeks & will continue some time longer recruiting from the *excessive* cares & *exhausting labors* attendant in *Governmental duties.* The affairs of the nation, meantime, are conducted by the remaining members of the cabinet. Your successor in office, [Branch] Archer, who is . . . *glorioso,* a good fellow, but not *overstocked* with judgement, hearing a short time since, that Arista[3] with four thousand Mexicans was on the Rio Grande, issued an all flaming Manifesto calling on all the good citizens to turn out in defence of their country etc., etc & ordering out *all the Militia* west of the Brazos. There was, of course, a great stir. In several counties every man turned out, & when it was ascertained that there was no necessity for the call, much dissatisfaction, of course, ensued. So you see the evil effects of your *resignation*. The worse consequences of the appointment of a man who is full of "plain Whiskey & water" & likewise, dearly loves to see his name at the foot of a publication which speaks of bleeding, country, invading-foes, worthless enemies, & etc., etc. Lamar has authorised Karnes to raise one thousand men to march to the Rio Grande, & has also ordered out all the vessels but one to cruise on the coast of Mexico. What all this portends, we do not yet know, but I shrewdly suspect that he has harkened to the solicitations of the Federalists, & that they will act in concert. They (the Federalists) are mustering in considerable force & entertain high hopes.

Politics are making but little stir, ie as regards the Presidential canvass, but there is some little excitement in several counties for the congressional election. Reily[4] is out for Harris [County] against Tomkins[5] & Cocke. I think he will be elected, though it is doubtful as he is a *gentleman*. Rusk has resigned[6] & is a candidate for Congress, & it is said he will run for President. This is all the news that was stirring, & most of that I expect you have heard before.

I have been very sick for the last five weeks, a severe spell of Bilious fever in Houston made me think seriously of trying *another* country, & I was confined to my bed nearly a week in New Orleans with a relapse. I am now recovering rapidly & hope with pure air & a little Sulphur water to return to Texas in the winter with renewed health & spirits.

What are you doing in Louisville? Reports says that you are renewing your suit to a certain lady who shall be nameless. General! I did not think you would be so rash! What! a Texian & in the midst of these hard times, & do you still believe that you will be successful?!! Tis a wilful *tempting* of *providence*, & you deserve *condignus* [suitable] punishment in the shape of a most awful kick. For my part, minded as I am in monetary matters, partially broken down in constitution, & laboring under the opprobrium which a residence in *our country* seems to throw indiscriminently [sic] on all, I shall not dare to speak to a woman this summer, & shall have the gratification, at least, of suffering nothing ostensibly, no matter what may be my private feelings. But, General, shd [should] you be successful, do not permit the wiles of woman, nor the lure of what they call society, to keep you in the States. We can't spare you in Texas, & these pretty little [illegible] . . . are too confined for a man who has once breathed the pure air of a great central Republic.

I am on my way to my plantation where I shall stay a few days &

then go on to Virginia, then back to Texas in November. If possible, I may probably pass through Louisville. If so, I shall see you, of course. I have much to say that the limits of a letter will not admit of being written. You must excuse this scrawl as the boat is under way & is shaking awful.

God bless you Your friend

R. Morris

1.   The steamer *Empress* was a new light-draft river boat that ran regularly between New Orleans and Louisville, Kentucky.
2.   Richard Morris was born in 1815 in Virginia. In 1838 he immigrated to Houston, Texas, and practiced law with James H. Davis. In 1840, after Davis died, Morris reestablished his law practice in Galveston. In 1841 President Lamar appointed him district attorney. Also that year, he married Mary Love, James Love's daughter. "Morris, Richard," *Handbook of Texas Online* [accessed November 3, 2004].
3.   Mariano Arista was born in 1802 in the city of San Luis Potosí, Mexico. He became the general of the Mexican Army of the North in 1839. In 1840 he crushed the federalists' attempt to establish the Republic of the Rio Grande. "Arista, Mariano," *Handbook of Texas Online* [accessed November 5, 2004].
4.   James Reily resided in Houston at the time this letter was written. See "Reily, James," *Handbook of Texas Online*.
5.   Augustus M. Tomkins practiced law in Houston and earlier served as a reporter for the Republic of Texas Senate. "Tomkins, Augustus M.," *Handbook of Texas Online* [accessed November 5, 2004].
6.   Rusk resigned as chief justice of the Texas Supreme Court on June 20, 1840, and made an unsuccessful bid for Congress. See "Rusk, Thomas Jefferson," *Handbook of Texas Online*.

Alexander Parker Crittenden to Albert Sidney Johnston

Galveston
Dec 10th 1840

[no salutation, only a diagram for playing chess by letter using a system of numbers and a challenge issued by Crittenden.]

Having waited a decent time, just sufficiently long to make you

feel anxious to hear the news of the country from good authority and to
feel duly grateful to any friend who will take the trouble to send it, I[1] now
commence a series of essays upon all subjects which have ever occurred to
the *mind* of man or even the *fancy* of woman—and in the course of them, I
hope to be able to remove many prejudices under which you labor, and by
force of argument, to instill many sound & necessary truths into your mind.
You are aware, that upon the subjects of Morality and Political Economy,
you have many antiquated and incorrect notions. You must be modern-
ized, and I flatter myself that no one could undertake your reformation
with greater prospects of success than myself. From the many conversations we have had, you must, of course, have discovered that my opinions
are entitled to great respect and that yours are generally erroneous. You
are, therefore, in a fit state of mind to receive instruction with humility
and to profit of it. In my next, I will discuss the comparative value
of honesty and money, and upset your old fashioned theory. I consider
that a subject of pressing importance in the present state of affairs.
By impressing upon your mind a few plain and generally received principles, I shall be doing you a maternal service. You are, at present, an
unarmed and defenceless man in the midst of armed crowds. I must put
a sword and shield into your hands, or you will fall a victim to excessive honesty.

　　　Now for the news:

　　　The Congress are now in full swing. Throwing down and building up, Retrenchment and Democracy is the watch word. They propose to
reduce the salaries of all officers of the government and to diminish their
number. They will probably abolish the office of Sect [Secretary] of the
Navy and Post Master General, placing those departments in the hands of
Clerks under the control of the Sect of War, at the same time, uniting all the
bureaus of the War Department into one. They talk of laying up the Navy
and reducing the Army, and at the same time, of commencing active hostilities against Mexico—with *volunteers*. Proud and independent in the midst of
poverty, they are about to recall the loan Commrs [commissioners]. The bill
for that purpose having already passed the House. All power is to be placed
in the hands of the people, and by way of commencement, they have made
the Chief Justices of the County courts elective by the mob. Considering it
an insult to the sovereigns that any of the acts of their representatives should
be concealed from them, they have made public all the proceedings of former

secret sessions and all the private correspondence of the departments with the loan Commrs.

The project of purchasing peace with Mexico through the intervention of England created something of a sensation. Of course, having been a member of the cabinet when the matter was discussed, you are acquainted with it. With Mexico, there is now no hope of peace. Treat, having given up in despair, left in the *San Antonio* for Galveston and died on the way. Our Navy are still on the Mexican coast. [Commodore Edwin] Moore (you have read of the mighty exploit) sent a boat to the shore for water without any communication with those in command, and of course, it was fired upon. Enraged at this *unexpected* insult to the flag, he gave orders to capture all vessels under the Mexican flag. The poor little Schooner *Ana Maria,* owned in Campeachy by a conspicuous Federalist and a warm friend of Texas & sailing under the express promise of the Commodore that she should pass unharmed, was accordingly seized, much to the delight of the Centralists, and sent in as a "lawful prize."[2] She is now claimed and I supposed will be given up. The capture was made by one of the Schooners during the absence of the Commodore. Had he been present, I presume she would have been released.

Canales has given up the cause and made his peace with the Centralists. I have not yet read the articles of the treaty [but] I suppose they are as rascally as could be expected from Mexican honor. Jordan, not being willing to be bought and sold, cut his way out of the country with the loss of a few men, and being reinforced, has gone upon an expedition upon his own hook. It is rumored that since their union, Canales and Arista have crossed the Rio Grande and intend a serious invasion.[3] You may believe it if you think proper.

The Comanches have had another drubbing with an actual loss of probably eighty or a hundred, and a newspaper loss of a hundred and fifty. Moore's victory has thrown Houston into the shade and destroyed all his bright anticipation.[4] Even another bulletin will fail to do away with the effect of this unfortunate success. Felix has ceased to be Felix and is forgotten—untalked of.[5]

Rusk is now the man. It has been suddenly discovered that he deserves well of the country, and it is proposed to reward him with the honor of a contest with the magnifico Sam. It is said that he will undoubtedly be the man. Burnet considered the contest hopeless and will withdraw. I *think*

Henderson with be Houston's *Deputy*.[6] It is an inference of my own from certain saying and doings of Henderson himself, though my opinion is unsup-
ported even by rumors. Henderson looks higher—I am much mistaken if
he has not marked out for himself a course which he thinks will, if skillfully
followed, lead to his successorship of the Hero of San Jacinto. His plan will
develope [*sic*] itself in the course of time. It is defective and will fail, or I am
much mistaken in my estimate of the fickleness of the *people*.

Dec 13th

I have just learned that Hemphill[7] is elected Chief Justice by a
majority of two over Webb,[8] and his salary reduced to 3,000 the same as the
other judges. All those elected last year to fill vacancies are to be legislated
out of office. Shelby is about to resign, [and] Robinson, I *think* and *hope*,
will succeed him. The bills to "close the Courts of Justice" & to "establish a
general bankrupt law" have been defeated by large majorities in the House.
The same body have appointed a committee to "inquire into the expediency
of enlisting 5,000 volunteers for the invasion of Mexico—the volunteers to
take whatever they can seize for pay and to be entitled each to one league
of land wherever they can take possession of it and hold it." Whether such a
bill can pass is very doubtful. Whether it will produce any effect, if passed, is
still more so. I send you a paper in which you may find something that will
interest you.

I am still in Galveston, but in a day or two shall leave for Washington [Texas] with my little family. I was much pleased with the County of
Montgomery, but not with the town, finding it impossible to get any kind
of accommodations there. I have determined upon making Washington my
home, provided always, I can raise sufficient funds to transport me there.
Money, you may recollect, was rather scarce when you left. It is now more so.
Business has not recommenced, nor will it for a year or two. Our streets are
desolate and one-fourth of the houses in the city unoccupied. I predict that
in six months from this time, the population of Galveston will not be one-
half of what it is at present. It is doomed almost to die and then to revive.

Morris and Doswell[9] have returned. They staid [*sic*] but a few hours
and then hurried on to Houston. Miss Mary Love is in exceedingly low spirits and in bad health. What can be the cause?

I have now cleared my budget of news. Having got rid of the rub-
bish, hereafter I will have at you in a fair field. Upon one point I shall be

exacting; every assault must be answered promptly. Your shafts directed to
Galveston will find me. For the present, I bid you goodbye.

Yrs truly
A. P. Crittenden
Genl A. Sidney Johnston
Louisville Ky

1. Alexander Parker Crittenden, a distant relative of John J. Crittenden, the
    Whig politician of Kentucky, was born in 1816 in Lexington, Kentucky. He
    was an able lawyer and lived with his mother, wife and children, and his sister
    in Galveston. He moved to California in 1848. The family followed two years
    later. In 1870 his paramour, Mrs. Laura D. Fair, shot him in front of his wife
    and children. See Charles F. Adams, *Murder by the Bay: Historic Homicide in
    and about the City of San Francisco* (Sanger, Calif.: Quill Driver Books, 2005);
    http://politicalgraveyard.com/families/10368.html.
2. The owner of the *Anna Maria* was John L. McGregor, the U.S. consul at
    Campeche and a personal friend of Commodore Moore. The vessel was cap-
    tured by the commodore's cousin, Alexander Moore.
3. Samuel W. Jordan joined the Texas Army in 1836 and fought during the revo-
    lution. In 1839 he participated in the military operations against the Chero-
    kee Indians in East Texas, where he undoubtedly befriended Albert Sidney
    Johnston. Later that year he resigned from the Texas Army and joined the
    Mexican federalists' attempt, under Antonio Canales, to form the Republic
    of the Rio Grande. In October 1839 Jordan defeated centralist forces at the
    Battle of Alcantra. In 1840 he defeated centralist forces at Saltillo, Mex-
    ico, then returned to Texas. In December 1840, around the time Alexander
    Parker Crittenden wrote this letter, Jordan, while visiting Austin, tried to kill
    Sam Houston with an axe. This action probably amused Albert Sidney John-
    ston's friends. See "Jordan, Samuel W.," *Handbook of Texas Online* [accessed
    December 31, 2006]. Crittenden was wrong. Canales and Arista did not cross
    the Rio Grande.
4. Commodore Moore in early June 1840 took the Texas Navy to sea. They
    blockaded the Mexican east coast, initiated an alliance with federalist leaders
    in the Yucatán, and captured the city of Tabasco. The TN *Zavala*, formerly
    the *Charleston*, participated in this action. In doing so the *Zavala* became the
    first steam-powered vessel to engage an enemy with hostile fire. See "Moore,
    Edwin Ward," *Handbook of Texas Online*.

5. Felix Huston left Texas in early 1841 and resumed his law practice in New Orleans and later, Natchez. See "Huston, Felix," *Handbook of Texas Online.*

6. Crittenden is referring to James Pinckney Henderson, who returned to Texas in 1840 and established a law practice in San Augustine.

7. John Hemphill was born in Blackstock, Chester District, South Carolina, in 1803. He came to Texas in 1838 and settled at Washington-on-the-Brazos, where he practiced law. In January 1840 he was elected judge of the Fourth Judicial District, thereby making him an associate justice of the Texas Supreme Court. "Hemphill, John," *Handbook of Texas Online* [accessed November 8, 2004].

8. At this time James Webb served as attorney general. See "Webb, James," *Handbook of Texas Online.*

9. Richard Morris was courting Mary Love, and James Temple Doswell was a merchant in Houston. See "Morris, Richard," *Handbook of Texas Online.*

Samuel Alexander Roberts to Albert Sidney Johnston

Galveston

Jany 17th 1841

Dear Genl:

I[1] think something once passed between us upon the subject of a correspondence during your absence, but what it was, I cannot now exactly call to mind, further than that "all communications addressed to you at Louisville would meet you there or be forwarded to your address in case you should be elsewhere." Acting thus, partly upon the implied, but contained, in the above observation, that an occasional interchange of letters would not be disagreeable, and partly from a more selfish motive, to banish the gloom which always makes war upon me when the East wind blows, accompanied as it always is, by a heavy fall of rain, but more than all, from a real desire to cultivate by friendly offices, the acquaintance (might I say the friendship) of one for whom I have *always* entertained the highest respect, and recently, the most unfeigned regard—acting, I say, from one or all of these motives, I am about [to] consecrate as gloomy an afternoon as you can well imagine by "breaking ground" and laying the "cornerstone" of an ediface [sic], the completion of which will depend upon you. This much by way of preface.

If I knew who your correspondents were in this country, or how long it had been since you had a complete detail of the occurrences most worthy of note, I should the better understand how to make my letter interesting. As it is, I shall confine myself to the most recent events, trusting that others may have supplied you with whatever has happened of interest up to about this period.

Of late, the all absorbing topic seems to be the apprehensive war with Mexico. Burnet, acting President,[2] has made two communications to Congress in both of which he states [with] no substance, that he has *certain* and *positive* information that we are to be invaded—and that the enemy for this purpose is concentrating his forces on the Rio Grande. By the last mail from Austin, we learn that Col Seguin[3] had just arrived express from San Antonio bringing information that the army was now actually encamped at San Patricio on the Nueces, twelve or fifteen hundred strong; that their foraging parties were collecting all the cattle in the neighborhood and that they had driven off Seguin's own cattle within *thirty miles* of San Antonio. Major Howard,[4] who is in command at S. Antonio, has sent an express to Austin with a requisition for ammunition, arms, men, etc.—which was *immediately* granted by a resolution of Congress. In fact, the war fever seems now fairly an epidemic, and Burnet sounds loudly the trumpet for the onset.

A "war bill" has been introduced, and by the last accounts was undergoing angry & violent discussion. Sam Houston has taken sides against it, and Felix Huston has come out in the papers with "*his plan*" again, which he says is "to call out the militia"!![5] Futile inexpedient, is he not. But to return to the war bill. The impression seems to be that it will pass, notwithstanding the opposition of Genl Sam Houston. I am sorry I cannot give you more of an outline of the bill. It contemplates, I am *told*, offensive measures, but of this I am by no means certain, and only give to you as the one act in this place.

I am truly sorry that at this critical juncture, you are not here, tho, I by no means intend to advise your return. In fact, I am still sceptical [*sic*] about war. In this, I confess, I am almost alone, and for that reason mistrust very greatly my judgement tho I still stick to it. My principal reasons for disbelieving are such as will readily suggest themselves to your mind, such as the poverty of our enemy, the season of the year, the unpopularity of the service & the consequent difficulty of getting troops willing to undertake the Campaign. If these, however, are not satisfactory altogether, even to my mind, and if it was not the recent treaty with England and the results which I expect from it,[6] I do not know that I should be so confident in my predictions.

Accompanying the treaty (which has gone up to Austin), was a dispatch for the British Minister at Mexico (Mr Packenham) with a letter from Genl Hamilton requesting that an armed vessel might be *immediately* dispatched with it, on its reaching this place. This will be done. It is said that this dispatch contains instructions to the British Minister, which will at once put an end to the war against this country. Now altho' this seems a round-about way of arriving at a conclusion, I, nevertheless, most firmly believe it. The influence which England possesses in the Councils of Mexico is well known, and that she will not fail to exert it, to secure the heavy debt due her, is not to be doubted. This Genl Hamilton knew, and it is rumored has availed himself of. Of course, the treaty is not yet made public, but some of its features are said to be known, the principal of which are that upon *condition* of the Rio Grande's being acknowledged [as] our western boundary, we [paper torn] England *our* portion of the Mexican debt. . . . [paper torn] . . . by a Geographical decision how fa . . . [paper torn] . . . to that portion of the Mexican territory if it had never been severed from the mother country. If this be true, it is easy to see how England is interested in establishing peace, but how it can be liked in this country, I know not.

The Congress, I believe, is getting on much as usual—unmaking what they have before made. Very little excitement seems to exist upon the subject of the Presidency. Houston & Burnet will doubtless be the only candidates, tho' your name and Rusk's are still frequently mentioned. Genl Lamar is at Doct Hoxey's[7] very ill, I hear, & I much fear will never be able to get any further. He started for the U S on account of his health, but broke down at the place above named. I think of going up to see him.

It was understood here some days ago that the election of Judge for this District was appointed to come off the week before the last. Since that we have had no intelligence from Austin. Robinson tells me that his friends inform him, he will certainly be elected.[8]

You probably heard of the loss of one of the Schooners; the other two are in port & the ship and steamer are expected in any day. Moore made the Federals pay him $25,000 in specie for his cooperation against Tabasco.[9]

At Mrs. Crittenden's, things go on as usual. You are not forgotten by any of them. We have got a few good jokes in which you figure at which we laugh & make merry, and our standing toast at our game suppers, which by the bye, we get up in a style that an Epicurean might envy, is "our absent friend, Genl Johnston." Our little society consists of Mrs. & Miss C[rittenden], Robinson, Jennings, now and then Parker (when he happens to be here), and your humble servant. When will you add on to the number?

But I must close. If you can make anything of this disjointed rambling scrawl, then will I commend your ingenuity and perhaps to ask it again the same way. Meantime, believe me your friend & obt svt [obedient servant].

S A Roberts
Genl A. S. Johnston
Louisville Kentucky

1. Samuel Alexander Roberts at this time served as the acting secretary of state. See "Roberts, Samuel Alexander," *Handbook of Texas Online.*

2. David G. Burnet, vice president, became acting president in December 1840, when President Lamar asked Congress for permission to seek medical treatment in the United States. He never left Texas, though, falling ill in Washington County, and he returned to office at the end of January 1841.

3. Juan Seguín was born in San Antonio in 1806. An active participant in the Texas Revolution, he defended the Alamo and commanded the only Tejano unit at the Battle of San Jacinto. He was the only Mexican Texan in the senate of the republic. In the spring of 1840 he resigned his senate seat and volunteered to fight for General Antonio Canales in his attempts to form the Republic of the Rio Grande. After Canales's defeat, Seguín returned to San Antonio and became that city's mayor. He arrived in Austin on December 24, 1840. "Seguín, Juan Nepomuceno," *Handbook of Texas Online* [accessed November 8, 2004].

4. George Thomas Howard was born in 1814 in Washington, D.C. He came to Texas in 1836 and joined the army. He remained with the army, commanding first at Galveston and later at San Antonio. He participated in the Council House Fight and the Battle of Plum Creek. "Howard, George Thomas," *Handbook of Texas Online* [accessed November 8, 2004].

5. Felix Huston's plan called for an attack on Chihuahua and the establishment of a colony west of the Nueces River. See "Huston, Felix," *Handbook of Texas Online.*

6. In November 1840 James Hamilton negotiated three treaties between Texas and Great Britain. The first dealt with commerce and navigation. In the second, Britain pledged to mediate a treaty that would secure Texas' independence from Mexico. In exchange, Texas would pledge to assume a portion of the Mexican debt contracted with Britain prior to January 31, 1835. The third treaty called for the Republic of Texas to forbid the African slave trade. Congress approved the first two in January 1841, but the third treaty did not arrive before the body adjourned. See "Hamilton, James," *Handbook of Texas Online*.

7. Dr. Asa Hoxey was born in Savannah, Georgia, in 1800. He moved to Texas in 1833 and was very active in the revolutionary movement. He signed the Declaration of Independence and participated in the siege of Bexar. Although he was a licensed physician in the United States, he never formally practiced medicine in Texas. "Hoxey, Asa," *Handbook of Texas Online* [accessed November 8, 2004].

8. Tod Robinson was not made district judge. See "Robinson, Tod," *Handbook of Texas Online*.

9. The schooners in question were part of the navy of the Republic of Texas. The *San Jacinto* went aground in the Arcas Islands in October and was destroyed by a storm. The other two schooners, *San Antonio* and *San Bernard*, were in port, and the steamer *Zavala* was expected to arrive from its operation in the Yucatán Peninsula.

James Love to Albert Sidney Johnston

N Orleans
Jany 31, 1841

My dear General

I received your letter yesterday and was really glad to hear from you even if it was short. Not on account tho' of its contents, but because I did want to hear from you.

Your notes are in the hands of Dr. Woods; the $2,000 to be paid him here, the other note will be placed in the Bank of Louisville to be paid the 1st day of August. This was the longest time I could get, and I hope it will be satisfactory.

I have been here two months, awaiting the arrival, or favorable intelligence from Burnley. I go tomorrow as I have remained the longest possible time, altho I have no doubt tomorrow will bring me news from him. Mary [is] with me and not very well . . . [paper torn] . . . and Mrs. Davis[1] are both a little [paper torn]. I have not been idle since I was here. My own affairs, scribbling for newspapers, trying to control legislation at home by constant letters to members, has left me little time for recreation.

Lamar will die. Burnet has thrust himself into Felix's hands[2] and proclaims war, "let the sword do its duty," he says. They will fail in their objects. The war fever will subside, or has subsided, and a war of invasion will not be attempted.

Whether we get the loan or not, the prosperity of Texas is brightening. Some seven or eight thousand slaves have gone there since October, and there is enough by emigration of the right kind. The recognition by England has done much service, and our people have gone to work.

The watch you gave me which I [paper torn] more than anything I had . . . [paper torn] . . . out of my pocket into the . . . [paper torn] . . . [whole bottom line missing] . . . horse, and I shall take care of him. The guns I wish you to send to the care of Bryan.[3]

Let me hear from you and come *home* as soon as you can. The call for President is not yet certainly fixed. A great many are dissatisfied with both Burnet & Houston, the latter less objectionable.

> Very truly Your friend
> James Love
> Genl A. Sidney Johnston
> Louisville Kentucky

1. Love is referring to Mrs. Mary Jane Hawkins Davis, widow of James H. Davis, who died prior to October 14, 1840.
2. At this time Felix Huston called for an invasion of northern Mexico as a way to force the Mexican government to recognize Texas independence. See "Huston, Felix," *Handbook of Texas Online.*
3. During the Texas Revolution William Bryan, a New Orleans commission merchant, provided Texas with financial assistance, supplies, and services. President Lamar appointed Bryan Texas consul in New Orleans. His actions as consul were critical in procuring the second Texas Navy. "Bryan, William," *Handbook of Texas Online* [accessed November 10, 2004].

James Love to Albert Sidney Johnston

Galveston
March 31, 1841

My dear General

I was really glad to hear from you, and we all would be glad to see you. The renowned Felix[1] has departed, not in the best of humor, and I do not think he will return. All your labors have been overturned, and the *material* you had provided with so much care will all be wasted. I am sorry you ever left the War Department, as I am sure the action of Congress has been founded on want of confidence in the administration of affairs.

Burnet has been suddenly and unexpectedly dethroned by the return of Lamar to Austin. They all said he was dying, [but] Mr. Henri[2] cured him with tobacco, and he has returned in better health than he has before had in Texas. I am glad he has gone back, as he is better than those he left behind. Burnet has fallen greatly since you left and will hardly make a show in the country. Hunt[3] and Menard[4] have both been nominated for *vice* [president] on the Island; Manifee,[5] Anson Jones,[6] and Genl Smith[7] all out, no one can say who will succeed.

Major Howard[8] is just here from San Antonio, says Dr. Booker arrived there from Camargo & reports 8,000 Mexicans under Arista in arms.[9] A Mexican arrived two days after with the same news, & both concur in saying they are for Texas. I do not believe it, but am of opinion that Arista is about to revolt from the Central party and intends his force for Mexico.

Norwood[10] ran over to Houston and did not take the lots. I have paid the notes, the one due in April as well as the one due next year. I thought it best to do so, as money could not be much lower & I did not think it prudent to risk the rise.

I paid Dr. Woods six hundred dollars for you. I had an indistinct recollection that Watrous[11] was to pay some & referred them to him for the balance.

Now altho money is at all times acceptable to a *Texan* (I spell it right), still I do not wish you either to be in a hurry or to make a sacrifice to pay it. I can wait.

My plan for engrossing *all* Galveston is beginning to operate. I will have it, I *think*, some time or other. I already have one-fourth of the stock[12] and $80,000 in land are to be paid in monthly . . . [paper torn] . . . for the wharf, which I will buy . . . [paper torn] . . . fall, unless those who furnish the money agree to certain other matters I have suggested [and] I believe they will.

We have a young daughter. What think you of that. Jo[13] is still a captain & complains that you did not send him the top. Mrs. L[ove] & Mary are well and so are all your friends here.

> Very truly yours
> Jas Love
> Genl A. Sidney Johnston
> [redirected in another hand]
> Louisville
> Ky

1. Shortly after the Battle of Plum Creek Felix Huston left Texas and established a law firm in New Orleans. He never returned to Texas. See "Huston, Felix," *Handbook of Texas Online.*

2. Perhaps Love is referring to S. W. Henry, who was a taxpayer in Washington County in 1840.

3. Memucan Hunt.

4. Michel B. Menard

5. William Menefee was born in 1796 in Knox County, Tennessee. He immigrated to Texas in 1830 and actively participated in the independence movement. He was one of the signers of the Texas Declaration of Independence. He was chief justice of Colorado County, and from 1837 to 1841, he served in the Texas Congress. In the 1841 elections, Edward Burleson defeated Menefee for the office of vice president. "Menefee, William," *Handbook of Texas Online* [accessed November 10, 2004].

6. At this time Anson Jones practiced medicine in Brazoria. He refused to run for vice president in 1841. See "Jones, Anson," *Handbook of Texas Online.*

7. Brigadier General James Smith was born on 1792 in Spartanburg County, South Carolina. He arrived in Texas in 1835 and built a plantation near Nacogdoches. He served in the Texas Army during the revolution. In 1839 he commanded a regiment at the Battle of the Neches. In 1840 he was elected brigadier general of the Third Brigade and was stationed on the frontier with Mexico. "Smith, James," *Handbook of Texas Online* [accessed November 10, 2004].

8. George Thomas Howard heeded calls for an expedition to Santa Fe, New Mexico. At the time this letter was written, he sought out volunteers and money for this operation. There is no record that he asked James Love to join the crusade. See "Howard, George Thomas," *Handbook of Texas Online*.

9. Dr. Shields Booker was born in South Carolina. He entered Texas prior to the Battle of San Jacinto and participated in it. After the war he served as a surgeon in the Texas Army and participated in the Battle of the Neches. He resigned from the army in July 1840 and promptly joined the federalist army from Mexico that tried to establish the Republic of the Rio Grande. He rode express from Camargo on the Rio Grande to San Antonio to deliver this report. The rumor of eight thousand Mexican troops massing on the Rio Grande turned out to be a false alarm. "Booker, Shields," *Handbook of Texas Online* [accessed November 12, 2004].

10. Nathaniel Norwood leased the Tremont House in Galveston in 1839.

11. Love and Johnston conducted several real estate transactions with John Charles Watrous. At this time Watrous served as an attorney for the Peters Colony and then the Texas Land and Emigration Company.

12. Love was a member of the Galveston City Company and speculated heavily in island real estate. See "Love, James," *Handbook of Texas Online*.

13. James Love's son "Jo" had been named Joseph Eve Love, after his brother-in-law, the U.S. chargé d'affaires to the Republic of Texas. See "Eve, Joseph," *Handbook of Texas Online* [accessed December 1, 2004].

Samuel Alexander Roberts to Albert Sidney Johnston

Galveston
April 1, 1841

My Dear Sir

I wrote to you not very long since, and I believe destroyed all the credit I might have hoped to have gained by telling you with most unfashionable simplicity, that it was to kill a dull hour as much as anything else, that I did so. You, I suppose, have defered [sic] your reply until you could be familiar with a similar *excuse*, which I take for granted has not yet presented itself. Ennui, to me I know, was a disease unknown until I became a "habitant" of this dull isle, and even now when I get awy [sic] from it, I am so busy *doing nothing,* that I can hardly find time to eat my dinner, much less keep up a correspondence with anyone of the male gender. I cannot, I imagine, be very different in this respect from many others. Your own observations and experience has doubtless furnished you with proof of the apparent paradox, that to have time for anything, every moment of our time must be seriously employed. When we have nothing to do, we do nothing; and when business presses us on every side, we accomplish many things that otherwise we never should have thought of. Is it not so? But I must not furnish you with too many excuses, or you may think I [am] endeavoring to demonstrate that you *ought not* to write.

The truth is, I was led to think of you this evening by a message of regard in which Miss Mary Love, with whom I have just parted, returned to me from you, and as I have gotten to my office too early for bed and too late for study, without knowing why or wherefore, I found myself scribbling away to you.

The public events are not of much moment, but as you are probably ignorant of them, I will endeavor to bring you up to the present time. The canvass for the Presidency has settled down between Houston & Burnet. Rusk's name is occasionally mentioned but he *will not* run. Burnet is unpopular to a degree unprecedented, I suspect, in the history of any public man in any country who has committed no crime. He will hardly get more than 1/3 and some think as low as 1/4 of the votes that will be polled at the next election. The consequence will, of course, be the election of Genl Houston almost by aclamation [*sic*]. And yet strange as it seem, he is not a popular man. The opinions are, among his friends (I mean the knowing ones) is that he might have been beaten easily. The only difficulty was to find a man around whom all the opposition would have been willing to rally. Burnet cannot carry his own friends, and it is said here, conducted affairs so little to Lamar's satisfaction during his (Lamar's) short absence as entirely to forfeit his support, if not his friendship. Of course, this settles *his* expectations. Rusk was equally obnoxious with Houston on account of his dissipated habits, to say nothing of many other, very cogent objections. You, I believe it is now pretty generally conceded, could alone have cleared all objections. You could have beaten Houston. That, you may recollect, was my opinion before you left here, and I am now confident of its correctness. I have conversed with many of your warm personal friends who think with me, & who deplore your absence at this time as unfortunate in the extreme.

The contest for Vice P will, I think, be between no less personages than "Memucan Hunt," Brig Genl, etc etc & *first* minister pleno. etc etc etc. and "Menard." Burleson's name has been mentioned, but he declines, I understand, as does also, W. G. Cook, who was nominated at Austin. Hunt is very active and Menard is doing nothing, but the knowing ones think Menard will beat him badly. God only knows how it will go. So much for the next elections.

Lamar has recovered his health in a great measure and has returned to Austin. The same people who had persuaded him to depart from that City only two months before, never was supposed to return again, without a single demand broken of [illegible], received him on his return with shouts & aclamations [sic]. *Varium et mutable semper* [ever fickle and changing].

Felix Huston has finally left us in *disgust*. His end, to use one of his own elegant similies [sic], suggested I suppose by the character of his associations, "he had *played the game out* and had fairly lost." He is now, I hear, in N. Orleans, abusing the country at a sound rate. Love may he continue to do so[!]

I dined yesterday at Col Love's. They speak almost positively of going to Kentucky in May, but I still think they will spend the summer here.

The alarmists are still endeavoring to make us believe the "Mexicans are coming," but it won't do.

Texas money is growing into the seasoned yellow leafs and must soon go out of circulation entirely. "7 for 1" is the rate now.

Parker Crittenden has just come down from Houston with his family and has gone today with Tod R.[1] to San Luis. I think maybe he will go there to live, but he is very undecided.

I had thought to make this letter interesting to you, but I have grown duller and duller until I have a great mind to—to—hi-ho—the fact is, I am so sleepy, I scarcely know what I am about. So good bye.

> Your friend & ob svt
> Saml A. Roberts
> Genl A. S. Johnston
> Louisville Ky

---

1. At this time Tod Robinson edited the San Luis *Advocate*. Crittenden continued to practice law in Galveston.

James Love to Albert Sidney Johnston

N. Orleans
April 22 1841

My dear General,

I am once again here and announce to you what you will have seen
in the papers, the successful negotiation of the loan. He has sold seven million
six percent bonds at 50 cts certain, if he procures the guarantee of the French
government, which he thinks he will, and which I believe he will by giving
them some comprehensive advantages in commerce, then at 90. In any event,
it gives us money enough and opens the tide of prosperity so long looked for.[1]

Our money is worth 35 here and will go up. Am I not a man of talents
in anticipating the payment of our debt, and are you not obliged to me for saving
you one hundred percent, and probably 300 on an eight thousand dollar debt.

Burnet is so flat that in six weeks I have not heard a man say he
would vote for him. Old Sam *is* lucky. Well, you have been here in adverse
times, come & see our prosperity. Things will go better and there will be
some room for the exercise of talent. Come when you may, I am sure you will
always find in me a friend.

Jas Love
Genl A. Sydney [sic] Johnston
St Louis Missouri

1. The "he" referred to in this paragraph is James Hamilton. Love's confidence
    was misplaced; the French loan was never completed. See "Hamilton, James,"
    Handbook of Texas Online.

James Love to Albert Sidney Johnston

Galveston
May 16th 1841

Dear General

Many problems have talked to me lately about the prospects of
your being a candidate for the Presidency. In every instance, as a prelimi-

nary, I have required that it should be already announced that Burnet was
no longer a candidate. It is now almost certain that it will be so announced.
Mayfield[1] is here and very anxious, and was sanguine about it. He undertakes
to have Burnet off; I [will have] to write to you about it. When the first is
done, then the other can be considered. I have made no promise or said
anything to commit you, but I thought it would be the means of . . . placing
your name advantageously before the public for the future if nothing else.
I do, however, believe if this thing had been done two months sooner, you
could easily have been elected. And I think now the prospect would be a fair
one. I would be the last to advise you to enter upon a doubtful contest, nor
as I am at present advised, do I think you should. But *if* it be your intention
to make this your home, I believe you ought to be here at once. It gives you
every advantage. Some of papers will take up your case; you will have credit
at least for magnanimity with old Sam. If you do not, it places you in a prominent position, and your excuse with his enemies may be that there was
not time.

The approbation of the loan brings about a new state of things here,
and those who feel identified with the country, whether in interest or ambition, should be on the spot. All should bring their influence to bear to have
things rightly done.

I cannot in a letter give all my reasons or make you understand the
state of affairs, but as a friend whose opinion I know you have some faith in,
I advise you to come.[2]

My family are all well and often speak of you. Mary and Mr. Morris are engaged, the time, I believe is not settled. I need not tell you I am
pleased. I have confidence in his honor and believe him to be a gentleman,
and this is all I ever require of anyone.

I send this to Louisville first & hope you will receive it soon and let
me hear from you.

Very truly your friend
Jas Love
Genl A. Sidney Johnston
Louisville Kentucky

If Genl J. is not at Louisville, to be forwarded to St. Louis

1.   James S. Mayfield was serving as "party chairman" for the Lamar faction and
      screening candidates. He served in Lamar's cabinet as the sixth secretary of

state, appointed in February 1841. See "Mayfield, James S.," *Handbook of Texas Online*.

2. Johnston resisted the pleadings of his Texas friends, probably because of financial problems in Kentucky and the fact that he was courting Eliza Griffin, though they did not marry until 1843. Johnston visited Texas after the September elections and returned to Kentucky in early 1842. "Johnston, Albert Sidney," *Handbook of Texas Online* [accessed September 20, 2004].

Alexander Parker Crittenden to Albert Sidney Johnston

Brasoria [*sic*]
June 21ˢᵗ 1841

Dear Genl

I'll try you yet once more. If this fails in extracting a reply, I'll give you up as incorrigible and imitate your silence for the future. I confess, I have been seriously uneasy about you for several months; rumors of the most alarming kind have been current in this country respecting your movements and intentions. It is said you are about concluding certain arrangements incompatible with a residence in so barbarous a region. That your political notions are changed—that you are determined henceforth to eschew republics and live under an absolute monarchy. These rumors have been confirmed by your non-arrival in this month according to promise. If they are true, your departure from Texas last year will have had a most remarkable effect upon your condition in life. Will have made you the governed instead of the governor, which you would have been had you remained.

Are you aware that you have lost the Presidency by the move? With the *glory* of beating the Hero of San Jacinto, too? to say nothing of the Satisfaction. Such I am convinced is the fact. Burnett [*sic*] & Houston are both unpopular—Burnett being the more odious of the two will be distanced. I have heard many persons from all parts of the Rep. speak of the coming election, and it seems to be the universal impression, that had you staid [*sic*] at home like a good boy, you would have had the honor to be chosen the head of this mighty government. I have heard it suggested, that your name should be announced without your consent, merely for the purpose of giving the gentlemen of the country an opportunity of exercising their privilege. Between the prsent [*sic*] candidates, it is hard to choose—it is almost a matter of indifference which is successful. I doubt whether more than 2/3s of the votes in the country will be polled.[1]

If the recent news be confirmed, that the negotiation of the loan is no negotiation at all, we have no need of Pres[iden]t. or Government. We must either break up in a row or take protection under the wing of the United States. The probability is we shall soon have peace with Mexico. We will then set up a claim to California and all the regions round about and make a formal offer of ourselves and our claims to Uncle Sam provided he will assume our little liabilities. I suppose *you* consider this treason?

You see by the superscription I have changed my domicile. I am in possession of the prettiest little tenement in the county—have the greatest quantity of fruits of every variety, and by the time you reach Texas, shall be very snugly fixed. My front porch is a glorious place for a game of chess, and my old board has withstood all the rude assaults & rough encounters of which it has been the scene. No one in this region has any science, and my victories are followed by no profit and entitled to no honor. I long for a right good fight with you. [Paper torn] you must brush up before you undertake me again. I'm replete with Philidos.[2] Consider this not only as an invitation, but as a challenge which cannot be declined honorably. If you need any more incitement, I'll call you a coward and declare that you fear to meet me.

What wonderful things have you accomplished during your stay[?] Have you erected a pyramid or an obelisk? or have you made yourself famous by publishing any of those speculations which used to occupy our time last summer? The existence of a natural sense of right and wrong for instance? Nothing very important occurs in this country nowadays. Occasionally there's a marriage or a birth to give life or the prospect of life to the dulness [sic] of the times. Dick Morris is unquestionably to marry Miss Mary Love this fall, so *they* say, and *they* ought to know. Doswell & Miss Eve[3] are engaged *sans doute*. Col Grey,[4] you know, is dead. Sam Roberts, you are aware, is Actg Secy of State, and will probably have the office and all the honors in full before long. When shall I hear from you[?]

> A. P. Crittenden
> Genl A. Sidney Johnston
> Louisville Ky

1. Crittenden was not the only Texan who encouraged Johnston to run for president against Houston. For an analysis of political support for a Johnston

presidency, see Donald Willett, "James Love, Albert Sidney Johnston, and Political Ambition, 1838–1841," *Southwestern Historical Quarterly* 109, no. 4 (2006): 531–46. Johnston's friends did not conduct a write-in campaign for the 1841 presidential election. Houston easily defeated Burnet, 7,508 to 2,574 votes.

2.   The word *philidos* refers to people who like to play chess, not necessarily well.

3.   James Temple Doswell married Evelina Stone Gray, the daughter of William Fairfax Gray, on June 22, 1842.

4.   William Fairfax Gray died in Houston on April 16, 1841, after suffering briefly from a severe cold caught during the spring session of court in Galveston, where he served as the clerk of the district court. See "Gray, William Fairfax," *Handbook of Texas Online*.

James Love to Albert Sidney Johnston

[Galveston?]
July 1 1841

Dear General

The return of Judge Webb[1] from Mexico two days since has produced some excitement amongst us. The Mexican Government refused to receive him or listen to any propositions based upon the separation of the *department* of Texas from Mexico. They reproach the British Government in set terms for offering to mediate between a free and slave holding people. They had not, I suppose, heard of the late importation of Africans into Jamaica. The popular feeling here is decidedly for war, and a strong effort is making to induce the President to order out the fleet at once, and to issue letters of Marque to privateers & both Judge Webb and Lipscomb[2] advocate it. I mention this to show you that it is something more than mere popular effervescence.

Arista[3] is evidently occupying a position in defiance of his government. He is making overtures to us, to be prepared, doubtless, for centralist . . . [entire line unreadable] . . . under his sanctions and his treatment to our people is highly courteous. His popularity is great, and the probability is that he is preparing the way for revolt in the event of Santa Anna's success which seems probable.

The expedition to Santa Fe[4] set out three weeks since. It is composed of 300 good men and true, well equipped, and well commanded. Commissioners are sent along, one of whom is to reside there.

The government committed a great error in its quarrel with Saligny.[5] It was unnecessary and certainly very impolitic. It is not improbable it has its effects upon the negotiations for the loan. A weak people should not submit tamely to indignity, but they certainly are not in a condition to provoke bad feelings.

In the letter I wrote to you, it was not my intention to advise you to be a candidate. The object of the interview with Mayfield,[6] and the promise of writing to you was just to induce the withdrawal of Burnet, and then to trust to the state of public feeling for bringing out . . . [entire line unreadable] . . . pronouncement before the people as you do, and I am confident had it not been for the mulish obstinacy of Burnet, you could and would have been elected with ease, even in opposition to Houston.

The money would be acceptable, but I can say now, as I have before said, make no sacrifice to pay it.

I suppose we shall not see you until fall. Many of your friends ask frequently when you are to return. Some entertain the opinion you have left us forever.

You know my opinion of the U.S. and that may be received as our answer to the McLeod affair.[7]

My family are all well and send to you their kindest wishes. I am a successful planter, the best crop & in the best order of any in Texas, so says good

Give my best greetings to my old friend Throckmorton.[8]

> Very truly your friend
> James Love
> Genl A. Sidney Johnston
> Louisville, Kentucky

1. James Webb, who served as secretary of the treasury, secretary of state, and attorney general under President Lamar, made his third and last journey to Mexico to secure recognition of Texas' independence during the Lamar administration. When Mexican authorities learned about his mission, they refused to receive him. See "Webb, James," *Handbook of Texas Online.*
2. Abner Smith Lipscomb was Lamar's former secretary of state. See "Lipscomb, Abner Smith," *Handbook of Texas Online.*

3. Rumors continued that General Mariano Arista planned to rebel against Santa Anna, but other than his trying to prevent Santa Anna's taking over the presidency from Bustamante, the rumors proved false. See "Arista, Mariano," *Handbook of Texas Online*.

4. On June 19, 1841, some three hundred merchants and adventurers set out for Santa Fe, New Mexico. Lamar, struggling to overcome the many disappointments of his years as president, bypassed Congress's authority and by executive decree sent the party to the upper Rio Grande. He hoped this action would divert the lucrative Santa Fe trade from Missouri to Texas and establish hegemony over the area claimed by the Republic of Texas since December 1836. Hugh McLeod commanded the armed party, and three commissioners—William G. Cooke, Dr. Richard F. Brenham, and José Antonio Navarro—represented the civil authority.

5. This refers to Jean Pierre Isidore Alphonse Dubois, the French chargé d'affaires to Texas and the embarrassment that developed from the colorful "Pig War," a dispute over damage to the Frenchman's personal effects caused by an innkeeper's unruly pigs. See "Pig War," *Handbook of Texas Online* [accessed November 12, 2004].

6. At this time James Mayfield served as President Lamar's secretary of state.

7. The "McLeod Affair" refers to the arrest and trial of Alexander McLeod, a Canadian citizen who in 1837 participated in the infamous "*Caroline* Affair," in which Canadian citizens crossed the border in 1837 and attacked and destroyed the American vessel *Caroline* and killed at least one American citizen. In November 1840 American officials arrested McLeod shortly after he crossed into the United States. They claimed that during the *Caroline* raid he murdered an American citizen. These charges so angered the British foreign secretary, Lord Palmerston, that a war scare between the two countries briefly flourished. McLeod's acquittal in an American court defused the situation and opened the door for the Webster-Ashburton Treaty of 1843. See Kenneth R. Stevens, *Border Diplomacy: The* Caroline *and McLeod Affairs in Anglo-American-Canadian Relations, 1837–1842* (Tuscaloosa: University of Alabama Press, 1989).

8. Love's reference is to Avis Throckmorton of Louisville, Kentucky.

PART II

"All That Emanates from Him
Is Falsehood upon Deceit"

THE HOUSTON YEARS, 1842-1845

When Mirabeau B. Lamar stepped down as president of the Republic of Texas, these letter writers believed that their country was headed in the right direction. Their boundaries were well protected. Their glorious little navy asserted command of the sea over the western Gulf of Mexico. Mexican military operations, over land or by sea against Texas, although possible, did not appear likely. The Indian question had been solved, or so they thought. The national economy continued to expand. Land prices rose and the population increased. And several European nations looked favorably at granting diplomatic recognition and signing mutually beneficial commercial treaties.

Of course, some problems existed. Mexico stubbornly insisted that Texas was an errant Mexican province in a state of rebellion, not a sovereign and independent nation. Many countries agreed with Mexico's view. The Republic of Texas government was virtually insolvent. Its treasury was bare, and the nation was unable to find a willing creditor. And the bills continued to mount.

After Albert Sidney Johnston resigned as secretary of war he returned to Kentucky to court his future second wife, Eliza Griffin, and to replenish his nearly depleted bank account. During Sam Houston's second term as president Johnston remained in the Bluegrass State but occasionally returned to Texas to examine his investments and visit his friends. During this time, 1842–1845, Johnston received letters from James Love, Albert Triplett Burnley, Alexander Parker Crittenden, Leslie Combs, Joseph A. Swett, Robert Holmes Chinn, James S. Mayfield, and William Pitt Ballinger. James Love continued to practice law in Galveston and manage his and Johnston's land holdings. Albert Triplett

Burnley split his time between his plantation in Mississippi and his land holdings in Brazoria County. Alexander Parker Crittenden continued to practice law in Galveston. Leslie Combs, a firm supporter of Texas independence, lived in Kentucky. Joseph A. Swett resided in Galveston. Robert Holmes Chinn practiced law in New Orleans. James S. Mayfield served in Texas' Sixth Congress and later participated in the Somervell expedition. William Pitt Ballinger arrived in Galveston in 1843 and studied law with his uncle, James Love. During the U.S.-Mexico War Ballinger served as Albert Sidney Johnston's adjutant.

On the eve of Sam Houston's second inauguration, news that the Mexican army had captured the members of the ill-fated Santa Fe expedition shattered these letter writers' dreams of shaping the destiny of Texas. This tense moment in Texas history marked the last in a series of tragic blunders that overshadowed the Lamar presidency. And President Sam Houston's refusal to avenge this blemish on Texas' honor initiated a systematic dismantling of Texan hegemony, autonomy, and independence, all undertaken by the Hero of San Jacinto.

Johnston and friends believed that Houston's refusal to try to free the Texan prisoners at Santa Fe amounted to a tacit abandonment of the republic's western boundary to either the Mexican government or the nomadic Plains Indians. It also sent a strong message to the governments of Mexico, Great Britain, and the United States that the new Texas executive would do little to defend his nation's limits. And when Houston terminated all attempts to negotiate loans from foreign governments, these men sensed that his call to slow down government spending was a clever ploy to weaken the government's ability to defend itself or its people. Stripped of any pretense of military might, Texas, they feared, would appear before the international community like a defenseless child looking for a foster parent.

Texas faced in rapid succession the Vásquez raid and the Woll invasion of 1842, and Houston's refusal to take any provocative action against these Mexican violations of Texan territory signaled a reversal of Lamar's aggressive military policy. Houston's handling of the Texas Navy—his orders to sell the ships and his branding of the crews and officers as pirates—conceded command of the sea to Texas' enemy and delivered a death blow to the once proud service. Under Houston's pacific policy, reasoned these letter writers, the Texas coast and port cities were now vulnerable to a Mexican naval blockade and bombardment. The traditional overland invasion route into the heart of Texas also beckoned Mexican forces. Without an army or a navy, how would Texas sustain its independence?

Under Houston's leadership these letter writers worried that Texas would once again become a Mexican province ruled by a vicious and bloodthirsty dictator. To these men Houston's reluctance to use military force to solve Texas' problems with Mexico was the act of either a coward or a traitor. They wondered if Houston's refusal to seek martial glory once again was driven by fear. They wondered if he was working with his old Mexican nemesis to destroy the Republic of Texas. They looked on in horror as the Hero of San Jacinto engaged in a macabre diplomatic dance of the dead with his old battlefield antagonist, Antonio López de Santa Anna. The Old Hero's prediction that an armistice with Mexico was forthcoming never materialized. Later, his intimation that the United States and Great Britain were pressuring Santa Anna to sign a treaty of peace that would recognize Texas independence likewise led to naught.

As Houston's second presidential administration drew to an end, Albert Sidney Johnston and friends watched their worst nightmare unfold. Their beloved Republic of Texas was all but gone. Its treasury was empty. Its currency was worthless, and its ability to repay its national debt was nonexistent. Because of Houston's adroit economic, political, and diplomatic maneuvers Texas could no longer defend itself from enemy attack. The army could not supply itself, and the militia no longer trusted Houston's leadership. The Texas Navy was in shambles. Its naval vessels, unfit for duty, rotted in Galveston harbor. Its sailors, unpaid and unsupplied since Houston came to office, had once proudly ruled the western Gulf of Mexico. Reduced to poverty, these wretched souls now begged for food and money from anyone who would listen to their pathetic pleas for help.

In the end Houston completely crushed Johnston and friends' dreams. Given this context, it is not at all surprising that Johnston and those who shared his views held a dismal opinion of Houston and his leadership. In a letter to Johnston dated December 13, 1844, James S. Mayfield stated flatly of Houston that "all that emanates from him is falsehood upon deceit."

By the end of Houston's presidency only the United States showed interest in the Republic of Texas. As Sam Houston prepared to hand over the presidency to his secretary of state, Anson Jones, American diplomats opened hurried negotiations with the prostrate republic. The United States offered to bring this independent nation into the Union as a territory. Houston happily agreed. However, the American president, John Tyler, and his followers could not muster the required two-thirds vote in the U.S. Senate to pass this treaty, so this first attempt to annex Texas failed.

James K. Polk's triumph in the presidential election of 1844 reenergized incumbent President Tyler's desire to annex the Lone Star republic. This time he carefully recounted his votes and noticed that he controlled enough "ayes" to pass a joint resolution that would annex Texas into the Union as a state. It passed, but all was lost. The dream was gone and the Republic of Texas was no more.

A. T. Burnley to Albert Sidney Johnston

New Orleans
Jany 28th 1842

My dear Genl

Your two letters of the 18th and 24th Inst were both recd only yesterday. I am pleased to see the spirit of Texas so much aroused, & I hope it will result in her placing herself in a condition to resist *aggression* at the least. Tho' I still cannot believe in a Mexican invasion, but we ought to be prepared for any game she may happen to choose to play at. You may pledge me to anything personal or pecuniary which may become a good citizen, & I will redeem the pledge.[1]

We have plenty of sympathy about the Santa Fe affair, but such is the horrid state of money matters here, that I think all hope of any pecuniary aid in the United States perfectly useless. You have seen how nobly old Kentucky has acted—her citizens have cause to be proud of her.[2]

I am sorry you have not closed the Hall purchase,[3] tho the knowing ones here say property of every sort must come down still lower, & the times become worse, if possible. I believe I could buy 30 to 40 or 50 negroes at 1, 2, & 3 years—paying a pretty good price, & giving good security for principal & interest, & I would do it, if I had paid my debts. But altho' I have paid all I owe until the 11th of Feby (when I owe $3,000), yet how I am to pay, that is more than I yet know, for I have not $50 to do it with, & until that question is settled, I cannot ask E[rwin][4] to make himself further responsible for me. Besides which, I owe 6 or 7,000 to others which must be paid soon, or I cannot keep up my credit to the point which would justify me, *in my own estimation,* in asking a friend to render himself responsible for me. Under these circumstances, I cannot move in attempting to purchase negroes from

E[rwin], Mrs. W[hite], or anybody else whereby a friend is to be involved with me until the preliminary question is settled, whether I can pay what he is already bound for.

I have two or three *ideas* about raising money, which in ordinary times I am sure I could realise, but as things now are, it is hard to tell what a man can do. Money can now be loaned out here perfectly secured at 18 & 20 perc[en]t.

As to the bill of articles for Col Love's house, Mr. Philips told me Capt Rawlings[5] promised to attend to it when he left [on] the *Neptune*, & therefore, I am uncertain whether he may not have carried the articles over, as the *Neptune* had not arrived at Galveston when your letter was written. But in addition to that, the *New York*[6] has more freight engaged than she can take, & worse than all, I actually have not the money to buy the articles. When the *Neptune* returns, if the things have not gone in her the last trip, I will try to procure & send them over, if I do not go over myself, tho' my affairs are too unsettled to fix a day for my departure yet.

How does my house come on?

To save trouble, I direct this letter to you or Love. It contains what I would say to either or both.

> In haste yr friend
> A T Burnley
> Genl A. S. Johnston or
>   Col Jas Love
> Galveston Texas

The things for Col Love, I will send certainly pr *Neptune.* ATB

1.   Texans were angry because members of the Santa Fe expedition had been taken prisoner in September on the outskirts of Santa Fe. The news reached Texas in December 1841, on the eve of Sam Houston's second inaugural. The Houston administration adopted an unpopular course of defensive action and did not aggressively pursue revenge or recovery of the prisoners. Rumors continued concerning a Mexican invasion.

2.   Louisiana and Kentucky residents were particularly excited about the capture of the Santa Fe expedition because at least two U.S. citizens, Amos Kendall, the editor of the New Orleans *Picayune*, and Franklin Combs, son of General Leslie Combs of Kentucky, were among the prisoners.

3. Warren D. C. Hall was born in 1788 in Guilford County, North Carolina. He first entered Texas in 1813 as a member of the Gutiérrez-Magee expedition. He settled in Texas in 1828 and was active in colonial affairs. He served briefly as secretary of war under the Burnet administration. Johnston and Burnley planned to buy the six-thousand-acre China Grove Plantation from Hall, who was about to lose it to creditors. The plantation was northeast of Brazoria between the Brazos River and Oyster Creek. It had been the headright of Hall and his brother, granted to them in 1824. Johnston entered a contract to assume the indebtedness, and Burnley agreed to supply the labor force. They planned to operate the plantation as absentee land owners. "Hall, Warren D. C.," *Handbook of Texas Online* [accessed November 15, 2004].

4. This refers to James Erwin of New Orleans.

5. This refers to Williams Rollins, captain of the *Neptune.*

6. The steamer *New York* was a 365-ton steam vessel with auxiliary sails. In 1837 Charles Morgan bought the ship and used it in the New York to Charleston, South Carolina, trade. Starting in 1839 Morgan transferred the ship to Texas, and it served as a regular packet between Galveston and New Orleans. In1840 Morgan refurbished the ship with sixty passenger staterooms and an elegant salon. http://www.gomr.mms.gov/homepg/regulate/environ/archaeological/19th_century.html. [accessed December 4, 2007].

Alexander Parker Crittenden to Albert Sidney Johnston

Brasoria [*sic*]
Feb 5ᵗʰ 42

My dear Genl

I want to know something about this *misfortune* which I hear has happened to Bob Wickliffe. What are the particulars? Is the fact true, and if true, what effect has it had, and will it have, upon his standing? I do not ask from idle curiosity; as you are aware, Bob and myself have not been friendly for a long time, and recently some new cause of difficulty has arisen. I have written him a severe caustic communication, one that will cut to the quick. But since this affair, I hesitate to send it. I cannot strike a fallen man. He has been a friend, and though he has done everything to excite me to enmity, I am not disposed to join with a pack of yelping curs to pursue him to destruction. So far from it, that were he fallen, I should forget the past and exert myself to defend him, to raise him up. Give me all the information you have on the subject, for by your report, I shall govern my course.

I am delighted to hear of your arrangements. You shall put me up a nice little cabin on your place, to be exclusively my own. You shall supply it with some half dozen books that I will name, a standing box of cigars (if they be not proscribed by the Supreme power), and a rifle—and in return, I will give you the pleasure of my company—a fair exchange? When do you come up? Where's friend Roberts? I wish you would suggest to him, that on the first of last April or May, a bet was made between us (of which he has a mem.) of a handsome suit of clothes, that in one year's time, Texas Treasury notes would not be worth more than five cents on the dollar. That was my position, and it is sustained. I have won the bet and shall feel no compunction in exacting the forfeiture *because* he was so very confident and positive at the time, as to be almost angry with me for supposing the possibility of such a thing, and deserves punishment for the temper he displayed; *because* he had had some of the Treasury pap[er] and, of course, has fattened upon it; and *because* my only cloth coat has grown exceedingly rusty that I see no chance of supplying its place but by levying contributions upon my inferiors in payment and foresight. Please request him to issue a "fiere facias"[1] to the best tailor, the most extravagant and ultra fashionable in New Orleans. You are interested in this, for how shall I venture to appear at Johnston Place in a jeans roundabout? Speaking of the Place—you'll have a billiard table? and a piano? and a nice little library containing Hooker's Eccelesiastical [sic] Polity; Burkes' works; Bacon's; Crabb's Synonymes [sic]; Diversions of Priestly; & Harris' Hermes?[2] Some good old brandy, too? And all kinds of fruit in their season? and a noble set of chess men? None of your fantastical, womanish red and white ivory toys, but solid, substantial, sedate masses of carved oak? With me at your elbow to suggest wants to you, I think you will soon be right comfortably fixed. All this is to be, provided these plaguy Mexicans will only let us alone, a thing they had better do if they could only see what was for their safety. But they are such fools, they'll run their heads into the fire half a dozen times before they'll be convinced it will burn. That's true philosophy, to make a multitude of experiments before establishing a principle, but its not policy. But I have great confidence in that lordly talk of Felissiums Huston about Anglo Saxons, flags, and towers of Montezuma, and all that. It's in their own style and comprehensible.

I want a copy of the "Artillery Tactics."[3] We have three pieces of artillery here—in what age made is unknown—short, stumpy, determined looking little bull dogs—that would have gone off of themselves on a campaign long before this only they had no wheels. We can easily mount them, or if we get right furious, can carry them without mounting. I think of organizing a regiment here, an "Invisible Legion" of light artillery, for the purpose of operating against the enemy in the thick timber where the Infantry can't penetrate. But I'm doubtful if it would not be better to establish floating batteries in the Brasos [sic] upon Genl Gaine's system?[4] I tell you what, Sir, I'll do something original to a certainty—a little beyond Sam Houston's novelty, that the best way to defend a country is to retreat out of it.[5] I have this war very much at heart and want to avail myself of it as a short cut to political distinction. I want to become a great statesman, a great Financier. I want to establish my character as a peaceable man by killing somebody. Ye Gods[!] What a prospect that man would have before him who could slay the arch fiend, Santa Anna! He might define his position mathematically thus—as a petty tribe of savages is to the great and enlightened community of Mexico, and as the *polished Santa Anna* to an *uneducated barbarian* (geometrical progression, mark you), so inferior should be the rank and reputation of Dick Johnson[6] to my own. If Dick Johnson, in spite of the colour of his family (which absorbs much of the lustre of his heroic deed), could become Vice President of the great republic, to what honors and office would I not be entitled?

Having, as is unusual with me, indulged in so much nonsense, I must apologise for having extended my note to such length. I assure you I have no disposition to persecute you, knowing as I do, that it only tries your patience without exciting any desire of revenge, that you bear such inflictions as this in silence. That blows and buffetings will not rouse you out of your lethargy more than entreaties and soliticitations [sic].

I leave you to *reflect* in *silence* upon the return which even a reasonable man might expect for the many favors with which I have honored you and subscribe myself.

> Your much neglected friend
> A P Crittenden
> Genl A. Sidney Johnston
> Galveston

1.   The Latin phrase *fiere facias* means "to cause it to be done." In law, it refers to a judgment for damages.

2. John Hooker (1554–1600) wrote *The Laws of Ecclesiastical Polity* (1594); Edmund Burke (1729–1797) was a British statesman, orator, and writer. Roger Bacon (1214–1294) was an English philosopher, and George Crabb (1778–1851) was an English legal writer and the author of the *Dictionary of English Synonymes*. The writings of Joseph Priestly (1733–1804), the British theologian and scientist, were contained in his *Diversions*. James Harris (1709–1780) wrote *Hermes* (1751), a learned work on language and grammar.

3. Alexander Parker Crittenden could have accessed a number of books on artillery tactics published between 1820 and 1842, including Samuel Cooper, *A Concise System of Instructions and Regulations for the Militia and Volunteers of the United States* (Philadelphia: Robert P. Desilver, 1836); United States War Department, *A System of Exercise and Instruction of Field-Artillery: Including Maneuvers for Light or Horse Artillery* (Boston: Hillard Gray, Little Wilkins, 1829); H. Lallemand and James Renwick, *A Treatise on Artillery* (New York: C. S. Van Winkle, 1820); or Robert Anderson and the United States War Department, *Instruction for Field Artillery, Horse and Foot: Translated from the French, and Arranged for the Service of the United States* (Philadelphia: Robert P. Desilver, 1839).

4. General Edmund Pendleton Gaines was born in 1777. He joined the U.S. Army in 1799 and fought in the War of 1812 and the Seminole War. He later served on the western frontier. He advocated an interlocking system of military railroads, turnpikes, and canals that could connect the frontier with population centers. He also advocated floating batteries to defend coastal cities and rivers from attack. "Gaines, Edmund Pendleton," *Handbook of Texas Online* [accessed December 4, 2007].

5. Crittenden, maybe in an attempt to provoke or flatter Johnston, poked fun at Houston's strategy during the Texas Revolution and his current strategy as president of the republic: to defend Texas passively, with local militia units, and not provoke a fight with the Mexican republic.

6. Richard M. Johnson of Tennessee had been Martin Van Buren's vice president, 1837–1840; his black housekeeper was the subject of much gossip, which diminished his reputation as the hero of the Battle of the Thames in 1813, where he had supposedly killed Tecumseh.

Leslie Combs to Albert Sidney Johnston

New Orleans
12 Feby 1842

Dear Genl

Your letter by the *Neptune* did not reach me till my 2nd return from Galveston. The suggestions I[1] made as to a simultaneous movement from Missouri & Texas were thrown out to be thought of only in case the *main* operation could not be accomplished. The *great war movement* spoken of.

I shall keep the latter constantly in mind if any feasible plan occurs to me of raising the *means.* I could find the men to make the *colony* west of the Nueces & ship & march them there or *elsewhere* as might be best do as to save us from the intervention of our government.[2]

I intend proceeding to Washington soon after my return to Ky & feel the pulse of our government, & if possible, raise a war storm. I have been preparing the way for a personal interview with Mr. Tyler which I hope may produce something. Write to me anytime before the 10th of March under cover to Honble [*sic*] John White, Washington City. After that to Lexington Ky.

I trust Hamilton was able to devise an acceptable project for Congress & that the Belgian may be satisfied.[3] I fear I cannot await Love's arrival, but if I do not, I shall leave my business to be closed by Burnley & Major Tilford[4] with him & trust nothing will prevent his early visit to this city. It is indispensible [*sic*] for me to have my hands *in my own hands to deposit in Bk* & show my friends in order not to be utterly crushed in my affairs. I have suggested a plan also to Burnley by which the [illegible] bill can be arranged. Were these matters off my mind, I could devote my energies to higher objects with some vigor & success, *But my wife & children must not starve.*

I am to see Lt Seegars[5] after breakfast. I will write by him to Co[mmodore]. Moore. Your Navy ought to have swept the gulf with a fiery broom long ago & the sooner it is now done the better. You may thus too, get respectable homages for Cooke[6] & his companions. On this point I shall urge our Government to act with *decisive* humanity and as becomes the great Christian power on this continent.

Burnley will, no doubt, write you fully about his affairs. If I can suceed [*sic*] in getting Mrs. White's negroes, I will join you & him in the Hall place.[7] By devoting all the proceeds, we could soon pay for land & negroes & have a very snug estate for a rainy day.

We have nothing from Mexico since Col Swett[8] left, except a note from my son advising me of his having been carried in chains before Santa Ana & after a brief course of interrogation, *released* & *honored* with a seat in the Dictator's carriage to the home of the American Minister.[9] He insists he never walked or endeavored to look prouder in his life than when thus inducted in fetters into the presence of "*Majesty*" as your President were to say. You will be gratified also to learn that in all their worst trials, sufferings, & apprehensions, the Old Kentucky Hunter's blood never gave way & that Frank neither flinched nor faltered. I hope he will remain till the other prisoners reach Mexico, so as to get Kendall[10] with him & report jointly *their* treatment & condition while captive.

After I had written this fact, I heard of the horrid affair on the *San Antone* last night & have since seen Capt Segers [*sic*]. He laments he was not aboard as he thinks he could have stoped [*sic*] the mutiny by shooting two or three of the leaders. He has arrested 5 or 6 of them & the whole police of New Orleans in after the others. The [U.S.] Revenue Cutter *Jackson* sent a guard aboard to aid him as soon as the affair was known. He speaks highly of the kindness & promptness of the naval and civil authorities here. He intends to ship a new crew & hopes to be at sea in a week. The Midshipmen are not dangerously hurt.[11]

I shall leave this open till Monday to give you more particulars.

Monday nothing new. I start to Ky in a few days & thence over the mountains.

Write me fully about matters & things—hopes, prospects, & fears of the future.

> I remain very truly yr fr & yr obs
> Leslie Combs

P S Remember me to my friends in Texas, especially McKinney,[12] Brewster.[13]

> Genl A S Johnson [*sic*]

1. General Leslie Combs was born in 1793 in Clark County, Kentucky. During the Texas Revolution Combs raised a regiment of Kentucky volunteers, but they never left the state. He was a well-connected Whig politician who strongly supported the Texas cause. He purchased more than $200,000 in Texas war bonds, which Texas never redeemed. His son Franklin was a New

Orleans merchant who participated in the Santa Fe expedition. http://www
.combs-families.org/combs/families/c-les.htm [accessed December 4, 2007].

2. Combs and Johnston seem to have adopted Felix Huston's plan to invade
Mexico and plant a colony west of the Nueces River. Combs is suggesting a
way to evade the U.S. neutrality laws.

3. President Lamar appointed James Hamilton to be a financial agent for the
republic and sent him to Europe to negotiate loans with various governments,
including Belgium. When Houston became president, he terminated Hamilton's mission. See "Hamilton, James," *Handbook of Texas Online*.

4. A Major John Tilford resided in Lexington, Kentucky, and served from 1835
until his death in 1851 as the president of the Northern Kentucky Bank.
http://www.rootsweb.com/~kyfayett/dunn/tilford_john.htm [accessed December 4, 2007].

5. Lieutenant William Seegars, of the Texas Navy, was the commander of the
schooner *San Antonio*, which had just arrived from a three-month cruise to
the Yucatán Peninsula to aid Mexican federalists in their cause. "Edwards,
John," *Handbook of Texas Online* [accessed December 4, 2007].

6. Combs hoped that Commodore Moore and the Texas Navy would seize Mexican hostages in order to secure the release of William G. Cooke and the other
Santa Fe prisoners.

7. "Hall place" refers to property owned by Warren D. C. Hall in Brazoria
County. He named this property China Grove Plantation and in 1843 sold
it to Albert Sidney Johnston and Albert Triplett Burnley. Apparently, Johnston, Burnley, and Combs originally hoped to purchase China Grove, but
Combs later backed out of the transaction. "Hall, Warren D. C.," *Handbook
of Texas Online*. See also Burnley to Johnston, January 28, 1842.

8. Joseph A. Swett, a native of Vermont, had practiced law in Houston and
Galveston since 1838 and had evidently been to Mexico, perhaps as an agent
for Combs.

9. The U.S. minister, Powhatan Ellis, secured the release of Franklin Combs and
others who could claim U.S. citizenship before the entire group arrived in the
Mexican capital.

10. George Wilkins Kendall was born in 1809 in Mount Vernon, New Hampshire. He was the founder and editor of the *New Orleans Picayune*. He joined
the Santa Fe expedition as a "guest" and was captured by Mexican troops
outside Santa Fe and marched to Mexico City. Like Franklin Combs, he
claimed American citizenship and soon was released by the Mexican government. When he returned to New Orleans, he chronicled his adventures in a

best-selling book titled *Narrative of the Texan Santa Fé Expedition*. "Kendall, George Wilkins," *Handbook of Texas Online* [accessed November 15, 2004].

11. On February 11 a portion of the *San Antonio*'s crew mutinied while Seegars was ashore. The crew complained that Seegars refused to grant them shore leave. Seegars feared that the crew would desert en masse. The mutineers attacked and killed the deck officer and wounded two midshipmen.

12. Thomas F. McKinney.

13. Henry Percy Brewster was born in 1816 in Laurens District, South Carolina. He arrived in Texas in April 1836, served as Sam Houston's personal secretary, and fought at the Battle of San Jacinto. After the war he served as secretary of war under interim president David G. Burnet. In 1840 he served as district attorney for the Second Judicial District. During the Civil War Brewster served as Confederate general Albert Sidney Johnston's chief of staff and was with the general when he died. "Brewster, Henry Percy," *Handbook of Texas Online* [accessed November 15, 2004].

Albert Triplett Burnley to Albert Sidney Johnston

New Orleans
Feby 14, 1842

My dear Genl.

Thinking it possible you may have returned to Galveston, I write I had hoped to be able to go over on the *New York* today, but I have found it impossible to arrange my affairs to do so.

The difficulty of the times surpasses anything you can imagine. No property will sell for half its value, & no credit will raise money. All confidence is gone. Banks & individuals are breaking every day & Mr Wisest [?] seems to think the worst has not come; that *all credit* will be abolished & property be reduced to one half of its present low value; [and] that your friend, Benton,[1] will slide into the Presidency on his hard money humbug, aided by his prejudice against the Bank.

My inability to meet all my engagements promptly has prevented me from *trying* to go farther in debt for negroes when I could only do so by asking my friends to go my security. I have not even talked to Erwin about his negroes. I could have bought 30 or 40 at a fair price on 1, 2, & 3 years credit, but I had not the courage to ask my friends to go my security, tho' I have every reason to believe they would have done it if I had asked them.

Mrs. White is not here, but at Washington. I have authorised Combs[2] (who is going on) to sound her about terms. If she will take the interest alone for 5 years, I believe I would ask Erwin to make the purchase secure to her. To Tucker, I have written nothing because I owe him $2,500, which I cannot pay. I have offered to sell the interest in Parker's Point,[3] but nobody has money to buy, & I am only waiting here to raise the money *indispensable to my moving at all* I hope to do so in time for the return of the *Neptune*.

I hoped you have got Hamilton & his schemes through. In the present aspect of affairs, all I have to say is sell land or anything you can from money & enter into no new engagements. If it be necessary to comply with out engagements, that we should carry out the trade with Hall,[4] of course it must be done if the Devil stood at the door, but if any modification of the contract is required which would certainly justify us in leaving off, I think you had better be off. For I am sure a year hence we can do better, & unless I can raise 12 or $15,000 in some way, I shall never be able to hold my head high enough to buy negroes without money, tho' I am still convinced I could do it if I could keep my credit as unimpaired as it now is but will not be for a month unless I can raise the money I want, which I see no certain prospect of doing.

If you will show this letter to Love, it will suspend the necessity of writing to him. I hope to be over in the *Neptune*.

> In haste yr friend
> A T Burnley
> Genl A. S. Johnston or
>   Col Jas Love
> Galveston Texas
> *New York*

1. Senator Thomas Hart Benton of Missouri was related to Johnston's first wife, Harriet Preston. The pair first met in 1827 at Benton's home.
2. General Leslie Combs.
3. Parker's Point was the plantation on Oyster Creek in Brazoria County that Burnley owned in partnership with James Love.
4. Warren D. C. Hall.

James Love to Albert Sidney Johnston

Galveston
March 31ˢᵗ 1842

Dear Genl

I write this in the hope it may reach you. We have not had a word from you since you left. We are, of course, entirely in the dark as to when, and how we may contribute to support you, or what might to be done.

One hundred and fifty volunteers arrived here on Wednesday from the United States [and] more will soon follow unless these already here become so disgusted with the state of things here as to discourage all of them. We thought at one time the President had made up his mind to an active prosecution of the war. He sent agents to the U.S. to raise troops, he appointed Daingerfield as government agent to attend to all things. He directed Somervell, as you will have learned, to cross the Rio Grande, his proclamation of blockade, and letters to Santa Anna all combined induced the belief.[1]

When we heard of troops returning and dispersing for want of orders to march, we were surprised, and still more so when we see not a single step taken to have troops sent west, or prepare them to be sent[.] The Secretary of War[2] has been here for some days. He does nothing, has issued no orders, says we must take Matamoros, but does nothing towards it. The volunteers from the U. States want action. They are already discouraged because they believe the President will take no step whatever to forward matters.

We shall hold a meeting tonight and take the first steps towards ending this state of things. We will send Burnley to him with resolutions and have his answer. Should he now back out, the next step will be resolutions for him to resign. The wish of the whole people, so far as I have heard, is in favor of prosecuting this matter to a close now.

Hockley has told me twice if you were here he would give you command and send you down to Corpus Christi to organize, and would forward troops to you. You will take this for what it is worth.

We shall have a press under way in two weeks, and for one, I feel determined to press the advance of troops, and make war upon his excellency until he does right. Is it not *awful* that this country should be cursed with such a man at such a time?

The *Lafitte*[3] returned yesterday, the *Wharton* went to sea fully equipped. Nothing later from Mexico. The English have refused to surrender the slaves taken in the *Creole*.[4] Thompson, the American Minister,[5] left N. O. for Mexico on Monday.

We are all well. I close by giving you an opinion. If you expect to hear from friends here, you must write to them.

Very truly yr friend
James Love
Genl A. Sydney Johnston
San Antonio

1. On March 5, 1842, a small force under General Rafael Vásquez occupied San Antonio. He stayed only two days, but most Anglo Texans fled the city, believing it was an invasion, not just a raid. Word of the attack reached Galveston on March 9, and James Love and others were appointed to a Committee of Vigilance. They sent agents to New Orleans to recruit men on their own responsibility. President Houston called up the militia and on March 25 sent William H. Daingerfield, secretary of the treasury, to New Orleans to secure munitions. On March 17, Alexander Somervell of Fort Bend, the senior militia general, was named commander of the troops and ordered to march toward the Mexican border. Houston's orders limited crossing the Rio Grande to Somervell's discretion. Also, on March 26, Houston ordered the *Wharton*, an eighteen-gun brig of war, to blockade Matamoros. "Vásquez, Ráfael," *Handbook of Texas Online* [December 4, 2007].

2. Secretary of War George W. Hockley was following Houston's orders. Houston favored only defensive action, not aggression against Mexico, a course unpopular in Galveston and San Antonio, where residents expected Mexican forces to attack. "Hockley, George Washington," *Handbook of Texas Online* [accessed November 17, 2004].

3. The *Lafitte*, the first steamer built in Texas, belonged to Thomas McKinney and Samuel May Williams. It was a shallow-draft sidewheeler designed for the Brazos River trade. Drawing only 3 feet, the *Lafitte* was 120 feet long and could carry three hundred bales of cotton. With worries about Mexico in the air, the vessel left Galveston on March 14 under the command of Captain John Wade and one hundred volunteers. They armed the vessel with a long cannon and two iron carronades. It cruised to Aransas Pass and, finding no Mexican troop ships, returned on March 30. "McKinney, Williams and Company," *Handbook of Texas Online* [accessed December 4, 2007].

4. The *Creole* was an American-owned slave ship. In 1841 a group of slaves who were in the process of being transported in the ship overpowered their captors and gained control of the ship, killed the captain, and sailed for the Bahamas. The United States demanded that the British return the ship and slaves to their owners. England refused and instead granted the mutinous slaves political asylum and manumission. This incident heightened Anglo-American discord and intensified the sectional conflict in the United States. http://www.jstor.org/view/00222992/dm990582/99p0523t/0 [accessed December 4, 2007].

5. President John Tyler named Waddy Thompson of South Carolina the United States' minister to Mexico, with special instructions to secure the release of the Santa Fe prisoners. Thompson replaced Powhatan Ellis. "Thompson, Waddy," *Handbook of Texas Online* [accessed December 1, 2004].

James Love to Albert Sidney Johnston

Houston
April 9, 1842

Dear General

Burnley and myself came up last night on our way to the plantation. B[urnley] will hold an interview with his Excellency today, and endeavor, if possible, to learn from him his views in the present alarming crisis. I met your letter here which was most welcome, its sentiments and your course in the exciting times west is just such as your friends expected and such as will result in honor to you. It is no time to squabble about procedures, nor do I believe, under the circumstances which have transpired, do I believe it would have been best for you to have been in, or assumed the command. Let the army become concentrated and then the whole matter will regulate itself.

It is useless now to go back and speak as I think of the occurences [*sic*] of the last month. The self will, imbecility, or some motive of our man has paralzyed [*sic*] the ardor of the people. He has sown dissention [*sic*] when there was unanimity. He has ruthlessly placed his country and the people who elevated him to his high station on the brink of a precipice from which all may be impelled. Bad as I think he has acted, still if he does not wilfully [*sic*] shut his eyes, I would even support him now if he pursues a course in any degree calculated to meet public opinion and public dangers.

We all feel the deepest sympathy for our frontier friends. At the first alarm we immediately prepared to assist them, we gave with a liberality never seen paper money, provisions, and all the munitions of war. We had ready for the field in three days 300 men; we wished to fly to their relief and fight battles beyond the settlements. If we have been prevented, it is not our fault, but his, at the door of him who never defended the frontier either from the Mexicans or the savages, and who now talks of people making corn when the farmer, who sinks [in] repose from the toils of the day, does not know but that before he rises, his dwelling may be in flames, his wife or children slain or worse than that, in captivity. You may tell them we are ready whenever we know what is to be done.

You will have heard of the satisfaction by the President after you left—the orders of blockade, the proclamation for war and invasion, his letter to Santana [Santa Anna], his orders to Daingerfield to raise troops. We were encouraged in the belief that his eyes were opened and that he would take measures or rather pursue them energetically to save his country. 300 troops have arrived from the U States and sent to Corpus Christi. Thousands are ready to come. There is enthusiasm for our cause and nothing but wisdom and decision wanting to close this contest in victory and in glory. At the same moment these same fellows are landing on our shores; they see no preparations for raising men to cooperate with them, no plan, no organization. They, as a matter of course, will soon become disgusted as well as our friends in the "states," and when the wolf does come sure enough, they will not believe us & then we must of necessity fight for existence or abandon the country. Whether Mexico intended to invade us *now* or not, must we not all be blind mices not to know that the preparation and excitement, the arrival of troops from the U States will motivate them immediately to organize their greatest power for the conflict. They find us unprepared and will they not be upon us[?] Can they be arrested before they reach the Brasos [sic], *if then*[?]

I judge of what the President intends by what his *toadies* say. They talk of raising corn, his wisdom, his moral attributes, his sagacity, his firmness, that it is not time, wait "till" fall, then they will say untill [sic] spring, and then again, raise corn, etc. etc. It reminds me that Nero fiddled whilst Rome was burning. If none but those who danced were the loosers [sic], I would not care, all, however, must share the common danger.

We remain firm and united on the Island. There is some giving way here. The boys who started and returned are not as anxious. They seem to be inclined to sustain the recall, but want of ardor and patriotism may be attributed to them.

You know we always are ready to lay hold of excuses for retrograde movements whether in war or other matters.

The *Wharton* has gone out. Yucatan has given Moore notice they no longer want his services, so says the American consul just arrived at N. O. The American Minister Thompson has just sailed for Mexico from N. O. It is said he will bring matters to a pass at once. I don't know.

It is a rumor recd various ways but which I cannot trace to an authentic source that two steam frigates have been purchased for Mexico.[1]

Genl Hamilton has ordered a battery of Paixhan[2] guns from N. Y. He says, if necessary, he will be down with the chivalry of the south and asks no higher station than to serve under you. I shall write to him today. Morris arrived this morning and left directly for home. He looked a good deal like a loafer.

Your letters and papers have been sent to Corpus Christi by Capt Everett who commands the Mobile Company.[3]

I have written to you frequently with the uncertain chance of your receiving them.

Times look squally with the U S and Great Brittain [sic]. The newspapers in the U S seem to think that G. B. is simulating Mexico to the contest with Texas.

No domestic news. We are all well. I think you should return as soon as you decently can. I see no reason for your remaining at the present.

> Sincerely and truly yr Friend
> Jas Love
> Genl A. Sidney Johnston
> at Sutherlands

If not there, Mr Sutherland[4] will please forward to him.

1. The rumors were true, and the two British-built steamers arrived in the fall under the command of British officers. The *Montezuma*, a wooden-hulled, 1,164-ton vessel built in London, was 203 feet long, had a 280-horsepower engine, and mounted two 68-pound swivel guns and six 42-pound Paixhans guns. The *Guadaloupe*, the world's first iron steamship and largest such vessel, was built by the Lairds Shipyard at Birkenhead. It was 788 tons, 183 feet long,

with 180-horsepower engines, and carried two 32-pound cannons and two 68-pound swivel guns. With the delivery of these vessels Mexico could truthfully boast that it possessed the largest and most technologically advanced navy in the Gulf of Mexico. "*Montezuma* Affair," *Handbook of Texas Online* [accessed January 27, 2007].

2. In 1822 French lieutenant Henri-Joseph Paixhans invented this smooth-bore light-weight cannon. These guns fired large exploding shells. James Hamilton left Texas in March 1842. http://www.globalsecurity.org/military/systems/ship/steam6.htm [accessed December 4,2007].

3. John R. Everett commanded a company of Alabama volunteers. They left Galveston on April 4 for Corpus Christi.

4. George Sutherland was born in 1787 in Virginia. He came to Texas in 1830 and settled on the Navidad River in Jackson County. He quickly became active in local affairs. During the revolution he joined the army and fought at the Battle of San Jacinto. In 1842 he participated in military operations against the invasions of Texas by Generals Rafael Vásquez and Adrián Woll. "Sutherland, George," *Handbook of Texas Online* [accessed November 17, 2004].

Albert Triplett Burnley to Albert Sidney Johnston

Houston
April 9th 1842

My dear General

Love has written you so fully today about matters & things in general, that I have little to say, but to thank you for yours of 3rd Inst.

I have been to see Houston today, but he was so surrounded [that] I had no opportunity for private conversation & shall call again this evening & if I can, will tell him what I think about public matters. My opinions coincide with yours in the main, but from what I hear here, I fear it will have little effect. He will do everything his own way, or prevent it from being done. *This* way can't be successfully adopted & consequently, the country must be greatly & permanently injured without some providential interference in our behalf, which we neither deserve or have a right to expect & besides, I believe any influence I might once have had with Houston is destroyed by the *evil association* I have kept up with *you* & *Love*. He suspects all my suggestions to be influenced by you two, & I believe does not wish to talk to me. We are establishing a press at Galveston which will deal him some blows that will make his bones ache if he persists in a policy to ruin the country.[1]

Believing that the whole enterprise of invading Mexico will fail in disgrace, I think you had better return home at once & let the whole responsibility fall where it ought.[2]

I intended to return to the United States this summer & expected to be able to raise some negroes. But the late invasion & continued uncertainty about everything will forbid success, & I expect prevent me from leaving Texas.

> A T Burnley
> Genl A. Sidney Johnston
> at Southerlands [sic] on
> the *Navidad*

1. The *Texas Times* was advertised in the Houston *Telegraph* on March 30 but did not actually publish its first issue until later that year. It was the successor of the San Luis *Advocate*. Ferdinand Pinckard remained its editor.
2. Johnston agreed with his friends and returned by April 25. See "Johnston, Albert Sidney," *Handbook of Texas Online*.

James Love to Albert Sidney Johnston

> Galveston
> August 29th [1842]

Dear General

I returned a week since from a visit of nearly a month to the plantations, and found everything there in better condition than I expected. The crops are good & would be fine but for the late heavy rains. I was sick yesterday, not well today, and look for an attack tomorrow, not exactly "chills," but nearly so. It is the effect of my stay in the Brazos bottom.

We are all tolerably quiet. The elections scarcely excite any interest whatever. That of Major General, the President has refused to order; he pocketed the bill and did not sign it. *He says Genl Houston has not settled his accounts.* What a miserable old wretch. You would have had no opposition, and what I hear from all quarters, it would have been useless.

Hunt[1] is out on the President and is writing a book. He [Sam Houston] in truth has but few friends. A letter Morris wrote Tankersley[2] about the assassination found its way to the President, enclosed to him as he says, by a *gentleman* from Galveston with the seal broken. He says he read it, enclosed it to Tankersley and denies having made the charge against Morris. Morris called on him for the name of the person who sent him the letter [but] he refused to give it. M told him he was just as bad as the others, & so they parted. Tankersley wrote him so & worse.

No men fighting. There are some Mexicans on the Nueces. Burleson is out against the Indians. The Santa Fe prisoners have arrived & generally left this. They were in the most destitute condition. Howard[3] is at my house sick. The volunteers from the states all gone home in no good humor with his Excellency.

Edmonds resigned, & Bryan is again consul.[4] Old *Sam* got his buggy.[5]

> Sincerely yr friend
> Jas Love
> Genl A. Sydney [*sic*] Johnston
> Louisville Kentucky

1. Memucan Hunt published a number of books, but none during this time period.
2. Benjamin F. Tankersley, a young lawyer from Virginia, was an anti-Houston man, as were Love and Morris.
3. George Thomas Howard was a member of the Santa Fe expedition who was imprisoned in Puebla, Mexico. He subsequently escaped and returned to Galveston on August 21. He must not have been too sick, for he joined the Somervell expedition that left San Antonio on November 25. See "Howard, George Thomas," *Handbook of Texas Online*.
4. When Sam Houston assumed the presidency for the second time he fired the Texas consular agent in New Orleans, William Bryan, a Lamar appointee, and replaced him with P. Edmonds. Upon examining the consular office's financial records Edmonds abruptly resigned. This forced Houston to reinstate

Bryan. See Alma H. Brown, "The Consular Service of the Republic of Texas," *Southwestern Historical Quarterly* 33, no. 3 (1930): 212–13.

5. In July 1841 Sam Houston ordered a buggy from McKinney and Williams. There were some rumblings that Houston favored these merchants.

Joseph A. Swett to Albert Sidney Johnston

Galveston

August 31, 1842

My Dear General

When you left, I promised you should hear occasionally from Texas, but I am sorry that I am unable to communicate to you any change for the better in the affairs of this country. The bill requiring the President to order the election of M[a]j[o]r General was held over by the President, and in the meantime, the Congress adjoined [adjourned], so that was lost. The law stands as it did. The western people are getting more and more uneasy & they talk loudly of all moving east of the Colorado.

The Pres[iden]t says he will "bring us all out right" and he is willing to receive either gratitude or abuse for his *great* and *good* exertions! Most of the volunteers have returned from the west and many to the United States. All are outraged against the Prest and many fellows who came in for a long time, took the liberty of addressing long communications to him in most of which he was openly charged with *lying* & other like practices, all which he took very philosophically.

The Santa Fe prisoners arrived here a week last Tuesday. Many on their arrival at Houston attempted to see Mr. Prest Houston, but he was *too unwell* to see them.

A few days ago, Capt E. McLean[1] *cowhided* Mr Butler, the lawyer, on the Tremont piazza. Butler, being a Christian, did not resist and has not resented it. Potter,[2] I think, is pretty sure of being elected from this county. Green has a fair chance of being elected from Brazoria[3]—the others, more doubtful, I am told. Mayfield had gone to Austin [and] Nat Watrous also has gone; one or the other is a candidate for that county.[4] The *Civilian* announced your name as candidate for Major Gen before it was known the law had failed. There would have been no doubt of the result, this Sam

Houston knew. Please remember me to Mr. Davis[5] and accept for yourself my most sincere professions of Respect and Esteem and believe

> Me most truly your obt Servant
> J. A. Swett
> Gen A. Sidney Johnston
> Louisville, Kentucky

1. Ephraim McLean was born in 1816 in Christian County, Kentucky. He was Thomas F. McKinney's nephew. He came to Texas from Missouri in May 1836 and went to work for his uncle. In 1839 he joined a ranger group and served in the Indian campaigns and spy companies. "McLean, Ephraim Walton," *Handbook of Texas Online* [accessed November 17, 2004].

2. Henry N. Potter was born in 1822 in Connecticut. He arrived in Texas in 1838 and settled in Galveston. The following year he was elected city attorney but served for only one month. In 1842 he represented Galveston in the Seventh Congress. "Potter, Henry N.," *Handbook of Texas Online* [accessed November 17, 2004].

3. Thomas Jefferson Green participated in the Somervell and Mier expeditions and spent time in Perote prison in Mexico. He returned to Brazoria County and represented it in the Eighth Congress. See "Green, Thomas Jefferson," *Handbook of Texas Online*.

4. Neither James Mayfield nor John Watrous was elected to office in 1842. Later in the year, however, Mayfield participated in the Somervell expedition. "Somervell Expedition," *Handbook of Texas Online* [accessed November 24, 2004].

5. This probably refers to H. W. Davis, who had been with Albert Sidney Johnston in Texas.

James Love to Albert Sidney Johnston

> Galveston
> Sept 13th 1842

Dear General

I do not consider that you deserve a letter at my hands, but still I write. The elections are over. We have not heard much as yet. Potter[1] reced [sic] here 235, Borden[2] 114, Bache[3] 114. Baker is elected.[4] Sherman is elected in Harris.[5] 54 majority over Henderson.[6] Lowery third. Col Warren is elected in Brazoria,[7] not certain whether Green or Robinson.[8] There was no ticket for Maj General for the reasons I gave you in a former letter.

The President has determined to remove to Washington[9] because Sherman was elected, and because the corporation of Houston refused to furnish offices. His Excellency is odious. On the application of the British and American ministers, he has taken off the blockade as far as relates to foreign vessels.

We like Capt Elliot[10] very much. He is frequently at my house, a plain and sociable man. From what I see and know, I believe the English ministers are earnestly engaged and endeavoring to get us peace.

There are no Mexicans on our borders.[11] Kinney[12] wrote Aubrey from Matamoros that Reyes was raising a force to attack Austin.[13]

Genl Burleson has gone out with a party of 70 against the Indians in the upper country. Col Hockley has resigned in disgust.[14] Hunt[15] was offered his place, but refused. What do you think of that? No one who regards his character would accept office under Houston.

We have had incipient rains since 13th July. The crops cut off one half, no prospect of its cessation.

Two German Counts[16] who brought letters from Genl Cass[17] are here on some scheme of colonization. They have dined with me. They are sensible men and speak our language. Com[modore] Moore is still at N. O., and I am afraid will not be able to get out. Exchequers are worth 70cts. Pinckard is afloat & his first No appears next week.[18] We have no fever on the Island and the country everywhere is healthy.

Howard[19] still is with us, he is convalescent. Cook[20] [sic] and McLeod[21] were about to fight a duel [but] they were arrested. Morris & Judge Eve[22] have raised a slander on me that I had chills, don't believe it.

I see nothing to prevent you being next President as everybody seems to be for you. All are well & send their regards. I hope to see you soon.

yr friend sincerely
Jas Love

Will you send me a newspaper containing the Ky returns of the elections?

Genl A. Sidney Johnston
Louisville Kentucky

[added lengthwise across the writing on the first page of the letter]

Nat. Watrous elected. Darnell[23] & Scurry[24] in S Augustine. Robin-son[25] in Brazoria. They have captured two Mexicans near Austin, who, on the credit of Indians, have been committing murders. They killed King & Dobson at Barton's Spring. They say there is a band of fifty on the Cibolo together with several Americans. A party has gone over, and I look for rare fun in the way of hanging.

We had a storm last night, the 18th, two churches flooded & many houses unroofed. McLean's Wharf[26] gone. I recd no damage.

1. Henry N. Potter.
2. Gail Borden Jr.
3. Richard Bache was born in Philadelphia, Pennsylvania, in 1784. He entered Texas in 1836 and later served aboard the TN *Zavala*. He moved to Galveston in 1842 and after his defeat served as the commissioner of the navy yard. Galvestonians later elected him their justice of the peace. "Bache, Richard," *Handbook of Texas Online* [accessed December 21, 2004].
4. Moseley Baker was born in Norfolk, Virginia, in 1802. His family moved to Alabama, and later he founded and edited the Montgomery *Advertiser*. In 1829 he was elected to the Alabama legislature and served as the Speaker of the House. He entered Texas, probably in 1833, and settled on Galveston Bay. He was an avid proponent of independence and fought at the battle of Gonzales, the "Grass Fight," the siege of Bexar, and the Battle of San Jacinto. He served in the First and Third Congress and was a charter member, along with James Love, of the Galveston City Company. In 1842 Houstonians elected Baker brigadier general of the militia, and he led a company of soldiers against General Adrián Woll's seizure of San Antonio. "Baker, Moseley," *Handbook of Texas Online* [accessed January 20, 2007].
5. Sidney Sherman was born in Marlboro, Massachusetts, in 1805. He entered Texas in 1835 as the captain of a company of Kentucky volunteers. At the Battle of San Jacinto he was the first Texan to use the battle cry, "Remember the Alamo." Harris County voters elected Sherman to the Seventh Congress. "Sherman, Sidney," *Handbook of Texas Online* [accessed January 20, 2007].
6. James Wilson Henderson was born in Sumner County, Tennessee, in 1817. He entered Texas shortly after the Battle of San Jacinto. After the revolution he settled in Harris County and worked as a land surveyor. He studied the law and was admitted to the bar. Shortly after the election defeat mentioned in

this letter he joined the Somervell expedition. "Henderson, James Wilson," *Handbook of Texas Online* [accessed January 20, 2007].

7. John Warren was born in Massachusetts in 1800. He first came to Texas in 1825 but later returned to the United States. The citizens of Brazoria County elected Warren to the House of Representatives in the Seventh Congress. "Warren, John," *Handbook of Texas Online* [accessed September 1, 2008].

8. Thomas Jefferson Green did not serve in the Seventh Congress. Tod Robinson was reelected by the citizens of Brazoria County to serve as a member of the House of Representatives in the Seventh Congress.

9. After the Vásquez raid on San Antonio President Houston insisted that Congress move the capital away from Austin, a town he never liked. Temporarily the government met in Houston, but a poll of citizens revealed that they did not support the request from the administration to furnish quarters, and the next session of Congress reluctantly met at Washington-on-the-Brazos, where Houston and the administrative offices had moved.

10. Charles Elliot, the only British chargé d'affaires to Texas (there were no consuls), served from June 28, 1842, until the summer of 1845, when Texas voted to join the United States. "Elliot, Charles," *Handbook of Texas Online* [accessed November 24, 2004].

11. This was not true. On August 30, 1842, a portion of the Army of the North under General Adrián Woll's command crossed the Rio Grande and marched toward San Antonio. They entered the city on September 11, two days before Love wrote this letter. "Woll, Adrián," *Handbook of Texas Online* [accessed November 24, 2004].

12. Henry Lawrence Kinney was born in 1814 near Shesequin, Pennsylvania. He arrived in Texas in 1838 and in 1839, in partnership with William B. Aubrey, established a trading business near present-day Corpus Christi, a city he helped to found. They quickly developed a prosperous illegal trade with northern Mexico. At the time of this letter rumors suggested that Kinney was a captive on parole in Matamoros. In late July his partner, William P. Aubrey, abandoned their trading post on the Nueces River after several Mexicans attacked their stockade. "Kinney, Henry Lawrence," *Handbook of Texas Online* [accessed November 17, 2004].

13. General Isidro Reyes succeeded Mariano Arista as the commander of Mexico's Army of the North.

14. George Washington Hockley was born in Philadelphia, Pennsylvania, in 1802. A protégé of Sam Houston, he entered Texas in 1835. He served as Houston's

chief of staff at the Battle of San Jacinto and as Houston's secretary of war and marine during both administrations. He did not support Houston's handling of the Mexican invasions and resigned his post on September 1, 1842. Three weeks later the new secretary of war and marine, Morgan C. Hamilton, appointed Hockley acting colonel of ordnance and engineer of the port of Galveston. See "Hockley, George Washington," *Handbook of Texas Online*.

15. Memucan Hunt.

16. Love may be referring to Count Joseph of Boos-Waldeck and Prince Victor of Leiningen, who came to Texas in 1842 in connection with the Society for the Protection of German Immigrants in Texas. For an excellent account of the early Germans in Texas, see R. L. Biesele, *History of the German Settlements in Texas, 1831–1861* (Austin: Von Boeckmann-Jones, 1930).

17. Lewis Cass was born in Exeter, New Hampshire, in 1782. He served in the War of 1812 and reached the rank of brigadier general. He served as Andrew Jackson's secretary of war from 1831 until 1836 and then as the United States' ambassador to France. "Cass, Lewis," *Handbook of Texas Online* [accessed January 25, 2007].

18. After the San Luis *Advocate* ceased publication, Ferdinand Pinckard moved the newspaper operation to Galveston and renamed his publication the *Galveston Texas Times*. Its first issue appeared on October 11, 1842. "*Galveston Texas Times*," *Handbook of Texas Online* [accessed February 5, 2007].

19. George Thomas Howard.

20. William G. Cooke.

21. Both Cooke and Hugh McLeod participated in the ill-fated Santa Fe expedition, and each spent time in a Mexican prison, Cooke in the Santiago prison and McLeod in the Perote prison. Cooke arrived in Galveston on August 10, 1842, and quickly volunteered to serve in the operations against General Adrián Woll. McLeod arrived in Galveston on August 21, 1842. Shortly after challenging Cooke to a duel, McLeod returned to San Antonio and completed Samuel A. Maverick's term as a member of the House of Representatives. Woll captured Maverick in San Antonio and sent him, ironically, to the Perote prison.

22. Richard Morris was Love's son-in-law, and Joseph Eve was his brother-in-law. Joseph Eve was born in Culpeper County, Virginia, in 1784. Around 1807 he moved to Kentucky, and in 1810, 1811, and 1815 he served in the state legislature. During the War of 1812 he reached the rank of colonel. After the war he was a state senator in Kentucky and a circuit court judge. An avid Whig, he supported William Henry Harrison. In 1841 President John Tyler

appointed him chargé d'affaires to the Republic of Texas. See "Morris, Richard" and "Eve, Joseph," *Handbook of Texas Online*.

23. Nicholas Henry Darnell was born in Williamson County, Tennessee, in 1807. He moved to Texas in 1838 and settled in San Augustine. He served in the Sixth and Seventh Congresses as a representative for that city. His colleagues elected him Speaker of the House on November 24, 1842. "Darnell, Nicholas Henry," *Handbook of Texas Online* [accessed January 20, 2007].

24. Richardson A. Scurry was born in Gallatin, Tennessee, in 1811. He moved to Texas in 1836 and participated in the Battle of San Jacinto. Citizens from San Augustine elected him to the Seventh and Eighth Congresses, and he served as the Speaker of the House from 1842 to 1844. "Scurry, Richardson A.," *Handbook of Texas Online* [accessed January 20, 2007].

25. Tod Robinson.

26. McLean's Wharf was constructed by Ephraim Walton McLean. He was born in Christian County, Kentucky, in 1816. He was Thomas F. McKinney's nephew. In 1836 he and James Prather McKinney, Thomas's younger brother, entered Texas and soon worked for McKinney and Williams. In 1837 he constructed a large palmetto wharf in Galveston. The 1842 hurricane destroyed it. See "McLean, Ephraim Walton," *Handbook of Texas Online*.

James Love to Albert Sidney Johnston

Galveston
Sept 22, 1842

Dear General

The Mexicans numbering 1300 under command of Genl Woll[1] captured Bexar on the 12th Inst. The circuit court was in session, the Judge,[2] Calhoun,[3] Jones of Gonzales,[4] Cunningham,[5] Luckie,[6] Maverick,[7] Ogden[8] and others making in all 53, are prisoners.[9] They had information the day before of the attack [but] it was doubted. They, however, prepared for defense, [and] gave one fire which was returned. Then they surrendered to a flag of truce sent in by the Genl. We have various rumors of a large force being this side the Rio Grande and in the immediate neighborhood of Bexar. Rumor heretofore had been so wide of the mark that I hesitate to say how far I believe. I will give them as they reached us yesterday. Clark Owen[10] has written that he sent out spies who reported 1000 at Goliad, & 1000 at another place.

Howard,[11] who lives near San Antonio, was with a party at Goliad of some
15 at a fandango.[12] They told him it was [an] invasion and a large force, that
Woll had issued a proclamation saying he would have dismissed the prisoners
if they had not fired on his troops; that the war was to be conducted on usage
of civilized nations, private property respected, etc.

Upon the news of the approach of the Mexicans, Hays,[13] Chevalie,[14]
and others had gone out to reconnoitre upon the two roads. Whilst out, the
Mexicans entered San Antonio from hills (north) and did not approach by
either road. They, on their return, found it occupied, & escaped. Hays fell
back to Seguin; Clark Owen is at Victoria with 150 men [and] the families
moving in.[15]

The President has issued his proclamation in his usual style, to punish the enemy for their "audacity," to drive them across the Rio Grande, etc
etc. He orders out troops west of Brazos; those below Washington to march
at once to the frontier, those above, by way of Austin. Other counties to
organize as a reserve. He directs them to report and march without further
orders and to elect, when assembled, their own commander.

News reached here from Matamoros three weeks since, from one
entitled to every credit, that an expedition was about to start to take Austin.
The President took no steps of preparation. The inference I draw from the
movement is that this force intended to make a dash on Austin and take
it. Being prevented by high floods, they fell down on Bexar, or that it is the
advance of an invading force to occupy Bexar, Goliad, etc., to fortify as a place
of deposite [sic], concentrate their forces, and make a grand move. I believe
the latter, because I do not think that Genl Woll would command a marauding party. He is the friend of Santa Anna, high in his confidence, the best officer they have. He is a Belgian[16] [and] all speak of him as a gentleman. Besides,
the steady preparation by Mexico for the last six months, makes it evident
to me, they will invade. If either of the rumors be true, that Owens spies saw
other forces or that Woll issued a proclamation, the invasion has commenced.

The terrible gale we had on the 18th has detained the boat. I shall
have nothing further to write you for three weeks as I do not expect additional intelligence before the boat leaves.

You will receive another letter from me by this boat (before written)[.] I offer no suggestions as to your course, whether you shall come at
once or await further intelligence. Calhoun & others have written that they
are well treated. There is also a rumor that they have been sent to Rio Grande.[17]

There seems to be great apathy in the people. They have been cheated and deluded by a fool or knave and have no confidence in him. The storm, the destruction of our crops, the invasion, the folly and wretchedness of a bad man has placed us in a position none need envy. If the next arrival confirms the opinion that we are invaded, I join the army at once and fight to the last.

> James Love
> Genl A. Sydney Johnston
> Louisville Kentucky

1. General Adrián Woll was born in 1795 in Saint-Germain-en-Laye near Paris. He entered Mexico in 1817 and fought for Mexican independence alongside General Santa Anna. He campaigned with Santa Anna during the Texas Revolution but did not fight at the Battle of San Jacinto. In June 1842 the Mexican government appointed him second in command of the Army of the North and head of the Department of Coahuila. The government ordered him to invade Texas, capture San Antonio, then reconnoiter the Guadalupe River to Gonzales. He captured San Antonio on September 12 but never completed the rest of his mission. See "Woll, General Adrián," *Handbook of Texas Online*. For more information on Woll's invasion of Texas, see J. Milton Nance, *Attack and Counter-Attack: The Texas-Mexican Frontier, 1842* (Austin: University of Texas Press, 1964), 297–408, 600–603.

2. The judge was Anderson Hutchinson. He was born in Greenbrier County, Virginia, in 1798. He entered Texas in 1840 and settled in the Austin area. The next year the government appointed him judge of the Fourth or Western District. He was holding court when General Woll captured San Antonio. Retreating Mexican forces removed Hutchinson to the Perote prison. Santa Anna released Hutchinson to Waddy Thompson, the American minister to Mexico. "Hutchinson, Anderson," *Handbook of Texas Online* [accessed January 26, 2007].

3. Nance, *Attack and Counter-Attack*, 600–603, does not name a "Calhoun" among the list of captured Texans.

4. William E. "Fiery" Jones was born in Georgia in 1808. He entered Texas in 1839 and settled in Gonzales County. He represented the county in Congress during 1841–1842. Waddy Thompson arranged his release from prison. "Jones, William E.," *Handbook of Texas Online* [accessed January 26, 2007].

5. General Woll listed John R. Cunningham as a lawyer. Taken prisoner by Mexican troops, he died near the Leona River from a fever he contracted earlier while in Houston. See Nance, *Attack and Counter-Attack*, 330.

6. Nance, *Attack and Counter-Attack*, 600–603, does not name a "Luckie" among the list of captured Texans.

7. Samuel A. Maverick was born in Pendleton, South Carolina, in 1803. He entered Texas in 1835 and was active in the Texas Revolution. He participated in the siege of Bexar and attended the constitutional convention as one of two delegates from the Alamo. In 1838 he settled in San Antonio and served as mayor. After the Vásquez raid he moved to Gonzales and returned to San Antonio to attend the district court. Retreating Mexican forces removed Maverick to the Perote prison. Santa Anna released Maverick to Waddy Thompson, the American minister to Mexico. "Maverick, Samuel Augustus," *Handbook of Texas Online* [accessed January 27, 2007].

8. Duncan Campbell Ogden was born in 1813 at Ogdensburg, St. Lawrence County, New York. He entered Texas in 1838 and joined the Army of the Republic of Texas. He later moved to San Antonio and opened a mercantile store with his old friend, George T. Howard. "Ogden, Duncan Campbell," *Handbook of Texas Online* [accessed November 24, 2004].

9. Nance lists fifty-two prisoners from San Antonio. Nance, *Attack and Counter-Attack*, 600–603.

10. Clark L. Owen was born in 1808 in Shelby County, Kentucky. He came to Texas in 1836, and in May 1837 he joined the Texas regular army with the rank of captain. At the time this letter was written, he commanded Texan forces at Victoria. "Owen, Clark L.," *Handbook of Texas Online* [accessed November 24, 2004].

11. This is likely George T. Howard. See "Howard, George T.," *Handbook of Texas Online*.

12. A fandango is a party or festive gathering.

13. John Coffee Hays was born in 1817 in Little Cedar Lick, Wilson County, Tennessee. He came to Texas in 1836 and served in the army. After the war he joined a company of rangers and patrolled between San Antonio and the Rio Grande. At the time of the Woll invasion Hays held the rank of captain. "Hays, John Coffee," *Handbook of Texas Online* [accessed November 24, 2004].

14. Mike Chavellie was one of the scouts in Captain Hays's ranger company. Woll approached San Antonio via an old trading road from Presidio that ran north of the headwaters of the San Antonio River.

15. When Woll occupied San Antonio, Captain Hays, along with fourteen other rangers, waited outside the city for approximately two hundred volunteers from Seguin and Gonzales, under the command of Mathew Caldwell, to arrive.

16. General Woll was actually born in Saint-Germain-en-Laye, France, in 1795. See "Woll, Adrián," *Handbook of Texas Online*.

17. The fifty-two captives were taken from Bexar on September 15 and crossed the Rio Grande eight days later on their way to imprisonment in central Mexico.

Robert Holmes Chinn to Albert Sidney Johnston

New Orleans
Tuesday Sept 27 1842

Gen A. S. Johnston
My Dear Sir

The long expected time has arrived—before you will receive this letter Galveston will be *invested* with the enemy and entirely ruinated [sic]. The *Picayune* that I[1] sent you will detail most of the particulars, but for fear that you may not receive it, I will write it over and state some that the *Picayune* does not say anything about, leaving it entirely to your kindness to excuse such mistakes as you will find in this letter.

Gen Woll invested with 1300 Mexicans San Antonio and took all the officers and the Bar of the Circuit Court there in session, with a No. of other Americans. Chavalier & Hays who were spies, were out and escaped.[2] Gen Houston ordered the men from the lower western counties on the coast to assemble at San Antonio and the upper counties on the Brazos and Colorado at Austin. Love & Morris, who was holding the Circuit Court at Galveston[,] were preparing for San Antonio as soon as the news was confirmed and Houston's orders were obeyed. Houston's Proclamation requests the other portion of the Texians to hold themselves in readiness. Yucatan and Tabasco have yielded to the Central Government,[3] and Commodore has sufficient information from Mexico to assure him that Galveston will be attacked by sea from the steam ships which are manned by English saylers [sic] & officers, and that in a very short time.[4] The very next news we may expect to hear from Galveston will be the final destruction. It is now partly destroyed by a hurricane; the water was nearly on Tremont and Bay. Commodore Moore is still here without the means of leaving. He cannot get off without money. His officers are dissatisfied, wavering as they say, between a severe sea battle on the Gulph [sic] and Mexican prisons or a dishonourable confinement in N. O. The most anxious and nervous persons I ever saw to meet the contest, although the Mexicans have the supremacy in point of naval force besides being manned by Englishmen.

Gen, to inform you that I would *rather* fight under you as a common soldier will be sufficient to insure me more kindness and attention than I could request as Colonel under any other Texian I ever saw. So you will please to let me hear from you at your earliest convenience.

With my best respects to your friends and the little Gen.

> I am yours very respectfully
> Robert H. Chinn
> Gen A Sidney Johnston
>   Louisville Kentucky [crossed
>   through in another hand]
> Shelbyville Shelby County care
> of George Hancock

M. B. Baker senator 3 maj. over Lawrence; Sherman rep from Harris; Pot. 100 maj Galveston; Tod Robinson from Bras. Election will be contested some 2 or 3 maj over Col Warren. Col L. P. Cook beaten in Travis; Sam Whiting opposed to Houston.[5] Mr. and Mrs. Doswell & Mrs. Gray living at Galveston. Mr. & Mrs. Nickolson, she used to be Maggy Stone, living in Houston.[6]

My love to Harrison Davis.

1. Robert Holmes Chinn was a resident of New Orleans and came to Texas in 1841 when he petitioned Lamar to be appointed chief justice of Brazoria County. He returned to the Crescent City and resumed his law practice and is listed in the city directory through 1846.
2. Mike Chavellie and John Coffee Hays were scouts for Texas forces outside of San Antonio.
3. This statement is not true. Centralist forces under General Pedro de Ampudia had laid siege to the city of Campeche but had not yet captured it.
4. Chinn's comment, when coupled with Crittenden's desire to overhaul some smooth-bore cannons and use them for coastal defense (see letter dated

February 5, 1842) and Love's claim in his April 9, 1842, letter that General James Hamilton had ordered Paixhans guns to defend Galveston from attack, suggests that coastal Texans strongly disagreed with President Houston's wait-and-see approach to national defense. For lowland Texans and residents of San Antonio that threat of Mexican attack was real. The two Mexican steam-powered warships that Chinn mentioned were the *Montezuma* and the *Guadaloupe*.

5.   Chinn added news of these election returns, as the newspapers had provided only partial returns from the election. However, Chinn's information was not totally correct. Sam Witting, the editor of the *Austin City Gazette* in 1839, at first supported Lamar then in 1840 began to attack his administration.

6.   James Temple Doswell and his wife, the former Evelina Gray, moved from Houston to Galveston and were accompanied by her widowed mother. Mrs. Gray's niece, Margaret Clayton Stone, had accompanied the Grays to Texas in 1838, and she married Ebenezer B. Nichols, the son of William Nichols, a native of New York, who had opened a jewelry store in Houston in 1838.

James Love to Albert Sidney Johnston

Galveston
April 10th 1843

Dear General

I have just returned from the plantation and have left everything in as prosperous condition as the seasons permit. Burnley's place very much injured by the overflow, the other not at all, *much less* water on it than yours, remember that. The last four days, the only summer weather we have had, [and] the garden for the third time begins to look well.

The most important item of intelligence is that which was brought by Judge Robison.[1] He has been released by Santa Anna and is the bearer of propositions as the basis of peace with Texas. They are such as in fact makes us independent except our acknowledgment of the sovereignty of Mexico. No one will agree to the terms, but I view them (if Santa Anna is at all sincere) as an opening for negotiation, which will end for the present in a truce and after, in peace. Yucatan as yet holds out, altho I yet entertain the opinion that she will fall. Affairs in central Mexico are in an unsettled condition, and the Dictator not yet firmly seated. The present is the most auspicious period to make a demonstration on the Rio Grande. Mexico is greatly exhausted in resources, [and] Yucatan occupies her time & resources. Santa Anna has his hands full at home, and we might march and take possession of all the northern frontier without the firing of a gun.

There is talk of a campaign, and Rusk[2] says he is determined to carry into effect the law of the last session. It seems that he and the President is not on good terms. He [Rusk] has appointed Mayfield Inspector General[3] who lately went to Washington [and] *demanded* Rusk's commission and received it.

I have a letter from Mayfield dated "Washington 11th March." He says Rusk wished to appoint you Adjutant General, or if the force is raised, that you should be the Brigadier. He says Rusk is your friend and will support you for the Presidency, and the East [East Texas] prefers you to any but Rusk. Whilst upon this subject, I may say that I saw Lipscomb[4] at Brazoria. He said if he wishes at all to be a candidate, he should not think of permitting himself to be announced without seeing you, and spoke very friendly. Those most opposed to Houston do not want Lipscomb and Burleson would, no doubt, oppose and best him. If he runs at all, it will be only by the consent of your & Burleson's friends. Lipscomb is no friend or candidate of Houston, and would publickly [sic] say he was opposed throughout to his administration of affairs since he was in. I have the opinion that Rusk will be a candidate, altho his most intimate friends say not.

If he [Rusk] is not a candidate, you can easily beat any other, and such is the general suspicion, and whether you wish it or not, you will, in a manner, be compelled to office. It is a thing to be remembered by you, that if a campaign is organized for the Rio Grande, and you not here to go with the forces, that you are a gone man. And also, if your mind is fully made up that your destiny is to be cast here, that it is indispensible [sic] to your future ambitious hopes that you be on the spot, and always on it. A day here brings forth important results and one who intends to exercise an important position in the country should always be ready to control or direct events. You have an influence, which if properly directed, will leave you nothing to ask in Texas.

It seems the Mier prisoners have escaped [and] several have already arrived. They rose upon their guards, disarmed them; they lost eleven of their number in the conflict, Dr. Brenham amongst them, who lost his life by precipitating himself on a bayonet. They were conducted north by Cameron to avoid military stations.[5] The boat arrived yesterday from Houston & brought a letter from Torrey to his partner here. He says he has recd a letter from his brother on the Rio Grande, who says they will be in a few days [and] that they are *equipping* themselves out in good style at the expense of the enemy. Is not all this wonderful[?] If other news arrives before the boat leaves, I will add it.

You may remember the conversation we had in Capt Elliot's[6] room a few days before I left on the subject of the purchase of Texas slaves by the British abolitionists. A movement has been attempted, mainly by Andrews of Houston,[7] & in which he connected Sam Williams, Elliot, Sydnor, & myself as committed to that policy. He came down there to lecture, [but] he was sent across to Va [Virginia] Point & warned off. He next went to my neighborhood. The excitement became so great that he has made up his mind to *leave*. Sam Houston & Reily are both implicated, whether justly or not I cannot say. I was on the Brazos when the agitation was here, and my conjecture is that the movement grew out of that conversation, altho I have not heard it alluded to. It was, I think, the beginning of an effort to give Great Brittain [*sic*] a control over us. The Capt [Elliot] disclaimed all con-nection with it as a matter of course.

Reily beat Bronnaugh less than 100 votes for Col in Harris. What think you of that!

Morris has not yet returned home. The Judge has been better for the last five days. The rest of us all well, and generally and severally, send their kindest greetings.

> Sincerely Your friend
> Jas Love

Let your friends know at once just what you want. If they have the same regard for you that we [have], they can relieve you from suspense & set you to work. Had I their means, I could start you back in 24 hours. They should not hesitate because your fame and fortune are both at stake, and it may be a long time before they might have such another opportunity of doing honor to themselves and to you. And if a lady is to come with you, the sooner she is initiated into our rough manners and *uncivilized* country, the better. Lessons taught early are best remembered.

> J L

You will consider everything as [a] report in relation to the prisoners except that they rose on their guards. The Mexican account is that 111 have been retaken. What has become of most of the others is not so certain. A few have got in that separated from the others.

I will endeavor to procure the printed statement of S[anta] Anna's proposition and enclose it.

> Genl A. Sydney [*sic*] Johnston
> Louisville Kentucky

1. James W. Robinson was captured by General Adrián Woll and taken to Mexico City. While imprisoned he began clandestine talks with Santa Anna about Texas independence. Santa Anna released Robinson with a set of proposals he desired to negotiate with the Texas leaders. Robinson arrived in Galveston on March 27, 1843, two weeks before James Love composed this letter. See "Robinson, James W.," *Handbook of Texas Online*.

2. In January 1843 Thomas Jefferson Rusk, over Houston's veto, was elected major general of the militia by a joint vote of the Texas Congress. Congress appropriated fifty thousand dollars for frontier defense. Houston supporters claimed that Rusk's election was a ploy to win military glory for the presidential race of 1844. See "Rusk, Thomas Jefferson," *Handbook of Texas Online*.

3. James S. Mayfield.

4. Abner Smith Lipscomb. The presidential election was scheduled for September 1844.

5. Ewen Cameron was born in 1811 in Scotland. He arrived in Texas with the Kentucky volunteers in 1836 and spent most of his time with the army. He participated in the Mier expedition and was captured by Mexican forces. During the prisoners' forced march to Mexico City Cameron orchestrated a failed escape that led to the famous "Black Bean Episode." Even though Cameron did not draw a black bean, President Santa Anna ordered him to be executed for leading the escape. The Mexican army executed him on April 24, 1843. "Cameron, Ewen," *Handbook of Texas Online* [accessed December 1, 2004]; "Black Bean Episode," *Handbook of Texas Online* [accessed February 6, 2007].

6. Charles Elliot was born in 1801 in Dresden, Saxony. A member of the British diplomatic corps, he arrived in Galveston on August 6, 1842, as British chargé d'affaires to the Republic of Texas. Johnston had visited Texas during the winter months of 1842–1843, as had A. T. Burnley, and the two proceeded with their plans to purchase plantations along Oyster Creek and the Brazos River. The group had met with Elliot and John S. Sydnor, auctioneer

of Galveston, and discussed a popular topic of the day: should British abolitionists not pay Texan slave owners if they felt so strongly about abolishing
slavery in Texas? See "Elliot, Charles," and "Sydnor, John S.," *Handbook of
Texas Online* [accessed February 1, 2007].

7. Stephen Pearl Andrews was born in 1812 in Templeton, Massachusetts. A
    lawyer by profession and an abolitionist at heart, he settled in Houston in
    1839. He devised a scheme to abolish slavery in Texas by purchasing the
    slaves and setting them free. Accused of stirring up discontent among the
    slave population, he was almost lynched after his home in Houston was
    mobbed. He was soon forced to leave Texas. After resettling in England, he
    attempted to raise money in the form of a loan from Great Britain to the
    Republic of Texas to buy Texas slaves and set them free. The Texas chargé
    d'affaires, Ashbel Smith, repudiated this remarkable offer. "Andrews, Stephen
    Pearl," *Handbook of Texas Online* [accessed November 24, 2004].

James Love to Albert Sidney Johnston

Galveston
April 22 1843

Dear General

It seems the United States has entered earnestly upon mediation
between Texas and Mexico. The minister here as that at Mexico[1] has been
instructed to remonstrate with both governments against the prosecution of
the war by marauding parties whether by way of retaliation or otherwise. The
tone and temper of their instructions are rather positive and very firm. I have
no doubt the principles laid down will be enforced, and as a consideration,
we shall not again, in my opinion, have war on a small scale, if at all.

Count Cramayel has recd a copy of instructions sent to the French
minister at Mexico.[2] They are equally strong and positive. The English
government has done the same. All this leads me to suppose that these
three great powers have come to the conclusion to close the contest. I feel
confident that we will not be troubled by them the present year, and by that
time we will have [a] truce, if not peace. You will understand that what I
have mentioned above is not to be used in a manner to compromit [*sic*] me
as a friend.

Dr. Hill, Secretary of War and Marine,[3] left here yesterday for

Washington [on the Brazos, Texas]. He said the President would appoint a commissioner to go to Mexico to negotiate with Santa Anna. He said, also, he was hastening back to prevent any warlike movement by Rusk to compromit [sic] the government, and I believe from Rusk's character for indecision, that they may so far influence him as to prevent any movement.

It seems that the President, when he sent the commissioners to N. Orleans to take possession of the fleet, took the precaution in the event of the Commodore refusing to give it up, to give them authority to call on the U.S. authorities for assistance to compel him, and also sent a proclamation to be published in the event of his having sailed, denouncing it without the authority by the government and piratical.[4] When the commissioners showed this authority to the Commodore, he offered if they would not take these steps, he would bring the fleet into port here [Galveston], go and see the President, and endeavor to prevail on him to permit him to sail. The *Neptune* left N. O. last Saturday; the passengers have got the news and several letters were recd from the officers stating the anchors were up, and they would positively sail on next day. They have not arrived. The Commodore has either concluded not to *call,* or the vessels have been detained by the U. States authorities. Should he come here, he will be arrested immediately and deprived of command. I believe if he is permitted once to hoist his flag on the Gulf, that he will go to [the] Yucatan and brave everything as the only means to save himself from disgrace.

I have heard nothing since I wrote of the prospect of getting up an expedition under Rusk. The boat from Houston will be in this morning, if it brings any news, I will endeavor to let you have it. We have had no further information from that portions of the prisoners who escaped and were under Cameron.[5] I fear they have been recaptured. I do not believe a word of the extraordinary story of their capture of Camargo and a bloody fight & killing 600 etc. brought by a mail carrier from the west who had it from a Mexican *just in.*

We are getting along in politics pretty much in the old way. There is rather a calm, even the *Brazos Farmer*[6] has become rather decent of late. Genl Lamar has returned and brought no assistance to the *Times.* I have made up my own mind to let it take its fate rather than further to make advances to sustain it. I will not injure myself further when so much apathy prevails with those who should feel as deep an interest in the cause of the country as I do.

Judge Eve[7] received by the *Neptune* the notification of his recall and the appointment of Wm. S. Murphy. He is a Democrat, I believe, and from Ohio, or it may be the late governor of Alabama, a Democrat. I do not recollect his first name, altho I served with him in Congress. The Judge's health is still precarious and I still think his days are numbered.[8] He speaks of visiting Ky in June, [but] I do not think he will ever leave the Island. Mary has a daughter, a week old, and is pretty well. All the rest of us are in excellent health.

Will you take the trouble to procure for me a list of the Congressional districts [of Kentucky] as arranged by the last legislature, and also the candidates in each so far as they have been announced.[?] We have heard that Mrs. Davis[9] has had the misfortune to lose her daughter. Is it so?

Gail Borden has resigned the office of Collector. It is, I believe to be put in *commission* that his Excellency may govern its receipts according to his fancy. What a beauty he is! Butler & Miss [Gibbs? paper torn] are to be married on Wednesday. So I have given you all the news foreign and domestic and will close.

Yr friend
James Love

Tell that young son of yours[10] I feel very much inclined to be a friend of his and shall feel most happy in assisting him in the prosecution of his hopes of ambition should he come to Texas. And by the time he shall assume the station of manhood, this will be the only country in which he can hope for distinction. As things now are in the U States, the greatest mind and highest talent are forced to become the slave of party, or remain honest in obscurity. There is a field here for talent and its exercise that is not, and will not be, open there.

Genl A. Sidney Johnston
Louisville Kentucky

1. Love is referring to his brother-in-law, Joseph Eve, the U.S. minister in Galveston, and Waddy Thompson, U.S. minister in Mexico.
2. Viscount Jules de Cramayel served as the French chargé for Texas during Saligny's absence from January 1843 to January 1844, and Baron Isidore E. J. B. Alleye de Cyprey had been the French minister to Mexico since 1839.
3. George Washington Hill was born in 1814 at Hill Creek, Warren County, Tennessee. He immigrated to Texas in 1836 and served as a surgeon in the

Texas Army. From January 1843 to December 1844 he served as President Houston's secretary of war and navy. "Hill, George Washington," *Handbook of Texas Online* [accessed November 24, 2004].

4. Sam Houston ordered James Morgan and William Bryan to sell the two vessels of the Texas Navy, the *Austin* and the *Wharton*, then in New Orleans. Morgan arrived in the Crescent City on February 25, but Commodore Moore was very persuasive and convinced him that the navy was in fighting shape and should not be sold. Morgan agreed with Moore and ordered Moore to take his fleet to the Yucatán. Bryan informed Houston that the fleet had not been sold as ordered. This act of disobedience enraged the president, and on March 23 he contacted American authorities and asked them to help apprehend Commodore Moore. Houston informed the world that he considered Moore and his crew to be pirates. "Morgan, James," *Handbook of Texas Online* [accessed February 2, 2007]; "Bryan, William," *Handbook of Texas Online*.

5. Ewen Cameron.

6. The *Texian and Brazos Farmer* was a weekly published at Washington-on-the-Brazos in 1842–1843 and edited by Thomas "Ramrod" Johnston. Its editorial leanings were pro–Sam Houston.

7. Joseph Eve, U.S. minister to Texas.

8. Judge Eve died in Galveston in June of that year.

9. Mrs. Mary Jane Hawkins Davis had returned to Kentucky.

10. This refers to William Preston Johnston, age twelve.

James Love to Albert Sidney Johnston

Galveston
May 7, 1843

My dear General

I recd your letter by the *Neptune.* We all were pleased to hear from you and equally regret that necessity should impose upon you a residence so remote from scenes where stirrings and exciting events that daily arise amongst us is so well calculated to engross the thought of a mind capable of appreciating and inciting great deeds.

The government of the U. States has in so many words said to Mexico, you shall not prosecute the war against Texas except it is in a manner usual with civilized parties and with "competent forces." These instruc-

tions were sent to Genl Thompson[1] & copies sent here, their date 3rd Jany
& 7th Feb. Genl Hamilton[2] by the last mail enclosed me a letter from Genl
Thompson of 18th March without comment. It states that there did not exist
the most remote possibility that Santa Anna would recognize the independence of Texas, that he would yield everything, separate legislature, judiciary,
etc., but would not listen to any overtures for peace except upon the reserva-
tion of sovereignty. Genl Thompson enters upon an argument to shun the
advantages that would arise to Texas and clearly gives his opinion it ought to
be accepted.

This letter, together with some other smaller indications, has led
me to believe that some negotiation is on the tapis [table, i.e., under consid-
eration] by which Texas is to be sold by Mexico to the United States in the
event of peace between Texas and Mexico which seems to be a *sui generis*.

Now all this does not accord exactly with the views of his [sic] Majesty's government, whose feelings and interest I know to be in favor of our
absolute independence for reasons we have often talked about. The United
States, in her known selfish policy, will never move a finger or expend a dollar to effect the greatest objects for us. She might so do if her interests were
in any manner involved. She will collect her *money* through the influence
of the Texas question & then leave us to our fate. On the other hand, Great
Brittain [sic] does not wish to see the extension of the U S influence or territory on this continent, and sees the great advantages given to commerce &
immigration by our independence, and in my opinion, will soon enter upon
this question earnestly, and finally bring it to a close. My diplomacy is now
directed towards that object; I have furnished facts and drawn inferences
which are on their way across the Atlantic in an official form, that in my
opinion, will do us good. I may also say that it is known to me that France
is uniting with Great Brittain [sic] upon this Texas question, holding the
same views from the same causes. That these movements may and probably
will excite the U States, I think is certain. And it is a matter by no means
improbable that this question, before it closes, may be the means of angry
altercation, if not of blows.

It is now certain that Commodore has gone down the Gulf. He
did not call and has Morgan on board. I fear he is too late to do good. Capt
Elliot, the cousin of the minister,[3] & son of Lord Minto[?], arrived the day
before yesterday in a vessel of war five days from Vera Cruz. He brought the
news that Mérida had fallen through the treachery of Genl Miñon.[4] They
were celebrating the victory when he left and published the account as offi-

cial. Mérida being the capital, its fall would, of course, be the subjugation of Campeachy, the last hope of the province. The last Mexican news from Campeachy could not be later than the 12th of April. The letter from the British Minister giving this news to Capt Elliot is 20th April. It is asserted that news has been recd in N. Orleans from Campeachy of the date of the 25th at which time nothing of that kind had occurred. If so, there is a hope that it is not true and that the probability is that Mexico has anticipated the victory. Santa Anna had issued a proclamation saying the money due the U. States must be paid on the 30th April, that his government did not have it, and intimates it must be raised by *voluntary* contribution. The want of money may have procured the capture of Mérida. A few days will decide the uncertainty.

The Mexican Secretary of State had issued a diplomatic note to foreign ministers in which he stated that Mexico would treat all foreigners who had entered Texas since the revolution as intruders, that she would not respect their rights, and will strip them of all their acquisitions. The British *chargé* answered this & said that he supposed that Mexico would be governed by the laws of nations on such subjects, that her Majesty's government had recognized Texas, and had official relations with her and would know how to take care of the interests of her subjects. He sent a copy of the circular and answer to Elliot.[5]

News has reached Mexico of the decimation of the recaptured prisoners. Maverick had before brought the news from Tampico. Señor Jesus returned from Corpus Christi last night and confirmed. It may be put down as true now, as being the consequence of Houston's letter that they entered the country without the authority of the government.

I have not heard anything of Rusk since I wrote you, and supposed his contemplated movement will evaporate in smoke. He has again been nominated in the East as President, the probability is that his reluctance will at last be overcome. The movements attempted in favor of Lipscomb have all failed. He is to be married on the 10th to Mrs. Bullock.[6]

There is no particular excitement in politics. The *Times* has ceased its publication, the whole expense had fallen on me, and I could not further sustain it. Lamar returned and has not contributed one dollar, so you and I are left to the mercy of mercenaries, and the country without a press of any independence.

Judge Eve is gradually sinking, he now suffers much from sore throat and swelled feet. The rest of us are well. I have had an attack & truth compels me to own to one severe chill.

Burnley goes up immediately and will give you all [the] news. What I have said about public affairs, altho' not intended to be strictly confidential, but not get into newspapers.

Yr friend

Jas Love

1. "Genl Thompson" was Waddy Thompson, the U.S. minister to Mexico.
2. When Houston became president he fired James Hamilton and refused to pay his salary for the time he spent in Europe negotiating loans and treaties with various countries. Hamilton's uncompensated service to the republic left him near bankruptcy and forced him to return to South Carolina. He did not return to Texas until 1855. See "Hamilton, James," *Handbook of Texas Online.*
3. Charles Elliot was captain of the HMS *Spartan.* See "Elliot, Charles," *Handbook of Texas Online.*
4. This information was incorrect. At this time, Mexican forces under General Pedro de Ampudia were laying siege to the city of Campeche.
5. A copy of this correspondence between Percy W. Doyle, the British chargé d'affaires, and Captain Charles Elliot may be found in the April 20, 1843, letter and is in Ephraim Douglass Adams, ed., *British Diplomatic Correspondence concerning the Republic of Texas, 1838–1846* (Austin: Texas State Historical Association, 1918), 183. José María de Bocanegra was the secretary of state of Mexico.
6. Abner S. Lipscomb married Mrs. Mary P. Bullock of Austin, his second wife. See "Lipscomb, Abner S.," *Handbook of Texas Online.*

James Love to Albert Sidney Johnston

Galveston

May 15th 1843

Dear General

The most extraordinary thing that has occurred since I wrote is the proclamation of the President denouncing Com[modore] Moore as mutinous, his acts piratical, and calls upon all friendly powers in Christendom to bring him in to be punished. You will probably see the proclamation published. The Com[modore] had repeated positive orders to report himself in person in arrest. I do not excuse him, but it surely is more than madness in the Executive to have taken such a course at the moment his enemies might be so important to the country. As it is, nothing but a most brilliant achievement can save the Commodore. We look most anxiously to hear from him tomorrow by the *Neptune*.

The President has also declared martial law west of the Nueces and appointed Capt Hays to arrest all who have no passports. The object of this unconstitutional exercise of power is no doubt, to give advantages to favorites in the way of trade.

I had a letter from Genl Green to you & myself dated the 19th ult. He gives it as his opinion that the decimation of the sev[en]teen was occasioned by the letters of the President disavowing that they went under orders.[1] This letter he wrote to Elliot with the request to be forwarded to the British Minister. He copied the letter & sent it. It seems strange it should have come to light through that channel. It is highly probable he had other correspondents.

They are holding meeting[s] in the East and nominating Rusk. I believe that it is understood that he will assent & only wants gentle coercion. Your name has been mentioned there, the letter writer say as an absentee, or rather as one whose citizenship is doubtful. You will ascertain the motive for this is to forestall public opinion & will doubtless have its effect. The prospects of Lipscomb are not bright, & do not seem to be improving. There is not as yet much excitement on the subject of the ensuing election. Dr. *James B. Miller*[2] has accepted the office of Sec Treasury. Terrell says he will resign immediately after the adjournment of the Supreme Court. I don't believe it.[3]

Our paper has stopped; I could not longer support it as I met with no aid. Pinckard[4] is going to the U. States. I am sorry we were compelled to discontinue it as it is much needed and would do much good.

I do not hear a word of Rusk's campaign. That seems to have died *the death*. He has done himself no credit in the affair.

The health of Judge Eve is bad, much worse than when you left altho the doctors say otherwise. I feel confident he will die. He speaks now of going to Kentucky in June.

Not more than twelve of the Mier prisoners have returned. Genl

Green's letter leaves only 20 unaccounted for & he says with the exceptions of those at Perote, it is not known where the rest are, Genl Thompson so informed him. Did I write you that Thompson's opinion was that Mexico would not in any state of case make peace upon the principle of independence? He so wrote Genl Hamilton who forwarded me the letter.

The *Brazos Farmer* gives you cut almost every number. I mention this only because I know you are philosophic and don't mind it. That stout son of yours would fight about it at any time before he is 35, after that, he would laugh at it. Tell him to learn to box, shoot pistols, and the sword exercise. He is just the age to begin, when he shall be a man, we will give him full exercise in Texas.

I note what you say about the opinions of us. I pity them, they are fast approaching rusticity and know not the glorious excitement of uncertainty.

> Your friends
> James Love
> Genl A. Sidney Johnston
> Louisville Kentucky

1. General Thomas Jefferson Green was a member of the Somervell expedition to the Rio Grande. When General Somervell retreated northward, Green joined the ill-fated Mier expedition and became its second in command. He surrendered to General Pedro de Ampudia and was incarcerated in the Perote prison. Green clearly blamed Sam Houston for the decimation of Texas troops in the infamous Black Bean episode. See "Green, Thomas Jefferson," *Handbook of Texas Online*.

2. James B. Miller was born in 1801 in Kentucky. He came to Texas in 1829 and was an active supporter of the Texas Revolution. In 1843 Sam Houston appointed him secretary of the treasury. "Miller, James B.," *Handbook of Texas Online* [accessed December 1, 2004].

3. George Whitfield Terrell was born in 1803 in Nelson County, Kentucky. In 1829, while Sam Houston was governor of Tennessee, he appointed Terrell to be that state's attorney general. Terrell entered Texas in 1837, and in December 1841 Houston made him attorney general of the Republic of Texas. "Terrell, George Whitfield," *Handbook of Texas Online* [accessed December 1, 2004].

4. Ferdinand Pinckard was the editor of the *Texas Times*. He invested, as did James Love, in the town of San Luis.

James Love to Albert Sidney Johnston

Galveston
May 22, 1843

My dear General

If the N. Orleans papers should have made their way to your remote region, you will now have learned the occurrence at Yucatan of matters highly important to Texas.[1] Since then, we have an arrival from Yucatan of the 10th bringing intelligence five days later. This vessel was sent up with dispatches from the Commodore and Col Morgan to the government and will remain for an answer which we look for tomorrow. Morgan avows his share in the enterprise in ordering the Com[modore] down, as he believed matters most partial to our safety depended on it. There has been no fighting between them from the fifth, the fleet in harbor becalmed, the enemies fleet outside. The greatest necessity prevailed for a breeze to enable them to go out and attack. I am confident as much as they express of their ability to capture the enemy's vessels if they can get at them. Ampudia,[2] to use Morgan's phrase, is in "hockety" [and] he is negotiating for surrender, cut off from sea, surrounded by land, he must fall, & this will be the end of the invading force numbering 5,000. How immensely important the result has been to Texas, and should we obtain possession of one steamer, which I think we shall, Mexico is at our mercy. What a commentary on the imbecility and misrule of Houston. I need not tell you there is but one feeling here, and had he committed murder, if victorious and brings in the enemies fleet, we would receive him in triumph. A public meeting was held last night summarily attended in which complimentary resolutions were passed highly complimentary to him, his officers, and Col Morgan. Stuart[3] attended, and even he has in an article disapproved the course of the President, *altho he thinks the President thought he was right.* The meeting requested Houston to rescind his proclamation of piracy against Moore. The decimation of the Mier prisoners and his denunciation of Moore and the navy has done him more injury than anything else.

Morgan writes that as soon as they have settled affairs there they will come up. A great many persons are writing letters approving all they have done. Ampudia has proposed to Gov Mendez[4] to yield to Yucatan any terms she asked, to unite and capture the Texan fleet, and then unite their forces for an immediate invasion of Texas. The governor answered him very indignantly and says it may suit Mexican faith to deceive allies and prove treacherous to them, but not the Yucatecos. It is a very handsome rebuke.

What a propitious time to make a dash at them in the Rio Grande. Rusk, however, seems asleep and I think no movement whatever will be made.

The President has declared martial law west of the Nueces.

I am confined at times on account of Judge Eve's health, and take but little interest in passing events. I do not think he will live ten days. He is rapidly failing and now much emaciated and confined to his bed. He has always been to me the most kind, disinterested, and sincere friend. I feel deeply for him.

We have no other news from the Mier prisoners. It is still positively asserted that Cameron[5] is in the Apache country with 100 and preparing in union with them for an attack on Mexican towns. I am incredulous.

We are all well and have no domestic news.

> Your friend
> James Love

I have seen several persons from the East [East Texas] lately [and] they all say particularly that Houston is unpopular there.

> J L
> Genl A. Sidney Johnston
> Louisville Kentucky

1. Love is referring to the arrival of the Texas fleet off the Yucatán coast. On May 16, 1843, the Texas Navy won a naval battle against Mexico's numerically and technologically superior navy. This action broke the centralist blockade of the port of Campeche. It was the only time in recorded history that sailing ships defeated steam-powered, iron-hulled warships. See "Texas Navy," *Handbook of Texas Online*. For more information on the Yucatán campaign see Jonathan Jordan, *The Lone Star Navy: Texas, the Fight for the Gulf of Mexico, and the Shaping of the West* (Washington, D.C.: Potomac Books, 2007), 250–62.

2. General Pedro de Ampudia, the centralist commander who had taken the Texan prisoners at Mier, had been moved with his large force to the Yucatán Peninsula.

3. Hamilton Stuart was born in 1813 near Louisville, Kentucky. He came to Texas in 1838 and quickly made friends with Sam Houston. At the time Love

wrote this letter, Stuart was the editor of the *Galveston Citizen*. The newspaper was a strong supporter of the Old Hero. "Stuart, Hamilton," *Handbook of Texas Online* [accessed December 1, 2004].

4. Santiago Mendez was the federalist governor of the Yucatán.

5. Ewen Cameron.

James Love to Albert Sidney Johnston

Galveston
June 1st 1843

Dear General

The proclamation, so far as I have learned, is condemned by everyone. His friends endeavor to justify him on the ground of the disobedience of the Commodore, but regret the publicity given to it by the President.

The vessel that brought dispatches from Morgan & the Commodore remained here about ten days. It is not known that he made any reply at all. Powers, the proprietor of the "Houstonian,"[1] (what has stopped) went down [and] it was believed he had dispatches. Since his departure, it is rather believed he had none. If he had any, he will not be permitted to leave the Commodore's ship. He spoke of going to Verra [sic] Cruz as well as Yucatan. Pinckard went down. We look with some anxiety for news from that quarter, much depends on it.

It seems to be understood that Rusk will be a candidate, if so, I think he will not have opposition. The friends of Houston evidently encourage his pretensions. A letter of his has been published at Austin, rather severe on Houston, which the official takes rather unkindly and says it must be a forgery. We have no certain news from the Mier prisoners, supposed to have escaped and under Cameron.[2]

The intelligence from the Rio Grande is that the Apaches are committing dreadful ravages there. They are said to number 3,000, and have with them forty or fifty Texans, and it is said they are on their way to Matamoros. We have no news from Santa Fe party. They are at that place by this time.

The ladies of Galveston held a meeting [and] passed complimentary resolutions to Morgan, the Com[modore Moore] officers, & crew, and sent a badge to the Col and officers with the motto "The gratitude of the ladies to their country's defenders."

We have been within a foot of being ruined by an overflow. Two days since the Brazos began to subside, as it is, a good deal of injury has been sustained on the rivers.

Judge Eve is yet alive. He has kept his bed the last two weeks. There is no hope for him.

Yr friend

James Love

Genl A. Sidney Joohston [sic]

Louisville Kentucky

1. The *Houstonian* was a tri-weekly newspaper that remained in circulation from March 1841 to May 1843. S. E. Powers was editor and proprietor. It favored Sam Houston's policies.
2. Ewen Cameron.

James Love to Albert Sidney Johnston

Galveston

June 26th 1843

My dear General

The most interesting piece of intelligence I have is that an armistice has taken place between Mexico and Texas. This event was announced a few days since by proclamation from your very good friend, the President.[1]

The matter was brought about by the British minister at Mexico, who dispatched a vessel of war with the intelligence, and to obtain the approval of Houston. Hostilities are not again to be commenced until after reasonable notice shall have been [made] to the British minister. It is believed that Williams and Hemphill will be appointed commissioners to negotiate a peace.[2] I am of opinion if terms of peace shall not be agreed on, that the armistice will not soon be broken and the beneficial effect to us almost equal to peace. I have strong hopes and fully entertain the opinion that for some time to come, we will have no war with Mexico.

The friends of his Excellency speak of it as a master stroke of state policy. I look upon it as the result of the singularly fortunate movement by Com Moore, and the consequent failure of Santa Anna's expected subordination of Yucatan. I happen to know all about the profound state policy of our distinguished chief, but still, if the country has the benefits that are certain to follow peace, if he were the Devil, he might have all the credit for what I cared. This don't suit your philosophy.

Kinney[3] escaped from Matamoras on the night of the 14th. He says a few hours before he left a vessel arrived bringing dates from Yucatan to the 8th that he heard read, letters from officers at Tampico which said that the *Guadaloupe* had been captured by the gun boats and that Ampudia had surrendered.[4] You will probably know before you receive this whether it be true as we have had no late arrivals from Yucatan.

Judge Eve died on the morning of the 13th at half past nine. He was interred next day at sea. He died as a philosopher should and retained his senses to the last. His funeral procession was composed, I may say, of the entire population, ministers, consuls, mayor, aldermen, all the military companies, citizens, and strangers. It is believed that it numbered a thousand persons. It was more gratifying to his friends from the fact that no effort whatever was made to get up a procession. It was a free and spontaneous offering of respect to the memory of a good man.

My wife, children, and *grandchild* have all had violent colds or influenza. Doswell and Mrs. Gray both ill of fever, the first one nearly well, the last improving for the last two days. The house has had somewhat the appearance of an hospital. I have been lame from a sprain. Bates married a young girl 16 years of age (Miss Cocke) and has gone to the states.[5]

We have no news from Santa Fe and have had no Indian depredations lately.

We are making large calculations from the effects of peace. Many talk of going to Europe to sell lands, etc. And those dreams of prosperity which have so often faded, may to some extent, be realized. I hope so. Tell that young son of yours never to think of girding on a sword. It is not only an useless weapon now, but will soon become most unfashionable. It may serve to tickle the vanity of a dandy, but will not most probably be used in honorable combat during his life.

Yr friend
Jas Love
Genl A. Sidney Johnston
Louisville Kentucky

1. The proclamation announcing an armistice pending negotiations for peace was published on June 15, 1843.

2. Sam Houston sent Samuel May Williams and George W. Hockley to Laredo via Matamoros to negotiate peace, but Mexican officials rebuffed these efforts. See "Williams, Samuel May," *Handbook of Texas Online*.

3. Love refers here to Henry Lawrence Kinney.

4. This rumor was not true.

5. Thomas Bates, clerk of the district court, married Mary L. Cocke on June 14, 1843.

James Love to Albert Sidney Johnston

Galveston
August 18 1843

My dear General

The contract with you and Hall[1] has been finally closed and I have accepted your & Burnley's notes for the amount agreed upon. It is something upward of $15,000. I did what I could to move the parties to let Hall have it, [but] they declined, and I had no alternative but to comply. I do not think you have made even a hard bargain, [but] it will become so unless you can provide hands to work it which I hope you will be able to do. We have splendid corn crops and very good cotton crops, equal to a bale of 300 lbs the acre, and all things considered, we can say that we are on rising ground with every prospect before us for material prosperity.

You have doubtless heard of the armistice. I believe I wrote you before about it. Since then, other dispatches have been received from Santa Anna. He is ready to name commissioners to negotiate, and has appointed Woll[2] to meet Texas commissioners at Laredo on 25th Sept to agree upon specific terms of armistice. Sam M. Williams and Col Hockley[3] have been appointed commissioners who will proceed to Laredo and thence to Mexico. I do not believe, nor is it expected, that Santa Anna will now agree to make peace on the principal [sic] of our independence, but it is believed that he will make a truce for several years which in the course of time will end in peace. From what I know, I do not entertain a doubt that he would gladly entertain any occasion to get clear of us altogether, but such is his position that he cannot grant independence to Texas without incurring consequences at home that he has no disposition to provoke.

Commodore Moore returned with the fleet a month since. A few days after, he recd his dismissal as a "murderer, pirate," etc. Lothrop was also dishonorably discharged.[4] The other officers with one exception resigned. The Govt discharged also the vessels now in the hands of the commissioner to carry into effect the secret act of Congress. They dare not sell the vessels here, and will not be permitted to take them out of port until Congress shall have met.

The Com and I have settled. He met Williams[5] in the street and was very abusive towards him. I sent him word if he meets me in a crowd, I would shoot him. He and Williams settled somehow. Attempts were made in my case, and I refused. He addressed a letter to me demanding an answer to one he wrote in May, 1842. I replied to his friend, I would not because it was insolent, [and] that before I could hold any communication whatever with him, it must be unconditionally withdrawn. He refused. I then stated and wrote to his friend [that] I wanted this matter settled soon as I wished to leave. He challenged, I accepted to fight at sundown on the beach with rifles at 40 paces back to back, to fire when you pleased and as you pleased. His friend and mine met when his decided, as mine made it a *sine qua non* [necessity], that he should withdraw his challenge and his letters. Mine agreed if he would write a gentlemanly letter, I will then answer. He did so, I asked for authority, he replied he was satisfied, he had been mistaken and had rather not give it, and so we ended, met, and spoke. My folks knew nothing of it, nor have I before given the particulars to anyone but Morris after it was settled. If compelled to fight, I intended to make a quiet matter of it, and since, I have not felt any disposition to gossip about it.

Hemphill is out as a candidate and will be supported by Houston. Rusk, after being considered a candidate for some time, has declined, he so wrote me. Tarrant, Mayfield, Sherman, Hunt, and Somerville are candidates for Maj General.[6] No one knows who will be elected and it matters not. It is said that Lamar will again be a candidate, but I would not be surprised if the race should be between those two. Dr Jones & Bache[7] are candidates here, the latter they expected to slip in for Houston. The Dr will beat him. Col Morgan and Henderson are candidates in Harris. The former is the candidate of the opposition, I don't believe in him.

The complexion of Congress is altogether uncertain. With any degree or effort and union, Houston might easily have been impeached. As it is, he may or not have a majority.

Our city continues to improve. A good crop will greatly move all our commerce and add greatly to our prosperity. Morris returned home from Washington circuit with fever. He is again well. All the rest of us in good health. There is not now a case of bilious Typhus or congestive fever on the Island, at least so says the physicians. There has not [illegible] this summer been a death from fever of any citizen residing in the city. Will your folks believe this[?]

I think you ought to return as early as you can in the fall because if you cannot make arrangements in Ky to work your place, opportunities may offer here. The ladies and self send their sincerest greeting.

> Your friend
> James Love
> Genl A. Sidney Johnston
> Louisville Kentucky
> Aug 20

Before I had the opportunity of forwarding the letter you will receive with this, I recd yours from Louisville. You will learn that I had just executed the contract for you on the purchase you had made. Townes[8] is here. The various interests in your notes prevents the possibility of a revision. I had labored diligently when last in Brazoria, and when the parties were here, to get clear of the contract for you. I exceedingly regret that you should have difficulty about it and if you can make the first payment, I believe you can, before another, sell the place or make arrangement with someone having negroes to join you in the purchase. I rented Mr. Read's place[9] to an emigrant having upwards of 20 grown hands. He wished to purchase it, [but] I would not sell it to him, but I do believe he would join you in the purchase. You will, however, see the necessity of making any sacrifices to make the first payment, otherwise it will be a source of perpetual annoyance to you. The place is amongst the best in the country and will always sell readily if not encumbered with notes due and unpaid. Surely a gentleman of your talent, appearance, and [illegible] can in that enlightened state get $3,000; if you cannot, foreswear the soil and the people and come where a gentleman never wants friends, or if he does, is sure to meet them.

Although you act wisely in your news about politics, still your friends regret that you have not been here. [With] Rusk out of the field, you would have doubled any man in Texas but Burleson who would have supported you warmly, so would Rusk. You will be convinced of your success when you learn that in all probability, Hemphill and Lamar will be the competitors.

I will attend to your tax bill tomorrow together with my own. Let me tell you, you are very much mistaken in your estimate of my industry. I have actually been so much engaged during the summer & spring in my own affairs that I love to work. They are so well regulated that it rejoices me to have something to do for another. And then to recommend a fellow that has chills, or grippe, and one that takes [illegible] to do business promptly is too bad. It only adds another evidence of the envy felt towards those who are never afflicted with those ungentlemanly diseases.

As I suppose you feel sympathy for Morris, I recommend to you as sovereign a decoction of Jerusalem oak[10] which has been so beneficial to him.

As a test of your industry, all I ask of you is to send me a Ky paper giving the returns of the elections, and if you are not sure to do it, ask your son to do so for me.

J L

The ladies here require that you should be most explicit on a certain subject, not, they say, as a matter of curiosity, but on account of the great interest they feel in your happiness.[11]

1. Albert Sidney Johnston purchased China Grove Plantation from Warren D. C. Hall.
2. General Adrián Woll.
3. George W. Hockley and Samuel May Williams sailed from Galveston during the second week in October and arrived at Matamoros. From there they journeyed up the Rio Grande to Sabinas, where they met with commissioners designated by General Woll. Hockley and Williams returned to Galveston on March 26, 1844, with a totally unacceptable protocol. Their negotiations failed because rumors of Sam Houston's negotiations for annexation to the United States reached Mexico. See "Hockley, George Washington," and "Williams, Samuel May," *Handbook of Texas Online*.
4. Commander John Lothrop commanded the *Wharton* at the Battle of Campeche.

5. Samuel May Williams and Commodore Moore exchanged a series of notes from July 21 to July 24 that gave basically the same account of Williams's dealings with Moore that Love provided.

6. Candidates for major general of the militia were Edward H. Tarrant, James S. Mayfield, Sidney Sherman, Memucan Hunt, and Alexander Somervell.

7. In the September 1843 elections to select members of the Eighth Congress, Dr. Levi Jones defeated Richard Bache for the Galveston seat in the lower house. See "Jones, Levi," and "Bache, Richard," *Handbook of Texas Online*.

8. Robert J. Townes was a lawyer in Brazoria who represented W. D. C. Hall in the sale of China Grove Plantation to Johnston. "Townes, Robert J.," *Handbook of Texas Online* [accessed March 12, 2007].

9. James Reed of New Orleans.

10. Jerusalem oak, *Chenopodium botrys*, has been used in nontraditional medicine as an antiasthmatic. It is also used in the treatment of catarrh. See http://www .ibiblio.org/pfaf/cgi-bin/arr_html?Chenopodium+botrys.

11. The ladies of James Love's household included his wife; his daughter, Mrs. Mary L. Morris; his wife's sister, the widow of Joseph Eve, Elizabeth W. Ballinger Eve; and Mrs. Millie Gray, the widow of William Fairfax Gray. They wanted to know all about the forthcoming marriage of Johnston and Eliza Griffin, which took place in October 1843.

James Love to Albert Sidney Johnston

Galveston
Nov 6th 1843

My dear General

We all congratulate you on your marriage. The greatest objection we have is that one [so] charming as the lady is believed to be, should have the power of taking from us so good and much esteemed friend as you are. We look upon it as a national affair, and have serious thoughts of bringing the matter before the U.S. government in order to compel the lady to make Texas her home. The curiosity of the ladies of my family is by no means satisfied. I thought the announcement either of the marriage or the day when it would come off would be sufficient, instead of that, it has only taken a different direction. It now is to see the lady, and I am most especially charged to say that they would be most happy to see you and her as our guests as soon as may be.

Your young friend Jo has by no means forgotten you. The salutary influence you exercised over him was not only beneficial at the time, but has in great degree controlled him ever since. It is even now only necessary to say to him that you would disapprove any particular act to make him disclaim it for the future.

Altho you have not said in direct terms you would not come visit Texas, I have taken up the suspicion that you would not. I regret this on many accounts. We have brought that miserable old reptile to bay,[1] and not withstanding the flourish of his friends and presses backed by the influence of the *armistice,* we have a majority against him in both houses. I am not sure but we will be able to pass a vote of impeachment against him, certainly so if we can get *at* the documents? Your aid would have been important. I am not satisfied to disgrace [him], but think the best interests of the country demand his utter proscription. He lately made a visit here on the express invitation of his followers. They tried several days to get up a petition for him to make a speech, [but] they failed to procure a respectable number and he did not speak. In an hour, we procured 75 respectable names inviting Lamar to dinner. Many persons refused to speak to him [Houston] and he left us mad.

I have not much to say about political matters. We are in a calm, the precursor usually of a storm. The jealousy of the U States will probably be of service. It will, I am confident, have the effect of driving British influence from amongst us. I have, however, not much faith in that *respectable* nation in which it is your misfortune at present to dwell, and believe so soon as she finds us free [of] the real or supposed design of her Majesty's govt, she will leave us to our fate.

We did not permit his Excellency to sell the Navy; the people gave *warning* to bidders.[2] Genl Sherman was elected by 2000 majority.[3] I wrote you a long letter on political matters by the "*Sarah Barnes*,"[4] and have not now sufficient leisure to write more on that subject now and will proceed to business.

The crops in the lower country have again been greatly injured by storms and the most incessant rain. A half is the most anyone will make. Under this state of case, I am confident you must place no reliance whatever on Col Hall for rent. It is doubtful whether he would have paid you with a good crop, and as it is, the only thing that can save him from immediate destruction is giving his crop as far as it will go. I do not know of any probability that induces the belief that Daingerfield can pay. If I had power [of attorney] from him, the two lots near the old office could be sold for $500 cash, but that cannot be had in time. There is an opportunity occasionally of selling one of the other lots that belong to us, but not in sufficient number, at any rate, to count upon it as a resource. The price of lots is on the rise but none are purchased except by those who wish to improve more on speculation or as an investment for profit. You will see from this that no reliance can be placed upon any means at my command to settle this debt. The state of my own affairs does not permit me to indulge my wishes as a sincere friend equally anxious to protect your honor or your interests. The first might be done by the risk of my person, the last only by money which I have no available means of acquiring. I have made great exertions to relieve Burnley in Texas [in order] that he might commence his business untrammeled. He owed $14,700 for the plantation, $4,000 for debts due by it. With the assistance of $2,000 he sent me of *our* money, I have paid all this, or will be prepared to pay what is yet due before January. At great inconvenience I have done this and consented to let all my claims rest for awhile altho I suffer greatly by it and have to provide for debts of my own that must be paid.

I have said he paid $14,700 for his plantation with all the improvements put on it, gin & house, etc etc. I have repeatedly offered to take $10,000 in cash or negroes. Could I have done this, I would have paid the $3,000 in negroes and removed his to Reed's place as he directed. I have written you before that if you were desirous of avoiding the purchase, you can only do so by paying the first payment promptly. I could have sold it once, but for that. No one has money to pay down & no one will purchase when it is encumbered with a debt due, and besides, the holders of a note due will not take another for it, but would send the note to the U. States for collection and still hold the land as security. Whatever I can do for you, I will. You know this. I write in candor that you may at once know the true state of case. If you do not come out this fall, what is to be done with the place[?] It is time now that this should be known in order to give anyone disposed to rent, time to arrange.

Although I have not the pleasure to know the lady whose fate is linked with yours for weal or woe, I beg you to present my kindest wishes for her undisturbed happiness, peace, and prosperity.

James Love
Genl A. Sidney Johnston
Louisville Kentucky

1.   The "miserable reptile" to which Love refers is President Houston.

2.   An auction scheduled for October 14 was postponed when several Galvesto-
     nians bid on the naval vessels in the name of the "people," and when Con-
     gress convened on December 4, it placed the navy ships in ordinary.

3.   Sidney Sherman won the September 4 election for major general of the mi-
     litia over a field of seven candidates with well over two thousand votes more
     than his nearest competitor, Edward H. Tarrant. See "Sherman, Sidney,"
     Handbook of Texas Online.

4.   The steamer *Sarah Barnes* left Galveston for New Orleans on September 24,
     1843, and the next day encountered a gale about forty miles south of the
     Sabine River. As a result, the vessel began to leak badly. The thirty-one pas-
     sengers and crew scrambled into a single yawl and two quickly improvised
     rafts of cotton bales, but less than a dozen survived the trip through the surf.
     The rest drowned, including the captain.

James Love to Albert Sidney Johnston

Galveston
May 10th 1844

My dear General

     I made a great effort to reach Galveston before you and Mrs. John-
ston left and was much disappointed that I did not see you. You cannot tell
how much I miss you. You were my only *crony*, and even ten pins is *flat* with
me since you left; I have not made my appearance there since.[1]

     I told you the fighting would begin so soon as you left. The Colo-
rado boys killed six of Houston's pet Indians who were taken in the fact of
stealing horses, or rather with stolen horses. Rossignol[2] has just returned from
Corpus Christi, and says on the 2nd of May, that nine Americans joined a
Mexican escort of traders from that place and encountered 45 regular [Mexi-
can] troops, killed eight & hung eight, the last done by the Mexicans. It
seems Canales is getting up another revolution,[3] bids defiance to the Govt.,
and says they will trade. On the other hand, Santa Anna has commissioned
five companies who are now ranging in that part of the country who are entitled to all the booty. They are likely to get none but blows. Walker[4] is just in
from San Antonio & returns today; he says that Hays[5] has laid his plans and
will have a fight before long.

I have seen many persons from different sections of the country since you left. There cannot be a doubt of Burleson's election by a large majority. Some meetings have been gotten up nominating P. C. Jack for Vice President.[6] It seems to take well and I believe his chance of success is fair.

The *Poinsett* steamer with a special agent to Mexico left this yesterday morning for Vera Cruz. The hope of the U.S. Govt now seems to be that they can accomodate [*sic*] matters with Mexico, and that all further action on that subject will be suspended in the U.S. Senate until the 3rd of June at which time they expect favorable news from Mexico. Its seems this is done to take from Mr. Clay & his friends their only objection. His letter did not reach us; its contents were noticed in the Bee.[7] If he defeats annexation, he has assumed a superiority that may overwhelm him. I have seen part of a speech from Cassius M. Clay; I wish you could send it to me as I wish to answer it for the benefit of my old friends in the mountains.[8]

The letters from Washington City are contradictory. Some assert the Treaty will be ratified without the consent of Clay, others think differently. We, of course, believe the one or the other as we are more or less sanguine. I have the opinion that it cannot pass unless Clay wills it.

As you may not know the precise terms of the Treaty, I will state them. Whatever you may hear, do not doubt the correctness of the information I give. The U. States pays $10,000,000 of the national debt which Sam will pay all. They will pay $100,000 to redeem Exchequers & pay unexpended balances. They pay $260,000 to Dawson for the Navy.[9] All officers now in commission except those in the Cabinet etc., to remain in office. We, of course, come in as a Territory. The Treaty is a good one for us, and everybody but the Europeans are for it.

I enclose you three letters. You will see that one of them was opened in N. O. by mistake. Mrs. Davis has kicked up a dust with the Genls, Commodores, Prsts, etc., but I believe she returns heart whole. I rather think she will not die a widow. I am of opinion she sometimes thinks there may be a man she would marry, and you know if a widow ever thinks about matrimony, she is a *gone case,* each succeeding day makes her less particular. Don't mention this treason as we are great friends, and I have no wish to have anyone of the sex flying at my ears.[10]

Mary's baby is very ill; I think its case doubtful, whooping cough, teething, & sore mouth combined has reduced it to a skeleton.[11] Tell that good wife of yours that we miss her very much, that she has left none but friends at Galveston, and that our folks often regret the absence of her pleasant face, and Jo languishes for Rory Alas [a ballad]. And tell that young son of yours that he has many competitors for the love of a mother he is so fond of, and that it will require all his efforts to hold the preeminence he now enjoys, and tell her from me, that with some slight tricks *from me,* I think she *will* make the best wife I know.

> Very sincerely & truly
> Your friend
> James Love
> Genl A. Sydney [*sic*] Johnston
> Shelbyville Kentucky
> per Maj Throckmorton

1. "Ten pins" is another name for the modern game of bowling. This sentence suggests that a ten pin alley may have existed on Galveston Island during the era of the republic.

2. Love may be referring to Charles Rossignol.

3. This was not true. Canales gave up his hopes of forming a republic in northern Mexico and joined Santa Anna, who appointed Canales as a brigadier general in the Army of the North but removed him from service in 1844. Love is probably referring to Canales's temporary dismissal from the Mexican army. See "Canales Rosillo, Antonio," *Handbook of Texas Online.*

4. Samuel Hamilton Walker was born on 1817 in Toaping Castle, Prince Georges County, Maryland. He came to Texas in 1842, joined the spy company of John Coffee Hays, and participated in the Mier expedition. He survived the Black Bean episode and imprisonment at Perote. In 1846, he helped Samuel Colt design what became known as the Walker Colt, the "six-shooter" technology that revolutionized the Texas frontier. "Walker, Samuel Hamilton," *Handbook of Texas Online* [accessed December 3, 2004].

5. John Coffee Hays.

6. Patrick Churchill Jack, the brother of William H. Jack, was a lawyer who lived in Houston. The frontrunner for the presidential election that was coming up in September 1844 was Edward Burleson, the favorite candidate of the Lamar faction. "Burleson, Edward," *Handbook of Texas Online* [accessed October 25, 2004].

7. The *New Orleans Bee/L'Abeille de la Nouvelle-Orléans* was a French-language newspaper that was first published in New Orleans on September 1, 1827. An

English section was added three months later. It was pro–Republic of Texas. See http://www.jefferson.lib.la.us/genealogy/NewOrleansBeeMain.htm.

8. Cassius M. Clay was campaigning for his kinsman Henry "Old Hal" Clay, but his abolitionist views became an embarrassment. Love intended to defend Texas slavery for the benefit of his friends in Knox County, Kentucky, where he formerly lived.

9. In 1838 the government of the Republic of Texas contracted Baltimore ship builder Frederick Dawson to construct six warships at a cost of $280,000. The Republic of Texas was unable to pay this bill. See "Texas Navy," *Handbook of Texas Online.*

10. Love is referring here to Mrs. Mary Jane Hawkins Davis.

11. Love is actually referring to his own grandchild, Mary Love Morris, age three.

James Love to Albert Sidney Johnston

Galveston
May 29th 1844

My dear General

Since I wrote, Houston made us a visit & advertised that he would make a speech in justification of his administration & upon the affairs of the country generally at Frosh's new building. The city was on the *qui vive* [alert], and everybody went, his friends to enjoy the triumph, his enemies to hear how it was possible for him to justify some of his acts. He spoke for half an hour and no applause. You know the man well to know that this did not suit him. Shortly after, he said something that this friends applauded, the others hissed. He said something else, anything but true, and had the presumption to ask "Is this not so?" "False, false, false," resounded from all quarters. He then said he was well informed a secret society existed here to act against him personally. "A lie, lie, lie, false as hell, false as hell, an infamous slander," etc etc was shouted from all sides, a scene of riot & confusion ensued, clubs drawn, shakes by the collar, and every indication of a conflict, & if so, you may guess his fate. I was on the outside of the crowd and after awhile was heard, & [I] begged they would listen without interruption as he would be answered. This restored order to a great extent. He then told the Buck story, "that's stale, stale, stale, we have heard that before, give us something else." Then he spoke of the fifty generals, 249 Cols., 360 Majors, 4 Captains, and some Lieuts he had discharged. "That's an old story, give us something new," said the boys. He floundered on for a short time and left the stand, passed out of the door immediately followed by about a dozen with little Rose on one side & Dr Wynn on the other, with shouts long & loud ringing in his ears, "Come back, Traitor, liar, Slanderer, and hear your infamous falsehoods crammed down your throat." His friends begged him to come back, he would not, went to his quarters, and to bed, & did not rise until he left on board the boat next day. When the riot was at its height, he turned pale and trembled; he thought, no doubt, that his day was at hand. I feared it and him the cause of my satisfaction. McLeod & Baker answered him, the last, literally speaking, demolished him. He has recd a severe blow on a most sensitive point in his character, his vanity & self confidence is deeply wounded, & he curses us most bitterly.[1]

Jack is a candidate for Vice President with some prospect of success. McLeod & Merriman are candidates for Congress, the latter rather noncommittal, altho he is for Burleson & Jack, and will probably be elected.[2]

A letter recd here yesterday from Kinney & Capt Stedman from Corpus Christi says that Arista & Canales are in rebellion and have two thousand soldiers under arms. The traders & forces sent by Mexico to prevent contraband trade have had several conflicts, all resulting in favor of the traders. Free trade, it is said, is the pretense for the insurrection. There is a rumor afloat in which I place no confidence that 1700 Mexicans are on the march to our frontier. If this insurrection should arise [and it] made a respectable head, it would be wise in us to assist them.

Three or four U States vessels of war have paid us a visit. The Home Squadron, I am told, is shortly to assemble here. Capt. Tyler is playing out his game with a strong hand. He will be a great bungler if he cannot get up a war before his time is out.[3] Was I him, I would do it or die. I would "head" some of your *cautious* politicians in the States. There are small politicians & small bullies, the latter can always get up a riot, and in the melee, very often are on the side of victory. I don't see why a *small* politician cannot do the same.

I do not wish you to make it public in that enlightened, moral, and virtuous community in which you sojourn, that the U.S. *chargé des affaires* [sic] and U.S. consul *pushed* each other in a barroom, that they have issued placards denouncing each other as liar, scoundrel, poltroon, etc. It is a beautiful illustration of the dignity and moral tone of a great nation, who feel so much horror at the base idea of political association with renegade Texans.

Mary's baby has been very ill, is now out of danger. Little Lucy is dangerously ill, whooping cough & a low, insiduous [*sic*] fever hard to subdue from the difficulty of administering medicine. She cannot walk. The rest of us are well. Present me most kindly to that *gude wife*[4] of yours and say that we have missed very much her customary visit and that if she considered it a compliment, that she has been more talked *of* than any lady in the land. We sent by Mr Davis the box of shrubbery.[5]

> Most sincerely & truly Yr friend
> James Love
> Genl A. Sidney Johnston
> Shelbyville Kentucky

1. Hugh McLeod and Moseley Baker, long opponents of Houston, replied to his speech. The supposed text of Baker's remarks is in the "Baker (Moseley) Letter, 1844," Center for American History, University of Texas at Austin.
2. Hugh McLeod and Frank Merriman, a lawyer in Galveston, were congressional candidates in the September election. McLeod, however, was elected from Bexar County, not Galveston. See "McLeod, Hugh," *Handbook of Texas Online*.
3. Love's sarcasm regarding President John Tyler refers to the fact that in 1813 a Virginia militia unit elected Tyler to the rank of captain. He did not see any combat during the War of 1812.
4. It was Mary L. Morris, Love's grandchild, and Lucy, his three-year-old daughter, who were ill. Eliza Johnston must have brought Sir Walter Scott's *Rob Roy* (1817) when she came to visit the Loves. The phrase "gude wife" abounds in the book, and in subsequent letters there are other references to the popular tale of the good-hearted outlaw, Rob Roy MacGregor.
5. Harrison W. Davis served as the conveyor of the shrubbery.

James Love to Albert Sidney Johnston

> Galveston
> June 10, 1844

My dear General,

An arrival from Corpus Christi on yesterday brought the news of a fight with the Comanches near that place. They had several conflicts which resulted in four killed [and] as many wounded on our part, 20 killed on theirs, and the loss of their cavalry, shields, horses, etc. They write also that a large body is in the neighborhood surrounding the Rancho on all sides. We have further intelligence to be relied on, that a general rising of the northern provinces has taken place and two thousand soldiers already in arms. It is asserted (altho I have seen no satisfactory evidence of the authority) that Arista heads the rebellion, if so, it will doubtless be serious.[1] Woll has taken the alarm and has gone to Monterey [sic] guarded by 400 cavalry. The obvious policy is to assist them, which I suppose will not be done by Houston.

The steamer *Poinsett* returned yesterday from Vera Cruz and did not bring any news favorable to the views of Capt. Tyler.[2] Santa Anna, it seems, is not willing to surrender any portion of country for *a consideration* as Nicol Jarvie[3] would say. Our affairs are getting into a state of most *beautiful* confusion as regards our diplomatic relations and we are likely to become a bone of contention between three Great Powers who look to their own interest without reference to ours. Whatever many have been the motive of Tyler I know not, his policy was certainly wise in endeavoring to affect annexation before the question could be agitated. It is much more easy to justify an act that has been done, than it is to convince it ought to be done. And had there been sufficient wisdom and patriotism in the U. States Senate to have ratified the Treaty, neither foreign nations or fanaticism at home could have disturbed the question. As it now is, it becomes not only a question for foreign interference, but produces a most exciting subject for political agitation and intrigue. I love the U. States and her institutions, I revere the memory of the great and good patriots who gave all for their country, but I very much fear that those institutions and principles of government which they in singleness of heart left to their posterity, have been lost sight of and are in danger of perishing in political intrigue for office.

The court martial for the trial of Com[modore] Moore assembled two weeks since. The Com filed some special pleas which were overturned. From those early decisions of the court, I think they will decide against him. I believe, however, that the proceedings will be spun out to an indefinite time, and probably no decision had before the meeting of Congress. Reily *is* a member of the court.[4]

There is nothing in the line of politics of any interest whatever. There is scarcely any excitement about the election, nor will any arise to any extent.

We have now in the harbor & in offing, the U. States vessels of War, Steamer *Union*, the *Vincennes*, *Somers*, & *Flirt*.[5] The city has been full of visitors all the summer; all this has given some animation to the place, or rather, more than usual.

The children are not yet well, both, however, are improving. They are very much emaciated. Morris has had another *chill*. I hope you have never told your son that you had chills, it would have a strong tendency to lessen the high admiration & strong filial reverence which so creditably to him seems to exist in his mind and manner towards you. Cassius seems to have made it a strong ground of ridicule against Caesar; it may have been his principal one in putting him to death. I have filled up my sheet and have no room to say more than to beg you to present me most kindly to Mrs. Johnston.

> Yr friend
> James Love
> Genl A. Sidney Johnston
> Shelbyville Kentucky

1. General Arista did not revolt.
2. Love is again referring to President John Tyler in a sarcastic vein.
3. In *Rob Roy* Nicol Jarvie is a Glasgow magistrate who is extremely pompous.
4. Congress ordered the court-martial over President Houston's strong objections. It met at Washington-on-the-Brazos on May 20, 1844, and lasted until the end of July. Sidney Sherman, the new major general of the militia, presided. Other jurists included Generals Alexander Somervell and Edwin Morehouse and Colonels Thomas Sypert and James Reily. All were Houston supporters except Sherman, who had been appointed by the Texas Congress. Congress charged Moore with neglect of duty, misapplication of money, disobedience of orders, contempt of the country, treason, and murder, but not piracy. Congress did not reveal its secret findings until December. The court acquitted Moore of all but four charges of disobedience and did not recommend any punishment.
5. In early 1844 President Tyler ordered a portion of the U.S. Navy's Gulf Squadron to take up station off the Texas coast and turn back any potential naval threat by Mexico against Texas.

James Love to Albert Sidney Johnston

Galveston
July 29, 1844

My dear General

You will perhaps have seen the newspaper accounts of Hays's fight with the Comanches. It is not exaggerated, altho it sounds like Romania.[1] You will also have seen the general news from Mexico. In addition to what seems to be the determination of Mexico from their public declarations, I can say they are concentrating munitions of war at Sabinas, baggage waggons [sic], etc. The late dispatches from Santa Anna to Houston declares the armistice at an end, & his determination soon to prosecute the war, & reproaches Houston with duplicity. If invaded now, it will doubtless result from the interference of the U. States who seems to sport with us & our affairs as may best suit their political strife. That Mexico is now backed by England, I have no doubt, & have as little that all their hope of success depends on the election of Mr. Clay, believing from his letters, that under his administration the U States will not interfere.[2]

We have not much excitement in our election. I believe Burleson will be elected altho it is not one of the certain cases. Anderson will beat Jack easily.[3]

We are in the midst of disease & death, sixty-five deaths in this month; eleven, some say seventeen on the 26th; ten yesterday; as many today & forty new cases. It is doubtless yellow fever arriving on the Strand & at Shaws's, and gradually extending.[4] Two thirds of the whole population have been attacked. This type is not malignant, as most all have recovered who were well provided & well attended. Genl Murphy, Consul Green, Sebring, the Editor, Street, Mrs. Judge Andrews, McFarlane & Mickey, I mention as acquaintances of yours who are dead.[5] Judge Franklin & wife, Shelby & wife, Cleveland & wife, Genl Hunt, Col Rhodes & son, Dr. Jones, McLeod, Rossignol are amongst those who have recovered.[6] No case in my family until this morning; Mrs. Love was attacked, mildly, I think, & so as not to create alarm. I expect to be attacked as I have been going night & day everywhere & altho not particularly brave, it became necessary in consequence of the great alarm of contagion, that an example should be set. It has done much good & now every poor family & fellow in the city is well nursed and medicined.[7] I am now as well as I ever was, but cannot expect to be the only one who will escape. McKinney[8] and myself take a nib at ten pins every day, good always for 120, and have been the only two I know that has neither been sick or frightened. No time to write more. Present me kindly to Mrs. J.

> Most sincerely Yr friend
> Jas Love

Our little daughter & Mary have recovered. They had a hard nib for life.

> Genl A. Sidney Johnston
> Shelbyville Kentucky

1. James Love may be referring to a battle in July 1844 on the Pedernales River where John Coffee Hays and fourteen other Texas Rangers, armed with the new Colt revolvers, attacked and defeated nearly eighty Comanche warriors. See "Colt Revolvers," *Handbook of Texas Online* [accessed September 6, 2008].

2. The news of the failure of the Treaty of Annexation reached Texas on July 3. Love and other Galvestonians feared an attack from Mexican vessels, unaware that internal Mexican problems prevented retaliation. Henry Clay's letters were designed to soothe Whig sentiments against a war with Mexico over Texas.

3. Anderson did beat Jack easily, perhaps because Patrick C. Jack succumbed to yellow fever on August 14, 1844, three weeks before the election. "Jack, Patrick Churchill," *Handbook of Texas Online* [accessed March 12, 2007].

4. Many believed that the yellow fever arrived on the United States' war steamer *Poinsett*. A popular notion of the day suggested that "fomites," or minute particles, and "miasma," or bad air that emanated from swamps, outhouses, and so forth, spread the disease. Galvestonians liked to think that the yellow fever existed only near the port area along the Strand and at Joshua Shaw's hotel. Peggy Hildreth, "The Howard Association of Galveston: The 1850's, Their Peak Years," *East Texas Historical Journal* 17 (1979): 36.

5. William S. Murphy, U.S. chargé, died July 13; U.S. consul A. M. Green died July 29; R. D. Sebring, editor of the *Galveston Weekly News*, died between July 26 and 31. Park G. Street was the operator of the Galveston to Virginia Point ferry. Mrs. Edmund Andrews's date of death is unknown. "Murphy, William Sumter," *Handbook of Texas Online* [accessed December 1, 2004].

6. Those who recovered included Benjamin C. Franklin and his wife, Bena; Anthony B. Shelby and his wife, Mary Ann; J. A. H. Cleveland and his wife;

Memucan Hunt; Elisha A. Rhodes, former U.S. consul to Texas in 1837 and his son James or William; Dr. Levi Jones; Hugh McLeod; and Charles Rossignol.

7.   Love evidently was a member of the Howard Association, a national society of civic leaders devoted to reducing crime and improving public health. Named for British philanthropist John Howard (1726–1790), the Howard Association was organized in New Orleans in the 1830s, and the movement had spread to Galveston by 1844. The men raised money to nurse, feed, and bury victims of the yellow fever epidemics. In some cases the members actually nursed the ill and set an example of unconcern in the face of panic. Most members were immune—usually having had the fever as a child. Hildreth, "Howard Association," 33.

8.   Apparently, Thomas Freeman McKinney and James Love enjoyed an occasional game of bowling.

James Love to Albert Sidney Johnston

Galveston
Aug 20 [1844]

My dear Genl

It is with a heart filled with sorrow that I announce to you the death of Morris last night of black vomit after an illness of five days. To us the loss is irreparable & you have lost a sincere friend. For two days he was aware of approaching dissolution and met his fate with more calm philosophy than any I have ever known. He retained his senses to the last. Poor Mary, now within two months of confinement, has & is sufering [sic] terribly. The rest of the family are well and there has not been a new case since Morris, & but two deaths in five days.[1]

I have not time to write but a word about your business. I had made an arrangement with Judge Andrews (who is dead) by which if $3,000 cash was advanced, the contract might have been rescinded. He had, as you know, the control of Merle's debt.[2] I believe I had another opportunity of doing the same thing. I wrote to Burnley generally of this, there was no necessity to speak of particulars. I do not know that I now could do anything of the kind, yet I fully believe if there was placed in N. O., subject to my draft, $3,000, that I could in the course of the fall, relieve you. In saying this, I wish to be understood that it ought not to be attempted until you fail in carrying out the contract by having the ability to work the place, and that I do not advise a sacrifice to raise the $3,000 upon this hope, but as a forlorn hope in a bad case.

The bell now rings, you will understand me.

> Yr friend
> Jas Love
> Genl A. Sidney Johnston
> Shelbyville Ky

1. Richard Morris, James Love's beloved son-in-law, died in Galveston on August 19, 1844, from yellow fever. See "Morris, Richard," *Handbook of Texas Online.*

2. Edmund Andrews of Brazoria County was the Texas agent for John A. Merle and Company of New Orleans. They held notes on China Grove Plantation contracted by Warren D. C. Hall that amounted to $4,663.18. In 1843 Johnston and Burnley assumed this encumbrance. Love managed to have the first payment, which was due on January 20, 1844, postponed until January 20, 1845, plus 10 percent interest since 1843. Thus, Johnston owed a little more than $5,000 to Merle. Johnston owed his creditors a total of $15,703.35. See Love to Johnston, February 1, 1845, Albert Sidney Johnston Collection, Howard-Tilton Memorial Library, Tulane University, for an exact breakdown of the total debt.

James Love to Albert Sidney Johnston

> Galveston
> Oct 29th 1844

My dear General,

I am just in receipt of your last letter and feel great concern at the representation you make of your affairs. It has cast a gloom over my own feelings most difficult to shake off. I need not repeat to you that I am ready to do all in my power to extricate you, but I really do not see how it can be done. The near approach of the time at which payment is expected is, of itself, a circumstance rather unfavorable to negotiation. I wrote you lately that it would be unwise to make any sacrifice to raise money founded on the opinion that I could settle it for you. But [I] say again as I before said, if the money can be procured without sacrifice, that it gives a certain basis for experiment that may end in rescission of the contract, probably with the entire loss of $3,000. I would, however, most earnestly advise you to come yourself, with or without money, as the best prospect of adjustment. You are highly esteemed in Brazoria, and if the debt is in that situation that it can be controlled by Townes, I am certain that he is disposed to befriend.[1] I am, however, of the opinion that he cannot, as many persons are interested in the collection. The death of Andrews may lessen the difficulty. The $5,000 or thereabouts due John A. Merle of N. O. could have been bought last spring at a rate not exceeding 50¢ on the dollar. Andrews was his agent. What change his death may make I cannot say, at all events, it would be well to see what can be done there.

I again say it is better for you to come, and a matter so important to you in future, is it not better to make everything else yield to the effort? And above all, if you do come, give no intimation that you do not expect to reside in Texas, a knowledge of that would increase the difficulty of settlement. And let me say, if you are to be as poor as you say, that it is much better to take your chance here than in Ky; there you may vegetate, here you may live after awhile. And besides, with advantages you possess of good character and good conduct in Texas, there is ever offering something for enterprize [sic] that you never will hear of in Ky. We have now had a *live* Prince, about such a man as you, a sociable fellow with plenty of money and great schemes for Germans, who *will* chase mustangs in the midst of Indians and says he will be ready for them.[2] I believe his first cargo is on the way; he says he will have ten thousand. It will be a hard case if a fighting man like you, should not fall in with a Prince, at least, he may expect to pick up a Duke or a Lord.

If your sword is never drawn until it shall be to repel a Mexican invasion for re-conquest, I fear it will rust in the scabbard unless such a step shall be sanctioned, or rather, set on foot by G. B. [Great Britain] in a crusade against slavery. Kennedy said yesterday, the fear of war with G. B. would prevent the U. States from acquiring Texas.[3] I told him he was a fool, and that closed the conversation.

I do not believe that the election in the U. States, let it terminate as it may, will promote annexation. The time for action has passed. There was wisdom in immediate annexation; the discussion and defeat of such a question with you is about one and the same. It seems that Mr. Clay's friends are confident of success. We shall see. I believe if he is defeated, his letter writing will have no little agency in bringing it about. He should have rested his case on his Raleigh letter and not confused it by explanations.[4] Old men will babble, it confirms me in an opinion long time expressed that they are not capable of any new or great original conception. They do very well like a mill horse in a beaten trace, [but] all new routes must be left to those more young with more mettle. They will often lose, but once in awhile, they will set the world in a blaze for good or evil as the case may be.[5] At 25, Bonaparte would have gained the Battle of Waterloo, at fifty, he was only fit to grumble at his diet.

We are all well & join in our best respects to Mrs. Johnston and yourself.

Yr friend

Jas Love

Genl A. Sidney Johnston

Shelbyville Ky

1. As a resident of Brazoria County, Robert J. Townes gained notoriety and local political power when in 1839 he led the movement to void some Mexican land titles. "Townes, Robert J.," *Handbook of Texas Online*.

2. Friedrich Wilhelm Carl Ludwig Georg Alfred Alexander, Prince of Solms, Lord of Braunfels, was born at Neustrelitz on July 27, 1812. In 1844 the well-connected prince promoted the immigration of German nationals to the Republic of Texas. He arrived in Galveston on July 1 of that year. His first German colonists arrived at Carlshafen (Indianola) in December 1844, then settled west of San Antonio. "Solms-Braunfels, Prince Carl of," *Handbook of Texas Online* [accessed March 12, 2007].

3. William Kennedy was the British consul in Galveston. Kennedy had published a two-volume work on Texas in 1841, *The Rise, Progress, and Prospects of Texas*, the result of an 1839 tour of Texas and the United States.

4. Henry Clay's letter writing, intended for publication in the Whig press, made his chances dimmer for the presidency. The "Raleigh letter," published in the *National Intelligencer* on April 27, 1844, equivocated over the annexation of Texas. He believed that the annexation of Texas should not be considered at present, but he implied that the topic could be broached at a later date. Subsequent letters during the summer, dated July 1 and 27, and a final one to the *Intelligencer* on September 23, tried to counter southern support for James K. Polk by stressing his fear that annexation might harm the Union. The Democrats, meanwhile, campaigned in favor of the annexation of Texas.

5. Henry Clay was sixty-seven years old at the time, while Love was only fifty.

James S. Mayfield to Albert Sidney Johnston

Washington [Texas]
Decr 13th 1844

Dear Genl.

I learn that you have arrived at Galveston with your "good woman."
I regret much that your business heretofore has so much drawn you from the
country. It was the purpose of many of your friends to have placed your name
before the public for the Presidency. I was assured from letters of Col Love in
the spring that you would not allow it under those circumstances. We centered on Genl Burleson who would not have opposed *you*, but who nevertheless, presents a certainty of election. The Congress is dead against Houston.
As yet, matters have progressed smoothly, but next week will be attended
with storms. Committees are beginning to scrutinize closely foreign and
domestic relations. Charges of traitorous action are being boldly professed.
Houston has feigned illness and retired, [and] all that emanates from him is
falsehood upon deceit. No subterfuge, as usual, is beneath him. I think the
hide will be torn off and the imposter exposed.

Let me have a line from [you]. My good wishes to Col Love & family, and be pleased to present me to your *charming wife,* as I know your good
luck must have [inkblot][led] you to such a Charm.

Your friend
J. S. Mayfield
Genl A Sidney Johnston
Galveston
Mr Moore

James Love to Albert Sidney Johnston

Galveston
March 30 1845

My dear General

I found yours of the 27th Feb. here on my return yesterday from a
visit of three weeks to Brazoria. Your place has been rented by Col Hall[1] to

Messrs Brown who are cultivating it very well and will have the fences all
well prepared. They are also making some improvement on the house, have
trimmed the trees, and have already given the place an improved appearance. They are also to build an improved cotton press of live oak. From all
I see, I have no doubt the place will be improved beyond the value of any
stipulated rent and will be in first rate condition for sale or cultivation the
ensuing fall. You have already made sacrifice and used energy to pay for this
place on your own responsibility. As the matter now stands, it is evidently
your interest, if it be *possible,* to pay up the balance at once, and take the
place entirely to yourself. There is no doubt in my mind that $3,000 cash
perhaps, in addition to the sum due from Dr. Jones, will liquidate the whole
debt. And I have as little doubt that either this year or the next, it would
realize to you $20,000 at least. The value of lands from Brigham's passing
yours to the mouth of Oyster Creek,[2] will be worth fifty p[e]r cent more
than any lands in Texas. They are preferable for sugar, cotton, rice, tobacco,
corn, and stock. Their convenience to tide water, the southern exposure, &
immense pasturage make them decidely [sic] preferable to any land I have
ever known. This place alone, if you could and chose to hold it, would be
an inheritance for your children that would give them sufficient wealth. You
have told me that your means were exhausted. You are known to have honor,
this should give you credit sufficient to procure that sum with the additional
security of the land. Do make another effort, I shall greatly regret to see it
pass from your hands at a time when every indication is favorable to holding
it. If, however, you shall decide otherwise, either from necessity or choice,
there is no earthly doubt that I can, this year, sell it for you at $15,000 and
have you relieved from every responsibility and receive a payment down for
your use, perhaps all the reserve in cash or negroes. Some half dozen wealthy
gentlemen from S. C. have visited us since you left. They all prefer that section of the country, and now that annexation is certain,[3] I feel confident that
in Brazoria County alone, in less than 12 months, there will be an addition
of 2,000 slaves. Dr. Jones has promised, and I believe he will during April,
pay the debt due you on the terms proposed. If he does not, I will endeavor
to have it arranged so as to pay as much as possible of the debt. It is better not to postpone liquidation too long; it always increases the difficulty
of adjustment.

　　We have some stir on the subject of annexation. The British &
French influence is brought to bear with every degree of energy. Dispatches
arrived for them both a few days since, and they started immediately for

Washington [Texas], altho Saligny[4] had just returned and had his baggage aboard the *N. York* to leave. Two days previous, dispatches had been
recd overland from Mexico. The opinion is, which I believe, that they are
empowered to offer unconditional independence. The day after they left,
Donaldson arrived, chartered a boat at $300, & pursued them in hot haste.[5]
Houston had been sent for by express, and all will arrive at Washington
[on-the-Brazos] about the same time. There is no doubt that the President
is opposed to annexation, and if any means can be devised by him to delay
or defeat it, he will attempt to do so.[6] We are watching him closely, and if
after an interview with the U. States minister, he refused to call Congress
and take the initiatory steps to ascertain the will of the people, we will take
the matter in our own hands, have a convention, unseat him, or hang him
if necessary to carry our purposes, and all that may abide by him. The feeling in favor [of annexation] is, in a manner, universal, west of the Brazos;
it is so also east of the Trinity. Those in pay of the Govt, the British influence, a few of the mercantile class, those who dream of conquest & military
glory in the future, those who have fled for crime and debt, will, of course,
oppose annexation.

It will all be unavailing, and altho the terms are hard, the people of
Texas will, by a large majority, four-fifths at least, accept of the terms & trust
to the justice of [the U.S.] Congress in future. We shall be prosperous beyond
the dreams of enthusiasm. The necessary expenditures of the U.S. Govt here
will alone give us a greater circulating medium than any people of the same
number on the continent. The *Whigs* may *theorize* on the right or wrong
of annexation, but that has but little weight upon the action of a popular
majority. Their cause in the U. States is irrecoverable. They will, of course,
join the abolitionists who will agitate for a time, but time will show that Mr.
Clay was right when he said that emancipation depended on the law of the
population. Such is the truth, and until that epoch, slavery will be useful and
profitable, which at last, is the cause of it, and it will expire when it is no
longer so and not till then.

I should be most happy to receive a letter from your young son, I
have a great regard for him independent of you. Five years since, you read me
a letter from him which left on my mind a most favorable impression. Tell
him not to fear the criticism of one fifty years of age, who has passed through
every stage of society and every state of existence from extreme poverty to
comparative affluence, and one who felt and acted alike under all circumstances, and one who, if he had not the power to advance the interest of

those coming after him, always had the disposition to do so. I sent him the book that he might learn a lesson, too apt to be perjorative [sic] in our intercourse with the world that there is a power advancing with mighty strides, I mean the power of intellect, that will overwhelm the pride of birth, family, station, and wealth, unless all these shall be united with intellect and recognize as the basis of superiority, *usefully only* and the greatest amount of good to the mass.

I would be happy, also, if I could be the means of convincing him that true eloquence, whether in speaking or writing, consists in the apt use of the most simple words that will convey the ideas. The highest compliment ever given an author was that he had written 30 pages of elegant and eloquent composition that did not contain one word of more than two syllables.

My whole family leaves on the 7th April for the U. S. I hope they may see you *en route*. My kindest regards to Mrs. Johnston, I wish her every blessing under the sun.[7]

> Yr friend
> Jas Love
> Genl A Sidney Johnston
> Shelbyville Kentucky

1. Warren D. C. Hall was the previous owner of China Grove Plantation.
2. The east bank of the Brazos was lined with narrow one-league tracts that extended from the river eastward and included Oyster Creek. The tract above Johnston's holdings, belonging to Francis Bingham, one of Austin's Old Three Hundred, extended almost to the Fort Bend County line. As the crow flies, Johnston's China Grove Plantation was about thirty miles above the mouth of Oyster Creek. See "Johnston, Albert Sidney," *Handbook of Texas.*
3. Word of the passage of the joint resolution on annexation reached Galveston on March 20.
4. Dubois de Saligny returned to Texas in January 1844 and served as the French representative until the annexation of Texas. See "Dubois de Saligny," *Handbook of Texas Online.*
5. Andrew Jackson Donelson, the nephew of President Jackson, received special instructions in Nashville to hurry to Texas with the proposal for annexation. He arrived at Galveston and raced toward Washington. He met the returning French and British ministers ten miles south of Washington-on-the-Brazos. He presented the annexation proposal on March 31. Donelson had been

named U.S. chargé in October 1844 and arrived November 10. "Donelson, Andrew Jackson," *Handbook of Texas Online* [accessed March 17, 2007].

6.   President Anson Jones agreed not to speak about British and French diplomatic maneuvering for ninety days. As a result, his friends did not know President Jones's position on annexation. Years later, in his collection of letters, there appeared annotations in his hand on letters from friends begging him to state publicly that he favored annexation all along. Most of his contemporaries believed that he opposed annexation. See "Jones, Anson," *Handbook of Texas Online.*

7.   Eliza Johnston was expecting her first baby, Albert Sidney Johnston Jr., born April 7, 1845, near Shelbyville, Kentucky. See "Johnston, Eliza Griffin," *Handbook of Texas Online.*

James Love to Albert Sidney Johnston

Galveston
April 25 1845

My dear General

I have to announce to you that the President has issued his proclamation calling Congress together on the 16ᵗʰ of June. His action has been tardy and reluctant, just in time, to use a Kentuckyism, to "save his bacon."[1] We have an overwhelming majority in the country in favor of annexation and you may consider the question settled so far as our action is concerned.

Ashbel Smith[2] has again gone to England to make apologies; He was *honored* by being burnt in effigy the other night in our city. The British and Govt party here made head against us here for awhile, but we have *floored* them.

We already feel the beneficial influence of the confidence inspired in our position, and a great rage is getting up for sugar lands. The last year's crop in Louisiana and the first here has in a great degree occasioned this. Some planters there last year having recd more than $500 the hund [hundredweight?]. I once again advise you to make everything yield to the payment of the balance due on the place this year. I feel perfectly certain before January you can sell the place for $25,000. I have refused $15,000, five of it in cash to be paid in the fall. I did not think it right to encumber it by an agreement to sell, when I knew it could be sold at anytime. The great advantage it has is that it is ready for sugar; very few places are on account of their freshness. I tried in April to get as much money as would buy $50 worth of cane to have planted there as a beginning for you. Take this matter in your own hands, as Burnley writes me that his affairs does not permit an advance of money. I do not rely certainly on Dr. Jones's mortgage, altho I hope to make it available.

Have you Lieut. Halthen's rifle[?] Burnley is authorized to draw on Doswell for the pay.

My family leaves in the morning for Ky. I wish Mrs. Johnston & yourself were here to stay with me. I think I could entertain you to your satisfaction, and your society would make me as happy as I could be in the absence of my own folks.

Yr friend
Jas Love
Genl A. Sidney Johnston
Shelbyville, Kentucky

1. About April 21, President Jones called for the Congress to convene on June 16, and later, for a convention to assemble in Austin on July 4 to consider propositions concerning the "nationality" of Texas. His action was forced by pro-annexation feeling, although he had promised to call the Congress into session "by June 20." See "Jones, Anson," *Handbook of Texas Online.*

2. Ashbel Smith was born in 1805 in Hartford, Connecticut. He entered Texas in 1836, shortly after the revolution. From 1842 to 1844 he served as the Texas chargé d'affaires to France and England. Anson Jones appointed Smith secretary of state. "Smith, Ashbel," *Handbook of Texas Online* [accessed December 16, 2004].

James Love to Albert Sidney Johnston

Galveston
June 26, 1845

My dear General

We have recd the news four days since from Washington [Texas] that the resolutions of our Congress in favor of annexation have passed unanimously. You will probably learn this before this reaches you as Capt Stockton[1] left immediately in the *Princeton*[2] to carry the news in all haste to Washington [D.C.]. I trust we shall have a quorum on the fourth of July, that this great act may be consummated by the immediate rept of the people on that great day. We shall after awhile have some curious developments from the anti-annexation party. The great ones victimized the small fry and have, to some extent, managed to free themselves from the odium of opposition and left their victims to bear it. They are restive under this and begin to show letters from Old Sam, etc. discouraging the measure. The truth is they badly miscalculated; they were silly enough to believe that the power of the Govt, Houston's supposed popularity, the foreign influence, and other causes would enable them to defeat it. Hence arose Smith's mission to England & Elliot's to Mexico. When Donaldson first had an interview with Houston and asked his opinion of annexation, he said the terms offered were infamous and would be rejected. He told many others he was opposed to it. He now seeks to change that impression & will probably succeed. Jones is altogether prostrate.

We have not yet heard the precise nature of the proposition sent from Mexico; it is announced publicly that they are very favorable. I am certain they are not and would not, in any state of case, be accepted by Texas. They are doubtless of that character intended to embarrass the question here, without, are nothing themselves. The President, so soon as Elliot returned & had an interview with him, announced the proposition to be favorable, and issued a proclamation for an armistice, a most extraordinary step when he had the distinct assurance of the U. States that during the pendency of the question, they would defend Texas.[3]

Majr [sic] Donelson had the authority to order the U. States troops here so soon as the convention shall have acted, and he will doubtless do so. The troops will not probably leave the old limits of Texas for a time. The plan is for Texans, before the measure is fully consumated [sic], to occupy the whole country to the bank of the Rio Grande and hand it over as ours. A month since, Com Stockton offered to furnish provisions for three months, munitions of war, etc., but Jones refused to act. I suppose we will have some fighting as I have no doubt that Mexico will concentrate all her disposable forces on & near the Rio Grande as soon as she knows annexation will take place. I do not believe, however, any serious difficulty will arise. Mexico will most probably heal her wounded honor in the reception of money.

I am not certain, but believe I wrote you I was elected to the [annexation] convention. So far as I have heard, I think we have a good representation: Hemphill, Lipscomb, Webb, Gov Runnels, Rusk, Henderson, Horton, Dr. Miller, Caldwell are among the number you know.[4]

We have had a most delightful season for the last 60 days. The thermometer has regularly stood at 87 on my mantle [sic] at noon and the breeze from the south. The crops of the country are splendid, the corn better than I have seen it. You have no idea of the number of persons looking at the country. The lower Brazos is in high favor for sugar. Your place can easily be sold in the fall if you do not conclude to pay for it & keep it. You had better come out & sell it. I saw Townes[5] lately [and] he entertains no doubt that the debt can easily be adjusted. I have not done anything with the mortgage; I hope to be able to do so, if not soon done, no discount ought to be made.

I trust you are relieved from apprehension for your young son and that Mrs. Johnston is in health. I beg you to remember me most kindly to her.

Yr friend
James Love
Genl A. S. Johnston
Shelbyville Kentucky

1. Commodore Robert Field Stockton was born on 1795 in Princeton, New Jersey. He joined the U.S. Navy in 1811 and served in the War of 1812 and in the war with Algiers.

2. Launched in 1842, the USS *Princeton* was the world's first screw-propelled naval steamer. It was designed by John Ericsson and Commodore Stockton. In February 1844 near Washington, D.C., the *Princeton* fired an experimental wrought-iron gun. It exploded and killed Secretary of State Abel P. Upshur, Secretary of the Navy Thomas Gilmer, two congressmen, and several crew members. Upshur and Gilmer, prior to their untimely deaths, had championed Texas annexation.

3. After receiving Elliot's message, Jones announced on June 4 that Texas and Mexico were at peace. See "Elliot, Charles," and "Jones, Anson," *Handbook of Texas Online.*

4. James Love is referring to John Hemphill; Abner S. Lipscomb; James Webb; Hiram George Runnels, a former governor of Mississippi who was living in Brazoria; Thomas J. Rusk; James Pinckney Henderson; Albert Clinton Horton; Dr. James B. Miller; and John Caldwell.

5. Love is referring to Robert J. Townes of Brazoria County.

James Love to Albert Sidney Johnston

Austin

July 8th 1845

My dear General

I reached this on the third, had an agreeable and pleasant trip saving and excepting the intense heat which stood in the shade on the 4th at 98. We organized the convention on the 4th by the election of Genl Rusk unanimously as President. He has not drank for a year and made a short, handsome address on taking his seat. Judge Lipscomb moved the appointment of a committee of 15, of which I was one, to draft an ordinance ratifying the annexation of Texas. This was soon reported, and it passed unanimously with one dissenting voice which was my colleague, Maj. Bache.[1] It was engrossed on parchment and signed by 56 out of 61 members, all that were present. I took some pleasure in signing it with a golden pen, a present from Hammeken.[2]

We then passed the necessary orders for the transmission of the ordinance, and then I offered a resolution to wear crape one month as a testimony of respect for the decease of Genl Jackson. Some of the Democrats opened their eyes that a Whig should dare to do a thing that they thought their exclusive right. I did it, however, with pleasure, for whatever may have been his political sins, he has been a true and faithful friend to Texas. The resolution was unanimously adopted and we then adjourned, not being willing to desecrate the day of Liberty with less glorious deeds.

We have since taken the necessary steps preparatory to entering upon the business of constitution making. The various subjects being referred to committee to report. There was some discussion today upon a resolution inviting the occupation of our frontier by the U. States troops; this business was unnecessary as the troops are already on their way, some by way of N. Orleans to Corpus Christi, the Dragoons overland. I know this to be so as I read the order given by Donelson to Genl Taylor. President Jones has thrown great obstacles in the way; the treaty he made with Mexico recognized that there was a disputed boundary, and after this, he issued a proclamation for an armistice. But for this, the U. States would not have hesitated to have taken possession of the Rio Grande. As it is, they cannot do so without placing themselves in an aggressive attitude, which on many accounts, they wish to avoid. We being in possession of Corpus Christi, they take possession of that, and I think somehow or other, they will continue to go to the Rio Grande. Genl Taylor is ordered now, if Mexico crosses that river in force, to drive her troops across it. This is something & shows they consider that a debatable land.

The convention is a body of greater talent, integrity, & worth than has before been assembled in Texas. I have been with them five days and have not seen anyone in the least degree excited from the use of spirits, and I verily believe we shall submit to the people a sound, sensible, and good constitution. If we do, it will add greatly to our future prosperity and happiness.

I left home with much reluctance, but I already begin to feel interest in our proceedings, and believe I shall be able to do some good. Whatever may be the political prejudices of members against me, I am sure to have their respect. My course of conduct is not to be prominent, but avail myself of circumstances to endeavor to effect my purposes. I made a short speech today in order to extricate the convention from some confusion, was listened to with respect, & stopped the debate by the adoption of what I recommended. I will try & not speak out of turn or season, and also try to win my way only that I may be useful. I have a great number of staunch friends; we will still have our might.

I am proposing to keep house in conjunction with Col. S. M. Williams; we have good brandy, wine, liquor, and other appliances. We shall be hospitable, even this may be of service.

This town [Austin] is in an utter state of delapidation [sic] and ruin. Where I once was entertained with hospitality, kindness, and with comforts, if not the elegancies [sic] of life, is now the habitation of the beast only. What does he deserve that brings ruin on hundreds for the wilfull [sic] gratification of his passion only? May God reward him according to his deeds is all the harm I wish him.[3]

> Your sincere friend
> James Love
> Genl A. Sydney Johnston
> Shelbyville Kentucky

1. Richard Bache, who was elected the justice of the peace for Galveston County in 1842, represented the island city at the annexation convention along with James Love. Bache was the only member of the convention who voted against annexation. "Bache, Richard," *Handbook of Texas Online*.

2. George Louis Hammeken was probably born in New York. In the 1830s he
    spent some time in Mexico as an agent for the Barings banking firm. He first
    came to Texas in 1835 but left for New Orleans when the Texas Revolution
    began. He returned after the war and became involved in railroad and canal
    building speculations. In the 1840s he became a commission merchant and,
    along with James Love, heavily promoted the city of San Luis. "Hammeken,
    George Louis," *Handbook of Texas Online* [accessed December 21, 2004].
3. Obviously, James Love blamed Sam Houston's abandonment of Austin dur-
    ing the Vásquez raid and the Woll invasion for that city's state of decline.

William Pitt Ballinger to Albert Sidney Johnston

Galveston Texas
September 17, 1845

Genl Johnston
Dear Sir,

The convention adjourned on the 28th of August. Col Love
returned home, remained only a few days during which he was constantly
employed, and left for Brazoria court. I[1] told him I intended sending you a
copy of the constitution, and he requested me also to write you a few lines
making apology for his own delay, and saying that immediately upon his
return, he would write you at length upon the condition of affairs.

Accompanying this, I enclose you the constitution, and I doubt
not that upon your examination of it, you will find cause of satisfaction and
rejoicing that it contains so many provisions which presage to the State of
Texas the blessings of safe government.

The representation of a people who have been for years almost
without the restraints of law, and whose sentiments I had supposed more
strongly imbued with the *ultra* democracy of the day, have avoided the most
of the evils which were to be apprehended from their causes, and adopted
what is, in the main, a wholesome organic system.

So far as my information extends, the constitution receives the
general approbation of the people and there will be no effort in any quarter
to raise objections to its adoption. Indeed, sir, I almost suspect that you, in
common with all those who have taken any interest in this matter, have suf-

fered yourself to be very much deluded by the opinions that there existed a party of government functionaries and their satellites here, who had opposed the union of Texas with the United States, and done all that they dared do to defeat the various measures for its consummation. You will regard it, however, as but another instance of the fallibility of all human judgement when you are convinced. So your charity or humility will perhaps render very easy that the objects and wishes of that party have been altogether misunderstood; that Genl Houston is the "father of annexation" and Dr Anson Jones and Ashbel Smith are its most consistent and zealous supporters.

Genl Henderson and Dr. Miller have been announced as candidates for governor. There is as yet no general indication of public preference, but I am led to believe that the former will be easily elected. The east will unite for him and he is not objectionable to the west. Col A. C. Horton[2] of Matagorda is a candidate for lieutenant governor. It seems to be the opinion that Houston & Rusk will be the senators.[3]

As one of the *on dit* [piece of gossip] here concerning our distinguished men, it may not be uninteresting to you to know that a personal encounter took place at Austin the day of adjournment of the convention between Genl Hunt and Col Mayfield. The latter made some remark (so the story goes) about Genl Taylor, the commander of the U.S. troops on the Nueces—which was positively contradicted by Genl Hunt, together with a warning that Col M. must be cautious how he talked of "a relation" of his. Mayfield slapped him in the face, a scuffle ensued, and the last intelligence of the affair was a note addressed by Hunt regretting that an injury to his hand prevented his demanding that immediate satisfaction recognized among gentlemen.[4]

The health of Galveston and of the country generally is good. Crops are fair though in some sections they have been impaired by the drought. We hear frequently from the ladies of the family; they are well and passing the summer agreeably.[5]

I request that you will present my very friendly regards to Mrs. Johnston, and that you will consider me as with sentiments of respect and esteem

> Yr friend
> William P. Ballinger
> Genl A. Sidney Johnston
> Shelbyville Kentucky

1. William Pitt Ballinger was born in 1825 in Barbourville, Kentucky. He came to Galveston in 1843 to study law with James Love, who was his uncle by marriage. During the U.S.-Mexico War he served as Albert Sidney Johnston's adjutant. "Ballinger, William Pitt," *Handbook of Texas Online* [accessed December 21, 2004].

2. Albert Clinton Horton was born in 1798 in Hancock County, Georgia. He arrived in Texas in 1835 and quickly became involved in the revolutionary movement. He recruited volunteers from Alabama known as the Mobile Grays. This unit served with Colonel James Fannin in South Texas. When Mexican troops captured and executed Fannin's army, Horton was on a reconnaissance mission. In 1842 he defended against the Vásquez raid on San Antonio. He attended the annexation convention. Texas voters elected Horton the first lieutenant governor of the newly formed state. "Horton, Albert Clinton," *Handbook of Texas Online* [accessed December 21, 2004].

3. On February 21, 1846, the state legislature selected Sam Houston and Thomas J. Rusk to serve as the state's senators in the U.S. Congress. There was a scattering of votes for other candidates, including two cast for James Love.

4. See below the series of correspondences.

5. The ladies were Mrs. Lucy Ballinger Love; her sister, Mrs. Betsy Ballinger Eve; Love's daughters Lucy, age four, and Mrs. Mary Morris; plus her two daughters and probably Joseph, age nine. They all visited the Ballinger home in Barbourville, Kentucky.

Memucan Hunt, James S. Mayfield, and Edward Burleson *correspondence*

[No. 1]
Aug 29th 1845

Hon J. S. Mayfield
Sir

Circumstances which transpired on yesterday afternoon compell [*sic*] me to demand an explantion [*sic*] of your conduct on that occasion.

(signed) Your obedient Servant
Memucan Hunt

[No. 2]
City of Austin
30th Aug 1845

Genl Memucan Hunt
Sir

Your note of the 29th inst was handed to me this day. In answer to which I have to say that on the afternoon of the day attended to by you, your language and bearing was considered offensive and impelled by the circumstances and occasion, I gave you a blow.

(signed) Very Respectfully
Your Obt Srvt
J. S. Mayfield

[No. 3]
City of Austin
Aug 31st 1845

Hon J. S. Mayfield
Sir

Your note per Genl Cazaneau[1] was duly received. I regret that its contents are not considered satisfactory.

In consequence of my disability to use my right hand, I am reluctantly compelled to defer for the present a demand for that satisfaction to which I am entitled under the circumstances.

(signed) Your Obt Srvt
Memucan Hunt

[No. 4]
Bastrop County
16th Sept 1845

Sir

I avail myself of the earliest opportunity after the restoration of my hand, the condition of which was referred to in my note of 31st ultimo, to demand of you the satisfaction due to me.

My friend, Genl Edward Burleson, is authorized to arrange the necessary preliminaries.

> (signed) Your Obt Srvt
> Memucan Hunt
> To Hon J. S. Mayfield
> Bastrop

> [No. 5]
> Bastrop
> Septr 17th 1845

Sir

I am constrained to defer answering the note you handed me on yesterday signed Memucan Hunt as a friend with whom I had confered [*sic*] and advised, touching the subject matter of that note, is not present. As early as I can be joined by him, which will be at the earliest period that he can be notified or that I can meet with another to substitute in his place, the note you handed me will be answered to and through you.

> (signed) Respectfully
>   Your Obt Srvt
> J. S. Mayfield
> To Genl Edward Burleson
> Bastrop

> [No. 6]
> Bastrop
> 18th Septr 1845

Col J. S. Mayfield
Dear Sir

In reply to your note of yesterday, I have to say that at any time previous to the 25th instant, I shall be in readiness to receive your answer to the note handed you by myself signed M. Hunt, dated the 16th instant, having made previously my arrangements to go into the woods and will be absent for sometime. Should it not be convenient for you to answer within the time above mentioned, you will please notify Genl Hunt any time after that time, so that he can avail himself of some other person who will act in my stead.

(signed) Very Respectfully
Your Obt Srvt
Edward Burleson

[No. 7]
Lagrange
Septr 27th 1845

Genl M. Hunt
Dear Sir

I send you this as a true copy of the last communication from May-field dated 23rd inst, though I did not receive it until the 25th. You can judge of it as you think proper. Immediately upon its receipt, I went to Lagrange where I was arrested one hour after my arrival upon the ground of an antici-pated difficulty between Mayfield and myself, though from the fact that no challenge had passed, we were both released the next morning. How it will terminate is yet unknown. The copy is as follows:

Col Mayfield's respects to Genl Burleson and desires to say, if insisted upon by Genl B that a response shall be made to him in reply to the note of Memucan Hunt, dated 16th inst before Genl B goes to the woods, that Col Mayfield then replies to Genl B as follows:

"First" Memucan Hunt is and has been a pensioner upon his country

"Second" That said Hunt is supported by and maintained by the charity of his personal friends and community without any visible means of employment to secure an honorable livelihood.

"Third" That said Hunt fills none of those social relations com-mon to Col Mayfield and for all and each of these reasons, said Hunt is not his equal

"Fourth" That none of these objections exist as to Genl Burleson, and any communication eminating [sic] personally from Genl B will be properly met

(signed) Mayfield
[signed by Edward Burleson]

[No. 8]
At Home
Septr 25th 1845

Col J. S. Mayfield
Sir

In accordance with the intimation given to you in my note of the 18th inst, I now notify you that all connection between Genl Hunt and myself has ceased so far as your offence and his are concerned. Of this fact, Genl Hunt is already notified, and whatever subsequent correspondence may take place between you and that gentleman must be conducted through some other medium than myself.

Should Genl Hunt think proper to designate that medium of communication, I presume he will [give] you due and proper notice of it.

Signed Very Respectfully
Your Obt Srvt
Edward Burleson

*This note was not sent to me by Genl Burleson, but shown to me by Genl Cazaneau at Galveston, and at my solicitation, he permitted me to copy it.

Signed Memucan Hunt

[In pencil and in the hand of Eliza G. Johnston]
All these papers I wish returned to me. EG Johnston

1. William Leslie Cazneau was born in 1807 in Boston, Massachusetts. He came to Texas in 1830 and opened a mercantile store in Matagorda. He joined the Texas Army in 1835. In 1839 Cazneau and Juan Seguín collected the remains of the Alamo defenders and buried them with military honors. That year he moved to Austin and was commissary general under the Lamar administration. He represented Travis County in the Seventh, Eighth, and Ninth Congresses and was a delegate to the annexation convention of 1845. "Cazneau, William Leslie," *Handbook of Texas Online* [accessed December 21, 2004].

James Love to Albert Sidney Johnston

Galveston
Sept 28th 1845

My dear General

I believe I am proverbial for not carrying into effect my good intentions. Amongst them I had contemplated to keep you regularly advised of every movement in our late convétion [*sic*], and of the affairs of the country in which I know you feel so deep an interest. When at Austin, I found myself of much more consequence than I had supposed, and called upon more frequently than was agreeable to perform a great deal of labor. And then I had company every day to dinner, and friends until late at night. I wrote once a week to my wife and daughter, as in duty bound. When that was done, I had no time but for short & hurried answers to letters recd.

It may surprise you to learn that I was a man of consequence in the convention, and *was popular*, and what will doubtless surprise you still more, I have recd a much greater share of applause from the people than I was entitled to. Circumstances made me prominent on some questions in which their interests were deeply concerned [and] I had success. They take the fact without inquiry, and without knowing the degree of talent exercised or the motive that controlls [*sic*]. I was unpopular with a large party without cause; I am popular with as little cause. So much for that which is so much sought after by those who wish to be prominent. It is acquired more frequently without merit and lost without cause. I have made up my own mind to rest on my laurels, and have resisted every effort to enter again into political life. I will, when I see you, give you a full history of matters and things. I have, to some extent, tasted the sweets of revenge, and have laid the train that, will at some day distant, perhaps enable to clear off all old scores.

There were many enquiries [*sic*] made for you in the most friendly manner, and almost everyone expressed for you sincere friendship. There is scarcely anything Texas would not do for you if you would place yourself in the situation to permit it. The general wish prevails that you may be Col of the new reg[i]m[en]t which it is supposed will be raised. You will have no competition for it. All the foremost men have told me if you wished the office, they would urge your appointment. The aspirants in Texas yield their claims to yours.

There is a great congregation of warriors, blacklegs, idlers, loafers, traders, and Mexicans at Corpus Christi. Genl Taylor has 4,000 soldiers there; six companies of Texas rangers under Hays have been mustered into service. They are teaching the U.S. officers and soldier[s] how to ride; the feats of horsemanship of our frontiersmen are most extraordinary. I saw one of them pick up from the ground three dollars each 50 yards apart at full speed, and pass under the horse's neck at a pace not much short of full speed. The Mexicans have eight thousand soldiers on the Rio Grande. It seems there is some difficulty amongst the generals, and the opinion is that Paredes, now in command, will rebel against the govt.[1] The Mexicans will not cross the river in force, nor will General Taylor advance. The Dragoons and one Regmt [of] infantry will be stationed at Lipantitlan.[2] The spies go out as far as little Colorado. A Mexican officer was detected in Taylor's camp, tried, and sentenced to death, [but] Taylor released him as not worth shooting.

The popularity of Genl Houston has recd a shock, and if opposition could be concentrated, he could easily be put down. Mercer's colonization[3] contract has greatly injured him. The charm is broken and no one can tell how low he may fall, altho it is not improbable he may fill a space for some years yet. Lamar is rather rising as a candidate for the Senate (U.S.); Henderson & Pillsbury[4] for Govr; Horton for Lieut Govr. Mayfield & Hunt, I suppose, have fought a duel before this. It originated in a street brawl at Austin before I left. M gave him a blow & called him coward. From what I know of the case, I think they will fight. H., I believe, will not be satisfied but with terms M. will not give.

I have a fine crop on the lower place. Had last week 110 bales picked out, expect to make, if the fall is favorable, 240. I have in crib 5,750 bushels corn, besides that which we have used since July. The crop yielded upwards of 50 bushels the acre. I have had branded this season 218 calves and some yet to brand. I can sell 3,000 bushels corn that will net 80 cents.

Your place has been well cultivated and has produced a fine crop. It is redeemed from its delapidated [sic] appearance. A screw has been put up. The fence yet needs amendment. I have had several propositions to purchase, [but] the powers I have are not sufficient to close a sale, nor if I had, would I do so without your advice. It is so obviously your interest first to make payment before you sell, that until I know whether you can effect the object in view of raising money, I would not sell. The debt may yet be paid at 50¢ or less; after sale, it will be at par. Let me, as a friend sincerely anxious for your interest, impress upon you the necessity of coming to Texas at the earliest possible moment, whether you sell or retain the place, it is necessary. I am satisfied if you do not wish to sell, you may put in the land with some one against negroes. It is also highly important that sugar cane should be planted this year, that a commencement be made, it would greatly enhance the value of the place.

I send your son a copy of the constitution in a newspaper; I have not been able to get it in pamphlet form. I also send him a copy in Spanish [and] with your assistance, if he will translate it, he will be a tolerable Spanish scholar, the pronunciations are literal. I will not forget my promise, but will write him someday.

I supposed Mrs. Love begins to think of returning. Will you write her a line & say when you will leave. She would, I know, be happy to give you all the trouble of escorting her to Texas. She is at Barbourville [Kentucky].

We have had no sickness in Texas this year, not a case of fever on the plantation all the year, no death of an adult in Galveston, but one. My kindest regards to Mrs. Johnston.

Your friend
Jas Love

1. On January 7, 1845, Mexico's congress named José Joaquín de Herrera president of Mexico. After the annexation of Texas President Herrera placed General Mariano Paredes y Arrillaga in charge of national defense. Rather than attack the American army in South Texas Paredes marched on Mexico City, deposed President Herrera, and declared himself president of Mexico.
2. Lipantitlan was a Mexican fort located about three miles from the city of San Patricio.
3. In December 1844 President Houston granted Charles Mercer a grant of land in central Texas. It was fraught with legal problems, however, and ultimately failed. "Mercer Colony," *Handbook of Texas Online* [accessed March 20, 2007].
4. Timothy Pillsbury was born in 1780 in Newburyport, Massachusetts. He arrived in Texas in 1837 and settled in Brazoria County. He was a member of the Fifth and Sixth Congresses and served as the chief justice and probate judge of Brazoria County. Defeated for governor, he was elected to the U.S. Congress in 1846. "Pillsbury, Timothy," *Handbook of Texas Online* [accessed December 22, 2004].

PART III

"So Let It Be"

STATEHOOD AND SECESSION, 1846-1861

Texas' annexation into the Union ended Johnston and friends' dream of living in the Republic of Texas. During this time period, 1846–1861, some of the earlier letter writers abandoned the Lone Star State and sought fame and glory elsewhere. Alexander Parker Crittenden and Tod Robinson, both infected with "gold fever," left for California. Thomas Rusk, Sam Houston, and Albert Triplett Burnley moved to the U.S. capital in Washington. Rusk and Houston served as Texas' first U.S. senators while Burnley founded a partisan newspaper. Other letter writers never entered Texas. Robert Holmes Chinn continued to practice law in New Orleans. General Leslie Combs remained in Lexington, Kentucky, until his death in 1881. The rest stayed in Texas. President Mirabeau B. Lamar took up arms during the U.S.-Mexico War and then returned to Austin as a state legislator. In 1857 he received an appointment as U.S. minister to Nicaragua and Costa Rica and served for twenty months. He died in Richmond, Texas, shortly after he returned from his diplomatic mission. Hugh McLeod participated in the U.S.-Mexico War and later spearheaded the construction of the Buffalo Bayou, Brazos, and Colorado Railway, the first railroad in Texas. When the Civil War commenced he helped to form the First Texas Infantry Regiment—Hood's Texas Brigade. He died during the war. Louis P. Cooke also participated in the U.S.-Mexico War and then settled in Brownsville. He died in 1849, a victim of cholera. Samuel A. Roberts retired to Bonham, where he practiced law and passionately defended the "peculiar institution" of slavery. He died in 1872. Memucan Hunt briefly served in the U.S.-Mexico War, after which he served one term in the state legislature. He spent the remainder of his life planning railroad routes into northern Texas. He died in 1856.

After helping to compose the first state constitution of Texas, James Love served as judge of the First Judicial District, an office he held for two years. In 1850, as a reward for his political counsel, President Zachary Taylor appointed Love clerk of the federal court in Galveston. He held this position until the secessionists declared independence from the United States. Shortly after he wrote the last letter in this collection Love headed north, intent upon serving as his old friend's aide. Heartbroken at Johnston's battlefield death, Love volunteered for the Eighth Texas Cavalry, the legendary Terry's Texas Rangers, and fought with the unit for two years. He returned home and continued his successful law practice in Galveston. After the war Texans elected him the first judge of the Galveston and Harris County Criminal District Court. He held this position until Radical Republican Reconstructionists removed him and many other former Confederate sympathizers from office as "impediments to reconstruction." Albert Sidney Johnston's old friend died in Galveston on June 12, 1874.

This section contains thirteen letters James Love wrote to Albert Sidney Johnston between 1846 and 1861. They commence with information about Albert Sidney Johnston's journey southward to fight against Mexico and end with his trip northward to fight against the United States of America. In between he fought the Mexicans, Sam Houston, unemployment, poverty, bankruptcy, political patronage, and military intrigue. He did not emerge from these fights victorious.

When the U.S.-Mexico War commenced Albert Sidney Johnston awaited his country's call to arms. When the U.S. Army did not request his services Johnston hurried south to Point Isabel and joined the First Texas Rifle Volunteers and soon became their commander. He fought valiantly at the Battle of Monterrey. After his enlistment expired, Johnston applied for a commission in the regular army. Even though the country desperately needed experienced field officers, Sam Houston used his political influence as a U.S. senator to quash Johnston's application. Deprived of any further martial experiences, the former Texas secretary of war returned to his plantation, China Grove, and embarked on three frustrating years as a poverty-stricken dirt farmer. The final result of this paladin-agriculturalist effort was a declaration of bankruptcy and the sale in 1849 of his beloved plantation. This warrior-hero struggled to stay out of debtors' prison until later that year, when the public elected General Zachary Taylor president. Johnston's friends, especially James Love and Albert Triplett Burnley, persuaded President Taylor to offer employment to his penniless former officer. At first Johnston refused, but mounting bills and a hungry family forced him to swallow his pride and accept this political patronage. For the next twelve years he followed his true calling as a soldier in the U.S. Army. A failure at everything except love and war, Johnston, on the eve of the Civil War, betrayed his country by fighting for his adopted homeland. Ironically, shortly after he received his last letter from his dear old friend, James Love, Johnston lost his life in a final, fateful confrontation with another West Pointer who also excelled only in marriage or military matters: Ulysses S. Grant. They met at a lonely field near an obscure Methodist church named Shiloh. Only Grant lived to see the sun shine the next day.

James Love to Albert Sidney Johnston

Galveston
June 15th 1846

Dear General

I understand a vessel arrived in the morning and I write you a line altho really, I have nothing to write. We have had no dates from N. Orleans later than the 4th inst, the same you had at P[o]r[t] Isabel by the *N York*.[1]

The information I have from Washington City leaves but little hope that you will receive the appointment of Colonel. One Regmt [regiment] has already been filled, and none from Texas higher than a captain, and I fear the other will be filled in the same way. It seems Genl Houston is in the ascen-dant at court, another evidence that the affairs of a great nation should never be given to a weak head. We will, however, soon see. It is also said that Houston will be one of the new Major Generals, and that it is intended to concede the war against Mexico to his management, with the view, doubtless, under the *edat* [éclat?] of a few victories, to make him President. This is said to be the design of one branch of the great Democratic party. I will, however, to the last, hope [for] better things for my country and of my countrymen.

Your friend
James Love
Genl A. Sidney Johnston
Texan Volunteers
Matamoros

1.   Eager for a command in the U.S. Army, Johnston moved his family to Galveston in early 1846. Despairing of action, he finally left Galveston in April to join General Zachary Taylor's command in Point Isabel as a volunteer. The United States declared war on Mexico on May 13, 1846. See "Johnston, Albert Sidney," *Handbook of Texas Online.*

James Love to Albert Sidney Johnston

Galveston
July 5th 1846

Dear General

Altho I know you are kept advised of everything here by Mrs. Johnston, I shall continue to write you occasionally. I congratulate you on your election, not so much on your own account, [but] as the certainty to my mind it will be better for the service.[1] Genl Lamar draws heavily on his friends, and I verily believe if his name had not been thrust forward as the anti-Houston candidate, we could have defeated Houston. You did right, certainly, to yield to him and support him.[2]

You will have heard that the Oregon question has been settled by treaty.[3] I have never anticipated so much danger of war with England for that country as there is likely to be about California. I do not think she will permit the U.S. to take that region without a contest. It is life or death to her Asiatic commerce. It is certain, to my mind, that G.B., as well as France, will now unite to use their influence to have the Mexican War brought to a close. They are aware the longer it exists, the farther we advance, and the worse it will be for Mexico. I am not in favor of the principle of acquiring territory by conquest, but if Mexico persists in her folly, it is not in human nature to give up all that shall be won. The Democracy are in some trouble at Washington; Allan resigned his office of Chairman of Foreign Relations in disgust on account of the Oregon treaty. They failed to elect their nominee, Lewis, and were forced to take McDuffie, no friend of the President.[4]

I am afraid you will have no opportunity for distinction, as I do not believe Mexico will give you battle on the frontier.[5] I do hope they may not treat until our soldiers shall see the *"Halls* of Montezuma," that you know, is an old brag, [and] I should like to see it fulfilled.

> Sincerely Yr friend
> James Love
> Col A. Sidney Johnston
> 1ˢᵗ Regmt Texan Volunteers
> Pt Isabel

1.   On June 6 Johnston joined Taylor's army at Point Isabel, near the mouth of the Rio Grande. In mid-June, shortly after Governor James Pinckney Henderson arrived, the Texas volunteers organized the First Texas Infantry Regiment and elected Johnston their colonel. See "Johnston, Albert Sidney," *Handbook of Texas Online.*

2.   Lamar was appointed inspector general of Taylor's army. "Lamar, Mirabeau Buonaparte," *Handbook of Texas Online.*

3.   On June 15, 1846, the U.S. Senate ratified the treaty with England to settle the Oregon boundary question.

4.   William Allen, a Democratic senator from Ohio, resigned as chairman of the Senate Foreign Relations Committee on June 15. On June 17 the Senate, after thirteen ballots, finally chose George McDuffie of South Carolina to replace Allen, thus bypassing Dixon H. Lewis of Alabama, who never received more than one vote.

5.   Johnston missed the first two battles of the U.S.-Mexico War: Palo Alto, on May 8, 1846, and Resaca de la Palma, on May 9, 1846. See "Johnston, Albert Sidney," *Handbook of Texas Online.*

James Love to Albert Sidney Johnston

> Galveston
> July 30, 1846

Dear General

Your letters by the *N York* was recd today. I tell you now, as I told you when we parted, not to waste your time in writing to me unless battles are to be fought and won, or when matters of some import is at hand. I can just as well tell here what you are going, and as I know your hands are full, I assure you, I shall feel no slight at your not writing frequently. The main thing is to write more or less everyday to your wife, and I shall hear enough of you to satisfy me as to your health and position, in both of which, you will permit me to say, I feel great interest.

I have made up my mind, however, that the day of glory for Texans now in service is very remote. You will not, of course, stay 12 months, & will be discharged, I suppose, at the end of three. What puzzles me is, that you should be ordered on when your time is almost out.

I will not at present censure the govt. They have certainly blundered and have occasioned a great waste of time and money. They fixed all time and manner at Washington without possessing any knowledge or information of the state of case. It was doubtless done over a "hasty plate of soup."[1] They have directed all these movements to that time and that manner—you were not to move before Sept and will not. Chihuahua, & Santa Fe, and the Rio Grand & Texas were all to be assailed by separate armies; Kerney [sic] has gone to Santa Fe, Genl Wool is here on his way to Chihuahua via San Antonio, where he will concentrate a larger force.[2] Tampico, Vera Cruz, Monterey, or some other point are all to be attacked at the same time, and when all these places are taken, if peace does not follow, the several forces are doubtless to make their way to Mexico. California, also, is to be subdued. I am no military man, but common sense teaches me when the capital is the object, the whole force should be directed there, minor conquests would follow without a fight. It is this grand scheme that has, doubtless, induced them to take no one for a less term than a year. I have no authority for my opinion but what I see of preparation, which I think warrants the conclusion.

Your Regmt is well reported of by all, more so than any other. I am glad of this on your own account as it will satisfy me to see you retire with credit, for it is certain you will be altogether overlooked by his Excellency.[3] Except for your preference for the military life, I should rejoice at this, as I know that not only you, but your lady wife, will after awhile be more happy in private life.

The Democracy will carry all their measures in Congress. The next pres[i]d[en]t election will be the grand & final battle on present issues. If the Whigs are beaten, new organizations will take place upon other questions. I do not remember any item of news to give you. The truth is, there is nothing stirring but talk of the war. We are all well and the health of the city is once more good.

Sincerely yr friend
James Love
Genl A. S. Johnston, Comdt
1ˢᵗ Regmt Texan Inftry

1. "Hasty plate of soup" was a popular phrase among those who poked fun at General Winfield Scott's pompous manners. Scott had at one point written to Secretary of War William L. Marcy that official dispatches had interrupted Scott's "taking a hasty plate of soup."
2. Love is referring to General Stephen W. Kearny, who led a column of troops from Fort Leavenworth, Kansas, to New Mexico. A second force, under General John E. Wool, marched from San Antonio to threaten Chihuahua but ultimately joined General Zachary Taylor's army in northern Mexico.
3. "His Excellency" is Love's sarcastic reference to Senator Sam Houston.

James Love to Albert Sidney Johnston

New Orleans
April 1ˢᵗ 1848

Dear General

I learn from home that Mr. Nuckols, the overseer, has been guilty of conduct on the plantation so different from what I expected, and so different from the views explained to him by Burnley and myself, that if true, I wish him at once to leave the place. It is not possible for me to come over and attend to this business personally, and I have taken the liberty of asking you, and also Col Hall,[1] to look into it for me. Dismiss him, should he have done things as regards the negroes, which both of you know I would rather never make a bale of cotton, than have done.

I learn amongst other things, that he whipped and caused Jim to be whipped in a cruel and excessive manner, and then had his back salted. Now I hold that no one fit to be an overseer would do this, nor shall anyone stay on the place that does it. I learn, also, he ordered Lucinda to the field when I expressly told him it was not to be done, and many other things which it is not necessary to detail.[2]

What I wish you and the Col to do is to look into this matter for me, and if the man is not properly and humanly conducted, to consider this as authority to take charge of it, and employ someone to go there until I return, which will certainly be in this month.

I shall come over immediately after my return and will talk with you about all things stirring in this country whether of law or politics. The contemplation of the atrocities [that] I hear that has been committed on this place, unfits me now to write of anything.

Dr. Davis, who succeeds Williams, will furnish everything needful for the place.[3] I mention this as Nuckols wrote him for supplies; we made the arrangements with Davis before we left.

My best respects to Mrs. Johnston.

> Yr friend
> James Love
> Genl A. S. Johnston
> China Grove Texas[4]

1. Warren D. C. Hall was the previous owner of China Grove Plantation. At this time he leased the land from Albert Sidney Johnston. See "Hall, Warren D. C.," *Handbook of Texas Online.*

2. The slave, Jim, age twenty-seven, is mentioned in the 1841 indenture between Love and Burnley. Lucinda, the mother of two children, is one of the slaves Love mortgaged to Nathaniel Ware in 1846. See Brazoria County Deed Records B, 539; D, 139.

3. Dr. Jesse J. Davis succeeded Henry Howell Williams & Company, a commission house in Galveston, and established J. J. Davis and Company. Henry Howell Williams had bought the commission business from his brother, Samuel May Williams, and Thomas F. McKinney in 1842, but financial difficulties forced him to retire to his establishment in Baltimore in 1848.

4. After he returned from the U.S.-Mexico War Johnston resided on his plantation, China Grove, in Brazoria County on Oyster Creek, about five or six miles north of Love's plantation. He moved his family to the modest dwelling there at the end of 1846, and for three years, until the close of 1849, struggled to make the farm successful.

James Love to Albert Sidney Johnston

N. Orleans
May 8th 1848

Dear General

I have thought ever since I have been in N. Orleans that I would write you by the first packet. My usual indolence has prevailed over my good intentions, but I have at least mustered courage to begin. In truth, I have been so beset with difficulties of one kind or another as to make it a hard matter to do anything not indispensible [sic].

Some two weeks since, I paid a visit with two friends to General Taylor at Baton Rouge, and we brought down with us the last letter, which you will have seen, more clearly defining his position as a politician. It has had a wonderful influence on the public mind, has greatly strengthened his cause, and increased his probabilities of obtaining a nomination from the Whig convention.[1] Such has been the [juggling?] more especially with Clay and his rabid partizans [sic], this nomination is essential even to make him a candidate. Altho, if left unbiased by politicians, I verily believe two-thirds of all the American people would vote for him.

This last letter of his, following as it did in so short a time Clay's last "pronouncement" (which is disapproved by all), was a severe blow.[2] The Democrats, as well as Clay Whigs, are confounded, and they now admit their hopes of success rests upon Clay's nomination.[3] Many letters had been recd here from members of Congress and others saying if Genl Taylor would define his position, he could beat Clay in the Convention and hence the visit to him which procured this celebrated letter. They cannot say Bliss writ [sic] it, because he was not there.[4] It bothers, I tell you, terribly.

The late news from N. York and Boston is quite favorable to the Genl's prospects, and every disposition seems to prevail to break the fetters in which Mr. Clay seems disposed to keep his friends bound.

We staid [sic] all day with the old "Hero," took bacon & cabbage for dinner, and staid for tea. I like him very much. He is just as apt to say a fellow is a liar or a rascal as anything else, altho he may have two epaulettes on his shoulder.

His friends here have urged me to attend the convention as delegate from Texas. I am hesitating, but am inclined to do so if I possibly can.[5] I suppose I must have made a good impression upon him as he has written a letter to a friend here saying a great many pretty things of me and wishes I may find it convenient to do so.

I abused old Houston pretty considerably and said as many kind things for you as I thought necessary. He spoke in high terms of you and is very much your friend. Now, if I go at all to the convention, it will be in the hope I may have some little influence in having him nominated, and if so, I am certain of his election, and then to free Texas from the domination of Houston in executive patronage.[6]

Public opinion with all parties is against the course pursued by the department towards Scott. Everyone has perfect contempt for Pillow. Worth and Duncan have both seriously injured themselves and the court of inquiry are universally execrated.[7]

I do not believe the prospects for peace are good. I don't think that Mexico will ever again fight in any other mode than guerilla [sic]. Many of her citizens are opposed to peace because they fear their own government after the withdrawal of our troops.[8]

All Europe has asserted her rights and a general repudiation of kings with the exception of England. She will sustain herself for a time, and perhaps forever, if she is progressive in reform and yields to the well grounded complaints of the people. Ireland is still a problem to be solved; my opinion is rebellion, if it exists there, will be suppressed, altho I am confident the Union will be repealed.[9]

Genl Taylor & his lady arrived here this morning on a visit of a few days. He is very much attended to. Genls Quitman, Lane, Cadwalader are here, or were here, yesterday.[10]

My best respects to Mrs. Johnston. I am sure I wish her and the babies all possible health and happiness.[11]

Yr friend

James Love

1. James Love, Logan Hunton, and Balie Peyton visited General Taylor on April 21, 1848, to urge him to write a letter they had composed. Earlier, they convinced Alexander Bullitt to publish this letter in the New Orleans *Picayune*. The letter explained Taylor's political beliefs and emphasized the general's desire to unite the Whig Party. The letter was addressed to Captain J. S. Allison, Taylor's brother-in-law, and dated April 22, 1848. The Whigs' nominating convention planned to assemble in Philadelphia in June.

Taylor's main rivals for the party's nomination were Winfield Scott, his colleague in the U.S.-Mexico War, and the party's perennial candidate and standard-bearer, Henry Clay. By this time Clay was seventy-one years old and quite unpopular with his party because of his vacillating position in 1844 on the annexation of Texas, a position that had caused him to lose to the Democratic nominee, James K. Polk. The letter appeared in the Galveston *News* on May 5, 1848.

2.   Clay's correspondence in 1844 had caused him trouble politically, and he had not learned from this experience. The Allison letter made Taylor the favorite to earn the party's nomination.

3.   The Democratic Party convention had assembled in May. It chose Senator Lewis Cass of Michigan as the party's standard-bearer.

4.   William Wallace Smith Bliss, a West Point graduate and Taylor's aide since 1842, married the general's youngest daughter, Betty, when the war ended. Fort Bliss is named for him.

5.   Love was unable to attend the Whig convention. No Whigs from Texas attended, and the Louisiana delegation cast Texas' four votes. See "Love, James," *Handbook of Texas Online.*

6.   Senator Sam Houston identified himself as a Democrat and used his power of patronage to prevent Albert Sidney Johnston from securing a military command from 1846 to 1848.

7.   Brigadier General Gideon Pillow, former law partner of and campaign manager for James K. Polk in his successful bid for the presidency in 1844, was a political appointee in the military and won little respect from anyone. As second in command to General Winfield Scott, he began a campaign to discredit his superior officer by inserting unsigned letters in newspapers in the United States belittling Scott's abilities and promoting his own. Brevet Brigadier General William J. Worth and his friend and junior officer, Colonel James Duncan of the artillery, joined the cabal, each with his own private political ambition. On November 12, 1847, Scott issued orders charging certain officers with scandalous conduct against a superior within enemy territory. Eventually all charges except those against Pillow were dropped. Instead of calling for a court-martial, Polk personally selected a court of inquiry to ascertain the facts and perhaps dispose of the embarrassing matter. Pillow was acquitted, and on January 13, 1848, General Scott was recalled, and though some of the Cabinet suggested the command be given to Zachary Taylor, Polk chose a Democrat, General William O. Butler. See Justin H. Smith, *The War with Mexico* (New York: Macmillan, 1919), 2:185–88, 434–38.

8. Mexico City residents welcomed the occupation of their city in September 1847. They feared reprisal from Mexican guerrillas, especially after the Mexican government in February 1848 signed the Treaty of Guadalupe Hidalgo. U.S. troops withdrew by June 12.

9. Besides the well-known revolutions of 1848 in France, Prussia, Austria, Belgium, and Italy, the Young Ireland Party also staged a futile uprising against Great Britain.

10. Love is referring to Generals John A. Quitman, Joseph Lane, and George Cadwalader.

11. Johnston and his wife had Albert Sidney Jr., age three, and Hancock McClung, born late in 1847, living at China Grove. See "Johnston, Albert Sidney," *Handbook of Texas Online.*

James Love to Albert Sidney Johnston

Galveston
May 23 1848

Dear General,

I reached home this morning and expect to have the pleasure of seeing you next week.

I regret it was not in my power without more sacrifice than I am in condition to make to go to the convention in Philadelphia, as I believe I could have been of some service to the old General. Great intrigue is going on with Clay's friends on one side and Scott's on the other to defeat his nomination. I am, however, of the opinion that he will receive it, and if so, his election is certain. I have seen many letters lately from members of Congress and others from Washington and other points in the North, and all represent his prospects as increasing. The Yankee states, it is said, will first vote for Webster and then for Taylor. I believe, also, from what I learned a few days before I left N. Orleans, that Mr. Clay's warm partizans [sic] in Ky begin to despair his success, but it is likely that many of them will, from sheer malice, take another candidate altho they know that Genl Taylor is most available. The truth is that most of those who are political partizans for the sake of office, only have misgivings that the old Hero is not so easily managed as they could wish, and of all his avowals, they dislike that most which says he will administer the government without reference to party.

The last news from Mexico is favorable to peace, as you will see from the last "News" which I send.[1] There cannot, however, be any certain calculation based on this news, and we know not now whether an insurrection the next day did not disperse Congress. We hope, however, peace will be made. We have won glory enough. President Polk has demoralized the army by countencing [sic], if not setting on foot, intrigues by juniors against superior officers. If I had power, I would dismiss from service every officer that had engaged in politics.

The failure of Burnley & Co will ruin him & his Va *friends* made them liable for $150,000, and from all I learn about the matter, they will lose full $100,000. I look upon the whole transaction as one of unparalleled baseness. Burnley does not bear his reverse philosophically, in fact, altho his demeanor is not changed perceptibly to the casual observer, I have been with him a great deal and he has talked freely to me. His situation will be bad, and he has many things to meet that will give him no little annoyance. I really am sincerely sorry for him and tell him it is a great pity he had not, like me, been in trouble all his life, if so, this small mishap could not in the least disturb him. I will, when we meet, have talk enough to do you a month.

> Yr friend
> James Love
> Genl A. S. Johnston
> China Grove

1. The last known *Galveston News* issue from May was dated May 5, 1848, the next issue being October 13. News from Mexico in the May 5 issue was not optimistic about the Mexican congress ratifying the Treaty of Guadalupe Hidalgo.

James Love to Albert Sidney Johnston

> Galveston
> June 1st 1849

Dear General

The letter from Burnley that you will receive today came to me unsealed with directions to read it, and also, the one from Tod.[1] You will see from the contents that your friends have not been idle, and if you entertain the proposition made in Burnley's, you had better answer it and send down your answer by one of the boys who can leave Saturday morning and get here before the boat leaves.[2] It will meet Burnley in N. Orleans where, if it be *possible*, I shall go on Sunday, but this is not to be counted on as certain by any means. I am not capable in such a case to express an opinion that should in any degree control you. It seems to me, however, that at present, it might place you in position to command credit or money that would enable you to pay for your place, which in ten years would be fortune enough for your children.

The overflow on the Miss. has been so disastrous, and its tendency every year to increase, that I have the opinion that all lands situated as yours must soon be in demand for sugar; and in the end, I have never doubted that Texas will force Lou[isiana] in a great measure to abandon its culture.[3] It is also to be considered if it does not suit you to be Pay Master, whether you will accept Burnley's proposition for the purchase of half his plantation in Miss. He would, without doubt, sell you his half of the one here at $25,000, bearing an interest of six per cent, and I think you could, without doubt, pay $2,500 per year besides interest after the present year. All these things, however, are to be considered by you as a matter of interest only, and when your mind is made up, I am prepared to act for you accordingly.[4]

I have felt great regret that I could not come up as I contemplated. The Judge was absent; I could not leave until his return as matters of daily occurrence in the office could only be done by him or me.[5] He did not return until last Thursday. Court is in session and I, of course, employed all day. He says after next week, I may go up, and go, if I choose, on Sunday to N. Orleans as he has business there also, provided I can get a competent clerk, which is doubtful. I have recd no letter from Burnley in relation to the subject of our conversation. I wrote him to Louisville with directions to forward to Washington if he was not there, and I presume it was forwarded after he left Washington. Before yesterday, I had not received a line from him since he left, nor had Doswell in N O when here a few days since.[6]

In all this matter I want to promote your interest and if you have time to reflect sufficiently to make up your mind, you had better at once make up your mind in time for this boat. The bootmaker will be with you on Friday. The boy sent down might get here on Saturday night. You may rest assured that I will come up the first possible moment I am at liberty.

Sincerely yr friend
James Love

P.S. I think it probable Ballinger may receive the appointment of U.S. D. Atto, a very important office for him.[7] Will you write a letter for him to Genl Taylor? Speak of his qualifications, morals, and any matter that may be calculated to do him service as you may think he deserves.

> J L
> Genl A. S. Johnston
> Brazoria

1. Tod Robinson moved to California later that year.
2. Albert Triplett Burnley had just returned from Washington, D.C., where he conferred with President Taylor. They discussed establishing a pro-administration press, later named the *Republic,* with Burnley and Alexander C. Bullitt, formerly of the *New Orleans Picayune.* The Burnley letter Love mentions, dated May 21, 1849, reported that the president first offered to give Johnston a job as either a federal marshal in Texas or as the customs collector at the port of Galveston. When Burnley insisted on a military appointment, Taylor suggested the paymaster's job until a field command became available. Burnley's letter resides in the Johnston Papers at the Kentucky Historical Society and is paraphrased in Roland, *Albert Sidney Johnston,* 154. During this period Johnston spent his time unhappily rusticating on his plantation at China Grove. He was unable to improve the property because of financial difficulties.
3. Sugarcane was first grown in Texas in 1828. Its cultivation as a commercial crop did not begin until the 1840s, however, partly because cane does not do well on newly cleared land and partly because Texas planters did not invest in sugar until the bollworm infestations, which began in the late 1840s, threatened cotton profits.
4. Johnston bought Burnley's interest in China Grove in 1843. By 1848, Johnston was unable to make payments. Creditors began foreclosure procedures in 1849. See "Johnston, Albert Sidney," *Handbook of Texas Online.*
5. As a reward for his support of Zachary Taylor, Love became clerk of the United States District Court in early 1849. John Charles Watrous was the district judge.
6. James Temple Doswell left Texas about 1845 for New Orleans, but he still maintained an office with the Galveston firm of Doswell, Hill & Company.
7. William Pitt Ballinger did not receive this appointment as district attorney.

James Love to Albert Sidney Johnston

Galveston
June 11, 1849

Dear General

No mail has left this for N. Orleans since I recd your letter to Burnley.[1] He was in N. O. a few days since with fair prospects of arranging his pecuniary liabilities with the Bank. I will address your letter in envelope to Doswell who will forward it, should he [Burnley] have left. I feel every confidence that he will arrange matters that you can purchase his interest in Parker's Point on such terms as will enable you to pay for it with the profits of the place, and make a surplus every year that will enable you to liquidate the debt due on your place.[2] That our sugar lands will be in demand in a short time I have no doubt, more especially so if we open an inland communication with the Brazos which I believe will be done.[3]

The plank necessary to fill your order could not be had here. It is ordered from the Sabine and will be here tomorrow and sent up the first boat. The furnice [furnace] is a small matter unless it shall be the means of delay. The labor of two or three days is all the difference between a large and small kiln of brick, when once at work. In this, however, as in every other matter, I wish you to exercise your judgement as it [is] doubtless better so as you can better judge on the spot the state of things. Make the engagement with Vogle or any other person that may be necessary to do everything complete. I have written to Burnley to send over five negro fellows 1st July. I suppose he will do so, if not, I shall endeavor to hire as many hands and send them up. The carts will be here by the 1st of July. I am endeavoring to have the mules purchased in N. O. They are so much larger and better, that I hope I may succeed, if not, I will send out the 1st of August and have the best purchase made that I can.[4]

I am sorry the boots did not fit, altho somewhat *dandyish,* yet when worn a short time, there is less of *surplus toe.* They were tens, a respectable boot of nines will not fit you as you will see when you receive them. I sent the hat a size larger than you wrote for as I recollected there was little difference in the size of our heads.

Col Bell is here with fair prospects of being elected governor.[5] He speaks of you in very warm terms of friendship. The Democracy are somewhat in a quarrel here about Pease; how it will end, I know not. A portion of them, whether a majority or not I don't know, are very much opposed to him and *all* the Whigs.[6]

> Yr friend
> James Love
> Genl A. S. Johnston
> Parker's Point

1. With this letter to Burnley, Johnston reluctantly agreed to take the proffered position of Texas paymaster for the army. He received the appointment in October and formally accepted in December. He served as paymaster from 1850 to 1855, traveling a regular route to Forts McKavett, Croghan, Chadbourne, Phantom Hill, Belknap, Worth, Graham, and Gates every two months. See "Johnston, Albert Sidney," *Handbook of Texas Online.*

2. Johnston was unable to buy Burnley's interest.

3. Since a large sandbar blocked the mouth of the Brazos River planters upstream found it more economical to ship their produce overland to Houston than use a water route to Galveston. In order to capture this lucrative trade Galveston merchants in 1850 financed a canal from the Brazos River through the shallow waters of the inland bays to Galveston. This canal produced limited success at the time but later became an integral part of the present-day Intracoastal Waterway system.

4. The brick kiln, furnace, planking, mules, and the need for extra field hands strongly suggest that Johnston was going to process sugar at his plantation in late 1849. His major biographers fail to mention such activity, however.

5. Peter Hansborough Bell was born in 1812 in Spotsylvania County, Virginia. In 1836 he came to Texas and fought at the Battle of San Jacinto. He served in the Texas Army and the Texas Rangers. He served under Captain John Coffee Hays and was a member of the Somervell expedition of 1842. When the U.S.-Mexico War broke out he joined the U.S. Army and served with distinction at the Battle of Buena Vista. He was elected governor of Texas in August 1849, defeating the incumbent, George T. Wood, and he served until 1853. "Bell, Peter Hansborough," *Handbook of Texas Online* [accessed December 30, 2004].

6. Elisha M. Pease was born in 1812 in Enfield, Connecticut. He came to Texas in 1835 and soon became involved in the revolutionary movement. He fought

at the Battle of Gonzales and helped to write the constitution of the Republic of Texas. After annexation he represented Brazoria County in the first three legislatures and authored the state's first probate laws. Later in 1849 he ran for the state senate and lost to John B. Jones. Pease contested the election results. The state agreed with Pease, who took the oath of office for the senate seat on November 9, 1849, just four days after Jones had been sworn in to the same office. "Pease, Elisha Marshall," *Handbook of Texas Online* [accessed December 30, 2004].

James Love to Albert Sidney Johnston

Galveston
Aug 23rd 1849

Dear General

I believe that everything goes up this morning that has been ordered that is necessary now for the progress of work. The plank is ready at Lynchburg and I supposed Callahan will send for it next trip.[1] Some of the iron and steel is not of the precise kind ordered, but as near as could be had. If not suitable, it will answer for some time for other purposes.

I have engaged Sherwood who takes up with him two carpenters.[2] He will go up by the next boat, that is, he will be ready in a week, at which time I hope to be able to come up. Court has not yet adjourned, but I believed that in two days, the important business will be done so that I may leave. The carts have not arrived which is vexatious. The barrel of oil, lamps, etc, have not been sent. There is time for that.

Col Coffee is here. He is sued in my court for $100,000 and more.[3] He will not be in condition to purchase until after the decision of that suit. He told me he had tried to induce some of his neighbors to come out, but had failed. I will not let any opportunity pass of proposing your place for sale. You have one great trouble only; it will be hard if you cannot be relieved from that. I am sure I will do my best to effect it.

The elections in Tennessee have gone for the Democrats. They have the Governor, a majority in the Legislature, and eight members of Congress. There will be no change in Ky if Marshal is beaten. News have been received that he is beaten, altho it is not certain. Alabama remains as it was. So does N. Carolina. A gain probably in Indiana by one member. The only accounts received are telegraphic, [and] not a word about the election for the convention in Ky.[4]

I enclose you all the returns received for Texas up to last night. Howard's election certain.[5] You may add to Bell's vote fully 800 votes for counties not [yet] received and precincts not heard from, but the only vote received east of [the] Trinity is that from Houston County, the town of Crockett, which you will see gives Bell 86 & Wood 125.[6] This is so favorable to him and so unexpected, that it induces me to believe his election certain. If I can get any additional word this morning, I will send it with this. The boat has come down from Houston & will doubtless have some other returns.

The wine and the corn has been recd. Molly & Bet are with their mother at Velasco. Miss Lucy is here and [in] their name, begs that their best respects and best thanks be given to Master *Syd* for a present so acceptable. The wine looks clear as pure water; one bottle will be tested here, the other I will send to N. Orleans. I feel so confident at its value that I wish it be tasted by a more practiced taste than my own. If it be so, it must be named Griffana.[7]

The city as yet continues entirely healthy, our family never more so. I trust that yours are equally fortunate. Judge Wooly died of cholera in Lexington,[8] the mortality there has been great. No names given lately, [but] I am credibly informed as many as 40 a day have died there. One day, everyone attacked died.

My best respects to Mrs. Johnston. Mrs. Love and Mrs. Eve both send their best wishes to Mrs. Johnston & to you.

> Your friend
> James Love
> Genl A. S. Johnston
> China Grove

[note on outside] The mail is not opened. I learn that Wood recd 3 to 1 in Nacogdoches.

1. Love may be referring to John J. Callahan, who lived in Harris County. Lynchburg was a small village at the confluence of Buffalo Bayou and the San Jacinto River. A sawmill operated there since the early 1830s.
2. James P. Sherwood was a carpenter who built many of the early private and commercial structures in Galveston.

3. Thomas J. Coffee, formerly a resident of Mississippi, resided in Brazoria County in 1850. Confirming the lawsuit is impossible because early U.S. District Court records were destroyed.

4. In the 1849 election William Trousdale, a Democrat, defeated the Whig candidate, Neil S. Brown, for governor of Tennessee. John J. Crittenden, the Whig candidate, won the governorship in Kentucky in 1848, so Love must be referring to the congressional race won by Whig candidate Humphrey Marshall (1811–1872), grandson of the historian and senator of the same name. Telegraph lines did not reach Texas until 1854, so the news was relayed by ship from New Orleans.

5. Volney Erskine Howard was born in 1809 in Maine. He was a former editor of a Democratic newspaper at Vicksburg, Mississippi. In 1840 his newspaper opposed a banking bill backed by former governor Hiram G. Runnels. In a duel that ensued Howard was seriously injured. After his defeat in a bid for a congressional seat he left Mississippi and practiced law in New Orleans. In 1844 he moved to San Antonio, where he represented Bexar in the constitutional convention of 1845 and the first legislature. In 1849 Howard won the congressional seat for the western district of Texas. "Howard, Volney Erskine," *Handbook of Texas Online* [accessed December 30, 2004].

6. George T. Wood was born in 1795 in Randolph County, Georgia. He brought his family to Texas in 1839 and built a plantation on the Trinity River. He soon became involved in politics and attended the annexation convention of 1845. He fought with distinction in the U.S.-Mexico War, and in 1847 he ran for governor and won handily. As the incumbent governor, Wood, who lived in San Jacinto County, was popular in eastern Texas while Peter Hansborough Bell, who lived mainly in San Antonio, appealed to westerners. "Wood, George Tyler," *Handbook of Texas Online* [accessed December 30, 2004].

7. Molly and Betti Morris, ages seven and four, were visiting friends at Velasco, the town on the east bank of the Brazos River, near its mouth, with their mother, Mary Love Morris. Lucy Love, age eight, was at home in Galveston. Eliza Griffin Johnston must have made the wine. See "Morris, Richard," *Handbook of Texas Online*.

8. Aaron K. Wooley was born in 1800 in Springfield, New Jersey. A contemporary of Albert Sidney Johnston, Wooley graduated from West Point. In 1827 he settled in Lexington, Kentucky, and from 1832 to 1839 he served in the state legislature. Upon concluding his legislative term he joined the faculty of Transylvania College and served as the Lexington circuit court judge. He died of cholera on August 3, 1849.

James Love to Albert Sidney Johnston

Washington City [D.C.]
March 4 1855

Dear General

I have this moment returned from the Senate and have the satisfaction to inform you that you have recd the appointment of Colonel of one of the new regiments to be organized under the law of this session. I give this on the authority of Genl Rusk who told me in the Senate Chamber.[1] Ben McCulloch is the Major, the only two appointments from [the] civil life, as I learn, of field officers. Ben has used every means in his power to be the Col. I believe that Davis and Genl Rusk obtained it for you.[2] The last had some embarassment [sic] as to McCulloch who is on the spot, and Rusk, of course, did not openly interfere, altho I have reason to believe he did all he could to place you in a high position before the President and wrote him a letter speaking of you, your services, and qualifications in the highest possible terms. I do not suppose I had it in my power to do you much service, but I did my best. I think you should write to Rusk.

When I saw you last, you said that such an appointment was the object of your ambition, and I, of course, congratulate you upon it. Whether Mrs. Johnston agrees with you, I do not know, but I feel sure she will not oppose your wishes.

A bill has passed appropriating $7,750,000 to pay off the Texas creditors pro rata provided Texas assents to it & releases the U.S. from all claims, and provided the creditors release Texas & the U.S. from further liability. The bill rejects the Texas scaled rate and pays pro rata according to the bond. It will give to each, as I understand, about 70¢ on the dollar. Texas also gets back some $300,000 she has already paid out. It was a very difficult matter to obtain the passage of this bill. It is to be hoped that the people of Texas will accept it, as I am perfectly certain no other bill will, for many years, pass Congress on this subject. The President was inclined to veto it; Guthrie dead against it.[3]

The bill for the benefit of the Texas Navy was lost in the House through a committee of conference. This was not right.[4] Congress has just adjourned, 12 o'clk Sunday, up all night.

Sincerely your friend
Jas Love

I write this not knowing that another will write you soon. I believe you are Col of Dragoons & know you will be stationed in Texas.

1. On March 9, 1855, President Franklin Pierce, a Democrat, appointed Johnston colonel of the newly formed Second Cavalry Regiment. The Texas legislature and Governor Elisha M. Pease had recommended Johnston. Thomas Jefferson Rusk and Sam Houston were the senators from Texas.

2. "Davis" is Jefferson Davis, President Pierce's secretary of war and Albert Sidney Johnston's future commander-in-chief of the Confederate army.

3. Congress passed the act to reimburse creditors on February 28; the sum included $6.5 million due bondholders of the republic and $1.25 million for damages suffered from Indian depredations. The Texas legislature accepted the offer in February 1856, and the scaled rate was seventy-seven cents on the dollar. Secretary of the Treasury James Guthrie, of Kentucky, favored passage of the bill and persuaded President Pierce not to veto it.

4. The problem of integrating Texas naval officers into the U.S. Navy was finally resolved with the Texas officers receiving five years' pay, providing they relinquished claims to rank in the U.S. Navy, where promotions were based on seniority. Jealous U.S. Navy officers, mostly former colleagues of Edwin W. Moore, were still lieutenants. They did not want a single person to attain captain's rank ahead of them.

James Love to Albert Sidney Johnston

Washington [D.C.]
June 8th 1860

Dear General

Geo T. Howard (Major Howard or Sam Howard) is here again to obtain a renewal of his transportation contract.[1] He says your endorsement before was of great service and would be again. He has made a great deal of money out of the contract; this has produced competition. He said that he knew you had always & under all circumstances been his friend, but he felt some delicacy in writing to you. I advised him to write. The departments here are disposed favorably towards him as one that has been reliable.

Now I suppose, you will be ordered to Texas as every Texan here is impressing upon the govt that you are the only officer that understands the system of Indian warfare. I intend to see Mr. Floyd and say the same thing because I believe that in one year after your arrival, no frontier man will have a shudder when he closes his door at night, provided the govt places the means in your power. It is better for you if you go there to have a friend who will aid you to the extent of his powers than one who cares not whether you succeed or fail.[2]

In the political world, it takes one of more talent than I have even to conjecture the end of the present difficulties that surround us. An ultra Democrat told me yesterday that in times like these, the disruption of the Whig party, altho they were wrong, was a national calamity because they were honest. The chances are that the Black Republicans will elect their candidate, & if so, and Sumner's speech is taken as the confession of faith of that party, farewell to the Union. You may read it, it is the most infamous of any I ever heard or read. I felt at the moment as if I would be doing God a service to stab him to the heart, and you know I am not violent. Govr Wise told me yesterday, [that] if it were possible to unite Va, North Car, Ky & Tennessee on a common national platform, they could easily control these United States or whip them into obedience.[3] I believe it, but how can it be done[?] He further told me that if the Baltimore Convention nominated one candidate and the cotton states another, Bell would carry Va.[4]

I pray you to present me most kindly to Mrs. Johnston & the boys. I hope yet I may see them before I die.[5]

Sincerely yr friend

James Love

1. After participating in the Santa Fe and Somervell expeditions and escaping from prison in Puebla, George Thomas Howard settled in San Antonio, where he was sheriff of Bexar County from 1843 to 1845. After fighting with distinction in the U.S.-Mexico War, he joined Duncan C. Ogden in the freighting business in 1848, a venture that was interrupted between 1850 and 1855, when Howard served in the Department of Interior as superintendent of Indian agents. He returned to the freighting business and served as a private contractor for the U.S. Army in Texas. See "Howard, George Thomas," *Handbook of Texas Online*.

2. In the spring of 1857 the government ordered Johnston to put down the Mormon rebellion in Utah. In early 1859 he finally received orders for a long requested leave of absence and journeyed to San Francisco to embark on the

sea voyage home. After a separation of three years Johnston returned to his wife and children in Louisville, Kentucky. He left the Second Cavalry in the hands of his second in command, Robert E. Lee. Texans hoped he would return to take command of the Texas frontier. Love planned to visit Secretary of War John B. Floyd to secure such an appointment for his friend.

3. Henry Alexander Wise, a former Whig congressman who became a Democrat before the election of 1848, served as governor of Virginia from 1856 to 1860.

4. John Bell of Tennessee was the presidential candidate of the Constitutional Union Party. The party was a coalition of former Whig Party and American Party members who did not approve of the Republican candidate or platform.

5. It is unlikely that Love saw Eliza Griffin Johnston or the children before he died on June 12, 1874. In November 1860 Johnston received command of the Department of California, and in December 1860 the Johnstons left Kentucky for New York, where they boarded a steamer for Panama and California. When Texas seceded, Johnston resigned his commission and moved his family to Los Angeles, where they stayed at her brother's home. She remained in California after her husband's death at the Battle of Shiloh on April 6, 1862. See "Johnston, Albert Sidney," *Handbook of Texas Online*.

James Love to Albert Sidney Johnston

Washington [D.C.]
June 11th 1860

Dear General

I like to be the harbinger of good news to you. Howard & I have just telegraphed to you that you would be the successor of Genl Jesup.[1] I have Howard's authority for saying that the Cabinet is in session & you have no competition. I do not exagerate [sic] when I say that I believe every officer in Washington is for you. This will make you a full Brigadier. Genl Jesup, when he supposed he would die, recommended you some time since. I learn, too, from reliable authority, that Genl Scott, who is so old he does not expect to live long, has filed in the Department of War his statement that you or Totten ought to be Commander in Chief in the event of his death, that Totten is too old, & recommends you.[2]

If I can add anything that may end in your own good opinion of yourself, it will be to say that Ben McCullough [sic] told me yesterday [that] he was rejoiced that you, instead of him, was appointed Col of the Regmt [Second Cavalry], as close observation in Utah, he believed that you was the best man that could have been sent there, and that he yielded to you in everything in the line of your duty as you had nobly performed it.[3] Take care, old fellow, or you will be President after awhile, a station that no honest man in these desperate days ought to hold, but I dare say that Madam (my very good friend, I hope) would have no objection in the White House to receive the Congress & their ladies.

I write you in full confidence that what I say will occur, but you must remember that the best grounded hopes may be disappointed in any Cabinet in these United States of late years.

Very Sincerely Yours
James Love

1. Thomas Sidney Jesup (1788–1860) had served as the U.S. Army's quartermaster general from 1838, when he organized the department, until his death in 1860. However, Secretary of War John Floyd named Joseph E. Johnson to the post, not Albert Sidney Johnston. Perhaps there was confusion over their names.

2. In 1860 General Winfield Scott was seventy-four years old and served as commander-in-chief of the army. Joseph Gilbert Totten, chief engineer and inspector of the United States Military Academy since 1838, was seventy-two.

3. Benjamin "Ben" McCulloch had been appointed one of two commissioners by President James Buchanan in 1858 to conciliate the Mormons, to force an end to the rebellion, and urge their acceptance of federal control. McCulloch visited Johnston's headquarters in May 1858. "McCulloch, Benjamin," *Handbook of Texas Online* [accessed December 30, 2004].

James Love to Albert Sidney Johnston

Galveston
Oct 14, 1861

Dear Genl

I regretted very much I did not see you when in Houston.[1] I had arranged to meet you there but unfortunately was passing a few days at Col Hall's, his wife being at my house, and so I missed the opportunity.[2]

I am rejoiced that you have the command of the army in Ky & Mo.[3] We all believe it will add a bright hope in your history. We have so much confidence that none of us for a moment doubt your success. Those states must be redeemed tho' oceans of blood shall be shed. You will have Terry & 1,000 [of] the bravest and best men upon earth. They are the best horsemen, the best shots, & bravest hearts upon earth. They will be more available in your service than in Va. Terrible will be the fate of those who meet them.[4]

Genl Hebert's proclamation is rapidly bringing soldiers here.[5] We have 38 companies now. This week will make the number 5,000, besides 500 reliable men in Galveston. Even I have a minnie [sic] rifle on my shoulder occasionally. We have no divisions in Texas; nearly all are under arms. Sibley's Brigade is about full, destined for New Mexico, I believe.[6] In northern & eastern Texas, a large force is on the way to McCulloch who somewhat beat Cottle by his surprise at Oak Hill.[7] It will be a good warning & perhaps lessen his vanity of his prowess. He is undoubtedly brave, his name too, everywhere but in western Texas, will be of service. Enough of him.

It was reported by telegraph from Houston the other day that Houston was dead [but] it is not true. He is yet in danger from typhoid, but is said to be better.[8]

I do not look with any confidence on the success of our defence of Galveston. We have too much space liable to attack, our preparations too incomplete to insure success. We have brave men to fight the battle, but I still think if attacked with all available force, our beautiful city will be laid in ruins. So let it be. Houston's late letter has united all our people that will fight at all.[9] The timid have left us here; the women & children are either gone or ready to go [at] the first alarm. All that is best for us.

I recd a day or two since a letter from John Morris (his address is Clarksville, Ten.). He said he had received a letter from Howard inviting him to Nashville.[10] His wife, when he wrote, had been & was at the point of death [and] this had prevented him from raising a regmt as he designed in Ky. He asked me to write you recommending him to you for an appointment on your staff. I wrote him today that I would do so, altho I deemed it altogether unnecessary, that a letter from him to you direct was better than one from any third party. I need not speak to you of his honor or his gallantry or his sincere friendship for you. I wrote this only because he asked me. Richard's daughter, Betti,[11] is at school at the female academy in Nashville. She writes had a hearty cry because the Professor would not take her to see you.

The friendship of the father is inherited by his children for you. If again in Nashville, do see the girl. It would be a proud feather in her cap.

All success, honor, and glory to you is the fervid prayer of an Old friend

James Love

It stirs my heart to hear of our success in Ky. I have long had an earnest wish to be there. Miserable poverty arrests my destiny. As God may judge me hereafter, I would freely lay down my life if I could strike one good blow for the redemption of my native state from the hands of the traitors that have betrayed her. If I met John J. Crittenden in conflict, I would prefer killing him to a Comanche. For him there is no excuse. He does know as well as I do, it is a war of life or death to the slave states. He does know it is one of liberty or subjection. He willfully betrays his class, his friends, and his country. His great mind & intellect does not admit the possibility that his judgement controls him. I trust he may go down to his grave, as he will, with the scorn and contempt of all those who most loved and admired [him]. Let his funeral oration be pronounced by the Yankee and not one of the southern birth attend his grave.

J L

1. Johnston had passed through Houston in September on his way to New Orleans to join the Confederate States of America's army. At the end of his leave in November 1860, he had accepted command of the Department of the Pacific headquartered at San Francisco, and Johnston and his family had arrived there in January 1861. Johnston was in command only three months before he resigned his commission. His reasons for resigning included the fall of Fort Sumter in April, questions about his loyalty, and the secession of Texas from the Union. In June he left his pregnant wife at her brother's home in Los Angeles and started overland with Captain Alonzo Ridley's company of southerners who had been living in California. They followed the army road through Yuma, Tucson, and El Paso. Johnston was fifty-nine years old.

2. Warren D. C. Hall lived on Galveston Island twelve miles west of the city. He owned a site on Lake Como, a large inlet near a landmark known as the Three Trees. This was near the 1819 site of an Indian village visited by the pirate, Jean Laffite. Hall lived there from 1856 until his death in 1867. Earlier

he had sold China Grove to Johnston. See "Hall, Warren D. C.," *Handbook of Texas Online.*

3. Jefferson Davis, president of the Confederate States, ordered Johnston to take charge of Department Number Two, which included northern Alabama, Mississippi, Louisiana, Tennessee, Arkansas, and the border states of Kentucky and Missouri. The Confederate government expected these border states at any moment to secede. Federal forces occupied northern Kentucky in September while Confederate Lieutenant General Leonidas Polk took Columbus, Kentucky, on the Mississippi River. Davis ordered Johnston to establish a long defensive line through Kentucky, from the Cumberland Gap to Bowling Green, Kentucky.

4. On September 11, 1861, Frank B. Terry organized Terry's Texas Rangers, a cavalry unit, at Houston, Texas. They joined Johnston's forces at Bowling Green, Kentucky. On December 17, 1861, Terry was killed during the unit's first engagement at Woodsonville, Kentucky. Many others fell in April 1862 at Shiloh, when Albert Sidney Johnston also died from a gunshot wound.

5. General Paul Octave Hébert became commander of the Texas Military District on August 14, 1861. He superseded General Earl Van Doren.

6. Brigadier General Henry H. Sibley, a former U.S. Army officer at Taos, raised thirty companies of men at San Antonio in order to capture New Mexico from the Union army and claim the Southwest for the Confederacy. Sibley's New Mexico campaign ended in disaster in mid-1862.

7. In early 1861, when the Texas secession convention was still in session, Ben McCulloch raised five hundred volunteers and, without firing a shot, captured the federal installation at San Antonio. He traveled to Montgomery, Alabama, and received a commission as brigadier general in the Confederate army. He formed the Army of the West and on August 10, 1861, soundly defeated the Union army at Wilson's Creek, about ten miles south of Springfield, Missouri. Most Texans disagreed with Love's analysis of the Battle of Oak Hill. See "McCulloch, Benjamin," *Handbook of Texas Online.*

8. Biographers of Houston and his wife fail to mention a bout with typhoid fever in 1861. The "Hero of San Jacinto" lived at his residence at Cedar Point on upper Galveston Bay. On March 16, 1861, he relinquished the office of governor of Texas, which he won in 1859, after he refused to take the oath of loyalty to the Confederacy.

9. The enemies of the "Old Hero" charged that he had conspired to incite civil war in Texas. In an effort to dispel these rumors, on September 12 Houston addressed a letter to the editors of the *Galveston Civilian*, a longtime supporter

of Old Sam. He denied allegations that he sought federal office or that he ever considered accepting President Lincoln's offer of federal troops to sustain him in office. See Llerena Friend, *Sam Houston: The Great Designer* (Austin: University of Texas Press, 1954), 340–49.

10. John Morris was the brother of Love's deceased son-in-law, Richard Morris.

11. Elizabeth E. Morris was born in 1844, two months after her father's death.

CHRONOLOGICAL LIST
OF THE LETTERS

NUMBER	DATE	SENDER	RECIPIENT
1	April 28, 1838	James Love	Albert Sidney Johnston
2	February 10, 1839	"	"
3	February 11, 1839	"	"
4	February 17, 1839	"	"
5	February 25, 1839	Albert Triplett Burnley	"
6	February 27, 1839	James Love	"
7	March 6, 1839	Albert Triplett Burnley	"
8	March 9, 1839	James Love	"
9	April 12, 1839	Albert Triplett Burnley	"
10	ca. June 1839	Charles Harrison	"
11	June 23, 1839	James Love	"
12	June 26, 1839	"	"
13	July 11, 1839	"	"
14	July 20, 1839	"	"
15	July 24, 1839	"	"
16	July 24, 1839	"	"
17	July 25, 1839	J. B. Ransom	"
18	September 17, 1839	James Love	"
19	September 20, 1839	Albert Triplett Burnley	James Love
20	November 6, 1839	James Love	Albert Sidney Johnston
21	November 14, 1839	James Reily	"
22	November 1839	Mirabeau Buonaparte Lamar	"

23	November 18, 1839	James Love	"
24	December 29, 1839	"	"
25	January 5, 1840	Albert Sidney Johnston	Sam Houston
26	January 12, 1840	James Love	Albert Sidney Johnston
27	January 24, 1840	"	"
28	February 22, 1840	Thomas Jefferson Rusk	"
29	March 1, 1840	James Love	"
30	April 17, 1840	Hugh McLeod	"
31	April 20, 1840	Louis P. Cooke	"
32	May 20, 1840	James Love	"
33	June 4, 1840	Tod Robinson	"
34	June 4, 1840	James Love	"
35	June 27, 1840	"	"
36	July 7, 1840	"	"
37	July 22, 1840	"	"
38	July 23, 1840	Richard Morris	"
39	December 10, 1840	Alexander Parker Crittenden	"
40	January 17, 1841	Samuel Alexander Roberts	"
41	January 31, 1841	James Love	"
42	March 31, 1841	"	"
43	April 1, 1841	Samuel Alexander Roberts	"
44	April 22, 1841	James Love	"
45	May 16, 1841	"	"
46	June 21, 1841	Alexander Parker Crittenden	"
47	July 1, 1841	James Love	"
48	January 28, 1842	Albert Triplett Burnley	"
49	February 5, 1842	Alexander Parker Crittenden	"
50	February 12, 1842	Leslie Combs	"
51	February 14, 1842	Albert Triplett Burnley	"
52	March 31, 1842	James Love	"
53	April 9, 1842	"	"
54	April 9, 1842	Albert Triplett Burnley	"
55	August 29, 1842	James Love	"
56	August 31, 1842	Joseph A. Swett	"
57	September 13, 1842	James Love	"
58	September 22, 1842	"	"
59	September 27, 1842	Robert Holmes Chinn	"
60	April 10, 1843	James Love	"

61	April 22, 1843	"	"
62	May 7, 1843	"	"
63	May 15, 1843	"	"
64	May 22, 1843	"	"
65	June 1, 1843	"	"
66	June 26, 1843	"	"
67	August 18, 1843	"	"
68	November 6, 1843	"	"
69	May 10, 1844	"	"
70	May 29, 1844	"	"
71	June 10, 1844	"	"
72	July 29, 1844	"	"
73	August 20, 1844	"	"
74	October 29, 1844	"	"
75	December 13, 1844	James S. Mayfield	"
76	March 30, 1845	James Love	"
77	April 25, 1845	"	"
78	June 26, 1845	"	"
79	July 8, 1845	"	"
80	September 17, 1845	William Pitt Ballinger	"
Exchange of notes	August–September 1845	among Memucan Hunt, James S. Mayfield, and Edward Burleson	

#1	August 29, 1845	Memucan Hunt	James S. Mayfield
#2	August 30, 1845	James S. Mayfield	Memucan Hunt
#3	August 31, 1845	Memucan Hunt	James S. Mayfield
#4	September 16, 1845	"	"
#5	September 17, 1845	James S. Mayfield	Edward Burleson
#6	September 18, 1845	Edward Burleson	James S. Mayfield
#7	September 27, 1845	James S. Mayfield	Memucan Hunt
#8	September 25, 1845	Edward Burleson	James S. Mayfield

81	September 28, 1845	James Love	Albert Sidney Johnston
82	June 15, 1846	"	"
83	July 5, 1846	"	"
84	July 30, 1846	"	"
85	April 1, 1848	"	"

86	May 8, 1848	"	"
87	May 23, 1848	"	"
88	June 1, 1849	"	"
89	June 11, 1849	"	"
90	August 23, 1849	"	"
91	March 4, 1855	"	"
92	June 8, 1860	"	"
93	June 11, 1860	"	"
94	October 14, 1861	"	"

NOTES TO PREFACE
AND INTRODUCTIONS

Preface

1. Her major publications included *Samuel May Williams: Early Texas Entrepreneur* (College Station: Texas A&M University Press, 1976); *Anahuac in 1832: The Cradle of the Texas Revolution* (Anahuac, Tex.: Fort Anahuac Committee of the Chambers County Historical Commission, 1982); *Juan Davis Bradburn: A Reappraisal of the Mexican Commander at Anahuac* (College Station: Texas A&M University Press, 1982); *Anglo-American Women in Texas, 1820–1850* (Boston: American Press, 1982); *The History of Baytown* (Baytown, Tex.: Bay Area Heritage Society, 1986); *Chambers County: A Pictorial History* (Norfolk, Va.: Donning, 1988); *The Samuel May Williams Home: The Life and Neighborhood of an Early Galveston Entrepreneur* (Austin: Texas State Historical Association, 1992); *The Cartwrights of San Augustine: Three Generations of Agrarian Entrepreneurs in Nineteenth-Century Texas* (Austin: Texas State Historical Association, 1993); *The History of Galveston Bay Resource Utilization* (Webster, Tex.: Galveston Bay National Estuary Program, 1993); *Lorenzo de Zavala: The Pragmatic Idealist* (Fort Worth: Texas Christian University Press, 1996); *Historic Brazoria County: An Illustrated History* (San Antonio: Lammert Publications, 1998); and *McKinney Falls: The Ranch Home of Thomas F. McKinney, Pioneer Texas Entrepreneur* (Austin: Texas State Historical Association, 1998).

2. Margaret's thesis is titled, "The Development of Slave Codes in Texas, 1821–1845" (University of Houston, 1969).

3. Margaret L. Henson to Connie Griffith, July 20, 1970, Margaret Swett Henson Papers, Texas Collection, Rosenberg Library, Galveston, Tex., hereafter cited as Henson Papers.

4. Connie G. Griffith to Mrs. J. Scott Henson Jr., August 19, 1970, Henson Papers.

5. Ann S. Gwyn to Margaret Swett Henson, June 16, 1978, Henson Papers.

6. Margaret S. Henson to Ann S. Gwyn, September 4, 1979, Henson Papers.

7. Ibid., September 28, 1978, Henson Papers.

8. Tulane University Library to Ms. Margaret S. Henson, June 6, 1979, Henson Papers.

9. Lloyd G. Lyman to Margaret S. Henson, December 18, 1979, Henson Papers.

10. Donald Willett to Kathleen Duncan, February 19, 2001, Henson Papers.

11. Quotes are from Margaret Henson's original introduction to the letters.

12. "Florida War" refers to the Second Seminole War (1835–1842), in which American troops suffered a defeat. "Runaway depositers" refers to the Panic of 1837. On May 10, 1837, in New York City, every bank stopped payment in specie (gold and silver coinage). The Panic was followed by a five-year depression that included the failure of many banks and high unemployment across the nation.

13. Quoted from Jimmie Hicks, "Some Letters of James Love," *Register of the Kentucky Historical Society* 63, no. 2 (April 1965): 132–33. Hicks found letters from James Love in the John J. Crittenden Papers, Manuscript Division, Library of Congress. The letter quoted is dated March 3, 1839.

14. Quoted from Hicks, "Some Letters of James Love," 132–33, letter of March 3, 1839.

Editor's Introduction, by Donald E. Willett

1. Margaret's original manuscript is in the Henson Papers at the Texas Collection of the Rosenberg Library in Galveston, Texas.

2. See William Preston Johnston, *The Life of General Albert Sidney Johnston: Embracing His Services in the Armies of the United States, the Republic of Texas, and the Confederate States* (New York: D. Appleton, 1878), 119, 155; and Charles P. Roland, *Albert Sidney Johnston: Soldier of Three Republics* (Austin: University of Texas Press, 1964), 117, 151–55.

3. See James Love to Albert Sidney Johnston, October 14, 1861, in this volume (all subsequent citations to such letters to Johnston refer to letters in this volume unless stated otherwise).

4. Regarding the campaign in 1841, see Donald Willett, "James Love, Albert Sidney Johnston, and Presidential Ambition in Texas, 1838–1841," *Southwestern Historical Quarterly* 109 (April 2006): 530–46. Regarding the later election campaign in 1844, see James Love to Albert Sidney Johnston, April 10, 1843.

5. See James Love to Albert Sidney Johnston, June 11, 1860.

6. See Charles F. Adams, *Murder by the Bay: Historic Homicide in and about the City of San Francisco* (Sanger, Calif.: Quill Driver Books, 2005).

7. See Albert Sidney Johnston to Sam Houston, January 5, 1840.

8. See James Love to Albert Sidney Johnston, May 20, 1840.

9. Ibid, August 18, 1843.

10. See Memucan Hunt to James S. Mayfield, August 29, 1845; James S. Mayfield to Memucan Hunt, August 30, 1845; Memucan Hunt to James S. Mayfield, August 31, 1845; Memucan Hunt to James S. Mayfield, September 16, 1845; James S. Mayfield to Edward Burleson, September 17, 1845; Edward Burleson to James S. Mayfield, September 18, 1845; James S. Mayfield to Memucan Hunt, September 27, 1845; and Edward Burleson to James S. Mayfield, September 25, 1845.

11. See Love to Lamar, April 14, 1840, in Charles Adams Gulick et al., *The Papers of Mirabeau Buonaparte Lamar*, 6 vols. (Austin: Von Boeckmann-Jones, 1921–1927), 3:372, and cited in Jimmie Hicks, "Some Letters of James Love," *Register of the Kentucky Historical Society* 63 (April 1965): 123. In this letter to President Lamar, Love referred to Houston as "a bloated mass of corruption."

12. Hicks, "Some Letters of James Love," 134–35.

Introduction, by Margaret Swett Henson

1. James Love to Albert Sidney Johnston, January 12, 1840, Mrs. Mason Barrett Collection of Albert Sidney Johnston and William Preston Johnston Papers, Special Collections Division, Howard-Tilton Memorial Library, Tulane University, New Orleans, La.

2. Charles P. Roland, *Albert Sidney Johnston: Soldier of Three Republics* (Austin: University of Texas Press, 1964), 9, 11, 16–18, 46, 49–52, 54.

3. Ibid., 55–80.

4. Ibid., 82–122, 125–39, 141, 151–54, 168–70, 185–86, 236, 241–47, 252–53.

5. *Telegraph and Texas Register (Houston)*, January 7, February 11, 1846.

6. The only study of early Texas politics that speculates about the roots of the Whig Party is James Alex Baggett, "Origins of Early Texas Republican Party Leadership," *Journal of Southern History* 40 (August 1974): 441–54.

7. James Alex Baggett, "The Constitutional Union Party in Texas," *Southwestern Historical Quarterly* 82 (January 1979): 257 (lists Love as a Constitutional Unionist); *Galveston Daily News*, June 12, 1874 (Love's obituary).

8. Llerena B. Friend, *Sam Houston: The Great Designer* (Austin: University of Texas Press, 1954); Tom Henderson Wells, *Commodore Moore and the Texas Navy* (Austin: University of Texas Press, 1960); Marilyn McAdams Sibley, "Albert Sidney Johnston in Texas" (MA thesis, University of Houston, 1961); Marilyn McAdams Sibley, ed., "Letters from Sam Houston to Albert Sidney Johnston in West Texas: Austin to Fort Chadbourne, March, 1855," *West Texas Historical Association Yearbook* 40 (1964): 121–45; Roland, *Albert Sidney Johnston*. In the summer of 2003 I visited the Howard-Tilton Memorial Library at Tulane University and double-checked the letters contained in this book. I also checked the list of people who used the Albert Sidney Johnston papers. The last name on the list was Margaret Henson.

Introduction to Part I

1. See James Love to Albert Sidney Johnston, April 28, 1838.

2   The exception is Albert Sidney Johnston to Sam Houston, January 5, 1840.

INDEX

The initials ASJ indicate Albert Sidney Johnston and the initials JL indicate James Love.

ISBN-13: 978-1-60344-145-2
ISBN-10: 1-60344-145-X

SOVEREIGN WEALTH FUNDS
IN RESOURCE ECONOMIES

SOVEREIGN WEALTH FUNDS IN RESOURCE ECONOMIES

Institutional and Fiscal Foundations

Khalid Alsweilem
and Malan Rietveld

Columbia University Press
New York

Columbia University Press
Publishers Since 1893
New York   Chichester, West Sussex
cup.columbia.edu
Copyright © 2018 Columbia University Press
All rights reserved

Library of Congress Cataloging-in-Publication Data
Names: Alsweilem, Khalid, author. | Rietveld, Malan, author.
Title: Sovereign wealth funds in resource economies : institutional and
    fiscal foundations / Khalid Alsweilem and Malan Rietveld.
Description: New York : Columbia University Press, [2018] | Includes
    bibliographical references and index.
Identifiers: LCCN 2017006011 (print) | LCCN 2017022373 (ebook) | ISBN
    9780231544993 (ebook) | ISBN 9780231183543 (cloth : alk. paper)
Subjects: LCSH: Sovereign wealth funds. | Natural resources.
Classification: LCC HJ3801 (ebook) | LCC HJ3801 .A47 2018 (print) |
    DDC 333.7—dc23
LC record available at https://lccn.loc.gov/2017006011

∞

Columbia University Press books are printed on permanent
and durable acid-free paper.
Printed in the United States of America

Cover design: Lisa Hamm

Contents

Acknowledgments

THE AUTHORS would like to thank a number of colleagues for their invaluable contributions, support and generosity in sharing their thoughts on sovereign wealth funds, fiscal rules, and the management of resource revenues. We started working and researching these topics together in 2013 as part of a research project at Harvard's Kennedy School of Government. We thank Ricardo Hausmann and Eduardo Lora of the Center for International Development, as well as Gary Samore and Graham Allison of the Belfer Center for Science and International Affairs, for their assistance in facilitating our research and for encouraging the engagement of ideas and expertise between scholars from these two centers at Harvard's Kennedy School. We also wish to thank Katherine Tweedie and Hendrik du Toit of the Investment Institute at Investec for their support of that project, as well as Angela Cummine of the University of Oxford for her contribution to the research.

We have benefited enormously from talking to several renowned experts and practitioners in the field of sovereign wealth management, institutional economics, and the fiscal challenges around the management of resource revenues. In this regard, we thank in particular Gordon Clark, Martin Feldstein, Jeffrey Frankel, Scott Kalb, Leonardo Maugeri, Adrian Orr, Francisco Monaldi, Meghan O'Sullivan, Patrick Schena, Martin Skancke, Ng Kok Song, Ted Truman, John Tichotsky, Craig Richards, Adam Dixon, Ashby Monk, Samuel Wills, Håvard Halland, and Amadou Sy. Professor Stanley du Plessis, the dean of Commerce Faculty at the University of Stellenbosch, offered invaluable and detailed comment on large parts of this book.

Finally, we thank Bridget Flannery-McCoy and Ryan Groendyk, our editors at Columbia University Press, for supporting the publication of this book and for their effort in producing the final manuscript.

List of Tables and Figures

SOVEREIGN WEALTH FUNDS
IN RESOURCE ECONOMIES

Introduction

THIS BOOK OFFERS an analysis of sovereign wealth funds as institutions for managing resource revenues. The increasing appeal of sovereign wealth funds is reflected not only in the growth in assets under their collective management, a number for which credible estimates vary between $6.5 trillion and $8.3 trillion (as of the end of 2015), but also in the proliferation of new funds. While the origins of the oldest sovereign wealth funds can be traced back to the mid-nineteenth century, and many of the largest and most famous of these funds emerged in the Middle East during the oil boom of the late 1970s, a significant acceleration in the establishment of new funds has occurred over the past decade

Despite their increasing popularity and prominence, the literature has struggled to arrive at a satisfactory definition of sovereign wealth funds. This reflects, in part, the diversity of the sovereign wealth fund landscape, which features institutions with a variety of funding sources (notably, resource revenue windfalls and excess foreign-exchange reserves) and operational models, as well as a myriad of objectives, including macroeconomic stabilization, saving, income and wealth diversification, and the funding of developmental projects. In this book, the focus is firmly on sovereign wealth funds that are funded through natural resource revenues, although we argue for the importance of clearly distinguishing within this group between funds that serve different functions. These include macroeconomic and fiscal stabilization, income generation or savings, and, as is increasingly popular, a range of strategic and developmental functions (table I.1 provides a list of sovereign wealth funds, with their inception year and main source of funding).

Most important, we argue, the full—and most fruitful—embrace of the sovereign wealth fund model by resource economies requires more than the mere establishment of a portfolio of financial assets funded from resource revenues. Rather, the sovereign wealth fund model is best understood as a component of a credible, countercyclical rule-based fiscal framework for resource revenues. The sovereign wealth fund model contributes significantly to improved economic performance if it is embedded in a system of rules that govern the flow of resource revenues into the fund and the flow of assets and income out of the sovereign wealth funds (variously designed). Finally, the principal–agent relationships involved in the delegated authority around the management of sovereign investment institutions require another set of rules and institutions that are the subject of the final part of the book.

The case for the analysis of the sovereign wealth fund model through an institutional lens rests in part on the increasing support in the literature on the resource curse for the importance of institutional quality in determining whether resource wealth promotes or undermines economic growth in the long run. We argue in this book (in line with recent scholarship on the resource curse) that the understanding of "institutions" in this context remains rather general. A more fruitful line of inquiry focuses on the cluster of institutional and policy reforms located around the management of natural resources. We present the sovereign wealth fund model as exactly this kind of institution.

A dominant question in the debates around sovereign wealth funds— which is also reflected in the literature on the relationship between institutions, growth, and economic prosperity more generally—pertains to the sequencing of institutional reforms. One argument suggests that targeted institutional reforms are either unlikely to occur or succeed in the context of weak general institutions. An alternative view is more sympathetic to the potential contribution of incremental institutional

TABLE I.1
Sovereign wealth funds

Government	Fund authority	Inception	Source of funding
Texas	Texas Permanent School Fund	1844	Oil and public land
Texas	Permanent University Fund	1876	Public lands
New Mexico	Land Grant Permanent Fund	1898	Minerals and public land
Kuwait	Kuwait Investment Authority	1943	Oil
Kiribati	Revenue Equalization Reserve Fund	1946	Phosphates
Saudi Arabia	Public Investment Fund	1971	Oil
New Mexico	Severance Tax Permanent Fund	1973	Oil and minerals
Wyoming	Permanent Wyoming Mineral Trust Fund	1974	Minerals
Abu Dhabi	Abu Dhabi Investment Authority	1976	Oil
Alaska	Alaska Permanent Fund	1976	Oil
Alberta	Alberta Heritage Savings Trust Fund	1976	Oil
Montana	Montana Permanent Coal Trust Fund	1978	Minerals
Oman	State General Reserve Fund	1980	Oil
Brunei	Brunei Investment Agency	1983	Oil
Abu Dhabi	International Petroleum Investment Co.	1984	Oil
Alabama	Alabama Trust Fund	1984	Oil and gas
Louisiana	Louisiana Education Quality Trust Fund	1986	Oil
Malaysia	National Trust Fund	1988	Oil
Norway	Government Pension Fund-Global	1990	Oil
Botswana	Pula Fund	1996	Diamonds
Gabon	Sovereign Fund of the Gabonese Republic	1998	Oil
Venezuela	Macroeconomic Stabilization Fund	1998	Oil
Azerbaijan	State Oil Fund	1999	Oil
Iran	National Development Fund	1999	Oil
Algeria	Revenue Regulation Fund	2000	Oil
Kazakhstan	Kazakhstan National Fund	2000	Oil

TABLE I.1 (*continued*)

Government	Fund authority	Inception	Source of funding
Mexico	Oil Revenues Stabilization Fund	2000	Oil
Trinidad and Tobago	Heritage and Stabilization Fund	2000	Oil
Abu Dhabi	Mubadala Development Company	2002	Oil
Equatorial Guinea	Fund for Future Generations	2002	Oil
Qatar	Qatar Investment Authority	2003	Oil
Russia	National Welfare Fund	2004	Oil
Sao Tome and Principe	National Oil Account	2004	Oil
Ras Al Khaimah	RAK Investment Authority	2004	Oil
Venezuela	National Development Fund	2004	Oil
Timor Leste	Timor-Leste Petroleum Fund	2004	Oil and gas
Chile	Pension Reserve Fund	2006	Minerals
Bahrain	Mumtalakat Holding Company	2006	Oil
Dubai	Investment Corporation of Dubai	2006	Oil
Libya	Libyan Investment Authority	2006	Oil
Mauritania	National Fund for Hydro-carbon Reserves	2006	Oil
Malaysia	Terengganu State Sovereign Fund	2006	Oil and gas
Chile	Social and Economic Stabilization Fund	2007	Minerals
Papua New Guinea	Papua New Guinea Sovereign Wealth Fund	2011	Oil and gas
Mongolia	Fiscal Stability Fund	2011	Oil and minerals
Ghana	Ghana Heritage Fund	2011	Oil
Ghana	Ghana Stabilization Fund	2011	Oil
Nigeria	Nigerian Sovereign Investment Authority	2011	Oil
North Dakota	North Dakota Legacy Fund	2011	Oil
Australia	Western Australian Future Fund	2012	Minerals
Angola	Angola Sovereign Fund	2012	Oil
Kazakhstan	National Investment Corporation	2012	Oil

TABLE I.1 (*continued*)

Government	Fund authority	Inception	Source of funding
Leading non–resource-based sovereign wealth funds			
Singapore	Temasek Holdings	1974	Fiscal appropriation
Singapore	Government Investment Corporation	1981	Foreign exchange reserves
Malaysia	Khazanah Nasional	1993	Various public revenues
New Zealand	New Zealand Superannuation Fund	2003	Fiscal appropriation
Australia	Future Fund	2004	Fiscal appropriation
South Korea	Korea Investment Corporation	2004	Foreign exchange reserves
Vietnam	State Capital Investment Corporation	2006	Various public revenues
China	China Investment Corporation	2007	Foreign exchange reserves
Brazil	Sovereign Fund of Brazil	2008	Various public revenues

reform. Our inclination is toward the latter view. A generally supportive institutional context increases the prospects that sound institutions for the management of resource revenues will endure. However, sovereign wealth funds and fiscal rules for resource revenues can—and, we argue, have—contributed to ameliorating a number of the common afflictions associated with the resource curse. Often, what Rodrik (2008) describes as "second-best institutions" set in motion a series of positive policy and institutional reforms—and we suggest that sovereign wealth funds can do this in the case of resource revenues.

Also of relevance to this discussion is evidence that the emergence of resource revenue windfalls tend to be associated with a subsequent deterioration in institutional quality. This raises the possibility that targeted reforms around the management of resource revenues, particularly in new resource producers without an inherited institutional structure that has been shaped by a long history of resource production, can contribute to avoiding a dynamic that might otherwise result in a further deterioration of institutions. Finally, it is far from the case that economies with otherwise sound institutions are in some way inoculated from the emergence of weak institutions for the management of resource revenues. This book identifies aspects of the institutional arrangements for sovereign wealth funds and resource revenues in locations such as Norway, Alberta, Chile, Alaska, and Wyoming that require reform—or at least have room for improvement.

As with most institutions, sovereign wealth funds are not "one-size-fits-all" solutions. Yet we show in this book that there is significant scope for tailoring sovereign wealth funds' functions and their consequent saving and spending policies to meet local requirements, based on the economic (and political) realities. Criticisms of sovereign wealth funds underestimate the degree of nuance and variation in the sovereign wealth fund model, as well as the extent to which resource-based sovereign wealth funds are designed to directly and indirectly address common afflictions associated with the resource curse—particularly those of an institutional or political economy nature. In line with Rodrik's notion of "second-best institutions" and the idea that sovereign wealth fund models themselves evolve and mature over time, we discuss fiscal rules and investment approaches that may be considered suboptimal but have the advantage of simplicity and can serve as intermediate steps toward more complex institutional arrangements.

The fledgling academic literature on sovereign wealth funds has already underlined the critical importance of institutional arrangements (or "governance")—notably, spending and savings rules, mechanisms for transparency and accountability, and rule-based investment strategies—to the effectiveness of sovereign wealth funds (see, for example, Bacon and Tordo, 2006; Humphreys and Sandbu, 2007; Das et al., 2009; Monk, 2009; Ang, 2010; and Frankel, 2012). We devote significant attention to these issues in the book, and argue in particular that the institutional arrangements or governance of fiscal rules, as distinct from their design, are often overlooked in discussions about sovereign wealth funds. Even the best-designed rule-based fiscal framework for resource revenues and sovereign wealth funds can be undermined by weak institutional arrangements.

Our discussion of sovereign wealth funds' fiscal rules reveals a wide range of institutional mechanisms through which this is achieved, ranging from constitutional mandates to legislative statues to presidential decrees to elements of custom (or informal institutions). Three models that have achieved some measure of success and durability provide valuable insights into the specification and governance of fiscal rules for managing resource revenues and sovereign wealth fund assets and income. Norway emerges as an example where the fiscal rule is governed through consensus and custom, Chile as one that champions the contributions of technocratic expertise, and the American state endowment model as one in which the fiscal rule is hardwired into the Constitution (albeit in an incomplete manner). We regard these three models as viable conceptual frameworks that can be tailored to fit with local requirements and realities.

The final section of the book focuses on the institutional aspects of the sovereign wealth fund model that pertain to the investment function, particularly various layers of delegated investment authority typically involved in investments of sovereign wealth funds. The section considers why and how to achieve a degree of operational independence from government for an investment management authority, how to clarify the roles and responsibilities of the various principals and agents involved in the delegated-authority model of investment, and how the governance and performance of the investment authority is strengthened by an embrace of rule-based investment policies.

Having made the case for operational independence in the management of long-term sovereign investment portfolios, the institutional question considered in this section deals with a familiar tension in public policy: balancing the desire for assigning operational independence to a technocratic institution (in this case, the investment authority of the sovereign wealth fund) with a degree of government control and oversight of such delegated authority. While the case for operational independence rests on compelling foundations in the case of sovereign wealth funds—including improved investment performance, addressing fears of a regulatory backlash from recipient countries, a desire to escape from public-sector pay scales to attract and cultivate internal human capital, and the political ring fencing of assets—the analysis indicates that independence is typically (and appropriately) a matter of degree. Independence is never absolute, and the exercise of discretionary powers by delegated sovereign investment authorities should be constrained by clearly articulated rules and demands for transparency and accountability.

This book argues that sovereign wealth funds can play a highly constructive role in the management of resource revenues. We reach this conclusion with the important caveat that the sovereign wealth fund model requires these funds to be embedded in a rule-based fiscal framework and institutional framework. The potential contribution of sovereign wealth funds alone to addressing or avoiding the resource curse should not be overstated. Nevertheless, when accompanied by well-designed and governed fiscal rules, as well as a clear institutional structure for the management of agency relationships that arise from delegated authority, the sovereign wealth fund model is a promising targeted institutional response to the widely understood problems of resource economies.

An Institutional Perspective on Resource Economies and the Role of Sovereign Wealth Funds

CHAPTER ONE

The Most Disadvantageous Lottery in the World

Historic Controversies Around Natural Resources and Economic Prosperity

THE RELATIONSHIP between natural resource wealth and economic prosperity has confounded economists for centuries. At first glance, the idea that an abundance of resources bestow anything other than benefits on their owners is counterintuitive. Natural resources are an essential factor of production, and their scarcity value might therefore be expected to greatly advantage countries and regions in which they are located. These advantages relate both to international trade and fiscal affairs, notably the revenue-generating capacity of resource-rich states. While the existence of a resource curse has gained increasing support in the postwar period, its counterintuitive nature is reflected by associated terms such as the "paradox of plenty" (Karl, 1997).

Scholarship around the resource curse has proliferated in recent decades, but this literature is but the latest in a centuries-old debate in economics that dates back at least as far as the very origins of the discipline. The Physiocrats and mercantilists of the eighteenth century agreed on little, but shared a basic understanding of economic prosperity that was rooted in the accumulation of natural wealth. Adam

Smith disagreed. In his view, the wealth of a nation derived from productivity-enhancing specialization with cooperation through markets. He argued that an undue obsession with resources and commodity accumulation undermines the development of a "commercial society," in which lasting economic prosperity resulted from specialized trade, manufacturing, and the efficient division of labor.

Intellectual traditions do not emerge in a historical vacuum, but are rather embedded in prevailing economic realities. Four major economic epochs signified major shifts in the history of economic thought around resource wealth: the Early Modern Era, the aftermath of the Industrial Revolution, the postwar period in the mid-twentieth century, and the aftermath of the oil shocks in the late 1970s. The latter culminated in the formal articulation of the resource-curse hypothesis. This literature and the vast theoretical and empirical literature that has accompanied its expansion are the focus of this chapter, as they frame and contextualize the central arguments advanced in this book. To underline the deep intellectual origins of the debate, however, we turn first to historical antecedents of the resource curse.

SUCH STRANGE DELUSIONS: HISTORICAL ANTECEDENTS TO THE RESOURCE CURSE

In intellectual traditions that predate the Industrial Revolution, natural wealth was synonymous with agricultural productivity and prowess. Agrarian productivity was regarded as obviously conducive—and indeed tantamount—to economic and social well-being. The Physiocrats, the first *économistes*, who influenced Adam Smith and the emergence of Enlightenment political economy, most famously regarded agricultural prowess as the cornerstone of economic progress. In most other leading philosophies of the Enlightenment, however, natural wealth assumed a wider meaning beyond agriculture.

Mercantilists and the Enlightenment

The moral philosophers of the Scottish Enlightenment, notably David Hume and Adam Smith, held a more qualified view of natural resources in relation to economic wealth than that of the Physiocrats and the bullionist tradition of mercantilism. Indeed, the Scottish Enlightenment political economists' opposition to the bullionist obsession with rare metals as the measure of wealth was a central criticism of that particular strand of mercantilist logic. While acknowledging the motivational power of the quest for silver and gold to the Iberian colonial expansion during the Age of Discovery, and the extent to which the promise of bountiful raw materials underwrote successive European nations' expansion into the New World, Smith was deeply critical of the irrationality that accompanied such pursuits.

"The same passion which has suggested to so many people the absurd idea of the philosopher's stone, has suggested to others the equally absurd one of immense rich mines of gold and silver," Smith ([1776] 1981:563) argued. Referring to Sir Walter Raleigh's fixation with the mythical city of El Dorado, Smith argued that so strong was the lure of resource riches, that "even wise men are not always exempt from such strange delusions." Smith was equally skeptical about the microeconomics of mining. No enterprise was "more perfectly ruinous than the search after new silver and gold mines"—indeed, for Smith, mining constituted "the most disadvantageous lottery in the world [in which] the common price of a ticket is the whole fortune of a very rich man" (Smith [1776] 1981:562).

The most prescient of Smith's insights on the subject of natural resources, however, pertain to the more general level at which resource wealth creates distractions and incentives that lead economic actors away from more productive endeavors. Smith's argument in this regard is an early articulation of "rent-seeking," an argument that has been applied with increasing frequency to the case of resource economies (as discussed in chapter 2). Even when observers understood full well that "the wealth of a country consists, not in its gold and silver only, but in its lands, houses, and consumable goods of all different kinds," once confronted with resource abundance, "the lands, houses, and consumable goods, seem to slip out of their memory; and the strain of their argument frequently supposes that all wealth consists in gold and silver, and that to multiply those metals is the great object of national industry and commerce" (Smith [1776] 1981:429). Late twentieth-century scholars would observe a similarly slippery grasp of economic beliefs in the face of large resource discoveries.

By the age of the industrial revolutions in Britain, Western Europe, and the United States, the concept of natural wealth shifted toward the direct uses of commodities, such as timber, coal, steel, cotton, copper, and rubber, in industrial processes. Both contemporary observers and subsequent scholarship has identified access to proximate natural resources as an unambiguous boon, and possibility a prerequisite, for economic development and industrialization in that era. The relative ease with which Western European nations accessed supplies of coal, steel, timber, and peat from domestic deposits, as well as peripheral geographies, such as the Baltics and their colonies, has been advanced by some scholars as a—and sometimes *the*—critical factor in determining why the Industrial Revolution occurred there rather than in other comparatively advanced societies of the period (for a recent articulation of this view, see Pomeranz, 2000; however, the argument dates back to Jevons, 1865).[1]

Escaping Backwardness: Natural Resources in Postwar Development Economics

The increase in the global trade in commodities in the late nineteenth century reduced the relevance of the geographic proximity to resources that prevailed during the Industrial Revolution. In the United States, trade in agricultural goods and industrial metals increasingly migrated toward formal exchanges, such as the Chicago Board of Trade and the New York Mercantile Exchange, to facilitate more efficient price discovery, risk management (including through the trading of commodity futures and options), and information sharing. Gradually, this mode of trade and market exchange became the norm across agricultural and nonagricultural commodities. On the demand side, rapid economic growth and global trade supported the expansion of commodities trading and production. The inter- and postwar periods of the twentieth century heralded significant growth in the demand for and trade in natural resources, driven by energy- and resource-intensive growth patterns, the rise in automobile usage, and postwar reconstruction efforts. Persistent breakthroughs in transportation (notably, the use of "super tankers," capable of transporting more than three million barrels of oil) and physical and financial infrastructure further promoted international commodities trading, as well as the globalization of supply and demand dynamics for most natural resources (World Trade Organization, 2010).

Of particular importance to the evolution of the literature on resources and economic development is the emergence during this period of a large number of developing countries as global suppliers of primary products and traded commodities. Consequently, natural resources featured prominently in the grand theories of economic development that emerged after World War II. The emergent field of "development economics" viewed the rapid modernization of poor countries as a distinct challenge and intellectual project, providing a fertile breeding ground for scholarship on the role of natural resources in the economic development of comparatively poor countries.

All the important contributors of this period—Walt Rostow, Albert Hirschman, Hans Singer, Raul Prebisch, Paul Rosenstein-Rodan, Ragnar Nurkse, and Arthur Lewis—addressed the role of the natural resource sector in relation to broader economic development and modernization. While offering contrasting visions of the means and pace through which modernization could be achieved, these theories had in common the belief that the key to economic development lay in moving away from the "backward" economic undertaking of extracting primary goods toward modern industry, characterized by higher skills, productivity, and real wages. Most of these modern development theories—still under the impression of the role of coal, steel, and other industrial resources in the industrialization of Europe and, subsequently, the United States—regarded abundant resources as a catalyst for economic development. Although resource wealth was not viewed as the key to economic prosperity, it was widely regarded as an advantageous starting point.

Rostow's influential stages-of-growth theory (1960), with its focus on investment and capital accumulation, viewed the extraction of primary goods as the most basic—or, to use his famous term, "backward"—modes of economic production. That said, resource abundance was regarded as critical to mobilizing the requisite savings, investment, and capital formation to advance through predetermined stages of economic development. Indeed, the often large rents and windfalls generated by resource wealth opened up the seductive possibility of "leapfrogging" certain stages of development in Rostow's view. Arthur Lewis's similarly influential two-sector model of economic development was built on the assumption that economic development required the release of surplus labor from the primary modes of production and its reallocation toward an urban, capitalist one (Lewis, 1954, 1955). In Lewis's view, this process would only be accelerated by an abundance of natural resources—indeed, he attempted to show how poor countries could still industrialize even when they were relatively resource poor. Following Rostow, Lewis believed an abundance of natural resources to be a means through which to accelerate an economic transition to modern, industrial capitalism.

A more dirigiste view of how natural resources should advance the goal of rapid economic development and modernization was contained in Rosenstein-Rodan's (1943) earlier "big push" model, and further expanded on by Nurkse (1961). To achieve "balanced growth," the big push involved state-directed investments funded by resource windfalls into other sectors of the economy that remained underdeveloped. Rosenstein-Rodan and Nurske argued that in the absence of massive, state-led investment, developing countries would get stuck in a low-equilibrium trap based on specialization in resource production. As with Rostow and Lewis, models in the big push tradition did not regard an abundance of resources as in any way detrimental to the process of modernization, for it merely strengthened the means to achieve balanced growth and modernization, and potentially sped up this process.

Albert Hirschman's (1958) emphasis on the "forward and backward linkages" between economic activities contained a more qualified view of the role of the resources sector in economic development. In his view, certain primary subsectors, such as agriculture, had relatively few linkages and were therefore not conducive to sustained development, whereas others, such as steel, were characterized by a myriad of such linkages, which could help spur development and growth. It is important to note that Hirschman, who cautioned against heavy-handed state planning and generally favored gradual economic reform and change, opposed Rosenstein-Rodan and Nurske's "big push" approach. Hirschman was more comfortable with what he regarded as inevitable periods of "unbalanced growth" and the piecemeal realization of forward and backward linkages that may stem from the extraction of natural resources. The distinction between Hirschman and the big push tradition with respect to the pace of economic transformation (and diversification)—as well as the state's role in this process, particularly through large-scale investments of resource rents—has remained a pervasive theme in resource-curse literature. This tension is one to which this book will return on a number of occasions, not least in the context of current debates around the scope and mandate of sovereign wealth funds.

The majority of postwar development economists, therefore, held a largely positive view of natural resources in relation to economic development, albeit as a potential catalyst for modernization and industrialization. For this reason, a broad consensus emerged in the 1950s that the comparatively resource-rich developing countries of Africa and Latin America faced better growth prospects and would achieve faster rates of economic convergence with the advanced economies than their counterparts in Asia (Easterly, 2001).

The most notable exception to this view was found in the work of Hans Singer and Raul Prebisch, two leading advocates of export-led industrialization, and more specifically, import substitution, as a means to achieve it and avoid the entrenchment of the dependent relationship developing countries had with their developed counterparts. Working independently of each other, Prebisch ([1949] 1950) and Singer (1950) observed that developing countries primarily exported natural resources (or "primary goods"). What later came to be known as the "Singer-Prebisch thesis" held that the terms of trade for primary-goods exporters would decline relative to those exporting manufactured goods. This argument was based more on the observation of (selected) historic price movements than theory: the most detailed theoretical argument for the Singer-Prebisch thesis was that the demand for manufactured goods was subject to higher income elasticity than that for primary products. As global incomes rose, the Singer-Prebisch hypothesis posited, the demand for manufactured goods would increase more rapidly than that for primary products, resulting in a long-run price differential that favored the producers of the former. The Singer-Prebisch thesis was, therefore, built around a testable hypothesis: the predicted secular decline in commodity prices relative to other goods and services—and this is where the hypothesis has run into some difficulty since its original formulation. Table 1.1 shows the dates, magnitude, and length of historic commodity cycles. The empirical evidence on long-term trends in global commodity prices is clearly dependent on the specification of the sample period. There is little evidence of the secular decline Singer and Prebisch predicted, however.

Although the once popular notion of general economic "super cycles" (often referred to as Kondratiev cycles after their pioneer, the Russian economist Nikolai Kondratiev) has been discredited, there is some evidence that the argument may remain relevant to commodity

TABLE 1.1
Historic commodity super cycles, 1788–2015

Start date	End date	Price-index change (nominal)	Length of cycle	Index
March 1788	December 1814	135%	26 years 8 months	Warren and Pearson
December 1814	February 1843	−62%	28 years 2 months	Warren and Pearson
February 1843	August 1864	208%	21 years 7 months	Warren and Pearson
August 1864	June 1896	−70%	31 years 8 months	Warren and Pearson
June 1896	April 1920	218%	24 years 0 months	Warren and Pearson
April 1920	June 1932	−80%	12 years 2 Months	CRB monthly
June 1932	January 1951	689%	18 years 6 months	CRB monthly
January 1951	July 1968	−40%	16 years 6 months	CRB monthly
July 1968	October 1980	215%	12 years 3 months	CRB monthly
October 1980	October 2001	−31%	21 years 0 months	CRB monthly
October 2001	June 2011	145%	9 years 8 months	Spot Index (Bloomberg)
June 2011	—	−48% (as of January 2016)	—	Spot Index (Bloomberg)

NOTES: Based on U.S. commodity price cycle, with contraction cycles in bold.
   CRB = Commodities Research Bureau.
SOURCES: Warren and Pearson (1933), Commodities Research Bureau, and Bloomberg.

prices. The demand for industrial commodities may be driven by slow-moving, structural dynamics in the global economy, such as the post-war reconstruction of Europe and the industrialization of China since the late 1970s, while the supply response to positive price incentives takes many years to reach the market (Erten and Ocampo, 2013). However, the detection of clear trends in commodity prices and cycles are fraught with problems of sample-period selection, as Frankel notes:

Studies written after the commodity price increases of the 1970s found an upward trend, but those written after the 1980s found a downward trend, even when both kinds of studies went back to the early 20th century. No doubt when studies using data through 2011 are completed some will again find a positive long run trend. This phenomenon is less surprising than it sounds. Real commodity prices undergo large cycles around a trend, each lasting twenty years or more. As a consequence of the cyclical fluctuations, estimates of the long-term trend are very sensitive to the precise time period studied. (Frankel, 2012:24)

While the empirical evidence has, therefore, not been supportive of the central predictions of the Singer-Prebisch thesis, it remains a noteworthy chapter in the historiography. Most fundamentally, it was the first in a long succession of arguments that emerged in the second half of the twenty-first century that supported the notion that resource wealth may be damaging to long-run economic prosperity.[2] The Singer-Prebisch worldview regarded natural resources not as a valuable geological gift in aid of modern capitalist development, but rather as a developmental challenge that had to be actively counteracted through government policies.

The sharp—and surprising, from the perspective of 1950s development economics—divergence in economic fortunes of developing countries since the 1960s has sustained interest in the possible developmental challenges associated with resource wealth. Contrary to the predictions of development economists, it was a succession of comparatively resource-poor Asian countries, rather than the more resource-rich countries of the Middle East, Latin America, and Africa, that emerged as the undoubted "growth champions" of the second half of the twentieth century (see figure 1.1).

Given that this divergence occurred over a long sample period, which included significant up- and downswings in both the global commodity cycle and in the prices of individual commodities, it is clear that a secular decline in the relative price of commodities, as suggested by the Singer-Prebisch thesis, cannot serve as an explanation for the relative underperformance of commodity-rich economies. Consequently, "studies based on the post-war experience have argued that the curse of natural resources is a demonstrable empirical fact, *even after controlling for trends in commodity prices*" (Sachs and Warner, 2001:828; emphasis in the original). The remainder of this chapter discusses the evolution of the large literature on the resource curse in the aftermath of the oil price shocks of the late 1970s.

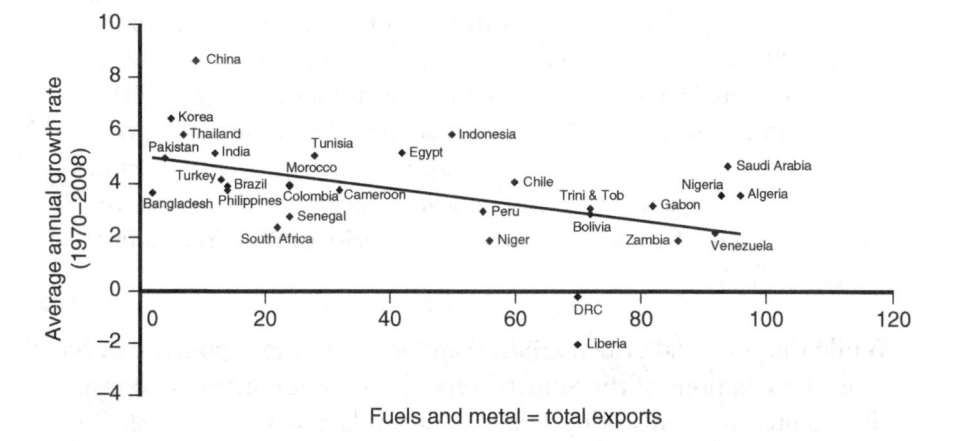

Figure 1.1 Developing country growth and resource exports, 1970–2008. Sources: Penn World Tables and World Development Indicators.

The Emergence of Dutch Disease

The 1970s oil price shocks provided the impetus for what would become a flood of new scholarship on the economics of resource wealth and windfalls. The context was the apparent difficulties encountered by a majority of oil-exporting countries in terms of capturing the full extent of anticipated benefits of this hugely positive terms-of-trade and fiscal shock, and particularly their painful adjustment to the aftermath of the boom, once commodity prices collapsed in the 1980s. The most enduringly influential work from this period would subsequently become known as the "Dutch disease" theory. Corden and Neary (1982) are often credited with the seminal paper on the subject, but in fact they consolidated a rapidly expanding theoretical literature, with critical earlier contributions by Van Wijnbergen (1981, 1984a, 1984b), Buiter and Purvis (1981), and Bruno and Sachs (1982).[3] The Dutch disease theory, which has seen a number of important refinements and adaptations, remains largely (and in most versions of the argument, solely) based on purely "economic" dynamics—that is, a theory that explains the underperformance of resource-rich countries in terms of a disequilibrium or market failure, without assigning a critical role to politics and institutions.

There are a number of subtle variations and elaborations within the Dutch disease tradition, but the common diagnosis of the disease involves the following symptoms: First, the discovery of a resource endowment results in a large windfall of public or private revenues, or both, and a surge in total investment and spending in the domestic economy. Second, a resultant shift in the allocation of capital and labor away from the traded-goods sector (where prices are set on the international market) occurs due to rising prices and more attractive returns in the nontradable commodities, goods, and services. Third, nominal and real frictions between the traded and nontraded sectors prevent them from clearing simultaneously, resulting in a real appreciation of the currency as prices rise in the nontradable sector (relative to the internationally cleared tradable sector). Ultimately, these dynamics are self-reinforcing, and if they continue long enough, a country either destroys its existing tradable manufacturing sector or fails to develop one in the first place.

Economists have questioned whether this sequence of events necessarily constitutes a disease. Why, for example, can a country not specialize in the production and export of natural resources, while allowing its resource earnings to strengthen the exchange rate and allow for cheap manufacturing imports from abroad, while also developing a thriving domestic service and nontraded goods sector? Is this not the exploitation of resource-rich countries' comparative advantage? The Dutch disease literature suggests a number of problems with this scenario. First, the short-term price volatility due to short-term exogenous shocks (such as adverse weather, conflict, and other supply disruptions), medium-term cyclicality, and long-term uncertainty of commodity prices and production volumes (due to geological factors and changing technologies) all make a reliance on commodity exports to pay for imports inherently destabilizing. The specialize-and-trade strategy requires stability and a steady stream of earnings from the export of resources to finance its imports. In practice, commodity prices and export earnings are extremely volatile, causing significant balance-of-payments shocks and painful adjustments, absent stabilizing policies and institutions.[4]

Most Dutch disease models further attribute positive externalities and specific developmental benefits to the manufacturing or tradable sector (much like the previously discussed growth models of development economists of 1950s). These models typically include the assumption that primary sectors have less scope for productivity growth, and less potential for increasing returns to scale than the manufacturing or traded sector (Van Wijnbergen, 1984a, 1984b; Krugman, 1987; Matsuyama, 1992). Similarly, it is often proposed that the manufacturing sector is more labor intensive (particularly during the early stages of development) than the primary sectors, implying the desirability of manufacturing for promoting full employment. "The Dutch disease can be a real disease—and a source of chronic slow growth if there is something special about the sources of growth in manufacturing," Sachs and Warner (1997) note.[5] In short, an abundance of natural resources can therefore be a curse if the manufacturing sector is modeled under non-neoclassical assumptions. While theories of the Dutch disease predate the official coining of the term the "resource curse," it remains a popular and influential explanation for the latter. The remainder of this chapter focuses on the emergence and evolution of this literature.

THE RESOURCE-CURSE HYPOTHESIS: WEAK- AND STRONG-FORM FORMULATIONS

Theoretical work on the Dutch disease continued to expand over the course of the 1980s in response to the dramatic rise in oil prices at the end of the preceding decade. However, the subsequent collapse in oil prices—during which oil markets remained vastly oversupplied for more than a decade and prices slumped to below ten dollars per barrel in the mid-1980s—provided further impetus for more general scholarship on the long-run relationship between resources and economic development. By the late-1980s and early-1990s, the adverse consequences of the poor management of resource booms and busts for economic performance were sufficiently apparent that the resource-curse hypothesis was formulated and increasingly accepted as received wisdom.[6]

There are different ways in which to interpret the resource-curse hypothesis. In its simplest articulation, the hypothesis holds that a large endowment of natural resources can be detrimental to economic prosperity, particularly in the long run. The strong-form version suggests that an abundance of natural resources results in lower growth than what would have been observed in the absence of such resources, either for a specific country or on average across countries. The weak form holds that although growth might still be positive in resource-abundant economies, it is often suboptimal—for example, lower than that predicted by a standard economic growth model. If we think about the difference between the strong- and weak-form versions of the resource-curse hypothesis in terms of a typical growth regression, the strong form would predict that the coefficient on an explanatory variable capturing resource wealth is negative, whereas the weak form merely suggests that it is insignificant.

The term "resource curse" is most frequently attributed to Richard Auty (1993), although an explicit association between resources and the idea of a "curse" was made five years earlier in a volume published by the World Bank, titled *Oil Windfalls: Blessing or Curse?* (Gelb, 1988). The latter study analyzed the extent to which a number of oil-producing developing countries had squandered an unprecedented positive terms-of-trade shock and the fiscal windfall that accompanied it during and after the 1970s oil price shocks. Gelb calculated that the countries in his study had consumed around two-thirds of these windfalls, with around half of revenues being invested in domestic public investment projects. Despite this massive increase in investment, "From 1974 to 1981 average growth rates were well below what would have been predicted by a simple neoclassical model, given the size of the investment boom. . . . Growth rates were even further below what would have been predicted by theories of capital- or foreign-exchange-constrained growth" (Gelb, 1988:136).

Gelb's contribution is seminal in the resource-curse literature, not least because it underlines the importance of the weak form of the resource-curse hypothesis, as articulated above. The important question about resource windfalls is most often not whether resource-rich countries register positive growth rates in the aftermath of positive terms-of-trade or revenue shocks. Moreover, it is not whether resource-rich countries grow faster than comparable countries with fewer resources. Given the massive increases in public investment and consumption that resource-rich countries generally experience following such booms, it is hardly surprising to observe higher growth rates in GDP (gross domestic product) than before the boom. The more fundamental question, implied in the weak form of resource-curse hypothesis, is whether resource-rich countries enjoy the economic benefits expected from the spending and public investment financed by resource windfalls, and whether resource-based growth dynamics can be sustained. Testing the weak form of the resource-curse thesis requires a comparison between observed economic outcomes (which may appear positive) and a notional or modeled, but ultimately unobservable, counterfactual. The construction of such counterfactuals is a topic to which we return in Part 2 of this book.

Empirical Evidence for the Resource Curse

Empirical support for the resource-curse hypothesis accompanied a major development in the broader literature on the macroeconomics of economic growth, namely, the use of "growth regressions." This research agenda, with important contributions from Barro (1991) and Mankiw and Weil (1992), attempted to identify the determinants of GDP growth in large cross-country samples, by regressing long-run growth on a set of determinants proposed in leading growth theories: savings rates, population growth, educational attainment, openness to trade, and so forth. In this vein, Sachs and Warner (1995, 1997, 1999, 2001) showed that resource wealth—measured as the share of resource in total exports (which, as discussed below, would later be revealed to be a rather problematic measure)—was correlated with lower economic growth, controlling for structural and other geographic and institutional attributes.[7] As such, they were the first authors to "confirm the adverse effects of resource abundance on growth on the basis of a worldwide, comparative study of growth" (Sachs and Warner, 1995). Sala-i-Martin (1997) provided additional support for this finding by identifying natural resource abundance as one of the ten most robust variables from (literally) millions of alternative growth-regression specifications.

These results had a profound effect on strengthening the intellectual support for the resource-curse thesis. Sachs and Warner claimed that natural resource abundance not only failed to have a positive effect on growth, but in fact that its effect was negative—that is, the coefficient on the resources-abundance regressor was, in fact, negative (as opposed to just not statistically significant). Unlike Gelb (1988), Sachs and Warner's finding therefore supported the strong form of the resource-curse thesis: resource abundance is a curse rather than a squandered opportunity. Sachs and Warner themselves emphasized this distinction between the strong- and weak-form versions of the resource-curse hypothesis (and their support for the former):

> [If] all that was happening was that the resource rents were consumed rather than invested, or that the investment that was done yielded low returns, then the path of GDP in natural resource abundant economies would be lower than it would have been in the same economies with optimal policies. But such economies would not neces-

sarily grow *slower* than other resource-poor economies. In other words, to explain the *negative* association we find . . . there must be something else going on beyond wasteful policies. (Sachs and Warner, 1997; emphasis in the original)

Sachs and Warner's scholarship was truly seminal, but it has not escaped criticisms around issues of measurement and methodology. The first of these was that the findings were subject to omitted variable bias. However, having provided regression evidence in favor of the resource curse after controlling for popular variables favored by four other empirical growth studies (including measures of initial income, macroeconomic policy, institutional quality, geography and education levels), Sachs and Warner (1997) showed that their finding survived the inclusion of nine additional regressors under multiple specifications. A second concern was whether the findings would be robust to alternative ways of measuring resource abundance, but the finding also survived under three alternative measures of resource abundance: the share of mineral production in GDP, the fraction of primary exports in total exports, and the amount of land area per person. Finally, critics questioned whether the results were biased by what Sachs and Warner called "an accident from the special experience of the Persian Gulf states"—a charge they also dismissed, "since most of these states drop out of regression samples for lack of data on other control variables" (Sachs and Warner, 2001:828).

The most enduring influence of Sachs and Warner's scholarship on the resource curse stems from their forceful rejection of institutional explanations. In various specifications and extensions of their regressions, institutional variables were repeatedly found not to be statistically significant, leading Sachs and Warner (2001:835–836) to conclude that institutional or political "explanations do not pass even a cursory look at the data." Moreover, even if econometric support could be found for the effect of natural resources on the formation of nondemocratic institutional and political characteristics, "there is unfortunately only weak evidence for an association between nonauthoritarian political systems and growth" (Sachs and Warner, 2001).

For at least a decade after the publication of Sachs and Warner's papers, a near obsession emerged in the resource-curse literature around whether institutions or the Dutch disease was a more important explanation for the resource curse. Sachs and Warner's finding directly challenged work that lay outside the confines of economics. Political scientists, for example, had long theorized the emergence of "rentier" and "clientelist" states as a particular form of state formation and political organization (particularly in the Middle East), and many of them suggested negative long-run economic implications of such arrangements. While their contribution was an empirical one, Sachs and Warner (1999) briefly discussed possible theoretical explanations for their famous finding by tentatively invoking the Dutch disease theory (to which Sachs had already made important contributions). As discussed in chapter 2, this Dutch-disease-versus-institutions (or economics-versus-politics) dichotomy has only recently softened due to the emergence of theoretical models and empirical evidence underlining important interactions between the two, as well as the recent literature's departure from attempts to explain the average, cross-country relationship between resources and growth.

Revisiting the Empirical Evidence: The Problem of Endogeneity

While the early criticisms of Sachs and Warner's empirical findings did not stick, a more recent one has. Recent scholarship has brought to light a number of problems associated with the interpretation and potential endogeneity of commonly used measures of resource abundance. In the early literature identifying the resource curse, the most commonly used measure of "resource abundance" was the share of natural resources to either GDP or total exports. However, this measure is in fact better interpreted as an indicator of "resource dependence"—an important, but entirely separate, issue—as it is not an exogenous measure of "resource abundance" or "resource wealth." Countries may have a low share of natural resources to total exports, not because they do not have an abundance of resources, but because they export many other products as a direct consequence of their economic growth and development.

To illustrate this point, consider the following thought experiment. Assume that Country A started off with a larger resource endowment than Country B in 1970. Country A then succeeded in developing a thriving manufacturing sector over the ensuing four decades, while Country B failed to do so. If we compare the share of resources to total exports of both countries in 2010, for example, the share of resources in Country A's total exports is likely to have dropped, as its share of manufacturing exports increased. Meanwhile, the share of resources in

Country B's exports is likely to have remained largely unchanged, given its inability to build a thriving manufacturing sector. Indeed, Country A's share of resources to total exports may be lower than that of Country B in 2010, given that the former's growth in nonresource exports effectively crowded out the share of resources in its total exports.

It would be a logical fallacy to conclude from this that Country B's higher share of resources to total exports, as measured in 2010, *led to* its possibly lower growth rate. As Frankel (2012:15) points out, "Industrialization may determine commodity exports rather than the other way around. The reverse causality could explain the negative correlation: those countries that fail at manufacturing have a comparative advantage at commodity exports, by default." The point is that a country can be resource abundant, while still having a low share of resource exports (that is, low resource dependence) because the rest of its economy has developed. Notable examples of such countries include Canada, Australia, Norway, and the United States. In short, the share of resources to exports (or GDP) can be endogenous to economic growth.

In an attempt to find an exogenous measure of resource wealth, scholars have used data on proven natural resource reserves (either in terms of total value, or per square kilometer or per capita). In theory, these measures, referred to in the literature as measures of "resource intensity," should provide a more accurate indication of resource wealth. Using various "resource intensity" measures to capture resource abundance, Brunnschweiler and Bulte (2008) conclude that the resource curse "may be a red herring," as their estimations show that "resource abundance positively affects growth and institutional quality," thus calling the entire resource-curse hypothesis into question.

However, these measures of resource intensity have also been found to be potentially endogenous to growth (and to other factors, notably the quality of institutions), as they reflect past resource discoveries that required costly investments in exploration and prospecting. Norman (2009), for example, argues that investment in exploration is endogenous to the rule of law, as private firms investing in costly exploration for resources want to know that they will be able to profit from any possible discoveries, rather than face the risk of appropriation once discoveries are made. Collier (2010) similarly links "investments in search" to the quality of institutions and the rule of law.[8] In their critique of Brunnschweiler and Bulte (2008), Van der Ploeg and Poelhekke (2009) argue that the endogeneity of measures of resource intensity undermines the former's findings. According to Van der Ploeg and Poelhekke (2009), evidence of the resource curse remains compelling, albeit through the generally neglected channel of excessive macroeconomic volatility in resource-rich countries (discussed in chapter 2).[9]

Ultimately, these endogeneity problems have continued to present challenges to empirical investigations of the effects of resource wealth on a variety of economic, political, and social outcomes—particularly when such investigations are conducted at the average, cross-country level. Efforts to overcome endogeneity problems have more recently turned to innovative econometric techniques that aim to resolve the problem in a statistical manner (using, for example, instrumental variables), rather than engaging in continued efforts to unearth exogenous measures. More generally, the empirical literature has evolved significantly in terms of the econometric treatment of the data since Sachs and Warner's original contributions.[10] As discussed below, these empirical innovations have provided support for more institutions-centric explanations for the resource curse, which were so forcefully rejected in the early empirical investigations of the resource curse.

THE RISE OF INSTITUTIONAL EXPLANATIONS AND THE CONDITIONAL RESOURCE CURSE

The gradual unearthing of the endogeneity problems in the early resource-curse literature, coupled with the introduction of econometric techniques that attempted to capture possible interactions between institutions, politics, and resource wealth, has resulted in support for institutional and political economy explanations. Indeed, such has been the ascendance of these arguments that Frankel's (2012) review of the literature concludes, "Of the various possible channels through which natural resources could be a curse to long-run development, the quality of institutions and governance is perhaps the most widely hypothesized."

Mehlum, Moene, and Torvik (2006) in particular present powerful empirical evidence in favor of institutional explanations for the resource curse. The authors' aims were boldly stated as investigating "the hypothesis that a poor quality of institutions is the cause of the resource curse and that good enough institutions can eliminate the resource curse entirely." They find strong statistical support for this hypothesis, arguing, "the main difference between the success cases and the cases of failure (in managing natural resources) lays in the quality of institutions" (Mehlum, Moene, and Torvik, 2006:1117). To underline their direct challenge to Sachs and Warner's rejection of the institutional explanations, Mehlum, Moene, and Torvik (2006) used not only the same econometric setup (with one noteworthy extension, discussed below) but also the same dataset as the original studies by Sachs and Warner (1995, 1997).

Mehlum, Moene, and Torvik's (2006) only innovation was the inclusion of an interaction term between measures of institutional quality and resource abundance.[11] Whereas the Sachs and Warner studies attempted to identify the effects of institutional quality and resource dependence (or in their original interpretation, resource abundance[12]) on growth separately, the inclusion of an interaction term tests the hypothesis that resource wealth is conducive to economic growth in the context of strong institutions and bad for growth in context of poor institutions. The interaction term was found to have a positive coefficient that was both economically and statistically significant, resulting in the conclusion that resource abundance is harmful to growth when the institutional quality is poor, but conducive to growth when institutions are strong. Therefore, countries that are simultaneously characterized by weak institutions and resource abundance are "doubly cursed."

Mehlum, Moene, and Torvik's (2006) work served a number of purposes in the evolution of the broader literature. First, it brought to the resource-curse literature the application of the institutions-centric perspective that had recently gained in ascendency in explaining other complex long-term economic patterns, and more specifically, questions in development macroeconomics.[13] Second, the evidence that resource abundance has a sharply differentiated impact on economic performance conditioned on the quality of institutions initiated a new emphasis on disaggregating the analysis between the "winners" and "losers" in the management of natural resources. Whereas studies based on evidence from cross-country growth regression attempted to identify the *average* relationship between resource abundance and growth, support for the institutional origins of the resource curse (and success stories) has led scholars down a more rewarding path of differentiation and country-specific analysis.

Finally, Mehlum, Moene, and Torvik's (2006) study underlined the importance of institutional quality at the time when resources are discovered (also known as "initial institutions")—bringing to the fore-front deep questions around the origins and sequencing of the institu-tional reform process. Proponents of this argument suggest that better initial institutions explain the success of Norway, Australia, and Canada in harnessing their resource wealth with striking success: large resource discoveries were made in the second half of the twenty-first century, when these countries had already developed highly supportive institu-tions. Similar conclusions have been presented in less obvious historical contexts, such as the mid-nineteenth-century California gold rush (Clay and Wright, 2005) and postindependence Botswana (Robinson, Acemoglu, and Johnson, 2003).

These arguments resonate with broader themes within institutional economics, most obviously with Douglass North's emphasis on path dependence and the deep historical foundations of differentiated eco-nomic performance, as well as with the analysis of economic historians (Wright and Czelusta, 2004, 2007) and political scientists (Karl, 1997) who were early proponents of the view that resource discoveries nega-tively impact the performance of economies with underdeveloped institutions—or "extractive" and "grabber-friendly" institutions, as posited by Acemoglu and Robinson (2012) and Mehlum, Moene, and Torvik (2006). A common theme in this literature is that the combi-nation of poor (extractive or grabber-friendly) initial institutions and resource abundance makes it more likely that resource revenues will be directed toward the benefit of a small elite.

CONCLUSION

The relationship between natural resources and economic prosperity is both complex and uncertain, and has confounded economists for centuries. The list of the largest producers of natural resources today includes some of the poorest and richest countries in the world. The role of resources in established historic theories of economic prosperity ranges from highly conducive and even essential to economic growth, to deeply detrimental. Despite contestation around the precise relation-ship between resources and economic prosperity and its measurement, economists' understanding has evolved in a number of illuminating ways. Compared with the uncritical acceptance of the resource curse that accompanied the findings of Sachs and Warner, the hypothesis is today maintained with considerable qualifications. The weak and contested average relationship between resources and economic performance has promoted a more fruitful emphasis on country- and context-specific factors that promote success or failure in harnessing resource wealth. The role and quality of institutions and political economy factors feature prominently in this discussion.

The modified, conditional restatement of the resource curse suggests that the quality of institutions, notably at the time of resource discovery, is particularly important. The earlier wholesale dismissal of the institutional link in the early resource-curse literature has been largely rejected. In particular, the conditional resource curse, with its emphasis on initial institutions, has important policy implications for developing countries with recent resource discoveries, many of which have weak and underdeveloped institutions. Weak institutions and resource windfalls are often a deadly combination, in which the latter reinforces the former, thereby greatly increasing the probability of poor long-run economic performance.

Chapter 2 focuses more narrowly on institutional and political economy challenges around the management of resource windfalls. The chapter also offers an account of the literature on institutions in economics that focuses on the process of institutional reform, and commonly observed forms and functions associated with high-quality institutions. This chapter and the one that follows form the theoretical backbone for the central argument advanced in this book: that sovereign wealth funds, if embedded in an accompanying rule-based system for fiscal policy, provide a promising—if incremental—institutional solution to widely observed failures in the management of resource windfalls. We therefore do not propose to offer solutions in the spirit of the "big push" models and other arguments offering quick and easy solutions to the problems confronted by resource economies. We are optimistic, however, that a sovereign wealth fund and a system of fiscal rules can make a meaningful contribution to their amelioration.

CHAPTER TWO

Getting to Denmark

Institutional and Political Problems of Resource-Dependent Economies

IN *POLITICAL ORDER and Political Decay*, Francis Fukuyama (2014) argues that the challenge that still confronts the majority of societies today is akin to that of "getting to Denmark"—that is, "an imagined society that is prosperous, democratic, secure, and well governed, and experiences low levels of corruption." However, the repeated failures in promoting these cornerstones of political order around the world and through history had underlined to the author (two and a half decades earlier) of the much-maligned "End of History" (Fukuyama, 1989), just how difficult and complex a task institution building is. "We don't understand how Denmark itself came to be Denmark and therefore don't comprehend the complexity and difficulty of political development," Fukuyama (2014:25) argues.

Fukuyama's comments bring to light a much-debated issue in economics: the timing, sequencing, and interactions of political, institutional, and policy reforms—that is, the challenge of escaping from an established set of institutions that are apparently not conducive to economic progress and political order. Recall that, as outlined at the end of chapter 1, scholars have identified the quality of institutions, particularly those prevailing at the time of resource discovery ("initial institutions"), as a robust predictor of the ability and inability of countries to harness their commodity wealth over the long run. Coupled with evidence that natural resources tend to erode the quality of already-weak institutions, the prospects for positive institutional reform appear bleak for economies that discover resources in the context of poor institutional quality, and perhaps even more so for economies whose poor institutions have become entrenched and reinforced by a history of resource extraction.

A more optimistic interpretation of the scholarship on the relationship between institutions, natural resources, and economic performance starts by shifting the lens of analysis from the general to the specific. The understanding of institutions in the empirical literature on the resource curse discussed in chapter 1 is based on what the literature refers to as "general" or "macro" institutions: the rule of law; security of contracts; the accountability, transparency, and efficiency of public institutions; and the extent of democracy and corruption. Depending on one's theory of change around institutions, it may be more fruitful to focus on a set of targeted institutional reforms that address specific political and economic problems associated with resource revenue management.

The second half of this chapter presents a discussion of the literature on institutional change, forms, and functions. Institutional change typically is—and should be—slow moving and incremental, with due attention to (political) incentive compatibility and the existing matrix of accompanying institutions. While there is an institutionally deterministic view that argues that institutional reforms need to be conducted in an all-encompassing, top-down manner, Acemoglu and Robinson have presented the counterargument (with specific reference to resource economies) as follows:

> The reform of [macro] institutions will be very hard because . . . it is typically not a coincidence that societies have unaccountable political systems, lack the rule of law and have low capacity states all at the same time. . . . A good place to start in reforming institutions is perhaps not the macro institutions of the whole society, but the nexus of institutions that surrounds natural resources . . . [which constitute] much more fruitful lines of policy reform than blaming the resource curse on just weak "rule of law" or lack of "checks and

balances"—even though both statements are likely true. (Acemoglu and Robinson, 2013b)

Similar calls for greater specificity around the institutions of resource-rich countries has issued by other scholars. Arguing that the literature on the "political economy of the resource curse . . . is still in its infancy," Torvik (2009) notes, "We still have a quite limited knowledge along which dimensions the resource-abundant winners and losers differ, and about what the mechanisms behind these differences are."

We propose a set of targeted institutions pertaining to the management of resource revenues that we believe can be feasibly implemented and sustained in the context of relatively poor general institutions. It is contended in this book that rule-based sovereign wealth funds are exactly the kind of targeted institutional reform that can address a number of the commonly observed political and economic problems surrounding the management of resource revenues. The adoption of a rule-based sovereign wealth fund model can arrest the further deterioration of institutional quality that has been found to accompany resource revenue management in the context of poor general institutions. As these revenues are in almost all cases fiscal in nature, our focus is on the analysis of the political economy of resource revenue management.

This chapter starts with a brief summary of the literature on the political economy problems in the management of resource revenues, which allows us to identify the specific issues that targeted institutional interventions need to address, and concludes with a discussion of the institutional economics literature that provides a conceptual framework to be used in the remainder of the book.

INSTITUTIONAL PROBLEMS IN RESOURCE REVENUE MANAGEMENT

The literature on the institutions and political economy of resource-rich economies addresses every conceivable link in the resource "value chain," from the point of exploration to decisions around the spending and investment of revenues. Collier (2007) popularized the concept of a resource value chain in his book, *The Bottom Billion:* the chain begins with exploration (the incentives and policies that promote or discourage exploration), followed by the taxation of resource extraction and sales, the public disclosure of the taxation regime, the management of volatile revenues, and the investment of these revenues.[1] In this chapter, the emphasis is on the institutional and political economy problems that result in particular from the last two links in this chain.

Rent-Seeking

Since their emergence in the 1970s, theories of rent-seeking behavior have become hugely influential in development economics (Tullock, 1967; Krueger, 1974). Rent-seeking describes efforts to manipulate the political and regulatory environment to capture "economic rents"— that is, income paid to factors of production in excess of their opportunity cost. Rent-seeking behavior allocates economic resources away from productive activities (value creation) toward an unproductive scramble for rents generated by existing economic value (rent-seeking). Rent-seeking promotes inefficiency and unproductiveness, as economic agents devote economic resources to efforts to grab a share of the existing wealth rather than trying to create new wealth.

The resource sector generates enormous rents and is therefore prone to pervasive rent-seeking behavior (Gelb, 1988; Collier, 2012; Frankel, 2012). The government typically plays a major part in the creation and distribution of these resource rents, as it typically has the power to award contracts for exploration and concessions for extraction, and impose taxes on resource production and profits. An important implication of the rent-seeking perspective for resource economics is that while traditional rent-seeking models can explain why these countries have underperformed their own potential (that is, the weak form of the resource curse thesis, as discussed in chapter 1), it cannot explain why they underperform resource-poor countries (as according to the strong-form version of hypothesis). Traditional rent-seeking models explain suboptimality (waste and inefficiency), but not outright negative economic performance.

Influential research by Tornell and Lane (1999) incorporated negative feedback mechanisms in their models to account for negative performance. This celebrated application of the rent-seeking argument to issues of resource economies introduced the idea of "feeding frenzy" around the capturing of rents emanating from the resource economy, which they call the "voracity effect." A resource boom results in more income being available for redistribution between a set of competitive and powerful domestic interest groups. In their game-theoretic setup, as each group demands higher transfers, a tax increase is required because capital is reallocated from the formal sector to the less productive informal sector, where it is safe from taxation. The higher tax rate required to offset higher transfers reduces the return on capital, which in their model can outweigh the direct effect of increased productivity and therefore lower growth. Hodler (2006) provides another significant contribution by linking a number of strands within the institutional literature: institutional quality is a key determinant of success in combating the curse, and is influenced by the degree of ethnic fractionalization, via the process of rent-seeking. Rent-seeking—and, more specifically, the related idea that governments can use the rents and revenues resources generate to effectively pay off interest groups—has also featured prominently in a number of theories linking resources to the (lack of) government accountability and the (short) length of political time horizons in the context of resource wealth.

Fiscal Financing, Accountability, and Forms of Government

Robinson, Torvik, and Verdier (2006) produced one of the most comprehensive theses on the interactions between abundant resource revenues, political accountability, and the origins of institutions. Their argument and empirical evidence suggests that governments that do not have to introduce socially tolerable and consistent systems of taxation but can instead finance themselves through resource revenues face reduced incentives to be accountable and responsive to their citizens. Consequently, they do not have a vested interest in the development of a thriving market-based, nonresource economy that is otherwise required to establish a taxable economic base and secure the fiscal sustainability of the state. In contrast, governments and ruling elites in nonresource countries have an incentive to promote the development of such a market-based economy, as it generates a multitude of corporate and individual taxpayers, thus providing a steady and stable source of fiscal revenue (in exchange for accountable governance and the provision of public goods).

In the Robinson, Torvik, and Verdier (2006) model, the existence of resources and their related rents increases the utility of holding political power for longer. As a result, political horizons are suboptimally short (from a social welfare perspective), as politicians change their policies in order to retain power. One manifestation of this is a bloated public sector, which establishes a vested interest in maintaining the status quo and is "paid off" through rents emanating from the resource sector. Unsurprisingly, a number of prominent studies have found strong evidence that resource abundance is associated with higher levels of corruption; even less surprising is the conclusion that resource abundance is more likely to be associated with high levels of corruption in countries with poor institutions (Mauro, 1995; Ades and Di Tella, 1999; Bhattacharyya and Hodler, 2010.

Robinson, Torvik, and Verdier (2006) and Auty's (2007) theory of "rent cycling" explain not only the existence of narrow patronage systems associated with a political elite, but also resonate with models of the forms governments take (or, in the language of political science, state formation) in the long run in resource-rich countries. Economic historians (Engerman and Sokoloff, 2000; Wright and Czelusta, 2004, 2007) have suggested that nonextractive societies developed institutions and foundations around the political state built on individualism, decentralization, accountable democracy, egalitarianism, and capitalism. Extractive societies, on the other hand, failed to develop along these lines, because centralized states and political elites had access to easy financing through a control of rents. This work also ties in with a significant theme in an older political science literature of resource-abundant and resource-dependent states, which has theorized the emergence of the durability of "rentier states" that assume a clientelist relationship with their citizens (Beblawi and Luciani, 1987; Ross, 2001; Wantchekon, 2002), of which "petrostates" are a specific, and acute, manifestation (Mahdavy, 1970; Karl, 1997). In this sense, the resource-curse literature has started the important and valuable task of describing the political-economy foundations of observed institutional outcomes (or certain types of state formation) rather than jumping straight to the deep, slow-moving institutional structures.

White Elephants: The Misallocation of Public Investment

The rent-seeking and broader political economy literature on the resource curse helps explain the prevalence of poor public investments financed by resource-related public revenue windfalls. Torvik (2009) suggests that one of the biggest intellectual puzzles surrounding resource-rich economies is why the massive domestic investments have not resulted in greater growth payoffs. Gelb (1988) calculated that around half of the windfall gains from the oil shocks in the 1970s were invested in domestic projects. As both these studies observe, any of the leading growth models in economics would have predicted much stronger growth on the back of such significant public investments.

There are a number of plausible arguments for why the anticipated growth failed to materialize, many of which draw on the previously discussed rent-seeking literature, as well as other insights from the broader Public Choice literature.[2] In his study of the Nigerian government's response to positive terms-of-trade shocks between 1972 and 1988, Gavin (1993) finds a "tendency for governments to invest in projects with high prestige or political payoff, but with little economic rationale." Similarly, Robinson and Torvik argue that resource-rich countries are more prone to investing in "white elephants"—that is, public investment projects with negative social surplus: "The higher the rents from holding office, the more economically inefficient investment projects can be and still be politically efficient" (Robinson and Torvik, 2005).

Excessive Volatility and Procyclical Policy

One of the leading explanations for the resource curse revolves around the extraordinary volatility of most commodity prices and the extent to which sharp and unpredictable fluctuations in value of their primary export products affect other macroeconomic aggregates in resource-dependent countries. So compelling and voluminous is this subset of the literature that it can be considered—as, indeed, Frankel (2012) does in his literature review—as an explanation for the resource curse in its own right. However, an insightful debate has developed in this literature around whether the underlying reasons for excessive volatility and procyclicality are due to market failures (specifically, some credit-market imperfection or constraint) or, as is now more commonly proposed, government failure (due to political economy factors).[3] Therefore, arguments around the observed excessive volatility and procyclicality of resource-rich countries are treated here as part of the political economy literature.

It is a stylized fact that commodity prices are more volatile than those of manufactured goods (Hamilton, 2009; Frankel, 2012; Jacks, O'Rourke, and Williamson, 2011). It has also been documented that many resource-dependent countries experience more generalized macroeconomic volatility, and moreover, have a strong tendency toward procyclicality (this point is widely made, but is central to the argument in Hausmann and Rigobon, 2003, and Van der Ploeg and Poelhekke, 2009). Finally, it has been shown repeatedly that such volatility "is detrimental to long-run economic growth and development, controlling for initial income per capita, population growth, human capital, investment, openness and natural resource dependence" (Ramey and Ramey, 1995). Van der Ploeg and Poelhekke (2009) have argued that the direct and indirect channels through which the volatility of natural resources negatively affect growth have been generally neglected in the literature—particularly the indirect channel through which resource exports "make already volatile countries more volatile and thus indirectly worsen growth prospects. . . . Ignoring the volatility channel may lead one to erroneously conclude that there is no effect of resources on growth."

The extreme level of volatility in commodity prices is powerfully illustrated by an anecdote about research conducted by James Hamilton on the statistical properties of time series of oil prices. Hamilton (2009) applied various possible statistical models to these time series, using different sample periods, and concluded that the oil price was best approximated by a random walk. This meant that starting from a price of $115 per barrel[4] in 2008 (the time of his writing), the best-guess estimate of where the real oil price would be four years hence was exactly the same price ($115)—the price series was a random walk, so there was an equal probability that the real oil price would be higher or lower than the starting price. Hamilton noted, however, that given the volatility and unpredictability of a random walk, it was also plausible that the price would be as high as $391 or as low as $34 per barrel. The range of this prediction, particularly his lower-bound number, seemed outlandish at the time, given the sharp and nearly unrelenting run-up in prices between late 2001 and 2008, which saw prices rise from around $30 per barrel to over $145 shortly before Hamilton wrote his paper. Conventional wisdom at the time suggested oil prices were going nowhere but up over the coming years (the commodities analysts of various Wall Street firms started talking about "$200+oil"). Ultimately, the real oil price registered at almost exactly the same levels in mid-2012— the end of Hamilton's "forecast" horizon—having dropped from $145 per barrel in June 2008 to $31 by the end of the same year.

Clearly, the challenges of macroeconomic policymaking in countries that rely almost exclusively on oil exports for foreign exchange earnings and oil taxes and royalties for fiscal revenues are staggering, given this level of exogenously determined volatility. Arezki, Gylfason, and Sy (2012) point out that for Nigeria (often the poster child for oil/resource dependence, but by no means unique in this regard), starting from a base value of $100 per barrel, the difference between a price of $50 and one of $150 is equivalent to a difference of 50 percent of GDP. It may be asking too much of macroeconomic policy to effectively stabilize the economy in the face of such volatility. Given the extreme volatility and uncertainty around resource prices and revenues, even the best-intentioned policymakers in resource-rich, and, perhaps particularly, resource-dependent, countries face a massive and often overwhelming information problem: it can be nearly impossible to identify whether a commodity-driven shock (whether positive or negative) is permanent or temporary, let alone how long shocks of the latter variety will last and how severe they will be.

However, there is plenty of evidence to suggest that not only is macroeconomic policy in resource-rich developing countries unable to provide countercyclical stabilization, but in fact, there is a tendency for policy to make things worse. Kaminsky, Reinhart, and Vegh's (2005) examination of procyclicality across a range of indicators, including fiscal policy, monetary conditions, and capital flows, found that "macroeconomic policies in developing countries seem to mostly reinforce the business cycle, turning sunny days into scorching infernos and rainy days into torrential downpours." Frankel (2012) also emphasizes the compounding effect of policy on volatility in resource-rich countries, arguing that government interventions "tend to exacerbate booms and busts instead of moderating them."

Nese (2011) examines the cyclicality of five fiscal measures in twenty-eight oil-producing developing countries during 1990–2009. The results suggest that the five measures—government expenditure, consumption, investment, nonoil revenue, and nonoil primary balance—are all strongly procyclical in the full sample. The procyclicality of fiscal spending is driven in large part by two large items in the budget: public investment projects and the civil service wage bill. Talvi and Vegh (2005) examine the evidence for a large number of developing and developed countries, and find that the resource-dependent developing countries in particular exhibit a "very low propensity to save out of what turned out to be a temporary shock . . . due mainly to the public sector's spending spree." Medas and Zakharova (2009) find evidence that oil windfalls are often spent on higher public-sector wages and tend to increase the number of people employed by the government, as well as indications that this increase is difficult to reverse when resource prices collapse. A number of studies draw attention to the fact that procyclicality tends to manifest across an even broader array of macro-economic variables in resource-rich countries (Hausmann and Rigobon, 2003; Van der Ploeg and Poelhekke, 2009). This literature finds that the exchange rate, capital flows, household spending, monetary conditions, bank lending, and credit extension and investment are all typically procyclical in resource-rich countries, and often more so than in comparator countries. Frankel (2012) finds that not only do developing countries on the whole tend to have more pronounced economic cycles than advanced countries but also that this is especially true of developing countries that are dependent on exports of oil, minerals, and other primary commodities.

Why are resource-rich and resource-dependent countries prone to macroeconomic volatility, and why do macroeconomic policies that should be countercyclical end up being procyclical? As noted earlier, the literature is divided into two broad camps, which essentially reflects neo-Keynesian and neoclassical foundations. The first category of explanations emphasizes the existence of market failures, particularly credit-market imperfection or constraint that encumbers the countercyclicality of (most fiscal) policy, by making it easier for government and other economic agents in resource-rich countries to lend during resource booms than to borrow during slumps (Gavin and Perotti, 1997; Kaminsky, Reinhart, and Vegh, 2005. Other authors have emphasized structural shortcomings or "missing markets" as factors that contribute to the volatility and procyclicality of resource economies. Hausmann and Rigobon (2003) and Van der Ploeg and Poelhekke (2009) argue that a lack of financial development makes risk management costly or impossible in volatile resource-rich countries (which as a corollary also leads to higher risk aversion among economic agents, thus reducing growth).

The second set of explanations emphasizes government failures due to political economy factors. The argument is that governments in resource-dependent countries should be able to anticipate their excessive exposure to exogenous volatility, that market imperfections will make it costly or impossible to borrow in hard times, and that the lack of financial sector development makes risk management prohibitively expensive for many economic agents. A rational response would, therefore, be to "self-insure," building up buffers during boom periods. Alesina, Tabellini, and Campante (2008) argue that to answer why such forms of self-insurance are very rare in developing countries, "one needs to consider the political arena" and that "procyclical and myopic fiscal policy stems from a political agency problem." The impact of political economy constraints (which are binding in the context of weak institutions) on volatility is implied in Tornell and Lane's (1999) famous voracity model: the absence of strong and credible legal-political institutions allows a multitude of powerful interest groups to compete for rents through the fiscal process, so that a positive terms-of-trade shock generates a disproportionate increase in fiscal redistribution; with available resources rising during boom periods, it follows that government spending will be prone to procyclicality.

Talvi and Vegh (2005) find empirical evidence to support the voracity effect to the extent that large fluctuations in fiscal revenues lead to procyclical fiscal policies. Alesina, Tabellini, and Campante (2008) develop a more elaborate model in which voters are able to observe the state of the economy (that is, identify a resource boom), but not the amount of government revenues appropriated as rents by the state apparatus. Due to corruption and a lack of government credibility, voters do not trust the government to save rents or invest them in productive assets, and therefore demand tax cuts and higher transfers. They describe this as "starving the Leviathan," which is a "second-best solution to an agency problem in an environment of corruption and imperfect information" (Alesina, Tabellini, and Campante, 2008). In the empirical section of their paper, they find support for the hypothesis that fiscal policy is more procyclical in countries where corruption is more widespread, particularly (and, in some specifications, only) in corrupt democracies, where corruption is combined with "reelection constraints." Frankel also emphasizes the compounding effect of policy on volatility in resource-rich countries:

> That developing countries tend to experience larger cyclical fluctuations than industrialized countries is only partly attributable to commodities. It is also in part due to the role of factors that "should" moderate the cycle, but in practice seldom operate that way: procy-

clical capital flows, procyclical monetary and fiscal policy, and the related Dutch Disease. If anything, they tend to exacerbate booms
and busts instead of moderating them. The hope that improved policies or institutions might reduce this procyclicality makes this one
of the most potentially fruitful avenues of research in emerging market macroeconomics. (Frankel, 2012:2)

Negative incentives in the political economy of resource-rich countries
are central to all models that develop an implied or explicit link between institutional quality and cyclicality (of fiscal policy or the general economy): political pressures to spend resource revenues are high
during boom periods, while the variability of the tax base generates
procyclical fiscal expenditure. The low propensity to save in boom
periods further results in contractionary fiscal policy during bad times
because there are fewer fiscal buffers available for smoothing the business cycle, thereby accentuating fiscal procyclicality.

THEORIES OF INSTITUTIONAL CHANGE

This book proposes that the sovereign wealth fund model can best be
understood as a targeted institutional innovation that seeks to address
a number of the most pervasive causes of the resource curse, specifically those founded in the political economy of managing resource revenues. It is instructive to consider, therefore, the critical importance
that "institutions" has come to assume in the discipline of economics;
what economists mean when they refer to institutions; and the extent
to which the literature has identified broad areas of consensus with
respect to the process of change around institutions, as well as the functions and forms they commonly assume. The remainder of this chapter
considers these largely theoretical issues regarding institutions, which
frame the argument advanced in the rest of the book that sovereign
wealth funds and fiscal rules are a promising institutional response
to the resource curse.

The Rise of Institutionalism in Economics

The ascent of the institutional lens in mainstream economics is fairly
recent. As Vernon Smith (2008) notes, for much of the twentieth

century neoclassical economics centered on developing "an institutions-free core." Gradually, economists have come to appreciate that, given the pervasive presence of transaction costs, the nature and extent (or "scope") of market-based behavior depends critically on various rules, norms, and incentives (collectively referred to as "institutions"). It is a testament to the influence of the study of institutions to the field of economics that the idea that "institutions matter" is today rather banal; indeed, Rodrik, Subramanian, and Trebbi's (2004) more forceful assertion that "institutions rule" seems more apt. Much of the growing influence of institutional analysis in economics is due to the emergence of the field of New Institutional Economics,[5] which is concerned with the form and function of institutions as sets of constraints.

The literature on institutions has long emphasized the gradual nature of institutional change, as well as the importance of context to institutional functions and design. North's seminal contributions to New Institutional Economics, for example, has drawn emphasis to the deep historic (and even cultural) foundations of social, political, and economic institutions, and understood that the process of institutional change is highly path dependent. This intellectual tradition has also frequently pointed out that transitions to what appear to be patently "better" institutions are often curtailed by political incentives for preserving inefficient institutions, the incompatibility of particular institutions with accompanying elements of the "institutional matrix," and the often high cost of institutional change. Finally, these insights have also led the understanding of institutions in economics to a greater emphasis on the functions that good institutions perform rather than the particular forms they are expected to take (although the chapter will also identify a set of general principles for institutional design).

Three major traditions within the field of New Institutional Economics can be identified: first, Douglass North's historical or dynamic analysis of the role of institutions; second, Oliver Williamson's "economics of governance"; and finally, the political economy of the Public Choice tradition, with its emphasis on contractual arrangements between governments and the governed. In North's oft-cited analogy, institutions are the "rules of the game," a set of "humanly devised constraints that shape human interaction" (North, 1990). The rules of the game are requisites for market-based exchange, which demands an (often elaborate) amount of certainty and information about the behavior of other players in the game and external factors that may affect the way the game is played. For Oliver Williamson, the overarching question was why certain forms of economic exchange took place through markets, while others were more efficiently conducted through institutions (or contracts). Williamson's "economics of governance" studied the nature and implications of different ways of arranging economic activity—such as public versus private ordering, vertical versus hierarchical structures, and the operation and organizational consequences of different legal systems.

In the Northian tradition, most forcefully continued through the scholarship of Daron Acemoglu and James Robinson, politics became a central area of analysis. North, for example, argued, "The whole development of the New Institutional Economics must be not only a theory of property rights and their evolution, but a theory of the political process, a theory of the state, and of the way in which the institutional structure of the state and its individuals specify and enforce property rights" (1986:233).[6] Later, North (1995) would argue that this task had in fact been achieved and that one of the ways in which New Institutional Economics had extended neoclassical theory was by "modeling the political process as a critical factor in the performance of economies."

Understanding and modeling the political process was also central in Public Choice theory, and in particular in the work of James Buchanan, who argued that economists "should cease proffering policy advice as if they were employed by a benevolent despot, and they should look to the structure within which political decisions are made" (1987:243). Buchanan (1975) described the required adjustment to mainstream economics as one of incorporating the "lens of contract" alongside the "lens of choice." It was not only the exercise of choice within constraints that mattered (as per the standard analysis of neoclassical economics), but also how those constraints were established— or the choice between constraints.

The early interest shown by North and Buchanan in issues of political agency in institutional economics has been reinforced by the more recent contributions of Daron Acemoglu and James Robinson (along with their frequent coauthor, Simon Johnson). One of the central arguments to emerge from this body of work is the primacy of politics in determining economic institutions and the way they operate:[7]

It is the political process that determines what economic institutions people live under, and it is the political institutions that determine how this process works . . . while economic institutions are critical for determining whether a country is poor or prosperous, it is politics and political institutions that determine what economic institutions a country has. (Acemoglu and Robinson, 2012:42–43)

This is the broad statement in favor of the explanatory primacy of politics, but Acemoglu and Robinson have also developed detailed theories around *why* political institutions are either "inclusive" or "extractive." Most of this work focuses on the political incentives for resisting transitions toward inclusive institutions. They point out, for example, that "political elites may block technological and institutional development, because . . . innovations often erode political elites' incumbency advantage, increasing the likelihood that they will be replaced" (Acemoglu and Robinson, 2006:129). These issues raise questions around the politically determined incentives and processes of institutional change, as well as differing views on the sequencing of institutional reforms, and the respective merits of and prospects for incremental, "bottom up" versus wholesale, "top down" modes of institutional change.

Politics and the Sequencing of Institutional Change

A central question about the process of institutional change pertains to whether the establishment of sound institutions has to be preceded (or at least accompanied) by political reforms, or, more specifically, whether good institutions require certain forms of political organization (notably, democracy and political contestation). In a famous paper on the subject, Glaeser et al. (2004) outline two intellectual traditions in the age-old problem of the sequencing of policy, political, and institutional reforms. One approach emphasizes the need to start with democracy and other checks on government—what was referred to earlier as general or macroinstitutions. The second approach holds that nondemocratic governments and rules can establish piecemeal institutional innovations (such as assigning and ensuring property rights, or adopting rule-based fiscal policy) as the result of a policy preference rather than a formal, or indeed informal, political constraint (Glaeser et al., 2004:271–272).

This distinction permeates every major debate in development macroeconomics, including that surrounding the resource curse. Glaeser et al. (2004) point out that there are significant similarities and agreements between both schools of thought,[8] and both views are clearly consistent with the broad notion that "institutions matter." However, they differ with respect to how these goals are to be achieved: the former emphasizes the role of general institutions in imposing political constraints on government, whereas the latter places greater faith in the ability of (unconstrained) leaders to implement and adhere to policies and specific institutional innovations as a matter of principle, good judgment, and benevolence. The disagreement pertains not so much to the relationship between these processes in the long run—a horizon over which the assumption of both sides tends to be that inclusive institutions are more durable and flexible. The debate is rather centered on different views as to the sequencing of policy, political, and institutional reforms from low-equilibrium conditions—that is, the debate is really about competing theories of change.

Acemoglu and Robinson often appear to occupy one end of the spectrum, characterized by the strongly prescriptive view that economic prosperity *requires* inclusive economic institutions, which cannot emerge in the absence of inclusive political institutions. Even with this causal framework in mind, however, they are careful to avoid the charge of politically determined institutional determinism. Given the wealth of historic examples (many of which are cited in their book) of countries that enjoyed periods of economic growth and "take-off" under conditions that can hardly be characterized as consistent with inclusive political institutions and open contestation for power,[9] Acemoglu and Robinson permit that "extractive economic and political institutions are [not] inconsistent with economic growth. . . . Extractive institutions that have achieved at least a minimal degree of political centralization are often able to generate some amount of growth" (2012:431). However, "growth under extractive institutions will not be sustained"— that is, inclusive political and economic institutions are a "requisite" for economic prosperity in the long run. Thus, even the most ardent supporters of the primacy of general (and political) institutions permit a great flexibility, both with respect to the different forms institutions may take and the sequence of reform.

At this point, it is instructive to return to the relationship between natural resources, institutional quality, and economic performance. Recall from chapter 1 the emphasis on long-run relationships: the question cannot simply be around whether countries with significant natural resources experience higher economic growth rates in response to a commodities boom or whether they grow faster than comparator countries with fewer resources in such periods. The deeper question, implied in the weak form of resource curse hypothesis, is whether resource-based growth dynamics can be sustained, particularly once transitory revenue booms fade. The question then becomes whether there are defining attributes of resource-dependent economies that encumber or prevent the gradual and progressive realization of the type of institutions commonly associated with sustained, long-run economic progress. If it is permitted that a gradual escape from a low equilibrium characterized by poor institutions is possible, including in resource-dependent economies, this opens up a more optimistic line of inquiry around piecemeal institutional reforms in the management of resource revenues that promote broader institutional development over time.

THE FORM AND FUNCTION OF INSTITUTIONS

Rodrik (2000) argues, "A strategy of institution building must not over-emphasize best-practice 'blueprints' at the expense of local experimentation . . . desirable institutional arrangements vary . . . not only across countries, but also within countries over time." The appreciation of context and history in the understanding of institutions has not rendered institutional economics silent on the commonalities of good institutions, but has led to an emphasis on the *functions* they perform rather than an obsession with their precise *forms*. This section starts with a discussion of common functions performed by institutions before presenting a number of broad principles for institutional design that are sufficiently general to permit Rodrik's notion of local experimentation and variation.

Establishing and Enforcing Property Rights

The scarcity (and in the case of many natural resources, finite supply) of economic resources often triggers distributional struggles and conflict for their control, particularly when property rights are not well defined and enforced. Institutions can contribute to managing and preventing such conflicts by preventing the reality or perception that the distributional struggle is systematically tilted in favor of "winners" at the expense of "losers." Even when property rights are well defined and societies are characterized by the rule of law, complementary institutions with the specific function of assisting in the management and prevention of conflict are frequently required (fiscal federalism and decentralization are prime examples).

Institutions that perform the function of conflict management are particularly important in countries characterized by acute ethnic fragmentation and sharp inequalities in income and wealth. As Rodrik (2000) notes, conflict, or even the threat of conflict, can "hamper social cooperation and prevent the undertaking of mutually beneficial projects." For economists, institutions that perform the function of conflict management are also important for the efficient and productive allocation of the factors of production. Social conflict is damaging to economic prosperity, "both because it diverts resources form economically productive activities and because it discourages such activities by the uncertainty it generates" (Rodrik, 2000).

Constraining the Arbitrary Exercise of Political Power

A well-understood tension underlying various theories of the state is that any entity powerful enough to create a system of property rights (and indeed other institutions) is simultaneously powerful enough to violate them (Weingast, 1995). The state typically enjoys a monopoly (or at least a significant comparative advantage) in the exercise and threat of violence and coercive power. On the one hand, this is why the state can credibly commit to enforcing property rights; on the other hand, requiring institutional constraints on the use of political power can result in the confiscation of property. Historically, robust institutions to constrain state and political power include constitutions and the rule of law, the separation of powers between various arms of government, political contestation, federalism, mechanisms that enforce transparency and accountability around government actions, and the transfer of powers otherwise vested in the state to independent authorities (for example, the conduct of monetary policy, financial supervision, and the management of public pensions). These institutional functions clearly resonate with the Western democratic traditions that emerged most prominently from the Enlightenment (but date back at least as far as Aristotle).[10] They are also typically the foundation for the argument outlined earlier for the primacy of inclusive general institutions.

Here too, however, alternative institutional arrangements can conceivably perform similar functions in constraining the arbitrary use of political power—after all, Fukuyama's "end of history" has not arrived.[11] The Chinese example again stands out as the case that demands explanation. Fukuyama (2012) argues that while China never developed the rule of law—that is, "an independent legal institution that would limit the discretion of the government"—the Chinese model, which he argues has essentially been maintained for two thousand years, "substituted for formal checks on power a bureaucracy bound by rules and customs, which made its behavior reasonably predictable." However, the absence of checks on power has created (and will arguably continue to create) a fundamental risk, with occasionally devastating consequences, which Fukuyama calls the "bad Emperor" problem: "While unchecked power in the hands of a benevolent and wise ruler has many advantages, how do you guarantee a continuing supply of good Emperors?" (52). Hence, while systems lacking formal constraints on the arbitrary exercise of political power can deliver positive results under very specific conditions, their inability to get rid of bad leaders—and, importantly, curb their discretionary powers while in office—remains a significant risk over the long run.

Once again, the point here is not that a fully fledged adoption of the rule of law and Western standards of transparency, accountability, and political contestation are an absolute prerequisite for economic progress, particularly from low-equilibrium points of departure. A number of historical episodes of economic growth and modernization under the tutelage of relatively unconstrained autocrats have resulted in an unscientific romanticism around the merits of benevolent dictatorships (Birdsall and Fukuyama, 2011). Ultimately, an emphasis on institutional functions underlines the importance of establishing mechanisms for political constraint. Rules, however contextually determined and nuanced, are an example of such mechanisms, and there are certainly examples where rules have been successfully implemented in nondemocratic environments.

Incentive Alignment

An emphasis on the incentive structures established by institutions is a central theme in New Institutional Economics: "Institutions provide the incentive structure of an economy; as that structure evolves, it shapes the direction of economic change towards growth, stagnation, or decline" (North 1991:97). In the context of decentralized economic organization, which relies on a myriad of principal–agent relationships, the study of agency relationships is a specific application of the tools of analysis of asymmetric information and incentive alignment. Given imperfect information between cooperating agents, "it takes resources to define and enforce exchange agreements. . . . In the context of individual wealth-maximizing behavior and asymmetric information about the valuable attributes of what is being exchanged (or the performance of agents), transaction costs are a critical determinant of economic performance" (North, 1991:98).

A number of factors can bring about agency problems and raise the cost of maintaining cooperative principal–agent relationships. The agent may have objectives that differ significantly from those of the principal, which become problematic if the pursuit of the agent's objectives undermines that of the principal. The contribution of institutional economics to the study of agency relationships has emphasized the importance of clearly defined contracts and other institutional "commitment technologies" that change the incentives confronting agents, so that it becomes in the agent's best interest to act in a way that is consistent with the achievement of the principal's objectives. In game-theoretic terms, successful institutions provide positive incentives for cooperation (and negative incentives for defection), thereby lowering the cost of decentralized exchange. The principal–agent framework is also a helpful and frequently used lens through which to analyze the role and functioning of government and its various institutions. Buchanan's "lens of contract" outlined earlier is particularly relevant here, as all contractual arrangements, whether between employer and employee or the state and the citizen, contain important elements of agency (Ross, 1973).

Promoting (Macroeconomic) Stability

The idea that markets do not always stabilize automatically—or, more to the point, that welfare gains can be achieved by efforts to speed up what might otherwise be a protracted return to equilibrium—is now widely accepted by almost all major intellectual and methodological traditions in the study of the business cycle (Romer and Romer, 2002). Policies and institutions aim to promote stability across at least three major dimensions: real economic activity, nominal variables, and the banking and financial system. While much of the attention in the literature falls on the positive role of countercyclical policy, notably monetary and fiscal policy (and the institutional underpinnings of such policies, as per Rodrik, 2004), it is clear that macroeconomic instability is also the result of institutional weaknesses—particularly at the extremes, such as during sovereign debt defaults and episodes of hyperinflation. An exclusive focus on the technical aspects of monetary and fiscal policy in their role in stabilizing the economy constrains the discussion to a purely technocratic and analytical exercise. Observed policy actions and frameworks can also be the proximate cause of instability, however, while institutions are the ultimate cause or "deep determinants" (Satyanath and Subramanian, 2004). Recent empirical studies have found strong support for institutions as the ultimate cause of both real (Rodrik, 1999; Acemoglu et al., 2003) and nominal instability (Satyanath and Subramanian, 2004).

A prominent theme in the literature on the economics of the business cycle is that monetary and fiscal policies (and indeed, stabilizing institutions) not only frequently fail to provide countercyclical forces but also are in fact procyclical: that is, they exacerbate the natural fluctuations in the real economy. This is particularly true in developing countries, suggesting that technocratic miscalculations and misapplications of policy tools are only part of the story, and that institutional weaknesses also warrant close scrutiny. As discussed earlier in this chapter, this is a particularly significant problem in resource-rich developing countries (Alesina, Tabellini, and Campante, 2008; Van der Ploeg and Poelhekke, 2009; Arezki, Hamilton, and Kazimov, 2011). A large part of the procyclicality of fiscal policy is still attributed to the political business cycle in the literature following the theoretical formalization of Nordhaus (1975). The adoption of rule-based fiscal institutions has been more staunchly resisted in the area of fiscal policy than in monetary policy, but offers a promising, if partial, solution to the observed tendency toward procyclicality—not least in highly volatile resource-dependent economies (Ossowski et al., 2008; Schmidt-Hebbel, 2012).

PRINCIPLES FOR THE DESIGN OF INSTITUTIONS

The argument against an emphasis on rigid institutional forms rests on three interrelated pillars. First, we do not know enough about the origins of and incentives for institutional change to make strong and realistic prescriptions. Second, an emphasis on specific institutional forms can naively ignore political agency, and the political use of institutions (that appear similar in form) is more important than their form. Third, support for specific institutional forms can be similarly ignorant of history and context, which brings to the fore questions regarding the compatibility of particular institutional forms with other elements of the institutional matrix and the most effective sequencing and pace of institutional reform. The consequent tendency to advance institutional functions over specific forms does not, however, render the literature completely silent on principles for institutional design, which are summarized briefly here.

Cost Efficiency

The overarching function of institutions is to reduce the costs that accompany information problems, uncertainty, and variously defined transaction costs. Logically, establishing and maintaining the existing institutions to reduce those costs cannot be more expensive to society than the losses associated with the problems that they aim to address. The cost-efficiency constraint applies across a number of dimensions: the cost of creating institutions (including adjustment costs), changing them in a dynamic setting, and the costs associated with the enforcement of institutions.

New Institutional Economics has focused on the prevalence of significant adjustment costs and path dependence to explain why apparently poor institutions persist. The historical reinforcement of a given set of institutional arrangements raises the cost of changing them. The cost of switching to an ostensibly better set of institutions, even if society is able to positively identify them, may be prohibitively expensive. The cost of adjustment is also a frequently invoked argument for gradualism: a piecemeal process of institutional change may reduce such costs, or at least spread the burden of carrying them over successive generations, while allowing other elements of the institutional matrix to adjust at a commensurate pace. Another theme pertaining to the costs associated with institutions is that the credibility of enforcement is inversely related to cost: again, commitment technologies are important to ensure that economic agents do not second-guess institutions and their enforcement. In the institutional apparatus of economic policy, the use of contingent rules as commitment technologies over the exercise of discretion has been proposed as a means to achieve credibility and reduce the cost of institutional enforcement.

Receptiveness

This chapter has repeatedly underlined the importance of context in the design and functioning of institutions. As noted above, it is a positive insight from New Institutional Economics that institutions change gradually due to the powerful effects of path dependence, but it is also a normative argument that piecemeal, gradualist reform is desirable, given not only path dependence and adjustment costs but also the intricacy and interwoven nature of the institutional matrix. However, it also follows from these positive and normative arguments that institutions *do* and *should* change, when both endogenous and exogenous events affect the functions they are required to perform. As discussed earlier, this dynamic understanding of institutions is due in particular to Douglass North.

Institutions can become obsolete if they do not adapt to changing contexts and changes to other elements within the institutional matrix. The New Institutional Economics literature suggests that institutions that are receptive to such changes have built-in mechanisms for receiving feedback and evaluation. The receptiveness of institutions touches on a range of structural political and economic features of a country— for example, the extent of judicial and legislative oversight (the separation of powers), the culture and public expectations with respect to the transparency of government institutions, and openness to global trade and competition. Even within open societies, however, some institutions are better than others at promoting feedback and evaluation— that is, receptiveness is also a matter of design.

Stability and Durability

One of the fundamental tensions in institutional economics is that while institutions should be receptive to dynamic change in the manner described above, they should also not constantly change—after all, the purpose of institutions is generally to bring a degree of predictability into otherwise higher uncertain economic exchange. Following the analogy of institutions as the "rules of the game," the quality of the game will suffer if players are uncertain about the rules. Ever-changing institutions can be a source of rather than a solution to instability, uncertainty, and unpredictability in economic life.

Political economic considerations provide additional reasons why durability is commonly associated with good institutions: they are often designed to outlive the time horizon or term of policymakers or politicians (for example, single terms or election cycles of four or five years). Political time frames are notoriously short, adding tremendous uncertainty and unpredictability to economic life in the absence of more durable, institutionalized rules of the game. Even in more benign policy contexts, rule-based policy frameworks can provide stability and continuity by avoiding cults of personality. The preceding discussion of the most important functions of institutions emphasized their role in reducing uncertainty, including securing property rights, curbing the arbitrary exercise of political power, and promoting economic stability. From these functions, it follows that institutions should be designed to be stable and durable, as it is the threat of unpredictable actions and outcomes in the preinstitutional state that often necessitates the establishment of institutions in first place.

Coherence

New Institutional Economics underscores the critical importance of situating specific institutions within the broader context of what North called the "institutional matrix" or the "institutional framework." Institutions and the organizations responsible for enforcing them cannot be analyzed and assessed in isolation, as they invariably form part of an "institutional matrix [that] consists of an interdependent web of institutions and consequent political and economic organizations" (North, 1991:109, emphasis added). Hall and Soskice (2003:17) emphasize that the effectiveness of the institutional matrix depends on "institutional complementarity"—the extent to which "the presence (or efficiency) of one [institution] increases the returns from (or efficiency of) the other."

Similarly, Rodrik (2002) argued that "different elements of a society's institutional configuration tend to be mutually reinforcing" and that the design and functioning of any particular institution has "repercussions for other parts of the institutional landscape." From an institutional design perspective, this point underlines the importance of considering whether a specific institutional change is productively paired with other elements within the (preexisting) institutional matrix. This has both positive and negative implications. Positively, certain institutional forms that would appear inefficient or ineffective in isolation can deliver positive results given the nature of the institutional matrix in which they are situated, and negatively, certain institutional forms that have worked well in a number of contexts can fail when implemented in an unsuitable and unsupportive institutional matrix.

Incentive Compatibility

Decentralized forms of economic organization invariably necessitate delegated interactions and principal–agent relationships. Well-designed institutions and contracts establish incentives for agents to act in a way that serves the interests of the principal, a feature that economists refer to as incentive alignment or incentive compatibility. Politics looms large over attempts to establish institutions that align incentives in public principal–agent relationships. In contexts where existing institutions are a tool for political patronage and security of office, it can be exceedingly difficult to align political incentives in favor of institutional reform. Recognition of the difficulty of aligning political incentives has been another source of support for gradualism in the process of institutional reform, notably from Rodrik (2008) and Acemoglu and Robinson (2013a). Rodrik, in particular, is sympathetic to the idea of suboptimal (or in his words, "heterodox" and "second-best") institutions, if these can be demonstrated to provide better incentive compatibility. Ultimately, good institutions take incentive alignment seriously and attempt to incorporate internal mechanisms to achieve this. At the very least, good institutions should not create a set of incentives that are clearly at odds with each other and the function the institution is tasked with performing.

CONCLUSION

Chapter 1 concluded with a number of observations regarding the increasing support for institutions-centric explanations for the observed divergence in economic performance of resource-rich economies. In this respect, the resource-curse literature reflects the broad ascendance of institutional analysis in economics in general and development economics specifically. The more granular perspective on the institutional and political economy problems in the management of resource revenues provided in this chapter is useful for a number of purposes. First, it enables a more fruitful discussion of piecemeal change around the cluster of institutions specifically involved in the management of resource revenues rather than general institutions. The focus of specific institutions opens up a more hopeful line of inquiry in pursuit of institutional interventions that help reduce the negative impact of resource revenue windfalls on general institutional quality. For economies with poor initial institutions, this establishes the possibility of achievable, piecemeal reforms, whereas for countries starting from a point of relative institutional strength (at the general or macrolevel), targeted institutions directed at resource revenue management can guard against a deterioration in general institutional quality due to the resource windfall.

Second, the more granular perspective on the specific institutions involved in resource revenue management is part of a generally insightful recent effort in the resource-curse literature to move away from understanding the average relationship between resources and economic performance toward a more country-specific approach. This has brought into sharper focus why certain countries appear capable of harnessing their resources in a positive way, while others fall victim to the resource curse. The quality of macroinstitutions is obviously an important factor, but even within the group of economies with sound meta institutions, there are relative successes (Alaska and Norway) and failures (Alberta in the 1980s and early 1990s); likewise, there are selected instances in which resource windfalls have been managed with a surprising degree of prudence in the context of weak general institutions (Timor Leste and Abu Dhabi).

This institutional framework will be employed in this book as a lens through which to make positive and normative assessments of sovereign wealth funds and their accompanying fiscal rules. However, one overarching theme from this chapter's theoretical discussion of institutions bears emphasis: the slow-moving nature of institutional reform, and the extent to which arguments in favor of the primacy of institutions in economics tend to pertain to long-run relationships. This is particularly important for any argument linking institutions to the resource curse, because—as argued in the preceding chapter—the latter is also best understood as a set of arguments regarding long-term economic relationships.

An important practical implication of this long-term, institutions-centric perspective on resource economies is that it calls into question the wisdom of many popular policy prescriptions, which suggest that capital-scarce developing economies in particular should invest windfall resource rents in large-scale infrastructure—in a manner not dissimilar to Rosenstein and Rodan's big-push model from chapter 1. Subsequent chapters, notably chapter 3, will return to the tension between gradualism and rapid transformation in policy debates around resource-dependent economies, particularly as it applies to the potential contribution of sovereign wealth funds. The contribution of sovereign wealth funds proposed in this book regards institutional and political economy constraints as fundamental to resource-dependent economies. Consequently, the institutional perspective on sovereign wealth funds calls for them to be embedded in a set of rules and supports a long-term, gradualist view of how resource revenues should be used in the process of economic development. The establishment of a rule-based sovereign wealth fund model for managing resource revenues is nothing more—but also nothing less—than part of the process of piecemeal reform and institutional change.

CHAPTER THREE

Guardians of the Future Against the Claims of the Present

*Sovereign Wealth Funds as an Institutional
Response to the Resource Curse*

IN HIS SURVEY on the resource curse, Frankel (2012) asserts that "there is no reason why resource-rich countries need fall prey to the curse" and identifies no less than ten common policy and institutional responses that "merit consideration" (an additional six interventions were deemed to have been failures) in addressing problems associated with various links in the resource value chain.[1] Of particular relevance to this book are three relatively recent items on Frankel's list that deal directly with the fiscal and institutional challenges of managing large, volatile, and temporary resource revenue windfalls: first, the avoidance of excessive spending in boom times through clearly defined counter-cyclical rules to govern the allocation of resource revenues; second, the establishment of commodity funds that are transparently and profes-sionally run, with rules to govern the payout rate and with insulation of the managers from political pressure; and third, the mandating of an external agent to provide transparency and freeze accounts in the event of a coup.

Combined, these three interventions reflect the growing acceptance of the role that rule-based sovereign wealth funds[2] can play in the prudent management of resource revenues. Progress has not been equal across all three areas: there is a far greater number of sovereign wealth funds than there are independent authorities managing them, while even fewer of them are managed within what could credibly be described as a rule-based countercyclical fiscal framework. Nevertheless, the combination of these three policy and institutional interventions today constitute "best practice" with respect to the management of resource revenues. In a growing number of cases, resource-based sovereign wealth funds have emerged as the national (and sometimes subnational) equivalent of endowed institutions, such as universities and charitable foundations, whose trustees James Tobin (1974) described as "the guardians of the future against the claims of the present," whose task it was to "preserve equity among generations."

The increasing appeal of sovereign wealth funds is reflected not only in the growth in assets under their collective management, a number for which credible estimates vary between \$6.5 trillion and \$8.3 trillion,[3] but also in the proliferation in new funds, as shown in figure 3.1. This increase in new sovereign wealth funds appears unlikely to end soon, with a geographically, politically, and economically disparate group of countries—including Israel, Lebanon, Colombia, Peru, Mon-

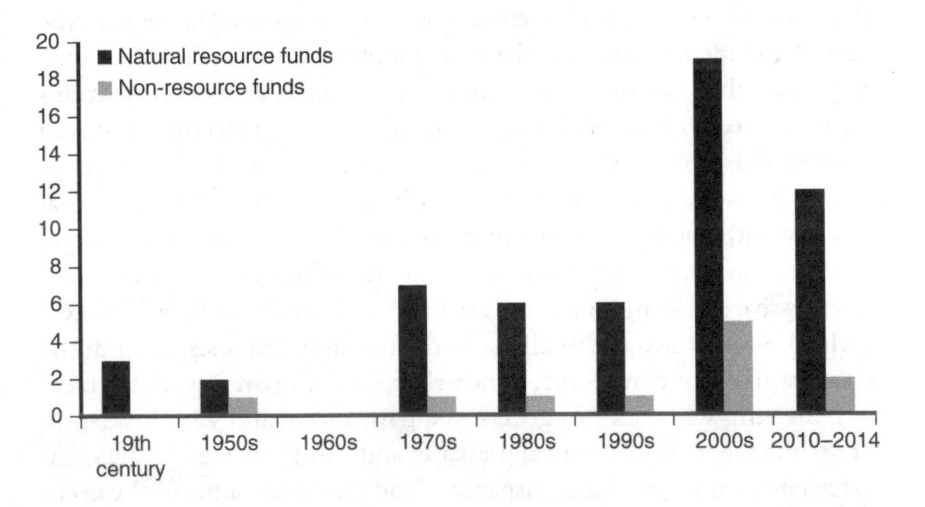

Figure 3.1 Number of new sovereign wealth funds by decade. Sources: Estimates based on SWF (Sovereign Wealth Fund) Institute data, Das et al. (2009), and fund documentation.

golia, Guyana, Niger, Uganda, Namibia, Zambia, and Tanzania—considering the establishment of funds to manage anticipated future resource revenue windfalls.[4]

This chapter discusses the historic emergence of sovereign wealth funds, which is framed predominantly in terms of a number of common functions they perform. What is striking about this discussion is the extent to which these functions emerge as a response to the economic and institutional causes of the resource curse. We also clarify a number of often misleading discussions around the definition and categorization of sovereign wealth funds. The chapter concludes with an assessment of the critiques that have been offered of the sovereign wealth fund model, and identifies a broad framework of analysis for the critical policy and institutional choices that surround this model.

DEFINING AND CATEGORIZING SOVEREIGN WEALTH FUNDS

While academic and regulatory interests in sovereign wealth funds are relatively recent phenomena, the funds themselves are not. The roots of one of the world's largest sovereign wealth funds, the Kuwait Investment Authority, for example, trace back to 1953 when its predecessor institutions were established under the British Protectorate to stabilize and invest its oil revenues. While the Kuwait Investment Authority is widely regarded as the first sovereign wealth fund (Kimmit, 2008; Balin, 2009), the true origins of the model date back to the permanent funds established in various American states, notably Texas and New Mexico, in the late nineteenth century to invest the proceeds generated on public land, notably from oil and gas production, to finance public spending needs, such as education, deferred maintenance on public investment projects, and the general budget.

The proliferation of interest in sovereign wealth funds has had the unfortunate consequence of imprecision in the use of the term itself.[5] Sovereign wealth funds are a highly diverse set of institutions that defy simple categorization, and consequently, definitions of sovereign wealth funds tend to be highly contextual. Broad definitions are typically suitable to general debates around issues of state investment, whereas narrower definitions are required when more specific issues are analyzed. For example, the literature that focuses on the regulatory and geopolitical implications of sovereign investors—much of which is concerned with the rise of "state capitalism" (Summers, 2007; Wolf, 2007; Kimmit, 2008)—has tended to adopt rather broad definitions, permitting the inclusion of a multitude of state-owned investment vehicles, such as public pension funds, state-owned enterprises, and development banks. On the other hand, discussions that focus on narrower questions—such as how sovereign wealth funds should shape their investment models to meet savings and intergenerational objectives and liabilities—have adopted more granular definitions that draw subtle distinctions between the various sovereign wealth fund models in operation.

The question of appropriate definitions is not an exclusively academic one, given the regulatory and political concerns that have been raised about the rise of state capitalism and state-owned investors. Sovereign wealth funds have been identified in this regard as potential instruments through which to advance a series of contentious national objectives, thus raising a range of risks around national security, industrial espionage, and investments in "strategic" assets and sectors (Cox, 2007; Summers, 2007; Truman, 2010). Summers (2007) argued that state ownership of sovereign wealth funds "shake[s] the capitalist logic" due to the possible "pursuit of objectives other than maximizing risk-adjusted returns," while Kimmit likened their impact to that of "public footprints in private markets." While the state-owned nature of these funds has been perceived as a threat in its own right, the obscurity of many sovereign investors with respect to the size of their asset under management, their portfolio composition, and their objectives and investment practices has compounded the concerns of recipient countries (Truman, 2010).

The threat of a regulatory backlash from investment-recipient countries (which essentially disappeared in the wake of the global financial crisis that started in 2008) resulted in the formation of an International Working Group of Sovereign Wealth Funds. This body subsequently established a set of Generally Accepted Principles and Practices, commonly referred to as the "Santiago Principles" after the Chilean capital where they were adopted, with an implied commitment to focusing on serving macroeconomic purposes; pursuing purely commercial investment objectives; and advancing accountability, transparency, and disclosure (International Working Group on Sovereign Wealth Funds,

2008).[6] However, a less appreciated consequence of the establishment of this group was its contribution to the definition and categorization of sovereign wealth funds. In the first instance, it required a degree of self-association with the concept of a "sovereign wealth fund" in order to participate in the group. Second, a number of funds that did not join the group took additional steps to assure national governments that are not (or do not regard themselves to be) sovereign wealth funds.[7]

Finally, the Santiago Principles also contained an actual definition of the term "sovereign wealth fund." As discussed above, however, the adopted definition is unsatisfactorily broad for any qualified discussion around sovereign wealth funds, which are defined as "special-purpose investment funds or arrangements that are owned by the general government" (International Working Group on Sovereign Wealth Funds, 2008). Clearly, this definition draws no distinction between sovereign wealth funds and a myriad of other types of investment institutions under government ownership—for example, social security funds, development banks, and even state-owned enterprises. Even the added qualification that sovereign wealth funds are "created by the general government for macroeconomic purposes [and] manage or administer assets to achieve financial objectives, and employ a set of investment strategies that include investing in foreign financial assets" fails to fully distinguish sovereign wealth funds from other public investment institutions, such as public pension reserves and central banks' foreign-exchange reserves.

To sharpen the definition, table 3.1 situates sovereign wealth funds within a broader sovereign-investor landscape consisting of the following types of institutions:

- *Classic sovereign wealth funds:* Stabilization and savings funds, established through the transfer of natural resource revenues, excess foreign-exchange reserves, or privatization windfalls. Note that there are further subcategories of funds within this grouping, as explained in greater detail below.
- *Central banks managing foreign-exchange reserves:* Monetary authorities hold foreign-exchange reserves in highly liquid fixed income securities and cash. While the distinction between sovereign wealth funds and central bank reserves appears obvious, it has been blurred in recent years by the accumulation in a number

TABLE 3.1
A typology of sovereign investors

Sovereign investor type	Sources of capital	Main functions	Typical investment models	Examples
Classic sovereign wealth funds	Resource revenues	Saving and growing capital for future fiscal needs (savings funds)	Saving and income funds: diversified portfolios with long-term horizons	Norwegian Pension Fund Global, Abu Dhabi Investment Authority
	Excess foreign-exchange reserves	Generating sustainable investment income (income funds)	Stabilization funds: liquid, fixed income–denominated portfolios	Revenue stabilization funds of Chile, Mexico, and Algeria
	Privatization proceeds	Promoting macroeconomic and fiscal stability (stabilization funds)		
Central banks	Foreign-exchange reserves	Held for exchange rate management and intervention purposes	Liquid, fixed income–denominated portfolios	National central banks
			Limited diversification into liquid equities and alternative assets	Some equity exposure: Swiss National Bank, People's Bank of China, and Hong Kong Monetary Authority
Public pension reserve funds	Earmarked fiscal provisions or surplus contributions, or both	Dedicated asset pools without short-term liabilities, promoting long-term solvency of national pension and social security systems (anticipation of rising entitlements)	Diversified portfolios with long-term horizons and ability to capture various long-term risk premiums	Australia Future Fund, National Pension Fund Korea, Government Pension Investment Fund of Japan, Canadian Public Pension Investment Board
Development banks, funds, and agencies	Government transfers, resource revenues, debt and-equity financing using own balance sheet	Investing in projects and sectors with high expected social and economic returns, particularly in context of financing gaps	Large variation in assets and portfolios, with assets that may include debt, public and private equity, infrastructure, land, and PPPs	National and regional development banks and agencies
		Degree of commercial versus developmental orientation differs		Sovereign development funds: Mubadala (UAE), Temasek (Singapore), Samruk-Kazyna (Kazakhstan), Khazanah (Malaysia)

NOTE: PPP = Purchasing Power Parity; UAE = United Arab Emirates.

of countries of massive reserve holdings that far exceed those needed for conventional policy purposes. Consequently, a number of central banks—such as the Swiss National Bank, the Hong Kong Monetary Authority, and the Dutch central bank—have embarked on the diversification of their reserves into equities and other riskier assets, *without* the additional institutional change of giving these assets to a separate sovereign wealth fund. Therefore, some "investment tranches" managed by central banks have become de facto sovereign wealth funds (Das, Mulder, and Sy, 2009).

- *Pension reserve funds:* Concerns over future public liabilities in countries facing long-term fiscal pressures due to deteriorating demographics have resulted in the establishment of pension reserve funds. The logic behind these funds is that their absence of current liabilities (they are pure reserve funds, without actual liabilities) enables them to assume greater investment risk in exchange for higher average returns. Consequently, they hold more diversified, risk-exposed portfolios than the underlying pension funds that they help prefund (Blundell-Wignal, Hu, and Yermo, 2008). Again, the distinction between pension reserve funds and sovereign wealth funds appears fairly clear, but in practice it is complicated by the desire of certain pension reserve funds (such as the Canadian Pension Plan) to actively disassociate themselves from sovereign wealth funds, while others (notably the Australian Government Future Fund and the New Zealand Superannuation Fund) are self-described sovereign wealth funds.[8]

- *Development banks, funds, and agencies:* There is a large and varied group of sovereign investors whose primary function is to invest in projects and sectors with high expected social and economic returns, particularly in the context of private-sector financing gaps. While institutions in the classic sovereign wealth fund model—whether of the saving or stabilization fund variety—have invested exclusively (as in the case of Norway, Abu Dhabi, Botswana, and Chile) or largely (as in the case of Kuwait and Alberta) in foreign assets, there is a growing tendency to include a domestic or developmental investment mandate, or both, within the ambit of a national sovereign wealth fund. The emergence of so-called sovereign development funds again blurs the definitional lines around sovereign wealth funds, as discussed in greater detail below.

As is evident from the categorization presented in table 3.1, once differentiated from other types of sovereign investors, sovereign wealth funds themselves can be categorized according to a number of interrelated criteria, including—

1. Investment mandates and styles: Based on the length of investment horizons, target returns, degree of portfolio liquidity and portfolio of diversification, and defined or implied risk tolerance.
2. Funding sources: For example, oil revenues, fiscal surpluses, privatization proceeds, or foreign-exchange reserves.
3. Functions: Including macroeconomic stabilization, intergenerational transfers and savings, income generation and revenue diversification, and domestic investment and diversification.

There is an intriguing parallel between the issues raised by the difficult task of defining and categorizing sovereign wealth funds and the distinction in the literature on institutional economics between the form and function of institutions. As discussed in chapter 2, the latter literature has increasingly emphasized the importance of institutional functions over forms. In keeping with this tradition, the following section discusses the most important functions performed by sovereign wealth funds. A full list of funds that meet the criteria to be considered sovereign wealth funds, based on the functions discussed below, is provided in table I.1 in the introduction to this book.

THE PRIMARY FUNCTIONS OF SOVEREIGN WEALTH FUNDS

The heterogeneity of sovereign wealth funds is reflected in the wide range of economic and political contexts in which they operate: sovereign wealth funds exist in some of the world's richest (Norway, Canada, and the United States) and poorest (East Timor, Nigeria, São Tomé and Príncipe, and Papua New Guinea) countries. Not surprisingly, sovereign wealth funds perform a wide-ranging set of functions, often in combination. It is useful to differentiate between primary and ancillary functions—the former are typically articulated in the formal mandates and objectives of the fund, whereas the latter are often of a more implicit nature.

The three most important functions of sovereign wealth funds relate to their role in (1) the *stabilization* of macroeconomic variables, (2) serving as a vehicle for the investment of accumulated public *savings*; and (3) the generation and diversification of fiscal income and national wealth (particularly in the case of resource-dependent countries). These three primary functions map into the three types of classic sovereign wealth funds: stabilization funds, savings funds, and investment-income funds. While the stabilization function is most commonly associated with sovereign wealth funds in countries with volatile resource revenues, the saving, income generation functions cut across both resource- and reserves-based funds (but have a particular meaning in the context of depleting natural resource wealth).

Macroeconomic and Fiscal Stabilization

The stabilization function is particularly important in resource-rich countries, and even more so in those that are also highly dependent on volatile resources for economic prosperity and government revenue. Resource-dependent economies face economic uncertainties on a number of fronts—commodity prices are extremely volatile, while production levels and the value of resource reserves are nearly impossible to predict over the medium to long term. Stabilization funds are a critical part of the policy apparatus for combatting general macroeconomic volatility, as well as more specific purposes such as stabilizing fiscal revenue, foreign-exchange earnings, and public investment.

In most cases, the stabilization function is performed by dedicated stabilization funds, which hold safe and liquid assets that can be used for intervention purposes when unanticipated shocks hit resource-dependent economies. Examples of such short-term stabilization funds include the Economic and Social Stabilization Fund in Chile, the Oil Stabilization Fund in Colombia, the Oil Revenues Stabilization Fund of Mexico, the Algerian Revenue Regulation Fund, and the Stabilization Fund managed by the Nigerian Sovereign Investment Authority.

Long-term investment-income funds (or, as they are called in the United States, "permanent funds"), which have more diversified portfolios that include more illiquid and risky assets, can also contribute to the stabilization of fiscal revenues if their annual investment income is significant compared with other public revenue sources. Examples where this is the case include Norway, Kuwait, Botswana, and Wyoming—where investment income is a significant and stabilizing source of fiscal revenue (without being linked to an explicit stabilization fund). Through either a liquid stabilization or an investment-income fund, sovereign wealth funds reduce the volatility of fiscal revenues by generating a stable alternative revenue stream that can also be countercyclical if the investment income is (at least partially) uncorrelated or even negatively correlated with the underlying resource revenue.

Note that the function of macroeconomic stabilization also played an important role in the accumulation of excess foreign-exchange reserve holdings that led to the establishment of reserves-based sovereign investment in a number of Asian countries in the aftermath of the Asian financial crisis of 1997–1998. Reserve accumulation has been described as a form of self-insurance against debt, banking and balance-of-payments crises, and the widespread economic instability that followed the crisis (Aizenman and Lee, 2006). While accumulated foreign-exchange reserves held for these purposes have typically remained under the control of national central banks, a portion of "excess" reserves has been transferred to dedicated sovereign wealth funds with a more long-term saving function (see below).

Long-Term Investment of Public Savings

Sovereign wealth funds are increasingly popular vehicles through which to achieve the kind of aims evoked by James Tobin's (1974) quote in the introduction to this chapter: acting as "the guardians of the future against the claims of the present." Savings funds facilitate a degree of intergenerational equity in the allocation of the benefits from national assets, preserving the claims of future generations to these assets from those of the present. This assumes special significance in the context of resource economies, as the finite and uncertain nature of resource wealth creates unique challenges in which the sovereign wealth fund transforms finite assets from depleting natural resources into permanent wealth in the form of a portfolio of financial assets.[9]

Sovereign wealth funds in both resource- and reserve-rich countries perform the function of investing accumulated public savings through diversified portfolios with long-term investment horizons and higher expected average returns. The motivations underlying the public savings that feed sovereign wealth funds in resource- and reserves-rich countries are, however, rather different. By transforming a depleting natural resource into a potentially permanent one in the form of an endowment of financial assets, a country can ensure that the level of public spending observed during the period of resource extraction can be sustained—or even increased—in its aftermath. Several commodity-based sovereign wealth funds, including those in Norway, Kuwait, Chile, Botswana, Alberta, and Alaska, have the stated objective of preserving resource wealth for future generations. Finally, concerns over the ability to prudently and productively spend and invest potentially massive resource windfalls (even when stabilized in the manner described above) has been part of the motivation behind the establishment of long-term savings funds in jurisdictions such as Abu Dhabi, Kuwait, Qatar, Botswana, and East Timor, as well as developed and industrialized economies, such as Norway (see discussion of the Dutch disease below).

The savings function has also gained increasing prominence in economies that accumulated excess foreign-exchange reserves. These assets were initially held almost exclusively in low-yielding, liquid assets, until after roughly a decade of rapid reserve accumulation resulted in increased awareness of the opportunity costs of holding low-yielding assets.[10] This opportunity cost of holding hundreds of billions of dollars in low-yield assets, coupled with the need to provision for anticipated future liabilities associated with demographic shifts, prompted the transfer of a share of accumulated reserve assets into more diversified portfolios with longer investment horizons and great risk tolerance, in pursuit of higher returns.

A striking similarity in the operational and institutional arrangements for the management of sovereign assets of both a reserves- and resources-based nature has therefore emerged. These similarities pertain to the objectives behind the establishment of different pools of sovereign wealth, the investment strategies adopted in pursuit of those objectives, and the separate institutional arrangements required for the effective management of these distinct pools. The stabilization funds of resource-rich countries are comparable to the conventional foreign-exchange reserve portfolios managed by central banks, while the savings and investment-income funds of resource-rich countries are the counterparts of the long-term investment funds established with excess reserves in a number of countries. The former are essentially buffer funds—insuring against external shocks (reserves-based funds) and revenue

TABLE 3.2

Comparing resource- and reserves-based sovereign wealth management

	Reserves-based sovereign wealth	Resource-based sovereign wealth
Liquid portfolio		
Primary motivation	Precautionary savings against shocks (debt, trade, financial crises)	Stabilization of volatile revenues and commodity price shocks
Management authority	Central bank	Ministry of Finance
Portfolio structure	Highly liquid, short-dated sovereign bonds and cash	Highly liquid, short-dated sovereign bonds and cash
Investment horizon	Short (0–12 months)	Short (0–12 months)
Long-term portfolio		
Primary motivation	Higher return on excess foreign reserve assets	Establishing an alternative source of wealth and fiscal income
Management authority	Dedicated investment authority (or dedicated unit in central bank if investment model is not too complex)	Dedicated investment authority (or dedicated unit in central bank if investment model is not too complex)
Portfolio structure	Diversified portfolio, with significant exposure to risk assets	Diversified portfolio, with significant exposure to risk assets
Investment horizon	Medium- to long-term (1–10+years)	Medium- to long-term (1–10+years)

volatility (resource-based funds), respectively—and therefore hold highly liquid, low-yielding assets. The latter are established to generate higher long-run average real returns and consequently hold more diversified portfolios with significant risk exposure.

To the extent that the management of these longer term and more risk-orientated portfolios—whether financed by resource revenues or excess foreign-exchange reserves—required different governance arrangements, operational structures and investment expertise, a number of countries created new, stand-alone institutions in the form of sovereign wealth funds. This often involved transferring assets away from their traditional locations in the treasury (in the case of resource revenues) and central banks (in the case of foreign-exchange reserves). The

Korea Investment Corporation and the China Investment Corporation, created in 2004 and 2007, respectively, are notable examples of the latter, while the National Oil Fund of Kazakhstan, the Pension Reserve Fund of Chile, and the Kuwait Investment Authority are examples of the former. Table 3.2 summarizes the similarities in the economics, operations, and institutional arrangements of managing resource- and reserves-based sovereign wealth.

Income Generation and Wealth Transformation

Resource-based sovereign wealth funds are often part of a process of transforming one source of wealth—natural resources—into another with more attractive properties—financial assets. Portfolio theory suggests that wealth, assets and income sources should be diversified to increase risk-adjusted returns (alternatively, to reduce the expected risk of the portfolio for a given level of return). If applied at the national level, this provides a rationale for the establishment of a sovereign wealth fund, which is an institutional mechanism through which (at least part of) natural wealth is transformed into financial wealth.

In the context of resource dependence, this transformative function of sovereign wealth funds assumes even greater urgency. Investment-income type sovereign wealth funds provide a supplementary—and, potentially, uncorrelated—source of public income to finance both capital and recurrent fiscal expenditures. The desire to transform the income source from commodities to financial assets arises for a number of reasons: the aforementioned volatility of resource-based revenues, a concern that resource revenues may be declining and therefore need to be replaced by a (potentially permanent) financial endowment, and a belief that financial assets may have a higher risk-adjusted return than natural assets.

In a speech titled "From Oil to Equities," Knut Kjaer, the former head of the Norwegian sovereign wealth fund, made the case that the continued transformation of oil wealth into financial wealth was the prudent thing to do for the sake of future generations, based on both return and risk considerations. It is clear that the interrelated concerns over intergenerational equity, risk, and return are all a part in the establishment of the Norwegian sovereign wealth fund, and the articulation of its role is transforming the country's sources of wealth and income:

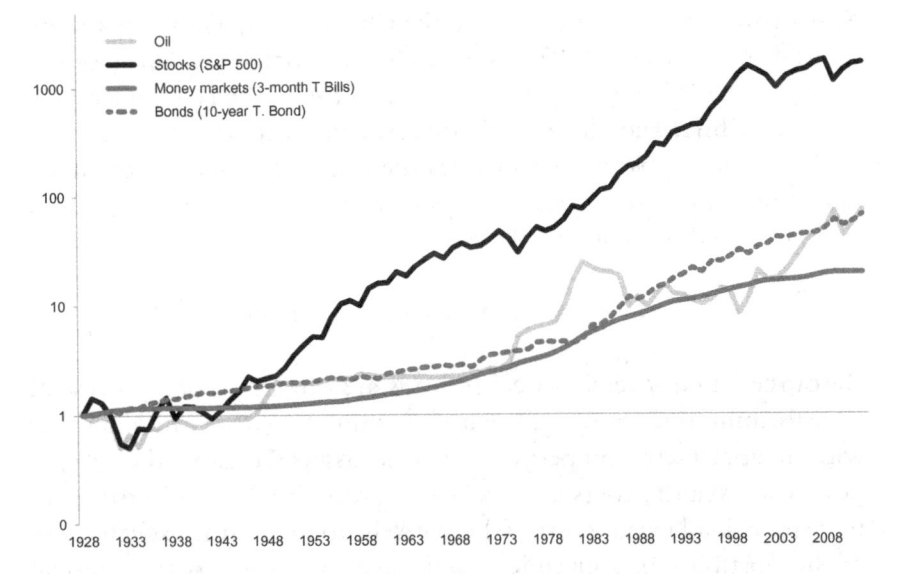

Figure 3.2 The cumulative total returns on financial assets and oil, 1928–2008. Source: Kjaer (2006); adapted using data from Bloomberg. The chart shows the cumulative total (nominal) returns on one dollar invested in financial assets and oil, respectively, starting in January 1928. Note that the vertical axis is horizontal.

The transition from oil in the ground to a broad portfolio of international equities contributes both to increasing the expected return on government wealth and reducing the associated risk . . . (the fund is) an instrument for diversifying government wealth and transforming income from temporary petroleum resources into a permanent flow of investment income . . . (it is for the) benefit of future generations that Norway succeeds in continuing the transformation/diversification of wealth into foreign financial assets. (Kjaer, 2006)

In making the case for the transformation of wealth from oil to equities, note the calculation of cumulative total returns (in nominal terms) on one dollar invested in stocks (proxied here by the S&P 500), bonds (proxied by U.S. ten-year Treasury bonds), and oil. Clearly judged purely on the basis of returns, financial risk assets (stocks) have outperformed oil. Oil has demonstrated a similar cumulative total return to that of U.S. Treasury bonds, but at a much higher volatility, evident in figure 3.2. However, Kjaer argued further that if one considers the

Value-at-Risk of Norway's total oil wealth (yet-to-be-extracted oil under the ground) relative to that of its financial assets (in the sovereign wealth fund), the risk-based argument for wealth transformation is similarly compelling. Arguing that if risk is measured as the standard deviation of the returns for the years 1900 to 2005, "the risk associated with the remaining portion of petroleum wealth is more than seven times higher than for the (sovereign wealth) fund," the risk associated with oil price volatility has, historically, been "more than twice as high as that associated with a well-diversified portfolio of international equities" (Kjaer, 2006).

As has been the case for a number of sovereign wealth funds that gradually increased their portfolios' allocation to risk assets, Norway's rising equity share (as well as its subsequent first moves into direct real-estate exposures) was hotly debated. However, as Kjaer argued, exposure to risk assets needs to be assessed in the context of the over-all portfolio and the fund's long-term investment horizon:

> The decision to invest in equities might have seemed bold . . . But was it really so? . . . [E]quities, much more so than petroleum, safe-guard the capital saved. Moreover, equities are real assets in that we acquire a stake in the world's production capacity. Fixed-income in-struments generate a reasonably stable return in the short term compared with equities. However, over a 100-year time horizon, which we must apply in this context, fixed-income instruments do not provide an absolute protection of real values. (Kjaer, 2006)

Naturally, not all stakeholders (including the financial media and poli-ticians, who both operate on much shorter time frames than the fund) are able or incentivized to adopt this holistic, long-term perspective. As Kjaer (2006) lamented, "It is somewhat paradoxical that oil wealth fluctuates enormously—without prompting frequent media headline coverage—while it only takes small changes in the Fund's balance to draw headline coverage and questions." Indeed, the establishment of a sovereign wealth fund introduces "headline risk to the extent that an unrecorded asset is converted into a portfolio that has a current value that can be gauged" (Kjaer, 2006).

The managers of the Norwegian sovereign wealth fund have tire-lessly engaged the media and other stakeholders in education efforts, pointing out that fluctuations in the fund's value are considerably smaller than the alternative of holding all of the country's wealth in the form of oil and gas. However, this work is never complete, and sovereign wealth funds around the world need to recognize—as Norway has done—the importance of a comprehensive and ongoing campaign of information sharing, education, and clear communication. Making the case for converting oil to equities will always remain a work in progress.

SECONDARY FUNCTIONS OF SOVEREIGN WEALTH FUNDS

A number of implicit functions of sovereign wealth funds emerge as extensions or underlying motivations for the primary functions discussed above—for example, the primary function of a sovereign wealth fund may be to save a share of resource revenues, but the reasons for savings may be related to a secondary function (such as avoiding the unsustainability or misallocation of investment financed from temporary resource boom). Other ancillary functions are entirely independent from—and possibly in conflict with—the primary functions outlined above, notably the increasingly popular role that sovereign wealth funds are expected to play in the domestic economy. It is particularly striking in light of the discussion of the resource-curse literature in Part 1 that many of the functions associated with resource-based sovereign wealth funds directly or indirectly address the most important causes of resource-related economic afflictions.

Domestic Economic Development: Infrastructure and Economic Diversification

Particularly among the sovereign wealth funds in developing countries, there is a growing tendency to give these funds a mandate for investing at least part of their capital in domestic assets that are expected to generate broader social and economic benefits. These investments run the gamut of public goods, but there has been a specific emphasis on physical infrastructure. The motivations for investments in domestic infrastructure include an apparent shortage in well-functioning physical infrastructure, evidence of a financing gap in the supply of infrastructure-related capital, a belief that infrastructure investments can generate high financial returns in the context of capital scarcity over a sufficiently long investment horizon, which a sovereign wealth fund has (at least in theory), and the argument that functional infrastructure is a prerequisite for economic growth and development, and therefore has a variety of social and economic returns outside of financial return considerations.[11]

Another dimension of the developmental function some sovereign wealth funds are tasked with is that of direct investment in certain industries and sectors that policymakers believe will promote economic diversification.[12] Among resource-rich countries, it is common for sovereign wealth funds with domestic investment mandates to invest in downstream industries related to the primary resource, such as refining and petrochemical engineering, to capture a greater national share of the resources value chain. Sovereign wealth funds in both resource- and reserves-rich countries have also been given mandates to invest in completely unrelated sectors, such as tourism, biotech, entertainment, and, particularly, financial services. In many cases, these investments are predicated on the belief that these sectors and industries are either labor intensive (thereby creating employment opportunities) or skills intensive (thereby subject to possible productivity and income gains).

Examples of sovereign development funds that combine domestic infrastructure development, the financing of other public goods, and diversification functions, include Bahrain's Mumtalakat Holdings, Vietnam's State Capital Investment Corporation, Abu Dhabi's Mubadala, Saudi Arabia's Public Investment Fund, and France's Fonds Stratégique d'Investissement. Singapore's Temasek Holdings could also be seen as a sovereign development fund, although it has graduated toward a more long-term wealth management approach that increasingly favors commercial objectives over developmental ones. Sovereign wealth funds with developmental functions differ in terms of their ranking of commercial and developmental objectives underlying such investments. Some are expected (at least de jure) to apply strict commercial criteria to domestic investments, based on their expected risk-return characteristics; while others explicitly take noncommercial objectives into account and are willing to forgo financial returns to pursue these additional objectives.

So pronounced has been the increased interest in domestic and developmental investment models, that sovereign development funds should arguably now take a position alongside sovereign saving, investment-income, and stabilization funds as the most important types of sovereign wealth funds. Similarly, domestic development may be elevated to a primary function of sovereign wealth funds. As argued in the remainder of this chapter, however, the governance and operational implications that accompany a domestic development function are sufficiently different from that of classic sovereign wealth fund models that it is useful to treat them as somewhat separate entities.

Preventing Dutch Disease and Maintaining Export Competitiveness

Sovereign wealth funds in both resource- and reserves-rich countries have been intrinsically linked with efforts to maintain export competiveness through the exchange rate channel. The Dutch disease remains one of the most popular explanations for the resource curse. By investing (part of) the proceeds from the extraction of natural resources in foreign assets, sovereign wealth funds help avoid an appreciation of the real exchange rate during boom periods in the commodity price or production cycle. Dutch disease effects are particularly acute in countries with limited absorptive capacity, due to an inflexible and unskilled labor market, infrastructure bottlenecks, and a lack of trade openness. A number of countries—including Norway, Botswana, and Chile—have made reference to the role of their sovereign wealth funds in avoiding the Dutch disease, and have, consequently, prohibited domestic investments by their sovereign wealth funds.

Preventing Waste, Corruption, and Poor Public Investments

Political economy factors are pivotal to the case for establishing a sovereign wealth fund. Evidence to suggest that the quality of public investment deteriorates during periods of (often unexpected) sharp increases in public revenue, spending, and investment, particularly in resource-rich countries (Gelb, 1988). By establishing a clear, rules-based framework for the management of resource revenues, sovereign wealth funds can reduce the rent-seeking associated with the revenue windfalls (Tornell and Lane, 1999; Torvik, 2002; Robinson, Torvik, and Verdier, 2006). Beyond these political dimensions, there is strong evidence that public investment is subject to significant declining marginal returns in the short run, particularly in the context of both economic and institutional capacity constraints (Pritchett, 2000; Berg et al., 2013; Presbitero, 2016). Finally, long-term public investments may be incomplete or their recurrent costs unfinanced if the revenue and export boom is reversed due to a decline in commodity prices or production.

These issues are particularly pertinent to countries with poor institutions at the start of the revenue boom, as very few countries have succeeded in building the requisite political and public investment processes to ensure that the windfalls are spent and invested in a sustainable, inclusive, and growth-enhancing manner. While sovereign wealth funds are no panacea to deep-rooted political and institutional problems, they can lengthen the horizon over which revenue windfalls are spent and invested in the domestic economy, thereby potentially improving the political incentives and avoiding the sharply declining returns on public investment in the short run. That is, sovereign wealth funds are an institutional "commitment technology" that allows the revenues from a resource boom to be spent and invested more gradually, as absorptive capacity constraints are lifted over time.

DEBATES ON THE APPLICABILITY OF SOVEREIGN WEALTH FUNDS FOR DEVELOPING COUNTRIES

The classic sovereign wealth fund model—which combines resource-based funding with stabilization, savings, and income-generation functions—has been criticized by a number of scholars who argued that this model is inappropriate for countries characterized by capital scarcity and large infrastructure investment needs (Van der Ploeg, 2008; Collier et al., 2010; Venables, 2010). Collier, for example, has argued that "the conventional model of a sovereign wealth fund" is inappropriate for poor countries, as "in a capital-scarce country it is unwarranted to accumulate long-term foreign investments" and that "the core objective should evidently be to finance domestic infrastructure" (Collier, 2012). Similarly, Collier et al. (2010) have argued that "an international sovereign wealth fund is not appropriate for a capital-scarce country [as it] is too conservative in that it precludes any near-term increases in consumption."

This criticism is informed by the view that the sovereign wealth fund model is based on the permanent-income hypothesis, a powerful theory developed by Milton Friedman (1957). Collier argues instead for an immediate surge in spending and investment in the aftermath of a resource revenue boom—beyond the level consistent with permanent-income type smoothing—even if that means a lower level of spending in the long run.[13] Collier and his coauthors' argument is that citizens of a country with a large resource discovery will be wealthier in the future, and that it therefore makes sense to spend the resource windfall up-front, to move the country toward its higher growth path faster: "The value to the society of consumption in the near term is considerably higher than consumption in the distant future when the economy has become fully developed. . . . It is therefore appropriate for a developing country to use some of its resource revenues to raise consumption up towards the level of the distant future, rather than to use them to raise the level of consumption in that distant future" (Collier et al., 2010:2). Collier (2010 and 2012) and Santiso (2008) provide enthusiastic support for sovereign development funds over investment income funds for capital-scarce countries with abundant resources, while Collier in particular promotes the idea of using such funds for investment in domestic infrastructure: not only will investment raise the country's growth potential, but the returns on these investments are high, given the capital scarcity (low capital–labor ratio) in these countries.

This critique is a significant challenge to the rising academic and policy support for—and increasing real-world embrace of—the "conventional" sovereign wealth fund model, not least because of Collier's standing in the fields of African economic development and resource economics. However, Collier and his coauthors' critique appears to wish away almost all the pervasive themes in the resource-curse literature, as discussed in Part 1, most notably the institutional and political constraints of efficient, large-scale public investment financed by resource revenue windfalls (which may also be temporary and subject to sharp reversals) and the Dutch disease and the inherent procyclicality of resource-rich economies. The second major objection is that Collier et al.'s (2010) criticism is essentially an attack on a straw man: not in one single case worldwide has the adoption of a sovereign wealth fund precluded an increase in consumption or forced governments to save all resource revenue without any access to investment income in return. Finally, Collier's argument relies on two would-be inevitabilities that have rarely been observed in the history of resource-rich poor countries: that future generations will be much richer than current ones, and that the return on domestic investments is by definition higher than that on international assets. These counterarguments are elaborated on in greater detail below.

Inaccurate Claims About the Allocation of Resource Revenues

Collier et al. (2010) contend that the conventional sovereign wealth fund model proposes "that *all revenue should go into the sovereign wealth fund*" and that this savings rule is "too conservative in that it precludes *any near-term increases in consumption*" (emphasis added). In practice, this is never the case. In most cases, domestic investment can still rise to a level consistent with that seen in high-growth developing countries in recent years, regardless of whether the country has a long-term investment income fund or not. The point of the conventional sovereign wealth fund model is that resource-rich countries tend to experience periodic revenue booms—which are of an unpredictable magnitude or duration—that generate rents in excess of what can be efficiently invested, given a range of economic, administrative, and institutional constraints that can only be progressively lifted (Berg et al., 2013; Presbitero, 2016).

By suggesting that the presence of a sovereign wealth fund moves all resource revenue–related public spending and investment into the future, Collier et al. (2010) are attacking a straw man version of these funds. In practice, governments with sovereign wealth funds typically transfer only a portion of their resource revenue windfalls to the fund. As discussed in chapter 5, governments typically specify a savings rule in the form of a certain percentage of revenues (for example, 30 percent of oil-related royalties) or hurdle-price for oil (for example, seventy-four dollars per barrel), suggesting that a significant share of resource revenue remains available for public spending and investment.

Domestic Returns Are Often Much Lower Than Predicted

As noted above, part of the argument for using resource revenues to ramp up public spending and domestic infrastructure development is based on the assumption that the return on domestic investment is higher than that on foreign investment. This is a common theoretical result in growth models with declining marginal returns to capital and a cornerstone of the "convergence" argument derived from them, as well as the idea that capital should flow to countries with low capital stocks or low capital–labor ratios (in search of higher marginal returns). However, it has been demonstrated with depressing regularity that neither convergence in economic growth nor the flow of capital from developed to developing countries are in any way inevitable: Pritchett's (1997) famous investigation of the evidence on convergence concluded that the reality was one of "divergence, big time," while the Lucas Paradox, in which capital flows "upstream" from emerging to advanced economies remains a puzzling phenomenon (Lucas, 1990).

Clearly, there are a host of complex factors, beyond the capital–labor ratio, that affect the rate of return on infrastructure investments in poor countries, including institutional factors. There is near universal recognition that the quality of institutions has a very significant bearing on the effectiveness of infrastructure investment on growth, as summarized by Esfahani and Ramirez:

> Institutional capabilities that lend credibility and effectiveness to government policy play particularly important roles in the development process through infrastructure growth. The effects indicate that countries can gain a great deal by improving investment and performance in infrastructure sectors. But, the exercise also implies that achieving better outcomes requires institutional and organizational reforms that are more fundamental than simply designing infrastructure projects and spending money on them. (Esfahani and Ramirez, 2003:471)

Given the insights from the resource-curse literature on the interactions between resources and the development of institutions, the assumption of high rates of return on infrastructure in resource-rich poor countries appears tenuous—particularly when combined with an unambiguous appeal for a rapid scale-up in such forms of investment.

The Impact of Institutional, Political Economy, and Public Choice Factors

Part of the appeal of sovereign wealth funds lies in the fact that if properly structured and governed, they reduce the "voracity effect" and a race-for-rents that accompanies a windfall revenue boom. Sovereign wealth funds are potentially powerful institutional commitment devices, establishing a framework of rules and guidelines for the difficult task of managing volatile and finite resource revenues. As noted in Part 1, the political and institutional challenges around resource revenue management is "probably the most active research field on theories of the resource curse currently, and will probably continue to be so for a while, simply because there are so many political-economy characteristics of resource-rich countries that still cry out for an explanation" (Torvik, 2009).

It is also highly questionable whether centralized policymakers will be able to successfully identify which infrastructure projects can be efficiently completed within the uncertain time frame established by a resource revenue boom. The Public Choice literature suggests that government officials face a variety of adverse incentives in arriving at these decisions. This story is consistent with Mehlum, Moene, and Torvik's (2006) conclusion that good institutions are crucial to the successful investment of resource revenues, as well as the empirical and theoretical work by Gelb (1988), Robinson and Torvik (2005), and Robinson, Torvik, and Verdier (2006).

Dutch Disease

The argument in favor of a scaled-up spending and investment boom financed by resource revenue windfalls is surprisingly oblivious to the risk of Dutch disease. The preceding point made the case for gradualism in domestic investment in light of anticipated institutional limits and bad political incentives, but the purely economic argument based on Dutch disease can be added to the case for a gradual scaling up of investment financed by a resource boom. In some sense, the fact that Collier is the leading authority associated with the criticism of sovereign wealth funds is highly surprising, given his personal scholarship on Dutch disease (and indeed all the above-mentioned problems with the spending and investment of resource revenues). Collier and Goderis (2007), for example, found "that a substantial part of [the resource curse] is explained by high public and private consumption, low or inefficient total investment, and an overvalued exchange rate." This amounts to very strong support from Collier for the Dutch disease hypothesis—and, moreover, for the role of inefficient spending and investment in causing it.

Lack of Rules and Fiscal Anchors

Collier's criticism of conventional sovereign wealth funds has also been directed at the International Monetary Fund, given the institution's support for the model. Responding directly to Collier's promotion of the sovereign development fund model as a more appropriate alternative for resource-rich poor countries, members of the Fund's Fiscal Affairs Department argued in a paper titled *Fiscal Frameworks for Resource Rich Developing Countries* that "development funds tend to fragment the budget process and policy decision-making, weaken the control of fiscal aggregates, as well as reduce the credibility and even the quality of the regular budget. Rather than looking for quick fixes, public financial management weaknesses need to be tackled holistically" (Baunsgaard et al., 2012).

Referencing Collier's contributions to the literature, the authors argue further that "the recent literature has emphasized the merits of using resource wealth to invest in physical assets with high yields in terms of nonresource productivity and growth (and nonresource fiscal revenue)," before adding, "Such a formulation, while theoretically sensible, is problematic from a practical perspective since it does not provide a meaningful anchor for fiscal policy" (Baunsgaard et al., 2012). The use of a sovereign wealth fund as a commitment device for spending and investing resource revenues—alongside other rule-based elements of the institutional matrix, notably a rule-based fiscal framework—establishes a more credible anchor for fiscal policy.

The Noninevitability of Growth and Rising Incomes

Collier's argument in favor of bringing the spending of resource revenues forward is made with an explicit recognition that it may mean lower average spending of these revenues over time. This reasoning rests on the argument that citizens of resource-rich poor countries will be richer in the future. There is, of course, nothing in the economic history of resource economies, which in fact includes massive investments in domestic infrastructure of the kind Collier proposes, to suggest that this is in any way inevitable, or even likely. The appeal to the supposed inevitability of rising incomes and future wealth is a way to dismiss concerns over intergenerational equity and sustainability once resources are depleted. If future wealth and prosperity is no longer regarded as a deterministic inevitability, intergenerational equity is yet another argument in favor of the conventional sovereign wealth fund model.

THE POLICY AND INSTITUTIONAL FRAMEWORK OF SOVEREIGN WEALTH FUNDS

It is useful to situate the discussion of sovereign wealth funds and the accompanying fiscal frameworks or rules in the context of the broader literature on institutions and the resource curse. In this book, our institutional analysis of sovereign wealth funds pertains not only narrowly to what may be called the "internal governance" of the fund—for example, the distribution of powers and responsibilities between its board of directors and its executive, and the fund's investment rules and policies—but we also focus on "external governance"—for example, the fund's independence from and accountability to government, its legal status (and its management authority), and its public disclosure and reporting policies. An obvious additional layer of analysis is that of "external governance"—for example, its independence from and accountability to government, the legal status of the fund (and its management authority), and its public disclosure and reporting policies. The institutional arrangements for the internal and external governance of sovereign wealth funds are discussed in detail in Part 3 of this book. Our institutional analysis of the sovereign wealth fund model extends further, however. Another critical additional layer for commodity-based sovereign wealth funds is the operation and governance of the fiscal framework—that is, the flow of funds into and out of the sovereign wealth fund, and whether these are discretionary, ad hoc, or rule based. Fiscal rules are discussed in Part 2 of the book.

The various levels of analysis for the sovereign wealth fund model—and indeed for the study of institutions in relation to resource economies in general—are depicted in figure 3.3. Note that most of the literature on the role of institutions and the resource curse (as described in chapter 1 and 2 of this book) are concerned with the first and second levels of analysis: macroinstitutions (the rule of law, government accountability, democracy, and so forth) and, to some extent, general fiscal institutions (resource financing of the state, rent-seeking, and so forth). As part of our effort to identify and analyze a more granular set of institutional

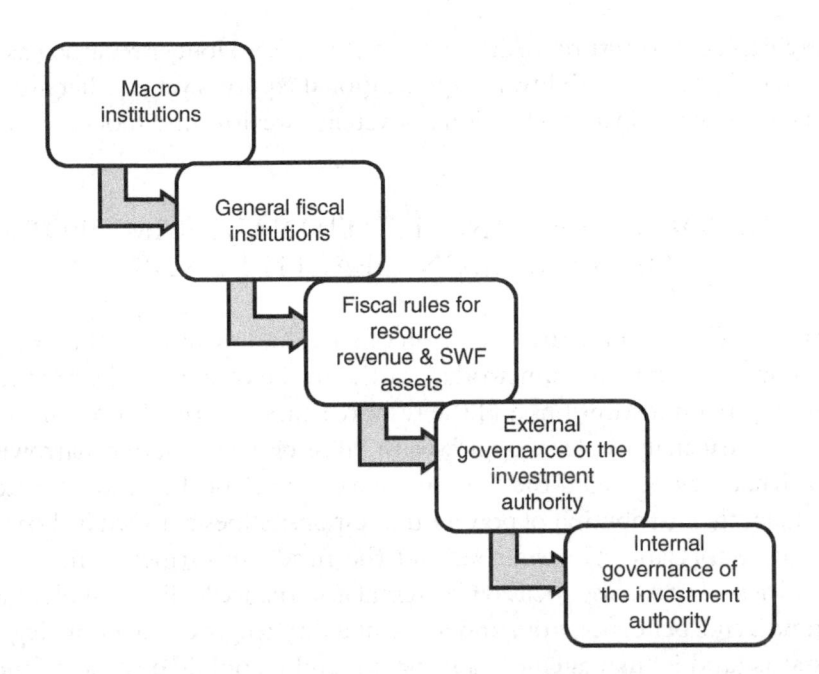

Figure 3.3 Levels of institutional analysis for sovereign wealth funds.

innovations around the management of resource revenues, we extend the analysis to the fiscal framework (or fiscal rules) for resource revenues and sovereign wealth fund assets and income (Part 2), and the external and internal governance of independent sovereign wealth fund management institutions (Part 3). The critical elements of the policy and institutional framework for the sovereign wealth fund model can be summarized as follows.

Fiscal Rules

All resource-based sovereign wealth funds need a mechanism through which to receive a portion of resource revenues to perform their stated functions. These mechanisms can be informal and discretionary, but in the interests of public accountability, predictability, and credible commitments, they are often rule based. Most savings mechanisms in operation today among resource-based sovereign wealth funds are based on very simple rules, such as a fixed percentage of resource revenues, a deviation from the past moving average of resource revenues, or as windfall revenues that arise when a commodity price exceeds a certain "hurdle price" (for example, seventy-four dollars per barrel for oil). If the country has a number of different sovereign wealth funds with stabilization, savings, or development functions (or a sovereign wealth fund with different subfunds or divisions), further rules may be required to allocate funds between the different funds. The following section will analyze a number of common savings rules, and make the case for a more dynamic rule that integrates savings, spending, and stabilization objectives in a single coherent and contingent rule-based framework.

In addition to a savings rule component, the fiscal framework or rule also generally includes a spending rule. Decisions about how to use the sovereign wealth fund's resources pertain to both its capital (or principal) and its investment income. Following the well-known "permanent fund" approach, several sovereign wealth funds, such as those in Norway and several American states, spend only the real returns generated on the fund's capital, while the latter is preserved in real terms into perpetuity or to meet or insure against major future spending needs. An alternative is to reinvest the fund's investment income to achieve a more aggressive buildup of assets managed by the sovereign wealth fund (perhaps before switching to a permanent fund approach, once the fund has reached a target level of assets under management). Both the sovereign wealth fund's capital and its investment income can be linked, implicitly or explicitly, to specific public spending needs on, for example, infrastructure, education, health, and pensions.

The Institutional Framework

The management of sovereign wealth funds often requires coordination between various parts of government and the public sectors, including government ministries (for finance, natural resources, and economic planning), the central bank, independent investment authorities, the parliament, and public auditors. Three key elements of any sovereign wealth fund's institutional framework are—

- *The governance of savings and spending rules and decisions:* The flow of funds in and out of sovereign wealth funds can be discretionary or rule based. The institutional dimension to these policies relates to who decides on these transfers under a discretionary arrangement and, under a rule-based system, who has the authority to set and potentially change the rules.

- *Position in the public sector and operational independence (external governance):* Who is responsible for the day-to-day operations and policy implementation of the sovereign wealth fund? Common arrangements are for the operational aspects of the fund to sit in the central bank, the Ministry of Finance, or in a dedicated investment authority (often depending on the operational complexity of the investment process). Generally, these decisions are made based on the nature of the fund's investment strategy and the concerns and sensitivity surrounding the possibility of political interference. To the extent that sovereign wealth funds of the saving and investment-income variety have long-term investment horizons and are expected to maximize investment returns, an institutional model characterized by operational independence is both popular and desirable.

- *Internal governance:* The sovereign wealth fund's internal governance structures—the rules and procedures that determine the powers and responsibilities of different groups in the organization—are also critically important. The success of the organization in performing the functions expected of it depends on clarity regarding the powers and responsibilities of the board versus the executive, the role and composition of the investment committee, and clear reporting lines within the organization. Of particular importance is an articulation of responsibilities and rules for the various elements of the investment process. The specification of a sovereign wealth fund's investment policy should reflect its stated functions, the government's needs and preferences, and the capacity, expertise, and unique attributes of the institution. The functions and implied (or explicit) liabilities of the sovereign wealth fund determine a number of characteristics: the fund's ability to gain exposure to different asset classes or risk factors, its investment horizon, target return, and risk limits. For either public disclosure purposes or for the clarity of the internal decision-making process, sovereign wealth funds' investment policies and strategies should ideally be consolidated in an investment policy statement and be governed by a set of rules.

CONCLUSION

This chapter has described the emergence of sovereign wealth funds, situated them within a broader landscape of public investment institutions, and categorized them based on a number of criteria, including funding source, investment styles, and most important, a range of common functions. The most important functions performed by sovereign wealth funds appear as a direct response to the common afflictions suffered by resource economies, as per the resource-curse literature discussed in chapter 2. There is significant variation within the broad sovereign investor landscape, as well as within the narrow grouping of sovereign wealth funds. This chapter therefore provided a typology of the different kinds of sovereign investors and sovereign wealth funds, with a specific emphasis on the variety of functions they perform and how these are determined.

There is significant scope for tailoring sovereign wealth funds' functions, policies around savings, spending and investments, and intragovernmental and internal governance arrangements to meet local requirements, based on the economic (and political) realities of the countries in question. Criticisms of sovereign wealth funds tend to underestimate or mischaracterize this degree of flexibility, as well as the extent to which resource-based sovereign wealth funds are designed to directly and indirectly address common afflictions associated with the resource curse. The remainder of this book addresses the critical elements of the policy and institutional framework for resource-based sovereign wealth funds, as identified at the end of this chapter.

CHAPTER FOUR

To Be Boring

Institutional Lessons from the Modern Monetary
Consensus for Sovereign Wealth Funds

MERVYN KING, the esteemed British central banker and monetary economist, once famously said the Bank of England's ambition is "to be boring" (King, 2000). While the extraordinary steps taken by central banks in the aftermath of the global financial crisis have cast doubts over achievability of this vision of abiding tedium, King's statement concisely captured the central tenets of a broad consensus around the appropriate institutional arrangements and policy frameworks of monetary policy. This consensus renders monetary policy so predictable, rule-based, and transparent that news of the latest meeting should be greeted by a collective shrug of the shoulders and a relegation to the back pages of daily newspapers. "Macroeconomic policy has, for most of our lifetime, been rather too exciting for comfort," King noted, adding that "our belief is that boring is best."

This chapter argues that the benefits of boredom are not unique to monetary policy. Indeed, the logic that resulted in the modern monetary consensus, and the case for boringness in monetary policy, can inform the design of other economic institutions and policy frameworks, notably those tasked with macroeconomic stabilization—and, in this specific case, sovereign wealth funds. A number of the world's best-governed sovereign wealth funds, such as those in Norway, Chile, Botswana, and the United States, reflect this basic insight. However, a seductive tendency remains in which sovereign wealth funds are viewed, on both positive and normative grounds, in exactly the opposite way: as mystical "power brokers" of the twenty-first-century global capital markets.[1] To frame and contextualize the discussion of the lessons from modern monetary policy from the policy and institutional arrangements of sovereign wealth in this chapter, we start with a brief discussion of the principal–agent problem, which characterizes both modern monetary policy and sovereign wealth funds.

THE BASIC PROBLEM: THE PRINCIPAL–AGENT RELATIONSHIP

Sovereign wealth funds are typically part of an elaborate system of delegated authority, the likes of which are widely studied in the economics of principal–agent relationships. A principal–agent relationship arises when one party (the principal) delegates authority or responsibility for achieving certain outcomes to a second party (the agent). Such agency relationships are pervasive in modern societies characterized by specialization and cooperation; however, they can introduce significant costs, particularly when the principal lacks the means to ensure that the agent behaves in a manner consistent with the advancement of the principal's objectives. As one of the leading authorities on agency economics observed: "Examples of agency are universal. Essentially all contractual arrangements, as between employer and employee or the state and the governed, for example, contain important elements of agency" (Ross, 1973).

A number of factors can bring agency problems to bear and raise the cost associated with the principal–agent relationship and cooperative economic arrangements. The agent may have objectives that differ significantly from that of the principal. This is particularly problematic if the pursuit of the agent's objectives undermines that of the principal. The economics literature, particularly contributions in the New Institutional tradition, has emphasized the importance of clearly defined contracts and other mechanisms that change the incentives confronting agents, so that it becomes in the agent's best interest to act in a manner consistent with the principal's objectives. In monetary policy, the adoption of an explicit, rule-based inflation-targeting regime, possibly complemented by clearly defined contracts for central bankers, is an example of a set of institutional arrangements that incentivize the agent (the central bank) to act in the interest of the principal (society). Inflation targeting focuses the central bank's attention on the maintenance of low and stable inflation over other policy objectives, and constructs a detailed institutional infrastructure promoting transparency and open communication regarding both the goals and the strategy pursued by the central bank (the agent) on behalf of the principal (society). In this sense, inflation targeting clarifies and reinforces the often implied contractual relationship underlying modern monetary policy (Svensson, 1997).

Agency problems also arise when principals are unable to clearly specify what their goals are or how the progress toward the achievement of its goal(s) may be measured or observed. Clearly, this compromises the process through which the principal may wish to ensure or incentivize that the agent acts in his best interest. It also complicates the monitoring of the agent's performance and track record, which is important in the context of accountability, particularly in a democracy. The literature has emphasized the importance of making the principal's objectives as clear and precise as possible. In a public policy context, this has resulted in the advocation and widespread adoption of explicit policy targets, which agents are tasked with achieving. Clearly defined numeric inflation targets are an example of this trend in the context of monetary policy. A final concern in the principal–agent tradition is that the behavior of the agent can be difficult, expensive, and sometimes impossible to monitor. Again, this complicates the monitoring process between the principal and agent. The literature has therefore emphasized the importance of transparency on the part of the agent in general, and in more applied settings on clear and practical mechanisms for promoting transparency (and, again, accountability in a democratic setting). In modern monetary economics, this is reflected in strong emphasis on transparency on the part of monetary authority (Dincer and Eichengreen, 2014).

In conclusion, the principal–agent framework is a powerful theoretical lens through which to analyze the incentive structures and institutional arrangements underlying devolved authority and decentralized decision making. The tools and solutions of principal–agent analysis have extensive applications in matters of public policy, notably in modern central banking.[2] Moreover, principal–agent concerns also permeate the field of finance and investment, given the myriad of agency relationships that arise from the extraordinarily high degree of specialization, cooperation, and decentralization in modern finance. The tools and solutions of principal–agent analysis are therefore particularly useful in the study of sovereign wealth funds. These funds are at the intersection of a number of fields in which principal–agent analysis is widely applied: general situations of devolved authority, decentralized public and macroeconomic policymaking, and highly specialized modern finance and investment. This chapter will frequently return to the question of how particular institutional arrangements can contribute to the resolution of agency problems related to sovereign wealth funds, and the extent to which the modern monetary consensus addresses these issues.

THE CENTRAL TENETS OF THE MODERN MONETARY CONSENSUS

Since the misadventures of the 1970s, a remarkable intellectual and practical consensus has been achieved around the appropriate institutional foundations and policy frameworks of modern monetary policy. This consensus reflects a synthesis in the historical disagreements between Monetarist and Keynesian schools of thought (Romer, 1993; Taylor, 1997; De Long, 2000). Above all, modern monetary policy, and the institutional framework in which it is nested, recognizes the appeal of institutional independence in the implementation of monetary policy, which has to be supported by explicit mechanisms for addressing ensuing agency problems. Consequently, the most important innovations in monetary policy since the 1970s include the specification of clear goals and targets for monetary policy, the establishment of mechanisms to ensure operational independence, the embrace of rule-based policy frameworks to enhance consistency and transparency, and considerably greater emphasis on transparency and openness in the conduct of monetary policy.

A detailed literature has emerged on each element of the consensus and surveys of this body of work feature subtle variations in emphasis. However, hardly any monetary economist or central banker today would quibble with any of the following six elements of the modern monetary consensus:

1. the primacy of *price stability as the long-run objective of monetary policy*, coupled with an understanding of the contribution that monetary policy can make to reducing output fluctuations;
2. the desirability of *central bank independence* in monetary policy, understood as "instrumental" or "operational" independence, while retaining goals dependence;
3. the expression of the central bank's objectives regarding *explicit policy targets* (or nominal anchors);
4. the use of *contingent rules*, which incorporate forward-looking information on the expected state of the economy, to achieve policy objectives and targets;
5. the importance of *institutionalizing the credibility* of the central bank; and
6. the need for ac*countability* in the monetary policy framework of instrument-independent central banks, with a resulting focus on *transparency*.

This list is very close to that compiled by Mishkin (2000), but makes the two uncontroversial additions of contingent rules and credibility.[3] The omission of these two elements by Mishkin is simply a matter of organization. The author does stress the importance of credibility, but under the discussion of nominal anchors (as have other synthesizing contributions to the literature, such as Blinder, 2000; Friedman, 2002; and Goodfriend, 2007). Similarly, the case for rules—with a critically important understanding of the desirability of their contingent nature—is no longer controversial, as evidenced by the detailed discussion of rule-based monetary policy in other synthesizing articles on modern central banking (Cecchetti, 1998; Woodford, 2002). While there is still some debate in monetary economics regarding the relative weight applied to "rules versus discretion," this traditional distinction has been considerably softened by the relatively recent emphasis on contingent ("state-dependent" or "dynamic") rules. Mishkin himself has acknowledged the consensus around the desirability of contingent rules, linking it to the idea that central banks operate under principles of "constrained discretion" (Mishkin and White, 2014).

LESSONS FROM MODERN MONETARY INSTITUTIONS FOR SOVEREIGN WEALTH FUNDS

The remainder of this chapter will assess the applicability to sovereign wealth funds of these six elements of the modern monetary consensus to the design of policy rules and institutional arrangements for central banks. The discussion will also be informed by the extent to which these elements and the institutional arrangements that follow from them match the principles for the forms and functions of institutions identified in chapter 2.

Policy Objectives and Institutional Mandates

If there is a binding theme in the modern monetary consensus, it is the emergence of a broad agreement around the appropriate goals of monetary policy. Greater clarity around both the power and limits of monetary policy informed all other institutional aspects of the consensus. The consensus reflects the understanding that monetary policy cannot affect (and therefore cannot target) real variables in the long run, and that the most significant contribution of monetary policy is the achievement of price stability (understood as low and stable inflation). The modern consensus also recognizes that monetary policy can contribute to reducing fluctuations in real variables (output and unemployment) in the short run and therefore can be used in part to stabilize short-run output fluctuations, albeit in a rule-based countercyclical manner (for reasons discussed below).

This understanding was achieved long after Milton Friedman (1968) famously warned that "the danger of assigning to monetary policy a larger role than it can achieve [is] preventing it from making the contribution it is capable of making." But Friedman's insight would prove remarkably prescient in understanding, first, that monetary policy is a powerful tool, and second, that misdirecting that power compromises its effectiveness. It took decades of piecemeal learning to arrive at an understanding of the appropriate goals and contribution of monetary policy, and following this, yet more time to develop a clearer vision of the supporting institutions (an emphasis on independence and credibility, rules and targets). The modern monetary consensus has been accompanied by arguably the most successful period in the history of monetary policy in the form of the "Great Moderation" in inflation and volatility of output since the early 1980s. Yet it is an open question as to whether this consensus will be shattered or reinforced by the events and aftermath of the global financial crisis that erupted in 2008.[4]

Advocates of sovereign wealth funds and of a particular set of institutional arrangements for these funds cannot (yet) rely on the kind of broad-based consensus. As is the case in monetary policy, however, debates around the objectives of institutions tasked with managing resource revenues can rely on decades' worth of empirical evidence and experience. Sovereign wealth funds emerged in response to long-observed problems in resource-rich countries. As discussed in chapters 1 and 2, the findings of the resource-curse literature are varied (and in some cases, still controversial), but a stylized list of problems in resource-dependent economies can inform the appropriate scope of sovereign wealth funds' functions and mandates (which are discussed in greater detail in chapter 3):

- *Volatility and procyclicality:* The exceptional volatility of commodity prices is well documented (Hamilton, 2009; Jacks, O'Rourke, and Williamson, 2011). Consequently, countries dependent on resources for fiscal revenue and export earnings are exposed to greater volatility in their fiscal policy, balance of payments and business cycles, and have a documented tendency toward procyclical fiscal policy.
- *Dutch disease:* Resource booms can result in a (temporary) loss of export competitiveness due to an appreciation of the real exchange rate and a demonstrably inefficient allocation of capital and other factors of production.
- *Weak institutions and political economy challenges:* That there is a negative correlation between resource abundance and institutional quality is not controversial (Mehlum, Moene, and Torvik, 2006; Robinson, Torvik, and Verdier, 2006). What is more contentious is the causality of this relationship, and explanations for the observed relationship. Regardless, as discussed in chapter 2, the association of resource windfalls with rent-seeking behavior, public investment in "white elephants," and unaccountable government and fiscal practices is well documented.
- *Intergenerational equity and the sustainability of public spending:* Sovereign wealth funds have been cast as a mechanism through

which to achieve a degree of intergenerational equity in the allocation of revenues derived from exhaustible or finite natural resources. The concern here is both moral (is it fair that the proceeds from finite resources are allocated to a particular generation alone?) and practical (can the level of public spending enabled by a resource boom be maintained both across the commodity cycle and on a more long-term basis once resources are depleted?).

These widely observed problems and the accumulated experiences of resource-dependent countries have been used to inform the scope of sovereign wealth fund objectives and institutional mandates. As discussed in chapter 3, these all involve the stabilization of volatile revenue and spending patterns, as well as savings to generate investment income for current or future purposes as a supplement to (and possibly as a replacement of) finite resource revenues.

These objectives—and especially an understanding of how they map into a clear institutional mandate—of sovereign wealth funds is not (yet) as widely accepted today as the price stability objective is for modern central banks with regard to monetary policy. However, the experience of monetary policy suggests a number of valuable philosophical insights. The first is the appreciation from Friedman (1968) that the undeniable contributions of public policies are undermined by exaggerated expectations. It is in the best interest of both the principal and the agent that there is a realistic view of both the power and limitations of certain policies and policy instruments. This understanding takes into account the technical constraints and epistemological limitations of policymakers: Friedman (1968) warned that the promise of "fine tuning" the business cycle by monetary policymakers had an "evocative" ring to it, which unfortunately bore "little resemblance to what is possible in practice." Similarly, there is no shortage of grandiose proposals for the tasks that sovereign wealth funds should set themselves, many of which bear little consideration of feasibility.[5]

If the objective of a sovereign wealth fund is to transform volatile and finite revenues from natural resources into a permanent and stable stream of income, saddling the institution with a variety of other mandates—popular additions include financing infrastructure and other public goods and services (such as health care and education)—risks undermining the achievement of this narrow, but immensely valuable, task. With a defined focus on the objectives of stabilization and income generation, a sovereign wealth fund contributes to social welfare in a number of important ways: it reduces the volatility of government revenues (and fiscal policy more generally), removes a number of the adverse incentives associated with revenue windfalls that result in poor governance and politics, and lengthens the horizon over which the benefits of natural resources are enjoyed.

In practice, there is a strong tendency to assign a range of policy goals to sovereign wealth funds, alongside those of stabilization and income generation—many funds have been tasked with allocating a share of their portfolio to domestic investments with anticipated social or economic returns rather than purely financial ones. While in theory social and economic returns do not rule out financial returns, great care needs to be taken in ranking the relative importance of different mandates, making sure different objectives are very clearly differentiated and articulated, and ensuring that the achievement of ancillary objectives do not compromise the primary objectives of an institution.

Operational Independence

Greater clarity over the appropriate objectives and contribution of monetary policy set in motion a number of institutional innovations that aimed to remove obstacles to their achievement. The most fundamental of these is the near universal acceptance of the benefits of operational independence in monetary policy. The case for operational independence rests on insights into the political difficulties of avoiding various inflationary biases when the monetary authorities are simultaneously tasked with achieving other policy objectives, particularly when they face incentives to stimulate output and employment in the short run. These biases arise under assumptions of perfectly benign intentions on the part of policymakers.

Kydland and Prescott (1977) identified a dynamic inconsistency that arises from the divergent long- and short-run effects of monetary policy on the real economy, which means policymakers are confronted with an exploitable short-run Philips curve and long-term monetary neutrality. Rational public expectations recognize that the monetary authorities have an incentive to exploit the short-run trade-off between inflation and output once low and stable inflation has been achieved. In a dynamic setting, however, this raises long-run inflation expectations and observed inflation above the socially optimal level (and raises the cost of achieving price stability). More immediately intuitive examples of inflationary biases are based on assumptions of outright malevolence on the part of government, such inconsistent behavior across the political business cycle (Nordhaus, 1975), and the generation of an inflation tax due to the pursuit of seignorage revenue (Alesina and Summers, 1993).

The argument for the operational independence of monetary authorities is based on the belief that independence enables a more credible commitment to behavior that resists these biases. The operationally independent central bank is conceived of as a more purely technocratic institution, capable of resisting the public and political pressures that result in higher than optimal inflation: with a primary objective narrowly defined as the achievement and maintenance of price stability, independent authorities are not as likely to be tempted to unduly exploit short-term trade-off and help ensure that public expectations of inflation do not arise in anticipation thereof.

The argument in favor of granting operational independence to sovereign wealth funds builds, in part, on the belief that the investment of resource revenues may be subject to similar biases unless it is to be removed and insulated from the political process. Empirical evidence has demonstrated that political intervention in the investment processes of public funds compromises investment performance (Mitchell and Hsin, 1997; Useem and Mitchell, 2000; Carmichael and Palacios, 2003). More specifically, empirical investigations of sovereign wealth fund investment behavior have identified that politically motivated domestic investments and direct political representation in their management structures lower returns (Chhaochharia and Laeven, 2008; Dyck and Morse, 2011; Bernstein, Lerner, and Schoar, 2013). Concerns about the effects of political influence on sovereign wealth funds' investment decisions have been raised in a more theoretical sense by other scholars (Das et al., 2009; Ang, 2010). Bernstein, Lerner, and Schoar (2013) have a number of important findings and observations. The authors suggest that "the more closely sovereign wealth funds are exposed to political influences, the more they might show major distortions from long-run return maximization," while "political involvement can either lead to misguided policy attempts to prop up inefficient firms or industries or [lead sovereign wealth funds to] engage in investment activities in industries, sectors or geographies that are 'hot.'"

Political biases manifest in a number of ways in the investment process of sovereign wealth funds (and other public investment institutions). First, from a theoretical perspective it is easy to understand how lower returns are generated by the misalignment between the short horizons of politicians and the longer horizons that sovereign wealth funds should assume in order to generate higher average returns. Models of distortions and misaligned incentives caused by the suboptimally short horizons of politicians have innumerable applications (Nordhaus, 1975). The adverse effect of short political horizons on long-term investment in resource-rich economies has been studied extensively (Gelb, Eifert, and Tallroth, 2002). Institutional arrangements that incentivize and ensure long-term horizons are, therefore, valuable.

In the specific area of portfolio management, a large body of research has demonstrated that while various rule-based investment policies and strategies, such as dynamic portfolio rebalancing, raise expected long-run returns, most investors have shorter de jure or de facto time horizons than those required for these approaches to pay off, thus limiting investors' ability to exploit these opportunities (De Long et al., 1990; Shleifer and Vishny, 1990). For sovereign wealth funds, political and public pressures can drive undue short termism, absent appropriate institutions that incentivize assessing investment objectives and performance over a longer horizon.

Political interference can result in "trend chasing." Trend-chasing investors have been variously described as "naïve" (Lakonishok, Shleifer, and Vishny, 1994), "popular" (Shiller, 1984), and "noise" (Black, 1986), with the common characteristic being that they "tend to get overly excited about stocks that have done very well in the past and buy them up, so that these 'glamour' stocks become overpriced" (Lakonishok, Shleifer, and Vishny, 1994). Political interference in the investment process makes trend chasing more likely for two reasons. On the one hand, politicians may apply undue pressure to pursue investments in prestige assets for political expedience and stature. On the other hand, sensitivity around political risk and exposure may result in an overly cautious or bureaucratic investment process, whereby even when trends are detected in a timely manner, organizational inertia results in "buying high and selling low."

Finally, particularly in the context of a potential lack of clarity around the goals of sovereign wealth funds, political influence may advance the pursuit of noncommercial objectives, either implicitly or explicitly. In addition to generating political and regulatory concerns on the part of recipient countries of sovereign wealth funds, such pursuits are also likely to undermine long-term investment performance, particularly if politicians favor "pet projects" that deliver high political returns rather than financial returns (or social utility, more generally). This risk is more pronounced if the sovereign wealth fund is to invest in the domestic economy, where the potential for investments with high political returns is significant.

The discussion of the incentive and governance problems around domestically and developmentally orientated sovereign wealth funds speaks directly to the frequent suggestions that these funds assume a more explicitly developmental function. Collier (2012) and Santiso (2008), for example, have proposed that developing countries should eschew more conventional sovereign wealth fund models in favor of "sovereign development funds" that provide public goods. While the merits of this proposal can be debated from a number of angles, it is uncontroversial to state that political pressure and direction could have a negative impact on the incentives under which a sovereign development funds operates—just as it does for other institutions and instruments of public investment, such as development banks, state-owned enterprises, and conventional fiscal spending and investment channels.

It has been suggested that sovereign wealth funds act as catalytic "anchor investors" in the development of nascent domestic debt or other capital markets, as environmental savior by providing funding for long-term investment in clean technologies and infrastructure (Stiglitz, 2012), and even as a potential "buyers of last resort" during the Eurozone debt crisis (Verma, 2012). There have also been concerns that sovereign wealth funds could be used as instruments of foreign policy or international relations (Summers, 2007; Kimmit, 2008). All of these noncommercial ancillary objectives of sovereign wealth funds, whether advocated or feared, raise the spectre of political influence, and risk transferring the political economy and incentive-based problems associated with the management and investment of resource revenues out of the budget process by simply transplanting them into the management of the sovereign wealth fund.

Of course, there is no guarantee that the operational independence of a sovereign wealth fund will guard against the above-mentioned biases—just as there are no guarantees that an independent central bank will always succeed in avoiding dynamic inconsistencies. Moreover, the government is not the only threat to prudent policy behavior. Faust (1996) has argued that the appointment of technocratic boards to conduct monetary policy is, at least in part, a solution to concerns that "rule by majority" would result in distributional struggles between debtors and creditors (and different income classes), which could undermine monetary prudence. A sovereign wealth fund is similarly subjected to the popular pressures from social agents with heterogeneous preferences around the trade-offs between saving and spending, and long-term returns and short-term stability. As observed by Alesina and Summers (1993), however, central bank independence at a minimum contributes to reducing political pressure (both from the government and the public) that biases policy toward inflation. The granting of operational independence to a sovereign wealth fund, if complemented by additional "commitment technologies" and appropriate transparency and accountability arrangements, can significantly contribute to the mitigation of similar biases.

Institutionalizing Credibility

The central importance of credibility on the part of policymakers is a cornerstone of modern monetary consensus. The theoretical work of the 1970s and the subsequent experience have greatly contributed to the realization that an *ex ante* commitment to price stability alone lacks credibility, because the monetary authorities have an incentive to renege on their commitment and exploit the short run trade-off between inflation and output, *ex post*. The emphasis on the credibility of central banks arises in large part due to the endogeneity of inflation expectations and price- and wage-setting behavior to the monetary policy process. This introduces a game-theoretic relationship between the central bank and wage- and price-setters. To avoid self-fulfilling inflationary spirals and reduce the cost of maintaining price stability, price- and wage-setters need to believe that the monetary authorities will do what they say they will do, rather than renege on previous promises. Absent credibility, the public constantly second-guesses the future behavior of policymakers, raising the cost of price stability by requiring higher interest rates in equilibrium.

The potential role of sovereign wealth funds and fiscal rules in managing public expectations and the behavior of economic agents in the context of commodity-driven volatility have not been discussed much in the literature. However, there are a number of channels through which agents would respond positively to the actions and credibility of a sovereign wealth fund. The resource-curse literature has identified a causal relationship running from the prevalence of corruption, rent-seeking, and volatility in resource-rich countries to the observed low levels of investment, particularly those of a long-term nature in these economies (Mehlum, Moene, and Torvik, 2006). A sovereign wealth fund may contribute to removing the incentives and scope for corruption and rent-seeking, while their role in reducing volatility is uncontroversial. The fiscal rule introduced and discussed in Part 2 of this book, as well as other rule-based policies that use sovereign wealth funds as a means to reduce the volatility of government spending, can contribute significantly to the management of medium- to long-term expectations by private agents in resource-dependent economies. To change expectations and behavior in a meaningful way, however, the sovereign wealth fund and the accompanying fiscal framework will need to achieve high levels of credibility. In the absence of such credibility, agents anticipate that the government will renege on its *ex ante* commitments to fiscal stability by saving an insufficient portion of revenues during "boom" periods, drawing down on assets unsustainably during "bust" periods, and deviating from a precommitted spending path.

An additional reason to emphasize the importance of credibility is more generic: sovereign wealth funds will, by design, be subject to considerable volatility, resulting both from their inherently volatile source of funding (under most fiscal models involving sovereign wealth funds, the volatility of commodity-based revenue and spending patterns are simply transferred from the budget to the funds—volatility does not magically disappear) and their investment behavior. With respect to the latter, note that an appropriately mandated and incentivized sovereign wealth fund (particularly a saving or investment-income type fund) will adopt a long-term and often countercyclical investment model—which allows it to harvest volatility premiums that other, more short-term investors are unable to capture.

Thus, as discussed in greater detail in Part 3 of this book, these funds *should* go through periods (sometimes lasting a number of years) of lower, and even negative, returns. In all cases, political and popular support will be essential to the sovereign wealth fund's effectiveness, or even its survival. Credibility and the ability to demonstrate that periodically lower investment returns are the result of exogenous market swings (to which the fund *wants* to be exposed in anticipation of higher long-run returns), rather than discretionary policy mistakes by the fund's managers, are critical in the fund's defense from inevitable attacks. Chapter 9 outlines how sovereign wealth funds can employ a number of established rule-based investment policies to, first, avoid behavioral tendencies toward dynamic inconsistencies, and second, protect themselves from attacks during periods of volatility and low returns.

An important lesson from monetary policy for sovereign wealth funds is the emphasis on institutionalizing—that is, depersonalizing— credibility. In monetary policy, there is a long-standing debate about the degree to which credibility is, can, and should be centered around individuals or a more elaborate institutional and rule-based policy framework. Alan Blinder (1997) famously argued that central bankers did not require rules and other "precommitment strategies" to achieve low inflation. Rather, all that was needed was the will to do the right thing. According to Du Plessis (2003), this view "disregards a fundamental insight of the institutional literature, i.e. that the benign decisions of any particular policymaker, or succession of policymakers offer no confidence that the next policymaker would continue in similar vein" (221). Vesting credibility in an institution—or, more specifically, the rules and principles that it is understood to follow—helps avoid the "cult of personality." It is not hard to see how such a cult can emerge around a sovereign wealth fund, particularly if the fund investment policies permit a relatively high degree of managerial discretion over investments. The investment world is famous for developing cults of personalities around would-be "investment gurus": a thriving cottage industry exists that attempts to replicate the investment philosophies and portfolios of celebrated investors.

A model of how institutionalized credibility can assist in avoiding the cult of personality is found in the leadership succession at the Norwegian sovereign wealth fund. Knut Kjaer, who became the reluctant spokesperson for the global sovereign wealth fund community during its emergence into the limelight in 2007, managed the fund since its inception. When Kjaer resigned in 2008 (at a time of great turmoil in the global financial markets), outside observers wondered how the transition to a new chief executive might impact the fund's investment strategy. Ultimately, however, the transition was a complete nonevent: the new chief executive, Yngve Slyngstad, simply stuck to the same rules and principles that guided the fund's investment approach under Kjaer's tenure. The fund has increased its exposure to equities and made its first ever allocations to real estate, but this diversification process—and importantly, the rules and principles that underpinned that process—was already underway before Slyngstad took over. It is unavoidable that the heads of a fund approaching a trillion dollars in assets will attract attention—but the extent of the Norwegian sovereign wealth fund's credibility, vested in the institution's rules and track record, rather than in the individual(s) that manage it, makes reporting on the fund rather boring.

It is clear that credibility has a very specific and important meaning in modern monetary policy, informed in large part by the endogeneity of price- and wage-setting behavior and expectations. Credibility is critically important to sovereign wealth funds as well. In the first instance, a credible sovereign wealth fund removes a number of well-documented obstacles to long-term investment in resource-rich economies by positively affecting expectations around corruption, rent-seeking, and volatility. Credibility is also important from a political economy perspective. An established track record of "doing what one said one would" provides essential insurance against political pressure during inevitable tough times. In this context, credibility might be better described as a tool toward "legitimacy"—a concept emphasized by noted scholars of sovereign wealth funds (Monk, 2009; Ang, 2010). The central banking literature has long since turned attention from a general emphasis on credibility to specific commitment mechanisms, notably explicit policy targets, operational rules, and accountability and transparency, which reduce the cost of establishing and maintaining credibility. This chapter now turns to the role of these three commitment mechanisms in advancing institutional credibility.

The Use of Explicit Targets

As is the case with credibility, the strong theoretical and practical support for the use of explicit targets in monetary policy is in large part based on the desirability and efficiency of anchoring endogenous inflation expectations. Indeed, the use of explicit targets in monetary policy is widely understood both as a means to achieving credibility and as a benchmark for assessing whether that credibility has been achieved. As Sterne (1999) noted, the adoption of explicit inflation targets are critical in "helping to define an institutional relationship between the central bank, the government and the population." Explicit policy targets are similarly critical to the political economy and institutional relationships surrounding sovereign wealth funds.

Perhaps the most important manifestation of this role is that it clarifies the fact that the government typically sets the policy target, while the delegated institution (the monetary authority or the sovereign wealth fund management authority) is granted the freedom and power to achieve it. Explicit rules promote communication and accountability, thereby reinforcing the credibility—or legitimacy—of the delegated institution. Based on a survey of the reasons for central banks' adoption of explicit targets, Sterne (1999) concludes that "policymakers use explicit targets because they find that it is better to have narrow objectives and explain misses, rather than having imprecise objectives that make success or failure difficult to measure."

This function of explicit targets has attractive applications for a public investment institution, such as a sovereign wealth fund. The use of various forms of targets is commonplace in the investment industry and there is no shortage of ways in which the investment objectives of a sovereign wealth fund can be clarified through the adoption of explicit investment targets. In the first place, the fund may adopt—or receive from the government—an explicit (long-run) target return, expressed in either nominal or real terms. The sovereign wealth fund's investment policies, decisions, and performance can be further clarified by the adoption and disclosure of an investment benchmark (in the form of a well-known index, combination of indexes, or reference portfolio), which the fund is expected to track with some acceptable degree of flexibility (in the form of a maximum tracking error). A narrow objective for a sovereign wealth fund could be further clarified through the specification of explicit (numeric) investment targets and asset-class benchmarks or a reference portfolio (see chapter 9).

From targets, a natural progression is to discuss a rule-based framework for policy implementation—that is, the game plan devised for hitting those targets. Monetary economics has moved away from stark "rules versus discretion" debates to a modern understanding of a middle group characterized by contingent or state-dependent rules (and "flexible" inflation targeting). This shift has important implications for the discussion of fiscal rules for resource revenues and the investment rules of sovereign wealth funds, as discussed below.

The Use of Contingent Rules

Economists' understanding of the respective merits of rules and discretion in the conduct of monetary policy has evolved considerably in the postwar era. Three distinct intellectual developments underline the piecemeal advances in understanding how rules—and in particular, what kind of rules—contribute to the credibility of commitments to avoid various inflationary biases, public understanding of the monetary policy process, and the accountability of independent central banks. The first development was the work of Milton Friedman in the 1960s around limits and dangers of activist countercyclical policy (and his advocation of a constant money growth rule). The second major development was the seminal contributions of the late 1970s by Sargent and Wallace (1975), Kydland and Prescott (1977), and Lucas and Sargent (1979), which emerged following the identification and increasing prominence of incentive-based dynamic inconsistency problems in policymaking. Finally, the work of John Taylor, Michael Woodford, and Lars Svensson has led to an important softening of the distinction between "mechanistic" rules and discretion. These contributions have underlined the fact that rules—including ones that are fairly simply specified—can take information on the current and expected future state of the economy into account. In monetary economics jargon, such rules are variously known as "contingent," "dynamic," or "state-dependent" rules.

Combined with an explicit policy target, the modern understanding of rules as outlined above constitutes what Woodford (2002) calls "principles of systematic conduct for institutions that are aware of the consequences of their actions and take responsibility for them." Emphasizing the fact that contingent rules and explicit targets by no means place policymakers in a straitjacket, Du Plessis (2003) notes that "the adoption of explicit targets has not implied a move to stark rules for monetary policy, but rather a move to a systematic framework for monetary policy that allows flexible implementation and transparent communication of policy decisions." While the expectations management aspect of contingent rules is of great significance to monetary policy given the endogeneity of price- and wage-setting behavior, there are more generic virtues of contingent rules that are relevant to the design of institutional arrangements for sovereign wealth funds.

These implications apply to both the fiscal rules that govern the flow of revenues and income to and from the sovereign wealth fund and the investment rules that guide the fund's investment policies.

With respect to fiscal rules, chapter 5 describes a number of simple savings rules for transferring a share of resource revenues to the sovereign wealth fund, which range from highly mechanistic (for example, fixed percentage rules, which apply irrespective of the state of the economy, resource revenues, or commodity prices) to less so (for example, reference price–based rules). Similarly, spending rules (flows of assets and income from the sovereign wealth fund to the budget) can be mechanistic (a fixed percentage draw) or contingent (based, for example, on the level of funding needed to maintain a stable government spending path). As noted in Part 2, the advantage of mechanistic fiscal rules is their simplicity, clarity, and ease of communication, whereas the advantage of more dynamically specified contingent rules is that they can be more stabilizing and countercyclical. A trade-off therefore exists between the benefits of the simplicity (but functional suboptimality) of mechanistic fiscal rules for sovereign wealth funds and the management of resource revenues, and the complexity (but superior functionality) of more dynamic, state-contingent rules. As noted in chapter 5, the latter can be—and, in practice, has been—used as an intermediary, second-best solution on the path toward more complex and dynamic state-contingent rules.

A parallel consideration of the merits of mechanistic versus contingent rules in the area of sovereign wealth funds pertains to their investment policies. As a starting point, it is clear that rule-based investing in a general sense is widespread among well-governed institutional investors, including some sovereign wealth funds. The investment equivalent of a Friedman-like k-percent rule is a very strict adherence to the benchmark, with low or zero tracking error, a standard measure of the extent to which the investor is allowed to deviate from the benchmark. With innovations in the investment industry in recent years, this kind of mechanistic rule has the benefit, in addition to being constraining (which has obvious attractive properties in certain contexts), of low costs. An index-tracking approach amounts to simply following the market, implying zero or minimal "active management" that seeks to outperform the market. The increasingly widespread embrace of passive, indexed investment strategies—which has long had considerable academic and empirical support—reflects the belief of many investors, both of a retail and institutional variety, that fees for active management (which are typically accrued whether "alpha" or market outperformance is achieved or not) or investments of "in-house" human capital in pursuit of outperformance are simply not worth the cost (see chapter 9).

The following chapter will outline how sovereign wealth funds might implement a number of established rule-based investment policies that strengthen their institutional foundations. Two important implications from the discussion around mechanistic versus more activist or contingent investment rules should be highlighted, however. First, the argument in favor of mechanistic strategies is much more compelling in the area of investment than it is for monetary policy. The burden of proof lies with those in favor of a more activist investment approach in pursuit of market-beating returns: a move toward more active strategies raises costs—monitoring costs, trading costs, management fees, technological infrastructure acquisition and maintenance, and investments in human capital—and introduces additional uncertainty into the investment process. Practically, these cost considerations are important for emerging sovereign wealth funds in countries with relatively small talent pools, experience, infrastructure, and expertise in investing. A new sovereign wealth fund needs to clear a high hurdle in the form of additional returns to justify active strategies, even if they are to be rule based. Over time, a sovereign wealth fund may accumulate sufficient human capital, technological infrastructure, and institutional credibility to pursue more skill-intensive active strategies or manage the complex oversight and manager selection processes that accompany allocating investment mandates to external managers.

The second implication is that part of these costs pertain to the need for more extensive governance and institutional arrangements when contingent rules, and particularly strategies that require a degree of managerial discretion, are pursued by sovereign wealth funds. Even if, as is desirable for all large institutional investors (let alone ones that manage public assets), the allocation to active strategies is governed by a robust rule-based framework,[6] the operation and interpretation of the rule needs to be explained and evaluated. Accountability mechanisms also have to become more elaborate, as the fund's managers have to account (to the board, political overseers, and the general public) for its pursuit of particular strategies and why deviations from benchmarks—which will inevitably be negative on occasion, sometimes for lengthy periods of time—occurred. Finally, active strategies raise the complexity of agency relationships between government, the fund's management, and external fund managers.

Ultimately, an overarching lesson from monetary policy is that all rule-based systems that govern processes involving at least some degree of discretion—whether it is the flow of funds to and from the sovereign wealth fund, or its investment policies—perform an important institutional function in both the *ex ante* internal decision-making process and the *ex post* evaluation of the performance of an operationally independent public institution. Du Plessis (2003) notes in relation to the role of rules in the evaluation of the monetary policy that "The 'normal' behavior of the central bank as well as its 'discretionary' decisions are, accordingly, rendered intelligible, and hence potentially transparent; and if potentially transparent, then potentially accountable." The case for constrained discretion, encapsulated in contingent rules, rests on the belief that gains can be made from incorporating information about the state of the world (or the commodity cycle or the financial markets), rather than relying purely on a stark, information-less rule. Often policymakers will be granted the power to interpret this information and act accordingly. This is as true for monetary policy as it is for active investing—hence, there will always be flexibility or discretion—in the interpretation and implementation of contingent rules. The existence of the rule establishes a benchmark through which both the policymaker and the public can understand the meaning and implications of the exercise of discretion.

Transparency and Accountability

The agency relationship established by the devolution of authority in the management of resource revenues requires institutional arrangements that promote and enforce accountability and transparency on the part of the agent. This is an entirely uncontroversial foundational assumption, which then shifts the discussion toward what kinds of institutional arrangements for transparency and accountability are appropriate and most important. In less democratic environments, the attention may be less on transparency and broad public accountability, but accountability to political elites (the king, the royal family, or a ministry) is nevertheless important.

The need for (and apparent lack of) transparency and accountability funds has been a major area of focus in both the literature and policy discussions on sovereign wealth funds. Demands and expectations for sovereign wealth fund transparency emanate from three sources. First, in line with the philosophy behind the accountability test and scores for central banks proposed by de Haan, Amtenbrink, and Eijffinger (1998), is an argument about addressing the "democratic deficit" that potentially arises from institutional independence: "A delegation of powers to unelected officials can only be acceptable in a democratic society if . . . (independent policy institutions) are one way or another accountable to democratically elected institutions" (3). Second, and more specific to sovereign wealth funds, are demands for transparency in particular, imposed by the international regulatory community or unilaterally by recipient country governments and financial supervisors. Finally, sovereign wealth funds, particularly when embedded in a clearly communicated rule-based fiscal framework, can enhance transparency, accountability, and predictability in the management of resource revenues—the absence of which is widely theorized as being associated with the resource curse. If this improvement is to be achieved, however, it follows that the objectives and operations of the sovereign wealth fund and its fiscal rule have to be openly communicated. In practice, a number of sovereign wealth funds fall far short of contributing to greater transparency and accountability in the management of resource revenues and windfalls (in fact, their secrecy may compound and reinforce the lack thereof).

One final observation regarding sovereign wealth fund transparency and accountability pertains to the type of openness that might be regarded as most important and impactful. Another way to cast this question is, Are there demands for transparency that can be damaging and are, therefore, legitimately resisted by sovereign wealth funds? Note that similar questions have been raised by leading central bankers and monetary economists in their field (Cukierman, 2007; Cruijsen, Eijffinger, and Hoogduin, 2008; Ehrmann and Fratzscher, 2008; Dincer and Eichengreen, 2014). When the most important contributions of sovereign wealth funds are believed to be in advancing stability and predictability in the management of volatile natural resource revenues, in providing a degree of separation in their management from the political progress, and in transforming a depleting asset (natural resources) into a sustainable and permanent one (a financial endowment), the most important elements of the previously discussed frameworks are those pertaining to "governance and objectives" and "fiscal rules" rather than, for example, high-frequency investment reports, such as quarterly reports. As Truman (2008) noted regarding his own demand for quarterly investment reports: "Views differ on the desirability of quarterly financial reporting. Some argue that it promotes too much focus on short-term returns."

Here, the importance of incentive compatibility and coherence with the institutional matrix, identified in chapter 2 as important characteristics of sound institutional design, enter the discussion. Simply put, the majority of sovereign wealth funds—particularly relatively new ones—still rest on flimsy institutional and political foundations, and are subject to frequent political attacks. Clearly, poor short-term investment returns, which are to be expected from long-term investors, can be a source of ammunition for opportunistic opponents of a sovereign wealth fund. These concerns are less pressing in contexts where other elements of the institutional matrix are already supportive of the role of the sovereign wealth fund (such as the rule of law, rule-based fiscal policy, and traditional respect for the independence of accountable economic institutions), as they are, for example, in Norway and Chile.

A consideration of the appropriate horizon for transparency and accountability is also warranted. Sovereign wealth funds with long-term investment horizons associated with saving and investment mandates should have multiyear, if not multidecade, investment horizons. As discussed in greater detail in the following chapter, the full and appropriate exploitation of this horizon suggests, and even requires, significant exposure to short-term volatility. A consistent theme in the finance literature relating to long-term investment is that this insight is difficult to understand and communicate, and that long-term thinking and a tolerance of short-term volatility is very difficult to incentivize. The question, therefore, is whether an emphasis on high-frequency financial reporting (monthly and quarterly) can be damaging to a nascent sovereign wealth fund, opening it up to undue political pressures, absent complimentary elements in the gradually realized institutional matrix, and preventing the establishment of incentives that promote a long-term approach to investment. In the area of investments, it is likely to be much more important that the sovereign wealth fund is accountable and transparent with respect to such elements as its long-term investment objectives, target returns, investment beliefs, rules, and strategies. More generally, it is self-evident that from a broad-based institutional perspective, demands for greater accountability and transparency around sovereign wealth funds' fiscal rules, ownership and reporting structures (internal and external governance), and ultimate policy functions and objectives are of a higher-order concern than whether or not the fund publishes a monthly or quarterly investment report.

CONCLUSION

This chapter assessed the extent to which the central tenets of the modern monetary consensus may be applied to the institutional arrangements for sovereign wealth funds. In doing so, the discussion frequently returned to the set of common principles for the form and function of sound institutions identified in chapter 2. The central importance of forward-looking expectations management plays a particularly significant role in the institutional arrangements of the modern monetary policy. This dimension, while not entirely absent in the area of sovereign wealth fund management (as argued throughout this book, sovereign wealth funds and fiscal rules can enhance the stability and predictability around the spending of resource revenues), plays a less central role. Nevertheless, the more generic institutional implications and insights from monetary policy are highly applicable to sovereign wealth funds.

The first is the importance of clarifying institutional mandates and objectives, which is important not only for accountability but also because it defines the appropriate scope of specific policies and institutions by emphasizing their optimal contribution and clarifying which social objectives lie beyond their reach. It was noted previously that there is currently less agreement on the appropriate objectives and mandates of sovereign wealth funds than there is for monetary policy. It is therefore critical to the process of institutional design for sovereign wealth funds that great care is taken to define, both positively and negatively, exactly what the functions, mandates, and objectives of sovereign wealth funds are—not least because this informs all other institutional arrangements.

The management of sovereign wealth funds shares with modern monetary policy institutions the characteristics of an agency relationship, established by the granting of operational authority to independent institutions to avoid well-known political biases and incentive problems that otherwise result in less stable, predictable, and broadly economically conducive policymaking. Operational independence has gained a particular understanding through the theory and practice of modern monetary policy—notably, it is typically accompanied by goal dependence and an elaborate set of complementary institutional arrangements that promote accountability and transparency. This chapter also noted the important lesson from the modern monetary consensus for sovereign wealth funds that results from an emphasis on institutionalized credibility—and the adoption of explicit targets and contingent rules as a means to reduce the costs associated with achieving such credibility (which in turn also promotes accountability).

PART TWO

Rule-Based Fiscal Policies for Sovereign Wealth Funds

CHAPTER FIVE

It's (Still) Mostly Fiscal

Simple Fiscal Rules for Accumulating Windfall
Resource Revenues in a Sovereign Wealth Fund

ACCORDING TO an old joke, the International Monetary Fund (IMF) so frequently identifies imprudent fiscal policy as the root cause of a country's economic problems that its acronym may as well stand for "It's Mainly Fiscal." As behooves an organization with such a moniker, the IMF has repeatedly emphasized that the role of sovereign wealth funds in resource-rich countries should be viewed as part of a broader rule-based medium- to long-term fiscal framework for managing resource revenues (Davis et al., 2001; Baunsgaard et al., 2012; IMF, 2015). In practice, however, the enthusiasm for creating sovereign wealth funds—an activity that is often accompanied by much political fanfare and vague references to the needs of future generations, job creation, and investments in infrastructure—is much greater than commitments to rule-based fiscal frameworks to govern how and when money flows into and out of the fund.

One of the central arguments we seek to advance in this book is that sovereign wealth funds alone have limited effectiveness if they do not form part of a broader fiscal framework that is rule based, constraining, and countercyclical. In assessing the potential contribution of sovereign wealth funds with respect to the management of resource revenues and preventing the resource curse, the conclusion to us is clear: it's still mostly fiscal. Absent accompanying fiscal rules, a sovereign wealth fund risks insignificance. When policymakers retain complete discretion over the allocation of resource revenues to and from the sovereign wealth fund over the commodity cycle, prospects for breaking the tendency toward procyclical fiscal policy are diminished. The absence of a rule-based fiscal framework makes it difficult to know whether enough assets have been transferred to the sovereign wealth fund during boom periods and there is risk of an unsustainable depletion of previously accumulated assets during bust periods.

This chapter discusses a number of simple savings rules, which establish basic benchmarks for transferring a share of resource revenues to a sovereign wealth fund, particularly during boom periods. These rules have the advantage of simplicity, but leave the question of how and when to draw on sovereign wealth fund assets and income—that is, a rule-based system for both the up- and downswings of commodity cycles. In this sense, they are what Rodrik (2008) referred to as "second-best institutions." For many countries, however, such second-best solutions would be a noteworthy improvement on current and historic practices. Moreover, simple savings rules may be thought of as an intermediary—and temporary—step toward the implementation of a more integrated and contingent fiscal rule that combines savings and spending decisions, and distinguishes between the stabilization and income-generating functions of a sovereign wealth fund.

SIMPLE ACCUMULATION RULES: A CONCEPTUAL OVERVIEW

Simple rules for accumulating a share of resource revenues in a sovereign wealth fund can be anchored to a number of macroeconomic variables, including the underlying commodity price(s) and a fixed percentage or moving average of total resource revenues. The first choice is whether the rule should be price- or revenue based. Conditioning the accumulation rule on revenues has the advantage that it incorporates a number of critical factors related to the resource economy, as total resource revenue is a function of both exogenous factors, such as the resource price, and aspects over which policymakers have at least some control, such as production levels and the taxes, duties, and levies imposed on resource extraction (and the efficiency with which they are collected). An accumulation rule anchored on commodity prices bases the savings process on factors that are exogenous to government policies, as governments typically have some control over production and revenue capture, but no influence on market-determined resource prices (unless, as has historically been the case in Saudi Arabia, the producer is so large that it enjoys some pricing power).

As noted earlier, the rules discussed in the first part of this chapter work best as a means toward accumulating financial assets in a sovereign wealth fund. They do not govern how accumulated assets may be split between the stabilization and savings functions of a sovereign wealth fund—or, indeed, how sovereign wealth fund assets and income are used at all). If the emphasis is, however temporarily, purely on the accumulation of financial assets (or, negatively, on the avoidance of unsustainable and inefficient spending increases during revenue booms), the following three types of rules may be considered (the main features of these rules are summarized in table 5.1).

Fixed Percentage Transfers

The simplest—to the point of being mechanistic—savings rules transfer a fixed percentage of resource revenues to a sovereign wealth fund. If strictly adhered to, such transfers are entirely agnostic to the state of the commodity price or revenue cycle, production levels, or the economy. A variation of this crude rule may be to introduce some explicit or implied "escape clause" that suspends the rule in response to a negative price or production shock.[1] In the absence of such an escape clause, these rules are potentially procyclical, as they oblige the government to transfer revenues even in years of unanticipated revenue shortfalls. However, they do have the advantage of being easy to communicate and difficult to manipulate, and they may be fruitfully combined with a stylizing or countercyclical spending policy.

Moving-Average Transfers

A more cyclically adjusted accumulation rule can be conditioned on deviations in resource revenues (or resource prices) in a particular year from its moving average of preceding years. For example, if a country receives $60bn in oil revenues in a given year, having on average received $50bn in oil revenues in the preceding four years, a rule may specify that the above-average $10bn should be transferred to a sovereign wealth fund. While this rule has the advantage of hardwiring countercyclical properties—transferring more revenues to the fund when prices and revenues exceed the average level of recent years, and vice versa—transfers can also be volatile during periods of sharp fluctuations in commodity prices and resource production (as shown below through an application to Saudi Arabia).

Rules based on deviations from a moving average also introduce some scope for manipulation. First, policymakers need to decide the period and weightings to use in applying the moving average, which potentially opens the door to a manipulation of these variables in order to make a greater share of resource revenues available for spending. Second, the rule can be applied symmetrically, allowing for both in- and outflows from the fund, depending on whether revenues are above or below the moving average, or asymmetrically, with positive transfers to the fund when revenues exceed their moving average, but no outflows from the fund when revenues drop below the average. A symmetric application will require the sovereign wealth fund to forego long-term returns, as it will need to maintain large liquid positions in order to be able to facilitate potentially large outflows in the event of a sharp drop in commodity revenues in a particular year.

Transfers Based on Reference Prices

Another potentially countercyclical type of savings rule is conditioned on deviations in the underlying commodity price from a specified reference price. Such reference prices may be established by the legislature, executive, or technocratic (and potentially independent) policymakers, most typically as part of the annual budget process. Under these sorts of rules, the government commits to transferring excess revenues that arise when the observed commodity price rises above the reference price, resulting in unanticipated windfalls. For example, if the government set a reference price of seventy-five dollars per barrel for oil in the 2014 budget and the average oil price for the year ended up being ninety dollars per barrel, 20 percent of the revenues are transferred to the sovereign wealth fund at the end of the year.

TABLE 5.1
Key features of simple accumulation rules

Type of rule	Operation	Advantages	Disadvantages	Examples
Fixed percentage	A fixed percentage of annual resource revenue is transferred to the SWF—for example, 10% or 20% of oil revenues.	Easy to communicate and monitor (if data for total resource revenues are available, accurate, and public).	Rule is mechanistic and does not respond to cyclical state of the economy or commodity prices/revenue—government still has to transfer a portion of revenues in a low-revenue year.[1]	Kuwait Investment Authority; Alaskan and Wyoming Permanent Funds
Deviation from moving average	Revenues are transferred to (and potentially from) the SWF when revenues are above (or below) their multiperiod moving averages.[2]	A more dynamic, counter-cyclical rule than the fixed percentage transfer rule. Does not require transfers to the SWF in periods of low revenue.	Difficult to communicate and monitor, and therefore open to abuse. Can generate volatile transfers to and from the SWF, complicating the fund's investment process.	Ghana Heritage Fund; Mongolia Fiscal Stabilization Fund (no longer operational)
Reference price	Revenue transfers are based on deviations from a predetermined reference price for the underlying commodity.	Can provide strong countercyclical force. Also allows government to better plan multiyear public spending programs, as unanticipated surpluses are saved rather than spent.	Rule is constantly open to manipulation in the absence of a binding commitment or institutional arrangement to set prudent (low) reference price. Transfers to/from the SWF can be large and unpredictable.	Nigerian Sovereign Investment Authority (nonbinding); State Oil Fund of Azerbaijan

NOTE: SWF=sovereign wealth fund.
1. Unless a separate escape clause is put in place to suspend transfers to the sovereign wealth fund in low revenue/price periods.
2. Rules are symmetrical if outflows from the fund are permitted when revenues are below average, and asymmetrical when only inflows are permitted.

This type of rule provides room to regularly adjust the accumulation rule by adjusting the reference price, and to pick a conservative, high-accumulation rule (low reference price) or low-accumulation rule (high reference price). As with the preceding rule based on a moving average, reference price–based rules can be applied symmetrically, permitting in- and outflows from the fund, based on positive and negative deviations from the reference price, or asymmetrically, only allowing inflows to the fund when the observed price exceeds the reference price. One important implication is that the strength of the government's commitment to saving will be reflected by its choice of a high or low reference price. This underlines the critical importance to the process and institutions through which the reference price is determined.

To gain an understanding of how these sorts of rules might operate in practice—as well as a sense of the savings that could have been accumulated during the most recent oil boom—we apply two of the above-mentioned rules to Saudi Arabia. The application is backward-looking, using data on actual oil revenues for the 2000–2013 period.

AN APPLICATION TO SAUDI ARABIA: STRUCTURAL FEATURES

Like most established oil producers, Saudi Arabia experienced significant growth in its level of oil revenues during the first decade and a half of the twenty-first century, until oil prices collapsed during the fourth quarter of 2014 (the sharp drop in oil prices in the aftermath of the global financial crisis proved to be short-lived, and was a very brief interruption of a trend of generally rising prices since the start of the century). Saudi Arabia's official data on oil revenues (in U.S. dollars) and the average price of oil for the period between 2000 and 2013 are shown in Table 5.2.[2]

Saudi Arabia has been the world's leading oil producer for several decades and is set to continue receiving significant revenues from oil for decades to come—its deposits of commercially viable proven oil reserves are unrivalled, and it is conceivable that Saudi Arabia will be able to maintain stable levels of oil production for decades to come. Moreover, Saudi Arabian oil is among the cheapest to extract worldwide, making it one of the most resilient producers in a low-price environment

TABLE 5.2

Saudi oil revenues and average oil prices, 2000–2013

Year	Total oil revenue (nominal US$bn)	Average oil price
2000	57.2	30.4
2001	49.0	26.0
2002	44.3	26.2
2003	61.6	31.1
2004	88.0	41.5
2005	134.5	56.6
2006	161.2	66.1
2007	149.9	72.3
2008	262.2	99.7
2009	115.8	62.0
2010	178.7	79.5
2011	275.8	94.9
2012	305.3	94.1
2013	276.0	98.0

SOURCE: International Monetary Fund (IMF) Article IV consultations, national sources, and author's calculations.

(a fact that featured prominently in Saudi Arabia's rhetoric and supply strategy during and after the late-2014 collapse in oil prices). In addition to its oil wealth, Saudi Arabia has amassed several hundreds of thousands of dollars in savings from previous revenue booms, held in foreign-exchange reserves and other official investment vehicles. Yet despite its natural and financial wealth, Saudi Arabia faces significant fiscal challenges in both the short and long term, as discussed below.

Savings at Risk of Depletion

The drop in global oil prices in the second half of 2014 resulted in large fiscal deficits and a decline in officially reported foreign-exchange reserves from more than $750bn at peak (in mid-2014) to $580bn as of the end of the first quarter of 2016. After more than a decade of rising oil prices and revenues, fiscal surpluses and growing reserves, the prospect of a sustained period of low oil prices after the 2014 collapse will put Saudi Arabia's savings from earlier oil revenue booms at risk of depletion. The IMF calculated that if total government spending rises at an annual compound growth rate of 4.5 percent, while oil revenues were on average 30 percent below the baseline forecast between 2014 and

2019 (where the baseline was simply an extrapolation of the preceding five years), the Saudi Arabian Monetary Authority (SAMA)'s assets would fall by around \$450bn by 2019. Both the observed and modeled depletion of reserves are a direct result of the absence of binding fiscal rules that constrain spending growth and establish a mechanism for using the earnings on accumulated assets in a sustainable way.

Oil Dependence: High and Rising

The Saudi economy and fiscal health remains highly dependent on oil. Moreover, oil dependence has risen persistently since the late 1970s, and is most apparent in relation to government revenue. Figure 5.1 shows the extent to which the share of total government revenue derived from oil has trended upward since the early 1990s and exceeded 90 percent in the last few years of the previous oil boom. Even in low oil price environments, oil's share of total revenue has remained above 80 percent. Exceptionally high oil dependence is also evident in the composition of Saudi Arabia's exports, where oil and its derivatives account for almost all the growth in Saudi exports since the mid-1990s. Crude oil accounts for around three-quarters of exports, while refined oil and petroleum gases account for an additional 10 percent (Hausmann et al., 2011).

Figure 5.1 Increasing fiscal dependence on oil. Source: Official data from the Saudi Arabian Monetary Agency.

As with many other dependent economies, foreign currency export earnings are particularly important for Saudi Arabian economic (and social) stability, as the majority of consumer and capital goods are imported. Moreover, the Saudi riyal is fixed to the dollar, which requires holding sufficient foreign assets at all times to maintain the fixed exchange rate. A substantial depletion of reserves could endanger the stability of the Saudi riyal peg.

Oil Price–Driven Volatility in Revenue, Debt, and Capital Spending

As a direct corollary of Saudi Arabia's dependence on oil, fiscal variables are volatile and medium- to long-term patterns are closely correlated with cyclical developments in the energy markets. The absence of countercyclical fiscal rules in Saudi Arabia is evident in the close connection between the share of capital expenditure in total expenditure to oil prices, as shown in figure 5.2. This suggests that when even Saudi policymakers have been able to maintain relatively stable spending growth throughout periods of short- and medium-term oil price volatility, the burden of adjustment has historically fallen heavily on the capital-spending component of the budget.

Note that capital spending as a share of total spending fell sharply when oil prices and revenue fell during the 1980s and early to mid-1990s,

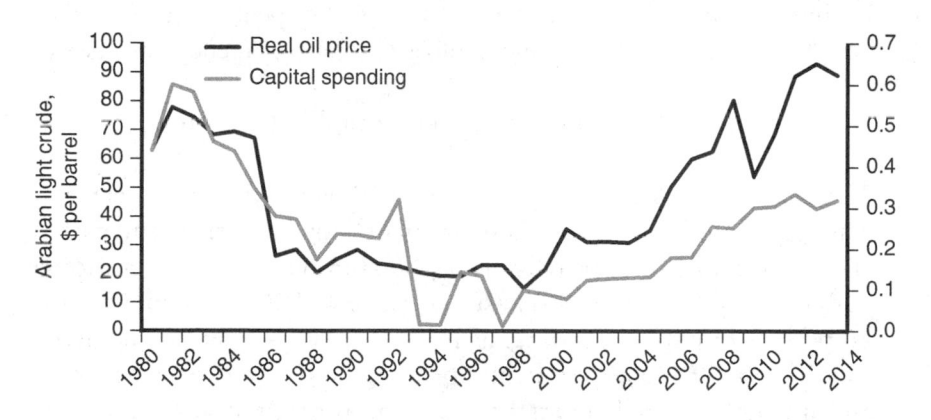

Figure 5.2 Oil price–driven cyclicality in capital spending. Source: Official data from the Saudi Arabian Monetary Agency.

and only partially recovered during the significant price and revenue boom from 2005 onward. Saudi Arabia's debt dynamics are similarly correlated with cyclical developments in oil prices. From the mid-1980s to the turn of the century, the Saudi Ministry of Finance issued a substantial amount of debt, as oil prices and revenues remained below the levels of the late 1970s. The debt-to-GDP ratio rose from very low levels to 103 percent of GDP by 1999. When oil prices and revenues rose again between 2005 and 2013, public debt was aggressively reduced to only 1.6 percent of GDP.

The Absence of Countercyclical Fiscal Rules and Anchors

The use of assets accumulated during previous booms to smooth out fluctuations in fiscal spending is not the problem—indeed, it is quite common and generally desirable in the context of resource-rich countries, as discussed in relation to the function of stabilization funds in chapter 4. However, such a policy requires a consistently applied countercyclical policy. While elements of such a countercyclical fiscal framework are in place, they remain at the discretion of policymakers, rather than being predictable and rule based. While the investment arm of the Saudi Arabian Monetary Agency can be described as a "quasi sovereign wealth fund"—its investment strategy and size (at peak) is comparable to that of the sovereign wealth funds of Norway, Abu Dhabi, and Kuwait—it is not as formally bound in a rule-based fiscal framework, and the majority of its assets are therefore exposed to fiscal pressures. In short, there are no time-consistent savings and spending rules for the use of oil revenues and the Saudi Arabian Monetary Agency's assets.

Long-Term Fiscal and Demographic Pressures

The major Saudi Arabian government spending categories are defense, education, and health care and social affairs; together, these three categories accounted for 80 percent of the 2015 budget. Across various budget categories, the public-sector wage bill is equal to around 40 percent of public spending, as more than 80 percent of employed Saudis work for the government. Spending on health care, education, and unemployment benefits have also been rising steadily, both in absolute and per capita terms, while spending on subsidies for the domestic use of fuel and food imports have also risen in line with growing demands and population trends. The composition of current spending, coupled with exceptional demographic pressures,[3] underlines the extent to which significant spending growth is to be anticipated in the coming decades in Saudi Arabia. Spending on defense and security will be difficult to reduce given the threat of regional insurgency, terrorism, and political tensions, and while there is potential to stabilize per capita spending on public-sector wages and entitlements, Saudi Arabia's demographics make it difficult, if not impossible, to reduce the growth in overall spending on these budget items (even assuming reductions in per capita spending on these items). Finally, while reductions to subsidies on fuel and food have long been identified as important areas for fiscal reform, again, Saudi Arabia's demographic profile suggests that even if the government pushes through politically unpopular reductions in per capita spending on these items, total spending on them will be difficult to contain.[4]

The structural features and long-term risks associated with oil dependence in Saudi Arabia described here inform the analysis of simple accumulation rules (as well as more complex fiscal rules, as discussed in the following chapter).

SIMPLE SAVINGS RULES IN PRACTICE: A COUNTERFACTUAL

In analyzing the potential accumulation of assets over the historic period in question, it is important to also consider the impact of financial market returns on these assets. The returns on a diversified global portfolio are a reasonable, low-cost benchmark for sovereign wealth fund investments, and can therefore be used to approximate a plausible set of investment returns on the accumulated assets. Such a portfolio can be constructed based on the following allocations: 25 percent in the S&P 500 Index (large market-capitalization U.S. stocks), 10 percent in the Russell 2000 Index (small market-capitalization U.S. stocks), 15 percent in the MSCI EAFE Index (twenty-one developed markets, excluding North America), 5 percent in the MSCI EME Index (emerging market equities), 25 percent in the Barclays Capital Aggregate Index (global bonds), 5 percent in the Barclays 1-3m Treasury (U.S. dollar money

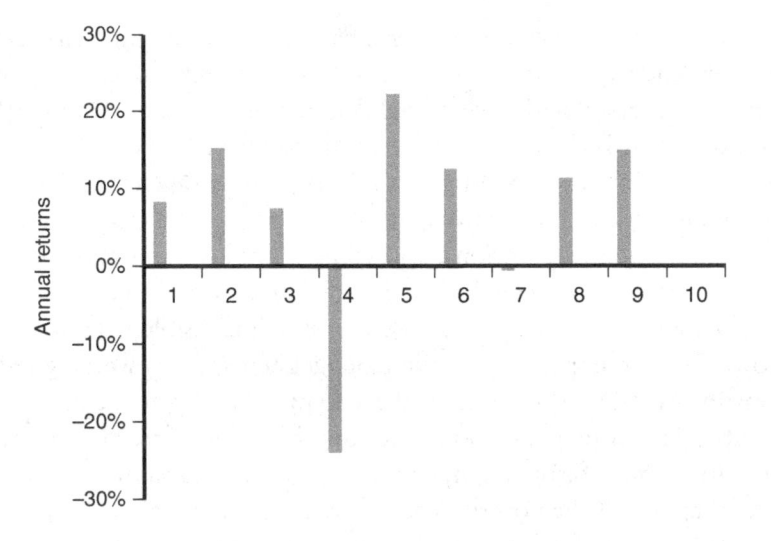

Figure 5.3 Annual returns on globally diversified portfolio, 2004–2013. Source: Bloomberg.

markets), 5 percent in the CS/Tremont Equity Market Neutral Index (global hedge funds), 5 percent in the Dow Jones/UBS Commodity Index (global commodities), and 5 percent in the NAREIT Equity REIT Index (a leading proxy for U.S. real estate). Annual returns on this portfolio are shown in figure 5.3. To isolate the impact of investment returns, this performance will also be compared with a stylized scenario in which the assets simply generate a fixed 5 percent annual nominal return.

Using actual data on recent Saudi Arabian oil revenues and financial market returns, we construct a number of counterfactual scenarios in which two simple rules are considered. The first is a moving-average rule under which transfers to the sovereign wealth fund (savings) are based on "upside" deviations in revenue from its four-year moving average. The second is a reference-price rule in which transfers to the sovereign wealth fund are based on upside deviations in the price of oil from a predetermined reference price, so that a percentage of revenues is proportional to the percentage difference between the actual price and the prespecified one. Note that the application of both accumulation rules is, therefore, asymmetric—the government transfers

TABLE 5.3

Key indicators of the moving-average rule, 2003–2013

Total oil revenues (US$bn)	2,006
Years yielding positive transfers	10 out of 11
Total transfers (US$bn)	413.0
Implied savings rate	20.6%
Fund assets by 2013 with fixed 5% return (US$bn)	716.5
Fund assets in 2013 with 60/40 portfolio return (US$bn)	829.7

NOTE: We start with an initial level of savings of $100bn in 2003, as Saudi Arabia had already amassed substantial savings by that point from previous boom periods.

money *to* the sovereign wealth fund only when revenues exceed the moving average or the oil price is above the reference price, but it does not transfer money *from* the fund back to the government when revenues or prices fall.[5]

Table 5.3 shows the outcomes for a counterfactual application of the four-year moving-average rule for Saudi Arabia. Recall that this rule requires the government to transfer to the sovereign wealth fund a share of oil revenues each year equal to its excess over that of the moving average of the most recent four years. Table 5.3 shows total oil revenues, the number of years between 2003 and 2013 in which the rule yields a transfer to the fund (that is, years in which revenue is above the moving average), the total value transfers, and the implied savings rate generated by the rule (transfers to the sovereign wealth fund as a percentage of total oil revenues). Figure 5.4 shows the growth in assets from 2003 to 2013 under the two return scenarios, based on actual diversified portfolio returns and a fixed 5 percent nominal return, respectively.

Note that from total oil revenues of just over US$2 trillion over the eleven-year period between 2003 and 2013, the moving-average savings rule would have resulted in a sovereign wealth fund portfolio by the end of 2013 of US$716.5bn, assuming a fixed 5 percent annual return, and US$829.7bn, assuming actual returns on a globally diversified portfolio. It is interesting to note that the lower end of this range is in line with the actual assets Saudi Arabia held by the end of 2013. That is, assuming a more aggressive investment strategy for the accumulated assets—in line with that of more established sovereign wealth funds—adds more than US$100bn in additional savings over a stylized fixed 5 percent return, given the generally healthy returns on financial

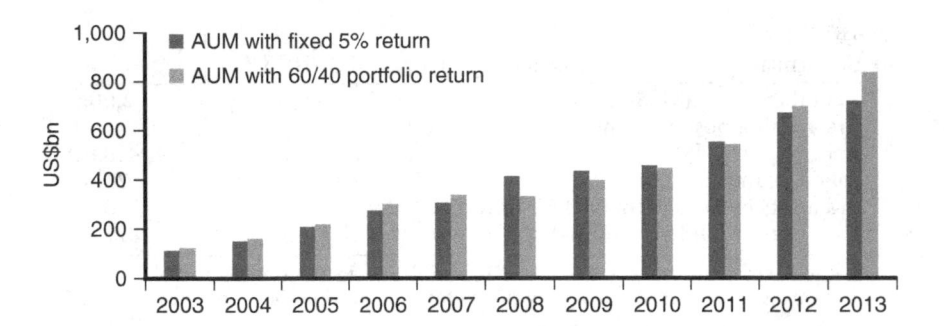

Figure 5.4 Total assets under a moving-average rule with investment returns.

assets over the period in question (the 2008–2009 financial crisis notwithstanding).

It is instructive to consider the hypothetical application of another type of savings rule in the Saudi Arabian case: a rule conditioned on a reference-price for oil. The key element in determining how conservative any such rule is—and therefore the size of transfers to the sovereign wealth fund—is the choice of a high or low reference price. The choice of a low reference price implies a conservative accumulation rule, and vice versa. To analyze the impact of different reference prices, we establish three plausible reference prices, established in 2000: $30, $40, and $50 per barrel, respectively (the observed average price for WTI crude oil for 2000 was $30.4). To inflation-adjust the reference prices, assume that it increases by 2 percent per annum, so that an initial $30 reference price for 2000 yields a $38.8 reference price in 2013, a $40 reference price in 2000 equals $51.7 in 2013, and a $50 reference price in 2000 equals $64.8 in 2013.

This provides for three inflation-adjusted reference-price paths: (1) a high-savings path, derived from a starting $30 reference price in 2000; (2) a medium-savings path, starting from a $40 reference price in 2000; and (3) a low-savings path, starting from a $50 reference price for 2000. A saving rule can be specified mandating the transfer of a percentage of revenues to the sovereign wealth fund equivalent to the percentage of a deviation of the actual price from the reference price—that is, if actual oil prices are 10 percent above the reference price in any given year (for example, $44 relative to a reference price of $40 for the year), 10 percent of total oil revenues would be transferred to the fund.

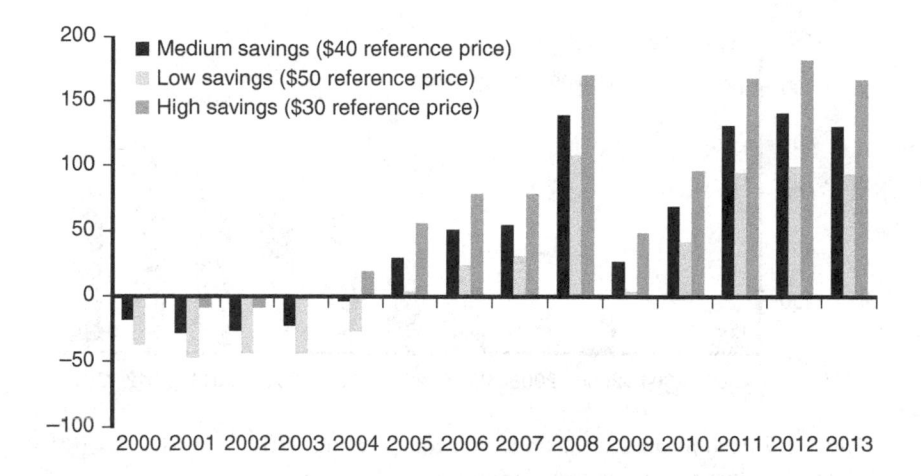

Figure 5.5 Annual transfers to the fund based on reference-price rules.
Note: All values are in nominal US$bn.

The difference between Saudi Arabia's actual revenues (based on the observed oil price) and the revenues consistent with these three price paths is shown in figure 5.5. Note that while figure 5.5 shows both positive and negative deviations in revenues, the asymmetric version of the rule would transfer assets to sovereign wealth fund only when the values are positive. It is striking that the medium-savings price path (using the $40 reference price for 2000), for example, does not result in any savings until 2005, given the relatively low oil prices during that period. Excess revenues, arising when prices are above the respective price paths, are dominated by four years—2008, 2011, 2012, and 2013—across all three specifications of the reference price.

As was the case for the moving-average rule analyzed above, the government would invest the assets transferred to the sovereign wealth fund, so that the accumulated assets would grow not only due to transfers but also through the compounding of investment returns on those assets. Assume that the government adopts the medium-savings price path and saves all resource revenues that arise when the actual oil price exceeds the price signaled by that price path in any given year. Figure 5.6 shows the results of such a rule with investment returns added.

The total accumulation of assets under this reference-price rule (assuming the medium-savings reference-price path described above) is

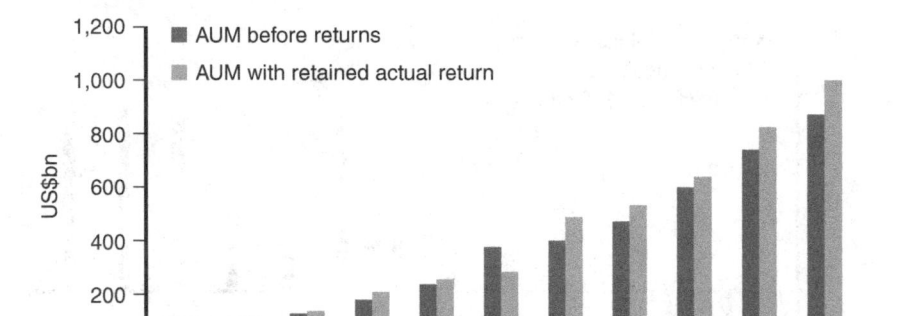

Figure 5.6 Accumulated assets under a medium-saving reference-price rule.
Note: All values are in nominal US$bn.

much greater than under the moving-average specification discussed previously. Out of a total of just over US$2 trillion in oil revenues over the eleven-year period between 2003 and 2013, the medium-savings reference-price rule would have resulted in a sovereign wealth fund portfolio of just over US$1 trillion, assuming actual returns on a passive globally diversified portfolio. This is roughly US$200–250 billion more than the total savings that Saudi Arabia did in fact accumulate over this period.

POLICY IMPLICATIONS

This chapter has introduced a number of simple saving or accumulation rules to govern the transfer of a share of resource revenues to a sovereign wealth fund. In particular, the focus was on simple rules for capturing excess or "windfall" revenues, through rules based on "upside" revisions from a moving average of past revenues or a predetermined reference price for oil. Examples of such rules were applied in a backward-looking manner to construct two counterfactual scenarios for Saudi Arabia for the period 2003–2013. The exercise showed that Saudi Arabia—and the same argument applies to other countries producing oil and other commodities that experienced a favorable price environment, particularly toward the end of the sample period—could have amassed significant assets over the period in question. With the combination of simple savings mechanisms for oil revenues (without requiring savings in years when revenues are down sharply) and the investment of those savings in a globally diversified financial portfolio, Saudi Arabia would have amassed a total of $830bn to $1 trillion by the end of 2013. This range suggests an additional US$200–250 billion in savings over the period from 2003 to 2013, relative to that generated by Saudi Arabia in practice. A number of more generic policy implications, relevant to all resource economies, can be drawn from the discussion and analysis in this chapter.

The Power of Savings in Boom Years

The application of the two basic savings rules to the Saudi Arabian case underlines how important and powerful it is to save a portion of revenues during boom periods (or even in single boom years) in which exceptionally high resource prices result in an unanticipated revenue windfall. For established resource producers who are dependent on resource revenues to finance the budget, implementing accumulation rules that are centered on such boom years should be relatively painless, as the government can maintain spending in low- or even average-revenue years, while only saving when resource revenues rise unexpectedly due to exogenous price movements. Resource revenue booms can, of course, also arise from an increase in production levels, particularly for emergent commodity producers. For new resource producers, even modest savings from rapidly rising revenues allow the government to not only somewhat graduate the scale-up in public spending and investment but also create a buffer fund with which to stabilize and endow future resource revenues. The point of simple savings rules, particularly those based on deviations from recent moving averages or a predetermined reference price, is that they commit governments to saving—rather than spending—unanticipated resource revenue windfalls.

The absence of (or lack of adherence to) even the most basic kind of savings rules discussed in this chapter often results in last-minute decisions to spend windfall revenues as they arise. Again, Saudi Arabia is a case in point. While Saudi Arabia did accumulate significant assets over this period, there was an equally pervasive tendency to spend a large part of the windfall revenues that arose. This is evident not only in the sharp rise in total government spending over the course of the last oil

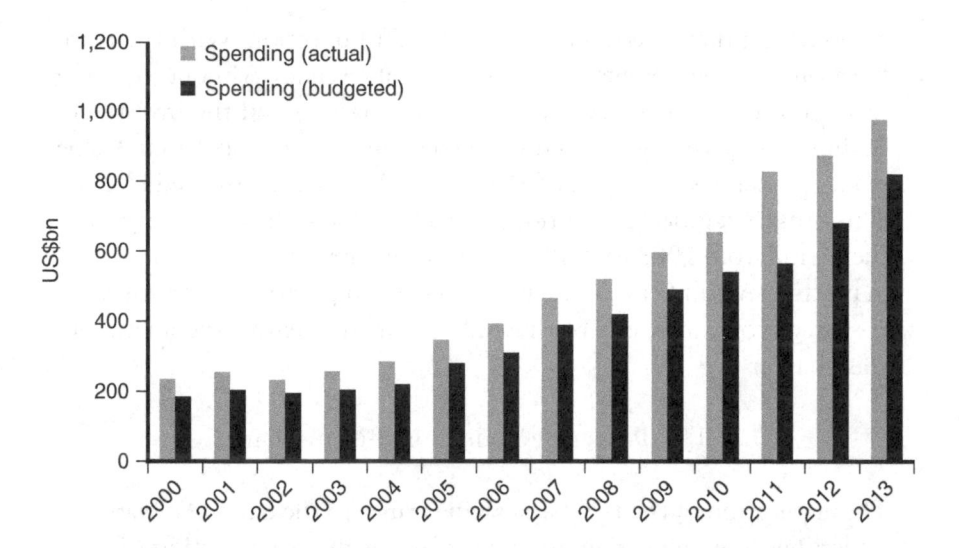

Figure 5.7 Actual versus budgeted total government spending. Source: Official data from the Saudi Arabian Monetary Agency.

revenue boom, but also in ad hoc increases in spending during this period. Figure 5.7 shows that actual spending was raised above the budgeted amount in every year since 2000, as oil revenues exceeded budgeted assumption (as well as in 2009, when revenues declined sharply). This suggests a procyclical and ad hoc fiscal response to oil revenue booms rather than a disciplined, rule-based approach to managing positive oil price and revenue shocks.

Reference-Price Rules Are Sensitive to the Chosen Price

Many countries, including Nigeria and Azerbaijan (and previously, Chile and Russia) have adopted a variant of the reference-price rule discussed above. This has been done both formally and informally, to guide the fiscal decision-making process around saving windfall revenues. The analysis in this chapter underlines a simple and intuitive fact about these rules: the commitment to save revenue during a windfall period can only be realized if policymakers establish a prudent reference price. A ten-dollar difference in the reference price may sound trivial, but it has a massive impact on the total amount of funds transferred to the sovereign wealth fund.

By way of illustration, consider the Saudi Arabian example discussed in this chapter. Saudi Arabia generated just over $2 trillion in oil revenue between 2003 and 2013. The use of three different reference-price paths, based on an oil price of $30, $40, and $50 per barrel in 2000 (and adjusted upward by 2 percent per year for inflation), resulted in total positive transfers of $500bn, $772bn, and $1,063bn, respectively, before adding in financial market returns. The sensitivity of the magnitude of savings to the specification of a reference price raises important questions around the process or mechanisms through which the reference price (or indeed other triggers for savings) is set: is it at the discretion of the Ministry of Finance, by an independent panel of experts, in consultation with the IMF, or according to a formula or model, and how frequently and on what basis are reference prices or reference-price paths revised and updated?[6] These are all critically important issues to consider with respect to the governance and institutional arrangements of the sovereign wealth fund and its accompanying fiscal rules.

Transfers Under Simple Rules Can Be "Lumpy"

The rules analyzed above, particularly the reference-price rule, can generate highly concentrated or "lumpy" transfers to the sovereign wealth fund. For example, years in which oil prices are below the reference price (generating no new transfers to the fund) can be followed by a single year in which the average oil price far exceeds the reference price, generating a very large transfer to the fund. In the scenario analyzed above, the overwhelming share of the total net transfers occur in only two boom periods, namely, 2008 and 2011–2013. While this is not necessarily a problem from the perspective of government spending, it does potentially complicate the long-term investment planning and strategy of the sovereign wealth fund. If this is the case, the government and policymakers may need to consider an additional mechanism to stagger transfers to the fund, enabling it to better plan the implementation of its investment strategy.

Symmetrical Versus Asymmetrical Rules

Unsurprisingly given the volatility of oil and other commodity prices over the sample period, there is a significant difference in total transfers under the versions of the accumulation rule that permits both in- and outflows (symmetrical) and ones that only allow for inflows (asymmetrical). For Saudi Arabia, under the medium-saving price path, a symmetric rule with in- and outflows from the fund would have yielded net transfers of $674bn, whereas an asymmetric rule with inflows only allowing for inflows in boom years would have resulted in $722bn in transfers. It is critical for policymakers to decide whether the fund's transfer rule applies in a symmetrical or asymmetrical manner. This is not only because it has a serious impact on the total net assets transferred to the sovereign wealth fund but also because the need to provision for potentially large (and unpredictable) outflows from the fund will impact the fund's investment strategy. With the possibility of outflows, the fund will have to hold a significant portion of its portfolio in liquid assets, which will lower its expected long-term average return.

CONCLUSION

This chapter has discussed a number of simple rule-based mechanisms for transferring public assets arising from natural resource revenues into funds, portfolios, and institutions that are able to invest these assets with a long-term investment horizon, with higher exposure to risk, and illiquidity in order to generate higher returns. After discussing a number of different types of accumulation rules, the chapter demonstrated the extent to which these rules would have resulted in the accumulation of significant assets in the case of Saudi Arabia between 2000 and 2013.

The policy implications outlined in this chapter are universal, however, and thus applicable to all resource-rich countries intending to embark on a transition period of accumulating assets with which to subsequently implement a more integrated and contingent fiscal rule that combines savings and spending decisions, and distinguishes between the stabilization and income-generating functions of a sovereign wealth fund. It can be very useful for new resource producers—or established producers moving toward the establishment of a sovereign wealth fund type model for fiscal policy—to implement simple accumulation rules that determine how much and when a portion of revenues are set aside to capitalize a new sovereign wealth fund. While mechanistic rules that set aside a fixed percentage of annual revenues are easiest to implement and communicate, more dynamic and cyclically adjusted rules are more desirable from an economic perspective—particularly in a dynamic setting across a boom–bust cycle in commodity revenues. In the chapter that follows, we discuss fiscal rules of a more complex nature that have more contingent properties and allow for the simultaneous evaluation of spending, saving, and stabilization decisions around resource revenues as part of an integrated fiscal framework. These more complex fiscal frameworks may follow as a logical evolution for the simple saving rules of the kind discussed in this chapter.

CHAPTER SIX

Integrated Fiscal Rules for Sovereign Wealth Funds

Spending, Saving, and Stabilizing Resource Revenues

THE PREVIOUS CHAPTER departed from the observation that sovereign wealth funds in resource-rich economies should be accompanied by fiscal rules. Absent a credible and sustainable fiscal framework—and an appropriate and in some way binding set of rules to govern the flow of resource revenues, investment income, and assets to and from the sovereign wealth fund—the contribution of these funds is at best uncertain. As such, chapter 5 discussed only one part—albeit a critical one—of the fiscal process for managing resource revenues, namely, savings. We analyzed a number of very simple rule-based mechanisms for saving a share of windfall resource revenues and providing initial capitalization for sovereign wealth funds. These rules treat the saving process as independent from those governing, for example, the level of resource revenue consumption over time, the use of sovereign wealth funds' investment income, and stabilizing transfers. In short, the sort of rules discussed in chapter 5 were isolated rather than integrated.

Beyond a certain level of asset accumulation, countries may look to adopt more sophisticated fiscal rules that consider these income streams and associated risks in a more integrated manner. This is exactly what the IMF has in mind with its recent emphasis not just on basic saving and spending rules for sovereign wealth funds but also on their integration into a "fiscal framework [that] should provide adequate precautionary buffers in countries that are vulnerable to high volatility and uncertainty of resource revenue; and could be supported by resource funds if they are properly integrated with the budget and the fiscal policy anchor" (Baunsgaard et al., 2016).

There are many ways in which such an integration between the sovereign wealth fund and the medium- to long-term fiscal framework may be achieved. However, sound rule-based fiscal frameworks for resource producers all share a number of institutional characteristics. The rule should be contingent—that is, it should have built-in feedback mechanisms that allow spending, savings, and stabilization dynamics to respond to unanticipated fluctuations in the resource revenues. Note that fiscal shocks to oil-producing, and particularly oil-dependent, economies arise from both unanticipated price and production developments, and may be of a cyclical and long-term nature. These are critical considerations to bear in mind when designing a medium- to long-term fiscal framework, and it is important to establish a system that does not rely too heavily on the limited ability of policymakers to forecast these cyclical and long-term trends. While allowing for some degree of flexibility, the rule should nevertheless still constrain policymakers in a manner that prevents time-inconsistent policies. The most obvious example of this is that the rule prevents spending an undue, unsustainable, and inefficient portion of a temporary resource windfall. More generally, a fully integrated fiscal rule should assist in enhancing the predictability of government actions with respect to the consumption of volatile and finite sources of fiscal income.

We start this chapter with a brief overview of conceptual and practical approaches to establishing an integrated fiscal framework for resource revenues and sovereign wealth funds. We then proceed to discuss a specific example of such a rule that builds on a framework proposed by scholars from the Center for International Development at Harvard Kennedy School. Finally, as in the previous chapter, we apply the rule in a backward-looking manner to the case of Saudi Arabia, discuss the results, and draw a number of general policy lessons.

APPROACHES TO INTEGRATED RESOURCE REVENUE MANAGEMENT

The design and implementation of an appropriate integrated fiscal framework for the management of resource revenues (and the assets and income from sovereign wealth funds funded by such revenues) depends critically on a range of local economic needs, characteristics, and preferences. The context-appropriate balance between using resource revenues and sovereign wealth funds for spending, savings, and stabilization are determined by, among a myriad of factors, the degree of fiscal dependence on resource revenues; the "spread" between the cost of borrowing and the expected return on financial assets; the anticipated horizon for resource production; an economy's level of development, existing capital stock, and infrastructure; its capacity to absorb revenue windfalls in the domestic economy; and, of course, its political economy and institutional characteristics. These "initial conditions" all factor into both positive and normative assessments of any integrated fiscal framework.

Unsurprisingly, given the diversity of resource economies, a large number of fiscal frameworks have been proposed and debated. Fiscal frameworks for resource economies are assessed and evaluated not only in terms of their narrow theoretical appeal but also on more pragmatic grounds, such as their simplicity, ease of communication, and robustness to changes in or deviations from projected input assumptions. A recent report from the IMF (Baunsgaard et al., 2012) provided an overview of the major conceptual approaches in practice among resource economies, which can be summarized as follows:

- *Permanent-income financing of nonresource deficits:* The idea is that the annual spending or consumption of resource revenues is limited to the perpetuity value of total resource wealth. In integrating this concept into a fiscal framework, the nonresource primary deficit can be financed indefinitely, if consumption of resource revenues is equal to the permanent income generated from resource wealth. Norway is the most famous adopter of this approach, and it defines permanent income (or the perpetuity value of resource wealth) as the sustainable real return on its petroleum-funded sovereign wealth fund (which the minister of finance believes to be 4 percent per annum). By defining the permanent consumption of oil wealth in terms of the assets held in the sovereign wealth fund rather than also adding in an estimate of yet-to-be-extracted proven oil reserves, Norway has adopted a more conservative "bird-in-hand" approach to valuing its oil wealth.

- *Modified permanent-income approaches:* The permanent-income financing approach can be modified in a number of ways, particularly to allow for a more "front-loaded" spending profile—a policy choice that may be justified in the context of capital-scarce developing countries with large resource assets. One modification is to depart from the above-mentioned "bird-in-hand" estimation of total resource wealth toward a "total wealth" approach in which the estimate of the value of yet-to-be-extracted subsoil assets are included in the conception of total resource wealth. Another modification is to allow for near-term debt financing in anticipation of future resource revenues or more general fiscal income (due to higher expected national wealth), or both—a classic intertemporal efficiency approach to fiscal sustainability and efficiency, as per Diamond (1965). In the context of resource-based wealth, modified permanent-income approaches can result in dramatic fluctuations in the estimate of wealth and permanent income, given the volatility of commodity prices and uncertainty around the commercial and geological viability of subsoil assets.

- *Structural balance approaches:* A number of countries attempt to establish a fiscal framework for resource revenues that delinks or decouples spending from cyclical fluctuations. In this regard, they are typically an extension of the kind of saving rules discussed in the previous chapter, but they add in a spending component based on estimates of the "structural" (that is, cyclically adjusted) fiscal balance. Resource price–based rules, such as Chile's fiscal rule, deal explicitly with resource price volatility by letting the overall fiscal balance move with the swings in resource revenue (Baunsgaard et al., 2012). As discussed in the previous chapter, the use of reference prices for the underlying commodity to define the structural fiscal balance can draw on a formula (such as a moving average), a parliamentary process, or (as in the Chilean case) an expert committee. Note that structural balance approaches are focused on stabilizing short- to medium-term cyclical adjustments to the spending or consumption of resource revenue, but "in principle [this] ignores exhaustibility issues" (Baunsgaard et al., 2012).

- *Nonresource current balance rules:* Another approach is to specifically earmark the consumption of resource revenues for capital expenditure rather than current spending. Under the nonresource current balance rule, both capital spending and resource revenue would be excluded from the fiscal targets (Baunsgaard et al., 2012). Clearly, this approach rests on the belief that the investment of resource wealth in physical assets with high yields in terms of nonresource productivity and growth (and nonresource fiscal revenue) raises the growth potential of a capital-scarce developing country. As discussed in chapter 4, Baunsgaard et al. (2012) argued that this approach "is problematic from a practical perspective since it does not provide a meaningful anchor for fiscal policy." It is also not clear why capital expenditure, such as large-scale public infrastructure investment, should be prioritized so prominently. Government expenditure on education and health, for example, is typically categorized as current expenditure (and is thus excluded from the nonresource current balance), and could have an even greater impact on potential growth. Baunsgaard et al. (2012) also argue that from a practical policymaking and governance perspective, a separate treatment of capital expenditure could result in "parallel budgets" and "provide strong incentives to camouflage recurrent expenditures as capital spending or to choose projects even if they may not produce strong benefits." Finally, a resource boom could lead to a capital expenditure boom and a budget that becomes volatile, procyclical, and ultimately unsustainable.

On their own, the rule-based frameworks above are principally concerned with either the question of the intertemporal allocation and consumption of resource revenues or with stability, cyclical adjustments, and the management of volatility. Of course, stabilization mechanisms are not incompatible with the long-term allocation frameworks (and vice versa), but they need to be introduced as "add-ons" or modifications to the respective framework as outlined above. The critical importance of precautionary savings and stabilization mechanisms rises with the degree of resource dependence. In the remainder of this chapter, we discuss and analyze an additional rule-based framework for resource revenues and sovereign wealth fund assets and income, which integrates savings, stabilization, and long-term consumption policy choices in a single framework.

AN INTEGRATED FISCAL RULE: AN INTUITIVE OVERVIEW

The integrated, rule-based fiscal framework discussed in the remainder of this chapter is based on the framework developed for Kazakhstan by Hausmann, Lora, and Lora (2014) that was subsequently extended and applied to a number of country cases in Alsweilem et al. (2015) and Lora, Rietveld, and Cuadra (2017). This framework starts with a major conceptual departure from the simple and more widely used savings rules and fiscal frameworks for resource revenues discussed earlier in this chapter and in the previous chapter. Rather than transferring a portion of resource revenues to a sovereign wealth fund *after* their allocation in the budget, the framework proposed here transfers all resource revenues to a sovereign wealth fund first. A distribution from the sovereign wealth fund to the budget is then achieved through a spending rule that generates a stream of revenue. An important function of the rule is that it decouples spending patterns from the cyclical volatility of revenues (by channeling revenue volatility through the sovereign wealth fund), while enabling the assets and income of the sovereign wealth fund to compensate for the long-term depletion of the resource.

The sovereign wealth fund in the rule consists of two subcomponents: a Stabilization Fund and an Investment-Income Fund. The convention in the literature on sovereign wealth funds is to simply refer to the latter structure as a "savings fund." However, a distinction between savings funds and investment-income funds made here clarifies an important point: pure savings funds preserve and accumulate assets for future use exclusively, while in addition to preserving assets over time (savings), an Investment-Income Fund also provides a steady (and potentially permanent) source of funds for current spending.[1] The Stabilization Fund's value fluctuates with the cyclical variation in resource revenues.

The spending rule proposed here includes transfers from both components of the sovereign wealth fund. Transfers from the Investment-Income Fund are based on its expected long-run real return, such as 5 percent per annum. This rule ensures that the fund is "inflation proofed"—that is, its capital is protected in real terms over the long run, as spending is based on the real rather than the nominal earnings potential of the fund. The revenue stream from the Investment-Income Fund is stable and predictable, and therefore contributes to the management of the volatility of resource revenues. The second component of the sovereign wealth fund, the Stabilization Fund, also makes an annual transfer to the budget and is based in part on the previous year's transfers and in part on the value of assets in the Stabilization Fund. Combined, the three revenue components—one from the Investment-Income Fund and two from the Stabilization Fund—anchor spending through the boom and bust periods of the commodity cycle (see equations below).

The need for an Investment-Income Fund arises in the context of declining long-term resource revenue (based on declining production) or raising spending needs, or both. When resource revenues are assumed to be permanent and the level of required spending is expected to rise in the long run, there is no need to transform natural wealth into permanent financial wealth, which means an Investment-Income Fund is not needed—the only challenge is stabilizing the volatility of that permanent wealth. In the more typical situation where resource revenues are expected to decline over time, the investment-income supplements—and, potentially, completely replaces—the depleting natural resource as a source of permanent income to the government. In this context, the share of annual resource revenues that are transferred to the Investment-Income Fund becomes a discretionary policy variable, reflecting the preferences of policymakers for trading off current for future spending.

If the objective is to stabilize the real level of spending during and after the depletion of the resource base, the fiscal rule and the percentage of revenues to be transferred to the fund can be set accordingly, using the best available information regarding the size and value of a country's resource endowment. Once resource revenues have ceased (due to the exhaustion of subsoil assets), the Stabilization Fund can be gradually depleted. The Investment-Income Fund will then stabilize at a permanent steady-state level in real terms, as there are no new resource revenue inflows "feeding" the fund, and it transfers only its real return to the budget (these dynamics are formalized below).

A final set of observations regarding this rule-based framework is institutional in nature. Separating the sovereign wealth fund into Stabilization and Investment-Income Fund components enables a differentiation between the management, investment mandates, and asset allocation of the two funds. The Stabilization Fund needs to hold more liquid assets, as its transfers (or implicit liabilities) are more volatile and unpredictable than those of the Investment-Income Fund, which only transfers its expected average long-run real investment return. The latter can have a much more illiquid and risk-orientated asset allocation, which raises its expected return, generating more revenue for government spending and investment in the long run. An Investment-Income Fund should also operate at arm's length from the government and the standard budget and fiscal process, as its mandate is to focus on long-term portfolio decisions in order to meet its target expected long-run average return.

Formalizing the Framework

Having provided an intuitive overview of the main dynamics of the proposed rule-based fiscal framework above, the key relationships can be formalized with a few simple equations. If a resource-dependent government is committed to stabilizing public spending, it should decouple spending from the volatility of underlying resource revenues. To achieve stability and sustainability, this commitment should be symmetric over the commodity cycle: the consumption of resource revenues needs to be constrained in boom periods, as this is what allows a steady level of spending in bust periods. To constrain spending in this manner, it can be anchored on a combination of some percentage of the previous year's spending and fixed percentage of assets held in the Stabilization Fund (which, as discussed above, receives *all* resource revenues). Such a spending rule can be specified as follows:

$$T_t = \alpha T_{t-1} + \beta S_{t-1} \qquad (1)$$

where T is an annual transfer from the fund to the government; S is the size of the Stabilization Fund; and α and β are fixed parameters <1

that indicate the respective weight given to each of the components, respectively, in stabilizing spending.

Through this equation, government spending is stabilized with plausible combinations of α and β. Suitable values for α and β that provide optimal solutions to the stabilization objective can be estimated, given certain assumptions regarding the distribution of future oil revenues and fund returns (for discussions of estimation techniques for the parameters in a forward-looking application of the rule, see Hausmann, Lora, and Lora, 2014, and Lora, Rietveld, and Cuadra, 2017). Under suitable parameters, the level of the Stabilization Fund will evolve according to the following identity:

$$S_t = (1 + r_t)S_{t-1} + X_t - T_t \qquad (2)$$

where r is the interest generated on the Stabilization Fund and X is the amount of resource revenue transferred to the fund. As per Equation (2), the Stabilization Fund's value is determined by its return and the net transfers (total transfers to the fund minus funds transferred to the budget to stabilize spending).

The manner in which this rule decouples spending from volatile resource revenues has a number of attractive features. It is not anchored on, and does not rely on, assumptions about future resource prices, production volumes, or total revenues in order to stabilize spending. If resource revenues go up during any particular year, the value of the Stabilization Fund will increase and the government will receive a fraction, β, of that increase in the following year. Should revenues stay the same the year after that, the government receives another fraction, $\beta(1+r)$, plus a fraction, α, of the increased transfers of the previous year. On the other hand, if revenues were to fall, the annual transfer to the Stabilization Fund would also fall only by a fraction, β, in the following year, with further adjustments in the subsequent years. The rule assures that transfers to the government (that is, the consumption or spending of resource revenues) adjust upward and downward gradually in response to often-dramatic annual changes in resource prices, production, and revenue. In that sense, the rule can be described as contingent (dynamic or state-dependent) in nature—a feature that was identified in chapter 4 as an important element in the current understanding of rule-based macroeconomic policy (and which was a shortcoming of a number of the more mechanistic savings rules discussed in chapter 5).

In the more likely scenario in which resource revenues are not permanent but rather subject to declines over the long run, the Stabilization Fund can no longer serve both the stabilization and savings functions, as the long-run decline in resource revenues leads to a depletion of the fund's assets. The transfers from the fund required to achieve stable spending draw increasingly heavily on withdrawals from the fund: if resource revenues are faced with a long-term downward trend, no possible combination of parameters α and β can achieve the stabilization objective indefinitely. Consequently, the establishment of an Investment-Income Fund, whose investment income over time replaces resource revenues as the source of permanent income, is required.

Assume that a fraction, φ, of total oil tax revenues is saved every year into the Investment-Income Fund (with the rest going to the Stabilization Fund), so that:

$$XE_t = \varphi X_t \tag{3}$$

where XE is the share of total revenue that is transferred to the Investment-Income Fund and φ can be interpreted as a flow "savings rate" for oil revenues. Over time, the size of the Investment-Income Fund will be determined by the following identity:

$$E_t = (1+i_t)E_{t-1} + XE_t - TE_t \tag{4}$$

where i is the return generated on the Investment-Income Fund and TE is the transfer obtained from the fund based on the size of the fund in the preceding year, multiplied by the fund's expected average long-term real return, δ:

$$TE_t = \delta E_{t-1} \tag{5}$$

Basing the size of the transfer from the Investment-Income Fund on the expected average long-term real return, δ, is a prudent strategy— and one that is widely used as the spending policy of foundations, endowments, and indeed sovereign wealth funds (assuming that expected return is realistic in light of the fund's asset allocation). Using the *average annual* return ensures a stable stream of income to the government; spending only *real* returns ensures that the fund's capital is not eroded by inflation and can be maintain indefinitely; and finally, focusing on the *long-run* return enables the fund to capture a number of premiums, such as volatility, value, and illiquidity premiums (discussed in chapter 9), which raise the expected return of the fund. If the transfers from the Investment-Income Fund are determined in this manner, it is important that the fund's *actual* average return over time is not lower than the *assumed* or *expected* average return—otherwise, the fund would be depleted or reduced, leaving a smaller endowment for future generations.

An important implication is that combining a Stabilization Fund and an Investment-Income Fund is a way to both stabilize and maintain the level of resource consumption *beyond* the resource production life cycle—and potentially into perpetuity. With the introduction of the Investment-Income Fund alongside the Stabilization Fund, the framework can simultaneously meet the stabilization and saving objectives. As in the case of the one-fund version of the framework, α and β can be chosen to stabilize transfers to the government from the Stabilization Fund. In turn, δ should correspond to the expected long-term return of the Investment-Income Fund, while the savings rate, φ, can be chosen to assure the desired accumulation of an endowment. The higher the savings rate, φ, the more willing policymakers are to accept a lower current or near-term level of spending from resource revenues in favor of transfers to future generations (and a higher level of permanent spending). A lower φ implies a greater preference for spending the resource revenue as it arises, thus leaving less of an endowment for future generations. In summary, the fundamental dynamics and features of this rule-based fiscal framework are as follows:

- The rule decouples spending from resource revenues so that volatility in spending is reduced and both positive and negative shocks to resource revenue are only passed through to spending in a stabilized and delayed manner. Volatility is effectively transferred to the fluctuating levels of the Stabilization Fund.
- This decoupling is achieved by basing annual spending on three sources: (1) a fixed percentage of the previous year's spending; (2) a fixed percentage of the value of the Stabilization Fund; and

(3) a fixed transfer from the Savings Fund, equal to its long-run average real return.

- The Stabilization Fund's size fluctuates in line with shocks to resource revenues. The fund's value increases when positive shocks to revenue occur, as the government is constrained by the fiscal rule from spending the excess revenue windfall immediately. Likewise, the Stabilization Fund decreases when negative shocks materialize, as the rule permits withdrawals from the fund to stabilize spending.

- The long-term growth of the Investment-Income Fund is determined by the size of transfers from annual resource revenues—a higher savings rate implies lower near-term spending in favor of higher future (and permanent) spending. As the Investment-Income Fund grows, it's annual contribution to the budget in the form of investment income (based on its expected long-run real return) supplements resource revenues—and potentially replaces it entirely on depletion of the resource.

- Finally, if the level of spending from the Investment-Income Fund does not exceed its long-run real return, its capital value will be preserved in real terms, meaning it becomes a permanent endowment and a source of permanent income across generations. Critically, in the context of finite resources, this enables spending to be maintained at a level commensurate with the level of savings, even once oil or other resource revenues diminish and ultimately cease.

The governments' preferences and political constraints have to be incorporated into the framework and the way key parameters are calibrated to specific circumstances. The basic assumption is that the government favors stability in spending, which, subject to certain feasibility constraints, determines the values for the stabilization parameters, α and β, of the spending rule.[2] Second, the government faces an intertemporal trade-off between current and future spending in determining the desired savings rate, φ. In short, the rule is sufficiently flexible that it can be parameterized or calibrated in a variety of ways that reflect a range of policy needs, preferences, and realities. As in the previous chapter, we apply the rule introduced here to the case of Saudi Arabia. As with the simple savings rules, it instructive to evaluate the integrated fiscal rule in a backward-looking manner, which the remainder of this chapter does by constructing a counterfactual in which Saudi Arabia adopted the fiscal rule at the end of 2004 (that is, the rule applied as of the 2005 fiscal year).

An Application to Saudi Arabia

To construct a counterfactual scenario in which the fiscal framework introduced in this chapter was adopted in 2004, we need to again make a number of input assumptions. First, we assume that Saudi Arabia held $300bn in previously accumulated assets at the end of 2004, which is in line with reported reserve holdings of the Saudi Arabian Monetary Agency at the time. We assume that these assets could have been split between a Stabilization and Invest Income Fund, so that the former held $100bn at the end of 2004, and the latter, $200bn. As was done for the previous chapter's analysis, the returns of the Investment-Income Fund are proxied by the annual returns generated by a globally diversified portfolio. Given the introduction of a Stabilization Fund in the integrated fiscal framework in this chapter, we assume that its annual return can be proxied by the observed yield on ten-year U.S. Treasury bonds. Oil revenue data are taken from official data released by the Saudi Arabian Monetary Agency (as per the previous chapter).

Recall that the fiscal rule provides for spending from three sources: (1) a fixed percentage (α) based on the previous year's spending, irrespective of the amount of revenues received; (2) a fixed percentage (β) transfer from the Stabilization Fund; and (3) income from the Investment-Income Fund, based on its expected long-run real return (δ). The exact parameterization of the fiscal rule depends on the realities and preferences confronting policymakers in each particular circumstance. Recall from the previous chapter the following trends and features of the Saudi economy:

- Oil dependence is high and rising;
- Revenue, debt, and capital spending are very highly correlated with cyclical movements in the oil price;
- Previously accumulated oil revenue reserves are at risk of depletions, as the budget breakeven oil price continues to rise; and
- Long-term spending pressures are rising (in particular, due to demographic pressures).

These structural features underline the importance to Saudi Arabia's long-term fiscal future of establishing a rule-based countercyclical fiscal framework of the kind introduced in this chapter. While Saudi Arabia has immense oil wealth and has managed to accumulate significant assets during the previous oil boom, fiscal spending remains highly correlated with oil prices and revenue, fiscal dependency on oil has risen considerably, and its ability to sustain steady increases in the level of government spending is questionable, absent interventions to diversify and grow the fiscal revenue base.

Given the high level of initial savings (as of the end of 2004) relative to spending, the spending rule can be calibrated for the Saudi Arabian counterfactual with high α and β values of 0.8 and 0.1, respectively, and with $\delta = 0.05$, based on the expected long-run real return of the Investment-Income Fund. In this way, the calibration of the parameters of the fiscal rule provides for a level of spending in 2005 ($92bn) that is exactly in line with actual spending during that fiscal year, establishing a sound base for comparison.

Figure 6.1 shows the comparison of actual government spending to that implied by the fiscal rule with two different savings rates, 20 percent and 40 percent. Note that the modeled profile of spending with a 20 percent savings rate is similar to that of actual spending, although spending growth is slightly more constrained in the former for the last few years of the sample. Total spending under the fiscal rule with 20 percent savings between 2005 and 2014 was $1.7 trillion versus the $1.8 trillion actually spent. Two important differences need to be highlighted. First, the actual (observed) spending shown in figure 6.1 is based on total revenue, which is of course dominated by oil revenue, but included around 10 to 15 percent of nonoil revenues over the period in question. In contrast, the modeled counterfactual spending profile is based on the consumption of oil revenues only (ignoring nonoil revenues, which could have been used to either raise the level of spending directly or to grow the sovereign wealth fund). A second difference lies in the much greater accumulation of assets during what was (with the benefit of hindsight) a significant, transitory boom in oil prices. Under the modeled fiscal rule with 20 percent savings, Saudi Arabia would have accumulated $1.393 trillion in total assets between the Savings and Stabilization Fund by the end of 2014, which is significantly more than the $750bn to $800bn that the Saudi Arabian Monetary Agency did in fact hold by the end of 2014.

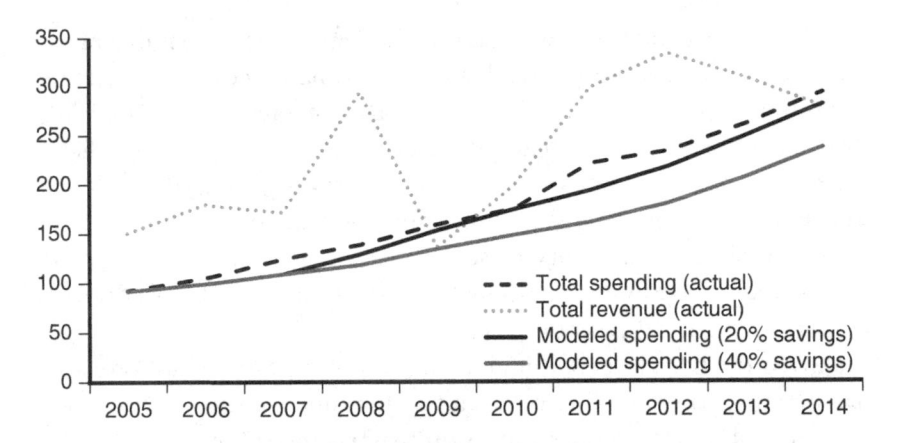

Figure 6.1 Counterfactual versus actual spending for Saudi Arabia.

Given the magnitude of the boom in revenues, it may have been prudent for Saudi Arabia to adopt a higher savings rate during this period, which would have constrained spending growth in the short term but would have resulted in a greater accumulation of saved assets (particularly in the Investment-Income Fund). Figure 6.1, therefore, also shows the modeled outcome with a 40 percent savings rate. Under the 40 percent savings rule, the total consumption of oil-based revenue and sovereign wealth fund income (and excluding nonoil revenues) would have been $1.48 trillion from 2005 to 2014, while total savings would have equaled an impressive $1.775 trillion.

A number of implications can be drawn from this counterfactual analysis for Saudi Arabia. Over the past decade, Saudi Arabia managed to accumulate savings from exceptionally high oil revenues in certain years, notably 2008 and 2011–2013, while at the same time raising its level of spending considerably. However, the analysis conducted in this chapter supports that of chapter 5 and suggests that the failure to implement a rule-based fiscal policy framework and formal sovereign wealth fund structures has been a missed opportunity. Saudi Arabia could have accumulated considerably more assets under the modeled fiscal rule. This greater accumulation would have been due not only to more constrained growth in public spending over the period but also to the compounding effect of a few years of high financial market returns (although it should be noted that, as in chapter 5, the sample period includes a period of sharp losses during the global financial crisis). To quantify the missed opportunity, the roughly $1 trillion in additional savings that would have accrued under the fiscal rule with a 40 percent savings rate would have generated an additional $50bn in permanent annual investment income that could be sustained into perpetuity. In light of the fiscal pressures that emerged in Saudi Arabia in 2015 and 2016 following the collapse of global oil prices, the opportunity cost of these foregone savings are striking.

Finally, note that the adoption of the fiscal rule, even under the most conservative savings assumption in which 40 percent of oil revenues are transferred to the Investment-Income Fund, still permits a significant increase in spending. Indeed, the consumption of oil-based revenue more than doubles from $92 billion in 2005 to $237bn in 2014 under this conservative specification of the rule. This is an important illustration of the fact that the fiscal rule proposed in this chapter does not preclude significant growth in public spending in the face of a sustained resource revenue boom, provided the level of assets in the Stabilization and Investment-Income Fund permits it.

GENERAL POLICY AND INSTITUTIONAL IMPLICATIONS

The discussion of integrated fiscal rules in this chapter has brought several policy and institutional implications to light. The benefits of integrated fiscal rules, along with their general policy and institutional implications, can be summarized as follows.

Trade-Offs in the Allocation of Resource Revenues

Trade-offs are pervasive in the allocation of resource revenues in any given period, as well as between their current and future use of those revenues. The fiscal rule proposed in this chapter helps to frame the trade-offs between the need for current spending, building buffers for stabilization purposes and creating an endowment for permanent income from a depleting resource source. Saving a portion of current revenue to create a Stabilization Fund and build a permanent endowment in the form of an Investment-Income Fund involves trade-offs that can be difficult to achieve politically. Yet the counterfactual application of the framework for Saudi Arabia demonstrated that fiscal rules and sovereign wealth funds do not always imply trade-offs as stark as those implied by their critics (see Collier et al., 2010). In the Saudi Arabian counterfactual, a significant increase in public spending was a realistic and prudent outcome in the context of rising oil revenue—despite the assumed adoption of a conservative and constraining fiscal rule that allocated as much as 40 percent of oil revenues to the sovereign wealth fund.

The framework usefully draws attention to the fact that stabilization policies for volatile resource revenues are mostly technical exercises (reflected in this chapter's framework in the identification of plausible values for α and β, given the relevant input), while choices around the intertemporal allocation of resource consumption over time are of a discretionary nature. In the rule-based framework introduced in this chapter, that discretionary choice or policy preference determines the value of φ. The value of φ determines the trade-off between current and future/permanent spending.

High-saving policies may be appropriate, or even required, in countries with declining revenues as well as those with increasing revenues. The narrative behind the case for savings differs, however. In the context of anticipated long-term declines in resource revenues, the Investment-Income Fund may need to grow over time to maintain spending levels once resources have been depleted—this is particularly true for countries that are fiscally dependent on resource revenues. On the other hand, in countries with rising resource revenues, high savings are typically both feasible (given that the rise in revenues is supplementary to the existing revenues) and prudent (given that it moderates an unduly rapid rise in spending in the context of absorptive capacity constraints).

In practice, policymakers can build a political consensus and public support for short-term sacrifices by explaining the cost of unstable public spending and the benefits of intergenerational transfers, thus ensuring the sustainability of resource-based spending and investment, and the long-term financing of public liabilities (such as pensions, education, and health care). The integrated fiscal rule discussed in this chapter allows policymakers to frame and quantify the constructive role that sovereign wealth funds, fiscal rules, and financial income can play in meeting these challenges.

The Importance of Adhering to Rules

The framework presented here is a rules-based one. The idea is that public spending is decoupled from the volatility of annual resource revenues and part of a depleting resource is made permanent through a set of rules. Rules are required to ensure dynamically consistent saving and spending policies, and to constrain policymakers' discretion, particularly when they face incentives for short-term behavior that is not consistent with long-term goals and principles of prudence. The design of the rules is embodied in the choice of—and adherence to—key parameters of the fiscal rule. For the framework to work as intended, it is essential that the government be able to adhere to the rules during difficult times. Political and legal safeguards are desirable institutional foundations for the fiscal rule (as discussed in detail in the following chapter) that make the fiscal rule resilient to changes in the political, economic, and financial environment. From an institutional perspective, the "governance" of sovereign wealth funds pertains not only directly to the fund itself, or even the institutions managing it, but also to the rules and institutional processes that govern the flow of funds in and out of the funds.

Separating Investment and Governance Models

The fiscal rule makes an important distinction between two types of sovereign wealth funds: a Stabilization Fund and an Investment-Income Fund. This distinction draws attention to the need to mandate the two funds to pursue investment models that are relevant to their respective functions. The Stabilization Fund needs to maintain sufficient levels of liquidity, as it needs to partially fund government spending annually (based on the stabilizing components of the spending rule, α and β). In years of sharp decline in resource revenues, the Stabilization Fund may need to contribute a significant amount of funding to the budget. By contrast, the Investment-Income Fund only contributes an annual amount equal to its expected average long-run real return.

It is therefore more important that the Investment-Income Fund benefit from its long-term investment horizon and other structural advantages to capture various risk premiums that raise expected and actual returns (as discussed in chapter 9). Care should be taken in the institutional design to ensure that the Stabilization Fund is sufficiently liquid to meet anticipated shortfalls, while the Investment-Income Fund should be protected from undue criticism for short-term losses and be evaluated and assessed in terms of its long-term strategy and performance. Just as the two funds need different investment models, so too do they require different management and oversight structures. The Stabilization Fund holds liquid assets, and can therefore be managed by the central bank (which typically has the capacity and experience to manage such assets in light of its management of the country's foreign-exchange reserves), or even directly by the national treasury.[3]

By contrast, the Investment-Income Fund is likely to have a more complex and diversified portfolio, which may require dedicated skills, capacity, and expertise that most likely extend beyond the experience of the central bank or the treasury department of the typical Ministry of Finance. Many governments have, in practice, handed the responsibility for managing such more complex portfolios to accountable, arms-length authorities that report to the government, parliaments, and/or the treasury. Delegated authority requires more extensive oversight and reporting structures than the operationally simpler Stabilization Fund (as discussed in chapter 8).

CONCLUSION

This chapter advanced the discussion of fiscal rules for sovereign wealth funds in the direction of integrated (and contingent) rule-based frameworks. The fiscal rule discussed in this chapter allows for saving, spending, and stabilization decisions to be assessed in a single, integrated framework. It is also contingent in the sense that the framework has automatic feedback mechanisms that allow spending levels to adjust, albeit gradually, to both cyclical and long-term variations in resource revenues.

This rule-based fiscal framework clearly underlines the importance of several institutional aspects of the sovereign wealth fund model. First, the chapter continues and expands this book's emphasis on the importance of well-designed fiscal rules that govern the flow of assets, revenue, and income to and from the sovereign wealth fund. In the following chapter, we will extend the analysis to the governance or institutional arrangements in place in a number of countries for establishing and potentially amending the fiscal rule. Second, the demonstration of the different role played by stabilization and long-term investment-income funds in the fiscal frameworks of resource-rich economies underlines the importance of an institutional separation between the two types of funds. In particular, this chapter helped to undermine the value of operational independence and a delegated authority in the management of a sovereign wealth fund's investments with long-term investment horizons and income-generating functions. The last two chapters in the book will discuss these issues in greater detail.

CHAPTER SEVEN

Governing the Fiscal Rule

The Design and Institutional Infrastructure of Fiscal Rules for Resource Revenues

WE ARGUE in this book that absent fiscal rules and a supportive institutional structure that governs the rules, the contribution of a sovereign wealth fund to improving the management of volatile and finite resource revenues is significantly reduced. When policymakers retain discretion in the allocation of resource revenues over the cycle, they are unlikely to break the historical tendency toward procyclicality. A rule-based fiscal framework helps ensure that a sufficient portion of windfall revenues are transferred to the sovereign wealth fund rather than consumed during boom periods and guards against an unsustainable depletion of previously accumulated assets during bust periods.

The institutional arrangements or governance of the fiscal rule is of underappreciated importance. Even the best designed rule-based fiscal framework for resource revenues and sovereign wealth funds can be undermined by weak institutional and governance arrangements. Moreover, rules and strong institutional arrangements to govern the fiscal rule are necessary precisely because fiscal rules are often most important exactly when it is easiest to break them—either during periods of significant windfalls or during periods of considerable fiscal pressure due to low commodity prices and revenues. Rules need to be applied—and indeed bind—in feast and famine.

In this chapter, we shift the focus from the design of rules to the institutional arrangements through which they are governed and enforced. The chapter reveals a wide range of institutional mechanisms for the specification and enforcement of fiscal rules, ranging from constitutional mandates to legislative statues to presidential decrees to elements of custom (or informal institutions, as per chapter 2). The examples discussed in this chapter are in no way exhaustive—in fact, they are biased toward systems that have worked reasonably well and have persisted. Three models in particular provide valuable insights into the specification and governance of fiscal rules for managing resource revenues and sovereign wealth fund assets and income: Norway, Chile, and the American state endowment model.

THE GOVERNANCE OF FISCAL RULES FOR RESOURCE REVENUES

There is a vast literature on the governance and institutional arrangements around fiscal rules (see, for example, Kopits and Symansky, 1998; Persson and Tabellini, 2004; Debrun and Kumar, 2007). The general theme from this literature (and the practical experience with fiscal rules) is not overly optimistic. Efforts to establish robust fiscal rules have suffered from at least three problems. First, the design of fiscal rules is complex. For example, the literature has identified the difficulty of determining whether optimal rules should bind on budget deficits, debt-to-GDP ratios, revenue, borrowing, or spending; whether and how cyclical adjustments should be taken into account; and whether the dynamics between fiscal policy at the federal and subnational levels undermine fiscal rules. The ability of politicians to resort to "creative accounting" around fiscal measures in relation to the fiscal rule is another common problem (Milesi-Ferretti, 2004). Moving from design to governance, it is clear that the "paradox of power" and dynamic inconsistency problems loom large over efforts to enforce and adhere to fiscal rules. Debrun and Kumar (2007) summarize the argument of fiscal rule skeptics in this regard, as follows: "There will always be circumstances in which scrapping or ignoring rules will be preferable for policymakers, suggesting a serious credibility problem. It follows from this argument that a credible solution to biased policies cannot be to suppress discretion but to find mechanisms through which it could be exerted more wisely" (481).

It is useful to think of three stylized mechanisms through which to achieve this goal. The first is to move critical elements of the fiscal process that are known to result in deficit biases and inefficient (and procyclical) spending from the realm of "in-period politics" to the "politics at the constitutional level," according to the language of Buchanan (1987) discussed in chapter 2. The second is to resort to external or third-party enforcement and expertise—that is, to technocratic (apolitical) opinion and analysis, or "rule by experts." Third, under specific conditions, the development of an institutionalized "custom," preferably arrived at through consensus, may work by establishing a sufficiently high cost of ignoring or bypassing a de facto rule. Of course, across all three mechanisms, deviations from the rule carry (political) costs, and the literature "emphasizes the role of democratic accountability as one natural mechanism through which deviations from the rule can be made costly," alongside that of market sanction (Debrun and Kumar, 2007).

The literature has also focused more narrowly on the application of fiscal rules in the context of resource revenues and the saving and spending rules of sovereign wealth funds (Davis et al., 2001; Ossowski et al., 2008; Baunsgaard et al., 2012; Schmidt-Hebbel, 2012). This chapter contributes to this literature by emphasizing the governance and institutional arrangements around fiscal rules for resource revenues, and framing this discussion in terms of the above-mentioned three mechanisms. This chapter identifies the American permanent-fund institutional model as an (incomplete) version of the "politics-at-the-constitutional-level" mechanism; the Chilean model as relying on "rule-by-experts"; and the Norwegian model as being founded on custom and consensus.

In discussing these rules and their institutional arrangements (along with the institutional shortcomings of otherwise reasonably designed fiscal rules in Kazakhstan, Nigeria, Ghana, and Timor Leste), we refer to the set of criteria for the design and function of good institutions identified in chapter 2. These features overlap with Kopits and Symansky's (1998) list of criteria for fiscal rules as articulated by Kyle (2014) in his analysis of Kazakhstan's fiscal rules. According to these criteria, good fiscal rules share the following characteristics (the compatibility of this list with the criteria for the design and function of good institutions in chapter 2 is apparent):

1. *Well defined:* Policy targets and the institutional setup to achieve them should be clearly defined. There should be as little room as possible for ambiguity in the operation of the rule.
2. *Transparency:* It should be possible to observe how the rule is intended to operate and for stakeholders to monitor its implementation.
3. *Adequacy:* The mechanisms envisioned in the rule should be capable of achieving the desired level of the target variable.
4. *Consistency:* The rule should be internally consistent as well as consistent with other policies and goals of economic policy.
5. *Simplicity:* The easier the terms in which the rule is defined are understood, the better.
6. *Flexibility:* The rule should be sufficiently flexible to deal with changing economic circumstances by, for example, containing adequate escape clauses and other built-in feedback mechanisms.
7. *Enforceability:* The mechanisms to enforce compliance must be clear, in particular with respect to the role of different institutions and public actors.

Clearly these criteria span both policy design and institutional aspects. While the emphasis and particular contribution of this chapter lies in analyzing the latter, the discussion below necessarily makes reference to aspects of the policy design of the rules themselves, as the design and governance of fiscal rules are often interrelated.

FISCAL RULES FOR RESOURCE REVENUES USING SOVEREIGN WEALTH FUNDS

Countries use a variety of approaches to determine the level and dynamics of transfers of resource revenues to their sovereign wealth funds (savings rules), as well as how to use the assets and income of their sovereign wealth funds (spending rules). In general, the savings rules tend to be better developed and more clearly articulated than spending rules. As with the design of the rules themselves, the institutional arrangements for implementing, monitoring, enforcing, and potentially amending rules varies significantly through the powers assigned variously to constitutions, statutory legislation, political consensus, ministerial/ executive policy, or informal customs.

Norway: Rule by Custom and Consensus

The sources of funding for the Norway Government Pension Fund Global include taxes and royalties generated from oil extraction. The fund also receives tax revenues on CO_2 emissions from petroleum production, and operating income and dividends from Statoil, the national oil company. The fund also reinvests earnings in excess of its mandated transfers to the budget. Accordingly, Norway saves and invests all of its oil revenues, minus a withdrawal equal to the estimated long-run real return of the sovereign wealth fund (4 percent per year), the latter being the spending component of the fiscal rule.

The process for allocating resource revenue starts with the transfer of all resource revenues to the fund—in the same manner as proposed in the fiscal rule introduced in chapter 6, but in combination with a spending rule that is more conservative. The spending rule allows for a transfer of investment income to the budget equal to 4 percent of the fund's total assets, based on what policymakers believe to be the sustainable amount of spending of resource revenues: the expected long-run average real return generated on the fund's capital. To ensure the sustainability of the fiscal framework, Norway formulates an annual budget under the assumption of having zero oil revenue—the so-called structural nonoil budget. This nonoil budget is permitted to run an average long-run deficit equal to the 4 percent transfer from the sovereign wealth fund. In other words, the sovereign wealth fund's investment income finances the nonoil deficit: the bigger the fund becomes, the larger the value transfer (based on a fixed 4 percent spending), and the larger the permitted sustainable nonoil deficit.

The most striking design aspect of the Norwegian rule is the large portion of resource revenues that is transferred to its sovereign wealth fund. Norway's level of economic development, quality of existing public infrastructure, and access to alternative sources of fiscal revenue— features that less-developed and more resource-dependent countries do not share—enable this highly conservative savings policy for oil revenue. Given its limited degree of fiscal dependence on resource revenues (nonoil revenues account for around 75 to 80 percent of revenue), its emphasis on a sustainable nonoil structural deficit, and the stable spending rule for sovereign wealth fund income, Norway does not need an additional stabilization fund and stabilizing transfer, as per the fiscal rule proposed in chapter 6. While the management of volatility is less of a concern for Norway, more oil-dependent economies have a greater need for such stabilization mechanisms.

In terms of institutional arrangements, a fiscal framework introduced in 2001 determines the flow of oil revenues into and investment income out of the Norwegian sovereign wealth fund. An underappreciated aspect of the much-lauded Norwegian model is that neither the savings nor the spending rule are legally binding, but rather emerged through a broad consensus around the need for prudence in spending oil revenues. The current rule-based approach enjoys the support of the Ministry of Finance, the Parliament, and Norges Bank Investment Management, but it is consensual, and can, at least in theory, be changed if the relevant parties agree.

The spending rule is the most likely element of such change, as it is based on the expected sustainable long-term real return of the fund. Given that the assets of the fund are invested in a largely passive manner, exogenous factors could lead to changes in expectations around what is a feasible and sustainable long-run real return. The Ministry of Finance, Norges Bank Investment Management, and external experts have agreed in recent years that a 4 percent annual real return is feasible, and is therefore an appropriate amount to transfer (as permanent income) back to government to finance the nonoil structural deficit. This remains a topic of debate, however. In late 2013, for example, the governor of Norges Bank suggested that it may need to be lowered to 3 percent due to lower returns in global financial markets (Olsen, 2012). Changing the spending rule in light of revised expected returns on the portfolio would involve external consultation and research, but is likely to be driven by the Ministry of Finance in consultation with Norges Bank Investment Management (possibly further requiring legislative approval, and certainly consultation). Thus far, an institutional bias toward preserving the 4 percent spending rule has been maintained, based on the view that an adjustment downward would establish a precedent to subsequently raise the return target and sustainable draw upward.

The institutional mechanisms that govern Norway's fiscal rule can, therefore, be described as characteristic of the custom-and-consensus model. In this regard, the governance of Norway's fiscal rule for resource revenues and the spending/savings rules for its sovereign wealth fund is, in fact, similar to those of various Middle Eastern jurisdictions, notably Abu Dhabi and Kuwait; however, the Norwegian model is further buttressed by exceptional levels of transparency and disclosure (which is lacking in these Middle Eastern countries). Consequently, the Norwegian fiscal rule meets all seven of the Kopits-Symansky criteria outlined previously, as well as the principles for the design and function associated with good institutions in chapter 2.

A possible objection to this assessment is that the Norwegian fiscal rule is not particularly flexible, given the transfer of *all* oil revenues to the sovereign wealth fund and the spending of a fixed percentage of investment income. However, the rigidity of the rule should be understood in terms of the country's specific fiscal needs. Resource revenues play a minor role in Norway's fiscal framework, certainly when compared with most other countries and subnational jurisdictions with sovereign wealth funds. Moreover, the fiscal rule is flexible in the most general institutional sense to the extent that the Norwegian Ministry of Finance frequently invites (publicly disclosed) external assessments of the merits of the fiscal rule, notably the Thøgersen Commission, which evaluated the rules-based fiscal framework in 2015.

Chile: Rule by Experts

The rules governing the flows in and out of Chile's two sovereign funds (and the funds themselves) were established by the Fiscal Responsibility Law, passed in 2006. The legal foundation of the strong rule-based saving and spending procedures means that there is little discretion vested in the hands of the Ministry of Finance to change them, absent a change in the law.

Chile is a prime example of a country that has adopted a two-fund structure of the kind proposed in chapter 6, although its fiscal rule works differently. The Chilean model combines a short-term stabilization fund (the Economic and Social Stabilization Fund [ESSF]) and a long-term savings/income fund (the Pension Reserve Fund). The rules for transferring revenue to and from the Chilean sovereign funds, particularly the ESSF, are inextricably linked to the "Structural Balance Rule," Chile's more general fiscal rule. The structural budget balance is the surplus or deficit, excluding automatic stabilizers—that is, the difference between expenditures and revenues that would be collected if the economy were operating at potential GDP.

Chile targets a balanced structural budget that allows for state-contingent fluctuations based on the output gap in the level of GDP and cyclical fluctuations in the price of copper (the country's primary export, which accounts for 10 to 20 percent of revenue). If the combination of the output gap and the deviation in the price of copper from expectations is positive, Chile is supposed to run a fiscal surplus, whereas if they are negative, a deficit is permitted. A unique institutional feature of the Chilean model, discussed in greater detail below, is its reliance on two "advisory committees" staffed by technocratic subject experts who calculate trends in GDP growth and the outlook for copper prices, respectively. These estimates are then used to calculate cyclically adjusted fiscal revenue and spending, and ensure that surplus fiscal income that arises due to cyclical factors are deposited into the sovereign wealth funds.[1] The Advisory Committee for Trend GDP consists of sixteen members, appointed by the minister of finance, and provides the ministry with medium-term projections for the growth rate of capital, the labor force, and productivity, which are then used to generate projections of trend GDP and the output gap. Similarly, the Advisory Committee for the Reference Copper Price, consisting of twelve members also appointed by the minister, provides projections for the long-term international price of copper (Schmidt-Hebbel, 2012).

While the (averaged) projections of the two committees are inputs into Chile's rule-based fiscal framework, built around the cyclically adjusted structural balance, the ministry "retains significant discretionary power in defining the methodology—equations and parameters—that determines the cyclically-adjusted fiscal balance rule" (Schmidt-Hebbel, 2012). The Ministry of Finance has, however, disclosed much of the details of its model, as well the minutes from the meetings of both advisory committees, which in practice limits the degree of discretion, as the ministry is held to account for any potential deviations from its models and rules. On the spending side of the rule, the provisions described in the previous section are established in law, which limits the scope for discretion or abuse of the sovereign funds—although there are provisions in the law for additional, discretionary savings to be authorized by the minister of finance during boom periods.

Given Chile's two-fund structure, it is important to understand the rule-based process that governs the allocation of savings not only to the Chilean sovereign wealth funds but also between them. The two-fund structure was established in 2007, replacing the Copper Stabilization Fund, a stabilization-only fund created in 2000. A minimum of 0.2 percent of the previous year's GDP must be deposited into the Pension Reserve Fund each year, and if the fiscal surplus exceeds this amount, the deposit amount can rise to a maximum of 0.5 percent of the previous year's GDP. Additional deposits to this savings fund structure can be financed with funds from the Economic and Social Stabilization Fund at the discretion of the minister of finance. The Economic and Social Stabilization Fund receives all remaining cyclically determined surplus fiscal revenue (Schmidt-Hebbel, 2012).

Transfers from Chile's Pension Reserve Fund and the Economic and Social Stabilization Fund are governed by different spending rules. The assets and investment proceeds from the Pension Reserve Fund can be used exclusively to pay for pension and social welfare liabilities. Current provisions differentiate between a spending rule until 2016 and a new process after that date. Until 2016, only the previous year's real return on the Pension Reserve Fund may be withdrawn (as per the investment-income fund component according to the rule in chapter 6—or the practice in Norway and American state permanent funds), while from 2016 onward, annual withdrawals from the fund cannot be greater than one-third of the difference between that year's pension-related expenditures and pension-related expenditures (adjusted for inflation) for 2008. The latter is thus simply a "spending cap" imposed on transfers from Chile's saving-cum-income fund. Withdrawals from the ESSF can be made to cover a cyclical budget shortfall, based on the calculations of the two expert committees, or at the discretion of the minister of finance to pay down debt ahead of schedule or to increase the asset base of the Pension Reserve Fund. The extent to which withdrawals from Chile's stabilization fund are governed by the structural balance rule puts the emphasis of Chilean fiscal policy on the need for countercyclicality and long-term sustainability (particularly the avoidance of unsustainable spending from temporary copper revenue–driven booms).

Two attractive features of Chile's fiscal rule are the manner in which it formally and unambiguously distinguishes between the stabilization and income-generating functions of its sovereign wealth funds, and the extent to which these funds are but a part of a larger, more comprehensive medium-term fiscal framework. The fiscal rule is not strictly constitutional, as it is imbedded in a simple Act of Parliament, which could in theory be overturned through the process of in-period politics. However, Chile's tradition of adhering to the rule and communicating policy to the public (as well as to the financial markets) at the hand of that rule has served to move much of the major considerations around fiscal policy to the level of constitutional politics—much as it has with respect to Chilean monetary policy (the country was an early adopter and leading innovator of central bank independence and inflation targeting).

The use of an independent committee of experts to determine the appropriate countercyclical stance of Chilean fiscal policy is laudable, although it is questionable how applicable this approach is to other developing-country and emerging-market contexts. Chile has a long and successful tradition of delegating authority for critical economic policy decisions to technocratic experts (as noted above, Chile has been an innovator around aspects of central bank independence). Technocratic proficiency—or "rule by experts"—is embraced and respected in a manner that is exceptional not only among emerging markets but indeed among all countries. While generally positive, the role of subject experts in relation to the fiscal rule in Chile does raise questions around the task of the expert committee that estimates equilibrium copper prices. Commodity prices, especially copper prices, are arguably too volatile and stochastic to expect even subject experts to make accurate assessments around the temporary and permanent shocks to prices.

In terms of the Kopits-Symansky criteria for evaluating fiscal rules, it could be argued that unreasonable expectations around the epistemological capacity of the committee establish a concern around the rule with respect to its "adequacy." It is not clear that "the mechanisms envisioned in the rule"—notably, the importance of the committee's findings as a critical input into the calibration of the fiscal stance—are fully "capable of achieving the desired level of the target variable." Alternative approaches to managing uncertainty around the temporary versus permanent nature of commodity price shocks on fiscal revenue would include the use of a moving average–based rule (see chapter 5) or a rule that channels a greater share of volatile copper revenues through the stabilization fund (see chapter 6). Finally, clarifications could be made with respect to the clarity and simplicity of the rule (including the transfer of assets between the two components of Chile's sovereign wealth fund), as according to the Kopits-Symansky framework.

American Permanent Funds: (Incomplete) Constitutional Rules

While permanent funds are used to manage a wide range of state-level revenues in the United States, there are funds investing public revenues garnered from natural resources in Texas, New Mexico, Wyoming, Alaska, and North Dakota.[2] These funds all perform the same overarching function of transforming a depleting asset in the resource deposits into a permanent form of wealth (capital held in a financial portfolio) and income (real returns generated on those financial assets). American permanent funds operate as both income- and intergenerational savings funds, in the same manner as Norway's sovereign wealth fund: first, they generate annual income based on the inflation-adjusted returns generated on the financial portfolio, and second, they ensure that this income-generating capacity is maintained for future generations by protecting the fund's capital (or principal) from both withdrawals and erosion through inflation.

As noted earlier, the savings rules associated with American state permanent funds are typically mandated by the state constitution. The capital or corpus of state permanent funds is similarly protected by the constitution (although rarely in real terms, leaving the process of inflation adjustment, or "inflation proofing" as it is referred to in the American context, open to statutory action or custom). Combined, these constitutional underpinnings establish the most binding and most difficult to overturn commitment mechanisms for savings of all sovereign wealth fund models in existence. The procedures for amending American state constitutions vary, but the hurdle is universally high, requiring a two-thirds or three-quarters super majority vote in both houses of the legislature, plus a popular vote. The governance and institutional arrangements for the use of funds earnings is, however, less binding. Perhaps due to the fact that very few American states can be regarded as fiscally resource dependent, there has historically been much less emphasis on stabilization funds and stabilization mechanisms for spending volatile resource revenues than on savings and investment-income funds (permanent funds).

The American permanent-fund model has its origins in Texas in the mid-nineteenth century, which, as argued in chapter 3, makes the state home to the oldest sovereign wealth fund in the world. The Texas Permanent School Fund and the Texas Permanent University Fund were established under the state constitution in 1876—only a decade after civilian government was restored in the state, following its cession from Mexico, the collapse of the autonomous Republic of Texas in 1846, and the turmoil of post–Civil War reconstruction. The Texas Permanent School Fund's predecessor, the Special School Fund, dates back even further, having been established by the State Legislature in 1854. While there are differences in every state's application of the model, the key elements of the Texan example are attractively simple and have since been emulated by a number of other states (and indeed by other countries). The savings rule is an earmarking of a fixed percentage of resource revenues to the permanent fund—typically defined as 25 to 30 percent of royalty and/or severance tax income on oil, gas, and coal, while the spending rule limits withdrawals from the permanent fund to its real returns (as per the Norwegian example). Both the percentage of resource revenue saved and the preservation of the capital of the permanent fund are typically enshrined in the state constitution, thus establishing high institutional hurdles to change. The savings rule under the typical American permanent-fund model can, therefore, be characterized as governed by politics as the constitutional level.

In Texas and New Mexico, the permanent funds are specifically earmarked for educational spending purposes. In the case of the Texas Permanent University Fund, the assets are in fact owned by the public university system, while the Texas Permanent School Fund, the New Mexico Land Grant Permanent Fund (also called the New Mexico Permanent School Fund), and the New Mexico Severance Tax Permanent Fund are part of the budget process, but investment income is dedicated to educational expenses (and, in New Mexico, to a lesser extent to maintenance on state hospitals, government buildings, penitentiaries, and water resources). In Wyoming, income from the largest permanent fund, the Wyoming Permanent Mineral Trust Fund, is not earmarked for specific budgeted priorities, but rather flows into the state's General Fund (earmarking would require a constitutional amendment), although the state does have a number of smaller permanent funds that are also funded through mineral royalties and are earmarked for educational purposes, notably the Common School Permanent Land Fund, the Excellence in Higher Education Endowment Fund. In the case of the North Dakota Heritage Fund, no payments from the fund have been made to date (as of 2015), and transfers are only expected to start in

2017 at the earliest, when the fund's interest and income will start to be rolled into the state's general budget. Money from the principal could also be spent in the future, if two-thirds of both houses of the state legislature approved (additionally, no more than 15 percent of the principal could be spent during any two-year period). Again, here the extent to which the constitutional underpinnings of the fiscal framework for the use of natural resource revenues, channeled through permanent funds, have largely removed the pervasive influence of in-period politics is striking.

The largest American state permanent fund, the Alaska Permanent Fund, has a famous spending policy. Whereas the saving policy and the protection of the fund's capital are guaranteed through a constitutional amendment established in 1976 (when the Alaska Permanent Fund was established), the use of the fund's earnings is a matter of policy, determined by custom and subject to legislative approval. The earnings of the Alaska Permanent Fund are formally separated from the capital (referred to as the "corpus") in the form of the Earnings Reserve. Although the two pools are invested in the same manner, the appropriation of money out of the Earnings Reserve is subject to legislative approval through a simple majority vote of 50 percent in both the State Senate and the House of Representatives. Since the early 1980s, an appropriation equal to 50 percent of the five-year moving average of the fund's earnings has been made to fund the Alaska Permanent Fund Dividend, a direct transfer to every citizen of Alaska (subject to minimum age and residency requirements). As a matter of custom, Alaskan State Legislatures have historically transferred part of the remaining balance of the Earnings Reserve back into the corpus to ensure that its capital is inflation protected. In summary, while the saving of part of Alaskan oil revenues through the permanent fund is governed by politics at the constitutional level, the spending of the fund's earnings (and the roughly 70 percent of oil revenues that are not transferred to the fund) are subject to in-period political processes.

This uniquely Alaskan spending policy has been a double-edged sword. The establishment of the Alaska Permanent Fund Dividend has had the consequence (intended or otherwise) of generating significant civic interest in the Alaska Permanent Fund, making it politically impossible for the legislature to raid the fund (which would require a change in the constitution). The downside is that it has limited the scope for fiscal adjustment, which is often needed in a state that derived more than 90 percent of state-level revenues from oil in most years since removing state income and sales taxes. In the aftermath of the 2014 collapse in oil prices, for example, the Office of the Governor of Alaska proposed a rationalization in the size of the dividend (which in 2014 equaled more than one-third of the state budget, excluding Federal transfers) and the use of part of the earnings to establish a rule-based budget transfer, but encountered fierce public and political resistance (Richards, 2015). The danger is therefore that the political economy established by public expectations of an ever-increasing dividend—the situation of the dividend and spending policy at the heart of the in-period political process—crowds out other important public spending priorities, such as education, health care, and infrastructure maintenance.

It is also important to highlight the merits and problems around the permanent-fund model's saving rules. As noted earlier, the savings rule component of the permanent fund model is built on a very simple, typically constitutionally enshrined, savings of a fixed percentage of resource revenues through the fund. In terms of the Kopits-Symansky criteria, therefore, this aspect of the rule scores well on the basis of "simplicity" and "consistency." The downside, however, is that when such savings rules are not combined with complementary stabilization mechanisms, they can be procyclical. In terms of the Kopits-Symansky criteria, they fall short with respect to "flexibility" (not being state contingent) and "adequacy" (being procyclical and failing to stabilize revenue volatility). The procyclicality of the fiscal rule is not a major practical problem in states where the budget is not reliant on resource revenues, as in Texas, New Mexico, and North Dakota. However, in Alaska (and to a lesser extent, Wyoming), where resource revenues account for a major share of revenue—in Alaska, oil revenues exceeded 90 percent of state revenues between 2010 and 2013—the fixed rule is problematic, given the absence of complementary stabilization mechanisms.

In Alaska, the component of the Earnings Reserve that is not used to fund the dividend, as well as other "buffer funds" such as the Constitutional Budget Reserve and the Statutory Budget Reserve, should in theory provide some offsetting stability in times of low oil revenues. However, these buffer funds are small in size relative to spending, and indeed total saved assets, and the use of their assets is not guided by a rule or established custom; instead, it is subject to legislative approval, and hence beholden to in-period political calculations and compromise. The above-mentioned fiscal reforms proposed by the governor in 2015 would adjust both the spending and saving mechanisms in a manner closely comparable to the fiscal rule presented in chapter 6—transferring almost all oil revenue (particularly the volatile components) to the Alaska Permanent Fund in exchange for a stable draw on the fund's investment income in order to fund the budget in a stable and sustainable manner (Richards, 2015). But the proposal has encouraged various path-dependent political obstacles, such as previously mentioned resistance on the part of legislators to reduce the size of the dividend and/or change the customary formula through which it is derived as well as the legislature's reluctance to effectively cede some of its de facto appropriation powers by being bound by a fiscal rule (Drummond, 2016; Walker, 2016).

In terms of the Kopits-Symansky criteria, Wyoming, and certainly Alaska in particular, would benefit from greater—and less politicized—recourse to stabilization mechanisms. In both states, stabilization funds do exist: Alaska has the Permanent Fund Earnings Reserve, the Constitutional Budget Reserve, and the Statutory Budget Reserve, while Wyoming has a Budget Reserve Account and the Legislative Stabilization Reserve Account. However, these funds can only be accessed after clearing various legislative hurdles, involving either a simple or absolute majority in both houses of the legislature.

In Alaska, where uncontroversial, rule-based access to countercyclical stabilization funds is most needed,[3] the observed reality is exactly the opposite: the use of and access to fiscal buffers are politically contentious, especially when it is most needed—during episodes of fiscal pressure when oil prices collapse. The use of the assets of the Earnings Reserve and the Statutory Budget Reserves, for example, requires a simple majority of 50 percent in both houses of the legislature, while the Constitutional Budget Reserve can only be accessed through an absolute majority exceeding 75 percent of votes in both houses—establishing inappropriately high political hurdles to the use of stabilization funds in times of fiscal crisis. Again, the fiscal rule therefore falls short in terms of Kopits and Symansky's criteria flexibility and adequacy.

Meaningful reforms around the role of stabilization funds, particularly for resource-dependent American states, would focus not only on growing the size of assets held in buffer funds relative to the level of annual spending in the budget, but more fundamentally on establishing clear rules for allocating resource revenues between the budget, the stabilization fund(s), and the permanent fund(s). The real institutional priority should be to depoliticize the flow of revenues in and out of these stabilization funds. Ideally, such reforms will be conducted as part of the establishment of a more dynamic framework (such as the fiscal rule introduced in chapter 6), which would improve the flexibility and adequacy of the rule, albeit at the expense of some loss of simplicity.

CONCLUSION

This chapter discussed the design and governance of fiscal rules currently used by a number of countries to determine the allocation of oil revenues and the use of sovereign wealth fund assets and income. The analysis of the rules actually used in practice allowed for an instructive comparison with the rule-based frameworks discussed in chapters 5 and 6. In general, the rule-based fiscal frameworks adopted in Norway and Chile come closest in design to the proposed framework of chapter 6: while their operation is different from that rule (and indeed from each other), they both integrate savings decisions with a concept of sustainable income from depleting resources. In both cases, the ultimate goal behind the rule is to constrain the spending of finite resource revenues in such a way that the budget does not become dependent on a depleting source of fiscal revenue.

Clearly, few countries are in the position of Norway in terms of the level of wealth and the quality of its institutions. The Norwegian model is thus applicable in the context of high levels of economic development, strong institutions, and the ability to draw on other sources of fiscal revenue outside of commodities. The state of Wyoming pursues a similar model to that of Norway—albeit on a more limited scale given that it consumes the majority of its resource revenues through the budget, and transfers only a percentage of resource revenues to its permanent fund. In Alaska, the same limited degree of savings applies, but to date the state has not used the earnings of the permanent fund to fund the budget (instead just earmarking half of it for a unique citizens' dividend scheme). Both Alaska and Wyoming would be well served by the addition of some stabilization mechanisms: either directing a greater share of volatile and depleting revenue through their permanent funds in exchange for a stable stream of investment income, or more directly through the establishment of larger and more rule-based budget stabilization funds.

The overarching message and purpose of this chapter is to underline the fact that without an at least marginally constraining fiscal rule to govern the flow of money into and from it, a sovereign wealth fund risks becoming little more than a repository of occasional discretionary exercises in fiscal prudence, prone to raids and unruly depletions when resource revenues collapse, as they inevitably do at some point. The chapter emphasized the importance of the institutional arrangements that govern the fiscal rule (as a distinct issue from the design of the rule itself). Three models of fiscal governance were discussed: the constitutional model (as practiced, incompletely, by most American permanent funds), the rule-by-experts model (as practiced in Chile), and the customary and consensual model (exemplified by Norway).

Once a credible medium- to long-term fiscal framework, governed by rules, has been established—with a sovereign wealth as an integral part of that framework—attention may turn to the key issues in the institutional arrangements around the management of the sovereign wealth fund's investments, such as how to achieve a degree of operational independence for the management authority, how to clarify the roles and responsibilities of the various principals and agents involved in the delegated-authority model of investment, and how the governance and performance of the investment authority may be strengthened by transparency, accountability, and an embrace of rule-based investment policies.

PART THREE

The Governance of Operationally Independent Sovereign Investment Institutions

CHAPTER EIGHT

Public Footprints in Private Markets

Institutional Arrangements in Delegated Sovereign Investment Management

ON NEW YEAR'S DAY in 2008, *Foreign Affairs* journal published an article on sovereign wealth funds authored by Robert Kimmitt, then serving as deputy secretary of the United States Treasury. Writing against a backdrop of increasing regulatory and political concerns in the West about the growing clout of sovereign investors from the Middle East, Russia, and Asia (notably, China), Kimmitt (2008) gave a balanced account of the benefits and concerns regarding sovereign investment from a recipient country perspective. "If these investments are economically, rather than politically, driven," Kimmitt noted, "recipient countries have a strong interest in providing an open, transparent, and predictable framework for sovereign wealth fund investment."

The article also contained a number of thinly veiled threats, suggesting that evidence of overt political intervention in the investment practices of sovereign wealth funds by their host governments would be met with strong regulatory retaliation. "Foreign governments could conceivably employ large pools of capital in non-commercially driven ways that are politically sensitive," Kimmitt argued, citing the concern that a government "could use its intelligence or security services to gather information that is not available to a commercial investor . . . [and that] a sovereign wealth fund could also obtain or extend financing at interest rates that a commercial investor could not." In addition to some of the specific concerns outlined by Kimmitt (and others), it is clear that the rise of sovereign wealth funds as a class of state-owned investors had potentially jarred with the foundational philosophy of free-market capitalism: "The US economy is built on the belief that private firms allocate capital more efficiently than governments," Kimmitt noted. The article ran under the evocative title, "Public Footprints in Private Markets."

While Kimmitt was articulating the recipient governments' apprehensions about the growth in state-owned investors, specifically sovereign wealth funds, a number of issues raised in the article are also of concern to the societies of host governments. In particular, the suggestion—and well-documented empirical evidence—that political intervention lowers the returns of long-term institutional investors is a concern, particularly in the context of long-term sovereign wealth funds with the explicit functions of saving, wealth transformation, and income generation. Operational independence and rule-based investing are of particular importance for savings and investment-income type sovereign wealth funds, and potentially less so for stabilization funds (given their short investment horizons and simple investment models) and sovereign development funds (where there is a case for alignment with political and strategic considerations).

This chapter considers institutional arrangements for the investment function of operationally independent sovereign investment authorities, while the last two chapters will focus on the analysis of asset allocation and rule- and contract-based investment policies. As noted in chapter 4, the operational independence of sovereign investment authorities establishes a principal–agent problem, and in the context of public institutions, a potential democratic deficit (much as it does in the case of operationally independent monetary, judicial, or regulatory authorities). Rule-based investment policies, along with more general governance principles of accountability and transparency, help reduce this deficit. This chapter starts by elaborating on the theoretical case and empirical evidence in support of operational independence for sovereign investment authorities, already briefly touched on in chapter 4. The second part of this chapter assumes a more positive approach, identifying how the institutional arrangements for delegated authority, which in the case of most sovereign wealth funds involves not just a simple principal–agent relationship but rather a chain of principals and agents, compares to established arrangements in other areas of institutional investment management.

THE CASE FOR OPERATIONALLY INDEPENDENT INVESTMENT AUTHORITIES

The most important reason for granting sovereign wealth funds a degree of operational independence from government owners is performance. As discussed in chapter 4, much as in the area of monetary policy, the independence of the investment authority in the case of sovereign wealth funds rests primarily on a belief that governments do not make good long-term portfolio investors—or, as Kimmitt (2008) noted, "Private firms allocate capital more efficiently than governments." The reasons for this view include misaligned incentives and horizons of politicians relative to the mandate of the sovereign wealth fund, and the need for technocratic expertise in long-term investment management. Again, these two arguments—political bias and the need for technocratic subject expertise—mirror the case of independent, technocratic policy boards or committees in the area of monetary policy.

As noted in chapter 4, there is a significant body of empirical evidence to suggest that political pressure and intervention reduces investor returns. The field of public-sector pension fund management, in which the investment policies, operations, and institutional functions are closely aligned with those of long-term sovereign wealth funds, provides a rich body of evidence. One of the leading areas of focus in the literature on public pension funds is on board composition and incentives. In the public pension fund world, boards are typically composed through a combination of elections (typically by plan members and beneficiaries), appointment, or ex officio status (Useem and Hess, 2001; Hess and Impavido, 2004). The general concern in relation to the public pension fund board pertains to ex officio board members, who are often political officeholders, and politically appointed members, with the assumption that beneficiaries have sufficient "skin in the game" to elect members who serve their best interests.

Political appointees, by contrast, are assumed (and observed) to face a conflict of interest, expressed in a tendency to favor investments with higher political, economic, and/or social returns, rather than pure return maximization. These investment activities run the gamut from favoring politically connected or local fund managers (if the board plays a role in manager selection), to prioritizing local or domestic investments with an inadequate or differentiated consideration of their expected risk–return dynamics, to subordinating the fund's investment performance in pursuit of other (politically rewarding) agendas, such as environmental and labor standards (Hess and Impavido, 2004). More generally, economists have modeled the negative impact on investment performance that arises due to misalignments of incentives (for example, the pursuit of politically beneficial outcomes rather than long-term returns), a mismatch in time horizons (with political horizons typically being shorter than that of an optimizing long-term investor), and the tendency toward "trend chasing" (De Long et al., 1990; Shleifer and Vishny, 1990; Lakonishok, Shleifer, and Vishny, 1994).

The empirical evidence on the links between board composition, the exercise of political pressure, and influence on public pension funds and investment performance provide strong support for the benefits of political independence. Useem and Mitchell (2000) find that an array of governance variables account for more than 20 percent of the variation in investment strategies pursued by 291 American state and local retirement plans (accounting for 80 percent of the country's pension fund assets), which in turn is a strong predictor of subsequent investment performance. More specifically, Mitchell and Hsin (1997) show that having a greater number of beneficiary representatives on the pension board reduces investment returns, which they argue is likely due to a lack of investment expertise.

A landmark study by Romano (1993) identified various conflicts faced by the board of trustees of public pension plans, with particular emphasis on what the literature refers to as "economically targeted investments," which according to a controversial United States Department of Labor definition are "investments selected for the economic benefits they create apart from their investment return to the employee benefit plan" (U.S. Department of Labor, 1994). The seductive argument in favor of economically targeted investments is that they offer rates of return comparable to those of other pension fund assets, while generating various positive externalities. Romano (1993) found that public pension funds are subject to political pressures to "tailor their investments to local needs, such as increasing state employment, and to engage in other socially desirable investing," and that the most wide-spread type of political pressure involved "demands to stimulate local economic activity directly by financing development projects that over-extended states cannot fund." The consequences of economically tar-geted investments on pension funds have been much debated, but largely found to be negative (Mitchell and Hsin, 1997; Nofsinger, 1998).

The public pension funds included in Romano's paper also demon-strated a tendency toward directing public assets toward companies with lobbying powers and significant campaign contributions. Romano found that the percentage of independent trustees directly improved investment performance measured by total return on plan assets, a finding that was robust even when controlling for asset allocation (which itself is widely found to be robustly correlated to board composition, as per Useem and Mitchell, 2000). Overall, "Public fund managers must navigate carefully around the shoals of considerable political pressure to temper investment policies with local considerations, such as foster-ing in-state employment, which are not aimed at maximizing the value of their portfolios assets" (Romano, 1993: 106).

Whereas the initial debate in the academic literature on public pen-sion fund governance focused on the distinction between (politically) appointed board members, who tended to advance the interests of plan sponsors (politicians), and elected members, who are either assumed or shown to better serve the interests of fund beneficiaries, the more recent literature has focused more on the respective merits of "repre-sentative" versus "professional" boards. The former typically includes nonsubject experts representing a range of stakeholders—the point is that, in the case of public pension funds, these may include elected board members (for example, union leaders and current beneficiaries) as well as appointed and ex officio members. Professional boards can also consist of a combination of appointed and elected members, but are by contrast selected on the basis of the specialist's subject knowledge and established professional criteria, qualifications, and experience. The for-mer has the alluring ring of democratic representation and inclusivity, while the latter promotes a closer alignment between the functions of a board and the skills required to perform them. The representative-versus-professional board literature suggests that the earlier distinction between elected and appointed boards (and board members) may be too simplistic. There is significant anecdotal and statistical evidence that a greater share of public pension fund board members drawn from and representing beneficiaries undermines performance, and that the skills and subject competence of the board are associated with improved investment performance (Mitchell and Hsin, 1997).

This development in the literature holds great significance for sovereign wealth funds, where a tendency toward "inclusive" boards may result from understandable democratic concerns. It is easy to see how the goals of inclusivity and representativeness trump board competence and skill—particularly in democratic political environments. Sovereign wealth funds and government-owned public pension reserve funds, such as the New Zealand Superannuation Fund and the Canadian Pension Plan Investment Board, do not have easily identifiable and organized members or beneficiaries. Consequently, there are no direct representatives of "beneficiaries" that, even theoretically, can promote their interests, and boards are almost always staffed or appointed by political officeholders. In some sense, then, these sovereign investors have an even higher hurdle to clear in ensuring that political pressures are not exerted on the investment authority through the board. The case for professional boards, with arm's length independence from government owners, thus becomes even more compelling.

Recent empirical investigations of sovereign wealth fund investment behavior have tended to mirror the findings from the public pension fund literature that politically motivated domestic investments and direct political representation in oversight and management structures lower returns. Concerns about the effects of political influence on sovereign wealth funds' investment decisions have been raised in a more theoretical sense by a number of scholars (Das et al., 2009; Ang, 2010), which statistical examinations generally (but not universally) support. Bernstein, Lerner, and Schoar's (2013) findings suggest a similar pattern among sovereign wealth funds as those observed by Romano (1993), Mitchell and Hsin (1997), and Useem and Mitchell (2000) in relation to public pension funds: exposure to political influences may introduce major distortions from long-run return maximization among sovereign wealth funds, such as "misguided policy attempts to prop up inefficient firms or industries" or investments in industries, sectors or geographies that are deemed to be "hot" (Bernstein, Lerner, and Schoar, 2013: 223). Their empirical evidence suggests that "politically influenced sovereign wealth funds also concentrate their funds in sectors that both have high price-to-earnings levels and then experience a drop in these levels, especially in their domestic investments. . . . Political pressures seem to force these sovereign wealth funds to use their funds to support underperforming local industries rather than build a savings buffer for the long run" (231–232).[1]

While the Bernstein, Lerner, and Schoar (2013) study is the most high-profile examination of sovereign wealth fund investment decisions and performance, a number of other studies raise similar concerns around political influence and biases in the investments of these institutions, as discussed in a survey of the literature by Megginson and Fotak (2015). Chhaochharia and Laeven (2008) construct a sample of 29,634 equity investments made by 27 sovereign wealth funds and a comparative sample of 38,880 equity investments by public pension funds in firms from 56 countries to examine whether the former demonstrate systemic biases compared with pension funds. They find that a bias toward investing in countries that share a common culture and religion is "particularly pronounced" among sovereign wealth funds compared with pension funds. Chhaochharia and Laeven's (2008) results also suggest that aspects of sovereign wealth fund investment strategies are at odds with portfolio theory and their long-term advantages, as they tend to chase past returns and hold portfolios that are poorly diversified both geographically and across industries (sovereign wealth fund portfolios are found to heavily overweight both oil companies and companies with large market capitalization). Similar results are reported by Dyck and Morse (2011), who also find evidence of portfolio concentration in financial services firms. Knill, Lee, and Mauck (2012) find a strong causal relationship between measured changes in the international political relationships of host and home countries and geographic investment patterns of sovereign wealth funds, to the extent that a deterioration in political relationships results in an increase in sovereign wealth fund investments, suggesting that sovereign wealth funds may be used as a political tool (or at least be influenced by changes in geopolitical relationships). A contrarian perspective is offered by Avendaño and Santiso (2011), who find that reported sovereign wealth fund investments do not differ greatly from those of privately held mutual funds, and conclude that fears regarding politically motivated investments by sovereign wealth funds are unfounded.

Regardless of whether political pressure or interventions do actually influence sovereign wealth funds, it is likely that concerns about such

perceptions by regulators in host countries have played a role in efforts
by home countries to proactively establish a degree of de jure independence. Consider, for example, the language around independence
adopted in the Santiago Principles: "A sound governance structure that
separates the functions of the owner, governing body(ies), and management facilitates *operational independence* in the management of the
sovereign wealth fund to pursue investment decisions and investment
operations *free of political influence* (International Working Group on
Sovereign Wealth Funds, 2008; emphasis added).

A more pragmatic reason for embracing a model of operational independence for the management of sovereign wealth funds includes a
need for "ring fencing" resource revenues, particularly in the context
of corruption and poor institutions, to protect against theft. Given their
size, complexity, and uncertain nature, resource revenues are often a
target of theft, while the tendency toward a "lack of transparency surrounding resource revenues . . . relaxes the disincentives to misappropriate funds" (Collier et al., 2010). While of course not offering any
guarantees that the sovereign wealth fund itself will not be raided—
or, even worse, become an instrument for kleptocrats to siphon off resource revenues into foreign bank accounts—the establishment of an
independently run sovereign wealth fund, subject to detailed disclosure requirements and formal oversight mechanisms, can at least increase transparency and introduce a number of logistical obstacles to
the plundering of assets. One concrete example of the latter may be to
have the assets of the fund administered or managed by the World
Bank's Treasury Department or the Bank for International Settlement
(BIS), with withdrawals requiring (for example), the signature of the
president, the finance minister, the minister for petroleum, the governor
of the central bank, and the chairman and executive of the sovereign
wealth fund, plus a statement of disclosure published by the World Bank
or the BIS (similar arrangements may be established in law and in contract with the fund's private-sector custodial bank).

Finally, another pragmatic reason for establishing an operationally
independent investment authority concerns the limitations and restrictions of public-sector pay scales. The need for hiring "in-house"
expertise—which can be prohibitively expensive for many sovereign
wealth funds—depends to a large degree on complexity, sophistication,
and degree of "active management" around the fund's investment strategy (as discussed in the following two chapters). The issue of compen-

sation for human capital in a public-sector investment context, particularly relative to the often very high earnings of people working in private-sector finance, has been analyzed in detail in the literature (Clark and Urwin, 2008; Bertram and Zvan, 2009; Ambachtsheer, 2011; Clark and Monk, 2013). For many sovereign wealth funds worldwide that face challenges around attracting and retaining talent—most notably due to the remoteness of their head offices and the limits of public-sector compensation relative to that of the private sector—the heavy use of external managers and investment consultants becomes a practical necessity, unless the fund invests exclusively in low-cost passive index type investments (Clark and Monk, 2013). One of the hallmarks of the much-lauded Canadian public pension fund model—which has been followed by a number of sovereign wealth funds—is the establishment of independent, professional investment institutions, which are not tied to implicit or explicit public-sector wage scales, but can establish their own compensation schemes to attract and incentivize internal managers.

ACHIEVING INSTITUTIONAL SEPARATION AND OPERATIONAL INDEPENDENCE

Having made the case for operational independence in theory, it is insightful to reflect on how an institutional separation between policymakers, legislators, and the management authority of sovereign wealth funds is achieved in a number of country cases. In reality, the independence advocated above is never absolute, but rather a question of degree. Moreover, the institutional arrangements between "principals" and "agents" in the case of sovereign wealth funds do not comprise a simple two-way relationship but are characterized by a chain of delegated authority. Most forms of institutional investing involve multiple layers of delegated authority and oversight—for example, between a board of directors/trustees and the executive, between the executive and internal/external fund managers, and so forth. In the context of sovereign wealth funds, additional layers are added: an independent appointed board of directors may report to a minister (or a higher "governing council" or "policy board"), which in turn reports to a parliament, a president, or a monarch (depending on the political context). Further down the chain of delegated authority, the often extensive use

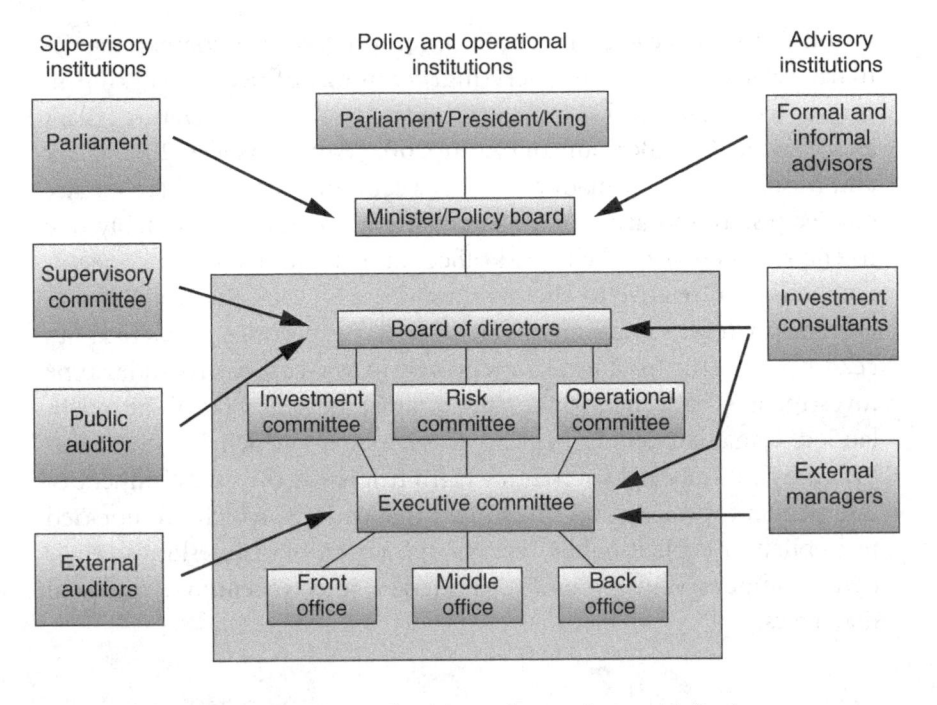

Figure 8.1 Institutional structure for delegated sovereign wealth fund management.

of investment consultants and external fund managers creates additional principal–agent relationships in the management of sovereign wealth funds, while expectations for public accountability add an often elaborate oversight infrastructure, involving a public auditor, a national regulator, external auditors, and sometimes a separate supervisory board (in addition to the board of directors).

The independence of the authority managing a sovereign wealth fund is therefore never absolute, but rather embedded in an institutional arrangement that enforces oversight and accountability. Naturally, in the context of a myriad of interlocking principal–agent relationships due to various levels of delegated authority, it is important that the institutional architecture provide clarity around the precise powers and responsibility of each principal and agent. Figure 8.1 provides an overview of a stylized institutional setup for delegated investment management of a sovereign wealth fund, while the discussion below outlines the most important tasks assigned to each element. Note that the figure shows the full scope of the most detailed institutional arrangement possible—in practice, as discussed below, it is possible to economize on this structure with some direct reporting lines and operational structures (as the case of Chile, in particular, illustrates).

The operational part of the structure, shown in the central box in figure 8.1, mirrors that of standard practices among institutional investors, such as public and private pension funds, endowments, and foundations, particularly the principal–agent relationship between the board and the executive, and their intersection through the various committees of the board (which typically includes executive board members). The executive management of the fund then manages internal teams, colloquially known as the front, middle, and back offices, responsible for portfolio management, risk management, and trade execution and processing, respectively.

The sovereign wealth fund simply adds additional layers of political ownership and accountability, as well as more detailed supervisory or oversight arrangements, than what is typically found in nongovernmental investment institutions, involving not only external auditors but also, for example, reports by the public auditor and parliamentary scrutiny by the minister or highest policy board (and sometimes more directly by the board of the sovereign wealth fund itself). In a small number of countries, parliamentary oversight is complemented by or delegated to a supervisory committee. Like most other institutional investors, sovereign wealth funds also make use of external advisors and managers, some providing assistance to the most senior policy institutions, others more directly on investment and operational matters to the board or executive of the sovereign wealth fund.

In practice, there is a significant degree of variation around this framework, as presented in figure 8.1. As noted earlier, it is possible to simplify and economize on this elaborate structure, particularly when the sovereign wealth fund is relatively small, and more important, if the investment strategy is very simple (for example, when investments are limited to passive, indexed strategies in liquid public markets) and highly transparent. Recall from the discussion in chapter 4 that the governance of sovereign wealth funds can be categorized according to external and internal dimensions: the former pertains to the institutional arrangements between the investment authority and its political owners (ministries, legislators, the president or kind, and the public at large), whereas the latter relates more narrowly to the structures operating within the investment authority, such as the distribution of authority and responsibility between the board and the executive, the adoption of rule-based investment policies, and so forth. Within a more elaborate institutional model in which delegated authority involves more than simple operational aspects, the two critical areas of differentiation in the overall governance structure are as follows:

"Supervisory Councils" versus "Policy Boards" in External Governance

The first major area of differentiation is the extent to which political officeholders exercise their authority over the management of the sovereign wealth fund in a manner that represents either a "supervisory council" or "policy board." In the supervisory council model, political representatives set the goals for the organization in comparatively broad terms, such as the articulation of the fund's purpose and legal standing, and then resolve to act mainly as an oversight body over the management authority, particularly its board (note that this may or may not be in addition to the supervisory committee, shown in figure 8.1 in the left-hand column). The management authority, through a combination of powers and responsibilities divided between the board and the executive, is then granted significant delegated authority to interpret this broad political mandate and articulate an appropriate investment policy (including, most critically, the fund's asset allocation).

In contrast, the more politically "hands-on" policy board model sees political officeholders, such as the minister of finance (often only this minister), other members of the cabinet, presidential appointees, and members of the legislature more directly involved with that articulation process, that is, more directly involved with the specification of the sovereign wealth fund's return targets, risk tolerance, and investment horizon (and, under most direct models, its asset allocation). Clearly, the supervisory council model assumes a higher degree of delegated authority and operational independence for the investment management authority of the sovereign wealth fund than the policy board model, although in practice the process may be more de facto consultative, involving the minister of finance (or broader policy board), the board, and the executive of the sovereign wealth fund.

Board- versus Executive-Centric Models
of Internal Governance

The second major distinction in the governance models of sovereign wealth funds pertains to the internal dimension—specifically, the distribution of authority and responsibility between the board and the executive. Management structures can be categorized as broadly board- or executive-centric, with the latter again implying a higher degree of delegated authority. The most common model sees the board responsible for the articulation of the fund's investment policy most critically, the fund's asset allocation. If the political body assumes a more supervisory role in external governance, as described above, the board will typically also have the authority to specify the fund's target return, risk tolerance, and investment horizon—as discussed in chapter 9, ideally through a publicly disclosed investment policy statement—which the executive is then tasked with implementing. Most typically, the board is also responsible for nominating or appointing the senior executive (sometimes subject to ministerial or parliamentary approval, or both).

In practice, however, the executive does have a role to play in the articulation of these critical aspects of the investment strategy—either through consultation to the board or, as is more common, by assuming any number of seats on the board. Typically, the chief executive officer will have a permanent seat on the board, but in the case of larger boards with greater executive representation, the chief investment officer and possibly the chief risk officer, chief financial officer, and the chief operating officer also serve on the board. The size of the board often becomes a practical issue in the management of the sovereign wealth fund (and other public investment institutions), given that the executive board members are typically joined by both appointed and ex officio board members. In such cases, common practice is to establish separate board-level committees, such as an investment committee (chaired by the chairman of the board and including the chief executive officer and chief investment officer of the fund), a risk or risk management committee, an audit committee, and an operational committee.

One of the most important factors in the relationship between the board and the executive is the degree of active management the board wishes to tolerate or encourage. Under more passive investment models, the executive's main responsibilities become administrative and operational in the sense that they implement a series of benchmark portfolios. More active investment models assume that the executive management can add value by outperforming a combination of benchmarks or by a low-cost reference portfolio, either through the executive's management of an internal investment team or its selection of above-average external investment managers. Benchmark- or reference-portfolio specification is the task of the board (or occasionally of a higher authority, such as a policy board, governing council, or minister), while active management and manager selection is that of the executive.

Governance Models and the Public Footprint

Decisions regarding the balance between supervisory versus governing models of political control for external governance, and between board- versus executive-centric models for internal governance, are made in part based on practical considerations around the cost efficiency of institutions. However, the outcome of these decisions also has a major bearing on the degree or perception of political influence on a sovereign wealth fund.

Naturally, if efforts are made to greatly reduce the "public footprints in private markets" left by sovereign wealth funds, the overall governance framework might be expected to gravitate toward a more supervisory council model for external governance (and possibly a more executive-centric internal governance model—or least one in which political representation or appointments, or both, to the board is limited). Alternatively, if political officeholders, such as the minister of finance, retain comparatively high levels of de jure authority over the sovereign wealth fund—as, in fact, they do in the case of both Norway and Chile, two widely lauded examples of sovereign wealth fund governance—concerns over the public footprint and political motivations behind the fund can be reduced by a combination of exceptional levels of transparency and disclosure, and simple, largely passive investment models.

The degree of political influence on a sovereign wealth fund can also be depicted as per figure 8.2, which is taken from an IMF paper on the governance of sovereign wealth funds (Al-Hassan et al., 2013). The fund's diagram depicts a stylized relationship between the "owner" of a sovereign wealth fund (that is, generally, the government and politi-

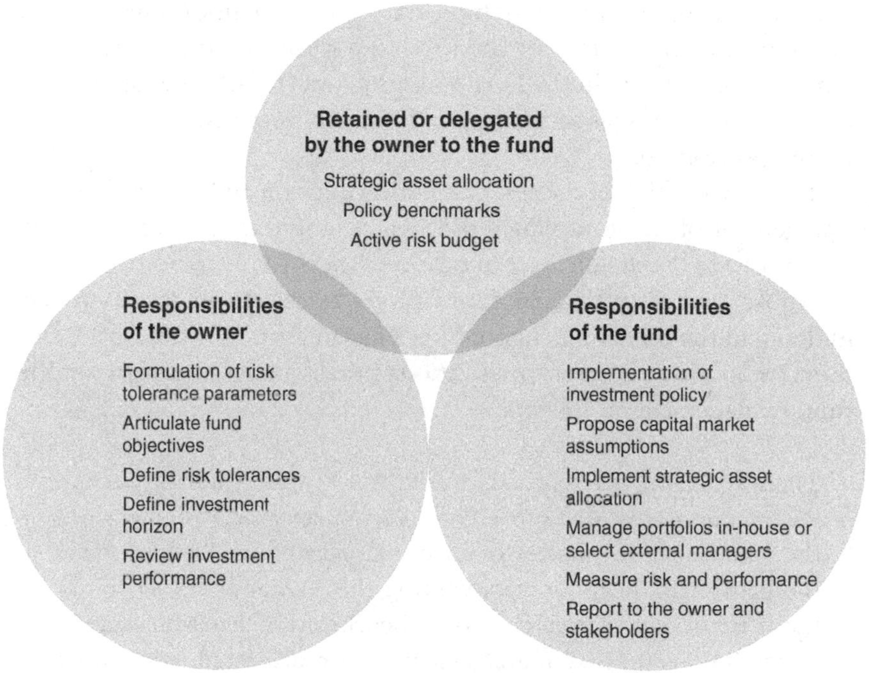

**Retained or delegated
by the owner to the fund**

Strategic asset allocation

Policy benchmarks

Active risk budget

**Responsibilities
of the owner**

Formulation of risk
tolerance parameters

Articulate fund
objectives

Define risk tolerances

Define investment
horizon

Review investment
performance

**Responsibilities
of the fund**

Implementation of
investment policy

Propose capital market
assumptions

Implement strategic asset
allocation

Manage portfolios in-house or
select external managers

Measure risk and performance

Report to the owner and
stakeholders

Figure 8.2 Roles and responsibilities in determining SWF (sovereign wealth fund) investment policy. Source: Al-Hassan et al. (2013).

cal officeholders) and the "fund" (that is, the delegated authority managing the fund). Without controversy, the responsibilities of the owner are depicted in broad terms: articulate the fund's objectives, define risk tolerances and the investment horizon, and review investment performance. Similarly, the articulation of the fund management entity's responsibilities includes a standard list of technical tasks: propose capital market assumptions, implement strategic asset allocation, manage portfolios in-house or select external managers, measure risk and performance, and report to the owner and stakeholder.

However, the key point is that figure 8.2 depicts the most critical long-term determinants of investment performance as open to being either "retained or delegated by the Owner to the Fund," with powers and responsibilities for fundamental decisions—strategic asset allocation, the specification of policy benchmarks, and the quantification of the risk tolerance (which Al-Hassan et al., 2013, refer to as an "active risk budget"). In the governance model depicted in figure 8.1, the most effective way to ensure and demonstrate limited political involvement in the investment policies of the sovereign wealth fund is for the government (or "owner" in the IMF's terminology) to delegate rather than retain these powers (as according to the supervisory council model discussed previously).

The "ownership" of the asset allocation decision and process is a critical element of the governance process, as long-term allocation (often referred to as "strategic asset allocation," or SAA) is by some margin the most important determinant of long-term returns (as discussed in detail in the following chapter). Al-Hassan et al. (2013) describe the different models and their implications in relation to sovereign wealth fund management, as follows:

> There are alternative approaches as to who "owns" strategic asset allocation decisions. In a more typical set-up approach, the owner of the fund, usually a ministry of finance, decides on the SAA, approves the benchmark portfolio representing the SAA and sets active risk limits for deviating from the policy benchmark. Operationalization of the SAA and active management is then delegated to the fund manager (this approach is adopted by Norway and Russia). In a less typical approach, the SAA decision is fully delegated to and owned by the fund manager (this approach is adopted by Singapore). In the former approach, the sovereign wealth fund's owner internalized the total risk of the policy benchmark, which represents on average about 80–95% of the overall risk, while the fund manager is responsible for the residual risk arising due to active management, and is held responsible for excess returns relative to the benchmark. In the latter approach, the fund manager is ultimately responsible for the total return of the fund, as well as for potentially substantial deviations from the stated return targets for long periods of time, with the fund owner not having direct control over investment outcomes. (18–19)

As noted earlier, some of the most celebrated governance models, such as those of Norway and Chile, follow what Al-Hassan et al. (2013) call the "typical model," in which the minister of finance retains de jure authority for long-term asset allocation decisions. The advantage of this approach is that it makes the ministry highly accountable for the long-term investment performance, risk, and return of the sovereign wealth fund—frankly, the minister has nowhere to hide if the fund underperforms and cannot blame the board or the executive of the fund for poor asset allocation decisions (unless the latter significantly deviates from the policy choices reflected in the minister's asset allocation). The potential downside to this approach is that it suggests an undue degree of political interference. In practice, however, the passive, uncontroversial, and consultative nature of the investment process (coupled with exceptional transparency) in cases such as Norway and Chile reduces concerns about the public footprint.

EXISTING SOVEREIGN WEALTH FUND GOVERNANCE MODELS

The governance arrangements for the management of a sovereign wealth fund described in the previous section is a stylized model. It is more elaborate than many of the existing models, which in practice economize on this infrastructure. As discussed earlier, within the most elaborate governance model, there is significant scope for both de facto and de jure variations in the allocation of authority and responsibilities. In particular, the degree of political influence of the fund may be expressed through the choice of whether political officeholders assume a more supervisory versus policy role (discussed previously in relation to the distinction between supervisory councils and policy boards), although the de jure powers of political officeholders under the latter can effectively be watered down or constrained by exceptional levels of transparency and disclosure, and the adoption of simple, largely passive investment models.

The Norwegian Governance Model

The Norwegian governance model most closely resembles the arrangement depicted in figure 8.1. The model is noteworthy for its involvement of a wide range of public institutions, each with clearly defined roles and responsibilities, as well as its exceptionally high reporting and disclosure requirements and practices. The most important institutions in the model are the Norwegian Parliament and the Supervisory Council as oversight institutions, and the Ministry of Finance, the Executive Board of the central bank (Norges Bank), and the senior management of a dedicated operational investment manager (under the auspices of the central bank), as the primary policy institutions. The distribution of core responsibilities and reporting lines around the Norwegian Pension Fund Global are as follows:

- The *minister of finance* determines the sovereign wealth fund's broadest strategic orientation, as reflected in its Strategic Asset Allocation. The ministry delegates all operational management and a degree of discretionary authority around the strategy and the selection of external managers to a dedicated investment authority within the central bank.
- The *central bank Executive Board* is the highest authority within the fund's operational management. It establishes the guidelines and strategic plans for the management activities of Norges Bank Investment Management (NBIM), a dedicated investment management unit within the central bank. The Executive Board is subject to an internal audit and is part of a governing structure for the management of the sovereign wealth fund that is separate from other aspects of the central bank (such as monetary policy and financial supervision). The board consists of eight members, with the governor of the central bank serving as chairman, and the two deputy governors as first- and second vice-chairman. The latter has a special responsibility for the sovereign wealth fund.
- *Norges Bank Investment Management (NBIM)* is a dedicated asset management department within the central bank and is the operational fund manager of the sovereign wealth fund (in addition to other public funds, including the central bank's foreign-exchange reserves). It implements investment strategy and exercises the small degree of active management that is permitted by the fund's owner. The team also performs significant research and analytical functions around the fund's asset allocation, external managers, and operational efficiency.

The above-mentioned three institutions form the core of the policy infrastructure in the Norwegian model. Clearly, the deep policy choices around the Norwegian sovereign wealth fund—notably its strategic asset allocation, but also the decision to pursue an "ethical investment" mandate, which results in the fund excluding investments in, for example, companies involved in the tobacco and arms industries, or deemed guilty of human rights violations and severe environmental damages—are the domain of the Ministry of Finance. The central bank's executive board is less of a policy board and more of an operational oversight body. Finally, the operational manager is also a largely operational authority, although it does exercise some limited and constrained discretion in attempts to outperform the benchmarks of the Ministry of Finance. Its discretionary powers and responsibilities have risen with the introduction of a difficult-to-benchmark real-estate investment mandate in 2011. In addition to the policy infrastructure, the Norwegian model makes provision for significant oversight and supervisory institutions, as follows:

- The *Norwegian Parliament* passes legislation governing the fund, approves the operational manager's annual budget, appoints a supervisory council, and reviews reports on the fund's guidelines, strategies, and performance prepared by the Ministry of Finance, NBIM, and auditors.
- The *Supervisory Council* supervises the central bank's activities (in general, not only those of NBIM). It has the right of access to information and investigative powers. The Supervisory Council reports to the Parliament, which also appoints its fifteen members. Appointments are for four-year terms with the possibility of reappointment twice. Every other year, up to half of the membership is reappointed or replaced. The chairman and deputy chairman are appointed for two-year terms.
- The *auditor general* performs an audit of the fund and the operations of Norges Bank Investment Management, and reports to the Parliament and the government. In addition, an external auditor is appointed and reports to the Supervisory Council.

As has been widely noted in the literature on sovereign wealth funds, Norway has exemplary governance structures (Das et al., 2009; Monk, 2009; Ang, 2010; Frankel, 2012). While other funds may find it difficult to implement similar structures given political constraints and local public-sector practices, the Norwegian governance structure rests on three characteristic features that are worthy of emulation: (1) a profound commitment to transparency and public disclosure that incorporates strategy, operations, and intragovernmental oversight; (2) the separation of powers and responsibilities across various stakeholders and public institutions; and (3) generating a stable consensus between these institutions through a highly consultative and representative process. Certainly, it cannot be argued that political officeholders are far removed from the investments of the Norwegian sovereign wealth fund—the minister of finance sets the strategic asset allocation—but, as discussed above, the transparency and simplicity of the fund's investment strategy and governance model allays concerns about undue political intervention.

The Kazakh Governance Model

The governance model of the National Fund of Kazakhstan is characterized by a high degree of centralized political authority, with the president serving as the highest reporting authority of the fund and as a member of its powerful Management Committee. The lack of independence of the Management Committee means that the political leadership, particularly the president and senior ministers, enjoy a high degree of control and discretionary power over the fund. The National Fund is also relatively nontransparent around key aspects (such as its detailed asset allocation and external audits) of its operations and performance (although less so than a number of sovereign wealth funds, particularly in the Middle East). The de jure governance structure for the National Fund of Kazakhstan is as follows:

- *The president:* Officially recognized as the highest reporting authority of the National Fund. The president created the National Fund and the Management Council, on which he sits, through presidential decrees.
- *The Management Council:* Consists of the president, the prime minister, key economic policy ministers, and other high-ranking officials (including representatives of the legislature). The Management Council sets all key governance, operational, and investment policies for the National Fund.
- *The minister of finance and the minister of oil and gas:* Jointly approve the list of petroleum sector companies whose taxes are deposited into the National Fund, while Parliament passes laws determining small variations in the amounts transferred from the fund annually.
- *National Bank of Kazakhstan:* Responsible for the day-to-day investment management of the National Fund. The central bank

selects and oversees the external managers of the fund's equity portfolios. In 2012, an independent unit was established within the central bank, called the National Investment Corporation, to manage part of the sovereign wealth funds' money (alongside other public funds).

- *External audits:* Applied to the central bank and include its activities in relation to investment of the National Fund's assets. The audits are not made public.

A particular feature of the institutional structure of the Kazakhstan fund is the formal recognition of the president as the highest reporting authority for the fund—something that is typically either strictly avoided, or only implicit, with other sovereign wealth funds. Much of the authority for establishing the National Fund's policies and investment strategy rests with the Management Council, which is headed by the president. Therefore, while the delegation of operational management to the central bank establishes some autonomy, the power vested in the Management Council—and, moreover, the president's prominent position on the council—does little to conceal the extent of political influence over the fund. Given the nature of Kazakhstan's institutions more generally, this structure is not surprising; it is also unlikely that a de jure independent or delegated-authority model would make much difference de facto (given the degree of centralized political control over various arms of government and state institutions). What is noteworthy is the fact that despite the formal authority of the president and other senior political officeholders over the National Fund, it appears that little actual intervention in the investment process has occurred (the strength of this observation is, however, weakened by the lack of transparency and independence around the fund—it is possible that the fund has made a number of politically inspired investments that are not disclosed externally).

The Chilean Governance Model

The Chilean governance model is noteworthy for three reasons: first, it is very simple; second, it is extremely transparent; and third, while the minister retains essentially all the de jure policy authority, there is a high degree of de facto reliance on the insights and expertise of an expert advisory committee. Both of Chile's sovereign wealth funds—its stabilization and savings funds—are under the jurisdiction of the Ministry of Finance, which develops investment policies and publishes monthly, quarterly, and annual reports on the funds' activities and performance. The Central Bank of Chile acts as the operational investment manager of the funds, but its role is relegated to an essentially operational one, given the decision of the Ministry of Finance to pursue a low-cost, passive investment strategy focused exclusively on tracking leading global stock and bond indexes. There are a number of other public institutions involved with the funds, particularly in advisory and oversight capacities. The roles, responsibilities, and reporting lines of these institutions are established by law for the Ministry of Finance, and by ministerial decree for the Central Bank (issued in 2006) and the Financial Committee (issued in 2007). The key institutions in the Chilean model are as follows:

- *The Ministry of Finance:* Determines investment and internal management policies for the sovereign funds, including their respective asset allocations, benchmark indexes, investment horizons, and risk budgets, while the General Treasury, Chile's revenue service, is responsible for accounting and preparing audited reports on the funds.
- *The Financial Advisory Committee for Fiscal Responsibility Funds:* A panel of experts, appointed by the Ministry of Finance, which provides advice on the funds' management and investment policies. The six members of the committee are selected by the ministry, and consist of local macroeconomists and financial experts, with overlapping tenures of two years. The committee meets on average every six weeks and its members are remunerated for attending these meetings. A secretariat for the committee is provided by the ministry, which also prepares technical reports on international financial conditions and financial performance of sovereign wealth fund investments. The Advisory Financial Committee releases its own annual reports and minutes from meetings, separate from those of the ministry. The transparent use of a technocratic advisory structure for the investments of the Chilean sovereign wealth funds mirrors that of the fiscal rule (as discussed in chapter 7, the fiscal rule draws on inputs from expert panels on trend GDP growth and future copper prices). Unlike the inputs (projections) from those two fiscal committees, the recommendations of the Advisory Financial Committee are not binding for the

minister of finance (Schmidt-Hebbel, 2012). However, the public release of the committee meetings' minutes, their annual report, and the frequency of their meeting schedule creates a high degree of public and political accountability, against which the policies and actions of the Ministry of Finance can be assessed.

- *The Central Bank of Chile:* Manages the funds' investment portfolios, with a portion delegated to external fund managers (around 35 percent of all assets of the Pension Reserve Fund, the country's savings fund). The central bank appoints and monitors the performance of external fund managers, who have few discretionary powers in deviating from the established index benchmarks. The central bank manages fixed income assets internally, while outsourcing some index-benchmarked investment mandates to external managers.

The simplicity and economy of the policy and operational dimension of the Chilean governance model is mirrored by a basic supervisory infrastructure. Given the passive, indexed investment strategy for both sovereign wealth funds, their operational management by the credible central bank, and transparency and accountability around policy and strategic decisions on the part of the Ministry of Finance and the Financial Advisory Committee, there is little need for an extensive arrangement of supervisory and oversight institutions, outside of the following:

- The *Chilean Congress* passed the legislation authorizing the funds and receives monthly, quarterly, and annual reports from the Ministry of Finance.
- The *comptroller general* performs an audit of the activities of the Ministry of Finance (including the fiscal rule and sovereign funds), and reports to the Congress. Independent *external auditors'* reports are included in the report of the General Treasury.

In some respects, the prominence of the Ministry of Finance in the institutional arrangements for the Chilean funds is an exception to the general tendency toward and desirability of autonomy for sovereign wealth funds, particularly long-term savings funds (in the Chilean case, the Pension Reserve Fund). However, this high degree of ministerial control is counterbalanced by exceptional transparency and disclosure, a very simple and nondiscretionary investment strategy, and a sovereign wealth fund strategy that is embedded in a rule-based fiscal framework. In the Chilean case, it could be argued that discretionary powers are not delegated to an independent authority, precisely because the rule-based framework and investment strategy does not permit much discretion in the first place—effectively, there is no power to be delegated, and no discretion to the constrained.

The Chilean example is the prime example of the keep-it-simple approach to sovereign wealth fund management and governance. It greatly economizes on the cost of operating and governing the country's sovereign wealth funds. The simplicity, built-in transparency, and accountability, and integration of the sovereign wealth funds with a broader rule-based fiscal framework are all highly attractive institutional features—indeed, it is a model with great relevance to other resource-rich developing countries, looking to establish policy, governance, and operational frameworks for their sovereign wealth funds.

American Permanent-Fund Governance Models

While there is a great deal of commonality in the funding rules and institutional objectives of American resource-based permanent funds, there is greater divergence with respect to the operational models and governance structures around their investment management function. There are essentially two models for managing American permanent funds: in most cases, the funds are managed (alongside other public funds) by an investment board within the state treasurer's office, while there is also limited use of dedicated independent investment authorities. The two most established and successful examples are the Alaska Permanent Fund Corporation and the University of Texas Investment Management Company. Both entities have well-developed governance structures, with a clear delineation between the board and the executive of the organizations, and their respective areas of authority and responsibility. In both cases, the comparatively large size of assets under management is a motivating factor behind the decision to incur the costs of a dedicated, independent management authority: the Alaska Permanent Fund, at roughly $52bn in assets under management (as of December 2015), is the largest sovereign wealth fund in the United States, while the University of Texas Investment Management Company manages $35 billion in assets (as of November 2015).

The more prevalent model for smaller American permanent funds is to retain investment management authority within a branch of the state treasury, typically through structures such as a state investment board or a state investment council. The model has the advantages of simplicity and cost: the state treasurer typically has an existing investment infrastructure in place to manage the state's cash flows, alongside existing debt and surplus asset structures (often including public-sector pension and benefit schemes). Adding the management administration and investment oversight of a new permanent fund to these entities' list of responsibilities may therefore be a logical step, albeit a potentially temporary one (until the assets under management are large enough to justify a dedicated investment authority).

State investment boards or councils are typically staffed by a small team of financial experts with a track record of prudent management of state assets. Given the complex asset allocation of most permanent funds (see below), state treasuries typically do not manage investments themselves, outside of passive cash and fixed income portfolios, but rather make extensive use of external managers and investment consultants. At first glance, this arrangement is at odds with the standard—and otherwise sensible—mantra on the governance of sovereign wealth funds, namely, that their investment operations should be removed, as far as possible, from executive officeholders (in this case, state treasurers). As in Norway and Chile, however, there are a number of mitigating factors that justify the choice of retaining the management oversight of permanent funds within the state treasury:

- First, the placement of these funds with the state treasuries has not come at the expense of transparency: rather, given American standards and expectations regarding accountable government, state investment boards and councils report frequently and extensively on their activities, investment performance, and internal decision making. Transparency helps offset potential concerns about undue political interference.
- Second, state investment boards and councils are staffed with officials that enjoy a high degree of public credibility, investment expertise, and specialist skills, and their appointment generally requires broad-based legislative approval (although of course there are no guarantees that this tradition will be adhered to at all times).
- Third, while the extensive use of external assets managers and professional investment consultants have the downside of costs (paid to in fees to fund managers) and governance (undermining true ownership of asset allocation decisions), it does protect against bad

decisions and abuse, as these private companies are very reputation-sensitive and bound by federal regulatory requirements to act in the best interest of their clients.

The placement of investment responsibility of permanent funds within the state treasury can be viewed as a pragmatic, second-best solution, which has certain governance (and cost) drawbacks, but at the same time brings the benefit of simplicity and insurance against really bad outcomes. In the coming years, some of the larger and more established American permanent funds may approach a size and level of maturity where consideration should be given to the establishment of dedicated investment authorities.

Irrespective of whether the funds are managed by the state treasury or dedicated independent authorities, a number of observations can be made about the common features of American permanent funds' investment models and governance processes. With the exception of the North Dakota Heritage Fund, which is still in its inception, American permanent funds have highly diversified portfolios (compared with, for example, the Norwegian and Chilean sovereign wealth funds). American permanent funds have significant allocations to illiquid alternative asset classes, such as infrastructure, private equity, real estate, high-yield credit, and hedge funds. While these asset classes can generate high returns and add the benefit of portfolio diversification, they are complex to manage, involve considerable risks, and incur high management fees when accessed through external managers.

Indeed, a defining characteristic of the American permanent-fund landscape is the extensive use of external asset managers and investment consultants. In part, the explanation for this is the observation that most American permanent funds face significant challenges around attracting and retaining talent, most notably due to the remoteness of their head offices in small state capitals, such as Juneau (Alaska), Cheyenne (Wyoming), and Bismarck (North Dakota).[2] Other challenges include the aforementioned limits of public-sector compensation relative to that of the private sector (Clark and Monk, 2013). As with their actual investment operations, American permanent funds tend to transfer a considerable amount of power and authority over asset allocation to external entities in the form of professional investment consultants.

As discussed in detail in the following chapter, academic research and past experience incontrovertibly demonstrate that strategic asset allocation, rather than short-term, "tactical" decisions, market "timing," security, and manager selection drive long-term portfolio returns. Asset allocation decisions are therefore at the heart of the policy choices around sovereign wealth fund investments, and the allocation of powers to determine asset allocation is at the heart of the governance structure. A potential downside to American state permanent funds' heavy use of investment consultants in asset allocation decisions is that it potentially dilutes the degree of ownership of these critical decisions by the entities ultimately charged with managing these funds—whether it be the boards of independent management authorities or investment councils housed within state treasuries.

The New Zealand Governance Model

New Zealand's sovereign wealth fund, the New Zealand Superannuation Fund, is a pension reserve savings fund. It invests funds specifically earmarked from current fiscal surpluses in anticipation of growing future pension system liabilities. In recent years, the fund has assumed an increasingly prominent leadership position within the global community of sovereign wealth funds, with an exemplary governance structure, exceptional levels of transparency and public disclosure (exceeding that of the much-lauded Norwegian sovereign wealth fund), and stellar investment returns—in October 2015, the chief executive officer of the fund was named the chairman of the International Forum of Sovereign Wealth Funds.

There are many lessons to be learned from the New Zealand sovereign wealth fund, notably from the comparison with the other sovereign wealth funds studied in this chapter, it is managed by the most independent investment authority (its use of a reference portfolio and risk-factor premiums to assess the fund's underlying risk-return exposure and the value added by active management is discussed in the following two chapters). The primary means through which this separation is achieved is the establishment of a powerful board, which itself delegates significant powers to the executive, and the depoliticized process for the appointment of the board, which established what the fund calls double arms-length independence.

The fund is managed by an independent investment authority, the Guardians of the New Zealand Superannuation Fund, which is established by law as an "independent Crown entity," which means that while the government has a controlling interest—for example, by owning a majority of the voting shares or through having the power to appoint and replace a majority of the governing members—the management authority is "legally separate from the Crown." The assets managed by the Guardians, however, belong to the Crown, that is, the government (New Zealand Superannuation Fund, 2015).

As the operational manager, the Guardians is overseen by a Board of Governors, which, according to the New Zealand Superannuation and Retirement Income Act of 2001, is appointed by the governor general on the recommendation of the minister of finance. Critically, the minister's recommendation follows nominations from an independent nominating committee (which the minister appoints) and consultation with representatives of other political parties in Parliament. The role of the independent nomination committee for board appointments is significant here, as it establishes the "first arm" of the double arms–length independence of the Guardians of the New Zealand Superannuation Fund. Board members are selected based on a detailed set of professional criteria—such as experience in corporate governance, senior management, risk management, global investments, and academic qualifications. Each board member is appointed for a term of up to five years and is eligible to be reappointed. There are no direct political appointees and no ex officio political officeholders on the board, which is designed by law to be small—consisting of five to seven members (New Zealand Superannuation Fund, 2015:31). In short, the board of the Guardians of the New Zealand Superannuation Fund is the embodiment of the "professional board," as opposed to the representative board model referred to earlier in the chapter.

The Guardians' governing legislation and the board charter define board responsibilities and matters delegated to management. Formally, the board is responsible for (1) supervising the management of the Guardians and the investment of the fund; (2) establishing the Guardians' objectives, corporate strategy for achieving those objectives, the overall policy framework, and monitoring management's performance; (3) ensuring that the fund's assets and the Guardians' assets are maintained under effective stewardship; and (4) ensuring that decision-making authorities within the Guardians are clearly defined and that all applicable laws are complied with (New Zealand Superannuation Fund, 2015:31). In the model of delegated authority, the most critical task of the board (outside of a generic role in supervising management and acting as an institutional buffer between management, the Ministry of Finance, and legislators) is that it specifies the fund's reference portfolio, which, as discussed in chapter 9, is simultaneously the articulation of the board's view on the appropriate balance between risks and excepted returns and the benchmark against which the added value of the Guardians is measured and assessed (the reference portfolio is a low-cost alternative to active management by the Guardians). This delegation of power from the government to the board for determining the reference portfolio is the second arm of New Zealand's double arms–length independence governance structure.

The final aspect of the New Zealand governance model is an extraordinary commitment to transparency, disclosure, and accountability. The list of policy and operational disclosures made by the fund is truly astonishing, including (but not limited to) quarterly, annual, and long-term benchmarking of active management performance by the Guardians against its reference portfolio (broken down in terms of risk factors and asset classes); a full list of the names and mandates of external managers; external consultant reviews (and the Guardians' response to these reviews); regular testimony before the legislature and frequent public presentations; a detailed breakdown of the fund's actual portfolio holdings; granular information on operational expenses, remuneration packages (including, for example, the chief executive's officer base salary and the calculation of his or her bonus), and travel expenses of the board members and the executive; and audits and financial statements. As mentioned earlier, the detail, quality, and frequency of disclosure and accountability by the New Zealand Superannuation Fund, its board, and its management authority establish a benchmark that not even the Norwegian sovereign wealth fund can match.

CONCLUSION

The chapter considered the ways in which countries have resolved a familiar tension in public policy: balancing the need or desire for operational independence for the manager or investor of sovereign wealth funds, while at the same time preserving a degree of government control and oversight of such delegated authority. While the case for operational independence is based on a number of compelling reasons—performance, fears of a regulatory backlash, a desire to escape public-sector pay scales, and the ring fencing of assets—this chapter has indicated that such in-dependence is typically a matter of degree. In all cases discussed in this chapter, with the exception of the New Zealand Superannuation Fund, the Ministry of Finance (or other political officers) retains at least de jure power to establish the most important determinant of the fund's investment policy, namely, its asset allocation.

When the institutional arrangements of sovereign wealth funds are compared with those of monetary authorities (as according to the framework established in chapter 4), an interpretation of the aforemen-tioned observation could be that while governments are willing to give the investment authorities responsible for sovereign wealth fund a high degree of operational independence, the principle of "goal depen-dence" is typically preserved. In the same manner that governments retain the power to establish the goals of monetary policy and explicit policy targets (such as a numeric inflation target), they generally wish to preserve the power to establish sovereign wealth funds' return tar-gets, risk tolerance, and asset allocation. In some cases, powers to ex-ercise some degree of constrained discretion around those targets are delegated down to the board and the executive, while the New Zealand example is comparatively extreme in that the government delegates major policy-setting powers to the board (which it, moreover, does not directly appoint).

Regardless of the exact institutional configuration of these powers, the examples discussed in this chapter show a generally high degree of public accountability from entities responsible for major policy choices (target returns, risk tolerance, asset allocation, and reference-portfolio selection) as well as entities responsible for investment implementation and operations. In a number of cases where the former remains under the control of the Ministry of Finance, such as Norway and Chile, concerns about potentially damaging political intervention in the invest-ments of the sovereign wealth fund are reduced by the full transparency of the ministry's policy choices, a high degree of public and expert consultation, and the adoption of uncontroversial investment policies. In the case of Kazakhstan, a lower level of transparency and the centralized concentration of power over the fund provide less comfort regarding the potential for political intervention in the fund's investment deci-sions. Finally, while the American permanent-fund model has delivered positive results over a number of years, the heavy use of consultants and external funds is not only potentially problematic from a cost perspective but also risks a dilution of institutional ownership of key decisions around these funds' asset allocation policies (which are typically fairly complex and risk orientated, with significant allocations to illiquid alternative asset classes).

Ultimately, there is a degree of cross-country variation in emphasis between delegated and centralized control over the investment policies and operations of sovereign wealth funds. The country-specific balance between political ownership of policy and delegated authority for investment operations is not only a function of the political system and characteristic of the countries but also of the degree of discretion permitted by the investment strategy—if the investment strategy itself is highly nondiscretionary, the discussion around the degree of delegated authority becomes less important, as there is essentially less power to delegate in the first place. For long-term investors, such as investment-income and savings type sovereign wealth funds, asset allocation (and its more sophisticated extension in the form of risk-factor allocation) is the fundamental determinant of long-term investment performance, and hence the most critical investment policy choice. The following chapter addresses the analysis of this policy choice, while the final chapter considers the use of various rule-based policies by accountable public investment authorities that potentially add value beyond the fundamental policy choices reflected in asset and risk-factor allocations.

CHAPTER NINE

Shadows and Siren Calls

Rules and Contracts in Delegated Sovereign Wealth Fund Investment Management

IN HOMER'S *The Odyssey*, Ulysses invents a cunning plan to resist the charms of the sirens. Upon learning that their song drove sailors temporarily insane, Ulysses instructs his men to tie his hands to the mast of the ship and for wax to be poured into his sailors' ears, to ensure that they cannot hear the sirens' song. Ulysses is able to listen to sirens, however, safe in the knowledge that, being bound to the mast, he is incapable of leading his ship astray. Although Ulysses faces a moment of crisis, as he too goes momentarily mad upon hearing the sirens and attempts to break free from the mast, the plan ultimately works and the ship proceeds safely on course to Ithaca.

Precommitment devices of this nature have come to be known as "Ulysses contracts" or "Ulysses pacts," and have wide-ranging applications. In medical practice, advance directives (or living wills) are a form of Ulysses contract, established to avoid confusion about whether decisions made by a patient during an initial state of health still apply when the patient has entered a different state of health. The use of Ulysses contracts is also common in the field of portfolio management as a means to "protect the portfolio from *ad hoc* revisions of sound long-term policy . . . when short-term exigencies are most distressing and the policy is most in doubt" (Ellis, 2013). Financial planners often force their clients to sign Ulysses contracts to avoid behavioral errors and irrational reactions to losses. Institutional investors similarly "tie their hands to the mast" through a set of publicly disclosed investment rules.

In matters of public policy, rules serve an additional function beyond precommitment: they are institutional devices that promote the accountability of public institutions that exercise delegated authority. Chapter 4 discussed the notion that transparent rules offer a way to distinguish between "normal" and "discretionary" decisions by public authorities with delegated powers (Du Plessis, 2003). This second function of rules assumes a degree of transparency (if not to the broad public, then to a selected nondemocratic audience or constituency, such as a ruling elite) around both the nature of the rule and discretionary policy actions that deviate from it. The rule gives practical meaning to the concept of accountability, as it provides a benchmark against which to monitor and assess discretionary actions that differ from the rule.

Chapter 4 discussed this function of rules in reference to monetary policy. An example from the practice of public investment can be found with the New Zealand Superannuation Fund, the country's sovereign wealth fund. The fund's "reference portfolio," established by its board, is the primary means through which the incremental contribution of its independent investment management team (the Guardians) is measured and assessed. In communicating this function of the reference portfolio, the fund's management refers to it as a "shadow portfolio," which they need to outperform in order for the investment management team to demonstrate "the value we are adding through our active investment strategies" (New Zealand Superannuation Fund, 2016).

The shadow or reference portfolio establishes a high hurdle: not only is it specified to be capable of meeting the fund's objectives over time (with an aggressive 80 percent allocation to equities), but it consists entirely of passive, low-cost, and listed investments that match the fund's long-term investment horizon and risk profile. The implication is that the reference portfolio is a notional low-cost, rule-based alternative to the more elaborate institutional structure that exists in practice, involving a board and an independent investment management institution. The fact that the shadow portfolio would still get the job done establishes clarity "on the 'hurdles' for active investments" by those exercising delegated authority (New Zealand Superannuation Fund, 2016). The well-paid and well-resourced team investing the fund's assets needs to demonstrate its worth by emerging—at least in the long run—from the shadow of their reference portfolio.

This chapter will consider a number of critical institutional arrangements that can be employed to govern the agency relationship between the "owners" of a sovereign wealth fund (the principal, such as a minister of finance or its own agent, the board) and an independent investment management authority (the agent). The discussion starts by framing these institutional arrangements in terms of the content of the most critical document—described here as a contract between the principal and agent—governing this agency relationship, namely, an investment policy statement, before proceeding to discuss the design and implementation of three specific rules that should form part of this document.

THE INVESTMENT POLICY STATEMENT: A CONTRACT BETWEEN PRINCIPALS AND AGENTS

Several uncontroversial principles in the resolution of agency problems are to reduce information asymmetries between the principal and the agent, to clarify the expected actions of agents, and to establish mechanisms for monitoring and measuring performance—ideally, in the form of a contract (Bolton and Dewatripont, 2005). In delegated asset management relationships in the field of institutional investment, the most common contract is an investment policy statement. This form of contract is used in a range of investment relationships, including private wealth management, when portfolio managers attempt to bind their clients to time-consistent policies (a Ulysses contract). They are particularly appropriate for long-term public investors, where there are established expectations of transparency and accountability.

The establishment (and periodic review) of a sovereign wealth fund's investment policy statement is usually an extension and clarification of a governing law. A number of foundational concepts—the function and purpose of the fund, the governance of the investment process, and possibly the articulation of the expected return of the fund through a numeric long-term return target, risk budget, and investment horizon—are really the domain of the principal. More granular elements of the investment policy statement can be arrived at through a more collaborative and iterative interaction between the principal and agent (most commonly through the board's investment committee, which includes representatives of both the principal and the agent). No matter how interactive the process is, good governance demands that the "buck stops" with the principal (or, specifically, the board) with respect to approval of the investment policy statement. The more collaborative elements include long-term asset allocation, the specification of benchmarks or reference portfolios, and a periodic rebalancing rule.[1] The most important elements of any sovereign wealth fund's investment policy statement are as follows.

- *Function and purpose:* As noted in chapter 3, clarity is required around whether the fund serves a stabilization or saving function, and beyond this, whether it is a fiscal or currency stabilization fund, and a future-generations or investment-income fund.
- *Governance of investment process:* The investment policy statement should clarify the distribution of powers and responsibilities of all the policy, operational, and supervisory institutions involved in the governance of the sovereign wealth fund, as per the various models discussed in chapter 8.[2]
- *Return objectives, risk tolerance, and investment horizon:* The most basic building blocks of any investor's investment strategy are a statement of the owner or principal's expectations of the fund's return, which cannot be contemplated without a concomitant statement of the fund's risk tolerance and investment horizon. These elements (particularly the latter two) are often missing from a sovereign wealth fund's governing framework, but agents benefit from having them clearly articulated. Asymmetric information and incomplete contracts are in neither the principal nor the agent's best interest.
- *Long-term asset allocation:* Chapter 8 identified that the allocation of power for these fundamental decisions generally serves as a litmus test for the degree of delegated authority in sovereign wealth fund management. The inclusion of the asset or risk-factor allocation in the investment policy statement is a useful device for managing agency relationships: based on historic data or capital-market assumptions, or both, the operational manager (and external advisors) can promote an asset and risk-factor allocation that is appropriate in light of the owner's return expectations. The principal may specify the asset allocation or reference portfolio in

terms of low-cost, passive, and tradable asset classes, leaving the agent to design and implement a more complex (and more costly) investment strategy in response.[3]

- *Benchmarks or reference portfolio*: Under a conventional strategic asset allocation approach, asset-class benchmarks are included as a means to measure and monitor the performance of the agent. For example, if the strategic asset allocation is expressed at 60 percent global equities and 40 percent global fixed income, the respective benchmarks for delegated management may be the MSCI World Index (equities) and the Citigroup World Government Bond Index. A more sophisticated risk-factor allocation approach—which looks through conventional asset-class labels— is best suited to the specification of a low-cost reference portfolio.
- *Rebalancing rule:* Periodic portfolio rebalancing is an essential part of long-term portfolio management. It can be achieved through a rule-based approach. As the principal, the owner or board of the sovereign wealth fund may simply insist on having a rebalancing rule, while giving the operational manager a degree of discretion in designing the rule.

Given the principal–agent relationship between the owner and the manager of a sovereign wealth fund, the investment policy statement serves as a contract between the principal (owner or the board that it appoints) and the agent (manager). The focus of this chapter is on the last three (the more interactive, and potentially controversial) items of the investment policy statement

THE IMPORTANCE OF LONG-TERM ASSET ALLOCATION

The literature on long-term portfolio choice distinguishes between strategic and tactical asset allocation (Cochrane, 1999b; Ibbotson and Kaplan, 2000; Ang, 2014). Strategic asset allocation is the process through which investors determine their long-run holding or weights to different types of assets, and is an articulation of an investor's desired exposure to expected risk and return. Strategic asset allocation can be described as a top-down, low-frequency decision *between* asset classes in contrast to bottom-up, higher-frequency choices *within* asset classes, based on attempts to select superior assets and avoid inferior ones (asset- or stock-picking), or to time the purchase and sales of specific assets based on perceived predictability in cyclical or mean-reverting asset price movements (market timing). An intermediate step is called "tactical asset allocation," which makes annual or semiannual "over- and under-weight" deviations from the strategic asset allocation, but still understood in terms of choices between, rather than within, asset classes (Ang, 2014).

The empirical literature on portfolio management has long underlined the overwhelming explanatory power of strategic asset allocation over observed investment returns. The seminal study in this literature, by Brinson, Hood, and Beebower (1986), found that more than 90 percent of the variation in investment performance is explained by strategic asset allocation. Since then, the discussion has evolved to examine the robustness of this finding to different sample periods, clarifying that it pertained to the variation in returns (rather than their levels), and a decomposition of cross-sectional and time-series dimensions of variation. Ibbotson and Kaplan (2000) unpacked the evidence across these two statistical dimensions. They found that 90 percent of the variation in investment performance within a single fund over time (a time-series question) and around 40 percent of the variation in investment performance between funds (a cross-sectional question) was explained by strategic asset allocation. Three-quarters of the variation in time-series returns is found to be due to market movement ("general asset allocation"), with the "remaining portion split roughly evenly between the specific asset allocation and active management" (Ibbotson, 2010). If the decision to be exposed to market volatility—which for Ibbotson (2010) amounts to holding stocks rather than cash—is interpreted as part of the asset allocation decision, the basic insight of Brinson, Hood, and Beebower (1986) stands: asset allocation is the dominant determinant of long-run investment performance for any particular fund.

Strategic asset allocation choices reflect deeply held policy preferences, whose importance to the long-term investment performance of a sovereign wealth fund are of a different magnitude than, for example, the ability to predict short-term movements in financial markets or select the "best" fund managers. There are two major conceptual frameworks through which the ultimate "owner" of a sovereign wealth fund's long-term investment policy may assess asset and risk-factor allocation choices. The simplest, and most widely used, way to arrive at a target or strategic asset allocation is based on conventional (liquid, publicly traded) assets classes, in which the variance of expected returns is the measure of the only source of risk: general, undiversifiable market volatility. Following this, many institutional investors add a range of alternative (illiquid, private-market) asset classes to the portfolio mix.[4] The bottom line of the risk-factor approach is that asset returns are rewards for exposure to a combination or "bundle" of risks, and that investors with an ability to be exposed to a number of well-identified risks have a myriad of ways to capture the rewards associated with them.

Simple Strategic Allocation Models Based on Traded Asset Classes

A useful starting point for a sovereign wealth fund is to focus on the efficiency that can be achieved by simply diversifying between stocks and bonds—described by Benjamin Graham (1949), the intellectual progenitor of long-term investment theory, as "the two major investment mediums." The allocation decision between stocks and bonds has been a mainstay of institutional and personal investors for at least a century. Indeed, leading sovereign wealth funds, including those of Chile, Botswana, and Norway, are simply diversified stock-bond investors.[5] A simple stock-bond allocation incorporates the theoretical insights of modern portfolio theory following Markowitz (1952); its subsequent expansion into the capital asset pricing model, or CAPM (Treynor, 1961; Sharpe, 1964; Lintner, 1965; Mossin, 1966); and the empirical evidence captured by the likes of Ibbotson and Kaplan (2000) and Ibbotson (2010).

The case for the simple model rests on both analytical and pragmatic grounds. Analytically, stock-bond allocations achieve a high degree of efficient diversification. Stocks confer equity rights to asset owners, with returns largely determined by profits and earnings, whereas bonds are debt instruments, with returns largely determined by interest payments and creditworthiness. Consequently, investors often distinguish between other types of assets having either bond- or equity-like returns (or some combination thereof). Empirically, leading bond indexes historically have among the lowest correlations of returns to leading stock indexes: emerging-market equities, absolute-return strategies, hedge funds, private equity, and real estate investment trusts all have higher historical correlations to U.S. equities than U.S. government bonds or a broad-based U.S. bond index (Leibowitz, Bova, and Hammond, 2010:10). So dominant are stock and bond allocations that a leading authority on factor investing classifies stocks and bonds as factors in their own right, and notes that "even without adding alternative asset classes, the equity-bond factor decision is the most important one . . . (as) it explains the majority of the variation in performance" (Ang, 2014:445).

Strategic asset allocation decisions are also influenced by more pragmatic constraints, which can be fruitfully analyzed through the lens of institutional economics. As public investors managing citizens' money, sovereign wealth funds may have a limited appetite for "headline risk." Default risk, which is a significant driver of returns on assets such as emerging-market credit and corporate bonds, are a major source of headline risk, and hence unsuitable for most sovereign wealth funds. Another practical consideration is whether the fund has sufficient institutional capacity to either manage operationally complex asset classes (for example, real estate, private equity, and infrastructure) in-house or through external managers (fees on alternative asset classes are much higher than those for liquid, traded assets).

Investments in private equity, real estate, and infrastructure, in particular, are operationally complex and expensive. They require, for example, direct engagement with the management of entities invested in and legal expertise to establish and negotiate contracts—in both instances because the assets are not traded on public markets or exchanges. These features raise the transaction costs associated with investing in private assets, which are much higher than those possible for investors in public assets, particularly with the proliferation of low-cost passive, index-based alternatives to active management in public markets.[6] Finally, to the extent that stocks and bonds are traded on public markets, they enhance transparency. Particularly for new sovereign wealth funds still in the process of establishing credibility, investments in private assets for which information on prices, risk, and performance is not easily scrutinized can be problematic. In contrast, publicly traded stocks, bonds, and indexes can be valued and monitored in real time, both by the fund and by external observers.

The normative prescriptions of modern portfolio theory and the CAPM are that all investors should hold the same efficient market portfolio, arrived at through a simple optimization based on expected means, variances, and covariances of stock and bond markets. A less risk-averse investor is *not* advised to hold a greater allocation of stocks, but rather to increase risk exposure by borrowing cash and investing it in the market portfolio—the same portfolio held by more risk-averse investors, only in smaller proportion relative to cash. Under modern portfolio theory, asset allocation only shifts when the investor believes that some permanent change in the covariance between stock and bond returns has occurred. The more challenging, and introspective, decision lies in determining how much exposure to market risk is suitable, given the investor's risk tolerance and risk-bearing capacity.

The efficient "market portfolio" is a theoretical construct. Its closest real-life approximation is the 60/40 portfolio (60 percent allocation to stocks and 40 percent to bonds), which is widely used as either an actual portfolio or benchmark—it is, for example, the benchmark of the Norwegian sovereign wealth fund (Chambers, Dimson, and Ilmanen, 2012). Cochrane (1999a) attributes the prominence of the 60/40 portfolio to the proximate market-capitalization weighting of the traded financial system: "The overall market is about 60% stocks and 40% bonds, so average levels of risk aversion, whatever they are, wind up at this value." In that sense, the 60/40 portfolio serves as a proxy for the market portfolio, and is also described as a balance portfolio.

Few investors strictly follow the recommendations of modern portfolio theory. Canner, Mankiw, and Weil (1997) describe an "asset allocation puzzle" according to which more risk-tolerant investors do not borrow to invest in the market portfolio, but rather simply increase their exposure to risk assets (equities), and vice versa. However, these deviations from theoretical advice have been explained at the hand of credit frictions, borrowing constraints, and the correlation of nonportfolio income to either stocks or bonds. In practice, a number of sovereign wealth funds—again, Botswana, Chile, and Norway are clear examples—have started with a bond-heavy balanced allocation and gradually increased their equity weighting (with maximum allocations of 70 percent to either asset class).

Advanced Asset Allocation Through Risk-Factor Models

Mean-variance analysis treats risk in a narrowly defined way. Risk is volatility, measured by the standard deviation or variance of an asset or a portfolio of assets. In reality, other risk dimensions enter the equation.

A multidimensional understanding of risk assumes that not all risks are the same to all investors. Once risk is defined across a range of dimensions, a more granular perspective can be gained regarding the different kinds of risk that investors either want exposure to, or alternatively, cannot afford to be exposed to (and are therefore willing to pay to avoid).

An insurance fund with contingent short-term liabilities (claims) has to assume a relatively short investment horizon and a preference (or need) for liquidity on at least part of its portfolio. If the fund is sufficiently capitalized and has the prospect of stable funding contributions over the long run, its managers can assume some degree of traditional volatility risk, as long as the assets are liquid and can be sold in the event of a large contingent payout. In contrast, a long-term sovereign investor, with a ten-year investment horizon, does not need as much liquidity—and can therefore demand compensation for exposure to that risk through an illiquid asset, such as real estate or private equity. The insurer, meanwhile, effectively "pays" or foregoes the additional illiquidity factor premium. A similar illustration can be made based on oil price exposure. Certain assets and asset classes have an inherent factor exposure to oil—for example, the currencies of oil-exporting countries (ranging from the Canadian dollar to the Nigeria naira), the stocks of oil-producing and servicing companies, and the bonds of the same countries and companies. This factor exposure driving at least part of the return on these assets is the oil price, and is distinct from the market-volatility factor. The sovereign wealth fund of an oil-importing country (Korea) is better placed to gain compensation for exposure to the oil price factor than a counterpart from an oil-exporting country (Kuwait).

The bottom line in the factor approach is that investors are rewarded for holding assets that are going to perform poorly under certain conditions, which Ang (2014) describes as "bad times." However, factor theory differs from the CAPM-inspired mean-variance approach to the extent that it recognizes that "bad times" or "risk" means different things to different investors. Whereas the CAPM has a single risk factor—market volatility (one beta)—multifactor theory assumes a range of risk factors (multiple betas). Multifactor theories have been gaining ground in terms of both academic theory and practice since a landmark paper on arbitrage pricing theory by Ross (1976) and the subsequent three-factor model of Fama and French (1992 and 1993).

Ross's contributions were mostly of a theoretical nature, while Fama and French's work added empirical support for and a parsimonious model of factor returns.

Multifactor theory extends the CAPM theory rather than revolutionizing it. Ang (2014) argues that the CAPM is a factor theory, albeit one with a single (which happens to be the single most important) factor. The following stylized list of lessons for the asset owner from the CAPM and multifactor theories, following Ang (2014:205) and Cochrane (1999a), underlines the similarities between these two workhorse theoretical models of portfolio theory, as well as the areas in which factor theory has introduced new subtleties.

Lesson #1: Diversify: Assess Exposure to a Factor, Not Individual Assets

The most important lesson of modern portfolio theory and the CAPM is that diversification is efficient. Combining assets that are not perfectly correlated in a portfolio provides the best possible return for a given level of risk (volatility), as it eliminates the inadequately rewarded idiosyncratic risk of individual assets. A diversified portfolio is still exposed to the most fundamental driver of returns: market (sometimes called "systematic") risk, which cannot be avoided through diversification. Investors need to determine how much exposure to market risk they are willing and able to bare.

Multifactor theories also conceive of the returns as compensation for bearing bundles of underlying risk factors. In competitive markets, the return on underlying factor-based drivers of asset returns are priced in equilibrium by the interaction of "buyers" and "sellers" of that particular factor exposure. Again, investors should avoid thinking about a portfolio's return in terms of individual assets, but rather as compensation for exposure to a range of risk factors, most efficiently accessed (or hedged against) by combining a variety of assets.

Lesson #2: Risk Tolerance Is Defined Relative to the Average Investor

The CAPM makes provision for heterogeneous agents. Investors have varying degrees of risk aversion, which determines the degree of exposure they hold to the market portfolio. The supply-and-demand of risk appetite determines the return on market volatility in equilibrium. The same logic applies in a multifactor world. Now the price of assets is determined by the balance of supply and demand for a range of risks, not just volatility. The different risk tolerances of heterogeneous investors—interpreted not just in terms of volatility but a range of risks—is what creates a market for trading assets that bundle together a number of fundamental, underlying risk factors.

In the CAPM, the average investor holds the market portfolio and the market portfolio only. Investors that are more risk tolerant than the average investor increase exposure to the market portfolio (through borrowing), and the more risk-averse investor reduces it (by holding more cash). Multifactor models apply the same logic across a range of risk factors: most investors do not want to hold large exposure to stocks that are highly cyclical, because their own wealth and income is correlated with the same risk factor. Hence, cyclical stocks tend to carry an additional risk premium over the broad index. If you differ from the average investor in terms of your willingness to hold cyclical assets, a healthy premium is (or should be) on offer. The task of the asset owner is not so much about finding great individual investments, but rather understanding its multidimensional nature of risk tolerance and sensitivity relative to the rest of the market: "Figure out what risks you do not face, but that give rise to an average return premium in the market because most other investors do face these risks" (Cochrane, 1999a).

Lesson #3: Returns Are Rewards for Bad Outcomes—Capture Them If You Can Tolerate Bad Outcomes

In both traditional and multirisk factor models, the expected return on assets is the reward for the fact that they are expected to perform poorly under certain circumstances—or as Ang (2014) refers to it, "bad times." The CAPM has a single definition for bad times: volatility. All investors dislike volatility—they just have differing degrees of willingness and ability to handle it. In multifactor models, "bad times" are more complicated; it is important to note that what one investor regards as really bad times might only be considered somewhat bad (or even positive) for another. It follows that assets that continue to pay off during periods widely regarded as bad times (that is, most investors dislike them strongly) will have lower expected returns. This goes back to the average investor point above: most investors prefer assets that are expected to be relatively stable for the economic cycle (such as high-dividend stocks and investment-grade sovereign bonds), rather than recession-exposed ones (high-yield credit, value stocks, and emerging-market equities). Hence, the expected return on the former is relatively low, as the demand for such assets are high.

Lesson #4: Risk-Factor Exposures Dominate Long-Term Returns

The general consensus, even among prominent advocates of exposure to a variety of risk factors (Swensen, 2000; Leibowiz, Bova, and Hammond, 2010; Ang, 2014), is that the market-risk factor is the dominant determinant of returns (which is why a simple stock-bond allocation is a good starting point). Empirical investigations of long-term investment performance using "factor screens" have found that additional factors explain the majority of returns that are left unattributed to the market-volatility factor (see Fama and French, 1993; Ang, Goetzmann, and Schaefer, 2009; Asness, Moskowitz, and Pedersen, 2013; and Ang, Brandt, and Denison, 2014). Risk-factor decomposition is merely a more sophisticated way of thinking about asset allocation than the traditional approach based on asset classes only.

There are a number of reasons why established sovereign wealth funds, in particular, should assess their return potential in terms of risk-factor exposure. The first is the above-mentioned emphasis on the long term: while idiosyncratic, nonfactor explanations for returns may be evident over short time periods, these tend to disappear and cancel each other out in the long run. Second, to the extent that idiosyncratic, nonfactor returns exist, they are typically exploitable only by a small number of fast movers in the market (before they are arbitraged away) and only on a relatively small scale. Sovereign wealth funds are typically comparatively slow-moving investors (with deliberately rule-based decision-making and execution processes, given their public nature), managing large portfolios, which limits the scope of exploitable nonfactor-based opportunistic investments (Ang and Kjaer, 2012).

Lesson #5: Focus on Risk-Factor Premiums That Have a Reason to Persist

There are sharply diminishing returns to attempting to uncover new factors. The market-volatility factor is dominant, and beyond this, the literature initially focused on only two additional factors to explain stock returns, "size" and "value" (Fama and French, 1992, 1993), and later added a more contested fourth factor, "momentum" (Carhart, 1997). These studies resulted in the so-called three- and four-factor models, which enjoy considerable academic support. Even for more complex global portfolios that include emerging markets and additional asset classes, Ang (2014) suggests that there are no more than ten academically supported factors in total. The most famous and uncontroversial tradable risk factors[7] are summarized in table 9.1. The discussion here is largely focused on the analysis of factor in equity markets, but factors exist across asset classes—indeed, as discussed below, the full embrace of the risk-factor approach calls for looking through traditional asset-class categories.

Note from table 9.1 that there are competing explanations for risk factors, ranging from those based on rational foundations to ones that require the assumption of behavioral irrationality. Moreover, it is not always clear whether risk-factor labels are accurate: Are the purported risks really independent of one another—for example, is the purported size factor simply compensation for illiquidity or default risk, or both? A general implication from the literature on factor theory is that the value factor enjoys the most support and is (along with the illiquidity premium) the most naturally applicable to long-term investors. Ang (2014) suggests criteria that investors can apply in identifying factors: First, factors should be supported by academic research. This threshold includes both theoretical underpinnings—which may be rational or behaviorally founded—and robust empirical evidence. Research may conclusively identify new factors, but this an extremely low-frequency event, which should be subjected to a significant burden of proof. It is important that the sample include significant periods of "bad times," when assets loaded with the factor in question perform poorly.

Second, factors should be expected to persist based on economic logic. Sustainable factors emerge as an equilibrium outcome due to the preferences (multidimensional risk tolerance) of heterogeneous investors: some investors, for example, are willing to have greater-than-average exposure to the economic cycle, and can consequently capture the value-factor premium by investing in value stocks that are undervalued relative to their long-term value, but more exposed to economic downswings. Others are less able to do so, and are hence willing to forgo premiums by eschewing value stocks. This supply–demand relationship

TABLE 9.1
Established tradable risk factors in addition to market volatility

	Description	Logic and explanations
Value	Difference in returns between "value" stocks (low price-to-book and earnings growth) and "growth" stocks (high price-to-book and earnings) stocks	Arguments in the rational paradigm include that firms with low price-to-book ratios have less flexible investment structures, and are hence more exposed to shocks (Cochrane, 1996; Zhang, 2005).
		Behavioral explanations include that investors overestimate or extrapolate from positive earnings momentum on growth stocks, and vice versa for value stocks (Lakonishok, Shleifer, and Vishny, 1994), or make mental accounting and framing errors around past losses on value stocks (Barberis and Huang, 2001).
Momentum	Captures effect of going long on a cross-section of stocks with past high returns and short stocks with past low returns	Momentum is largely explained on behavioral grounds. However, rationalist theories suggest that momentum is related to (and dependent on) monetary policy regimes and liquidity cycles—that is, "momentum" may in fact be concealing other factors, notably liquidity and macro factors (Pastor and Stambaugh, 2003).
		Behavioral arguments include trend-chasing investor behavior and irrational exuberance (or irrational panic), or "overreaction," as per Barberis, Schleifer, and Vishny (1998).
Size	Difference in returns between small- and large-market capitalization stocks	Rational explanations suggest that companies with small market capitalizations tend to be less liquid, at higher risk of default, and possibly more exposed to market and economic downturns—again, the small-cap premium may in fact be a proxy for other risk factors.
		Behavioral arguments suggest that investors overemphasize large-cap stocks due to headline effects and benchmark inclusion.
Credit	Differences between yield on bonds by AAA and sub–Investment Grade issuers	Explanations are largely rational: excess returns are compensation for the risk of default, which is a risk distinct from market volatility and other risk factors.
Liquidity	Additional returns on less liquid stocks and bonds, and other assets.	Explanations are largely rational: excess returns are compensation for the fact that less liquid securities and assets may not be tradable at will and have higher transaction costs.

can be assumed to persist in perpetuity, thereby preserving the value factor.

Finally, exposure to the factor must be achievable and cost-effective. Typically, this means that a factor must be tradable and, all things equal, this criteria strongly favors liquid markets. Ang (2014) points out that investing in illiquid, private-market instruments (such as private equity) is not the only way to capture the illiquidity premium: investors wishing to gain exposure to the illiquidity factor premium can also "overweight" less liquid stocks in a benchmark or index, while short-selling more liquid ones. This may prove to be a more tradable and cost-effective way of capturing the illiquidity factor than investing in private-market assets. Most factors can be harvested (or hedged against) in a variety of manners, not least through increasingly popular, low-cost factor indexes.

SPECIFYING BENCHMARKS AND REFERENCE PORTFOLIOS

The case for active management—the argument that investors can "outperform" the market through the expression of various forms of "talent," such as a persistently superior market, the ability to identify pricing anomalies (mispricing) *ex ante*, and security selection (picking "winning" securities)—enjoys limited academic support. Many unresolved controversies remain between adherents of efficient markets, for whom the appearance of above-benchmark returns are really just the result of luck or disguised (factor) risk taking, and those who believe markets exhibit not only periodic episodes of irrationality, but that those episodes are systematically exploitable in order to generate excess returns. Despite these philosophical differences, there is significant agreement on two empirical facts around the degree of efficiency in financial markets and the costs involved with trying to outperform them: (1) the most liquid and well-researched markets that approach efficiency and gains from active management are rarely, and certainly not reliably, realized over successive periods (over and above returns on risk factors); and (2) when excess returns are indeed generated in a liquid market, it is generally eroded by management and performance fees.[8]

Despite this evidence, most asset owners—and their agents—continue to believe in investment and expenses in pursuit of outperformance. If the asset allocation process is simple, based on leading asset classes (most public assets, as per the stock-bond portfolios described earlier, but also permitting allocations to alternative asset classes, such as real estate and private equity), the common practice is to simply select any one of a number of published country-specific and cross-country aggregate benchmarks per asset class. As with the underlying asset allocation process associated with this approach, the use of common public asset-class benchmarks is suboptimal, but defendable on the basis of simplicity and pragmatism.

More established sovereign wealth funds should, however, do better. Multiple risk-factor models suggest that the traditional focus on asset-class labels, while not exactly flawed, can paint an incomplete picture of the true sources of risk and return in a portfolio. The ability to look through asset-class labels and identify the combination of underlying risk factors associated with an investment improves investors' abilities to assess the risk-return implications of an investment. This has implications for the way in which the performances of operationally independent operational managers (and their own external manager) are evaluated, as well as for the way portfolio decisions are made across asset classes, using a reference-portfolio approach.

A practical application of factor theory in the context of delegated asset management is a recognition that third-party managers should not be allowed to simply harvest established factor premiums (that are not captured by leading market capitalization–based indexes) and claim that the ensuing outperformance of the index benchmark is evidence of the purported benefits of active management. This is not a hypothetical concern, but one that cuts to the core of the practice of delegated asset management. In the largely positive evaluation of the Norwegian sovereign wealth fund, Ang, Goetzmann, and Schaefer's (2009) empirical analysis, for example, found that the fund pays external managers for capturing a series of factor premiums that could be accessed at a fraction of the cost through factor-adjusted indexes:

> Overall external equity management has enjoyed a modest level of success, but the active returns of external fixed income funds have been very poor . . . large exposures of active external returns to systematic factors suggest that active external management has not reflected a large component of unique management ability. . . . Much

of the behavior of the Fund's small active return can be explained in terms of systematic factors. Our recommendation is that these exposures are, in general, appropriate but that they should be brought into the benchmark and that the Fund's average exposure to these factors should be a "top-down" decision rather than emerging as a byproduct of "bottom-up" active management. (Ang, Goetzmann, and Schaefer, 2009: 20)

For large asset owners, the bottom line of the ascent of risk-factor theory, and the concomitant proliferation of low-cost factor indexes, is that the decision to own a risk factor is a deeply introspective decision, taken by the senior leadership of the institution, based on a fundamental assessment of multidimensional risk tolerance, rather than something the asset owner should pay for through active management. Active management and investment talent, if it does exist and claims added value, needs to do so *in excess of* risk-factor exposures. Practically, this means active mandates need to be assessed relative to factor-adjusted benchmarks rather than generic, broad market index benchmarks. As Ang noted in an article coauthored with the former head of the Norwegian sovereign wealth fund, Knut Kjaer, "factor indices are the best way to benchmark active portfolio managers: if momentum or volatility risk can be done cheaply, then why should we pay 2-20[9] for a hedge fund manager to do it?" (Ang and Kjaer, 2012: 8).

The multiple risk-factor approach can be used to analyze specific investments and assess whether the (expected) return is commensurate with the asset's underlying risk exposures. The example of private equity is instructive, not least because it is one of the most popular methods of diversification for long-term investors (often through extremely expensive third-party funds and delegated managers). Private equity has higher expected returns than listed equity, although the dispersion of private-equity returns is much wider than that for liquid assets. But what are the risk factors underlying this higher return expectation? Even less risky leveraged buyout–style private equity (as opposed to venture capital) bundles together an extraordinary combination of risk factors. At a minimum, it includes the traditional CAPM market-risk factor (which is pervasive—and in this case directly impacts the asset due to the valuation of "exits" from private holdings), interest rate risk (private equity structures are typically levered), the size premium, default risk, and illiquidity risk (private equity funds typically have multiyear holding periods).

Given their long investment horizons, sovereign wealth funds may be well positioned to capture a number of these risk premiums. Private equity may indeed be a suitable investment. However, a factor-based decomposition of returns enables the investor to answer four interrelated and fundamental questions in an informed way: (1) What are the underlying risk factors that determine an investment's expected return? (2) How am I placed (relative to the average investor) to be exposed to these risk—how am I different? (3) Are the expected returns on a particular investment sufficient compensation for exposure to its bundles of underlying risk factors? and (4) Are there other, more cost-effective ways of capturing these premiums?

To assess the merits of a range of assets through a multiple risk-factor lens, some of the world's most sophisticated institutional investors have adopted the so-called reference- or total-portfolio approach. Under this approach, long-term asset allocation and the incremental contribution of active management are assessed through a reference portfolio (or policy portfolio), rather than a combination of rigid, asset class–specific benchmarks.[10] As stated earlier, a reference or policy portfolio is a low-cost portfolio, based on passive exposure to liquid assets, which would still be expected to meet the fund's target returns at an acceptable level of risk. It serves as an alternative or shadow portfolio to the more active and discretionary one managed by the operational manager.

Using this approach, the case for a private-equity investment needs to be made in the context of a reference portfolio—that is, against investments in other asset classes rather than against other rivalling private-equity investments alone. The proposed private-equity investment has to be broken down into its underlying risk-factor drivers of expected return. It is clear that the investment will contain, at the very least (for ease of exposition) an equity component (private equity is still equity) and a debt component (private equity transactions are levered, for argument's sake by 30 percent). Typically, private equity will not be included in the reference portfolio (which is a low-cost, passive shadow portfolio that the fund's managers are trying to outperform), which means the board needs to break the private equity deal down into equity and bond components.

A $100m private-equity investment mimics a "long" equity position valued at $130, combined with a "short" $30m bond position (to account for borrowing). The addition of the private-equity asset will increase the equity exposure of the total portfolio and reduce the bond component of the actual portfolio relative to the reference portfolio (Ang, 2014). Consequently, the approval of the private-equity investment by the board would require selling a significant share of the fund's liquid equity positions to restore the portfolio's balance of equity and bond exposure in line with the reference portfolio (it could also combine selling equity with buying more bonds, if new cash is available).

The factor-based reference-portfolio approach has both analytical and governance implications. Analytically, all investments are broken down into underlying risk factors and matched to the exposures reflected in the reference portfolio. The governance implication is that the board assesses the merits of each investment, not within the narrow confines of a private-equity silo (which operates independently of the equity or bond silos), but rather in cost–benefit terms in relation to the overall portfolio. The board has to determine whether funding a private equity investment is justified based on the fact that it has to be funded by selling exposure to the asset classes reflected in the reference portfolio.

Finally, the reference portfolio approach is also an effective tool for assessing the value added (or not) by the discretion granted to the operational manager—and for keeping the manager accountable in an intelligible way. Returning to the example of the New Zealand Superannuation Fund, it is insightful to note the central role its reference portfolio plays in public accountability of its operational manager, the Guardians of the New Zealand Superannuation Fund. The Guardians have argued that the "reference portfolio approach is first and foremost a governance construct designed to facilitate clear decision making and accountability of decisions" (Brake et al., 2015).

The fund has one of the longest de facto and de jure investment horizons in the world, given its complete absence of liabilities: it is simply trying to maximize a pool of assigned capital by a target date, well into the future when the portfolio will be used to fund future pension liabilities. Consequently, the fund has an aggressive "equilibrium" reference portfolio, established by its board, consisting of 80 percent exposure to equities and 20 percent to fixed income. Again, the reference portfolio is a low-cost, passive portfolio that contains only traditional asset classes and reflects an appropriate risk level for the fund, given its function (Brake et al., 2015).

The Guardians may (and do) deviate from the reference portfolio using a number of rule-based active strategies, but it needs to show that it is adding value (net of the human capital and operational costs associated with having the Guardians in the first place). The most noteworthy of these active strategies is the embrace of a top-down dynamic asset allocation, called "strategic tilting," which is based on two of the Guardian's stated investment beliefs: (1) there is a (small) degree of predictability in asset returns due to mean reversions, and (2) investors with a long-term horizon can outperform more short-term focused investors (because they have the patience to wait for mean reversion to occur over an uncertain horizon).

Strategic titling, which is similar to the tactical asset allocation discussed earlier but operates at a lower frequency, implies "tilting" asset class holdings relative to their weights in the reference portfolio, according to their relative expected returns over near- and medium-term horizons. The strategy involves the use of modeled and statistical inputs, overlaid with discretionary judgment by the Guardians. The strategy is not for the faint of heart—or not for the type of investor whose board or underlying owner does not have the patience to wait for the strategy to pay off. The Guardians note:

> Strategic tilting is a "contrarian" strategy that may imply an extended period of losses relative to long-run benchmarks. Being underweight an asset class [*sic*] in a bull market or overweight in a bear market can bring enormous pressure to unwind the strategy. Perhaps the worst possible outcome for a fund would be to abandon a position when valuations for an asset class prove to be extreme after the fact. For this reason, it is imperative that the Fund's board is committed to the strategy—both from the perspective of buying into the investment beliefs behind the strategy, and being willing to defend the strategy in periods when it underperforms. Having consistent investment beliefs bolsters the collective courage to stay the course. (New Zealand Superannuation Fund, 2014)

Strategic tilting, combined with investments in asset classes not captured in the reference portfolio that the Guardians believe are subject to a degree of inefficient pricing, and effective trade execution (which the Guardians call "portfolio completion") are the three "value-adding strategies" the Guardians employ in an effort to outperform the reference portfolio. The fund's 2015 *Annual Report* reflected on the fund's performance over the five years since it moved away from a conventional strategic asset allocation approach with asset class–based benchmarks toward the reference-portfolio approach: they found that 70 percent of the Guardians' actual portfolio mimics that of the reference portfolio, implying a 30 percent discretionary deviation. Whereas the reference portfolio generated an average annual return of 13.2 percent, the discretionary actions of the Guardian contributed an additional 3.65 percent per year on average—equal to NZ$4.55bn, or more than US$3bn (New Zealand Superannuation Fund, 2015:53). Clearly, at least over the five-year period in question, the gains associated with the delegated discretion granted to the Guardians, assessed relative to its reference-portfolio alternative, have outweighed the costs.

RULE-BASED PORTFOLIO REBALANCING

Strategic asset or risk-factor allocations are the *target* long-term weighting of different asset classes or risk factors in a portfolio. In reality, the constantly diverging returns on the various assets in the portfolio mean that the target weight is rarely achieved, absent interventions by the investor. For example, without periodic adjustments back to the target asset allocation, the long-run outperformance of equities over bonds will result in a higher effective allocation to equities over time than that of the original target weight in the strategic asset allocation. If the strategic asset allocation is indeed appropriately specified at the outset, this upward drift in the portfolio's equity holding would be undesirable—for example, reducing diversification and increasing the risk of the portfolio. Portfolio rebalancing ensures that the fund's overall portfolio is periodically returned to its targets. In doing so, a rebalancing rule precommits the investors to countercyclical investments that prevent "arbitrary actions of changing asset allocations in response to short-term noise" (Ang, Goetzmann, and Schaefer, 2009), and earns a rebalancing premium if asset prices revert to mean.

Rebalancing rules are an example of a Ulysses contract applied to portfolio management. The idea that rebalancing institutionalized countercyclical investing will result in additional investment returns when asset-class returns revert to mean is a proposition for which there is qualified support over the long run (Cochrane, 1999b; Barberis, 2000). Ang (2014:145) argues that rebalancing is related to the idea of the benefits of diversification, which is often described as a rare "free lunch," as applied to long-term investing: "Diversification gets you a benefit in one period, but this diversification benefit dies out if you do not rebalance." Rebalancing enjoys considerable academic support of both an empirical and theoretical nature, and is widely adopted by practitioners (Samuelson, 1969; Merton, 1969; Ang, 2014:144–147).

Both for the purposes of internal decision making and to promote accountability and transparency (particularly in the context of public investment institutions), it is useful to have rules and institutional arrangements that are clear in and of themselves and that advance clarity around the actual policymaking process and objectives of the institutions. Norway's sovereign wealth fund has been active in explaining the merits and mechanics of its rebalancing rule to the public and key constituents, testifying on the rule before Parliament and publishing white papers and notes on its design and operation. Holding a diversified portfolio and implementing dynamic rebalancing are rare "free lunches" that have a significant effect on long-run investment returns. As Mark Wiseman, the former chief executive officer of the Canadian Pension Plan Investment Board, noted:

> We consistently rebalance our portfolio to 65% equities and 35% fixed income. This is a brilliantly simple methodology that all investors, in my view, should employ. . . . We don't know when [the equity markets] are going to rally or turn bearish, so we just say what we want is to be consistent in keeping that 65% equity weighting through the cycle. That is a very, very powerful self-leveling mechanism. You're buying on the way down and selling on the way up. . . . [This] creates fantastic discipline. (Quoted in Zawalsky, 2012: n.p.)

Rebalancing should be a fundamental part of any long-term strategy of a sovereign wealth fund, regardless of its level of sophistication and expertise. Rule-based rebalancing does not require great skill—it "merely" requires a sound rule and conviction to ensure adherence to the rule when the pressure mounts. An investor who cannot stomach diversified exposure to market volatility and cannot specify and adhere to a rebalancing rule should not attempt more elaborate investment strategies, such as investments in illiquid alternatives (private equity, hedge funds, and infrastructure) and active market-timing or security-selection strategies.

CONCLUSION

This chapter has identified how a number of rule-based policies and contractual arrangements can be employed to manage the agency relationship established between the owner and the manager of a sovereign wealth fund. The rules and contracts discussed in this chapter—the collaborative establishment of an investment policy statement as a governing contract between the principal and the agent, a long-term asset allocation framework, the adoption of asset-class benchmarks or reference portfolios, and finally, dynamic portfolio rebalancing rules—all enjoy considerable academic and practitioner support. They are essential elements of institutional arrangements for the delegated nature of sovereign wealth fund investment management.

Rules perform two functions in the execution of investment mandates by sovereign wealth funds. First, in the spirit of a mast-bound Ulysses, rule-based investment strategies are voluntary precommitments to charting a steady course through periods when incentives and behavioral tendencies might lead to actions that are inconsistent with long-term objectives. Long-term investors should take advantage of the benefits of their extended investment horizon (compared with that of the average investor) by capturing the rebalancing premium, in addition to more complex and uncertain factor premiums. Periodic rebalancing is a way of establishing a degree of countercyclical investment, as it avoids "arbitrary actions of changing asset allocations in response to short-term noise" (Ang, Goetzmann, and Schaefer, 2009) and helps "protect the portfolio from *ad hoc* revisions of sound long-term policy . . . when short-term exigencies are most distressing and the policy is most in doubt" (Ellis, 2013: 55).

The second function of rule-based investment strategies is to promote and give substance to the accountability of sovereign wealth funds as public institutions managing assets on behalf of the citizenry. The investment policy statement, rebalancing rules, and a reference portfolio or asset allocation framework with associated disclosure of benchmarks establish observable counterfactuals to the actual, discretionary

portfolio management decisions of the sovereign wealth fund's delegated manager. While many sovereign wealth funds have failed to
adopt—or at least publicly disclose—such rules and contractual arrangements, a small number of them are at the vanguard of global
best practices around the governance of delegated investment authority, providing institutional benchmarks other sovereign wealth funds
can aspire to emulate.

CHAPTER TEN

Summary

IN THIS BOOK, we offer an analysis of the sovereign wealth fund model as an institutional response to various well-documented challenges associated with the management of revenues arising from natural resources. Our analysis emphasizes that adoption of the sovereign wealth fund model involves much more than the mere establishment of a fund. Most fundamentally, the full embrace of the sovereign wealth fund requires the adoption of a rule-based fiscal framework. We argue that the sovereign wealth fund model is best understood as a component of a credible, countercyclical rule-based fiscal framework. The sovereign wealth fund model can contribute to improved economic performance if it is complemented by—or embedded in—a system of rules that govern the flow of resource revenues into the fund, and the flow of assets and income out of the sovereign wealth fund. Finally, we argue that this model typically requires the construction of what is often an elaborate institutional infrastructure to govern the fiscal rule and the agency relationships associated with the management and investments of sovereign wealth funds.

Our analysis proceeds from our reading of the literature on the relationship between natural resources and economic performance that, first, underlines the historical and cross-sectional variation in economic performance of resource economies, and, second, emphasizes the central importance of institutions in determining whether resource wealth promotes or undermines economic growth in the long run. We argue that the understanding of institutions in this context remains rather general, and that a fruitful line of inquiry therefore focuses on a more concentrated cluster of institutional reforms located around the management of the fiscal revenues generated from natural resource extraction. We present and analyze the increasingly popular "sovereign wealth fund model" as exactly this type of targeted institutional reform.

THE RESOURCE CURSE, INSTITUTIONS, AND SOVEREIGN WEALTH FUNDS

The relationship between natural resources and economic prosperity is complex. Today, the list of the world's top ten producers of oil includes some of its poorest and some of its richest countries. Moreover, it is ahistorical to suggest that an abundance of natural resource wealth implies an inevitable disposition to poor economic performance, given the critical role such forms of wealth played in the historic economic emergence of the West. While the so-called resource curse phenomenon enjoys significant empirical and theoretical support, we point out that it has been conditioned and qualified in a number of ways. The erstwhile uncritical acceptance of the resource-curse hypothesis, which emerged in the 1980s and early 1990s, has been replaced by a more nuanced and conditional understanding of the average relationship between resources and economic performance. This has resulted in an emphasis on country- and context-specific factors that promote either success or failure in harnessing resource wealth. The role and quality of institutions and political economy factors feature prominently in this discussion, as does an emphasis on "resource dependence" rather than "resource abundance."

Whereas the early resource-curse literature was particularly dismissive about the role of the quality of institutions in explaining the differentiated economic performances of resource economies—preferring instead institutions-free economic models, notably the Dutch disease—institutional explanations have gained prominence and support in recent years. Most important, however, institutions-centric explanations for the resource curse are no longer presented in direct opposition to more fundamentally economic ones (such as the Dutch disease), but rather attempt to account for the interactions between resource windfalls, the quality of general institutions, specific institutions relating to the management of resources, and the quality of economic policies.

Chapter 1 provides an account of the historic ambivalence economists have demonstrated about the economic benefits and potential disadvantages of natural resources. The chapter discusses in some detail the emergence of the Dutch disease and resource-curse literatures in the 1980s and early 1990s. The chapter concluded with a discussion of the manner in which institutions-centric explanations for the observed divergence in economic performances of resource economies have gained prominence. The understanding of institutions, particularly in the empirical literature, is a deliberately general one, however, focused on what is often described as "meta" or "macro" institutions, such as the rule of law, the specification and enforcement of property rights, and the level of corruption. The emerging frontier of the literature is bringing more narrowly defined and resource-specific institutions into view—a development to which this book contributes.

Chapter 2 proceeds with a discussion of the institutional and political economy challenges around the management of resource windfalls. Given the prominence of "institutions" in the literature on resource economies and the management of resource revenues more specifically, the chapter also presents theories of institutional change and reform, as well as general principles around common forms and functions of institutions. Chapter 1 and 2, therefore, form the theoretical backbone for the central argument advanced in this book: that sovereign wealth funds, if embedded in an accompanying rule-based system for fiscal policy and rule-based and contractual principal–agent relationships, provide a promising—if only partial—institutional solution to widely observed failures in the management of resource windfalls. An important overarching theme is an appreciation of the slow-moving nature of institutional change and the extent to which arguments in favor of the primacy of institutions in economics tend to focus on long-run relationships. This is particularly important for any argument linking institutions to the resource curse, because the latter is also best understood as a set of arguments around long-term economic relationships.

A practical implication of this long-term, institutions-centric perspective is that it calls into question the wisdom of many policy prescriptions for the resource-dependent developing countries, particularly as it applies to potential contributions of sovereign wealth funds.

A powerful and seductive intellectual tradition, which started with Rosenstein-Rodan's big-push model in the 1950s, suggests that governments in resource-dependent poor countries should use commodity windfalls to promote rapid and dramatic economic transformation. Today, many development economists are the intellectual heirs of Rostenstein and Rodan in arguing that resource windfalls are a means through which to achieve such a transformation, economic diversification, and development. This tradition typically argues for the strong hand of the state in the escape from a number of perceived "development traps," with resource revenues providing otherwise scarce capital through which to achieve it.

The institutionalist argument in favor of sovereign wealth funds presented in this book takes a different view of resource-based economic development. This view suggests that big-push models, particularly as they assign such an aggressively activist role for the state in investing resource revenues, tend to underestimate the institutional and political economy constraints on efficient and sustainable public investment financed by resource revenues. The contribution of sovereign wealth funds proposed in this book regards these institutional and political economy constraints as fundamental to resource-dependent economies. Consequently, our institutional perspective on sovereign wealth funds calls for them to be embedded in a set of rules, and supports a more gradualist view of how resource revenues should be used in the process of economic development.

Chapter 3 presents sovereign wealth funds as a response to common challenges associated with the resource curse, and discusses various approaches to defining and categorizing these institutions. The chapter underlines the significant variation in the landscape of sovereign wealth funds, and provides a typology of the different kinds of sovereign wealth funds based on the various functions they perform. An important distinction is made between stabilization funds, with short-term investment horizons and the function of macroeconomic and fiscal stabilization, and more long-term savings- and income-generating type sovereign wealth funds, which diversify the fiscal base of resource-dependent economies and transform depleting assets into permanent wealth in the form of a financial endowment.

As with most institutions, sovereign wealth funds are not "one-size-fits-all" entities: there is significant latitude for tailoring sovereign wealth funds' functions, policies around savings, spending and investments, and intragovernmental and internal governance arrangements to meet local requirements, based on economic (and political) realities. Criticisms of sovereign wealth funds underestimate this flexibility, as well as the extent to which resource-based sovereign wealth funds are designed to directly and indirectly address common afflictions associated with the resource curse (identified in chapters 1 and 2).

Chapter 4 finds that the central tenets of the modern monetary consensus can be usefully applied in aiding the construction of an institutional framework for sovereign wealth funds. The major, and truly significant, breakthroughs in the conduct of monetary policy since the early 1980s are largely institutional in nature—and we identify a series of parallels and lessons from the modern monetary consensus for the less-established sovereign wealth fund model. The first area of overlap is the importance of clarifying institutional mandates and objectives, which are not only important for accountability but also define the appropriate scope of specific institutions, identifying their optimal contribution and clarifying which social objectives lie beyond their reach. Especially because there is currently less agreement around the appropriate objectives and mandates of sovereign wealth funds than there is for monetary policy, it is critical to define, both positively and negatively, exactly what the functions, mandates, and objectives of sovereign wealth funds are.

The management of sovereign wealth funds further shares with modern monetary policy institutions the characteristics of a classic agency relationship, established by the granting of operational authority to independent institutions to avoid well-known political biases and incentive problems. Operational independence has gained a particular understanding through the theory and practice of modern monetary policy—notably, it is typically accompanied by goal dependence and an elaborate set of complementary institutional arrangements that promote accountability and transparency. A similar understanding appears warranted in the area of sovereign wealth funds (further explored in the final section of the book). Further parallels to and lessons from modern central banking for the sovereign wealth fund model are drawn in chapter 4, including the emphasis on institutionalized credibility and the adoption of explicit targets and contingent rules as a means to reduce the costs associated with achieving credibility (while also promoting public accountability). The institutional framework established in the second section is used to evaluate fiscal rules and the management of the agency relationships around sovereign wealth funds in the remainder of the book.

FISCAL RULES

Having argued that a full and meaningful understanding of the sovereign wealth fund model requires that it be understood as part of a rule-based fiscal framework, the second part of the book is devoted to normative and positive assessments of saving and spending rules. These rules govern the flow of resource revenues into sovereign wealth funds, and the transfer of these funds' assets and investment income to the budget (or other earmarked purposes). With a few notable exceptions, there is significant scope for improving the fiscal rules surrounding sovereign wealth funds, and achieving greater integration of sovereign wealth fund savings and spending policies with a broader countercyclical fiscal framework. A more typical arrangement is to combine either ad hoc or highly mechanistic savings rules with simple spending rules for investment-income funds and poorly designed (or, again, ad hoc) transfers from stabilization funds.

Chapter 5 discusses a number of simple rules for saving a share of revenues arising from natural resource revenues through transfers to a sovereign wealth fund structure. These rules—variously based on a fixed percentage of resource revenues, deviations from a set reference price for the underlying commodity, or a similar deviation from a moving average of prices or revenues—are simple to the point of being crude. While they therefore have the attraction of simplicity and the ease of communication, they make no attempt to distinguish between the use of accumulated assets for stabilization—saving and income-generation purposes in particular—or, generally, how savings in the sovereign wealth fund may be integrated with a broader fiscal framework, as discussed above. They are therefore best understood as accumulation rules, most relevant to a potential period prior to the establishment of a more comprehensive fiscal framework. Another reason for studying these simple saving rules is that while clearly suboptimal, they are closer to current practice among global sovereign wealth funds than more complex, integrated fiscal rules (while, as the chapter demonstrates, a number of resource-dependent countries have failed to implement even such basic savings rules or processes during the most recent oil boom).

Chapter 6 introduces and applies a more integrated fiscal rule that combines spending, stabilization, and saving decisions for oil revenues in a single framework. The framework is based on a spending rule that anchors oil-derived spending—or, more precisely transfers from the sovereign wealth fund to the government—on a function of the previous year's spending and the balance of assets in the sovereign wealth fund, consisting of a stabilization- and investment-income fund component. The rule can be characterized as contingent, as it incorporates automatic feedback loops between fluctuations in resource revenues and the level of oil-derived spending (that is, transfers from the sovereign wealth funds): when oil revenues increase, the rule permits a gradual upward adjustment in spending, permitted due to an increase in the size of the sovereign wealth fund (and vice versa).

The fiscal rule underlines the trade-off between a rapid ramp-up in public spending financed by resource revenues ("front-loaded spending") and the accumulation of a significant pool of financial assets in the stabilization fund and the investment-income fund, which transforms a depleting natural asset into a source of permanent wealth and income. The trade-off between current spending and the creation of a stabilization fund is not that acute (beyond the initial accumulation with which to establish the fund), but the establishment of an investment income fund involves more substantial reduction in the level of short-term spending in order to establish the endowment and maintain permanent spending. A number of resource-rich countries have already accumulated such assets during previous commodity booms. These countries essentially already have the financial building blocks in place to successfully implement this fiscal rule—or some other form of integrated fiscal rule.

This part of the book concludes with a discussion and categorization of the governance of existing fiscal rules. The countries analyzed in chapter 7 cover a range of economic and political contexts, including some of the world's richest countries—Norway, Chile, and the United States of America—and reveal a wide range of institutional mechanisms for the specification and enforcement of fiscal rules, ranging from constitutional mandates to legislative statues to presidential decrees to elements of custom (or informal institutions, as per chapter 2).

The chapter identifies the American permanent-fund institutional model as an incomplete version of the "politics-at-the-constitutional-level" mechanism; the Chilean model as relying on "rule-by-experts"; and the Norwegian model as being founded on custom and consensus.

In general, the rule-based fiscal frameworks adopted in Norway and Chile come closest to the proposed fiscal rule: although their operation is different from the rule in chapter 6 (and indeed from each other), they both integrate savings decisions with a concept of sustainable income from depleting resources. In both cases, the ultimate goal behind the rule is to constrain the spending of finite resource revenues in such a way that the budget does not become dependent on a depleting source of fiscal revenue. The state of Wyoming pursues a similar model to that of Norway—albeit on a more limited scale given that it consumes the majority of its oil, gas, and coal revenues through the budget, sending only a percentage of resource revenues to its permanent fund. In Alaska, the same limited degree of savings applies; however, to date the state has not used the earnings of the permanent fund to fund the budget (instead just earmarking half of it for a unique citizens' dividend scheme). Both Alaska and Wyoming would be well served by the addition of some stabilization mechanisms: either directing a greater share of volatile and depleting revenue through their permanent funds in exchange for a stable stream of investment income, or more directly through the establishment of larger and more rule-based fiscal stabilization funds.

THE GOVERNANCE OF DELEGATED INVESTMENT AUTHORITIES

The final institutional aspects of the sovereign wealth fund model discussed in this book pertain to various elements of sovereign wealth funds' investments and the delegated investment institutions involved in this part of the model: why and how to achieve a degree of operational independence from government for the management authority; how to clarify the roles and responsibilities of the various principals and agents involved in the delegated-authority model of investment; and how the governance and performance of the investment authority may be strengthened by rule-based investment policies.

Having elaborated on the case for operational independence in the management of long-term sovereign investment portfolios, chapter 8 considers the ways in which countries have resolved a familiar tension in public policy: balancing the desire for operational independence on the part of an investment authority of sovereign wealth with a degree of government control and oversight of such delegated authority. While the case for operational independence rests on compelling foundations— investment performance, fears of a regulatory backlash, a desire to escape from public-sector pay scales, and the ring fencing of assets—chapter 8 indicates that independence is typically a matter of degree. In all cases discussed in this chapter, with the exception of the New Zealand Super-annuation Fund, the Ministry of Finance (or other political officers) retains at least de jure power to establish the most important determinant of the fund's investment policy, including, for example, its long-term asset allocation.

When the institutional arrangements of sovereign wealth funds are compared with those of monetary authorities (as according to the framework established in chapter 4), an interpretation of this observation could be that while governments are willing to give the investment authorities responsible for sovereign wealth funds a high degree of op-erational independence, the principle of "goal dependence" is typically preserved. In the same manner that governments retain the power to establish the goals of monetary policy and explicit policy targets (such as a numeric inflation target), they generally wish to preserve the power to establish sovereign wealth funds' return targets, risk tolerance, and asset allocation. In some cases, powers to exercise some degree of dis-cretion around the establishment of those targets are delegated down to the board and the executive, while the New Zealand example is com-paratively extreme in that the government delegates all major policy-setting powers to the board (which it, moreover, does not directly appoint).

In a number of cases where major investment policy decisions remain under the control of the Ministry of Finance, such as in Norway and Chile, concerns around potentially damaging political intervention in the investments of the sovereign wealth fund are reduced by transpar-ency around the policy choices of the ministry (or other political owners), a high degree of public and expert consultation, and the adop-tion of uncontroversial and rule-based investment policies. In the case of Kazakhstan, a lower level of transparency and the concentration of power over the fund provide less comfort around the potential for future political intervention in the fund's investment decisions. Finally, while the American permanent-fund model has delivered positive results over a number of years, the heavy use of consultants and external fund managers is not only potentially problematic from a cost perspective but also risks a lack of clarity around the ultimate institutional ownership of critical policy decisions, notably the funds' long-term asset allocations.

There is a significant degree of observed cross-country variation in emphasis between delegated and centralized control over the investment policies and operations of sovereign wealth funds. The country-specific balance between political ownership of investment policies and delegated authority for investment operations is ultimately not only a function of the political system and institutional characteristics of the countries but also of the degree of discretion permitted by the investment strategy in the first place: if the investment strategy itself is highly nondiscretionary, the discussion around the degree of delegated authority becomes less important, as there is essentially less power to delegate.

The final chapter of the book identifies a number of rule-based policies and contractual arrangements that can be employed to manage the agency relationship established between the owner and the manager of a sovereign wealth fund, under governance models that assume the delegation of discretionary powers from the principal (government) to an agent (the delegated sovereign investment authority). Rules and contracts perform two functions in the execution of investment mandates by sovereign wealth funds. First, rule-based investment strategies are voluntary precommitments to charting a steady course through periods when incentives and behavioral tendencies might lead to actions that are inconsistent with long-term objectives. The second function of rule-based investment is to promote and give substance to the accountability of sovereign wealth funds as public institutions managing assets on behalf of the citizenry.

The chapter proposes the collaborative establishment of an investment policy statement as a governing contract between the principal and the agent. For long-term investors, such as investment-income and savings-type sovereign wealth funds, long-term asset allocation—and its more sophisticated extension in the form of risk-factor allocation—is the fundamental determinant of investment performance, and hence the most critical investment policy decision. Whether determined by the minister of finance, a governing board of political officeholders, or an independent board, this long-term target weighting lies at the heart of the policy decisions pertaining to the investments of sovereign wealth funds and is an articulation of deep-seated policy preferences for the balance of risk and return.

Chapter 9 suggests that many existing sovereign wealth funds have mirrored other long-term institutional investors by keeping it simple and adopting the tried and tested balanced-portfolio approach based only on exposure to traded (or listed) stocks and bonds. As their risk tolerance increased over time, a number of sovereign wealth funds gradually increased the share of equities in their portfolios—in a manner that matches the workhorse benchmark portfolio for long-term institutional investors, namely, the 60/40 equity-bond portfolio. This basic, if limited, approach to long-term asset allocation achieves a significant degree of portfolio diversification and provides long-term capital a near-efficient allocation to the most pervasive determinant of portfolio returns: market volatility. It is a simple investment policy model for sovereign wealth funds to follow, particularly during their inception phase, when the focus is more typically (and appropriately) on the aforementioned fiscal framework.

More established sovereign wealth funds might embrace increasingly sophisticated and multidimensional asset allocation models and analytical tools. An emerging frontier in asset allocation is the risk-factor approach, which has been cautiously adopted by the world's most sophisticated and established sovereign wealth funds. The risk-factor approach attempts to look beyond the most basic specification of the fund's strategic asset allocation in terms of the asset classes to one that focuses on underlying risk-factor allocation. The basic logic is that investors are compensated for their exposure to a wide range of risk factors (in addition to the market-volatility factor of traditional portfolio theory), or, conversely, pay a premium (or an opportunity cost in terms of foregone return premiums) for holding assets that effectively hedge against these risk factors.

A risk-factor approach serves a number of important institutional functions in the context of long-term investment. First, it is a complete and comprehensive way of analyzing the long-term return potential of, and the unique opportunities available to, a sovereign wealth fund. Second, it is a useful lens through which to view both portfolio construction and case-by-case investment decisions: looking through traditional asset classes, which are simply bundles of underlying risk factors, the investor can determine the best way to gain desired factor exposure. Finally, factor-adjusted benchmarks and performance measures hold third-party managers to higher account, making it impossible for them to claim the harvesting of factor premiums to be the purported benefits of active management and investment talent. Chapter 9 suggests an initial focus on a small set of factors that enjoy considerable empirical and theoretical support, have a long empirical track record, and can be captured in a cost-effective manner. A focus on value and illiquidity factor premiums is an obvious point of departure for sovereign wealth funds with long investment horizons.

Chapter 9 further considers two additional rule-based contractual arrangements between the principal and its agent in the form of an independent investment authority managing a sovereign wealth fund's assets. The first of these is the specification of performance benchmarks through which to assess the contribution of investment discretion. In the case of simple asset allocation frameworks, common practice is to select a set of asset class–specific indexes as benchmarks; however, it was argued that the more sophisticated risk-factor approach to long-term asset allocation is best accompanied by the specification of a reference (or policy) portfolio. Finally, the chapter discusses and analyzes the specification of a dynamic portfolio-rebalancing rule, which institutionalizes a degree of countercyclical investment on the part of the agent, who might otherwise succumb to dynamically inconsistent behavior.

This book adopts a sympathetic stance on the contribution that sovereign wealth funds can offer in the management of resource revenues. This conclusion is based on the understanding that sovereign wealth funds are embedded in a comprehensive, rule-based fiscal framework, and that they are accompanied by an often-elaborate institutional framework (quite often in the still-emergent real-work implementation of the sovereign wealth fund model, these aspects remain limited or incomplete). The potential contribution of sovereign wealth funds, particularly when narrowly defined as simply a portfolio of assets funded from a resource revenue windfall, should not be overstated. When accompanied by supporting fiscal rules and a sound institutional structure, however, the sovereign wealth fund model is a promising targeted institutional intervention to the by now widely understood problems of resource economies.

Notes

1. THE MOST DISADVANTAGEOUS LOTTERY IN THE WORLD

1. For authoritative accounts of this argument, as well as extensions to the industrialization and economic ascendance of the United States, see Habakkuk (1962), Wright (1990), and Wright and Czelusta (2004, 2007).

2. The enduring interest in an idea that has so clearly been discredited is in part due to its influence on economic policies. The Singer-Prebisch hypothesis was embraced by the United Nations, particularly its Commission for Latin America and the Caribbean, an organization in which Singer and Prebisch held prominent advisory and leadership positions, respectively. Given the historic context in which the thesis gained prominence—on the cusp of the decolonialization of large parts of Africa and Asia—its popularity with newly empowered independence leaders is unsurprising. The thesis appealed to nationalist notions of economic sovereignty, reduced dependence on (and exploitation by) a global economic "core" dominated by former colonial powers, and visions of rapid social and economic modernization through state-directed industrialization.

3. Van Wijnbergen developed many of the original insights in his doctoral thesis at the Massachusetts Institute of Technology, awarded in 1980 (some of the confusion over the credit for the Dutch disease theory relates to delays between the awarding of his PhD and the subsequent publication of articles from it in leading academic journals). The idea was, however, already being discussed in nonacademic circles: the term "Dutch disease" was coined in an article in *The Economist* (1977) magazine describing the dynamics that led to the decline of the manufacturing sector in the Netherlands after the discovery of an offshore natural gas field in 1959.

4. The volatility and uncertainty of natural resource prices, and indeed a number of key macroeconomic aggregates in resource-dependent countries, are popular explanations for the resource curse in their own right, without integrating volatility and uncertainty into a broader Dutch disease model (Van der Ploeg and Poelhekke, 2009).

5. Sachs and Warner (1997) acknowledge that the assumption of higher positive externalities in the manufacturing sector is based mostly on broad observations rather than on "micro-level evidence" and "Therefore it remains somewhat speculative" (7). Another non-neoclassical assumption is the implicit or explicit belief that resource producers face credit constraints that prevent them from borrowing during unanticipated drops in resource revenues.

6. The resource-curse literature has been surveyed extensively elsewhere. Torvik (2009) and Frankel (2012) provide extensive accounts of leading theories, empirical evidence, and policy proposals around the resource curse. Van der Ploeg's (2011) survey is more narrowly confined to formal economic models explaining the resource curse, while Ross (1999) and Collier (2010) assess arguments that focus on institutional and political economy explanations.

7. Sachs and Warner are famous for advancing an understanding of a broad range of geographic factors as critical to growth, including countries' latitudinal position (typically measured as distance of the capitol from the tropics, which they argue provides a good proxy for susceptibility to debilitating tropical diseases) and direct access to coastline.

8. Collier and Goderis (1997) further note that any indicator that is expressed as a ratio of GDP is by definition endogenous to GDP growth: "Government policies and institutions are very likely to affect the ratio of commodity exports over GDP through the denominator (GDP)" (12). The same could be said of measures that are expressed as a ratio of total exports, which could be affected by the countries' trade policies and openness to trade.

9. Van der Ploeg and Poelhekke's (2009) criticisms of Brunnschweiler and Bulte (2008) are extensive and devastating, and include purported evidence of "an unfortunate data mishap, omitted variables bias, weakness of the instruments, violation of exclusion restrictions and misspecification error" (Van der Ploeg and Poelhekke, 2009: abstract).

10. The criticisms of Sachs and Warner's worked briefly outlined in this chapter pertain to potential measurement flaws, while still assuming that the general econometric setup of the growth-regression framework is sound. Of course, there have been important fundamental criticisms of the growth-regression approach as utilized in the 1990s. For more fundamental critiques of the growth-regression approach, see Mankiw (1995) and Easterley (2005).

11. Mehlum, Moene, and Torvik's (2006) measure of institutional quality is an unweighted average of five commonly used indexes: a rule of law index,

a bureaucratic quality index, a corruption in government index, a risk of expropriation index, and a government repudiation of contracts index.

12. Recall that the endogeneity of the measure of resource abundance used by Sachs and Warner means that the findings of both studies should be reinterpreted as a statement about the consequences of resource *dependence* rather than resource *abundance.*

13. The list of significant contributions in this extraordinarily fertile area of research since the start of the twenty-first century is a long one. However, the continued expansion of New Institutional Economics (North himself had numerous scholarly contributions on issues of development) into the major questions of development gained considerable impetus with such publications as Acemoglu, Johnson, and Robinson (2002); Glaeser et al. (2004); and Rodrik, Subramanian, and Trebbi (2004).

2. GETTING TO DENMARK

1. This framework has since become a reference for a multitude of other organizations working on natural resource governance, including the Natural Resource Governance Institute (formerly Revenue Watch Institute), the World Bank, and the Extractive Industries Transparency Initiative.

2. Of course, there are more technically economic reasons for this, particularly those relating to the volatility of resource revenues, which results in damaging "stop-start" public investment cycles, procyclicality, and sharply diminishing marginal returns to public investments during boom periods. These issues are discussed below, with a particular emphasis on the possible interactions between these economic outcomes and political economy factors.

3. Recall also that part of the Dutch disease argument includes volatility and procyclicality. In these models, the real exchange rate, public and private consumption and investment, and wages in the nontraded sector *all* increase procyclically.

4. Hamilton (2009) used the price for West-Texas Intermediate Crude oil.

5. The first use of the term "New Institutional Economics" is attributed to Williamson (1975).

6. This focus on politics in North's later work is a matter of emphasis rather than a dramatic change in his scholarship. Already in *Structure and Change in Economic History,* published in 1981, North discussed the difference between what he called the "contract theory" versus the "predatory theory" of the state (1981:20–27).

7. Acemoglu and Robinson (2012) study is a grand synthesis of more than a decade's worth of acclaimed scholarship and is intended for a general, popular readership. The arguments contained in it are based on a large body of

more technical work, most prominently a series of articles published in the top-ranked journals in economics and political science: Acemoglu and Robinson (2000, 2006, 2008) and Acemoglu, Johnson, and Robinson (2001, 2002).

8. Glaeser et al. (2004) contend that arguments for the primacy of general institutions were emphasized by Montesquieu, Adam Smith, and the Public Choice and New Institutional Economics literatures, while the view that is more supportive of the possibility of enlightened and benevolent authoritarianism is traced by the work of political scientists Seymore Martin Lipset and Adam Przeworski, with empirical support from Barro (1999).

9. The example of Chinese growth since the 1970s is the elephant in the room. Acemoglu and Robinson (2012) argue that China cannot sustain its recent growth trajectory absent political reforms. Other obvious examples of growth takeoffs under noninclusive political institutions include South Africa, Chile, Singapore, South Korea, and Taiwan.

10. In chapter 16 of *Politics*, Aristotle advocates in favor of the rule of law, in opposition to Plato's notion of the philosopher king who is above the law: "It is more proper that law should govern than any one of the citizens: upon the same principle, if it is advantageous to place the supreme power in some particular persons, they should be appointed to be only guardians, and the servants of the laws" (Aristotle, 1853).

11. In his recent book, *The Origins of Political Order*, Fukuyama tones down the "end of history" language significantly, but still maintains that the modern political order requires three institutional characteristics: a strong and capable state, the state's subordination to a rule of law, and government accountability to all citizens. The tension described here is apparent from Fukuyama's first two characteristics.

3. GUARDIANS OF THE FUTURE AGAINST THE CLAIMS OF THE PRESENT

1. As discussed previously, Collier (2007) promoted the idea of a resource value chain that starts with the incentives for exploration and ends with the management, and indeed investment, of resource revenues.

2. Frankel mentions "commodity funds," which is a subset of sovereign wealth funds, as discussed below. Commodity funds (or natural resource funds) account for the majority of sovereign wealth funds, both in number and assets under management, and for the bulk of the growth in new funds since 2000, as shown in figure 3.1.

3. The exact measurement of sovereign wealth fund assets is complicated by delays in reporting, the assessment of market-to-market gains and losses, a

lack of transparency and disclosure among a number of the world's largest funds, and, not least, by uncertainty and inconsistencies regarding definitions and whether or not certain investors should be categorized as sovereign wealth funds.

4. A number of subnational jurisdictions, such as Saskatchewan and the North West Territories in Canada, and American states, such West Virginia and Pennsylvania, may be added to this list.

5. The first use of the term "sovereign wealth fund" was in Rozanov (2005).

6. This structure was subsequently remodeled as the International Forum of Sovereign Wealth Funds when it assumed an autonomous governance structure and facilitated regular meetings between these funds.

7. The Canada Pension Plan (CPP), for example, has gone to great lengths to distance itself from sovereign wealth funds. In December 2007, the chair of the CPP Investment Board noted, "Neither the Canada Pension Plan nor the CPP Investment Board, which manages the assets of the CPP, meet the definition of a Sovereign Fund," adding, "At stake for the CPP Investment Board would be its ability to compete for global investments if it is incorrectly categorized as a sovereign fund" (Cook-Bennett, 2007). Despite these efforts, the CPP is still commonly included in discussions on sovereign wealth funds.

8. The Norwegian sovereign wealth fund, the Norway Pension Fund–Global, may be included in this list; however, the link to the funding of future public pension liabilities has not been formally or legally defined (despite the fund's name). The Norwegian fund is, therefore, better categorized as a classic sovereign wealth fund of the investment-income variety (as it makes an annual transfer, based on its real return, to the budget).

9. Economists have theorized these issues for centuries, from Jevons's (1865) *The Coal Question*, which raised the prospect of British empirical decline due to dwindling coal supply, to Hotelling's (1931) study on the efficient rate of resource extraction, to Solow's (1974) and Hartwick's (1977) examination of issues of intergenerational justice and efficiency in the extraction of finite resources and the investment of their proceeds.

10. Academics have attributed the accumulation of reserves to two primary motivations: "mercantilism" and "self-insurance." The former relates to the desire to maintain a favorable exchange rate to stimulate export growth and suppress the demand for imports, while the latter arises from the need to hold foreign assets in order to prevent or handle balance-of-payment, foreign debt, and currencies crises (Aizenman and Lee, 2006).

11. These observations are very much in keeping with so-called post-2015 development agenda and the emphasis on financing for development by the likes of the World Bank and the United Nations.

12. As noted below, many sovereign wealth funds in resource-rich countries contribute in an indirect way to diversification by preventing or combatting

Dutch disease and an appreciation of the real exchange rate, which undermines the competitiveness of their tradable goods sector.

13. Ironically, Collier is one of the leading forces behind the *Natural Resource Charter*, a list of "best practices" for the management of natural resources. Precept 8 (Principle 3) of the charter states: "Effective utilization of resource revenues requires that domestic expenditure and investment be built up gradually and be smoothed to take account of revenue volatility."

4. TO BE BORING

1. "Power brokers" is the phrase use to describe sovereign wealth funds in a well-publicized report by McKinsey & Company (Farrell et al., 2007). An in-depth feature in *Euromoney* described how the secrecy of many of the world's largest sovereign wealth funds has single-handedly established an aura of mystique around them: "The strategies and dimensions of Gulf sovereign wealth funds are an arcane subject made more mysterious by the lack—apart from Abu Dhabi's fund—of published annual reports" (Wright, 2012).

2. Principal–agent analysis is, unsurprisingly, a mainstay of the fields of Public Choice, New Institutional Economics, and monetary economics.

3. Mishkin (2000) adds that a central bank should also have the goal of financial stability, which is a valid and uncontroversial addition in the context of the role of central banks generally, but falls outside the core focus on monetary policy (although the role of monetary policy in financial stability has reemerged more as a point of debate in the aftermath of the 2008 global financial crisis).

4. Some observers are concerned that the hard-won battles that led to instrument independence and rule-based policymaking will be (or have already been) forgotten (Taylor, 2010). Alternatively, one could argue that the fact that neither deflation nor rapidly rising inflation has occurred—and that inflation and inflation expectations have remained anchored around most central banks' implicit or explicit targets, despite the biggest financial crisis since the Great Depression and unprecedented monetary and fiscal easing—is a further indication of remarkable advances in monetary policy.

5. These problems include, but are not limited to, greatly exaggerated expectations of the sophistication of sovereign wealth funds' investment models and strategies.

6. In designing contingent rules that govern active investment strategies, sovereign wealth funds should bear in mind an important lesson from monetary policy: monetary economists have recognized that specific targeting rules are typically sub-optimal in each specific context, but in practice the futile search for optimal rules has been replaced by a search for ones that are most robust to various specifications of the economic structure (see especially Svens-

son, 2003a, 2003b). The global financial markets are prone to periodic regime shifts and temporary deviations from long-standing structural features and asset correlations—what is important is to identify rules that govern the active allocation process that are robust to various plausible financial conditions and relationships rather than those that are optimal in the strict sense for a particular structure.

5. IT'S (STILL) MOSTLY FISCAL

1. The specification of an escape clause, while introducing a measure of countercyclicality, opens up the savings process to political abuse, particularly if the policymakers have a high degree of discretion in determining when the escape clause is to be activated.

2. Oil price data is the average annual dollar per barrel spot price for West Texas Intermediate, provided by the U.S. Energy Information Administration.

3. Due its "youth bulge," demographic pressures in Saudi Arabia have been analyzed at length as a major long-term concern. According to official data published by the Saudi Arabian Monetary Agency, more than 70 percent of the population was below the age of forty in 2012.

4. The rapid growth in the domestic use of oil, in light of subsidies, has been widely studied and is the source of some of the most pessimistic forecasts of Saudi Arabia's long-term fiscal outlook (Lahn and Stevens, 2011).

5. The government does have other policy options for insuring against downside risks to revenues, such as hedging against a drop in oil prices in the option market. For example, the government can secure a floor price by buying options to sell oil at sixty dollars per barrel. Mexico has adopted this approach to managing downside risks to revenue (Frankel, 2012).

6. The moving-average rule considered above, while conditioned on revenue rather than price, is an example of a formula-based mechanism for implementing the rule. The moving-average approach could easily be adapted to apply to price movements, too.

6. INTEGRATED FISCAL RULES FOR SOVEREIGN WEALTH FUNDS

1. The Investment-Income Fund in the framework described here could also be called a "permanent fund," as per the public finances of American states, or an "endowment fund," as per the convention in the literature on universities and charitable foundations.

2. The argument for stable spending rests on a number of well-established theoretical pillars. This may derive from an ethical concern with intergenerational equity, or from the permanent-income and life-cycle approaches pioneered by Friedman (1957) and Modigliani and Brumberg (1954), respectively. Preferences for, and the general desirability of, stable public spending are also standard building blocks in literature on the macroeconomics of the business cycle (Blanchard and Fischer, 1989), and the microeconomics of household utility (Deaton, 1991).

3. That said, a number of countries, including Kuwait, Botswana, Chile, and Nigeria, with a sovereign wealth fund structure that involves more than one type of fund, have preferred to assign responsibility for the management and investment of the entire fund to a single authority.

7. GOVERNING THE FISCAL RULE

1. A third advisory committee, the Advisory Financial Committee for Fiscal Responsibility Funds, provides guidance and assessments to the ministry regarding the investments of the sovereign wealth funds. The role and function of this committee is discussed in subsequent chapters.

2. This list could also include funds in states such as Alabama, Louisiana, Oregon, and Montana. These states are, however, not included in the analysis here, as they are smaller in size, and their funding sources are comingled with other forms of state income.

3. In recent years, Wyoming has generated around 30 to 40 percent of revenue from a combination of oil, gas, and coal; around 30 to 45 percent from sales taxes; and 15 to 20 percent from investment income from their Permanent Funds. Alaska is much more resource dependent: in the years preceding the collapse in oil prices (2011–2014), oil revenues exceeded 90 percent of the state's fiscal revenues. Even with the collapse in oil prices, oil accounted for approximately 79 percent of revenues in 2016 and is expected to account for 67 percent in 2017 (Petek, 2015; Richards, 2015).

8. PUBLIC FOOTPRINTS IN PRIVATE MARKETS

1. P/E levels refer to the price-to-earnings ratio, the most commonly used measure for valuing a company. P/E ratios or levels measure a company's current share price relative to its per-share earnings.

2. An obvious solution to this purely geographic problem is to establish in-house investment teams outside the state in major global financial capitals, such as London and Singapore—or even just in other American locations, such

as New York, Chicago, Boston, or San Francisco. Indeed, most sovereign wealth funds and large public pension funds—notably the sovereign wealth funds of Norway, Singapore, Korea, and the Middle East, as well as the largely internally managed Canadian pension plans—have done this to great effect. However, proposals to do so by American state permanent funds have generally met with fierce political and public opposition.

9. SHADOWS AND SIREN CALLS

1. If the investment model is comparatively simple, permitting limited discretion by the agent, the principal may author the majority of the investment policy statement, as it reduces the agent's role to a largely administrative one.

2. The investment policy statement might include an articulation of what is expected from external managers and how they will be selected, monitored, and evaluated. External managers may be selected due to the operational and budget constraints of the agent, a belief in the existence of investment talent, or because the external management fee structure is sufficiently low to justify external reliance rather than building internal investment capacity and infrastructure. The investment policy statement can be used to clarify these issues and to establish a ranking of factors that enter the selection, monitoring, and evaluation process (for example, fees, performance, track record, human resource and capacity building).

3. An increasing number of investors include an articulation of "investment beliefs" in their investment policy statement. The reason is that beliefs around the efficiency versus occasional irrationality of financial markets, the value of external asset managers and their ability to generate "alpha" (excess returns over the benchmark), and the degree of predictability and mean reversion in assets and asset classes have implications for the strategies pursued by the operational manager (for example, a belief in mean reversion bolsters the case for periodic rebalancing, much as a belief that certain markets behave [predictably] irrationally bolsters the case for pursuing active management strategies around market timing).

4. The term "alternative assets" covers many different types of assets of which the common characteristic is that they are traded in private, not public, markets.

5. Norway's sovereign wealth fund in 2011 diversified beyond stocks and bonds into real estate, to a maximum of 10 percent of its portfolio, but has yet to increase its effective weight to the asset class to the target level as of 2016.

6. Public exchanges for trading in debt and stock instruments emerged as a way to reduce transaction costs. More recently, passive index products for public stocks and bonds, including exchange-traded funds, serve a similar function.

7. The literature has distinguished between two broad types of factors, although the difference can become blurry. The first group of factors is called "fundamental" or "macro" factors; these are based on macroeconomic developments, such as economic growth, demographics, and productivity, which affect all assets albeit in varying degrees. The second group is called "dynamic," "tradable," or "style" factors, which can be actively traded in the market by going long or short in different groups of assets, and for which there typically exits a supply–demand relationship based on differing abilities and appetites for exposure to the underlying risk (Ang, 2014).

8. The articles contained in the symposium on "The Growth of the Financial Sector" in the spring 2013 edition of the *Journal of Economic Perspectives*, particularly Cochrane (2013) and Malkiel (2013), provide excellent summaries of the consensus around the empirical literature on the value of pre- and postfee active asset management. The previously mentioned disclosure of "investment beliefs" by long-term institutional investors, such as the New Zealand Superannuation Fund, typically reflects these points.

9. The term "2-20" is industry jargon for the widely used fee structure of a 2 percent flat fee on assets under management, plus 20 basis points on returns over the benchmark.

10. The pioneering formal adoption of this approach is credited to the Canadian Public Pension Investment Board, and has since been pursued (to varying degrees) by other sovereign wealth fund investors, including the New Zealand Superannuation Fund, the Alaska Permanent Fund, and Singapore's Government Investment Corporation, along with other venerated long-term investors, such as the United Kingdom's Universities Superannuation Scheme.

References

Acemoglu, D., S. Johnson, and J. Robinson. 2001. "The Colonial Origins of Comparative Development: An Empirical Investigation." *American Economic Review* 91 (5): 1369–1401.

——. 2002. "Reversal of Fortune: Geography and Institutions in the Making of the Modern World Income Distribution." *Quarterly Journal of Economics* 117 (4): 1231–1294.

Acemoglu, D., S. Johnson, J. Robinson, and Y. Thaicharoen. 2003. "Institutional Causes, Macroeconomic Symptoms: Volatility, Crises, and Growth." *Journal of Monetary Economics* 50 (1): 49–123.

Acemoglu, D. and J. Robinson. 2000. "Why Did the West Extend the Franchise? Democracy, Inequality, and Growth in Historical Perspective." *Quarterly Journal of Economics* 115 (4): 1167–1199.

——. 2006. "Economic Backwardness in Political Perspective." *American Political Science Review* 100 (1): 115–131.

——. 2008. "Persistence of Power, Elites and Institutions." *American Economic Review* 98 (1): 267–293.

——. 2012. *Why Nations Fail: The Origins of Power, Prosperity and Poverty.* New York: Crown.

——. 2013a. "Economics Versus Politics: Pitfalls of Policy Advice." *Journal of Economic Perspectives* 27 (2): 173–192.

——. 2013b. "The Resource Curse and Institutions: Getting More Specific." June 27. http://whynationsfail.com/blog/2013/6/27/resource-curse-and-institutions-getting-more-specific.html.

Ades, A. and R. Di Tella. 1999. "Rents, Competition, and Corruption." *American Economic Review* 89: 982–993.

Aizenman, J. and J. Lee. 2006. "Financial Versus Monetary Mercantilism: Long-Run View of the Large International Reserves Hoarding." IMF Working Paper 06/280. International Monetary Fund, Washington, D.C.

Alesina, A. and L. Summers. 1993. "Central Bank Independence and Macroeconomic Performance: Some Comparative Evidence." *Journal of Money, Credit and Banking* 25 (2): 151–162.

Alesina, A., G. Tabellini, and F. Campante. 2008. "Why Is Fiscal Policy Often Procyclical?" *Journal of the European Economic Association* 6 (5): 1006–1036.

Alsweilem, K., A. Cummine, M. Rietveld, and K. Tweedie. 2015. "A Comparative Study of Sovereign Investor Models: Institutions and Policies for Managing Sovereign Wealth." Discussion Paper. Belfer Center for Science and International Affairs and Center for International Development, Harvard Kennedy School, Cambridge, Mass., April.

Ambachtsheer, K. 2011. "How Should Pension Funds Pay Their Own People." *Rotman International Journal of Pension Management* 4 (1): 18–25.

Ang, A. 2010. "The Four Benchmarks of Sovereign Wealth Funds," September 21. http://ssrn.com/abstract=1680485.

——. 2014. *Asset Management: A Systematic Approach to Factor Investing.* Oxford: Oxford University Press.

Ang, A., M. Brandt, and D. Denison. 2014. "Review of the Active Management of the Norwegian Government Pension Fund Global, Norwegian Ministry of Finance." Oslo: Norwegian Ministry of Finance.

Ang, A., W. Goetzmann, and S. Schaefer. 2009. "Evaluation of Active Management of the Norwegian GPFG." Oslo: Norwegian Ministry of Finance.

Ang, A. and K. Kjaer. 2012. "Investing for the Long Run." Netspar Discussion Paper No. 11/2011-104. Network for Studies on Pensions, Aging, and Retirement. http://dx.doi.org/10.2139/ssrn.1958258.

Arezki, R., T. Gylfason, and A. Sy, eds. 2012. *Beyond the Curse: Policies to Harness the Power of Natural Resources.* Washington, D.C.: International Monetary Fund.

Arezki, R., K. Hamilton, and K. Kazimov. 2011. "Resource Windfalls, Macroeconomic Stability and Growth: The Role of Political Institutions." IMF Working Paper 11/142. International Monetary Fund, Washington, D.C.

Aristotle, translated by E. Walford. 1853. *Politics.* London: Henry Bohn.

Asness, C., T. Moskowitz, and L. Pedersen. 2013. "Value and Momentum Everywhere." *Journal of Finance* 68 (3): 929–985.

Auty, R. 1993. *Sustaining Development in Mineral Economies: The Resource Curse Thesis.* London: Routledge.

——. 2007. "Rent Cycling Theory, the Resource Curse, and Development Policy." *Developing Alternatives* 11 (1): 7–13.

Avendaño, R. and J. Santiso. 2011. "Are Sovereign Wealth Funds Politically Biased? A Comparison with Other Institutional Investors." In *Institutional Investors in Global Capital Markets*, ed. Narjess Boubakri and Jean-Claude Cosset, 313–353. Bingley, U.K.: Emerald Group.

Bacon, R. and S. Tordo. 2006. *Experience with Oil Funds: Institutional and Financial Aspects.* Washington, D.C.: World Bank, Energy Sector Management Assistance Program.

Balin, B. 2009. "Sovereign Wealth Funds: A Critical Analysis." The Johns Hopkins University School of Advanced Industrial Studies. Accessed September 23, 2009. http://ssrn.com/abstract=1477725.

Barberis, N. 2000. "Investing for the Long Run When Returns Are Predictable." *Journal of Finance* 55: 225–264.

Barberis, N. and M. Huang. 2001. "Mental Accounting, Loss Aversion, and Individual Stock Returns." *Journal of Finance* 56 (4): 1247–1292.

Barberis, N., A. Shleifer, and R. Vishny. 1998. "A Model of Investor Sentiment." *Journal of Financial Economics* 49 (3): 307–343.

Barro, R. 1991. "Economic Growth in a Cross Section of Countries." *Quarterly Journal of Economics* 106 (2): 407–443.

Barro, Robert J. 1999. "Determinants of Democracy." *Journal of Political Economy* 107 (1): 158–183.

Baunsgaard, T., M. Villafuerte, M. Poplawski-Ribeiro, and C. Richmond. 2012. "Fiscal Frameworks for Resource Rich Developing Countries." *IMF Staff Discussion Notes*, May 16, SDN/12/04, Washington, D.C.

Beblawi, H. and G. Luciani. 1987. *The Rentier State.* New York: Croom Helm.

Berg, A., R. Portillo, S. Yang, and L. Zanna. 2013. "Public Investment in Resource-Abundant Developing Countries." *IMF Economic Review* 61 (1): 92–129.

Bernstein, S., J. Lerner, and A. Schoar. 2013. "The Investment Strategies of Sovereign Wealth Funds." *Journal of Economic Perspectives* 27 (2): 219–238.

Bertram, R. and B. Zvan. 2009. "Pension Funds and Incentive Compensation: A Story Based on the Ontario Teachers' Experience." *Rotman International Journal of Pension Management* 2 (1): 30–33.

Bhattacharyya, S. and R. Hodler. 2010. "Natural Resources, Democracy and Corruption." *European Economic Review* 54 (4): 608–621.

Birdsall, N. and F. Fukuyama. 2011. "The Post-Washington Consensus: Development After the Crisis." *Foreign Affairs*, March-April, 45–53.

Black, F. 1986. "Noise." *Journal of Finance* 41: 529–543.

Blanchard, O. and S. Fischer. 1989. *Lectures on Macroeconomics.* Cambridge, Mass.: MIT Press.

Blinder, A. 1997. "What Central Bankers Could Learn from Academics—And Vice Versa." *Journal of Economic Perspectives* 11 (2): 3–19.

———. 2000. "Central-Bank Credibility: Why Do We Care? How Do We Build It?" *American Economic Review* 90 (5): 1421–1431.

Blundell-Wignall, A., Y. Hu, and J. Yermo. 2008. "Sovereign Wealth and Pension Fund Issues." OECD (Organisation for Economic Co-operation and

Development) Working Paper on Insurance and Private Pensions, No. 14. Paris: OECD.

Bolton, P. and M. Dewatripont. 2005. *Contract Theory.* Cambridge, Mass.: MIT Press.

Brake, S., D. Iverson, J. Cheung, and C. Worthington. 2015. "How We Invest." White Paper. 2015 Reference Portfolio. New Zealand Superannuation Fund, Auckland, July.

Brinson, G., L. Hood, and G. Beebower. 1986. "Determinants of Portfolio Performance." *Financial Analysts Journal* 42 (4): 39–48.

Brunnschweiler, C. and E. Bulte. 2008. "The Resource Curse Revisited and Revised: A Tale of Paradoxes and Red Herrings." *Journal of Environmental Economics and Management* 55 (3): 248–264.

Bruno, M. and J. Sachs. 1982. "Energy and Resources Allocation: A Dynamic Model of the 'Dutch Disease.'" *Review of Economic Studies* 51: 845–859.

Buchanan, J. 1975. "A Contractarian Paradigm for Applying Economic Theory." *American Economic Review* 65 (2): 225–230.

——. 1987. "The Constitution of Economic Policy." *American Economic Review* 77: 243–250.

Buiter, W. and D. Purvis. 1981. "Oil, Disinflation, and Export Competitiveness: A Model of the 'Dutch Disease.'" In *The International Transmission of Economic Disturbances Under Flexible Exchange Rates*, ed. J. Bhandari and B. Putnam, n.p. Cambridge, Mass.: MIT Press.

Canner, N., N. G. Mankiw, and D. Weil. 1997. "An Asset Allocation Puzzle." *American Economic Review* 87 (1): 181–191.

Carhart, M. 1997. "On Persistence in Mutual Fund Performance." *Journal of Finance* 52 (1): 57–82.

Carmichael, J. and R. Palacios. 2003. "Managing Public Pension Funds: A Framework." Paper presented at the Second Public Pension Fund Management Conference, World Bank, Washington D.C., May.

Cecchetti, S. 1998. *Current Issues in Monetary Economics.* Edited by H. Wagner. Heidelberg: Physica-Verlag.

Chambers, D., E. Dimson, and A. Ilmanen. 2012. "The Norway Model." *Journal of Portfolio Management* 38 (2): 67–81.

Chhaochharia, V. and L. Laeven. 2008. "Sovereign Wealth Funds: Their Investments Strategies and Performance." CEPR Working Paper No. 6959. Center for Economic Policy Research, London.

Clark, G. and A. Monk. 2013. "The Scope of Financial Institutions: Insourcing, Outsourcing and Off-shoring." *Journal of Economic Geography* 13 (2): 279–298.

Clark, G. and R. Urwin. 2008. "Best-Practice Pension Fund Governance." *Journal of Asset Management* 9 (1): 2–21.

Clay, K. and G. Wright. 2005. "Order Without Law: Property Rights During the California Gold Rush." *Explorations in Economic History* 42 (April): 155–183.

Cochrane, J. 1996. "A Cross-Sectional Test of an Investment-Based Asset Pricing Model." *Journal of Political Economy* 104 (3): 572–621.

———. 1999a. "New Facts in Finance." *Journal of Economic Perspectives* 23 (3): 6–58.

———. 1999b. "Portfolio Advice for a Multifactor World." *Journal of Economic Perspectives* 23 (3): 59–78.

———. 2013. "Finance: Function Matters, Not Size." *Journal of Economic Perspectives* 27 (2): 97–108.

Collier, P. 2007. *The Bottom Billion.* Oxford: Oxford University Press.

———. 2010. *The Plundered Planet.* Oxford: Oxford University Press.

———. 2012. "How to Spend It." Working Paper No. 2012/05. United Nations University, Helsinki, Finland.

Collier, P. and B. Goderis. 2007. "Commodity Prices, Growth, and the Natural Resource Curse: Reconciling a Conundrum." Working Paper Series 274. Centre for the Study of African Economies, Oxford.

Collier, P., F. Van der Ploeg, M. Spence, and A. Venables. 2010. "Managing Resource Revenues in Developing Economies." *IMF Staff Papers* 57 (1): 84–118.

Cook-Bennett, Gail. 2007. "Take a Closer Look Before Calling My Fund Sovereign." *Globe and Mail*, December 10.

Corden, W. and J. Neary. 1982. "Booming Sector and De-industrialization in a Small Open Economy." *Economic Journal* 92 (December): 825–848.

Cox, C. 2007. "The Rise of Sovereign Business." Gauer Distinguished Lecture in Law and Policy at the American Enterprise Institute Legal Center for the Public Interest by Chairman Christopher Cox, U.S. Securities and Exchange Commission, Washington, D.C., December 5.

Cruijsen, C., S. Eijffinger, and L. Hoogduin. 2008. "Optimal Central Bank Transparency." CEPR Discussion Paper No. 6889. Center for Economic Policy Research, London.

Cukierman, A. 2007. "The Limits of Transparency." CEPR Discussion Paper No. 6475. Center for Economic Policy Research, London.

Das, U., Y. Lu, C. Mulder, and A. Sy. 2009. "Setting Up a Sovereign Wealth Fund: Some Policy and Operational Considerations." IMF Working Paper WP/09/179. International Monetary Fund, Washington, D.C.

Davis, J., R. Ossowski, J. Daniel, and S. Barnett. 2001. "Oil Funds: Problems Posing as Solutions?" *Finance and Development* 38 (4). International Monetary Fund, Washington, D.C. http://www.imf.org/external/pubs/ft/fandd/2001/12/davis.htm.

Deaton, A. 1991. "Saving and Liquidity Constraints." *Econometrica* 59 (5): 1221–1248.

Debrun, X. and M. Kumar. 2007. "Fiscal Rules, Fiscal Councils and All That: Commitment Devices, Signaling Tools or Smokescreens?" In *Fiscal Policy: Current Issues and Challenges*, 479–512. Papers presented at the Banca d'Italia workshop held in Perugia, Italy, March 29–31.

De Haan, J., F. Amtenbrink, and S. Eijffinger. 1998. "Accountability of Central Banks: Aspects and Quantification." CentER Discussion Paper Series No. 9854. http://dx.doi.org/10.2139/ssrn.1307581.

DeLong, J. B. 2000. "The Triumph of Monetarism?" *Journal of Economic Perspectives* 14: 83–94.

DeLong, J. B., A. Shleifer, L. Summers, and R. Waldmann. 1990. "Noise Trader Risk in Financial Markets." *Journal of Political Economy* 98: 703–738.

Diamond, P. 1965. "National Debt in a Neoclassical Growth Model." *American Economic Review* 55 (5): 1126–1150.

Dincer, N. and B. Eichengreen. 2014. "Central Bank Transparency and Independence: Updates and New Measures." *International Journal of Central Banking* 10 (1): 189–259.

Drummond, H. 2016. "Raiding the Permanent Fund Threatens Alaska's Economy and Future." *Alaska Dispatch News*, May 17, 2016.

Du Plessis, S. 2003. "An Institutional Assessment of Inflation Targeting as a Framework for Monetary Policy." PhD dissertation, University of Stellenbosch, South Africa, December.

Dyck, A. and A. Morse. 2011. "Sovereign Wealth Fund Portfolios." Chicago Booth Research Paper No. 11-15. Accessed February 2011. http://ssrn.com/abstract=1792850.

Easterly, W. 2001. "Benevolent Autocracy." DRI Working Paper No. 75. New York University, May.

———. 2005. "National Economic Policies and Economic Growth: A Reappraisal." In *Handbook of Economic Growth*, ed. P. Aghion and S. Durlauf, vol. 1, chap. 15. Amsterdam: Elsevier.

Economist. 1977. "The Dutch Disease." November 26, 82–83.

Ehrmann, M. and M. Fratzscher. 2008. "Purdah: On the Rationale for Central Bank Silence Around Policy Meetings." ECB Working Paper No. 868. European Central Bank, Frankfurt.

Ellis, C. 2013. *Winning the Loser's Game: Timeless Strategies for Successful Investing*. 6th ed. New York: McGraw-Hill Education.

Engerman, S. and K. Sokoloff. 2000. "Institutions, Factor Endowments, and Paths of Development in the New World." *Journal of Economic Perspectives* 14: 217–232.

Erten, B. and J. Ocampo. 2013. "Super Cycles of Commodity Prices since the Mid-Nineteenth Century." *World Development* 44 (3): 14–30.

Esfahani, H. and M. Ramirez. 2003. "Institutions, Infrastructure, and Economic Growth." *Journal of Development Economics* 70 (2): 443–477.

Fama, E. and K. French. 1992. "The Cross-Section of Expected Stock Returns." *Journal of Finance* 47 (2): 427–465.

——. 1993. "Common Risk Factors in the Returns on Stocks and Bonds." *Journal of Financial Economics* 33 (3): 427–465.

Farrell, D., S. Lund, E. Gerlemann, and P. Seeburger. 2007. "The New Power Brokers: How Oil, Asia, Hedge Funds, and Private Equity Are Shaping Global Capital Markets." McKinsey Global Institute, London, October.

Faust, J. 1996. "Whom Can We Trust to Run the Fed? Theoretical Support for the Founders' Views." *Journal of Monetary Economics* 37: 267–283.

Frankel, J. 2012. "The Natural Resource Curse: A Survey." In *Beyond the Resource Curse*, ed. B. Shaffer and T. Ziyadov, 17–57. Philadelphia: University of Pennsylvania Press.

Friedman, B. 2002. "The Use and Meaning of Words in Central Banking: Inflation Targeting, Credibility, and Transparency." NBER Working Papers No. 8972. National Bureau of Economic Research, Cambridge, Mass.

Friedman, M. 1957. *A Theory of the Consumption Function.* Princeton, N.J.: Princeton University Press.

——. 1968. "The Role of Monetary Policy." *American Economic Review*, 58 (1): 1–17.

Fukuyama, F. 1989. "The End of History." *The National Interest*, Summer, 5.

——. 2011. *Origins of Political Order: From Prehuman Times to the French Revolution.* New York: Farrar, Straus and Giroux.

——. 2012. "China's 'Bad Emperor' Problem." *The American Interest*, May 28.

——. 2014. *Political Order and Political Decay.* New York: Farrar, Straus & Giroux.

Gavin, M. 1993. "Adjusting to a Terms of Trade Shock: Nigeria 1972–88." In *Policymaking in the Open Economy*, ed. Rudiger Dornbusch, 172–219. Oxford: Basil Blackwell.

Gavin, M. and R. Perotti. 1997. "Fiscal Policy in Latin America." In *NBER Macroeconomics Annual 1997*, ed. Ben Bernanke and Julio Rotemberg, 11–72. Cambridge, Mass.: MIT Press.

Gelb, A. 1988. *Oil Windfalls: Blessing or Curse?* New York: Oxford University Press (for the World Bank).

Gelb, A., B. Eifert, and N. Tallroth. 2002. "The Political Economy of Fiscal Policy and Economic Management in Oil-Exporting Countries." World Bank Policy Research Working Paper 2899. Washington, D.C., October.

Glaeser, E., R. LaPorta, F. López-de-Silanes, and A. Shleifer. 2004. "Do Institutions Cause Growth?" *Journal of Economic Growth* 9 (3): 271–303.

Goodfriend, M. 2007. "How the World Achieved Consensus on Monetary Policy." *Journal of Economic Perspectives* 21 (4): 47–68.

Graham, B. 1949. *The Intelligent Investor.* New York: Harper.

Habakkuk, H. 1962. *American and British Technology in the Nineteenth Century.* Cambridge, Mass.: Cambridge University Press.

Hall, P. and D. Soskice. 2003. *Varieties of Capitalism: The Institutional Foundations of Comparative Advantage.* Oxford: Oxford University Press.

Hamilton, J. 2009. "Understanding Crude Oil Prices." *The Energy Journal* 30 (2): 179–206.

Hartwick, J. 1977. "Intergenerational Equity and the Investment of Rents from Exhaustible Resources." *American Economic Review* 67 (5): 972–974.

Hassan, A. Al-, M. Papaioannou, M. Skancke, and C. Sung. 2013. "Sovereign Wealth Funds: Aspects of Governance Structures and Investment Management." IMF Working Paper WP/13/231. International Monetary Fund, Washington, D.C., November.

Hausmann, R., C. Hidalgo, S. Bustos, M. Coscia, S. Chung, J. Jimenez, A. Simoes, and Y. Yildirim. 2011. *The Atlas of Economic Complexity.* Cambridge, Mass: Puritan.

Hausmann, R., E. Lora, and J. Lora. 2014. "A Spending Rule for the Oil Income." Report to the Government of Kazakhstan. Unpublished memo, Kennedy School of Government, Harvard University, Cambridge, Mass., January

Hausmann, R. and R. Rigobon. 2003. "An Alternative Interpretation of the 'Resource Curse': Theory and Policy Implications." In *Fiscal Policy Formulation and Implementation in Oil-Producing Countries,* ed. Jeffrey Davis, 12–44. Washington, D.C.: International Monetary Fund.

Hess, D. and G. Impavido. 2004. "Governance of Public Pension Funds: Lessons from Corporate Governance and International Evidence." In *Public Pension Fund Management,* ed. A. Musalem and R. Palacios, 49–89. Washington, D.C.: The World Bank.

Hirschman, A. 1958. *The Strategy of Economic Development.* New Haven, Conn.: Yale University Press.

Hodler, R. 2006. "The Curse of Natural Resources in Fractionalized Countries." *European Economic Review* 50: 1367–1386.

Hotelling, H. 1931. "The Economics of Exhaustible Resources." *Journal of Political Economy* 39 (2): 137–175.

Humphreys, M. and M. Sandbu. 2007. "The Political Economy of Natural Resource Funds." In *Escaping the Resource Curse,* ed. M. Humphreys, J. Sachs, and J. Stiglitz, 194–233. New York: Columbia University Press.

Ibbotson, R. 2010. "The Importance of Asset Allocation." *Financial Analysts Journal* 66 (2): 18–20.

Ibbotson, R. and P. Kaplan. 2000. "Does Asset Allocation Policy Explain 40, 90, or 100 Percent of Performance?" *Financial Analysts Journal* 56 (1): 26–33.

International Monetary Fund. 2015. "The Commodities Roller Coaster: A Fiscal Framework for Uncertain Times." *Fiscal Monitor*, October, Washington, D.C.

International Working Group on Sovereign Wealth Funds. 2008. "Generally Accepted Principles and Practices ('Santiago Principles')." Santiago, Chile, October. http://www.ifswf.org/santiago-principles-landing/santiago-principles.

Jacks, D., K. O'Rourke, and J. Williamson. 2011. "Commodity Price Volatility and World Market Integration Since 1700." *Review of Economics and Statistics* 93 (3): 800–813.

Jevons, W. 1865. *The Coal Question: An Inquiry Concerning the Progress of the Nation and the Probable Exhaustion of Our Coal Mines*. London: Macmillan.

Kaminsky, G., C. Reinhart, and C. Vegh. 2005. "When It Rains, It Pours: Procyclical Capital Flows and Macroeconomic Policies." *NBER Macroeconomics Annual* 19: 11–82.

Karl, T. 1997. *The Paradox of Plenty: Oil Booms and Petro-States*. Berkeley: University of California Press.

Kimmit, R. 2008. "Public Footprints in Private Markets." *Foreign Affairs* 87 (January/February): 119–130.

King, M. 2000. "Balancing the Economic See-Saw." Speech to the Plymouth Chamber of Commerce and Industry's 187th Anniversary Banquet, April 18. www.bankofengland.co.uk/publications/ speeches/2000/speech82.htm.

Kjacr, K. 2006. "From Oil to Equities." Speech given at the Norwegian Polytechnic Society, Oslo, November 2.

Knill, A., B. Lee, and N. Mauck. 2012. "Bilateral Political Relations and Sovereign Wealth Fund Investment." *Journal of Corporate Finance* 18 (1): 108–123.

Kopits, G. and S. Symansky. 1998. "Fiscal Rules." IMF Occasional Paper 162. International Monetary Fund, Washington, D.C.

Krueger, A. 1974. "The Political Economy of the Rent-Seeking Society." *American Economic Review* 64 (3): 291–303.

Krugman, P. 1987. "The Narrow Moving Band, the Dutch Disease, and the Competitive Consequences of Mrs. Thatcher: Notes on Trade in the Presence of Dynamic Scale Economies." *Journal of Development Economics* 27 (1–2): 41–55.

Kydland, F. and E. Prescott. 1977. "Rules Rather Than Discretion: The Inconsistency of Optimal Plans." *Journal of Political Economy* 85: 473–491.

Kyle, S. 2014. "Mineral Revenues and Countercyclical Macroeconomic Policy in Kazakhstan." Department of Applied Economics and Management Working Paper, No. 180170. Cornell University, Ithaca, N.Y.

Lahn, G. and P. Stevens. 2011. "Burning Oil to Keep Cool: The Hidden Energy Crisis in Saudi Arabia." Royal Institute of International Affairs (Chatham House), London, December. https://www.chathamhouse.org/sites/files/chathamhouse/public/Research/Energy%2C%20Environment%20and%20Development/1211pr_lahn_stevens.pdf.

Lakonishok, J., A. Shleifer, and R. Vishny. 1994. "Contrarian Investment, Extrapolation, and Risk." *Journal of Finance* 49 (5): 1541–1578.

Leibowitz, M., L. Bova, and P. Hammond. 2010. *The Endowment Model of Investing: Return, Risk, and Diversification.* Hoboken, N.J.: Wiley Finance.

Lewis, A. 1954. "Economic Development with Unlimited Supplies of Labor." *Manchester School* 22 (May): 139–191.

——. 1955. *The Theory of Economic Growth.* London: Allen and Unwin.

Lintner, J. 1965. "The Valuation of Risk Assets and the Selection of Risky Investments in Stock Portfolios and Capital Budgets." *Review of Economics and Statistics* 47 (1): 13–37.

Lora, E., M. Rietveld, and M. Cuadra. 2017. "A Fiscal Rule for Managing Resource Revenues Through a Sovereign Wealth Fund." Center for International Development Working Paper. Harvard Kennedy School of Government, forthcoming.

Lucas, R. 1990. "Why Doesn't Capital Flow from Rich to Poor Countries?" *American Economic Review* 80 (1): 92–96.

Lucas, R. and T. Sargent. 1979. "After Keynesian Macroeconomics." *Quarterly Review*, Federal Reserve Bank of Minneapolis, Spring, 1–16.

Mahdavy, H. 1970. "The Patterns and Problems of Economic Development in Rentier States: The Case of Iran." In *Studies in the Economic History of the Middle East*, ed. M. A. Cook, 428–467. London: Oxford University Press.

Malkiel, B. 2013. "Asset Management Fees and the Growth of Finance." *Journal of Economic Perspectives* 27 (2): 97–108.

Mankiw, G. 1995. "The Growth of Nations." *Brookings Papers on Economic Activity* (1): 275–310.

Mankiw, G., D. Romer, and D. Weil. 1992. "A Contribution to the Empirics of Economic Growth." *Quarterly Journal of Economics* 107 (2): 407–437.

Markowitz, H. 1952. "Portfolio Selection." *Journal of Finance* 7 (1): 77–91.

Matsuyama, K. 1992. "Agricultural Productivity, Comparative Advantage, and Economic Growth." *Journal of Economic Theory* 58 (2): 317–334.

Mauro, P. 1995. "Corruption and Growth." *Quarterly Journal of Economics* 90: 681–712.

Medas, P. and D. Zakharova. 2009. "Primer on Fiscal Analysis in Oil-Producing Countries." IMF Working Paper WP/09/56. International Monetary Fund, Washington, D.C.

Megginson, W. and V. Fotak. 2015. "Rise of the Fiduciary State: A Survey of Sovereign Wealth Fund Research." *Journal of Economic Surveys* 29 (4): 733–778.

Mehlum, H., K. Moene, and R. Torvik. 2006. "Institutions and the Resource Curse." *Economic Journal* 116: 1–20.

Merton, R. 1969. "Lifetime Portfolio Selection Under Uncertainty: The Continuous Time Case." *Review of Economics and Statistics* 51: 247–257.

Milesi-Ferretti, G. 2004. "Good, Bad or Ugly? On the Effects of Fiscal Rules with Creative Accounting." *Journal of Public Economics* 88 (1–2): 377–394.

Mishkin, F. 2000. "What Should Central Banks Do?" *Federal Reserve Bank of St. Louis Review* 82 (6): 1–13.

Mishkin, F. and E. White. 2014. "The Federal Reserve System's Role in the Global Economy: An Historical Perspective." Paper presented at the Federal Reserve Bank of Dallas, September 18–19.

Mitchell, O. and P. Hsin. 1997. "Public Sector Pension Governance and Performance." In *The Economics of Pensions: Principles, Policies and International Experience*, ed. Salvador Valdes Prieto, 92–126. Cambridge: Cambridge University Press.

Modigliani, F. and R. Brumberg. 1954. "Utility Analysis and the Consumption Function: An Interpretation of Cross-Section Data." In *Post-Keynesian Economics*, ed. Kenneth K. Kurihara, 388–436. New Brunswick, N.J.: Rutgers University Press.

Monk, A. 2009. "Recasting the Sovereign Wealth Fund Debate: Trust, Legitimacy, and Governance." *New Political Economy* 14 (4): 451–468.

Mossin, J. 1966. "Equilibrium in a Capital Asset Market." *Econometrica* 34 (4): 768–783.

Nese, E. 2011. "Is Fiscal Policy Procyclical in Developing Oil-Producing Countries?" IMF Working Paper WP/11/171. International Monetary Fund, Washington, D.C.

New Zealand Superannuation Fund. 2014. "Investment Beliefs." New Zealand Superannuation Fund, Auckland, October. https://www.nzsuperfund.co.nz/how-we-invest/beliefs.

———. 2015. *2015 Annual Report*. Auckland, New Zeakand.

New Zealand Super Fund. 2016. "Reference Portfolio." Accessed April 2, 2017. https://www.nzsuperfund.co.nz/how-we-invest/reference-portfolio.

Nofsinger, J. 1998. "Why Targeted Investing Does Not Make Sense." *Financial Management* 27: 87–96.

Nordhaus, W. 1975. "The Political Business Cycle." *Review of Economic Studies* 42 (1): 169–190.

Norges Bank Investment Management. 2012. *Annual Report: 2012.* Olso, Norway.

Norman, C. 2009. "Rule of Law and the Resource Curse: Abundance Versus Intensity." *Environmental Resource Economics* 43 (2): 183–207.

North, D. 1981. *Structure and Change in Economic History.* New York: Norton.

——. 1986. "The New Institutional Economics." *Journal of Institutional and Theoretical Economics* 142: 230–237.

——. 1990. *Institutions, Institutional Change, and Economic Performance.* Cambridge: Cambridge University Press.

——. 1991. "Institutions." *Journal of Economic Perspectives* 5 (1): 97–112.

——. 1995. "The New Institutional Economics and Third World Development." In *The New Institutional Economics and Third World Development*, ed. J. Harriss, J. Hunter, and C. M. Lewis, 17–26. London: Routledge.

Nurkse, R. 1961. *Problems of Capital Formation in Underdeveloped Countries.* New York: Oxford University Press.

Olsen, O. 2012. Address by Governor Oystein Olsen to the Supervisory Council of Norges Bank and invited guests, Norges Bank, Oslo, Norway, February 16.

Ossowski, R., M. Villafuerte, P. Medas, and T. Thomas. 2008. "The Role of Fiscal Institutions in Managing the Oil Revenue Boom." IMF Occasional Paper 260. International Monetary Fund, Washington, D.C.

Pastor, L. and R. Stambaugh. 2003. "Liquidity Risk and Expected Stock Returns." *Journal of Political Economy* 63 (2): 642–685.

Persson, T. and G. Tabellini. 2004. "Constitutional Rules and Fiscal Policy Outcomes." *American Economic Review* 94 (1): 25–45.

Petek, G. 2015. "How Might the Oil Price Plunge Affect U.S. States' Credit Quality?" Standard & Poor's Ratings Services, January 27.

Pomeranz, K. 2000. *The Great Divergence: China, Europe, and the Making of the Modern World Economy.* Princeton, N.J.: Princeton University Press.

Prebisch, R. (1949) 1950. "The Economic Development of Latin America and Its Principal Problems." United Nations Economic Commission for Latin America (ECLA) conference, Havana, May 1949 (in Spanish); reprinted 1950 (in English), *Economic Bulletin for Latin America* 7 (1): 1–22.

Presbitero, A. 2016. "Too Much and Too Fast? Public Investment Scaling-Up and Absorptive Capacity." *Journal of Development Economics* 120 (1): 17–31.

Pritchett, L. 1997. "Divergence, Big Time." *Journal of Economic Perspectives* 11 (3): 3–17.

——. 2000. "The Tyranny of Concepts: CUDIE (Cumulated, Depreciated, Investment Effort) Is Not Capital." *Journal of Economic Growth* 5 (20): 361–384.

Ramey, G. and V. Ramey. 1995. "Cross-Country Evidence on the Link Between Volatility and Growth." *American Economic Review* 85 (5): 1138–1151.

Richards, C. 2015. "A Sound Fiscal Future: Recommendations for the Sustainable Utilization and Management of Alaska's Financial Assets." Governor's Financial Opportunities Working Group, Anchorage, Alas., October.

Robinson, J., D. Acemoglu, and S. Johnson. 2003. "An African Success Story: Botswana." In *In Search of Prosperity: Analytic Narratives on Economic Growth*, ed. Dani Rodrik, 80–119. Princeton, N.J.: Princeton University Press.

Robinson, J. and R. Torvik. 2005. "White Elephants." *Journal of Public Economics* 89: 197–210.

Robinson, J., R. Torvik, and T. Verdier. 2006. "Political Foundations of the Resource Curse." *Journal of Development Economics* 79: 447–468.

Rodrik, D. 1999. "Where Did All the Growth Go? External Shocks, Social Conflict and Growth Collapses." *Journal of Economic Growth* 4 (4): 385–412.

——. 2000. "Institutions for High-Quality Growth: What They Are and How to Acquire Them." *Studies in Comparative International Development* 35 (3): 3–31.

——. 2002. "Feasible Globalizations." NBER Working Paper No. 9129. National Bureau of Economic Research, Cambridge, Mass.

——. 2004. "Institutions and Economic Performance: Getting Institutions Right." *CESifo DICE Report* (Ifo Institute for Economic Research at the University of Munich) 2 (2): 10–15.

——. 2008. "Second-Best Institutions." *American Economic Review* 98 (2): 100–104.

Rodrik, D., A. Subramanian, and F. Trebbi. 2004. "Institutions Rule: The Primacy of Institutions Over Geography and Integration in Economic Development." *Journal of Economic Growth* 9 (2): 131–165.

Romano, R. 1993. "Public Pension Fund Activism in Corporate Governance Reconsidered." *Columbia Law Review* 93: 795–853.

Romer, C. and D. Romer. 2002. "The Evolution of Economic Understanding and Postwar Stabilization Policy." In *Rethinking Stabilization Policy*, Federal Reserve Bank of Kansas City, 11–87.

Romer, D. 1993. "The New Keynesian Synthesis." *Journal of Economic Perspectives* 7 (1): 5–22.

Rosenstein-Rodan, P. 1943. "Problems of Industrialization of Eastern and South-Eastern Europe." *Economic Journal* 53 (210/211): 202–211.

Ross, M. 1999. "The Political Economy of the Resource Curse." *World Politics* 51 (1): 297–322.

——. 2001. "Does Oil Hinder Democracy?" *World Politics* 53 (3): 325–361.

Ross, S. 1973. "The Economic Theory of Agency: The Principal's Problem." *American Economic Review* 63 (2): 134–139.

——. 1976. "The Arbitrage Theory of Capital Asset Pricing." *Journal of Economic Theory* 13: 341–360.

Rostow, W. 1962. *The Stages of Economic Growth.* London: Cambridge University Press.

Rozanov, A. 2005. "Who Holds the Wealth of Nations?" *Central Banking* 15 (4): 52–57.

Sachs, J. and A. Warner. 1995. "Natural Resource Abundance and Economic Growth." NBER Working Paper Series No. 5398. National Bureau of Economic Research, Cambridge, Mass.

——. 1997. "Natural Resource Abundance and Economic Growth." Center for International Development and Harvard Institute for International Development, Harvard University, Cambridge, Mass.

——. 1999. "The Big Push, Natural Resource Booms and Growth." *Journal of Development Economics* 59 (1): 43–76.

——. 2001. "Natural Resources and Economic Development: The Curse of Natural Resources." *European Economic Review* 45: 827–838.

Sala-i-Martin, X. 1997. "I Just Ran Two Million Regressions." *American Economic Review* 87 (2): 178–183.

Samuelson, P. A. 1969. "Lifetime Portfolio Selection by Dynamic Stochastic Programming." *Review of Economics and Statistics* 51: 239–246.

Santiso, J. 2008. "Sovereign Development Funds: Key Financial Actors of the Shifting Wealth of Nations." OECD (Organisation for Economic Cooperation and Development) Emerging Markets Network Working Paper. Paris: OECD.

Sargent, T. and N. Wallace. 1975. "Rational Expectations, the Optimal Monetary Instrument, and the Optimal Money Supply Rule." *Journal of Political Economy* 83, 241–254.

Satyanath, S. and A. Subramanian. 2004. "What Determines Long-Run Macroeconomic Stability? Democratic Institutions." IMF Working Papers 04/215. International Monetary Fund, Washington, D.C.

Schmidt-Hebbel, K. 2012. "Fiscal Institutions in Resource-Rich Economies: Lessons from Chile and Norway." Working Paper 416. Pontifical Catholic University of Chile, Santiago, Chile.

Sharpe, W. 1964. "Capital Asset Prices: A Theory of Market Equilibrium Under Conditions of Risk." *Journal of Finance* 19 (3): 425–442.

Shiller, R. 1984. "Stock Prices and Social Dynamics." *Brookings Papers on Economic Activity* 15 (2): 457–498.

Shleifer, A. and R. Vishny. 1990. "Equilibrium Short Horizons of Investors and Firms." *American Economic Review* 80: 148–153.

Singer, H. 1950. "U.S. Foreign Investment in Underdeveloped Areas: The Distribution of Gains Between Investing and Borrowing Countries." *American Economic Review* 40: 473–485.

Smith, A. (1776) 1981. *An Inquiry Into the Nature and Causes of the Wealth of Nations.* Indianapolis, Ind.: Liberty Fund.

Smith, V. 2008. *Rationality in Economics: Constructivist and Ecological Forms.* Cambridge: Cambridge University Press.

Solow, R. 1974. "Intergenerational Equity and Exhaustible Resources." *Review of Economic Studies* 41 (29): 29–45.

Stern, G. 1999. "The Use of Explicit Targets for Monetary Policy: Practical Experience of 91 Economies in the 1990s." *Bank of England Quarterly Bulletin,* August, 272–281.

Stiglitz, J. 2012. "Sovereign Wealth Funds: Distinguishing Aspects and Opportunities." In *Sovereign Wealth Funds and Long-Term Investing,* ed. P. Bolton, F. Samama, and J. Stiglitz, 26–31. New York: Columbia University Press.

Summers, L. 2007. "Funds That Shake Capitalist Logic." *Financial Times,* July 29.

Svensson, L. 1997. "Optimal Inflation Targets, 'Conservative' Central Banks, and Linear Inflation Contracts." *American Economic Review* 87 (1): 98–114.

———. 2003a. "Inflation Targeting: Should It Be Modeled as an Instrument Rule or a Targeting Rule?" *European Economic Review* 46: 771–780.

———. 2003b. "What Is Wrong with Taylor Rules? Using Judgment in Monetary Policy Through Targeting Rules." *Journal of Economic Literature* 41: 426–477.

Swensen, D. 2000. *Pioneering Portfolio Management: An Unconventional Approach to Institutional Investment.* New York: Free Press.

Talvi, E. and C. Vegh. 2005. "Tax Base Variability and Procyclical Fiscal Policy in Developing Countries." *Journal of Development Economics* 78 (1): 156–190.

Taylor, J. B. 1997. "A Core of Practical Macroeconomics." *American Economic Review* 87: 233–235.

———. 2010. "Does the Crisis Experience Call for a New Paradigm in Monetary Policy?" CASE Network Studies and Analyses No. 402.

Tobin, J. 1974. "What Is Permanent Endowment Income." *American Economic Review* 64 (2): 427–432.

Tornell, A. and P. Lane. 1999. "The Voracity Effect." *American Economic Review* 89 (1): 22–46.

Torvik, R. 2002. "Natural Resources, Rent Seeking and Welfare." *Journal of Development Economics* 67: 455–470.

———. 2009. "Why Do Some Resource-Abundant Countries Succeed While Others Do Not?" *Oxford Review of Economic Policy* 25 (2): 241–256.

———. 2012. "The Political Economy of Reform in Resource-Rich Countries." In *Beyond the Curse: Policies to Harness the Power of Natural Resources*, ed. R. Arezki, T. Gylfason, and A. Sy, 237–256. Washington, D.C.: International Monetary Fund.

Treynor, J. 1961. "Market Value, Time, and Risk." Unpublished manuscript.

Truman, E. 2008. "A Blueprint for Sovereign Wealth Fund Best Practices." Peterson Institute for International Economics, Policy Brief 8-3, Washington, D.C.

———. 2010. *Sovereign Wealth Funds: Threat or Salvation?* Peterson Institute for International Economics, Washington, D.C.

Tullock, G. 1967. "The Welfare Costs of Tariffs, Monopolies and Theft." *Western Economic Journal* 5: 224–232.

United States Department of Labor. 1994. "Interpretive Bulletin 94-1." Washington, D.C., June 28.

Useem, M. and D. Hess. 2001. "Governance and Investments of Public Pensions." In *Pensions in the Public Sector*, ed. O. Mitchell and E. Hustead, 132–152. Philadelphia: University of Pennsylvania Press.

Useem, M. and O. Mitchell. 2000. "Holders of the Purse Strings: Governance and Performance of Public Retirement Systems." *Social Science Quarterly* 81 (2): 489–506.

Van der Ploeg, F. 2008. "Challenges and Opportunities for Resource Rich Economies." OxCarre Research Paper 2008-05. Oxford.

———. 2011. "Natural Resources: Curse or Blessing?" *Journal of Economic Literature* 49 (2): 366–420.

Van der Ploeg, R. and S. Poelhekke. 2009. "The Volatility Curse: Revisiting the Paradox of Plenty." DNB Working Paper 206. Netherlands Central Bank, Research Department, Amsterdam.

Van Wijnbergen, S. 1981. "Optimal Investment and Exchange Rate Management in Oil Exporting Countries: A Normative Analysis of the Dutch Disease." Mimeograph, World Bank, Washington, D.C.

———. 1984a. "Inflation, Employment, and the Dutch Disease in Oil-Exporting Countries: A Short-Run Disequilibrium Analysis." *Quarterly Journal of Economics* 99 (2): 233–250.

———. 1984b. "The 'Dutch Disease': A Disease After All?" *Economic Journal* 94: 41–55.

Venables, A. 2010. "Resource Rents; When to Spend and How to Save." *International Tax and Public Finance* 17 (4): 340–356.

Verma, S. 2012. "China's CIC Quashes Europe Bailout Talk. Again." Emergingmarkets.org, published online on February 13, 2012.

Walker, B. 2016. "Costs of Delaying Alaska's Fiscal Fix Are Too Great." *Alaska Dispatch News*, May 14.

Wantchekon, L. 2002. "Why Do Resource Dependent Countries Have Authoritarian Governments?" *Journal of African Finance and Economic Development* 2 (1): 57–77.

Warren, G. and F. Pearson. 1933. *Prices*. New York: John Wiley.

Weingast, B. 1995. "The Economic Role of Political Institutions." *Journal of Law, Economics, and Organization* 11 (1): 1–31.

Williamson, O. 1975. *Markets and Hierarchies, Analysis and Antitrust Implications: A Study in the Economics of Internal Organization*. New York: Free Press.

Wolf, M. 2007. "The Brave New World of State Capitalism." *Financial Times*, October 16.

Woodford, M. 2002. *Interest and Prices: Foundations of a Theory of Monetary Policy*. Princeton, N.J.: Princeton University Press.

World Trade Organization. 2010. *World Trade Report: Trade in Natural Resources*. Geneva: World Trade Organization.

Wright, C. 2012. "Middle East: The Shadowy World of Gulf Sovereign Wealth." *Euromoney*, November. http://www.euromoney.com/Article/3111056/Middle-East-The-shadowy-world-of-Gulf-sovereign-wealth.html.

Wright, G. 1990. "The Origins of American Industrial Success, 1879–1940." *American Economic Review* 80: 651–668.

Wright, G. and J. Czelusta. 2004. "The Myth of the Resource Curse." *Challenge* 47 (March-April): 6–38.

——. 2007. "Resource-Based Growth Past and Present." In *Natural Resources: Neither Curse nor Destiny*, ed. D. Lederman and W. Maloney, 183–211. Stanford, Calif.: Stanford University Press.

Zawalsky, M. 2012. "Interview with Mark Wiseman." *Ivey Business Review*, April 3. http://iveybusinessreview.ca/cms/2271/interview-with-mark-wiseman-full.

Zhang, L. 2005. "The Value Premium." *Journal of Finance* 60 (1): 67–104.

Index

Page references in italics indicate tables and figures.